ULTIMATE COMICS
SPIDER-MAN

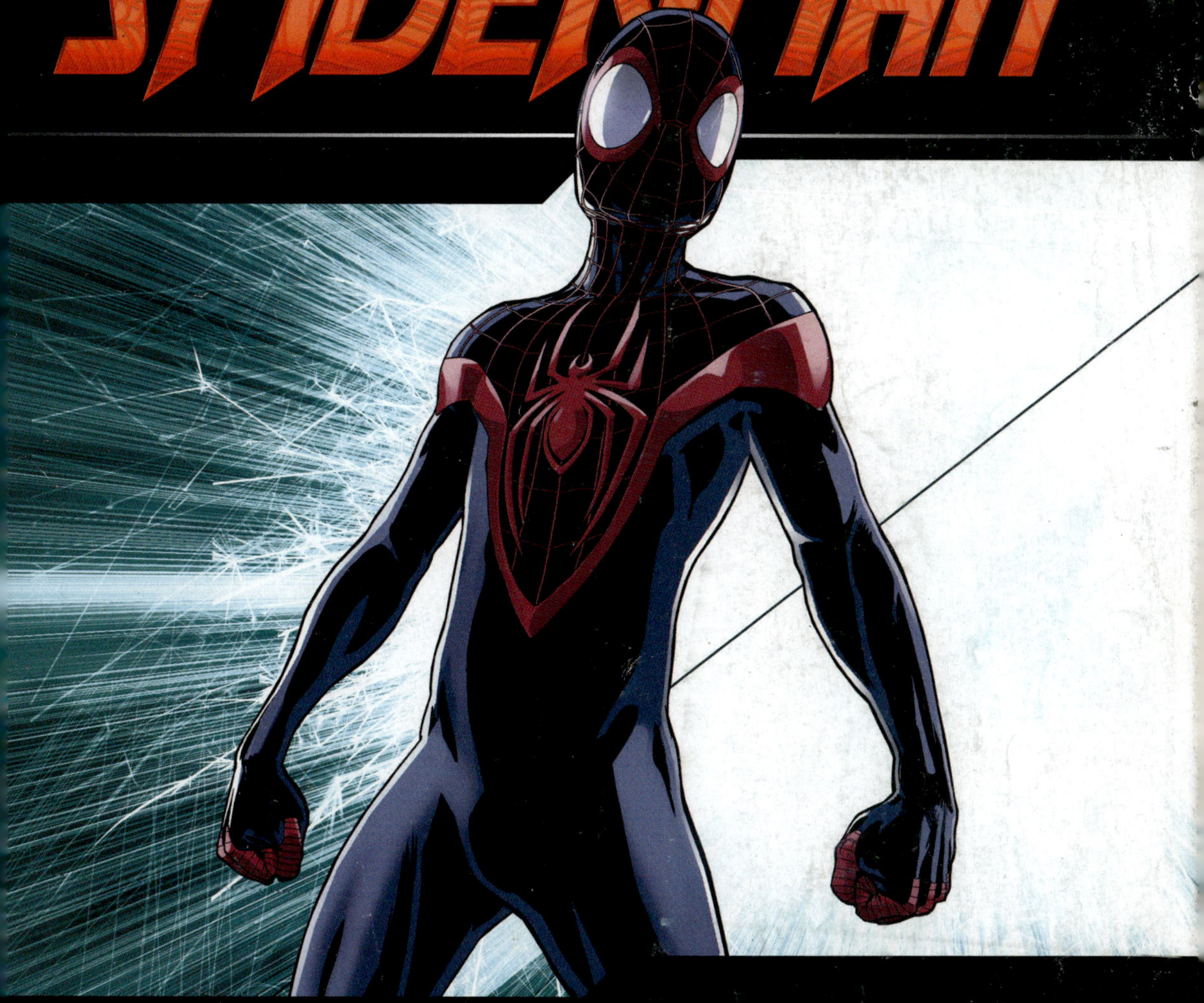

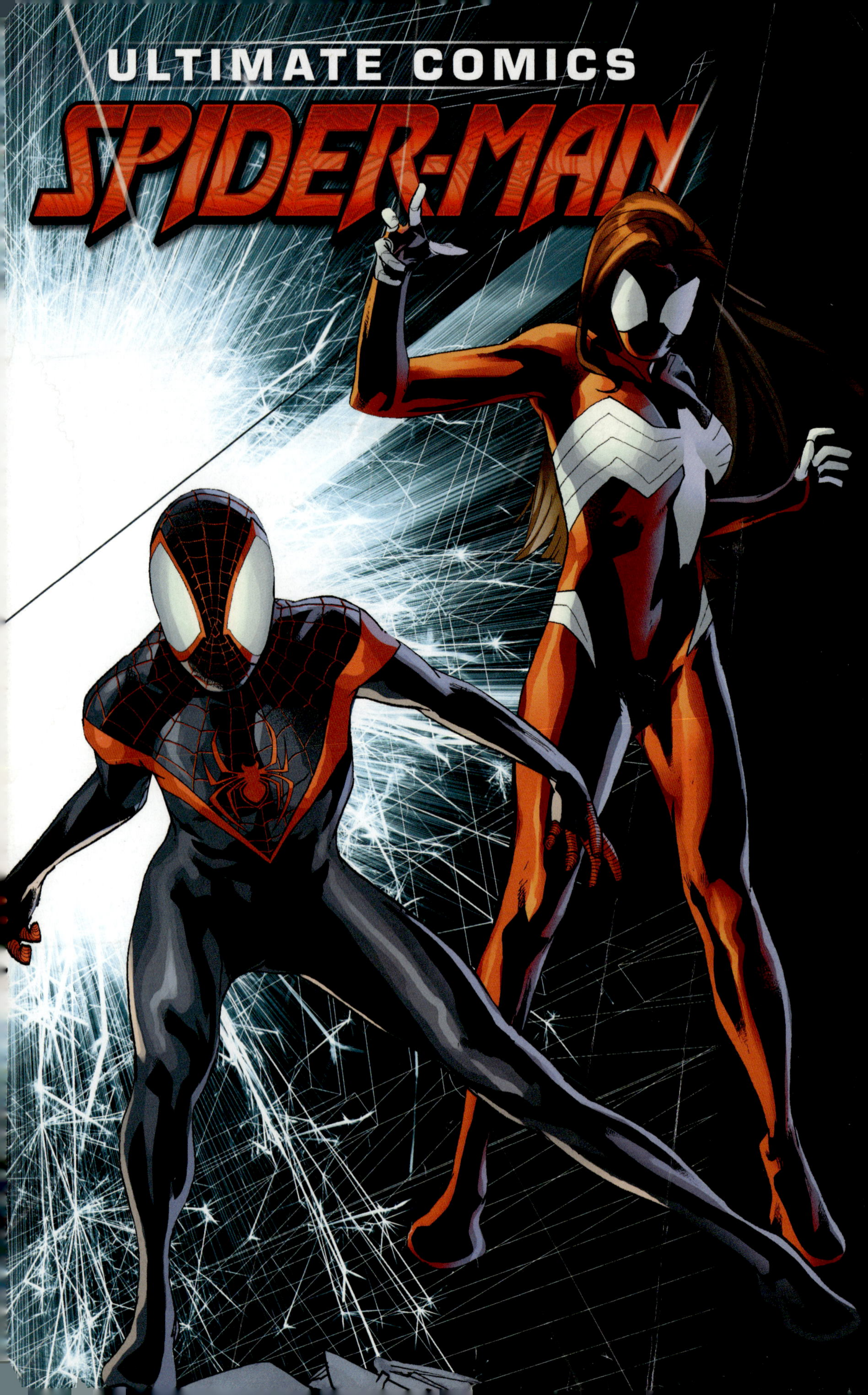
ULTIMATE COMICS
SPIDER-MAN

ULTIMATE COMICS SPIDER-MAN #13-28 & #16.1

WRITER: **BRIAN MICHAEL BENDIS**

ARTISTS: **DAVID MARQUEZ** (#11-15, #16.1, #18 & #23-28),

PEPE LARRAZ (#16–17) & **SARA PICHELLI** (#19–22)

COLORIST: **JUSTIN PONSOR** WITH PAUL MOUNTS (#28)

LETTERER: **VC's CORY PETIT**

COVER ART:

KAARE ANDREWS (#11), **JORGE MOLINA** (#12-15),

DAVID MARQUEZ & **RAIN BEREDO** (#16, #18, #24-25 & #28),

DAVID MARQUEZ & **JUSTIN PONSOR** (#16.1, #23 & #26-27),

SARA PICHELLI & **RAIN BEREDO** (#17, #19 & #21-22)

AND **SARA PICHELLI** & **CHRISTINA STRAIN** (#20)

ASSISTANT EDITORS: **EMILY SHAW** & **JON MOISAN**

ASSOCIATE EDITOR: **SANA AMANAT**

SENIOR EDITOR: **MARK PANICCIA**

SPIDER-MAN CREATED BY **STAN LEE** & **STEVE DITKO**

COLLECTION EDITOR: JENNIFER GRÜNWALD

ASSISTANT EDITOR: SARAH BRUNSTAD

ASSOCIATE MANAGING EDITOR: ALEX STARBUCK

EDITOR, SPECIAL PROJECTS: MARK D. BEAZLEY

SENIOR EDITOR, SPECIAL PROJECTS: JEFF YOUNGQUIST

SVP PRINT, SALES & MARKETING: DAVID GABRIEL

BOOK DESIGNER: JAY BOWEN

EDITOR IN CHIEF: AXEL ALONSO

CHIEF CREATIVE OFFICER: JOE QUESADA

PUBLISHER: DAN BUCKLEY

EXECUTIVE PRODUCER: ALAN FINE

MILES MORALES: ULTIMATE SPIDER-MAN ULTIMATE COLLECTION BOOK 2. Contains material originally published in magazine form as ULTIMATE COMICS SPIDER-MAN #13-28 and #16.1. First printing 2015. ISBN# 978-0-7851-9779-9. Published by MARVEL WORLDWIDE, INC., a subsidiary of MARVEL ENTERTAINMENT, LLC. OFFICE OF PUBLICATION: 135 West 50th Street, New York, NY 10020. Copyright © 2015 MARVEL No similarity between any of the names, characters, persons, and/or institutions in this magazine with those of any living or dead person or institution is intended, and any such similarity which may exist is purely coincidental. **Printed in the U.S.A.** ALAN FINE, President, Marvel Entertainment; DAN BUCKLEY, President, TV, Publishing and Brand Management; JOE QUESADA, Chief Creative Officer; TOM BREVOORT, SVP of Publishing; DAVID BOGART, SVP of Operations & Procurement, Publishing; C.B. CEBULSKI, VP of International Development & Brand Management; DAVID GABRIEL, SVP Print, Sales & Marketing; JIM O'KEEFE, VP of Operations & Logistics; DAN CARR, Executive Director of Publishing Technology; SUSAN CRESPI, Editorial Operations Manager; ALEX MORALES, Publishing Operations Manager; STAN LEE, Chairman Emeritus. For information regarding advertising in Marvel Comics or on Marvel.com, please contact Jonathan Rheingold, VP of Custom Solutions & Ad Sales, at jrheingold@marvel.com. For Marvel subscription inquiries, please call 800-217-9158. **Manufactured between 8/7/2015 and 9/14/2015 by R.R. DONNELLEY, INC., SALEM, VA, USA.**

10 9 8 7 6 5 4 3 2 1

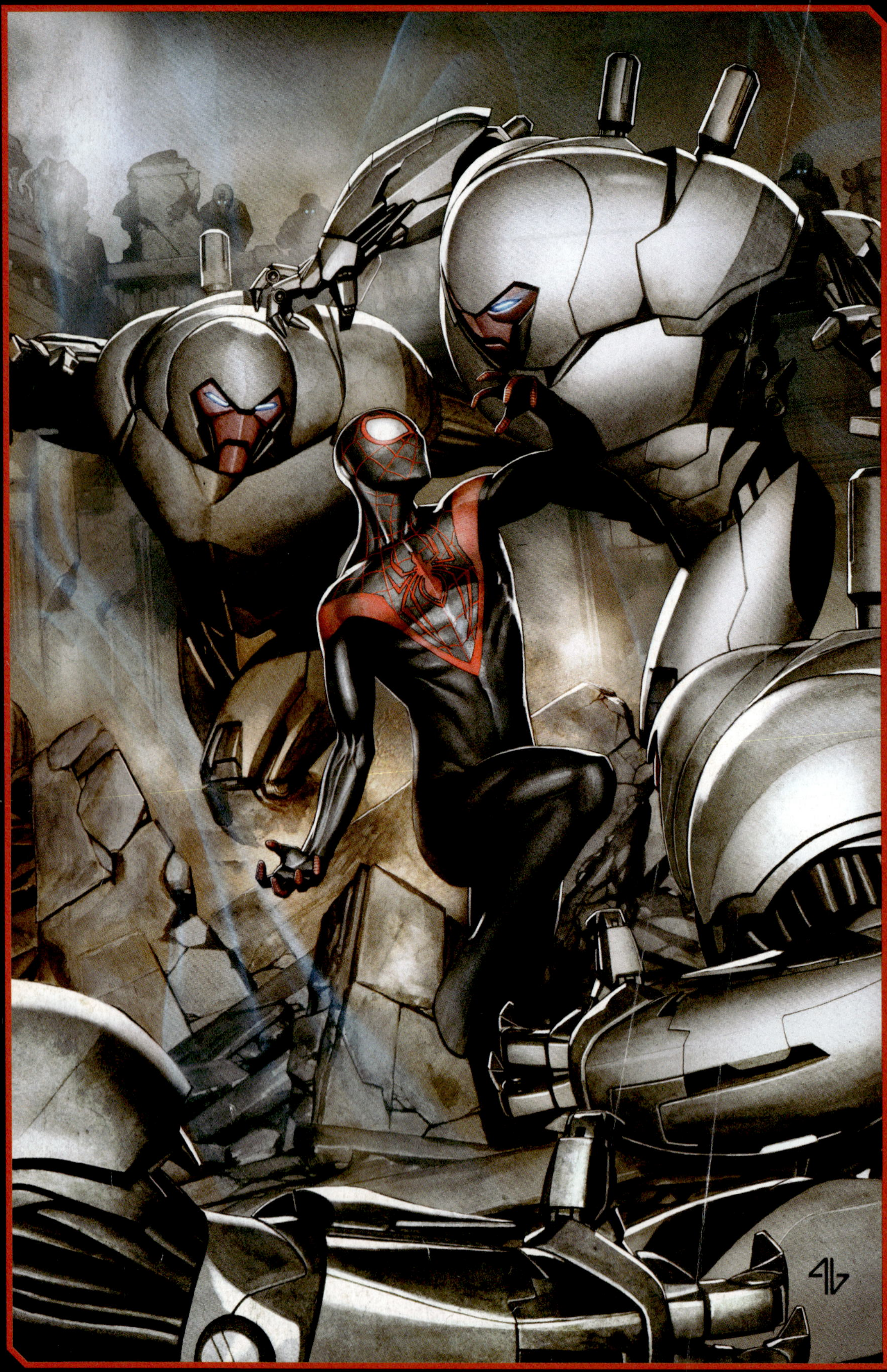

#13 VARIANT BY ADI GRANOV

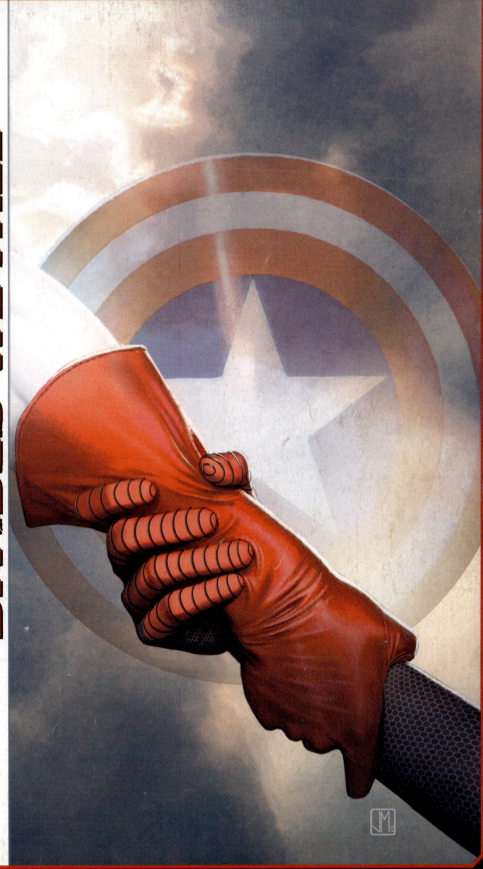

DIVIDED WE FALL

MONTHS BEFORE PETER PARKER WAS SHOT AND KILLED, GRADE-SCHOOLER MILES MORALES WAS ABOUT TO START A NEW CHAPTER IN HIS LIFE AT A NEW SCHOOL--WHEN HE WAS SUDDENLY BITTEN BY A STOLEN, GENETICALLY ALTERED SPIDER THAT GAVE HIM INCREDIBLE ARACHNID-LIKE POWERS.

ULTIMATE COMICS
ALL NEW SPIDER-MAN

SPIDER-MAN

GANKE

Washington is decimated.

The government is a mess.

The Southwest is in chaos.

States are seceding from the union.

America is falling apart.

Spider-Man commits murder?

DIVIDED WE FALL

CAPTAIN AMERICA

IRON MAN

S.H.I.E.L.D. SITUATION MAP:

[Anti-government militia hot spots]

Montana, N. Dakota
S. Dakota, Wyoming
Arizona, New Mexico
N. Carolina, S. Carolina,
Georgia

[Eastern seaboard control zone]

New England,
New York,
New Jersey,
Delaware,
Washington, D.C.,
Maryland,
Virginia

secured by National Guard under emergency powers committee

[the West Coast]

California, Oregon
Washington

status unknown

[Great Lakes states]

Minnesota,
Wisconsin,
Michigan,
Illinois,
Indiana, Ohio

status unknown

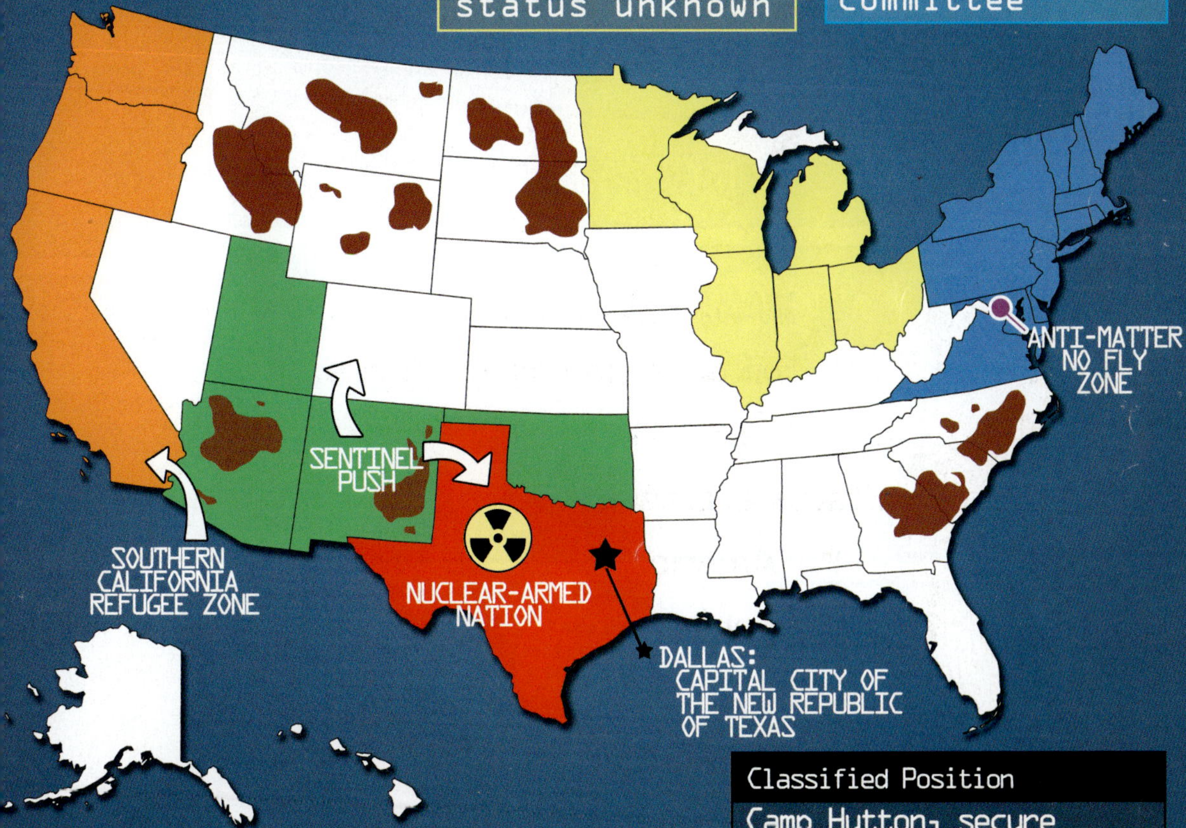
ANTI-MATTER NO FLY ZONE
SENTINEL PUSH
SOUTHERN CALIFORNIA REFUGEE ZONE
NUCLEAR-ARMED NATION
DALLAS: CAPITAL CITY OF THE NEW REPUBLIC OF TEXAS

Classified Position

Camp Hutton, secure location of the President of the United States

[Sentinel-controlled no-man's-land]

New Mexico, Arizona
Utah, Oklahoma

abandoned by the U.S. government

[The New Republic of Texas]

Texas

declared state independence

ALL STATES SHOWN IN WHITE ARE U.S. GOVERNMENT-CONTROLLED ZONES

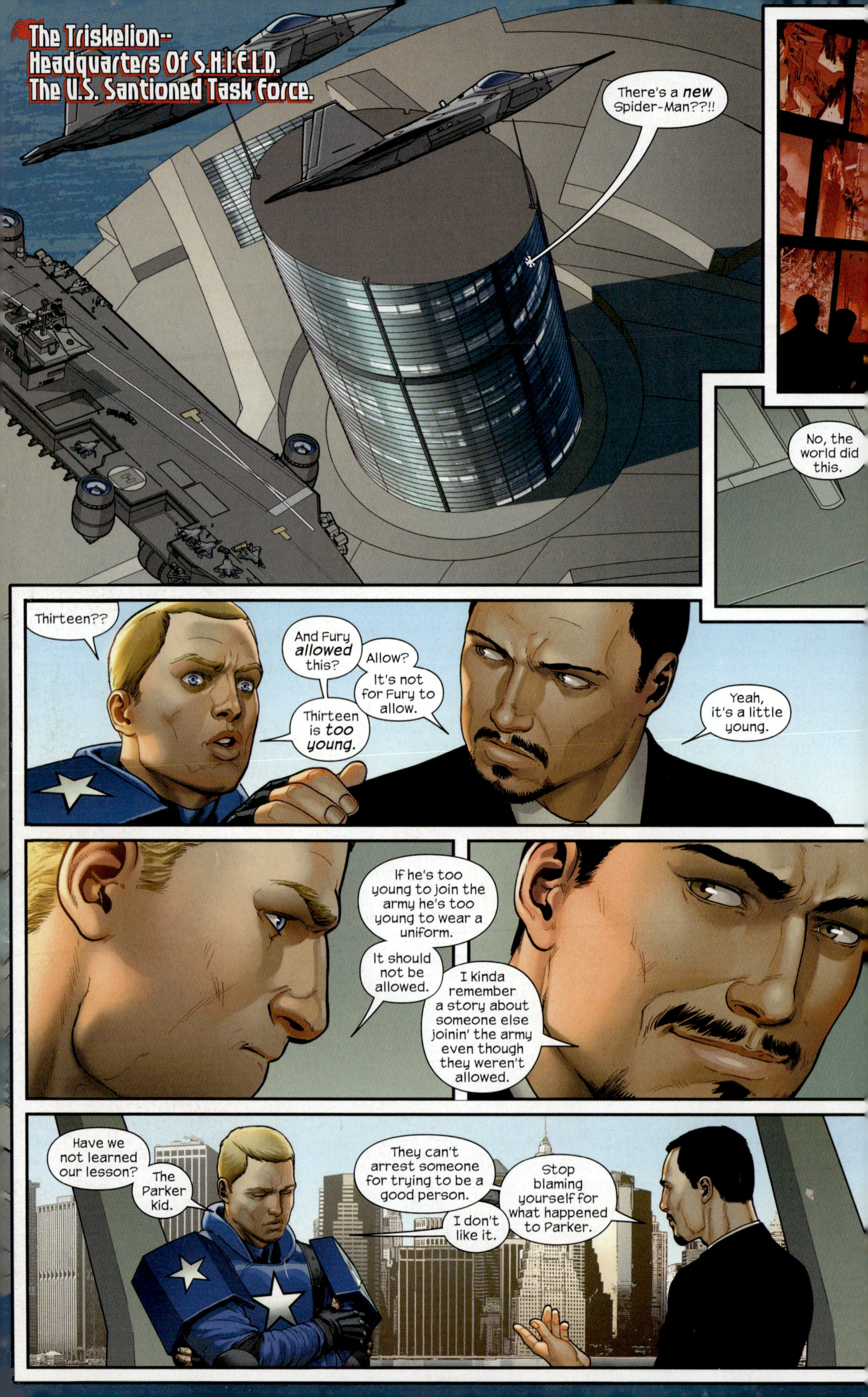
The Triskelion--
Headquarters Of S.H.I.E.L.D.
The U.S. Santioned Task Force.
There's a *new* Spider-Man??!!
No, the world did this.
Thirteen??
And Fury *allowed* this?
Allow? It's not for Fury to allow.
Thirteen is *too young.*
Yeah, it's a little young.
If he's too young to join the army he's too young to wear a uniform.
It should not be allowed.
I kinda remember a story about someone else joinin' the army even though they weren't allowed.
Have we not learned our lesson?
The Parker kid.
They can't arrest someone for trying to be a good person.
I don't like it.
Stop blaming yourself for what happened to Parker.

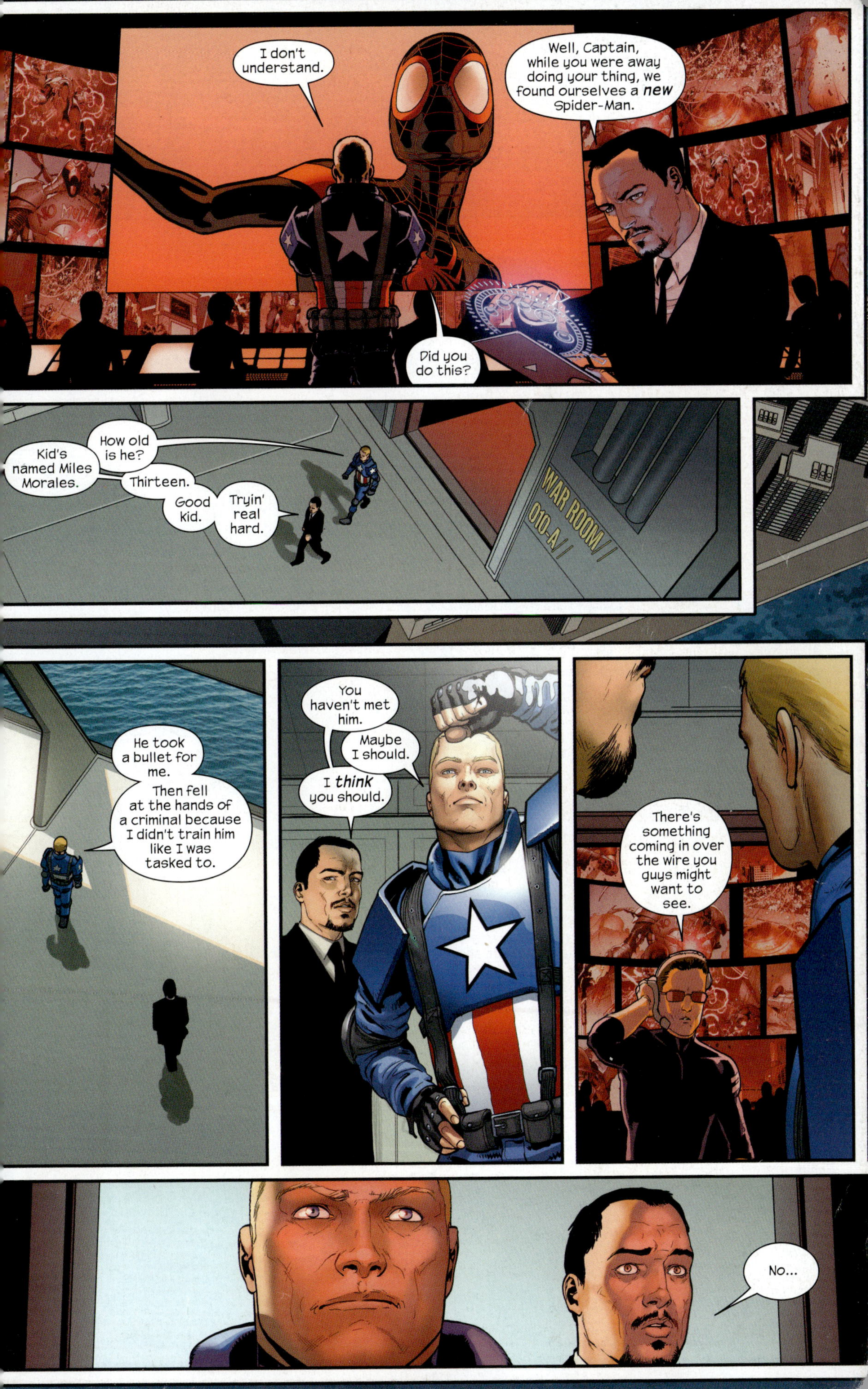
I don't understand.
Well, Captain, while you were away doing your thing, we found ourselves a new Spider-Man.
Did you do this?
How old is he?
Kid's named Miles Morales.
Thirteen.
Good kid.
Tryin' real hard.
WAR ROOM//
010-A//
He took a bullet for me.
Then fell at the hands of a criminal because I didn't train him like I was tasked to.
You haven't met him.
Maybe I should.
I think you should.
There's something coming in over the wire you guys might want to see.
No...

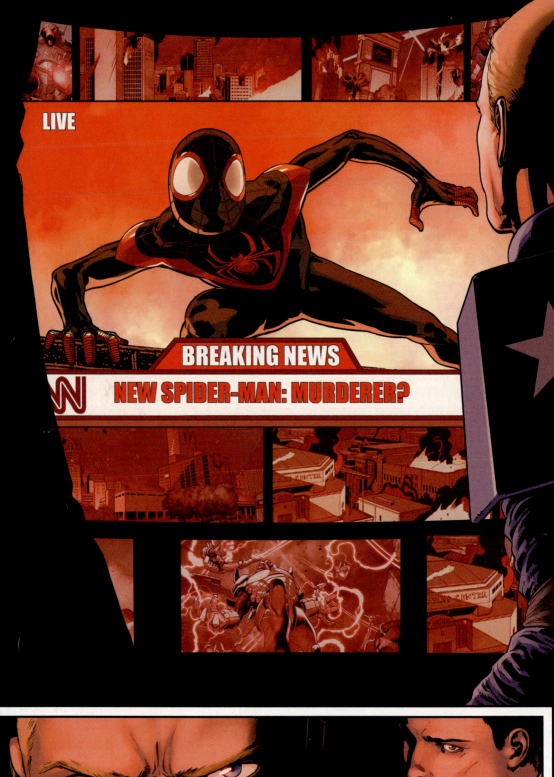

LIVE

BREAKING NEWS

NEW SPIDER-MAN: MURDERER?

I'll go talk to him *now.*

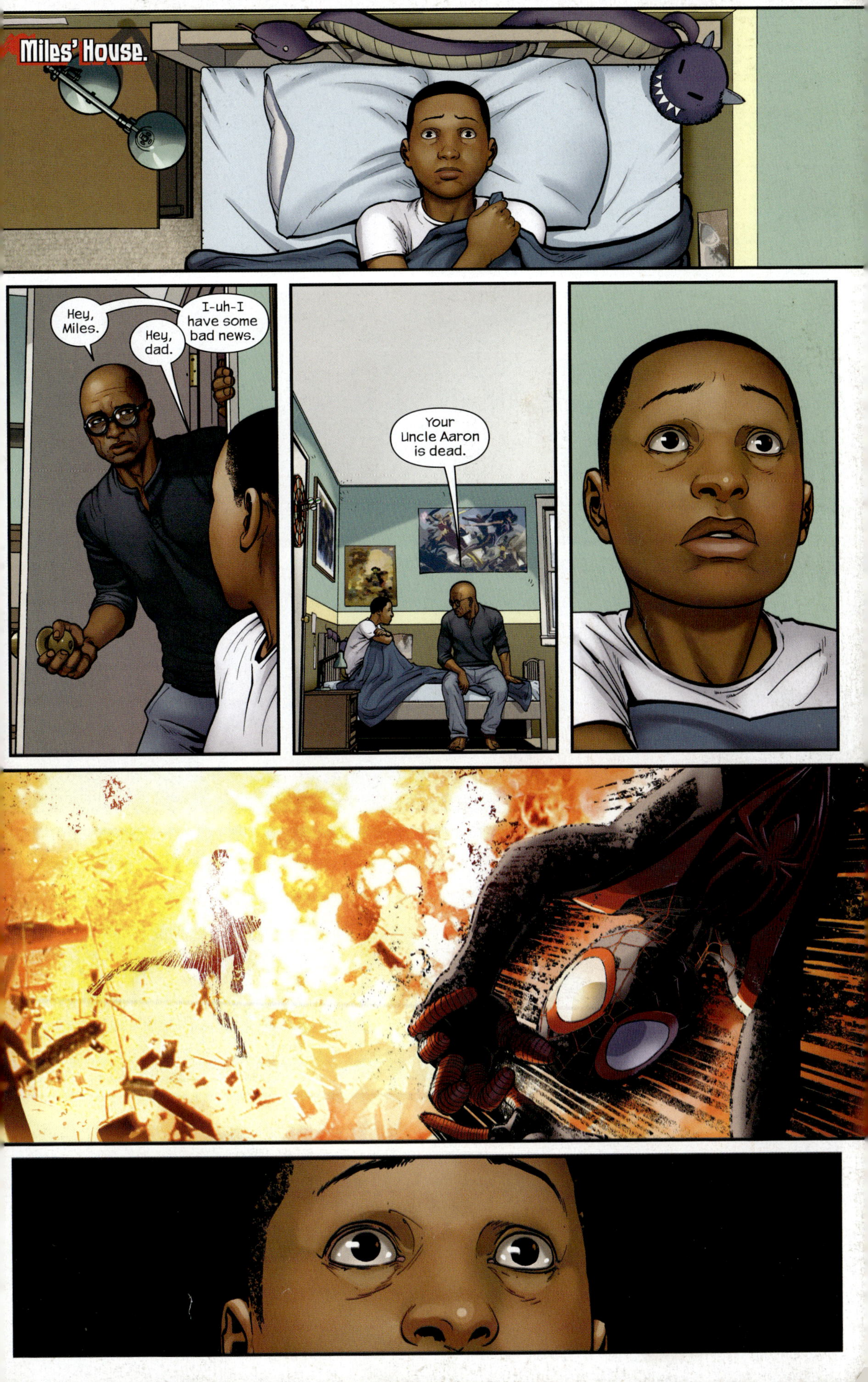
Miles' House.
Hey, Miles.
Hey, dad.
I-uh-I have some bad news.
Your Uncle Aaron is dead.

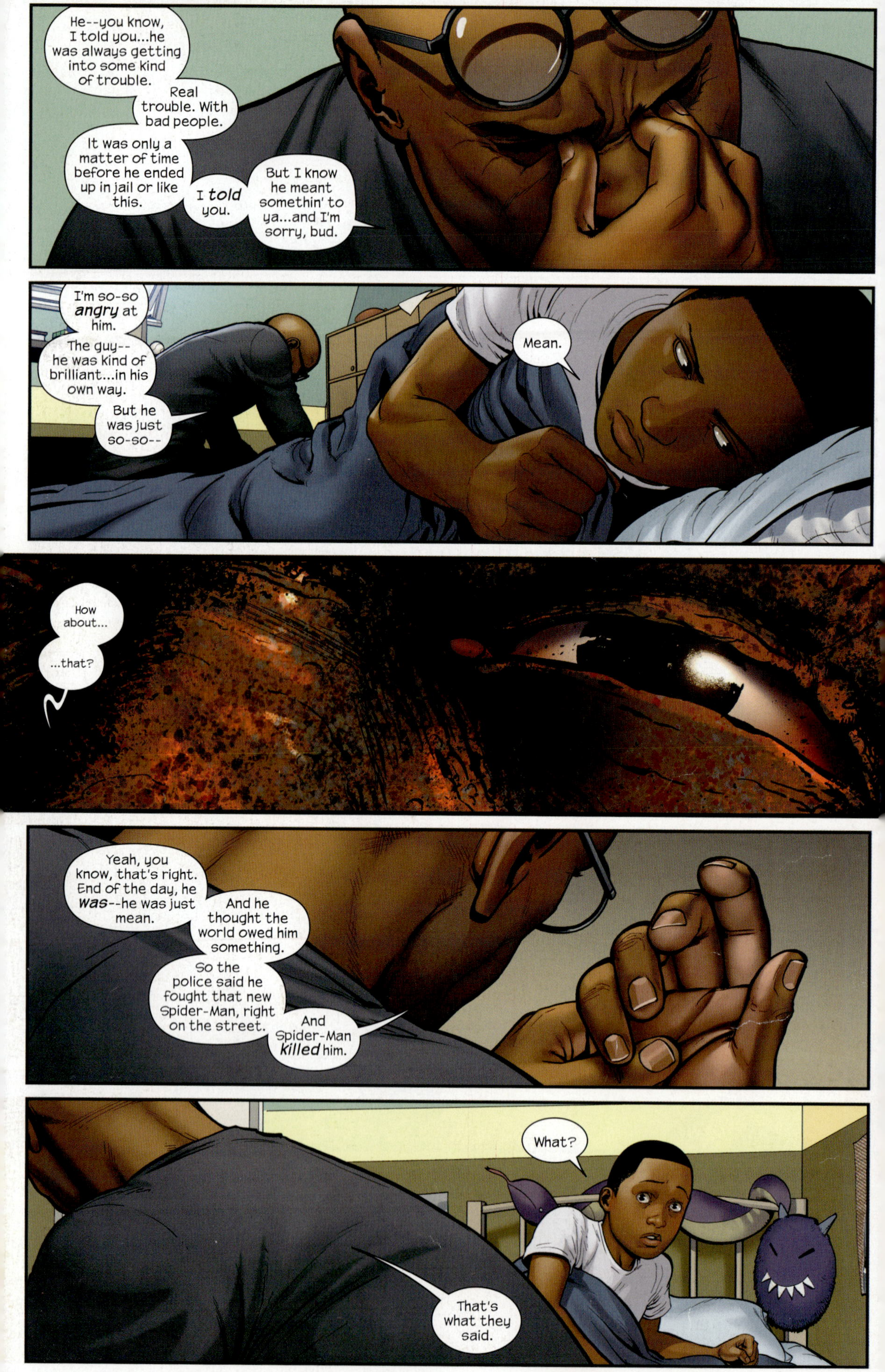
He--you know, I told you...he was always getting into some kind of trouble.
Real trouble. With bad people.
It was only a matter of time before he ended up in jail or like this.
I *told* you.
But I know he meant somethin' to ya...and I'm sorry, bud.
I'm so-so *angry* at him.
The guy--he was kind of brilliant...in his own way.
But he was just so-so--
Mean.
How about...
...that?
Yeah, you know, that's right. End of the day, he *was*--he was just mean.
And he thought the world owed him something.
So the police said he fought that new Spider-Man, right on the street.
And Spider-Man *killed* him.
What?
That's what they said.

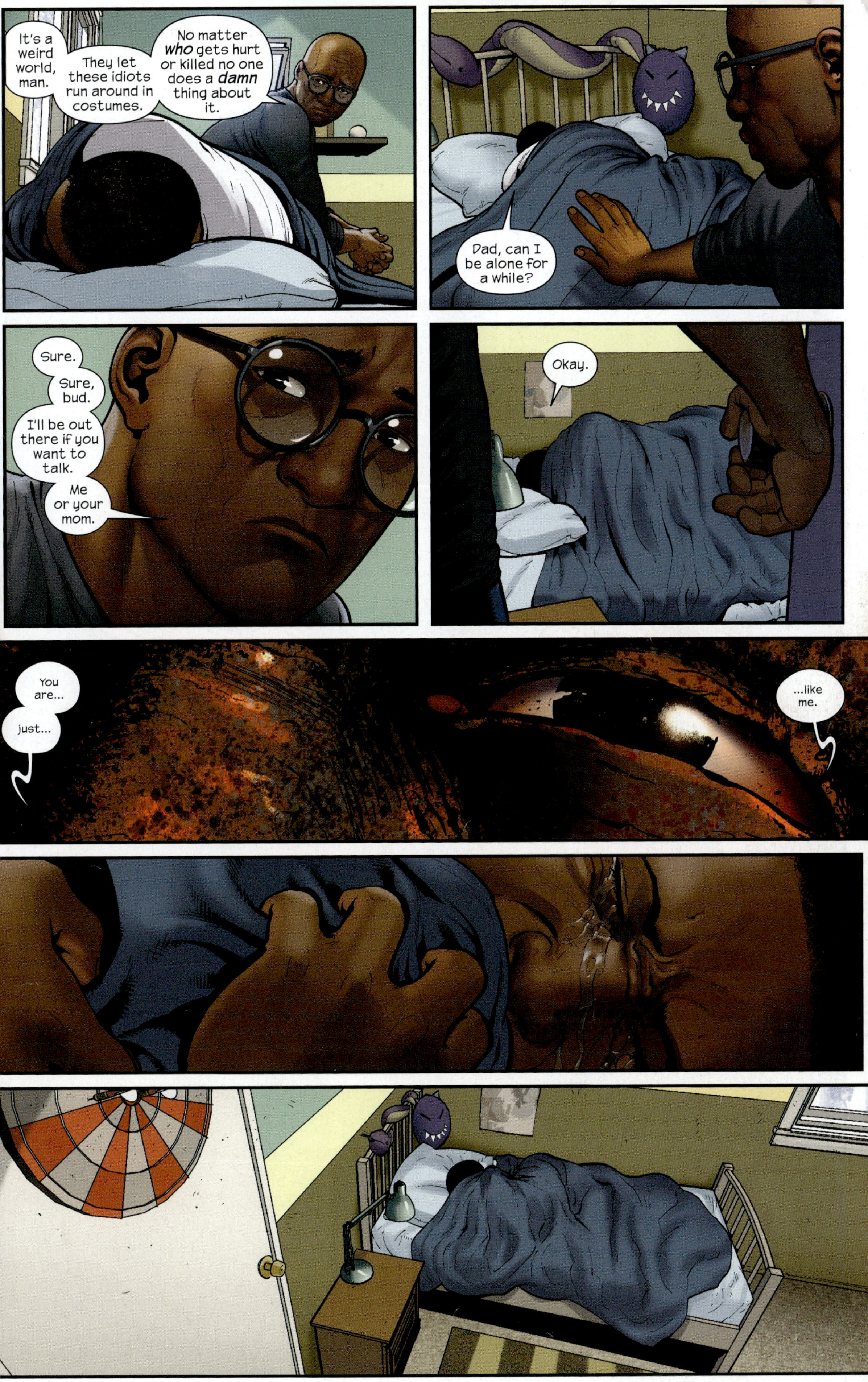
It's a weird world, man.
They let these idiots run around in costumes.
No matter who gets hurt or killed no one does a damn thing about it.
Dad, can I be alone for a while?
Sure.
Sure, bud.
I'll be out there if you want to talk.
Me or your mom.
Okay.
You are...
just...
...like me.

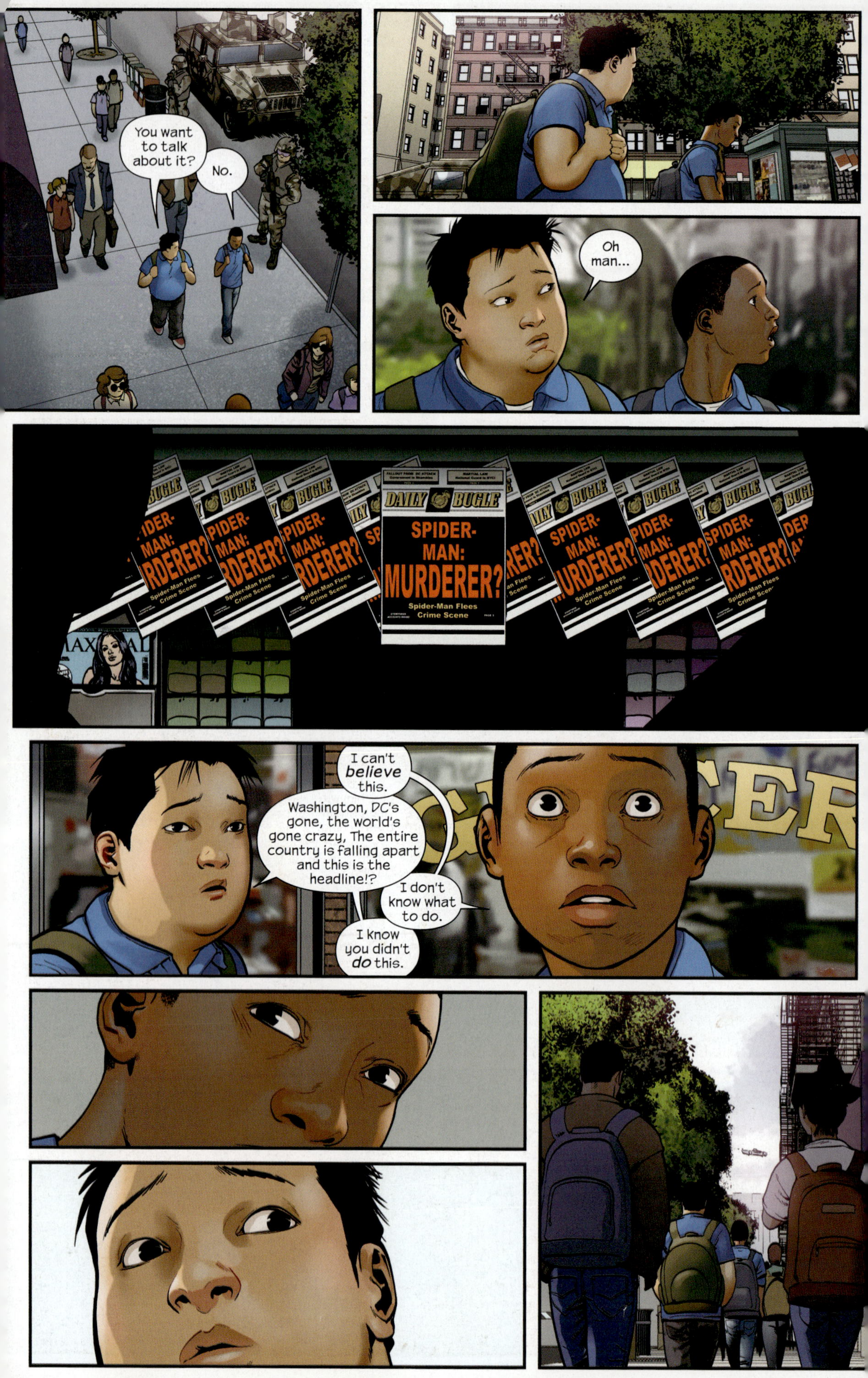

You want to talk about it?
No.
Oh man...
DAILY BUGLE
SPIDER-MAN: MURDERER?
Spider-Man Flees Crime Scene
I can't *believe* this.
Washington, DC's gone, the world's gone crazy, The entire country is falling apart and this is the headline!?
I don't know what to do.
I know you didn't *do* this.

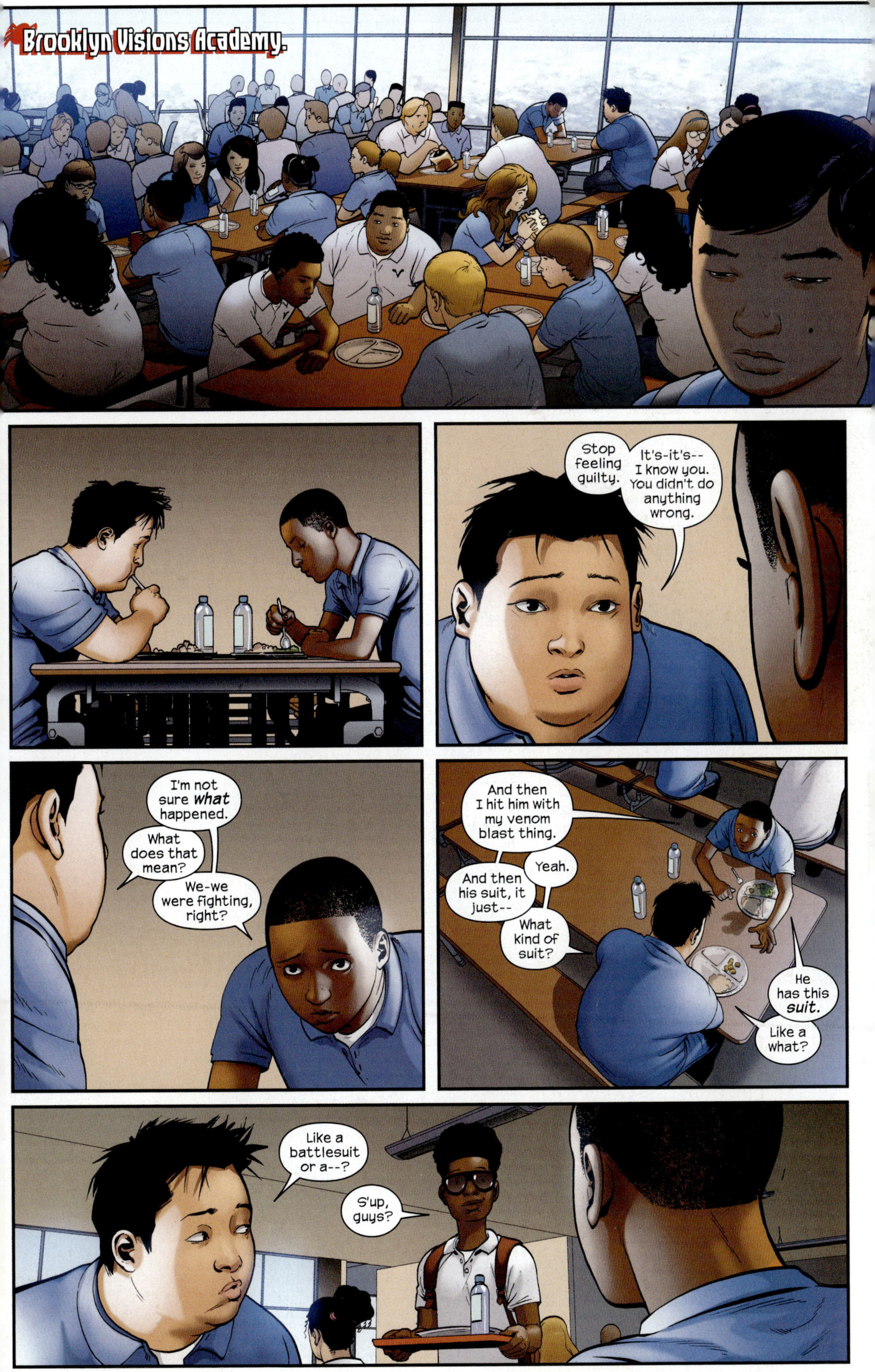
Brooklyn Visions Academy.
Stop feeling guilty.
It's-it's-- I know you. You didn't do anything wrong.
I'm not sure *what* happened.
What does that mean?
We-we were fighting, right?
And then I hit him with my venom blast thing.
Yeah.
And then his suit, it just--
What kind of suit?
He has this *suit.*
Like a what?
Like a battlesuit or a--?
S'up, guys?

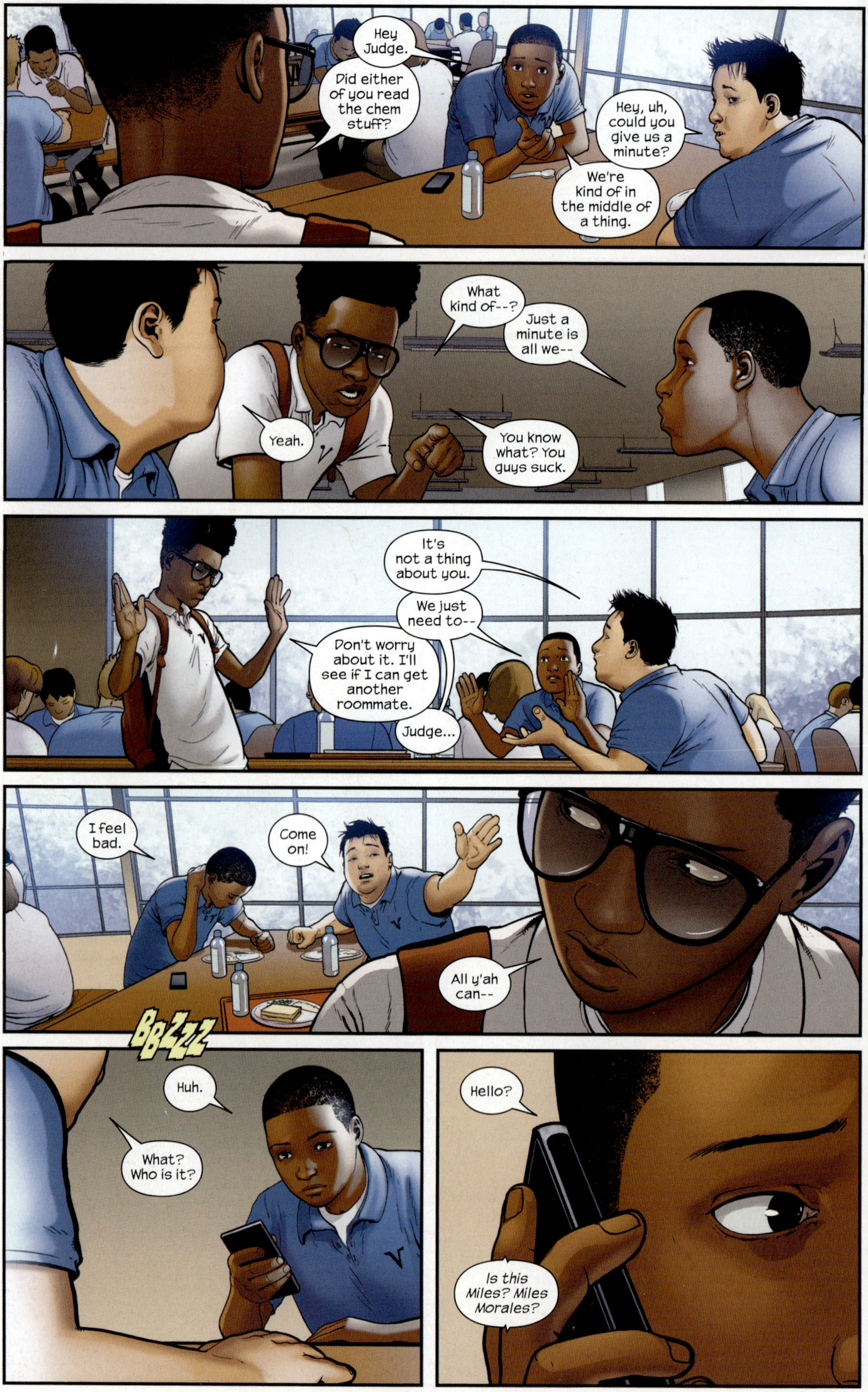
Hey Judge.
Did either of you read the chem stuff?
Hey, uh, could you give us a minute?
We're kind of in the middle of a thing.
What kind of--?
Just a minute is all we--
Yeah.
You know what? You guys suck.
It's not a thing about you.
We just need to--
Don't worry about it. I'll see if I can get another roommate.
Judge...
I feel bad.
Come on!
All y'ah can--
BBZZZ
Huh.
What? Who is it?
Hello?
Is this Miles? Miles Morales?

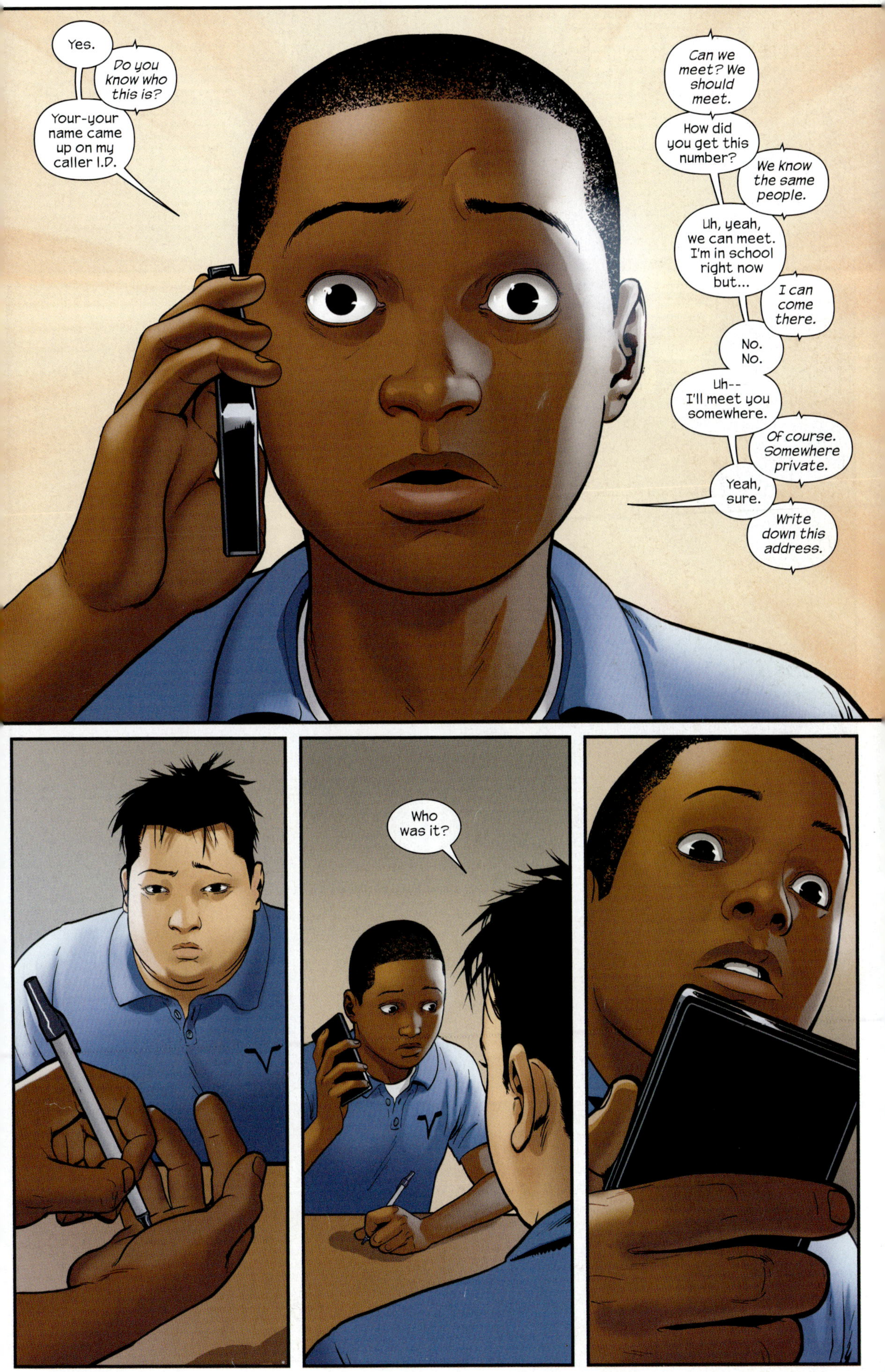
Yes.
Do you know who this is?
Your-your name came up on my caller I.D.
Can we meet? We should meet.
How did you get this number?
We know the same people.
Uh, yeah, we can meet. I'm in school right now but...
I can come there.
No. No.
Uh-- I'll meet you somewhere.
Of course. Somewhere private.
Yeah, sure.
Write down this address.
Who was it?

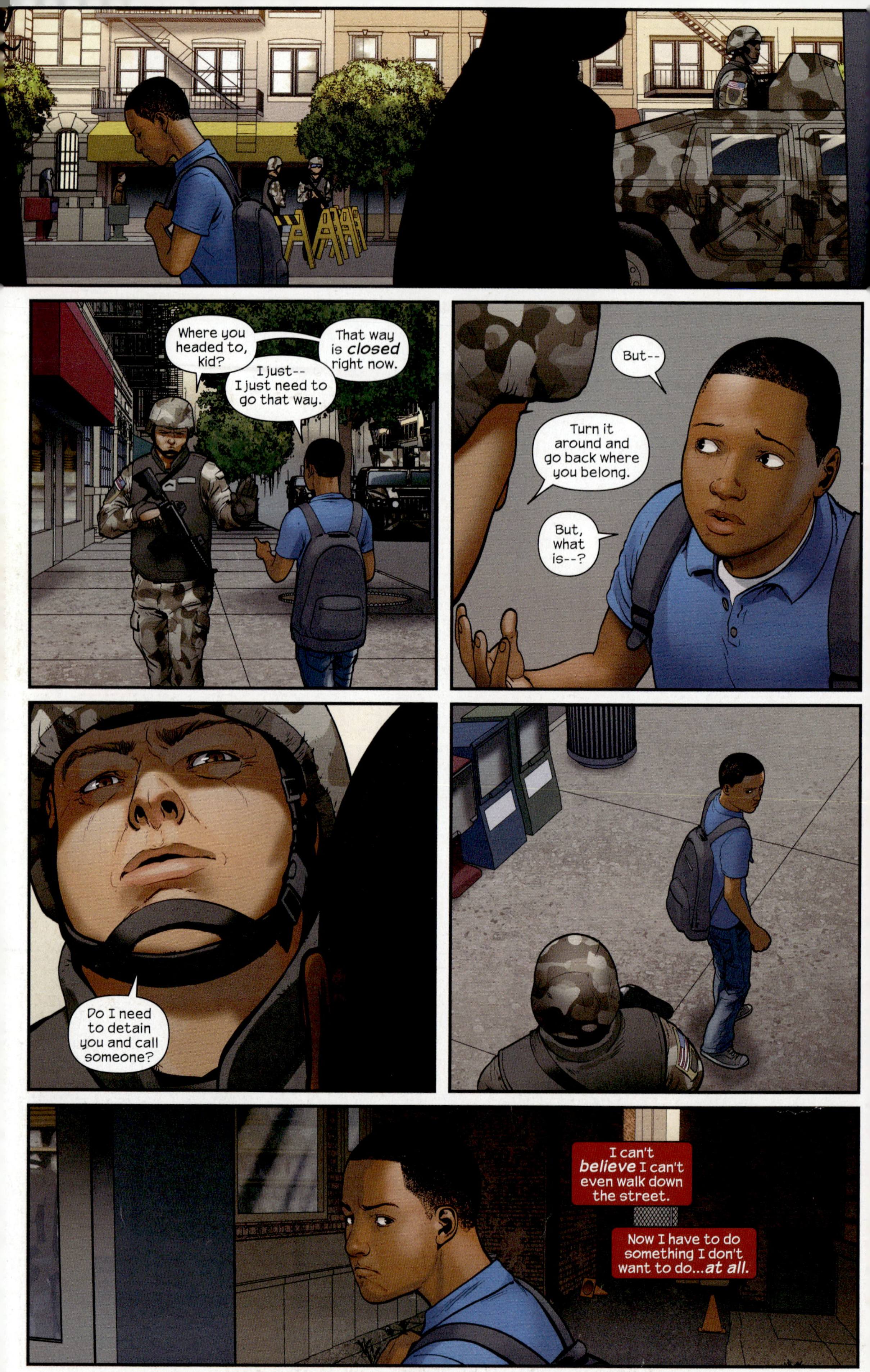
Where you headed to, kid?
That way is *closed* right now.
I just-- I just need to go that way.
But--
Turn it around and go back where you belong.
But, what is--?
Do I need to detain you and call someone?
I can't *believe* I can't even walk down the street.
Now I have to do something I don't want to do...*at all.*

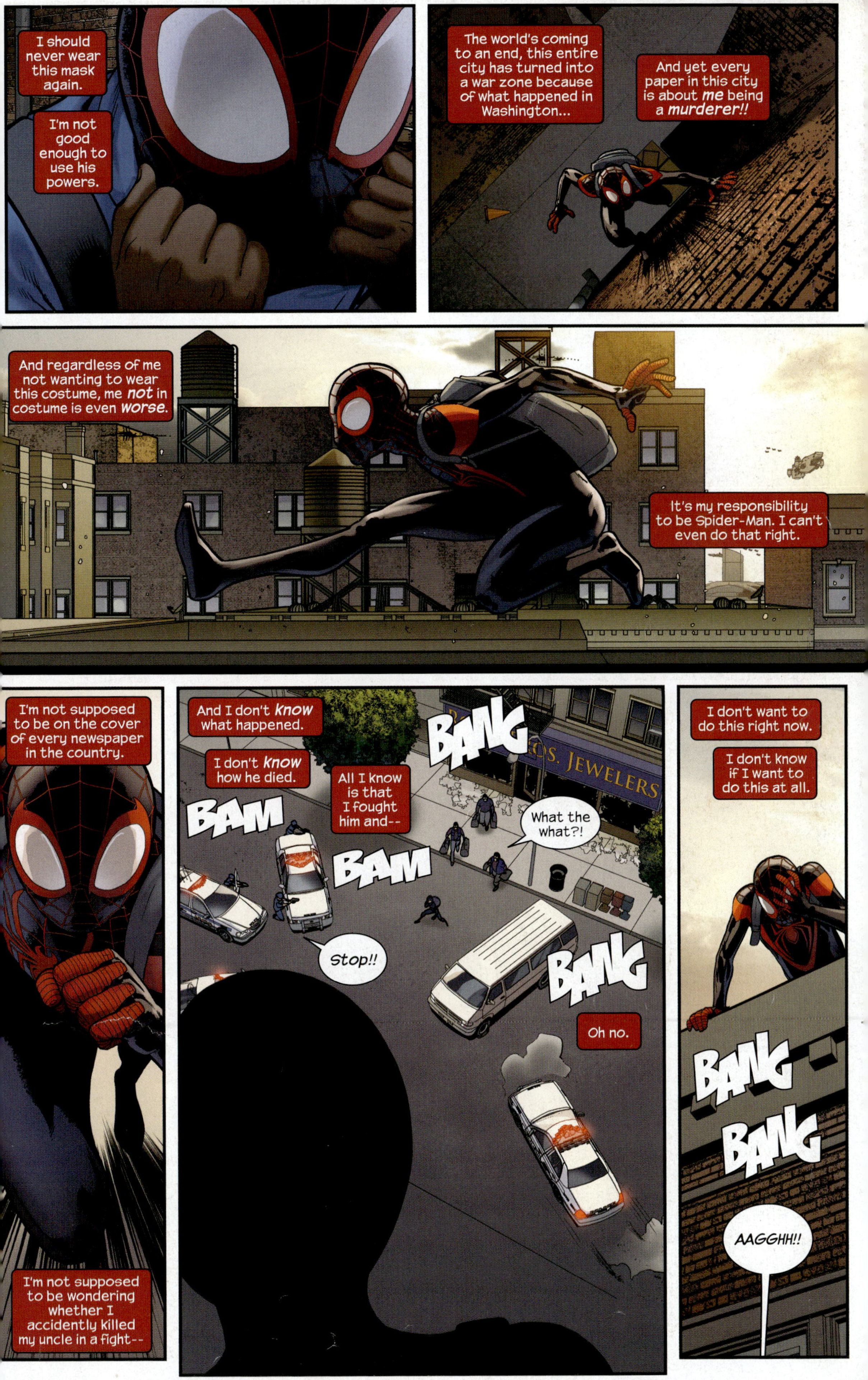
I should never wear this mask again.
I'm not good enough to use his powers.
The world's coming to an end, this entire city has turned into a war zone because of what happened in Washington...
And yet every paper in this city is about *me* being a *murderer!!*
And regardless of me not wanting to wear this costume, me *not* in costume is even *worse.*
It's my responsibility to be Spider-Man. I can't even do that right.
I'm not supposed to be on the cover of every newspaper in the country.
I'm not supposed to be wondering whether I accidently killed my uncle in a fight--
And I don't *know* what happened.
I don't *know* how he died.
All I know is that I fought him and--
BANG
JEWELERS
BAM
What the what?!
BAM
Stop!!
BANG
Oh no.
I don't want to do this right now.
I don't know if I want to do this at all.
BANG
BANG
AAGGHH!!

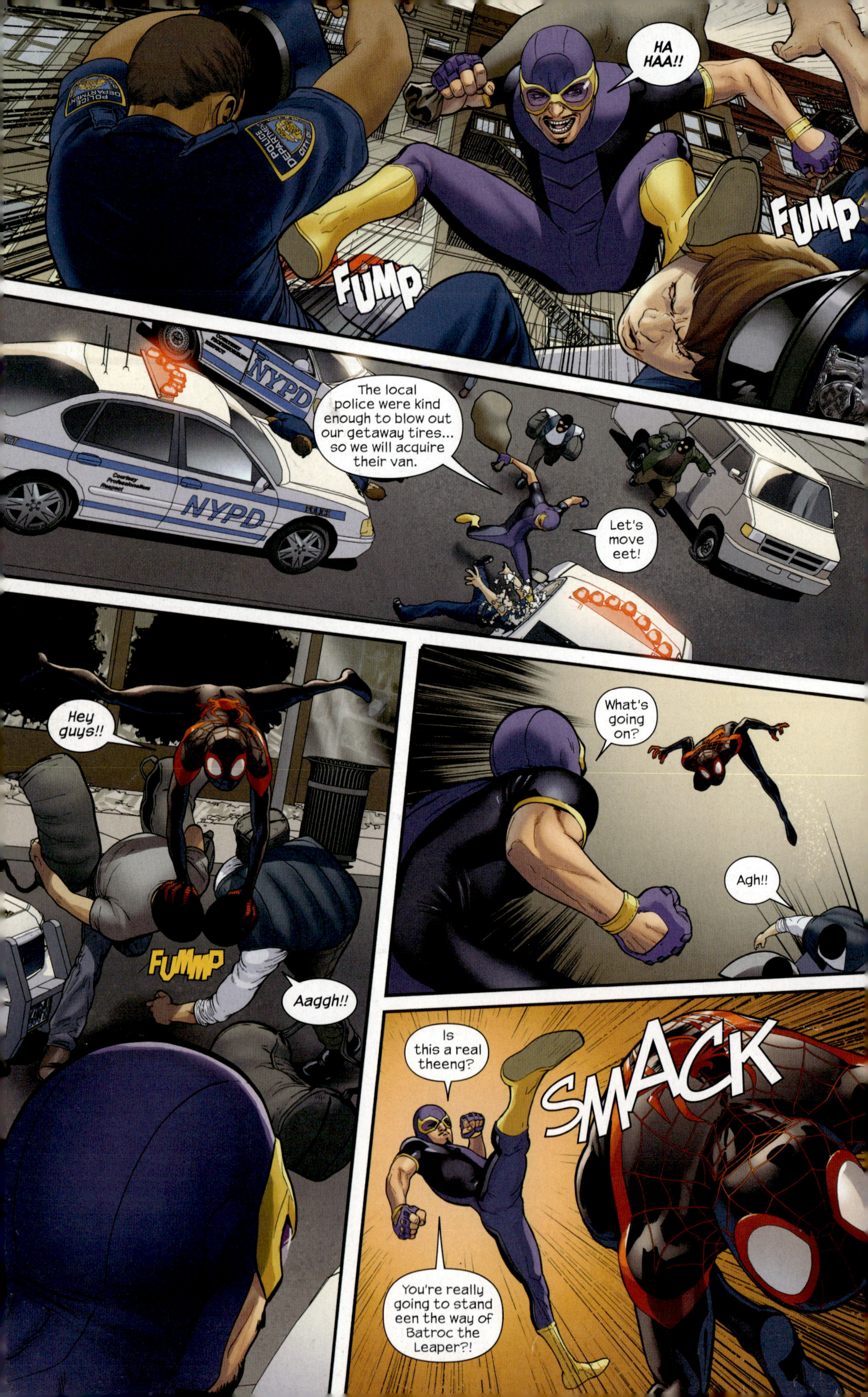
HA HAA!!
FUMP
FUMP
NYPD
NYPD
The local police were kind enough to blow out our getaway tires... so we will acquire their van.
Let's move eet!
Hey guys!!
FUMMP
Aaggh!!
What's going on?
Agh!!
Is this a real theeng?
SMACK
You're really going to stand een the way of Batroc the Leaper?!

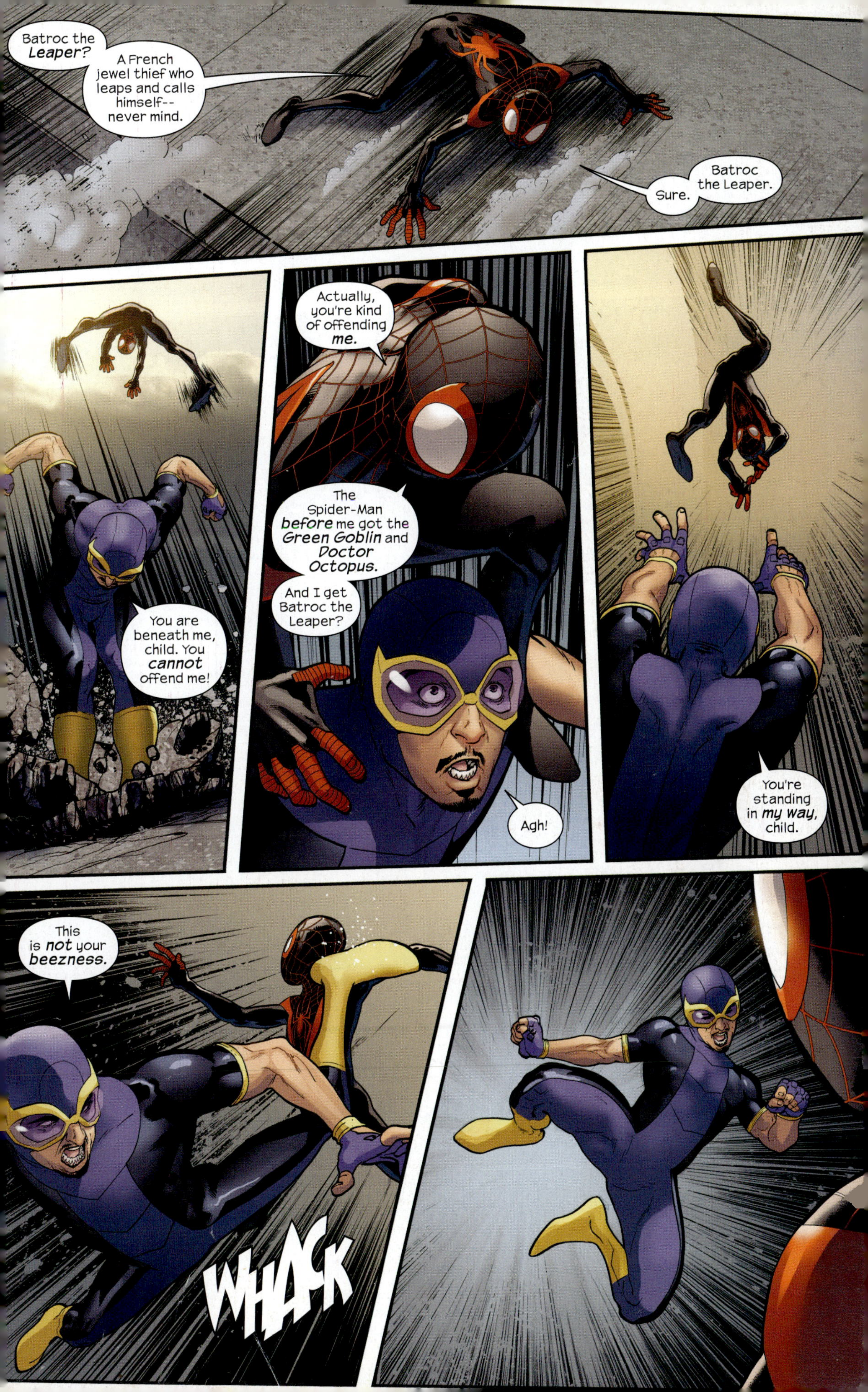

Batroc the *Leaper?*
A French jewel thief who leaps and calls himself-- never mind.
Sure.
Batroc the Leaper.
You are beneath me, child. You *cannot* offend me!
Actually, you're kind of offending *me.*
The Spider-Man *before* me got the *Green Goblin* and *Doctor Octopus.*
And I get Batroc the Leaper?
Agh!
You're standing in *my way,* child.
This is *not* your *beezness.*
WHACK

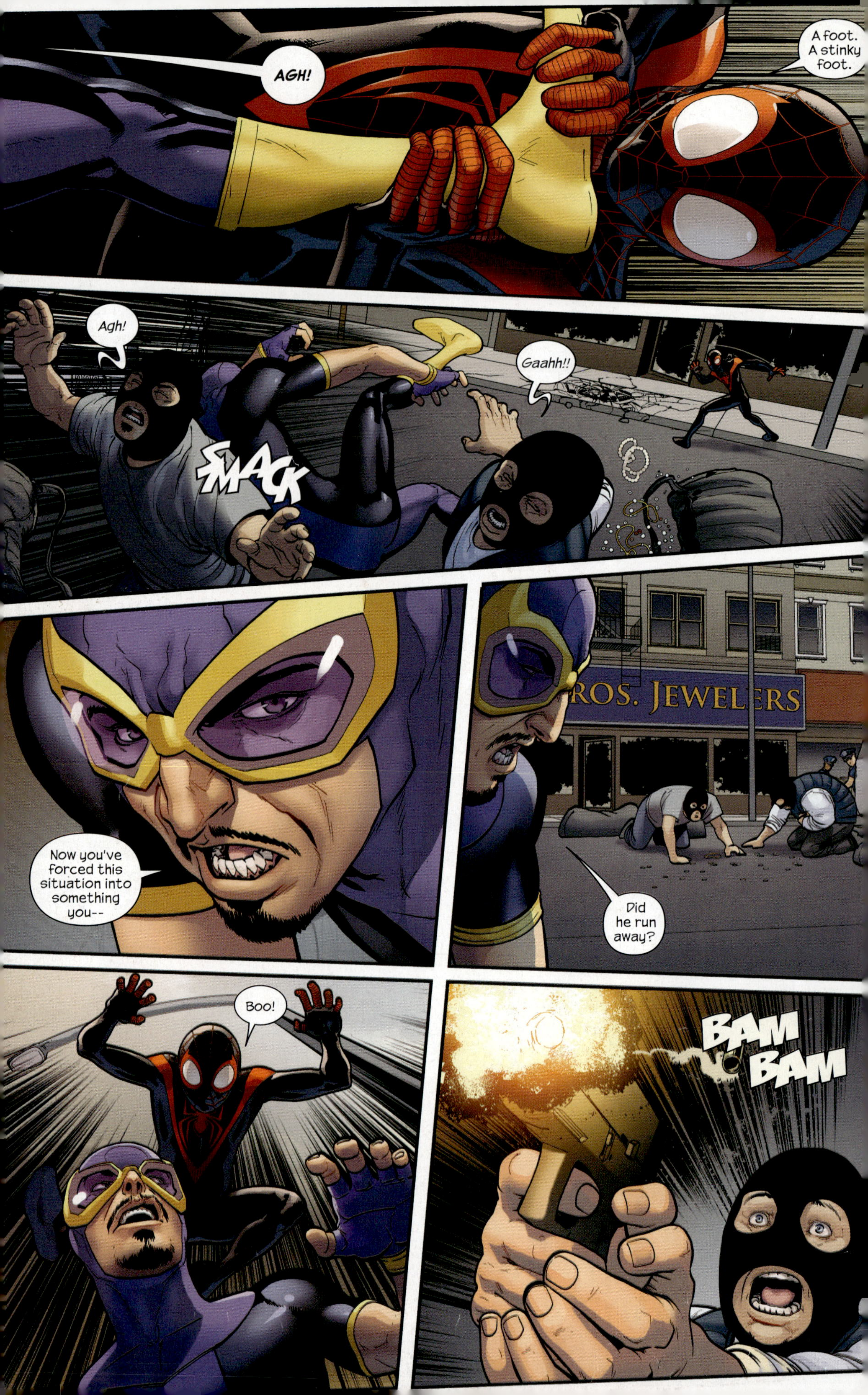
AGH!
A foot. A stinky foot.
Agh!
SMACK
Gaahh!!
Now you've forced this situation into something you--
ROS. JEWELERS
Did he run away?
Boo!
BAM
BAM

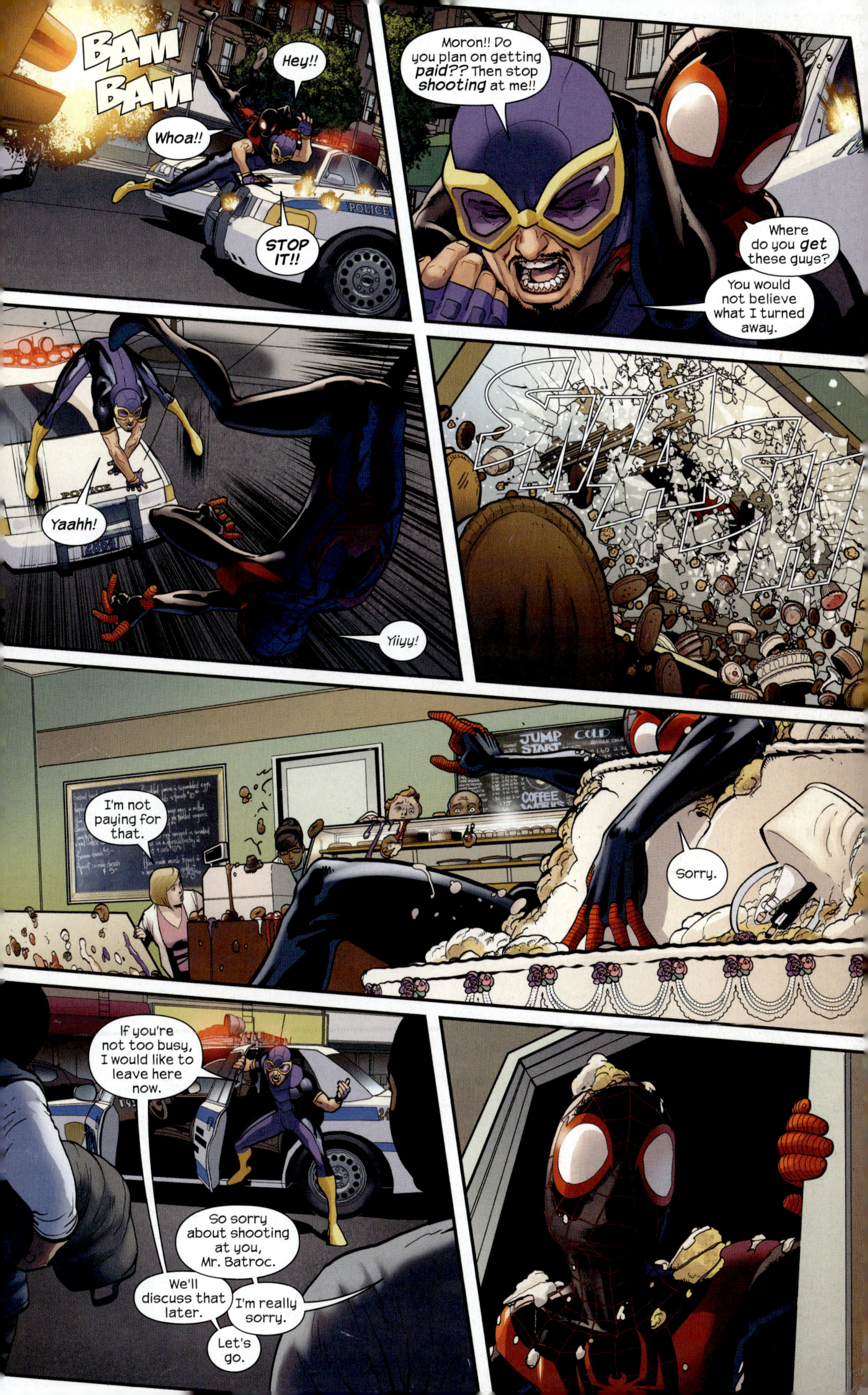
BAM BAM
Hey!!
Whoa!!
STOP IT!!
Moron!! Do you plan on getting paid?? Then stop shooting at me!!
Where do you get these guys?
You would not believe what I turned away.
Yaahh!
Yiiyy!
I'm not paying for that.
Sorry.
JUMP START
COLD
COFFEE
If you're not too busy, I would like to leave here now.
So sorry about shooting at you, Mr. Batroc.
We'll discuss that later.
I'm really sorry.
Let's go.

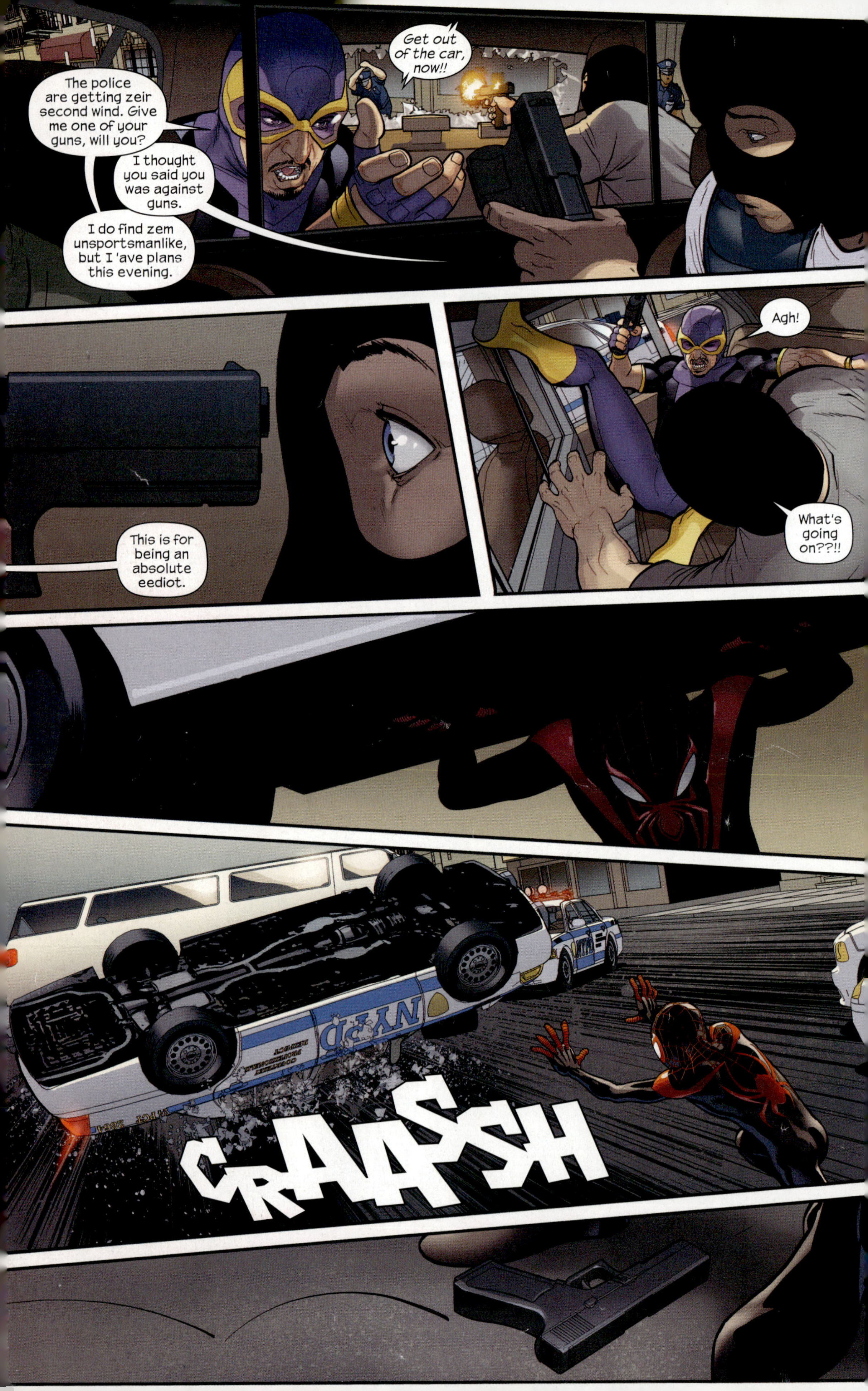
The police are getting zeir second wind. Give me one of your guns, will you?
Get out of the car, now!!
I thought you said you was against guns.
I do find zem unsportsmanlike, but I 'ave plans this evening.
This is for being an absolute eediot.
Agh!
What's going on??!!
CRAASH

Don't you pick up that weapon!

Hands on your head.

But--

TAKE OFF THAT MASK!!

I was the one that stopped the--

SHUT YOUR MOUTH!!

You have the right to remain silent!!

I didn't *do* anything.

You're *wanted* for murder!!

BAM BAM

Jeez Louise!!

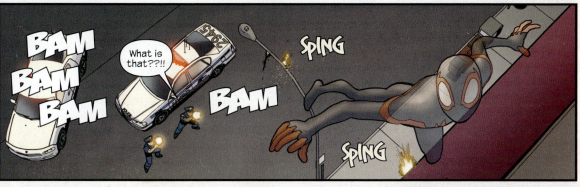

BAM BAM BAM

What is that??!!

SPING

BAM

SPING

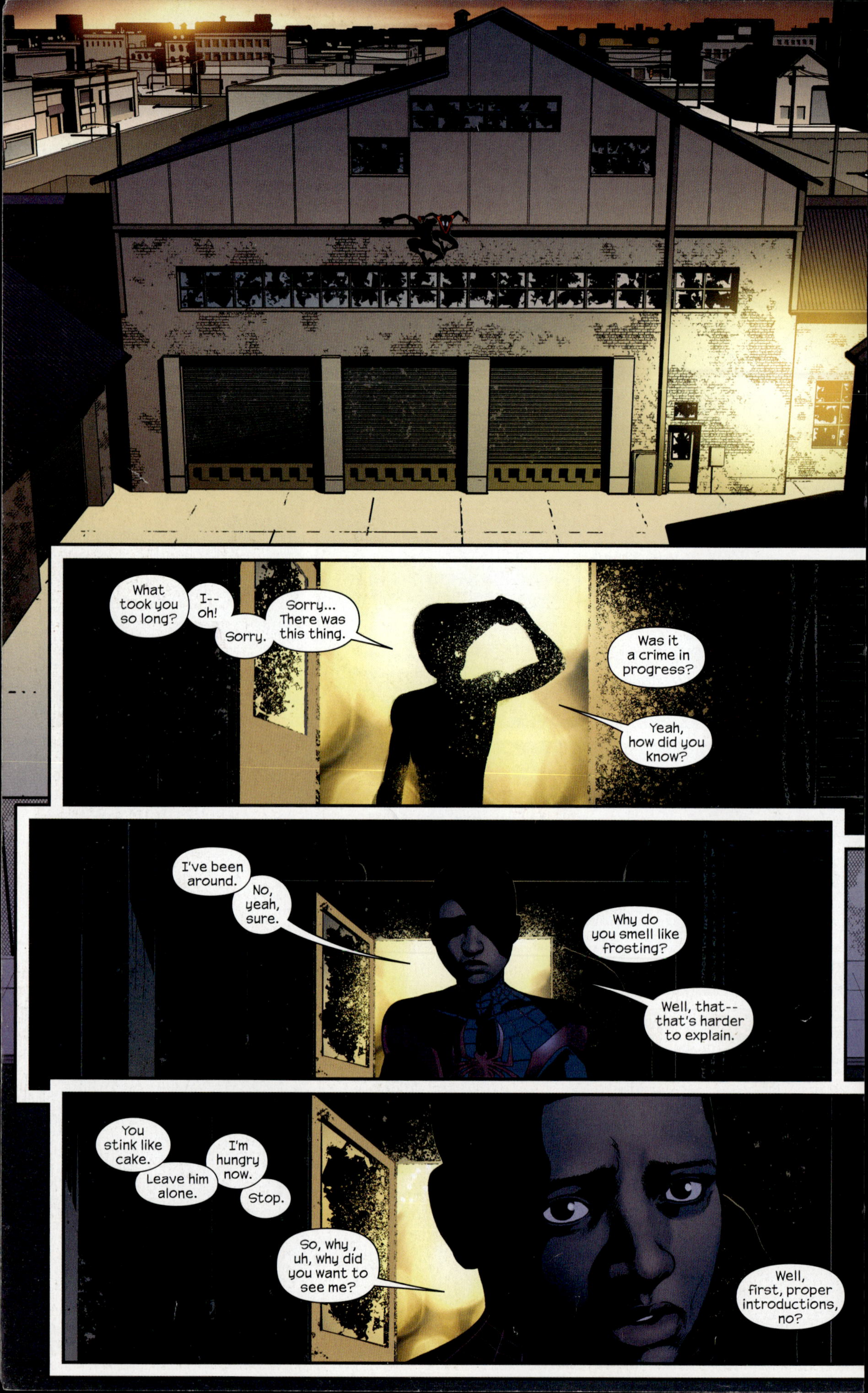
What took you so long?
I-- oh!
Sorry.
Sorry... There was this thing.
Was it a crime in progress?
Yeah, how did you know?
I've been around.
No, yeah, sure.
Why do you smell like frosting?
Well, that-- that's harder to explain.
You stink like cake.
Leave him alone.
I'm hungry now.
Stop.
So, why, uh, why did you want to see me?
Well, first, proper introductions, no?

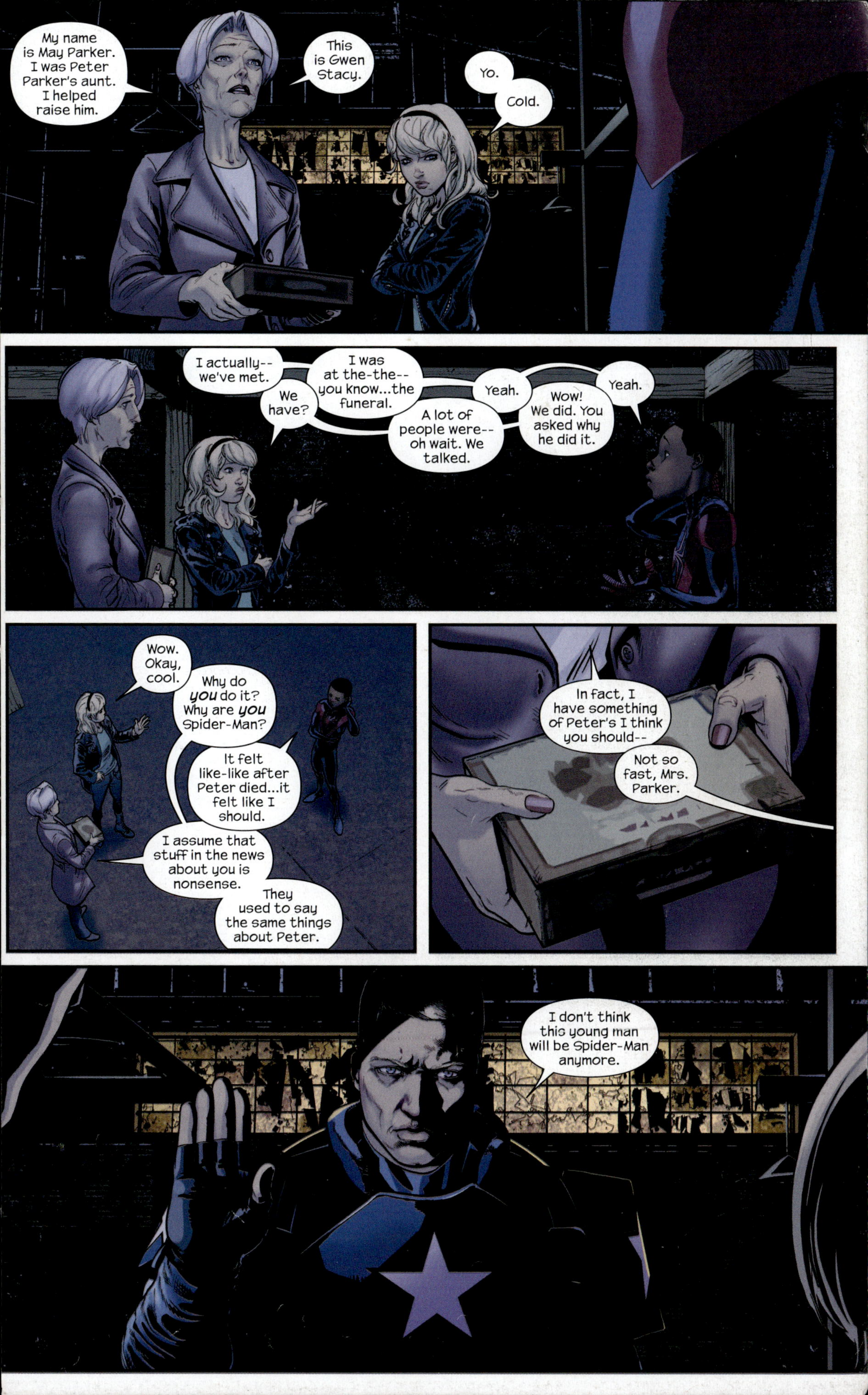
My name is May Parker. I was Peter Parker's aunt. I helped raise him.
This is Gwen Stacy.
Yo.
Cold.
I actually--we've met.
We have?
I was at the-the--you know...the funeral.
A lot of people were--oh wait. We talked.
Yeah.
Wow! We did. You asked why he did it.
Yeah.
Wow. Okay, cool.
Why do ***you*** do it? Why are ***you*** Spider-Man?
It felt like-like after Peter died...it felt like I should.
I assume that stuff in the news about you is nonsense.
They used to say the same things about Peter.
In fact, I have something of Peter's I think you should--
Not so fast, Mrs. Parker.
I don't think this young man will be Spider-Man anymore.

DIVIDED WE FALL!

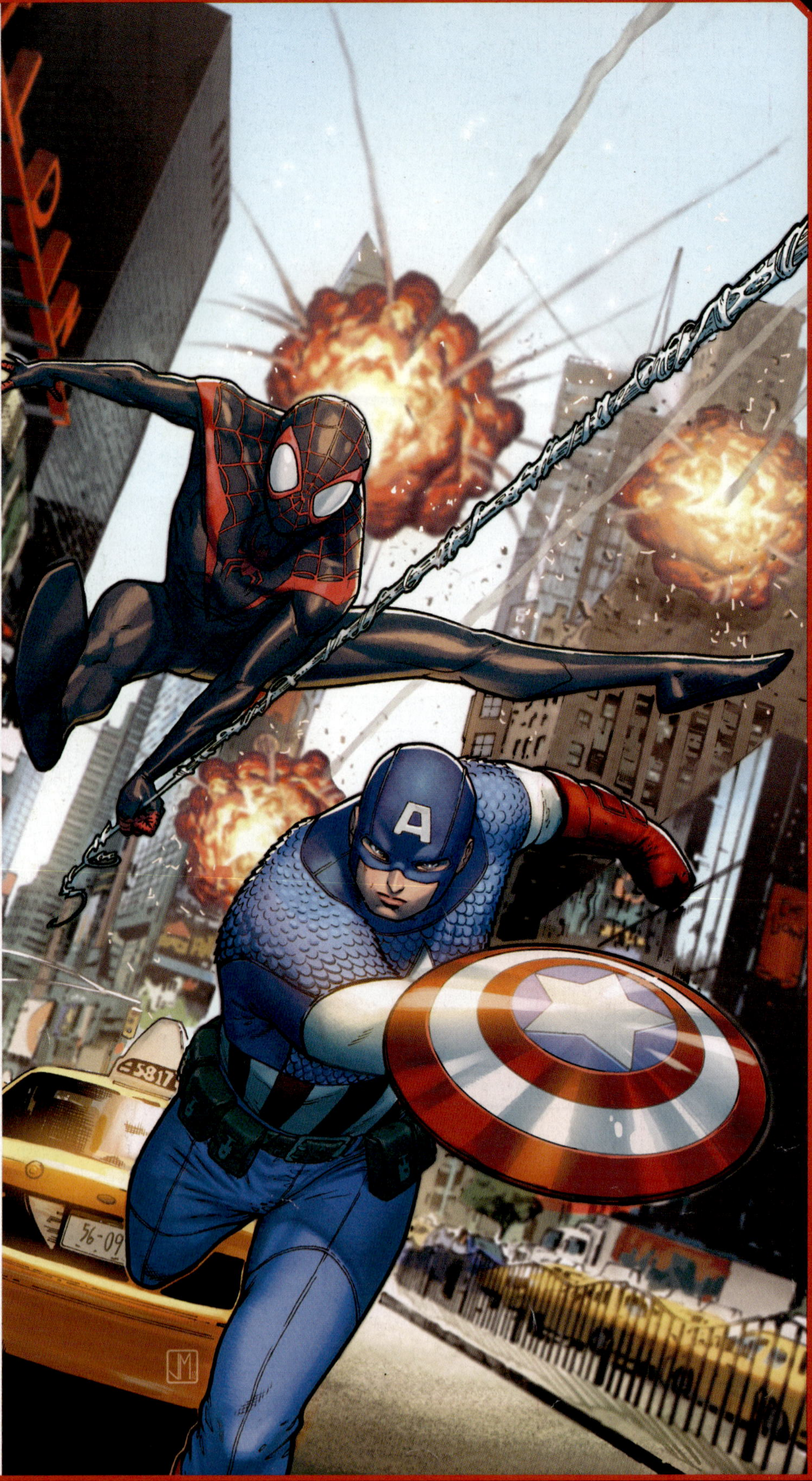
5817
56-09

S.H.I.E.L.D. SITUATION MAP:

[Anti-government militia hot spots]

Montana, N. Dakota, S. Dakota, Wyoming, Arizona, New Mexico, N. Carolina, S. Carolina, Georgia

[Eastern seaboard control zone]

New England, New York, New Jersey, Delaware, Washington D.C., Maryland, Virginia

secured by National Guard under emergency powers committee

[the West Coast]

California, Oregon, Washington

status unknown

[Great Lakes states]

Minnesota, Wisconsin, Michigan, Illinois, Indiana, Ohio

status unknown

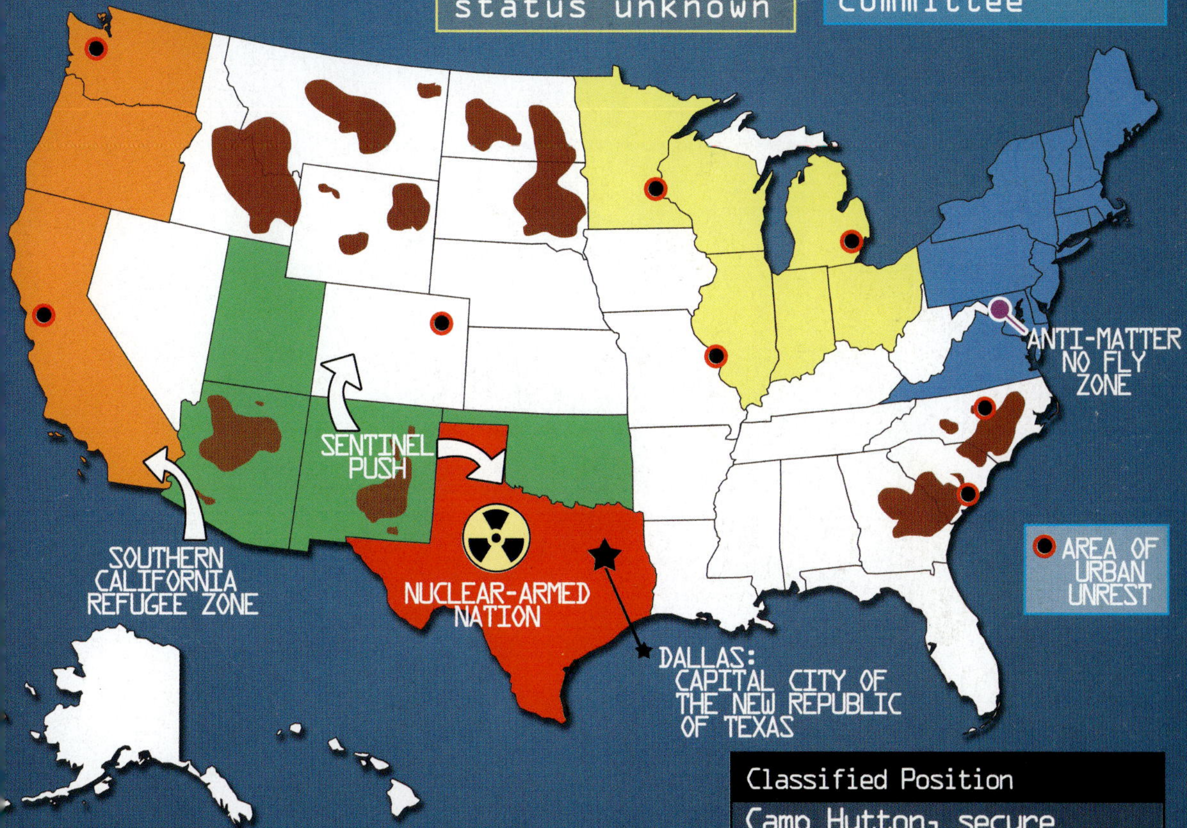
ANTI-MATTER NO FLY ZONE
SENTINEL PUSH
SOUTHERN CALIFORNIA REFUGEE ZONE
NUCLEAR-ARMED NATION
DALLAS: CAPITAL CITY OF THE NEW REPUBLIC OF TEXAS
AREA OF URBAN UNREST

Classified Position

Camp Hutton, secure location of the President of the United States

[Sentinel-controlled no-man's-land]

New Mexico, Arizona, Utah, Oklahoma

abandoned by the U.S. government

[The New Republic of Texas]

Texas

declared state independence

ALL STATES SHOWN IN WHITE ARE U.S. GOVERNMENT-CONTROLLED ZONES

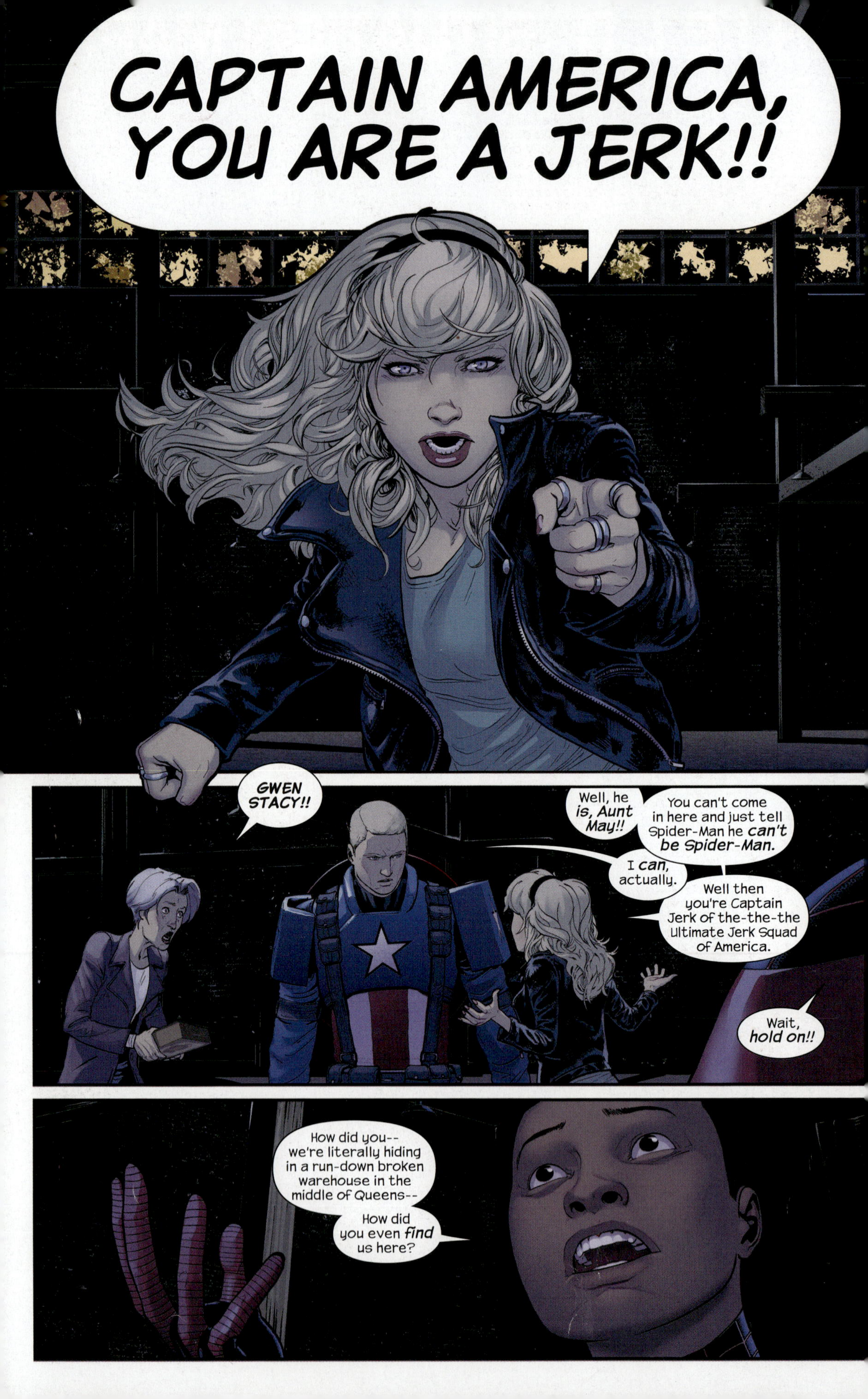
CAPTAIN AMERICA, YOU ARE A JERK!!
GWEN STACY!!
Well, he is, Aunt May!!
You can't come in here and just tell Spider-Man he can't be Spider-Man.
I can, actually.
Well then you're Captain Jerk of the-the-the Ultimate Jerk Squad of America.
Wait, hold on!!
How did you-- we're literally hiding in a run-down broken warehouse in the middle of Queens--
How did you even find us here?

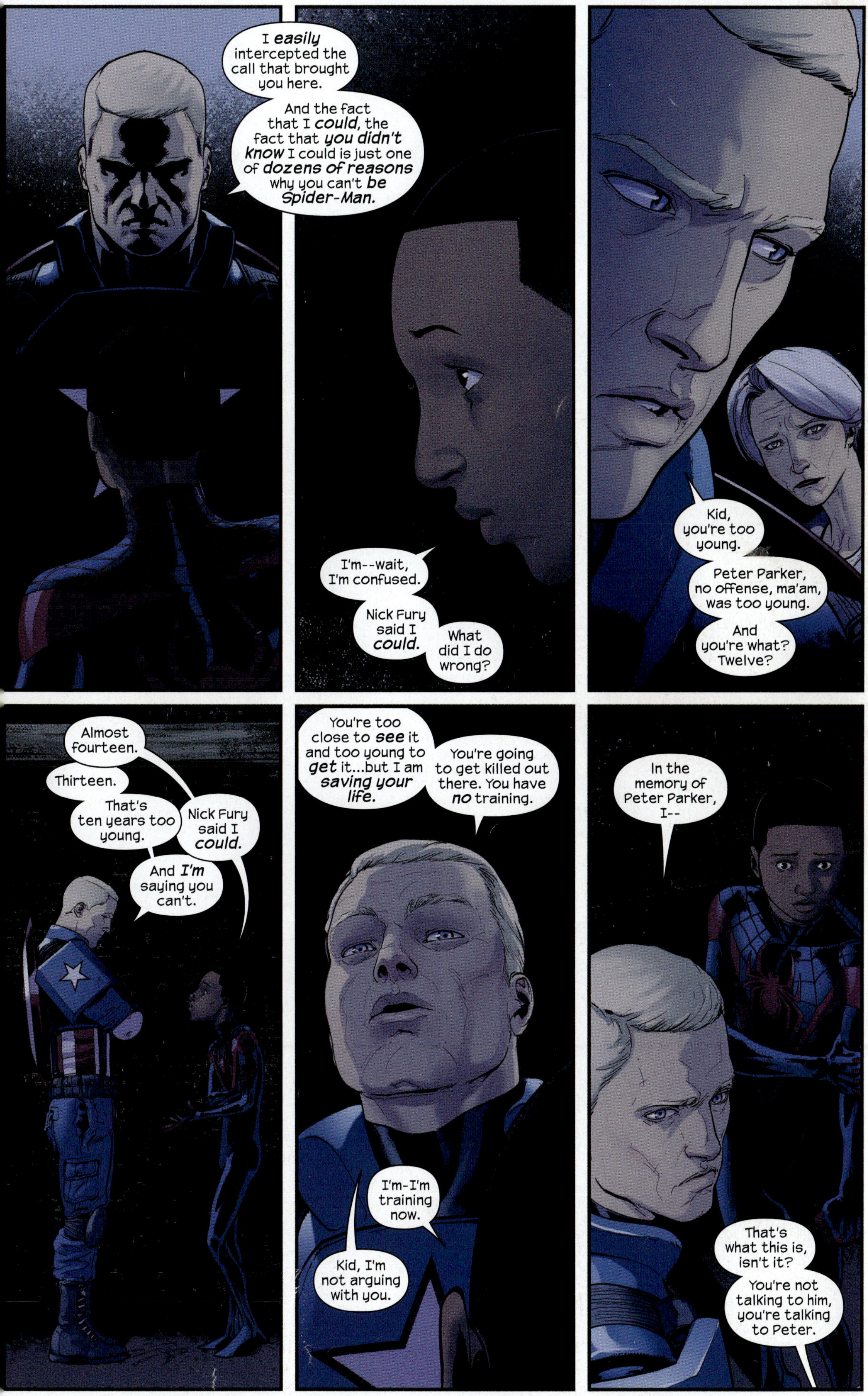
I easily intercepted the call that brought you here.
And the fact that I could, the fact that you didn't know I could is just one of dozens of reasons why you can't be Spider-Man.
I'm--wait, I'm confused.
Nick Fury said I could.
What did I do wrong?
Kid, you're too young.
Peter Parker, no offense, ma'am, was too young.
And you're what? Twelve?
Almost fourteen.
Thirteen.
That's ten years too young.
Nick Fury said I could.
And I'm saying you can't.
You're too close to see it and too young to get it...but I am saving your life.
You're going to get killed out there. You have no training.
I'm-I'm training now.
Kid, I'm not arguing with you.
In the memory of Peter Parker, I--
That's what this is, isn't it?
You're not talking to him, you're talking to Peter.

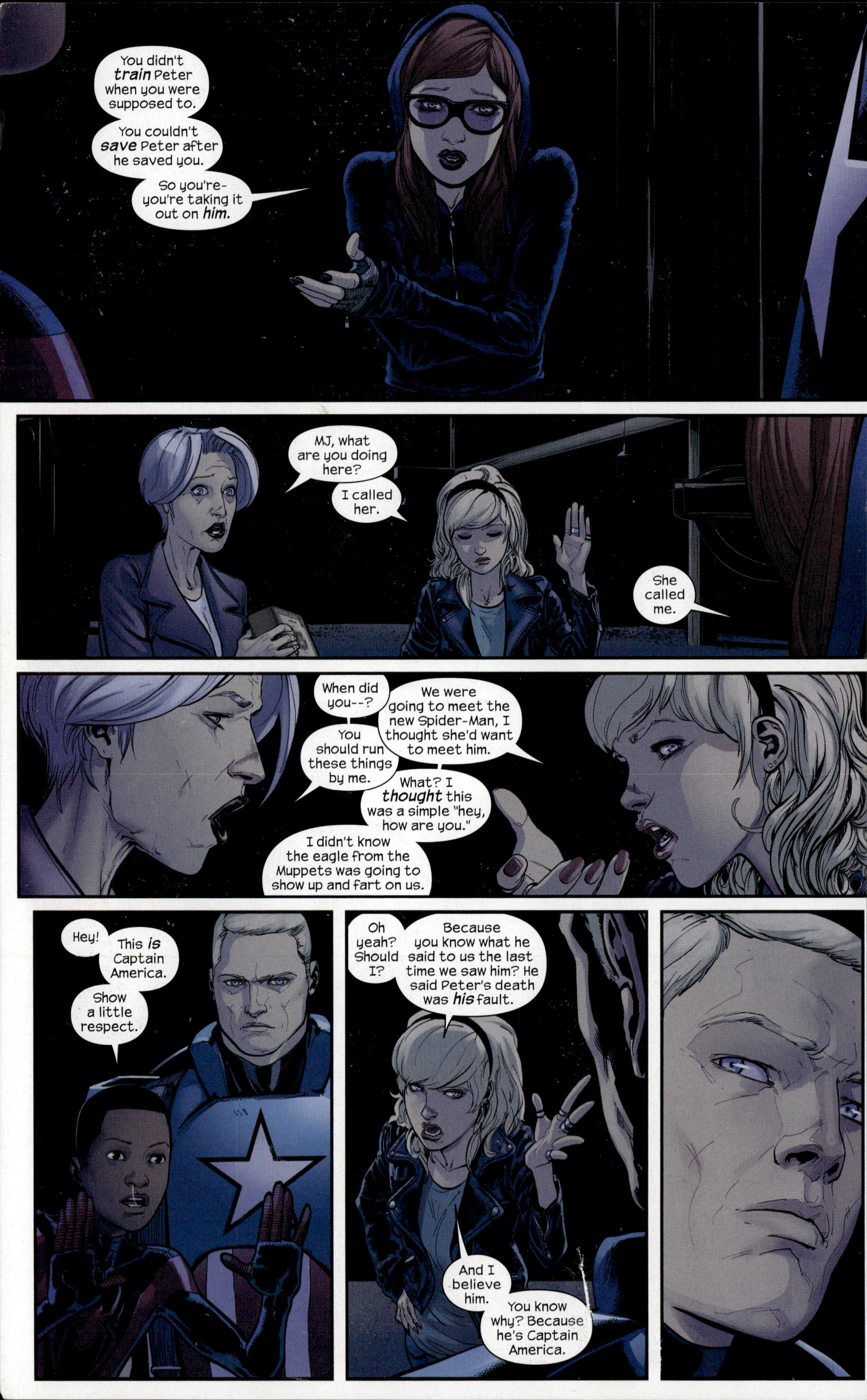
You didn't *train* Peter when you were supposed to.
You couldn't *save* Peter after he saved you.
So you're- you're taking it out on *him.*
MJ, what are you doing here?
I called her.
She called me.
When did you--?
You should run these things by me.
We were going to meet the new Spider-Man, I thought she'd want to meet him.
What? I *thought* this was a simple "hey, how are you."
I didn't know the eagle from the Muppets was going to show up and fart on us.
Hey!
This *is* Captain America.
Show a little respect.
Oh yeah? Should I?
Because you know what he said to us the last time we saw him? He said Peter's death was *his* fault.
And I believe him.
You know why? Because he's Captain America.

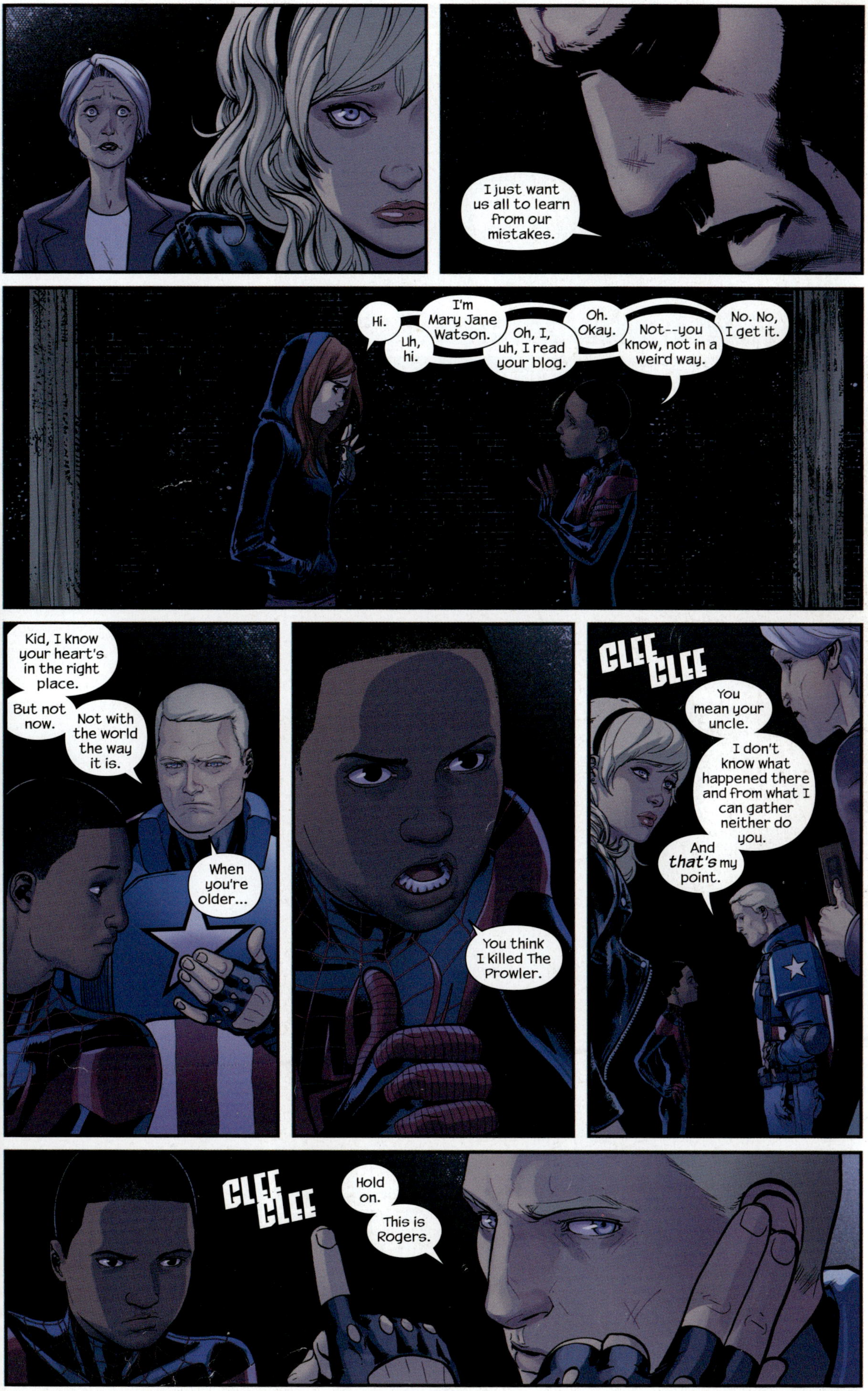
I just want us all to learn from our mistakes.
Hi.
I'm Mary Jane Watson.
Uh, hi.
Oh, I, uh, I read your blog.
Oh. Okay.
Not--you know, not in a weird way.
No. No, I get it.
Kid, I know your heart's in the right place.
But not now.
Not with the world the way it is.
When you're older...
You think I killed The Prowler.
CLEE CLEE
You mean your uncle.
I don't know what happened there and from what I can gather neither do you.
And that's my point.
CLEE CLEE
Hold on.
This is Rogers.

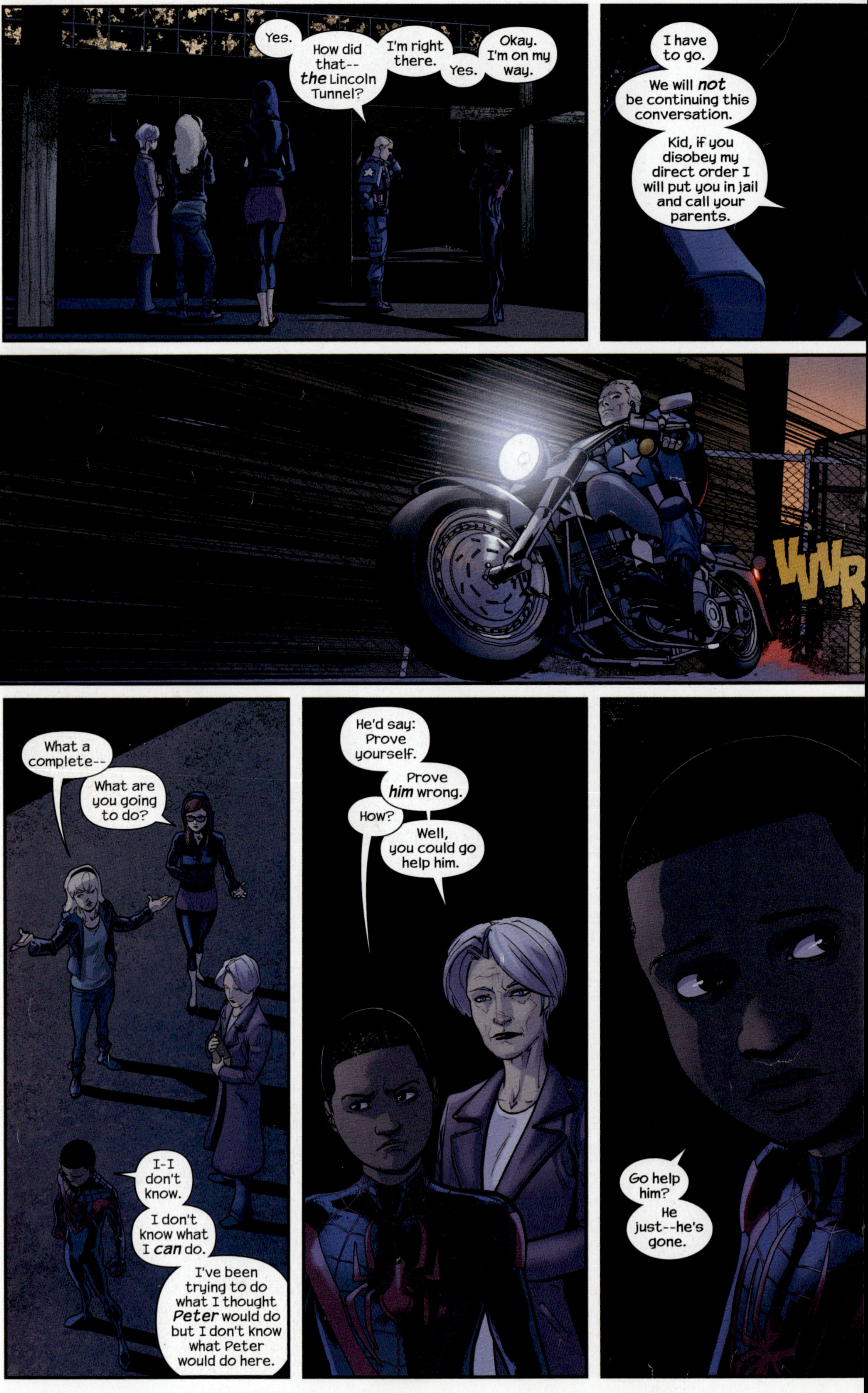
Yes.
How did that-- the Lincoln Tunnel?
I'm right there.
Yes.
Okay. I'm on my way.
I have to go.
We will not be continuing this conversation.
Kid, if you disobey my direct order I will put you in jail and call your parents.
VVVR
What a complete--
What are you going to do?
I-I don't know.
I don't know what I can do.
I've been trying to do what I thought Peter would do but I don't know what Peter would do here.
He'd say: Prove yourself.
Prove him wrong.
How?
Well, you could go help him.
Go help him?
He just--he's gone.

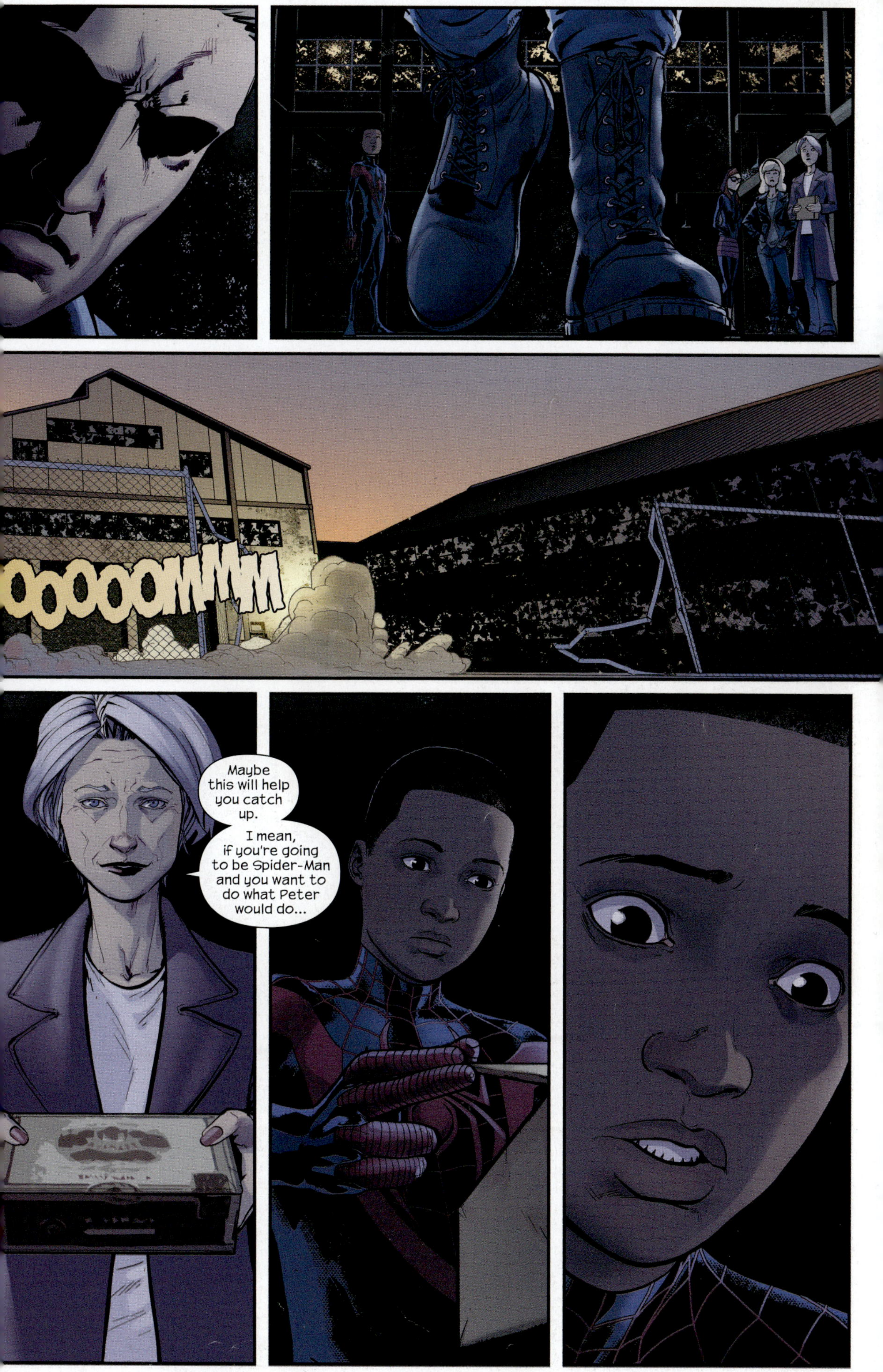
OOOOOMMMM
Maybe this will help you catch up.
I mean, if you're going to be Spider-Man and you want to do what Peter would do...

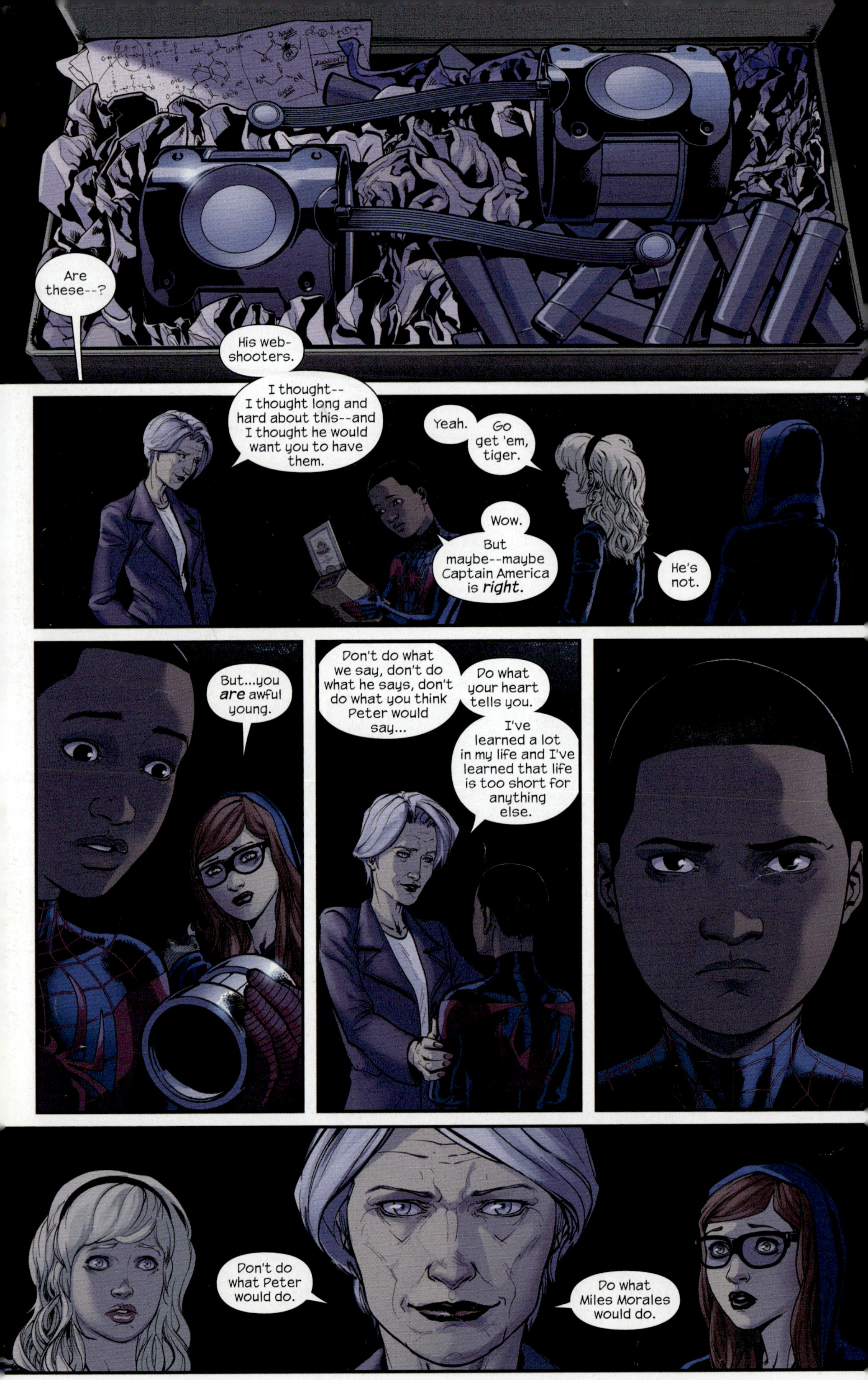
Are these--?
His web-shooters.
I thought-- I thought long and hard about this--and I thought he would want you to have them.
Yeah.
Go get 'em, tiger.
Wow.
But maybe--maybe Captain America is *right.*
He's not.
But...you ***are*** awful young.
Don't do what we say, don't do what he says, don't do what you think Peter would say...
Do what your heart tells you.
I've learned a lot in my life and I've learned that life is too short for anything else.
Don't do what Peter would do.
Do what Miles Morales would do.

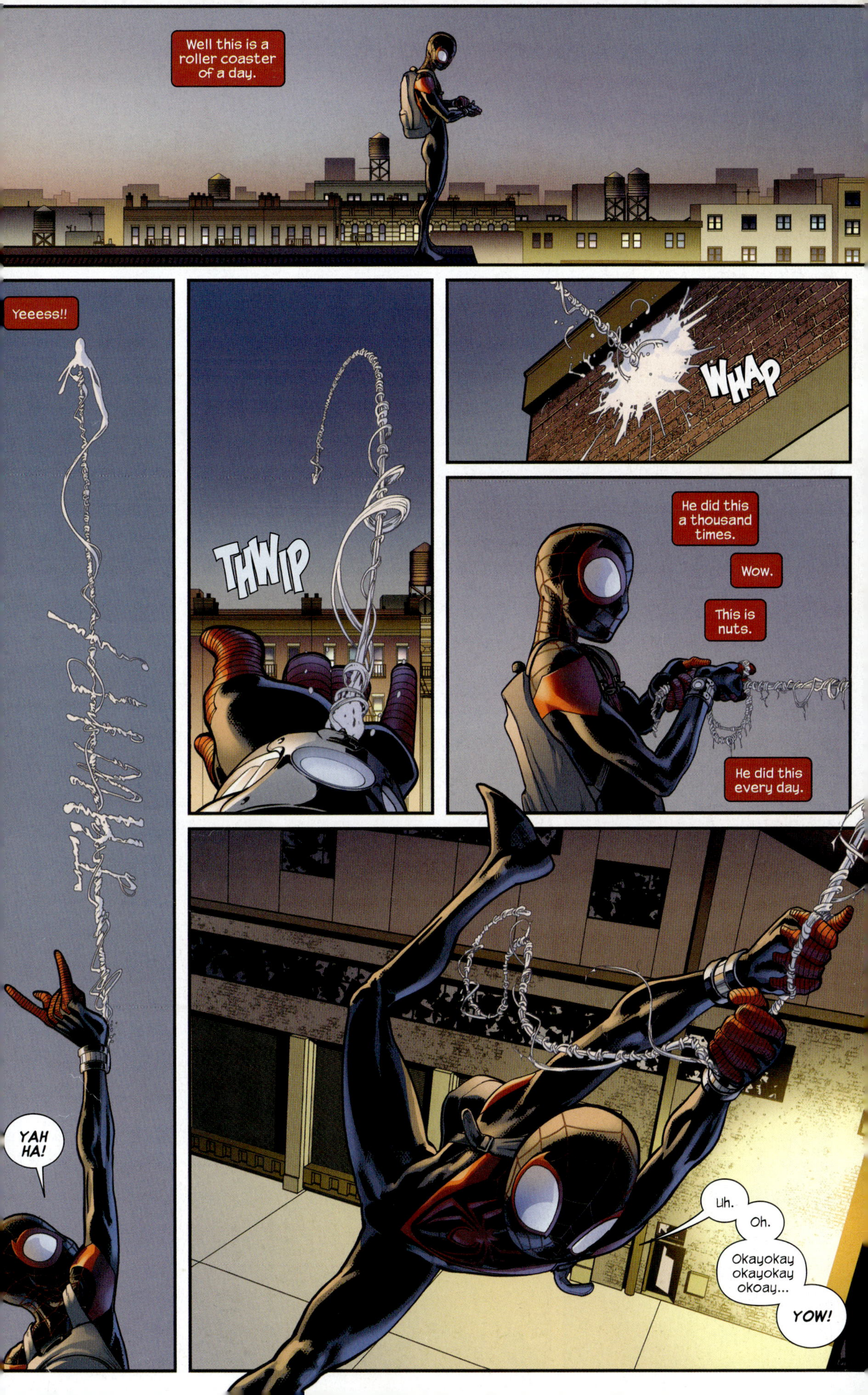
Well this is a roller coaster of a day.
Yeeess!!
YAH HA!
THWIP
WHAP
He did this a thousand times.
Wow.
This is nuts.
He did this every day.
Uh.
Oh.
Okayokay okayokay okoay...
YOW!

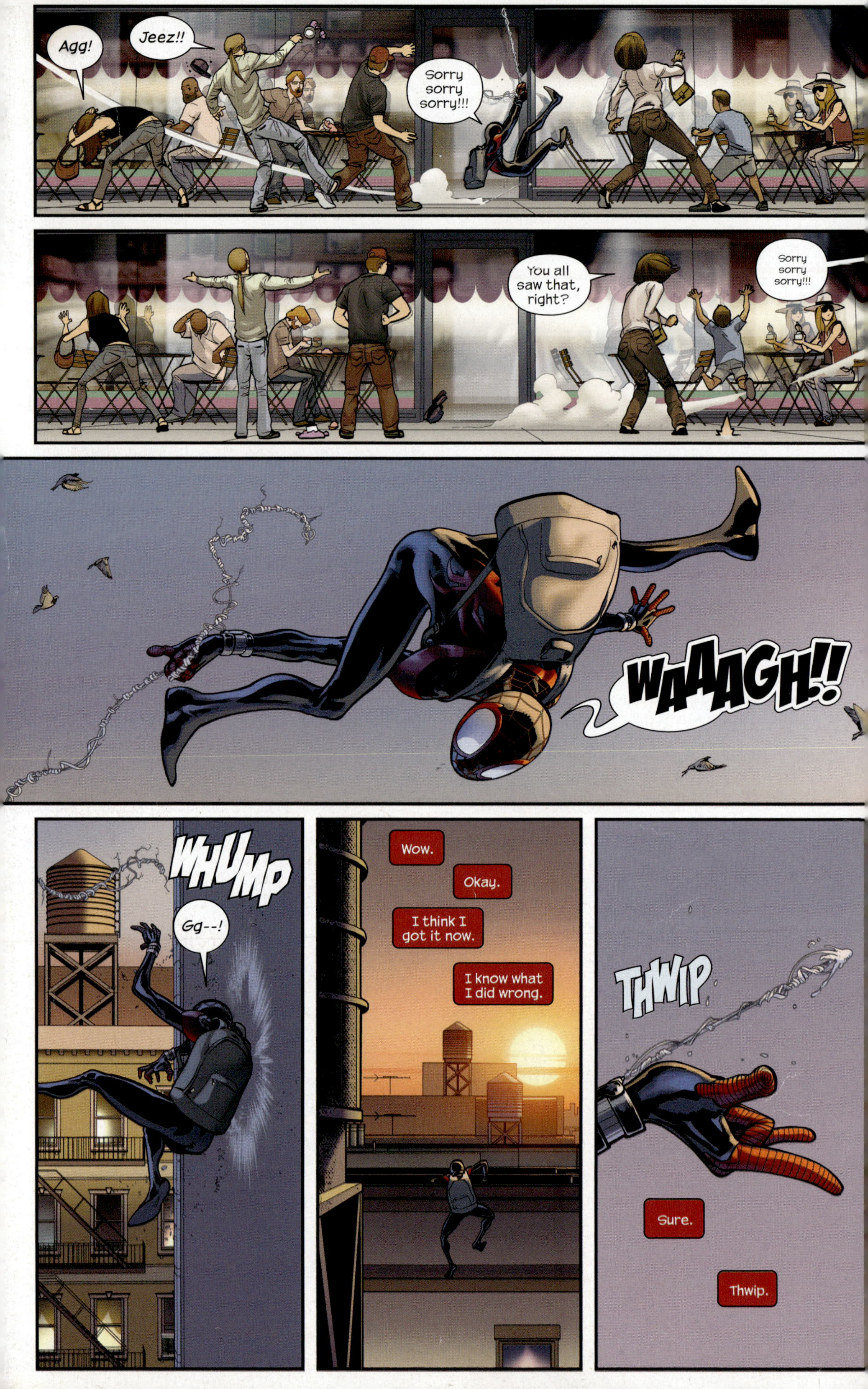
Agg!
Jeez!!
Sorry sorry sorry!!!
You all saw that, right?
Sorry sorry sorry!!!
WAAAGH!!
WHUMP
Gg--!
Wow.
Okay.
I think I got it now.
I know what I did wrong.
THWIP
Sure.
Thwip.

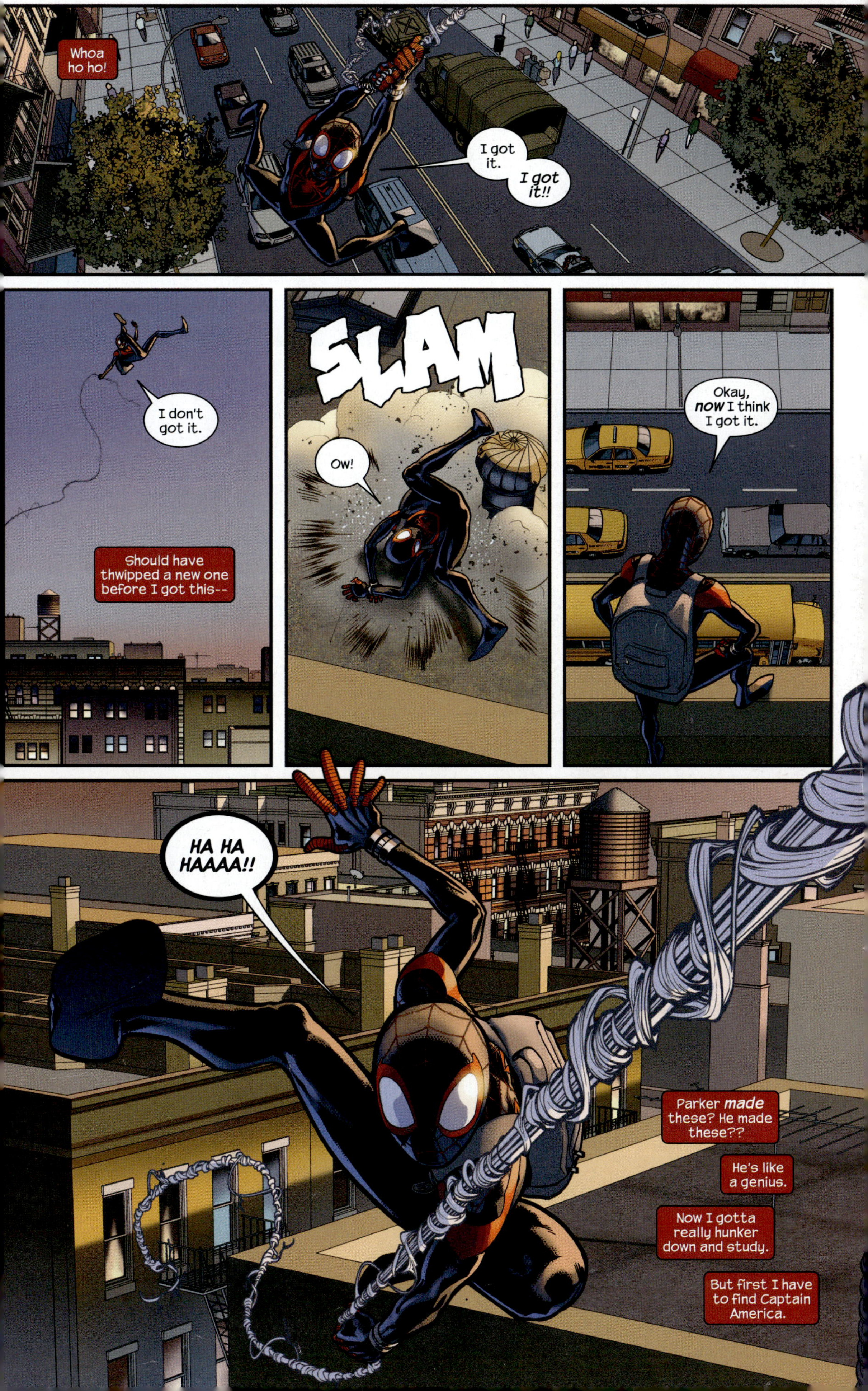
Whoa ho ho!
I got it.
I got it!!
I don't got it.
Should have thwipped a new one before I got this--
SLAM
Ow!
Okay, now I think I got it.
HA HA HAAAA!!
Parker made these? He made these??
He's like a genius.
Now I gotta really hunker down and study.
But first I have to find Captain America.

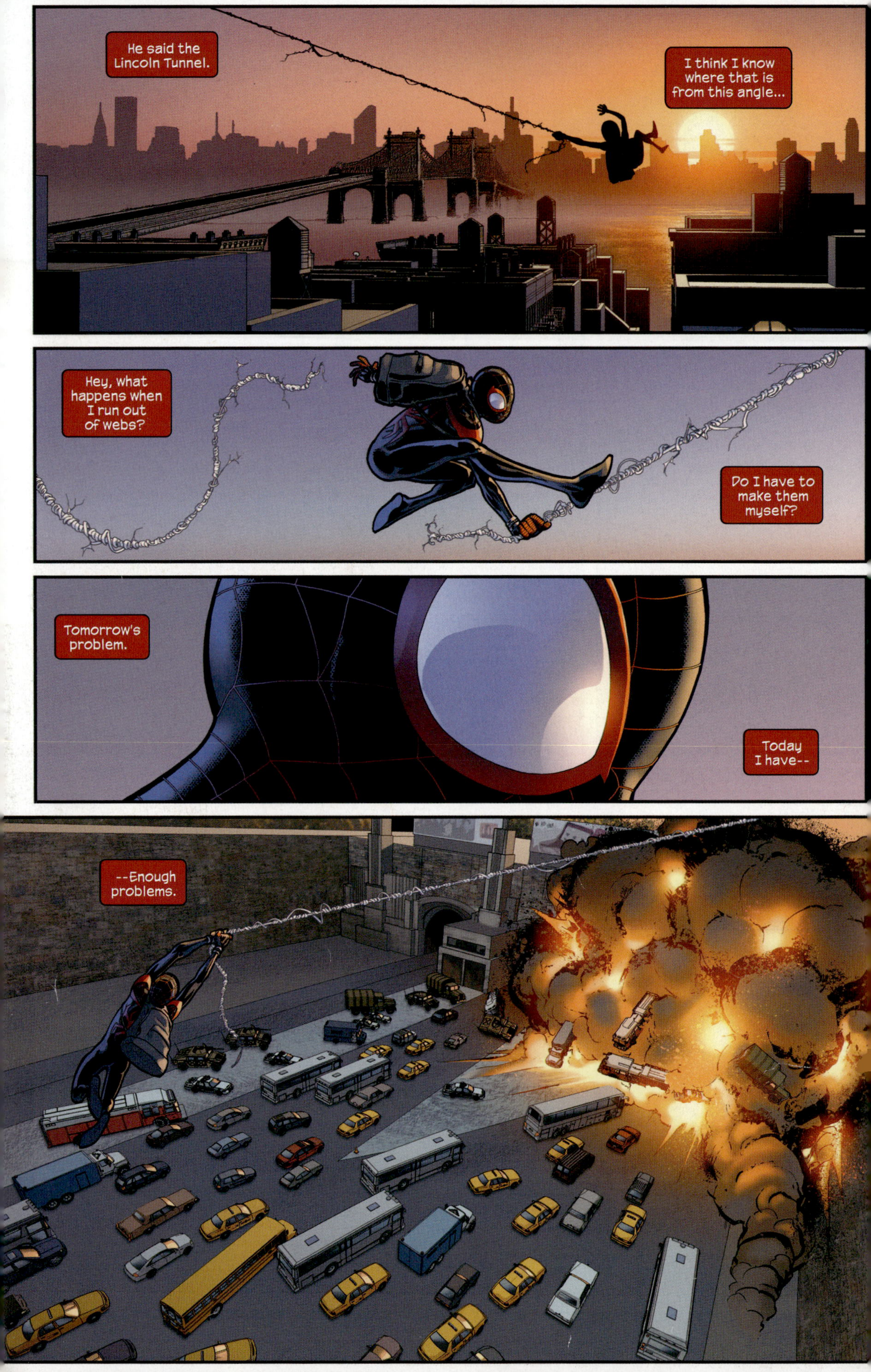
He said the Lincoln Tunnel.
I think I know where that is from this angle...
Hey, what happens when I run out of webs?
Do I have to make them myself?
Tomorrow's problem.
Today I have--
--Enough problems.

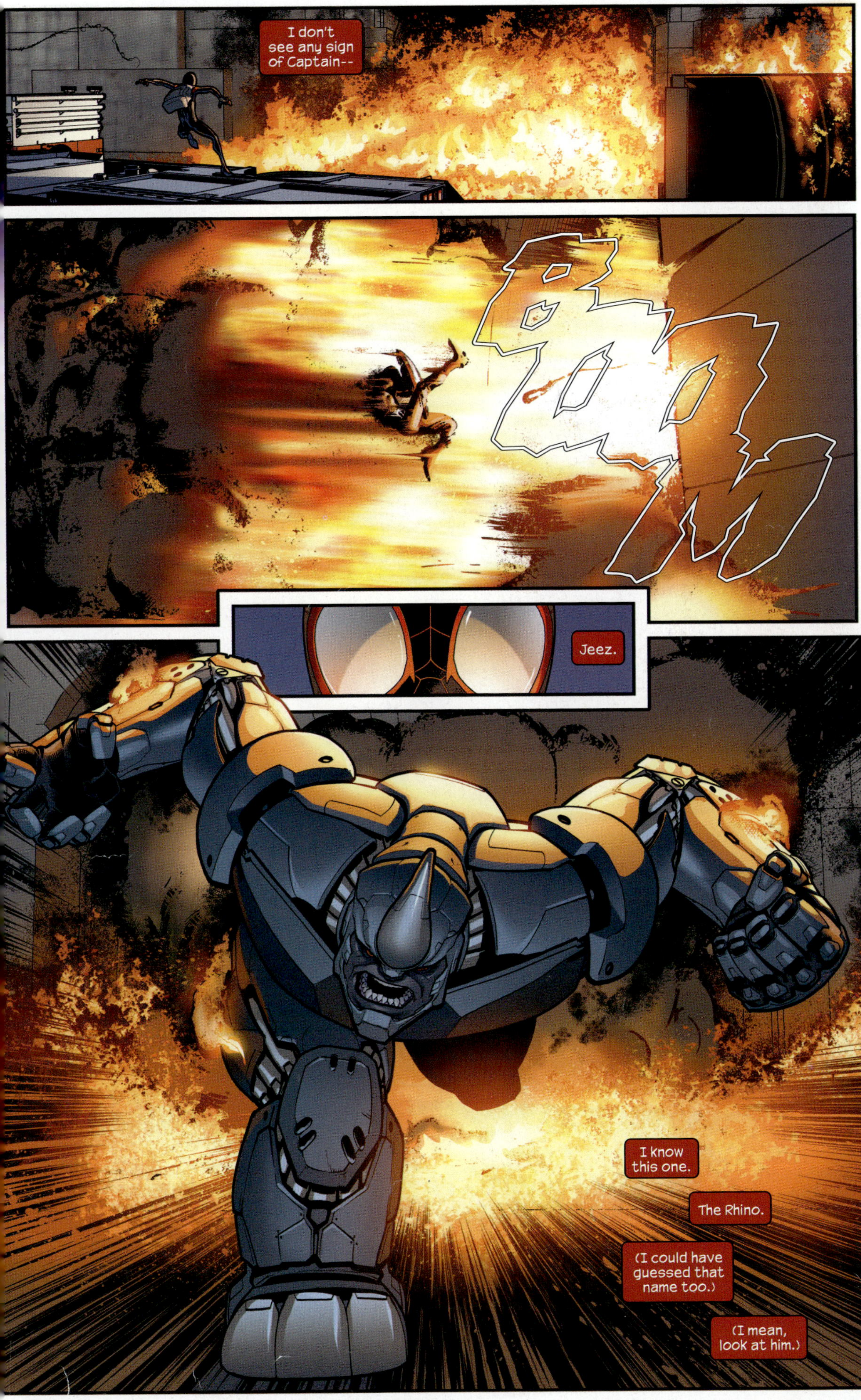

I don't see any sign of Captain--
BOOM
Jeez.
I know this one.
The Rhino.
(I could have guessed that name too.)
(I mean, look at him.)

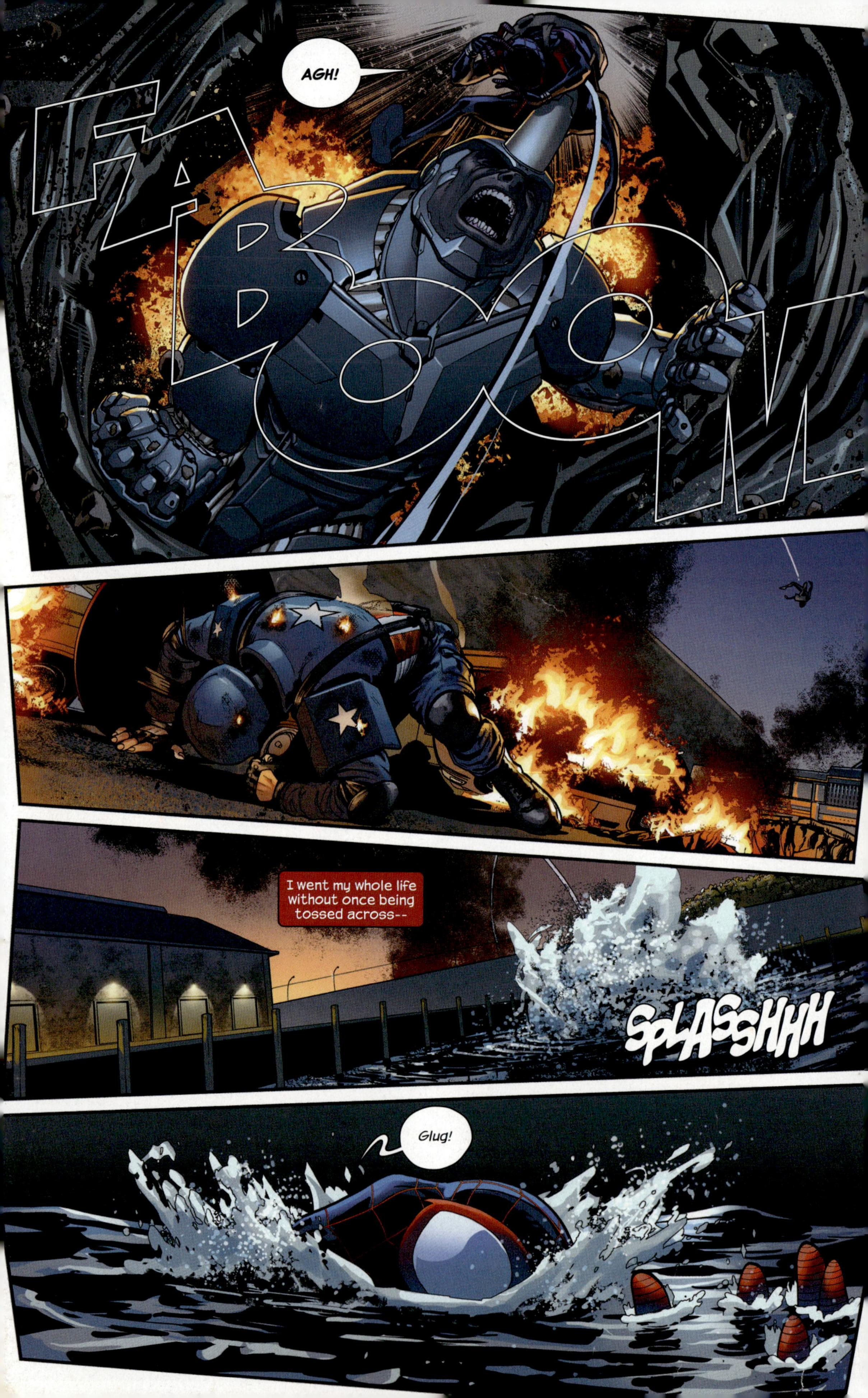
AGH!
FABOOM
I went my whole life without once being tossed across--
SPLASSHHH
Glug!

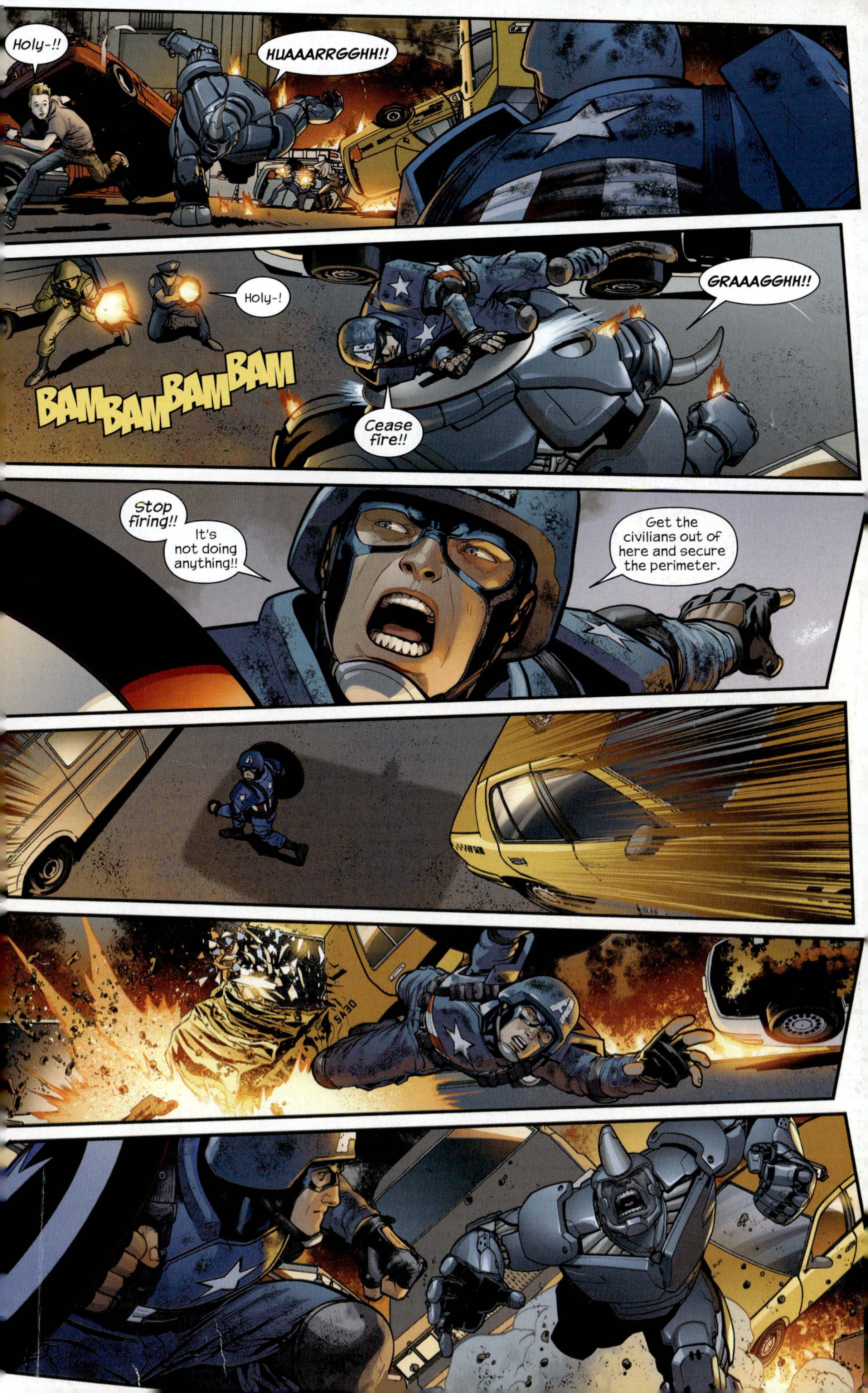
Holy-!!
HUAAARRGGHH!!
Holy-!
GRAAAGGHH!!
BAMBAMBAMBAM
Cease fire!!
Stop firing!!
It's not doing anything!!
Get the civilians out of here and secure the perimeter.

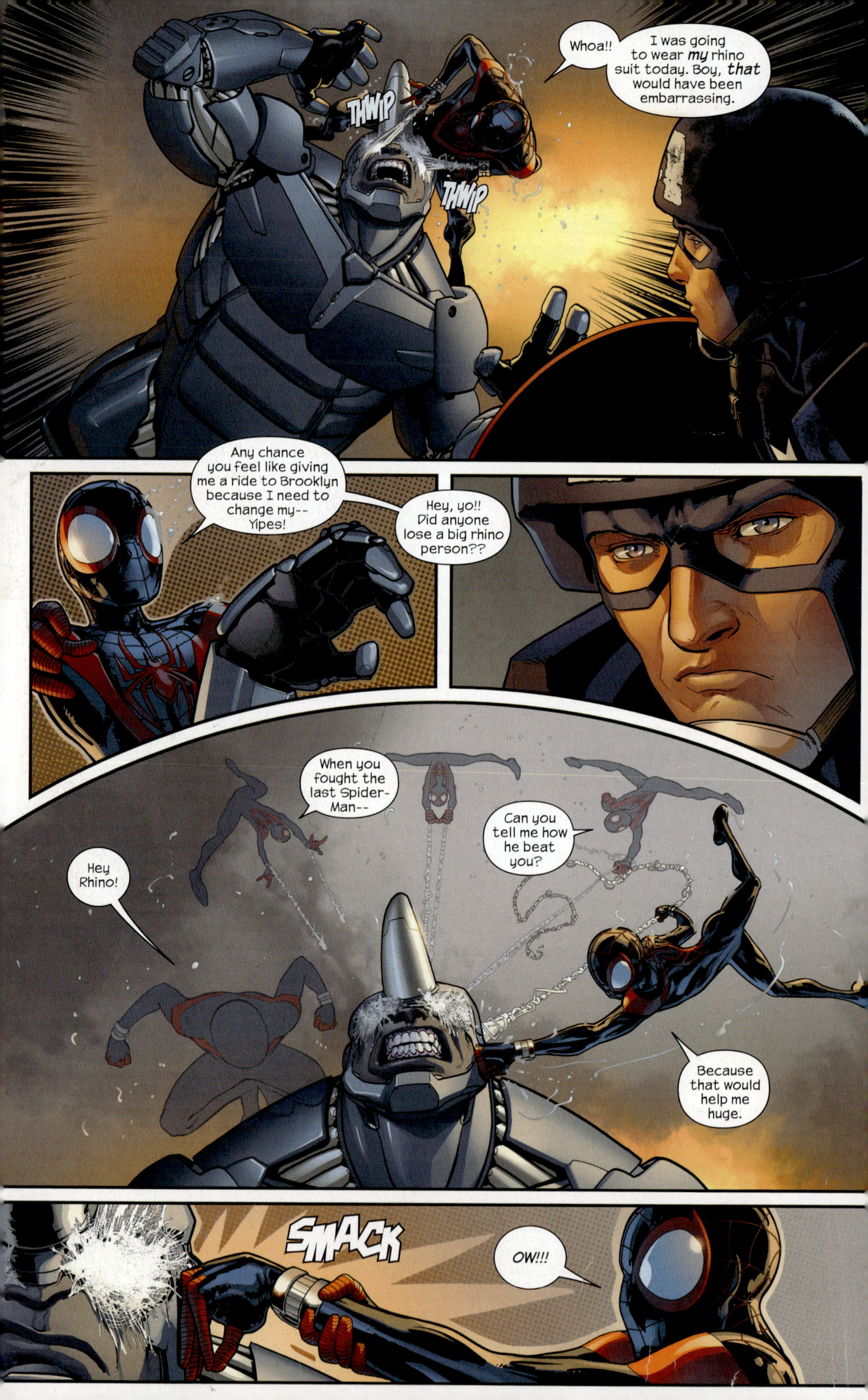
THWIP
THWIP
Whoa!!
I was going to wear *my* rhino suit today. Boy, ***that*** would have been embarrassing.
Any chance you feel like giving me a ride to Brooklyn because I need to change my-- Yipes!
Hey, yo!! Did anyone lose a big rhino person??
Hey Rhino!
When you fought the last Spider-Man--
Can you tell me how he beat you?
Because that would help me huge.
SMACK
OW!!!

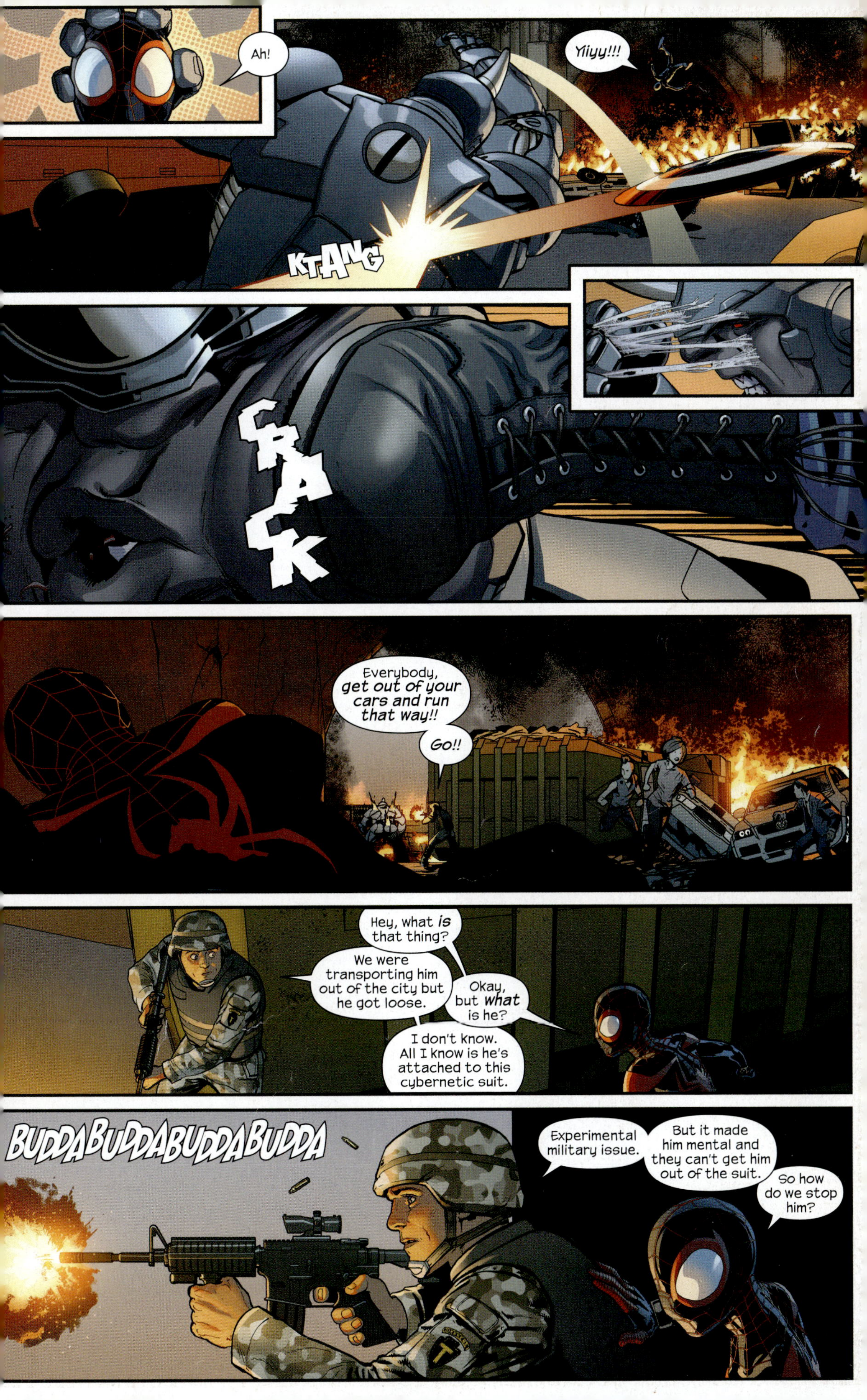
Ah!
Yiiyy!!!
KTANG
CRACK
Everybody, get out of your cars and run that way!!
Go!!
Hey, what is that thing?
We were transporting him out of the city but he got loose.
Okay, but what is he?
I don't know. All I know is he's attached to this cybernetic suit.
BUDDABUDDABUDDABUDDA
Experimental military issue.
But it made him mental and they can't get him out of the suit.
So how do we stop him?

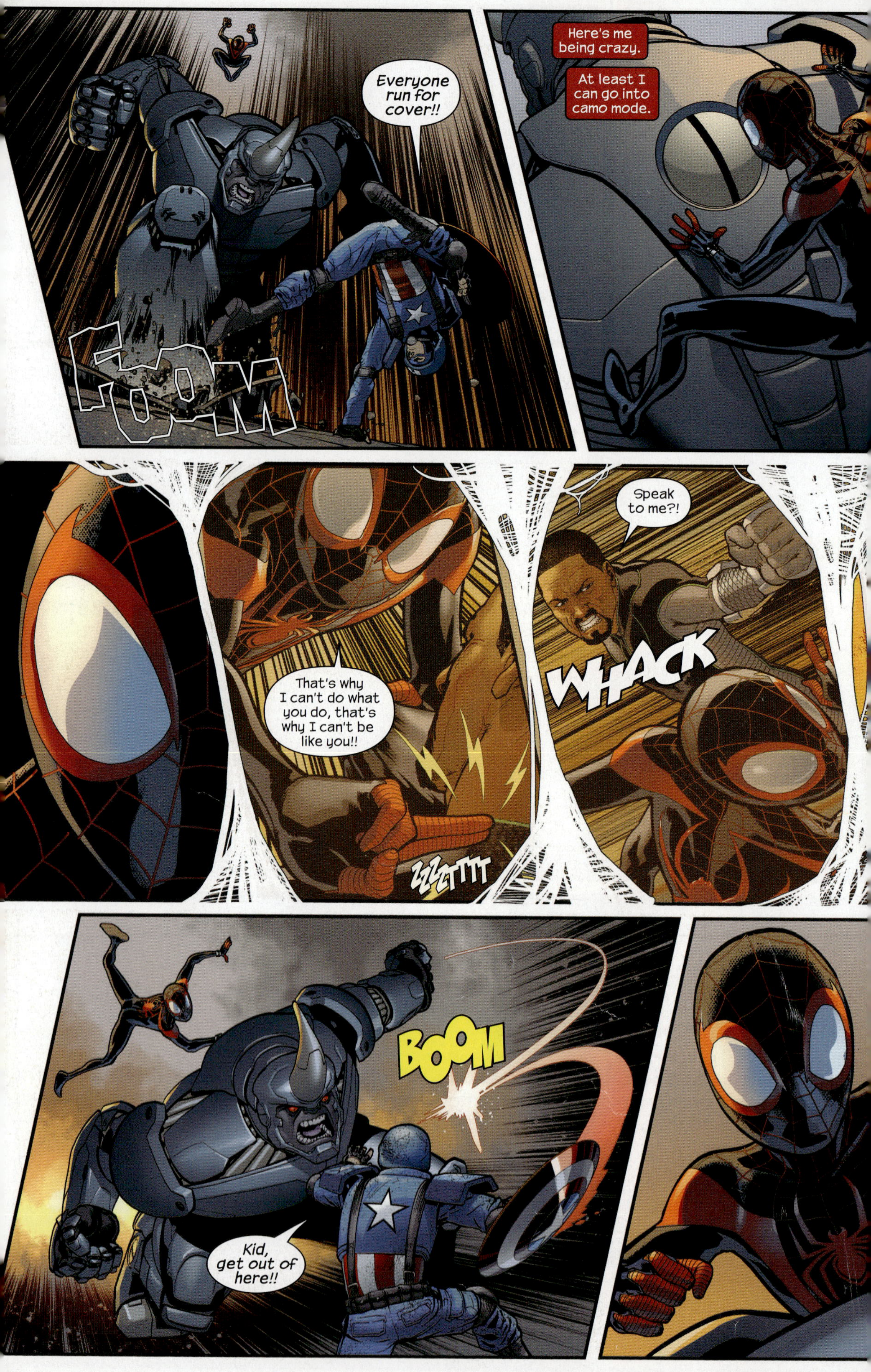
Everyone run for cover!!
FOOM
Here's me being crazy.
At least I can go into camo mode.
That's why I can't do what you do, that's why I can't be like you!!
ZZZZTTTT
Speak to me?!
WHACK
BOOM
Kid, get out of here!!

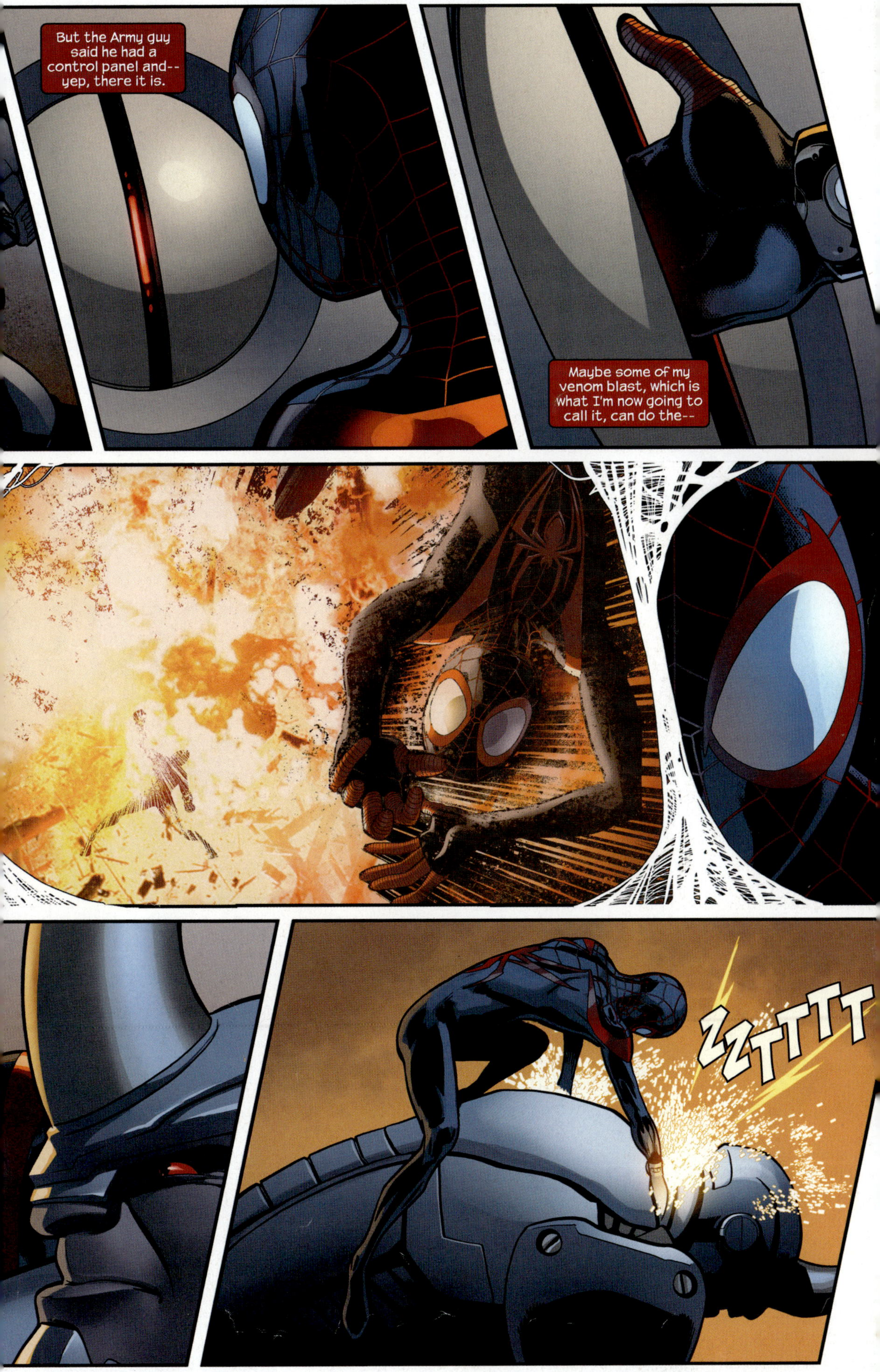
But the Army guy said he had a control panel and--yep, there it is.
Maybe some of my venom blast, which is what I'm now going to call it, can do the--
ZZTTTTT

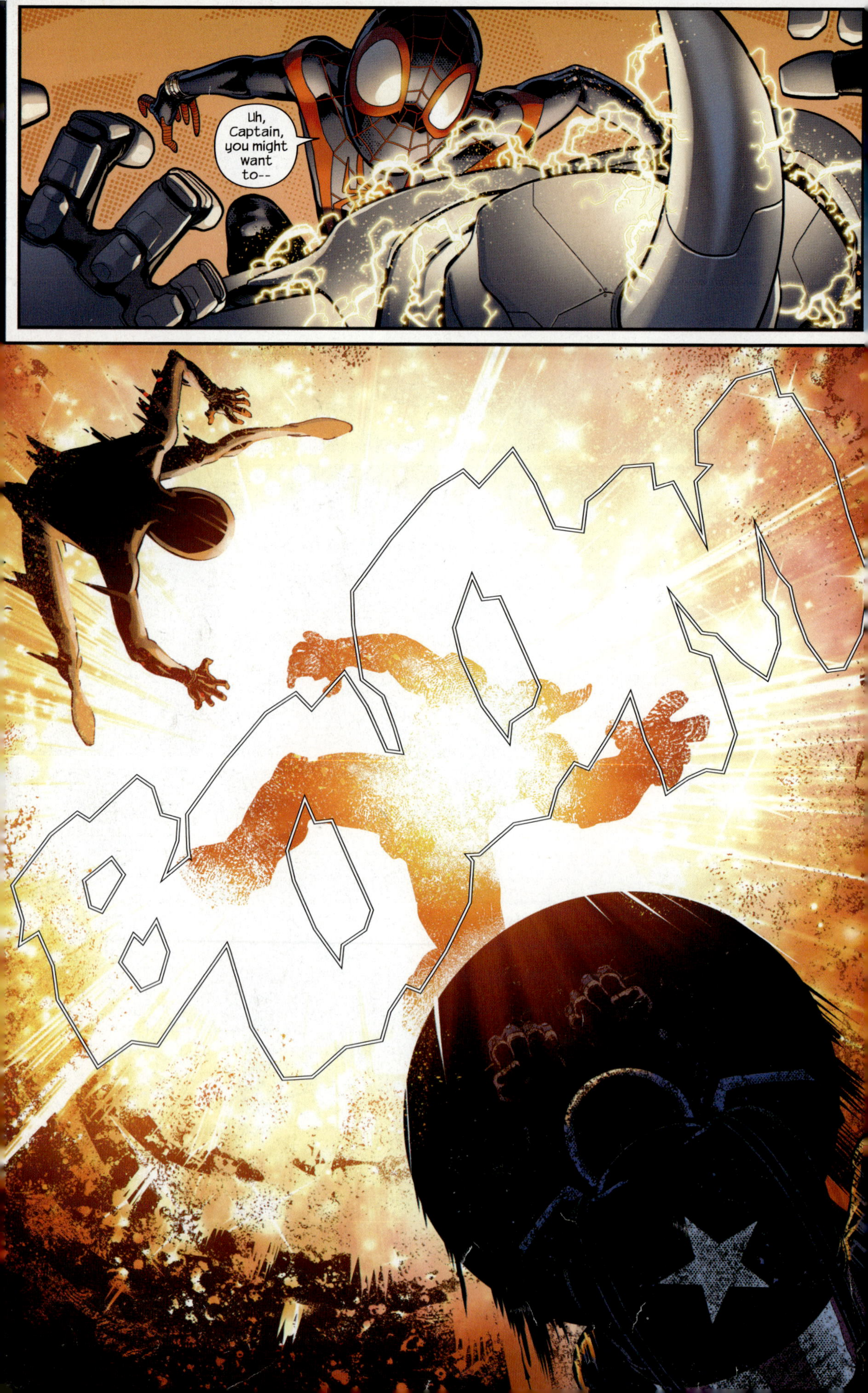
Uh, Captain, you might want to--
BOOM

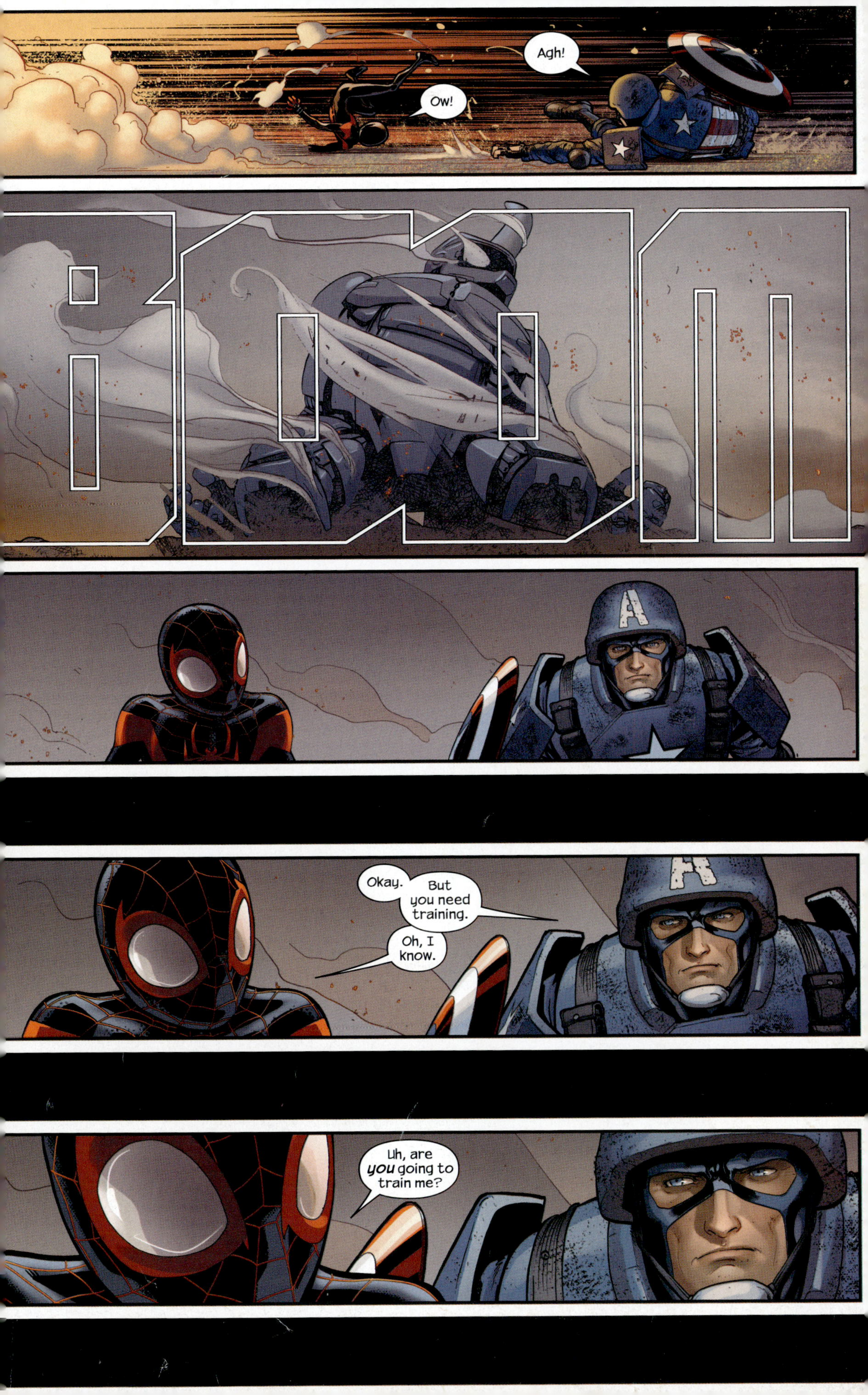
Agh!
Ow!
Okay.
But you need training.
Oh, I know.
Uh, are *you* going to train me?

UNITED WE STAND

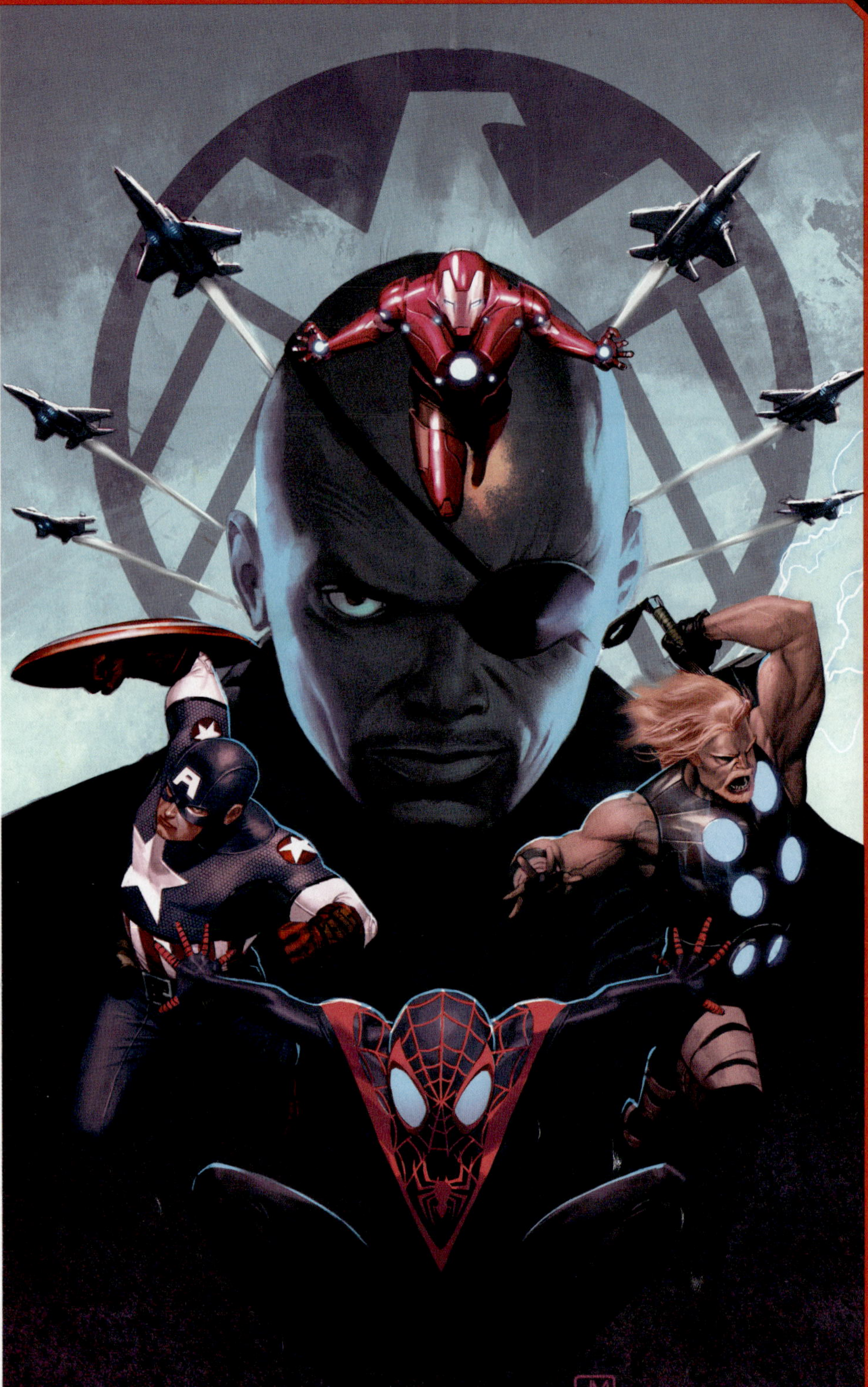

S.H.I.E.L.D. SITUATION MAP:

[Anti-government militia hot spots]

Montana, N. Dakota, S. Dakota, Wyoming, Arizona, New Mexico, N. Carolina, S. Carolina, Georgia, Idaho

[Eastern seaboard control zone]

New England, New York, New Jersey, Delaware, Washington D.C., Maryland, Virginia, Pennsylvania

secured by National Guard under emergency powers committee

[the West Coast]

California, Oregon, Washington

status unknown

[Great Lakes states]

Minnesota, Wisconsin, Michigan, Illinois, Indiana, Ohio

status unknown

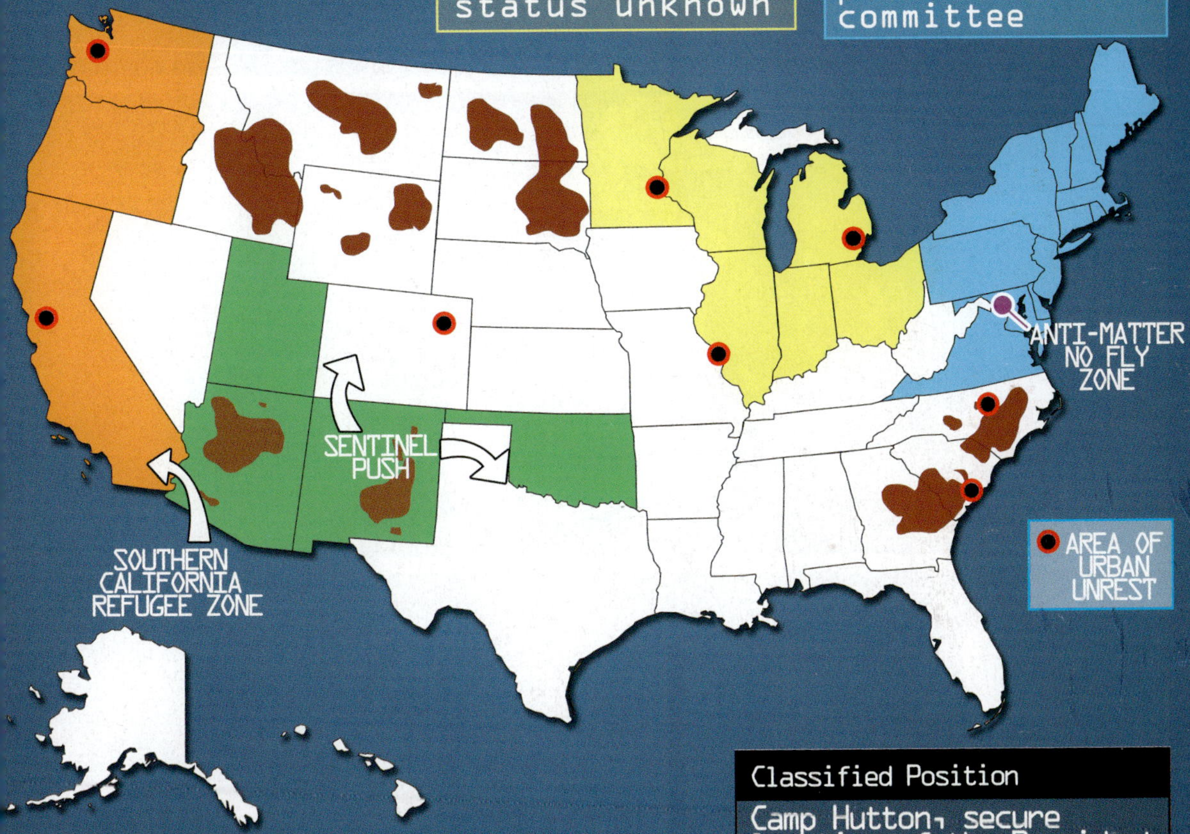
ANTI-MATTER NO FLY ZONE
SENTINEL PUSH
SOUTHERN CALIFORNIA REFUGEE ZONE
AREA OF URBAN UNREST

Classified Position

Camp Hutton, secure location of the President of the United States

[Sentinel-controlled no-man's-land]

New Mexico, Arizona, Utah, Oklahoma

abandoned by the U.S. government

ALL STATES SHOWN IN WHITE ARE U.S. GOVERNMENT-CONTROLLED ZONES

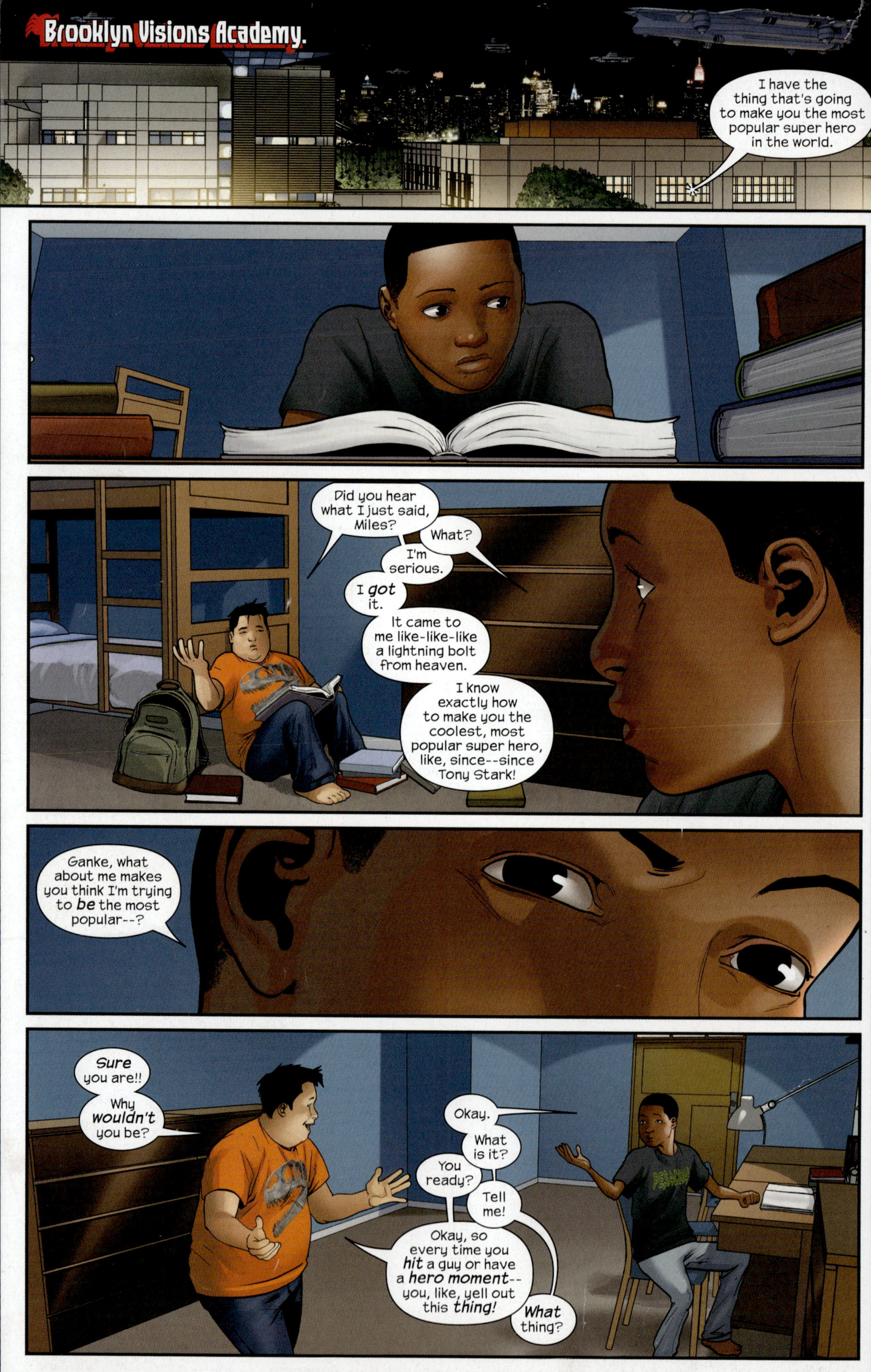

Brooklyn Visions Academy.
I have the thing that's going to make you the most popular super hero in the world.
Did you hear what I just said, Miles?
What?
I'm serious.
I got it.
It came to me like-like-like a lightning bolt from heaven.
I know exactly how to make you the coolest, most popular super hero, like, since--since Tony Stark!
Ganke, what about me makes you think I'm trying to be the most popular--?
Sure you are!!
Why wouldn't you be?
Okay.
What is it?
You ready?
Tell me!
Okay, so every time you hit a guy or have a hero moment--you, like, yell out this thing!
What thing?

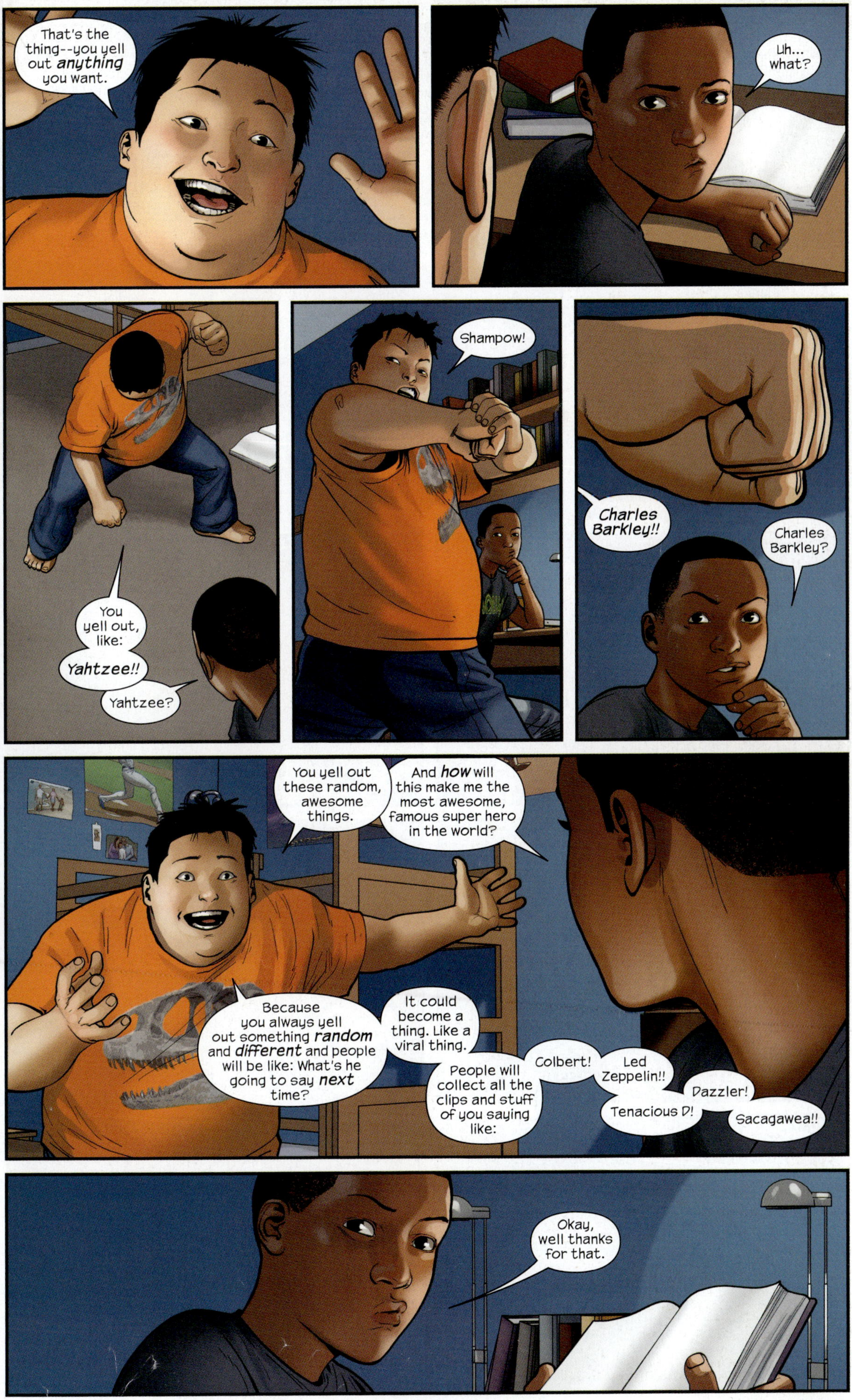
That's the thing--you yell out *anything* you want.
Uh... what?
You yell out, like:
Yahtzee!!
Yahtzee?
Shampow!
Charles Barkley!!
Charles Barkley?
You yell out these random, awesome things.
And *how* will this make me the most awesome, famous super hero in the world?
Because you always yell out something *random* and *different* and people will be like: What's he going to say *next* time?
It could become a thing. Like a viral thing.
People will collect all the clips and stuff of you saying like:
Colbert!
Led Zeppelin!!
Tenacious D!
Dazzler!
Sacagawea!!
Okay, well thanks for that.

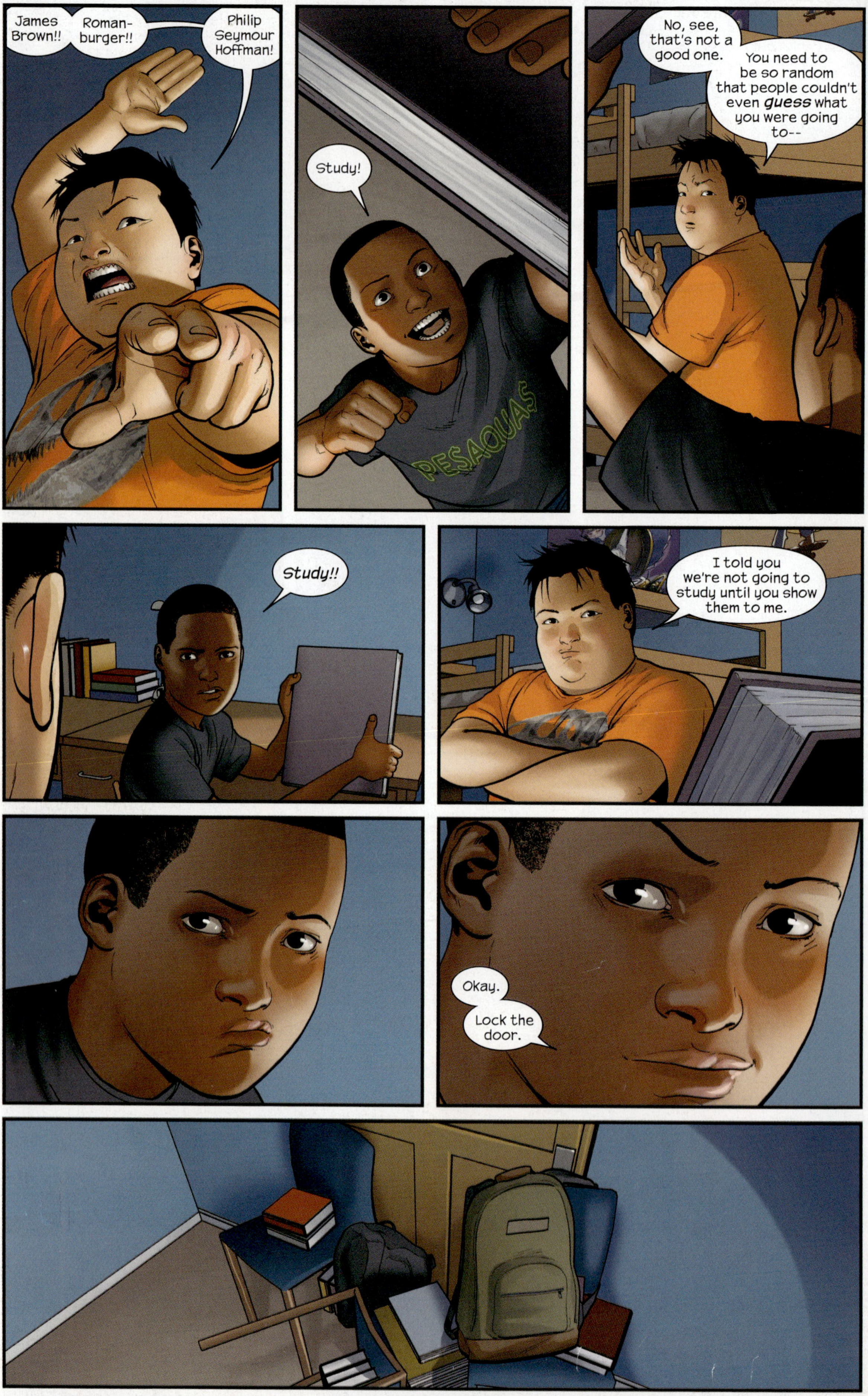
James Brown!!
Roman-burger!!
Philip Seymour Hoffman!
Study!
PESAQUA$
No, see, that's not a good one.
You need to be so random that people couldn't even *guess* what you were going to--
Study!!
I told you we're not going to study until you show them to me.
Okay.
Lock the door.

Wow.

Right?

The web shooters.

And his aunt just *gave* them to you?

Yup.

And these were *his*? These were the actual ones *he* wore?

And he *invented* them.

How do you do *that*?

I think he might have been some kind of genius.

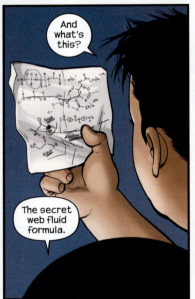

And what's this?

The secret web fluid formula.

So we have to make more?

When this runs out.

Uh-oh.

I was hoping that's where you would come in.

Me? You're the smart one.

I mean, I--I don't-- I can't!

If you can make a Death Star out of Legos using your own designs...

Yeah.

But-but-but chemistry.

THWIP

Oops.

Hey! Hey, why won't this door open?!

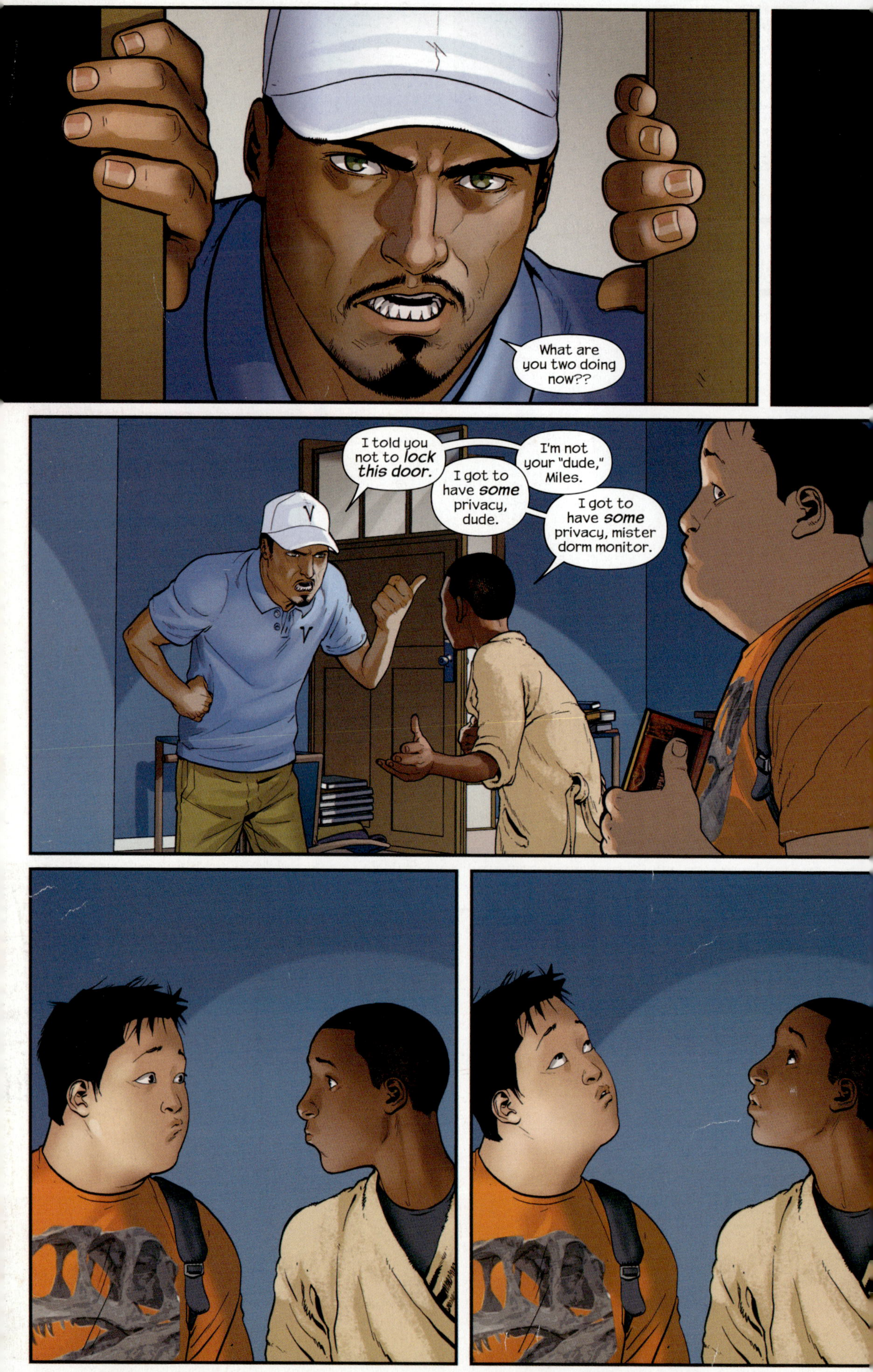
What are you two doing now??
I told you not to lock this door.
I got to have some privacy, dude.
I'm not your "dude," Miles.
I got to have some privacy, mister dorm monitor.

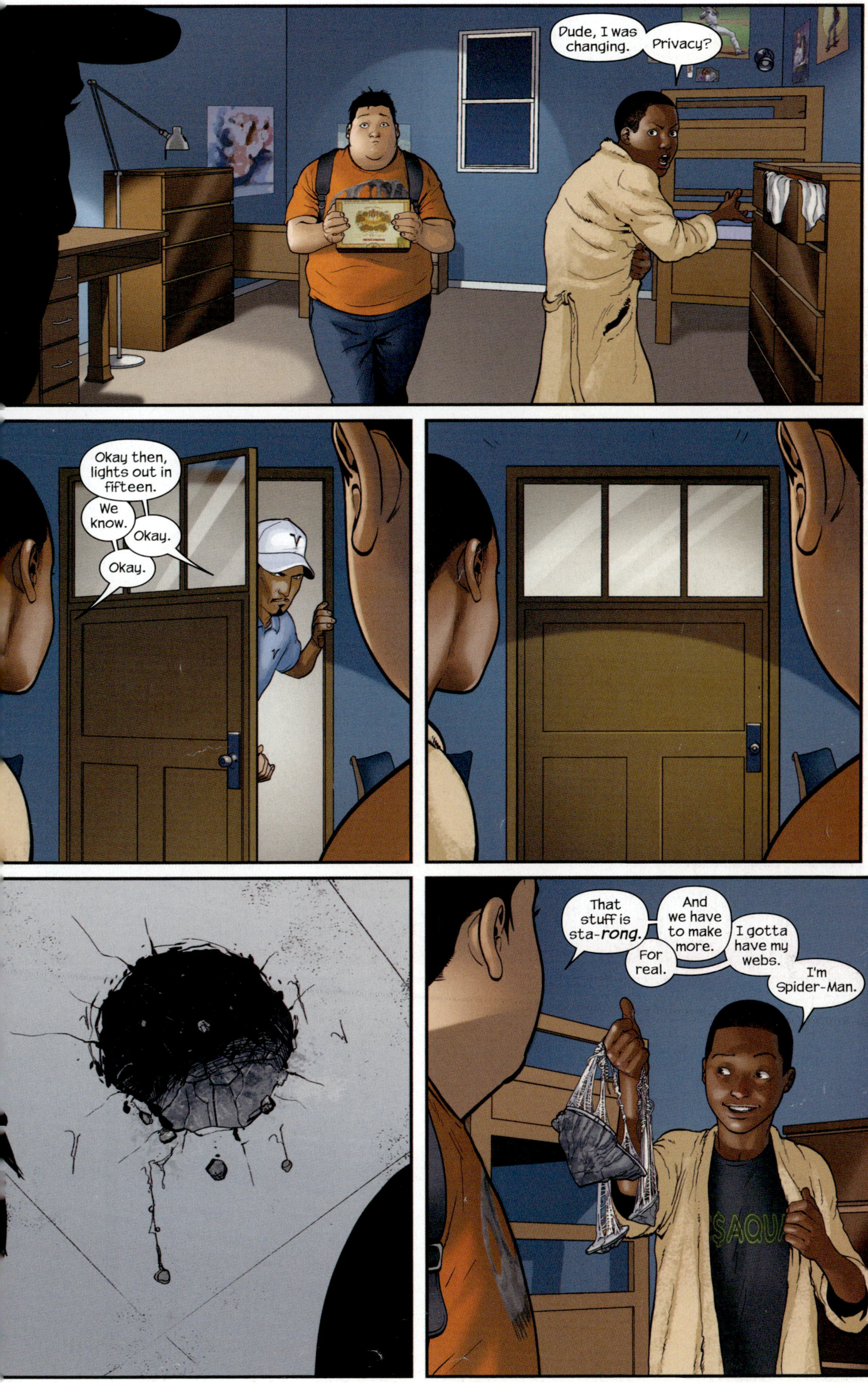

Dude, I was changing.
Privacy?
Okay then, lights out in fifteen.
We know.
Okay.
Okay.
That stuff is sta-*rong.*
For real.
And we have to make more.
I gotta have my webs.
I'm Spider-Man.
$AQU

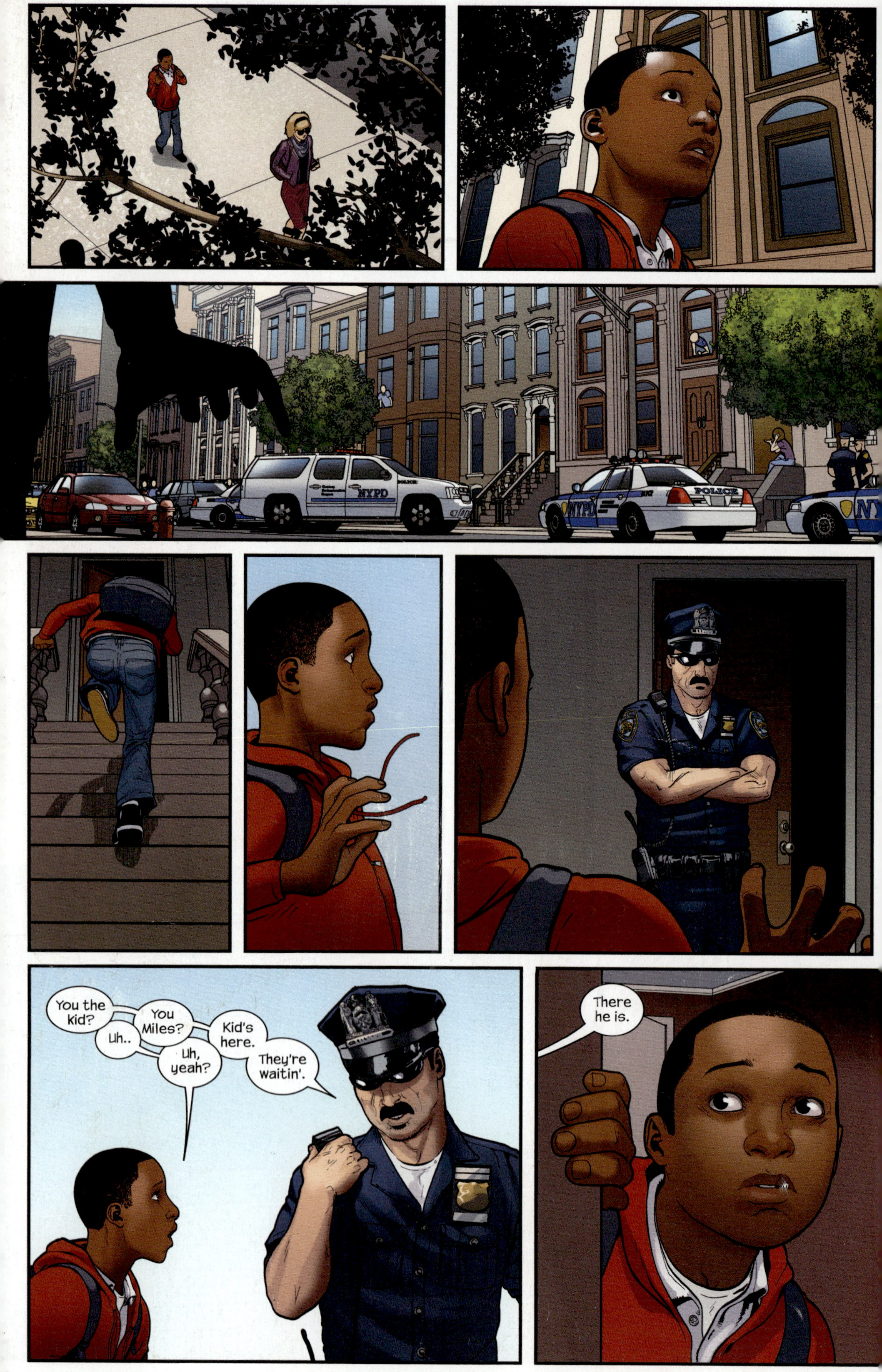
You the kid?
Uh..
You Miles?
Uh, yeah?
Kid's here.
They're waitin'.
There he is.

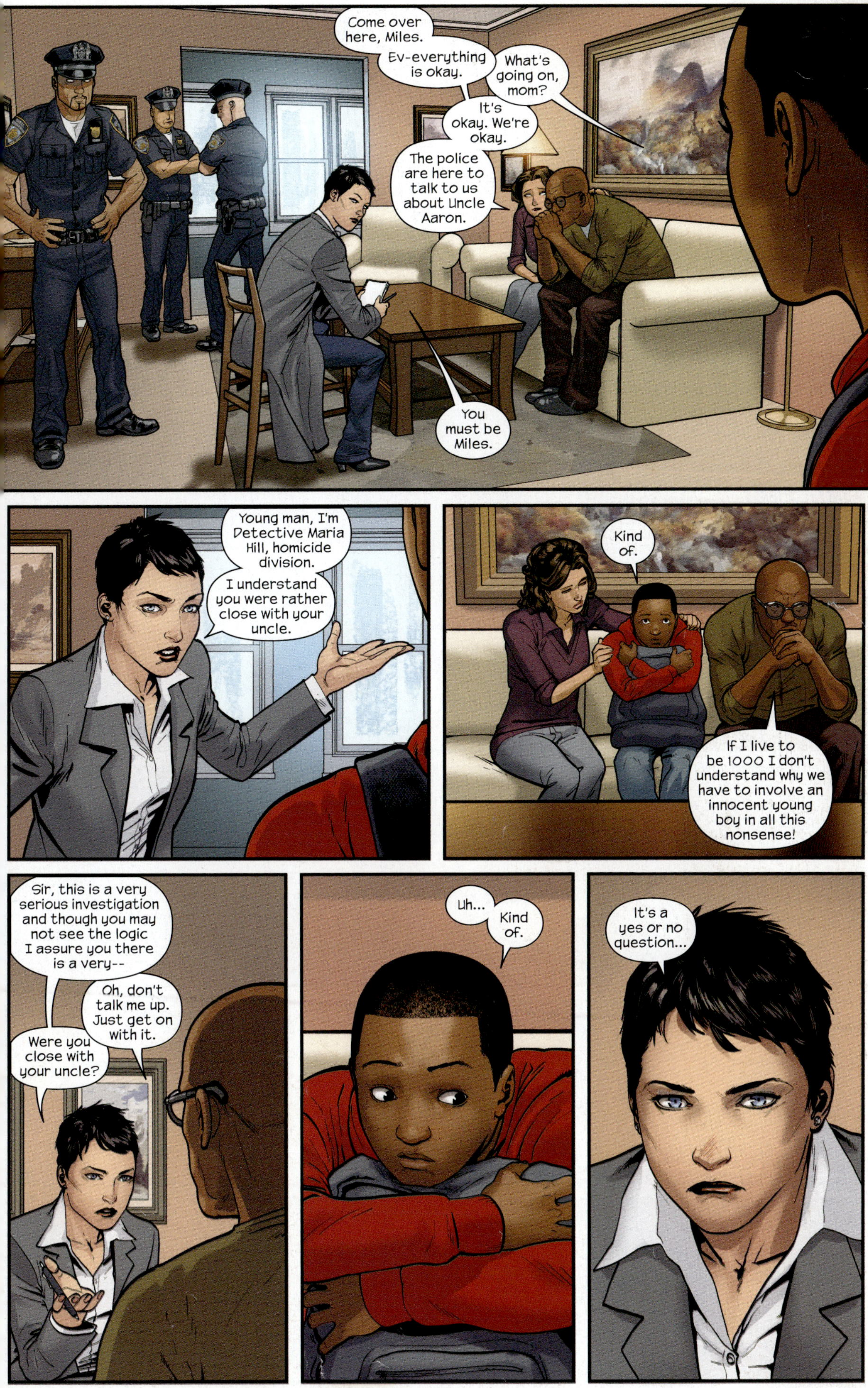
Come over here, Miles.
Ev-everything is okay.
What's going on, mom?
It's okay. We're okay.
The police are here to talk to us about Uncle Aaron.
You must be Miles.
Young man, I'm Detective Maria Hill, homicide division.
I understand you were rather close with your uncle.
Kind of.
If I live to be 1000 I don't understand why we have to involve an innocent young boy in all this nonsense!
Sir, this is a very serious investigation and though you may not see the logic I assure you there is a very--
Oh, don't talk me up. Just get on with it.
Were you close with your uncle?
Uh...
Kind of.
It's a yes or no question...

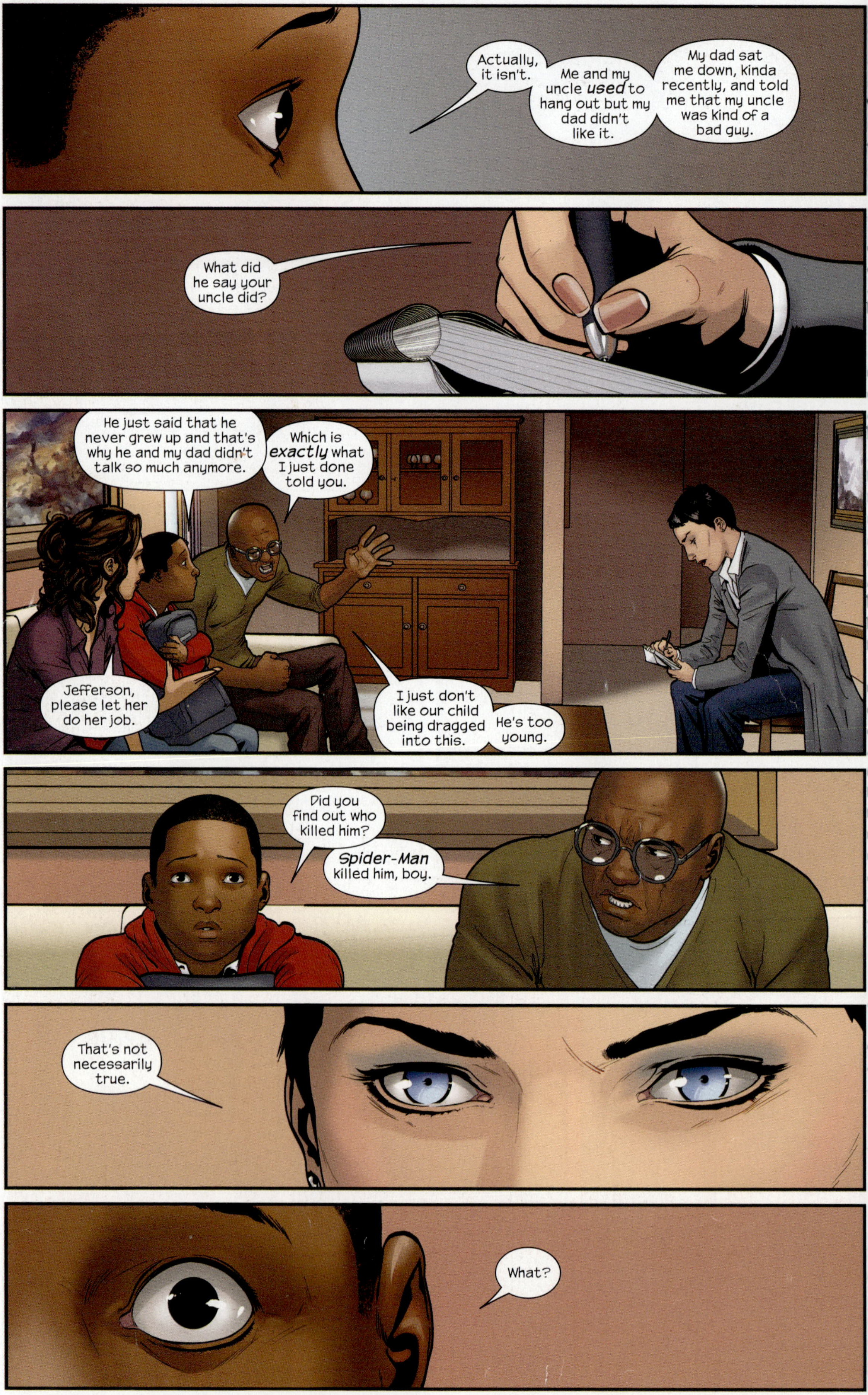
Actually, it isn't.
Me and my uncle *used* to hang out but my dad didn't like it.
My dad sat me down, kinda recently, and told me that my uncle was kind of a bad guy.
What did he say your uncle did?
He just said that he never grew up and that's why he and my dad didn't talk so much anymore.
Which is *exactly* what I just done told you.
Jefferson, please let her do her job.
I just don't like our child being dragged into this.
He's too young.
Did you find out who killed him?
Spider-Man killed him, boy.
That's not necessarily true.
What?

Your uncle had stolen some technology that he didn't know how to use...

And according to the coroner's report the tech was broken and backfired on him.

That's what killed him.

So it--it *wasn't* Spider-Man?

Uncle Aaron accidently killed *himself?*

We're still investigating.

Someone should--should, like, tell the news that it wasn't him, uh, Spider--

Well, my 13-year-old son doesn't know anything about any of this and he doesn't need to know what you're telling him.

(Filling his mind up with nonsense.)

Sir, your brother, the Prowler, was a master thief.

For years, he had a very specific agenda and a very specific modus operandi.

He knew *exactly* how far to push situations and he knew *exactly* how to dance between the raindrops of our legal system.

So for him to, all of a sudden, decide to announce his candidacy to be the *kingpin* of New York...

It just doesn't make sense.

He wasn't a "kingpin" kind of guy.

So the question is, why now?

Why all of a sudden does this master thief think himself a godfather?

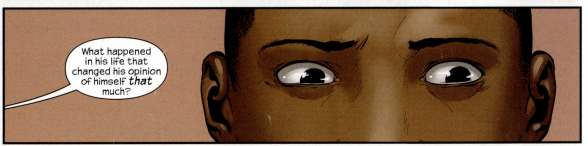

What happened in his life that changed his opinion of himself *that* much?

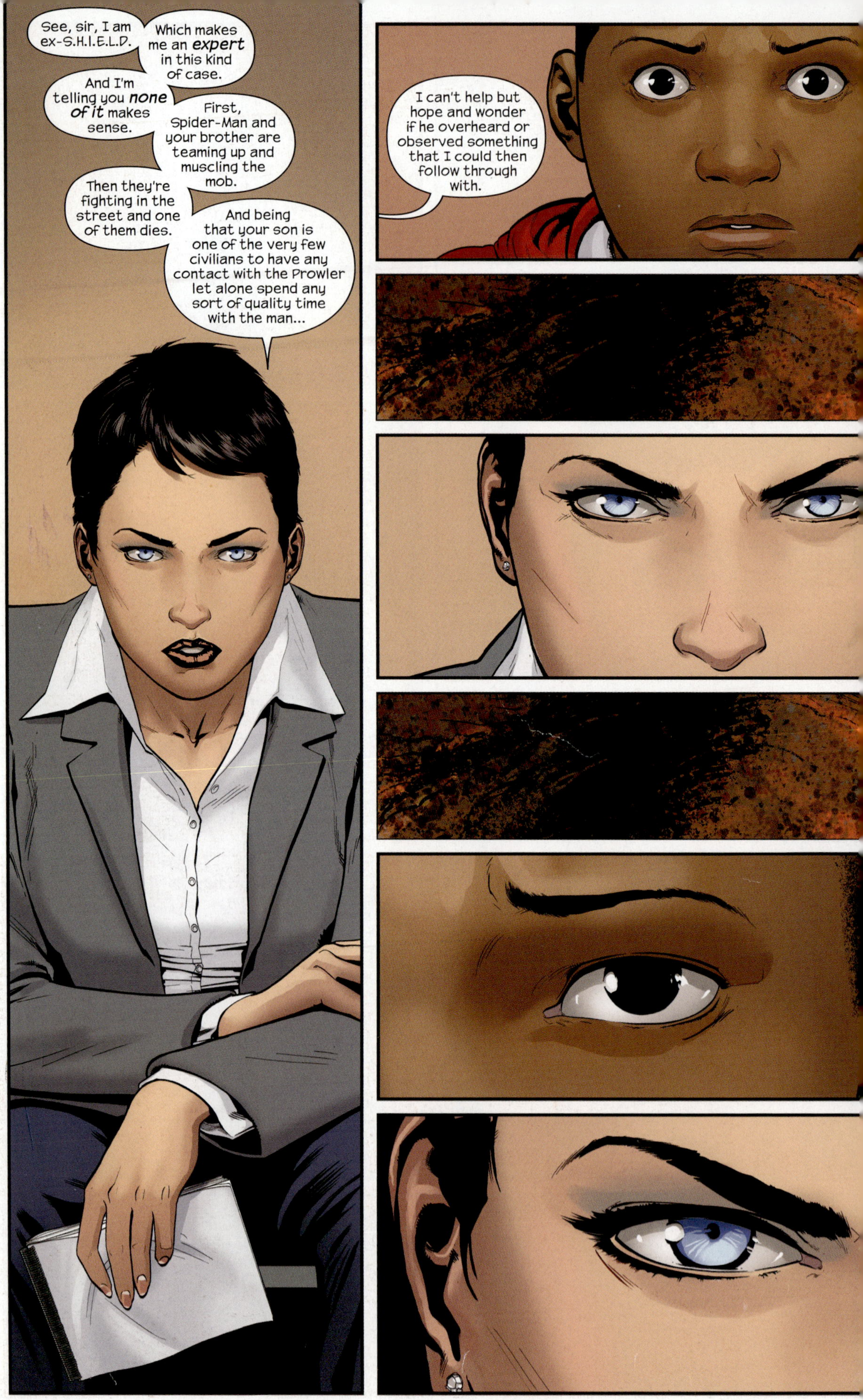
See, sir, I am ex-S.H.I.E.L.D.
Which makes me an *expert* in this kind of case.
And I'm telling you ***none of it*** makes sense.
First, Spider-Man and your brother are teaming up and muscling the mob.
Then they're fighting in the street and one of them dies.
And being that your son is one of the very few civilians to have any contact with the Prowler let alone spend any sort of quality time with the man...
I can't help but hope and wonder if he overheard or observed something that I could then follow through with.

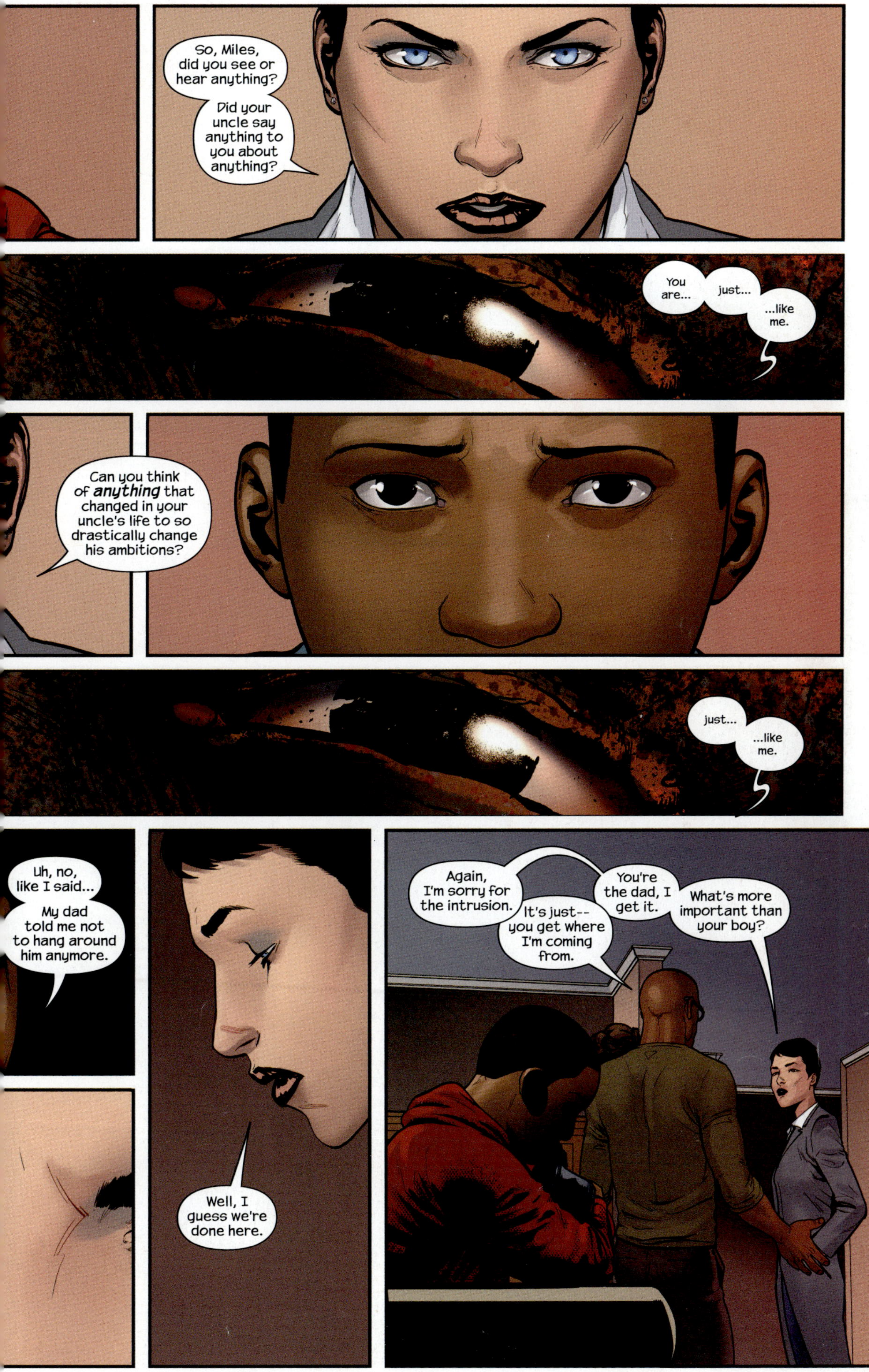
So, Miles, did you see or hear anything?
Did your uncle say anything to you about anything?
You are...
just...
...like me.
Can you think of *anything* that changed in your uncle's life to so drastically change his ambitions?
just...
...like me.
Uh, no, like I said...
My dad told me not to hang around him anymore.
Well, I guess we're done here.
Again, I'm sorry for the intrusion.
It's just-- you get where I'm coming from.
You're the dad, I get it.
What's more important than your boy?

Dude, that's *huge!!*

Uh... stop hugging me.

I, uh, I got an iPad. **So, yeah...**

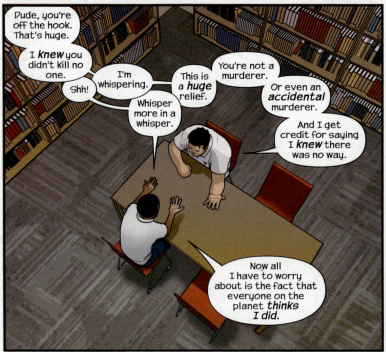

Dude, you're off the hook. That's huge.

I *knew* you didn't kill no one.

Shh!

I'm whispering.

Whisper more in a whisper.

This is a *huge* relief.

You're not a murderer.

Or even an *accidental* murderer.

And I get credit for saying I *knew* there was no way.

Now all I have to worry about is the fact that everyone on the planet *thinks* I did.

All students, all classes, please report to the auditorium for an important announcement!!

Announcement?

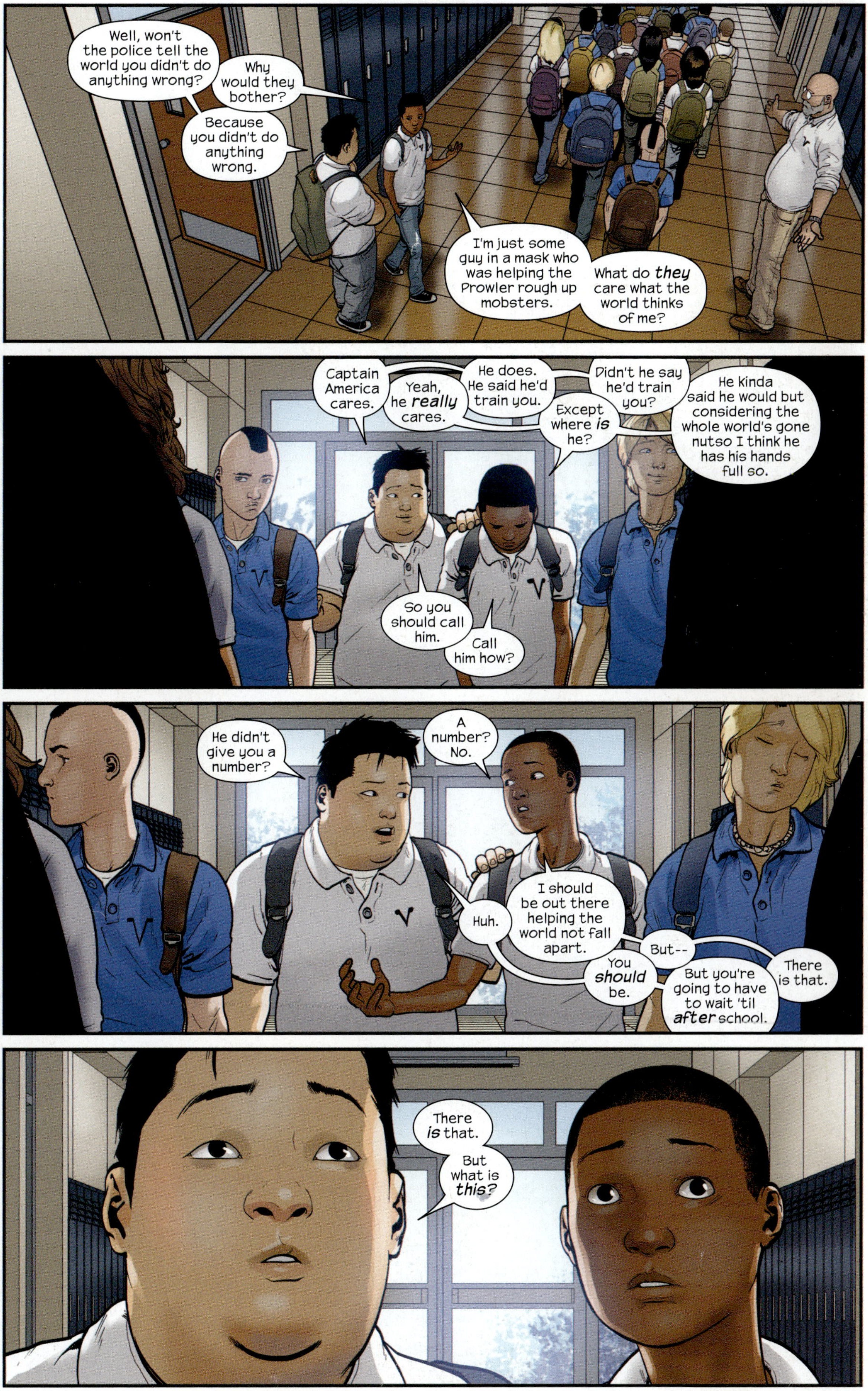
Well, won't the police tell the world you didn't do anything wrong?
Why would they bother?
Because you didn't do anything wrong.
I'm just some guy in a mask who was helping the Prowler rough up mobsters.
What do *they* care what the world thinks of me?
Captain America cares.
Yeah, he *really* cares.
He does. He said he'd train you.
Didn't he say he'd train you?
Except where *is* he?
He kinda said he would but considering the whole world's gone nutso I think he has his hands full so.
So you should call him.
Call him how?
He didn't give you a number?
A number? No.
Huh.
I should be out there helping the world not fall apart.
But--
You *should* be.
There is that.
But you're going to have to wait 'til *after* school.
There *is* that.
But what is *this?*

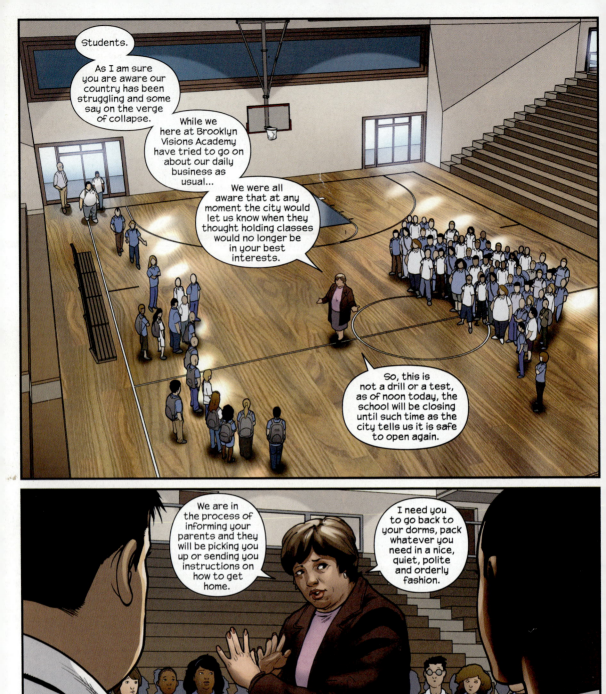

Students.

As I am sure you are aware our country has been struggling and some say on the verge of collapse.

While we here at Brooklyn Visions Academy have tried to go on about our daily business as usual...

We were all aware that at any moment the city would let us know when they thought holding classes would no longer be in your best interests.

So, this is not a drill or a test, as of noon today, the school will be closing until such time as it is safe to open again.

We are in the process of informing your parents and they will be picking you up or sending you instructions on how to get home.

I need you to go back to your dorms, pack whatever you need in a nice, quiet, polite and orderly fashion.

We will let you know when we are back to business as usual.

But for now, the first order of business is to stay safe.

Wow. This--this is good news.

For who?

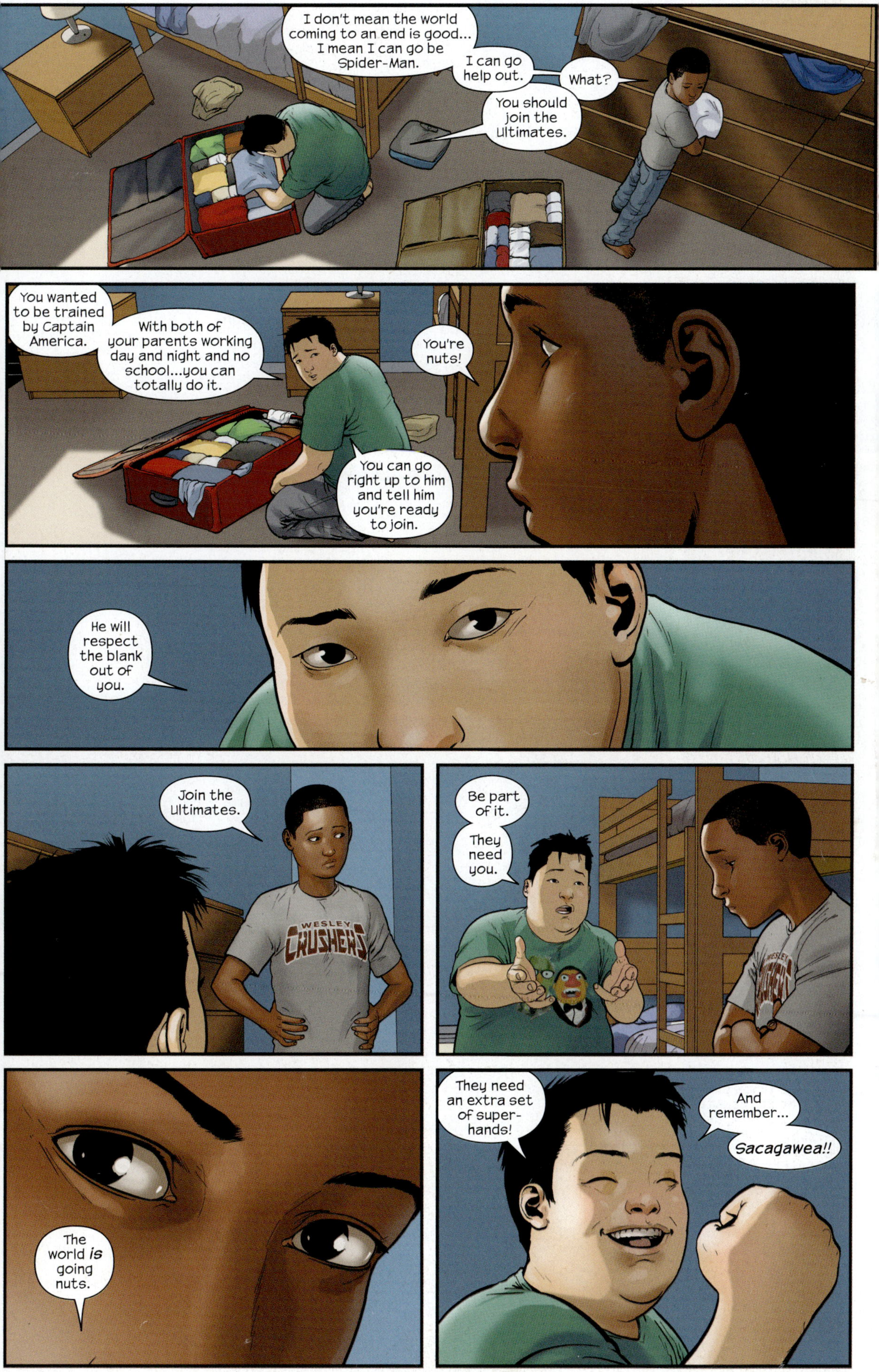

I don't mean the world coming to an end is good... I mean I can go be Spider-Man.
I can go help out.
What?
You should join the Ultimates.
You wanted to be trained by Captain America.
With both of your parents working day and night and no school...you can totally do it.
You're nuts!
You can go right up to him and tell him you're ready to join.
He will respect the blank out of you.
Join the Ultimates.
WESLEY CRUSHERS
Be part of it.
They need you.
The world *is* going nuts.
They need an extra set of super-hands!
And remember...
Sacagawea!!

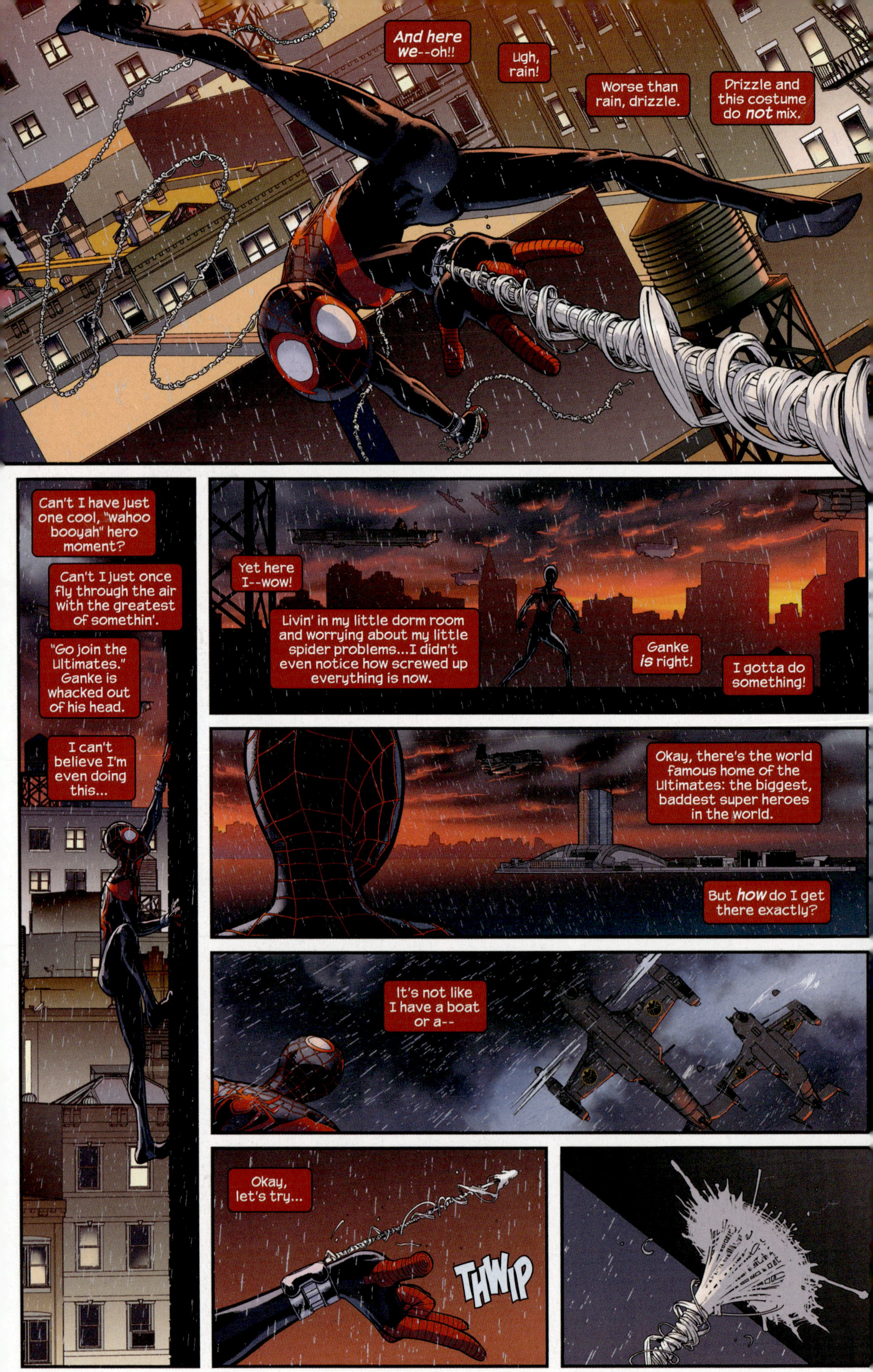
And here we--oh!!
Ugh, rain!
Worse than rain, drizzle.
Drizzle and this costume do *not* mix.
Can't I have just one cool, "wahoo booyah" hero moment?
Can't I just once fly through the air with the greatest of somethin'.
"Go join the Ultimates." Ganke is whacked out of his head.
I can't believe I'm even doing this...
Yet here I--wow!
Livin' in my little dorm room and worrying about my little spider problems...I didn't even notice how screwed up everything is now.
Ganke *is* right!
I gotta do something!
Okay, there's the world famous home of the Ultimates: the biggest, baddest super heroes in the world.
But *how* do I get there exactly?
It's not like I have a boat or a--
Okay, let's try...
THWIP

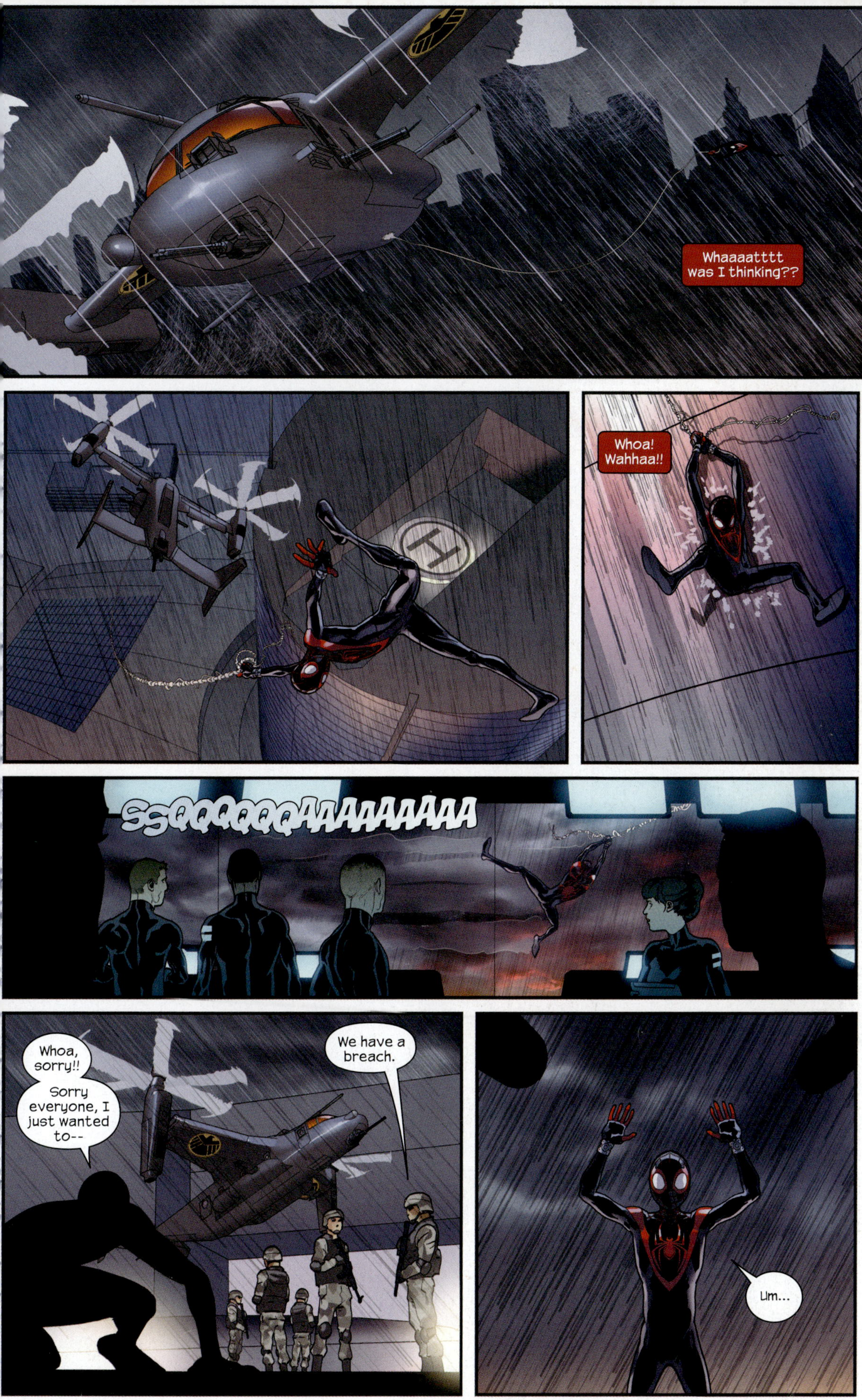
Whaaaatttt was I thinking??
Whoa! Wahhaa!!
SSQQQQQAAAAAAAAA
Whoa, sorry!!
Sorry everyone, I just wanted to--
We have a breach.
Um...

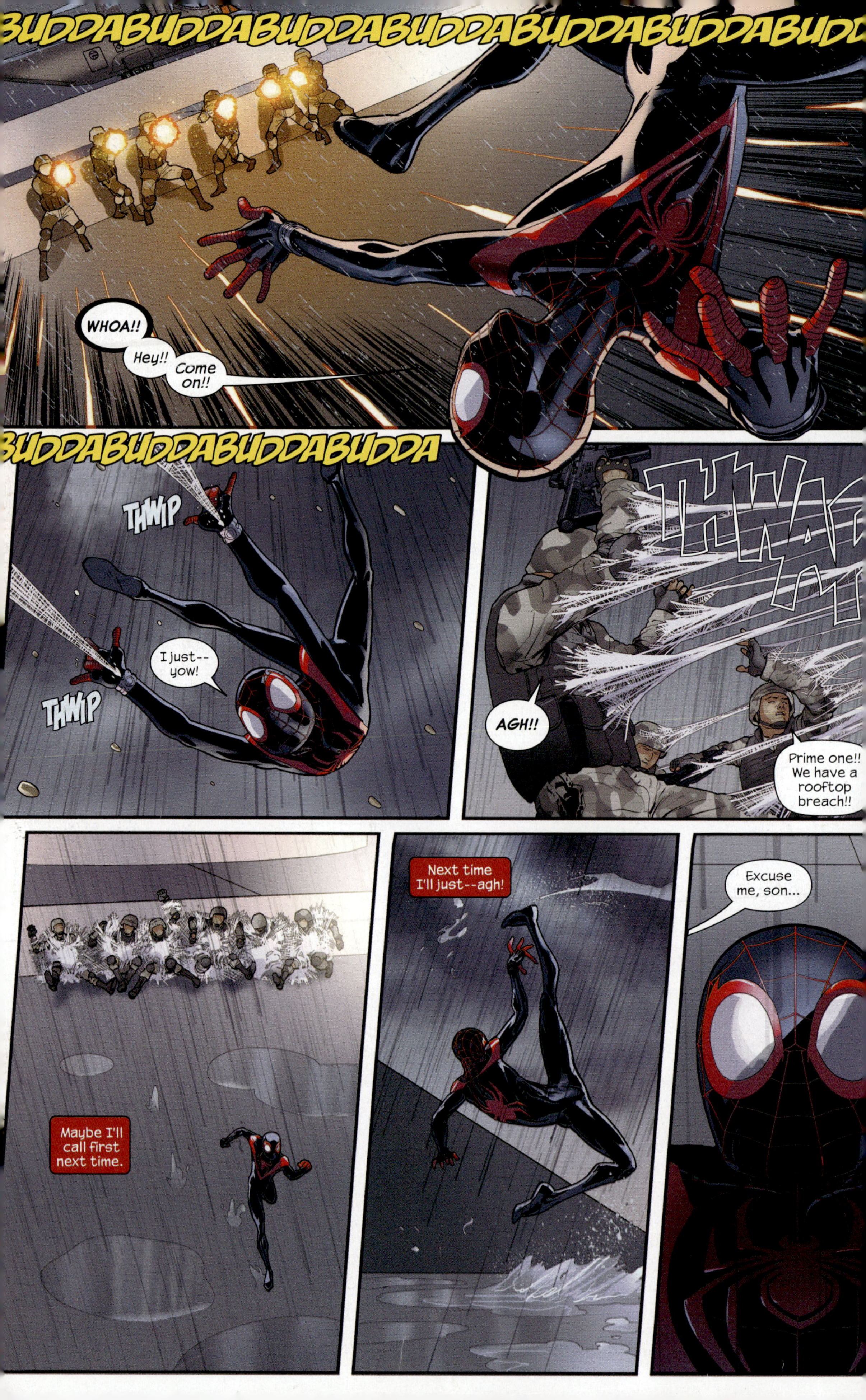
BUDDABUDDABUDDABUDDABUDDABUDDABUDD
WHOA!!
Hey!!
Come on!!
BUDDABUDDABUDDABUDDA
THWIP
I just-- yow!
THWIP
AGH!!
Prime one!! We have a rooftop breach!!
Maybe I'll call first next time.
Next time I'll just--agh!
Excuse me, son...

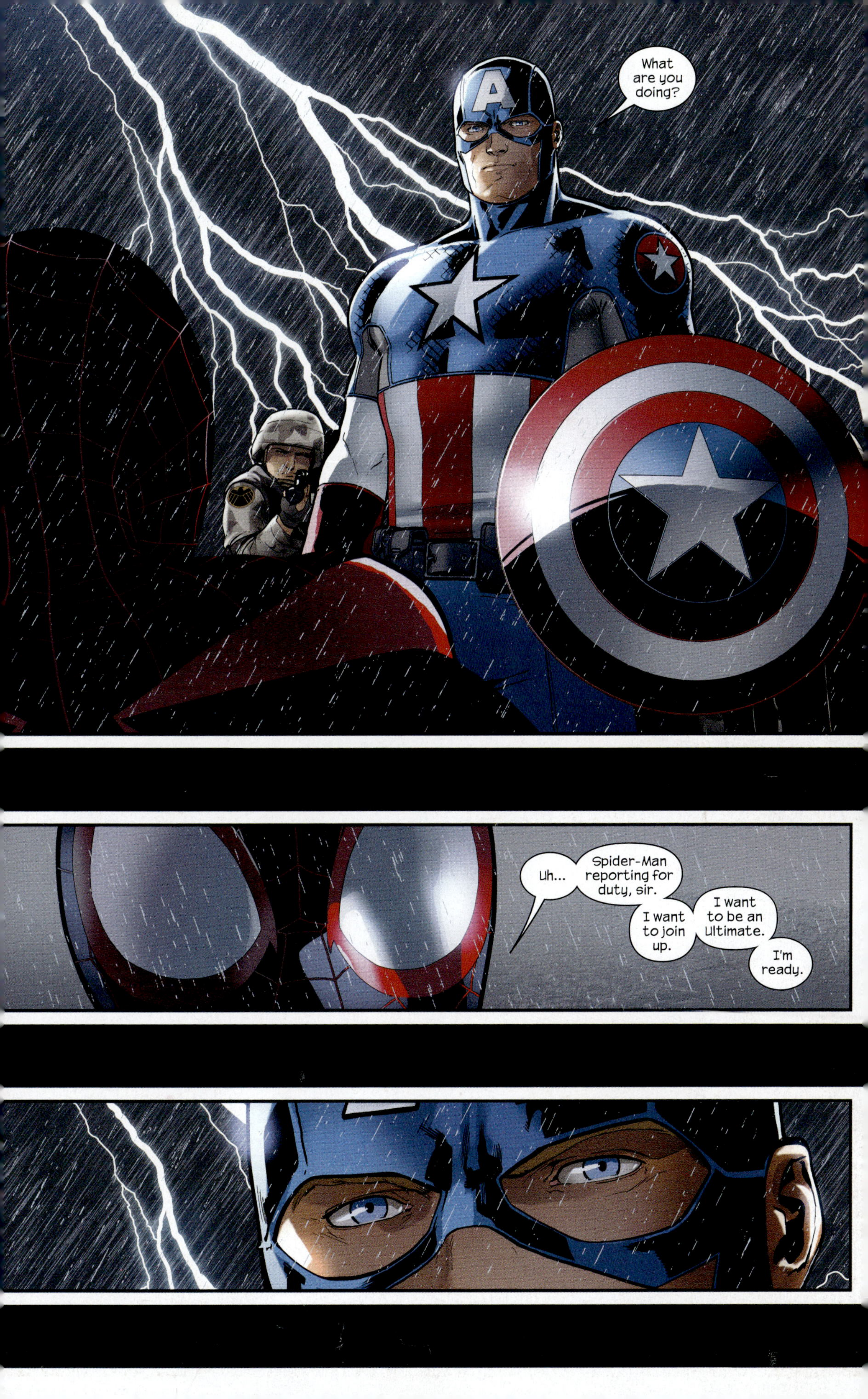
What are you doing?
Uh...
Spider-Man reporting for duty, sir.
I want to join up.
I want to be an Ultimate.
I'm ready.

UNITED WE STAND

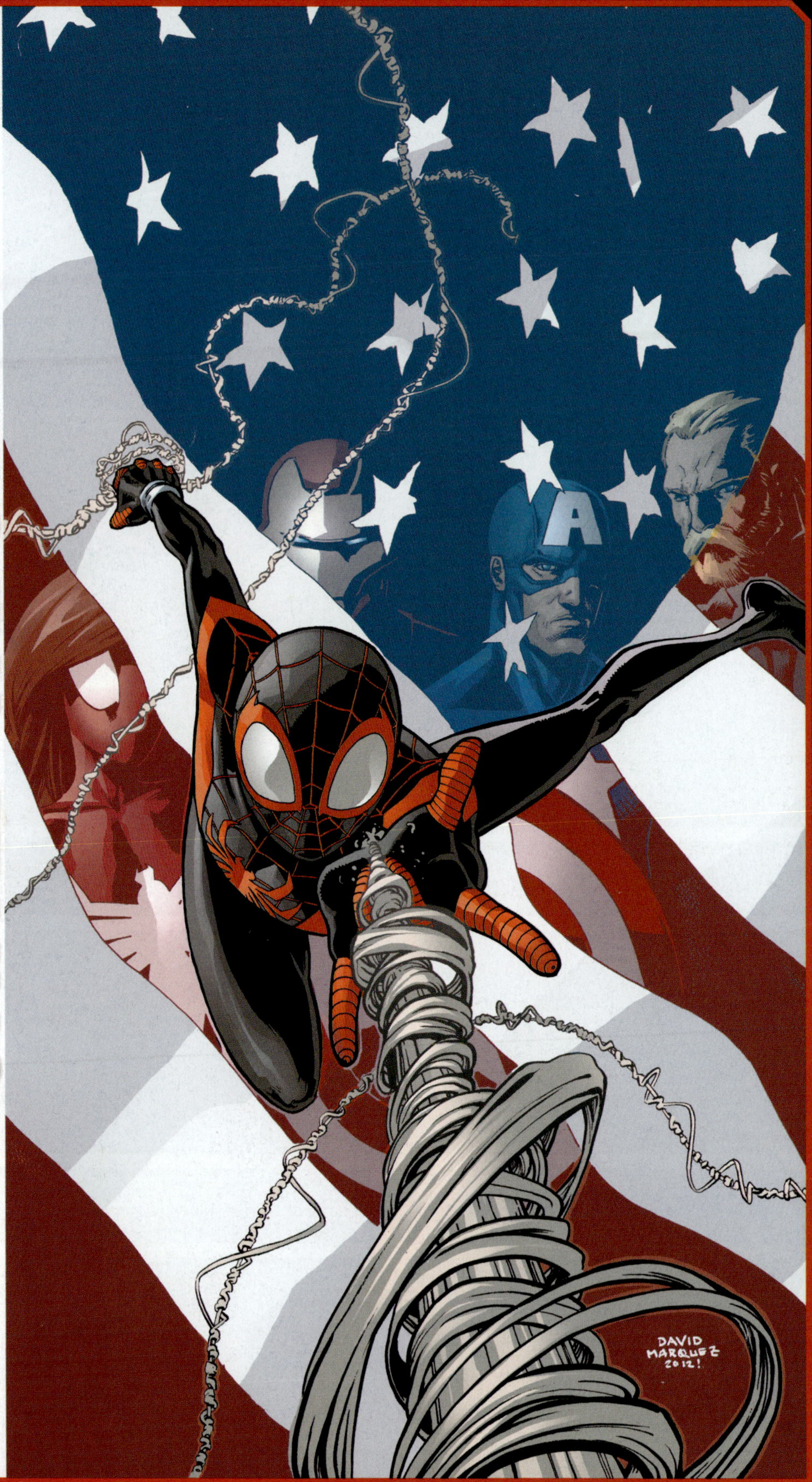
DAVID MARQUEZ 2012!

S.H.I.E.L.D. SITUATION MAP:

[Anti-government militia hot spots]

Idaho, Montana,
N. Dakota, S. Dakota,
Arizona, New Mexico,
N. Carolina,
S. Carolina, Georgia

[Eastern seaboard control zone]

New England,
New York,
New Jersey,
Delaware,
Washington, D.C.,
Maryland,
Pennsylvania,
Virginia

secured by
National Guard
under emergency
powers
committee

[The West Coast Nation]

California, Oregon,
Washington

Independent nation

Wyoming

status unknown

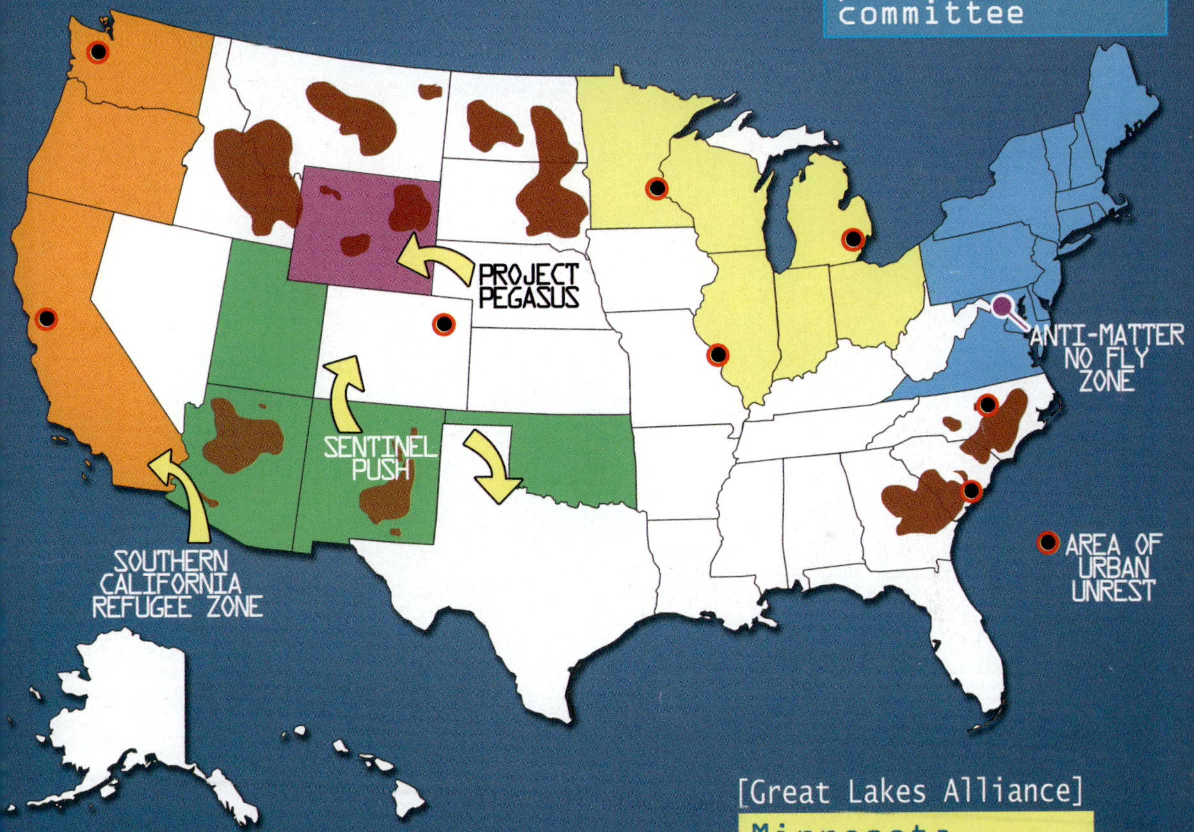

PROJECT PEGASUS
ANTI-MATTER NO FLY ZONE
SENTINEL PUSH
SOUTHERN CALIFORNIA REFUGEE ZONE
AREA OF URBAN UNREST

[Great Lakes Alliance]

Minnesota,
Wisconsin,
Michigan,
Illinois,
Indiana, Ohio

Independent
nation

[Sentinel-controlled no-man's-land]

New Mexico, Arizona,
Utah, Oklahoma

abandoned by the
U.S. government

ALL STATES
SHOWN IN WHITE
ARE U.S. GOVERNMENT-
CONTROLLED ZONES

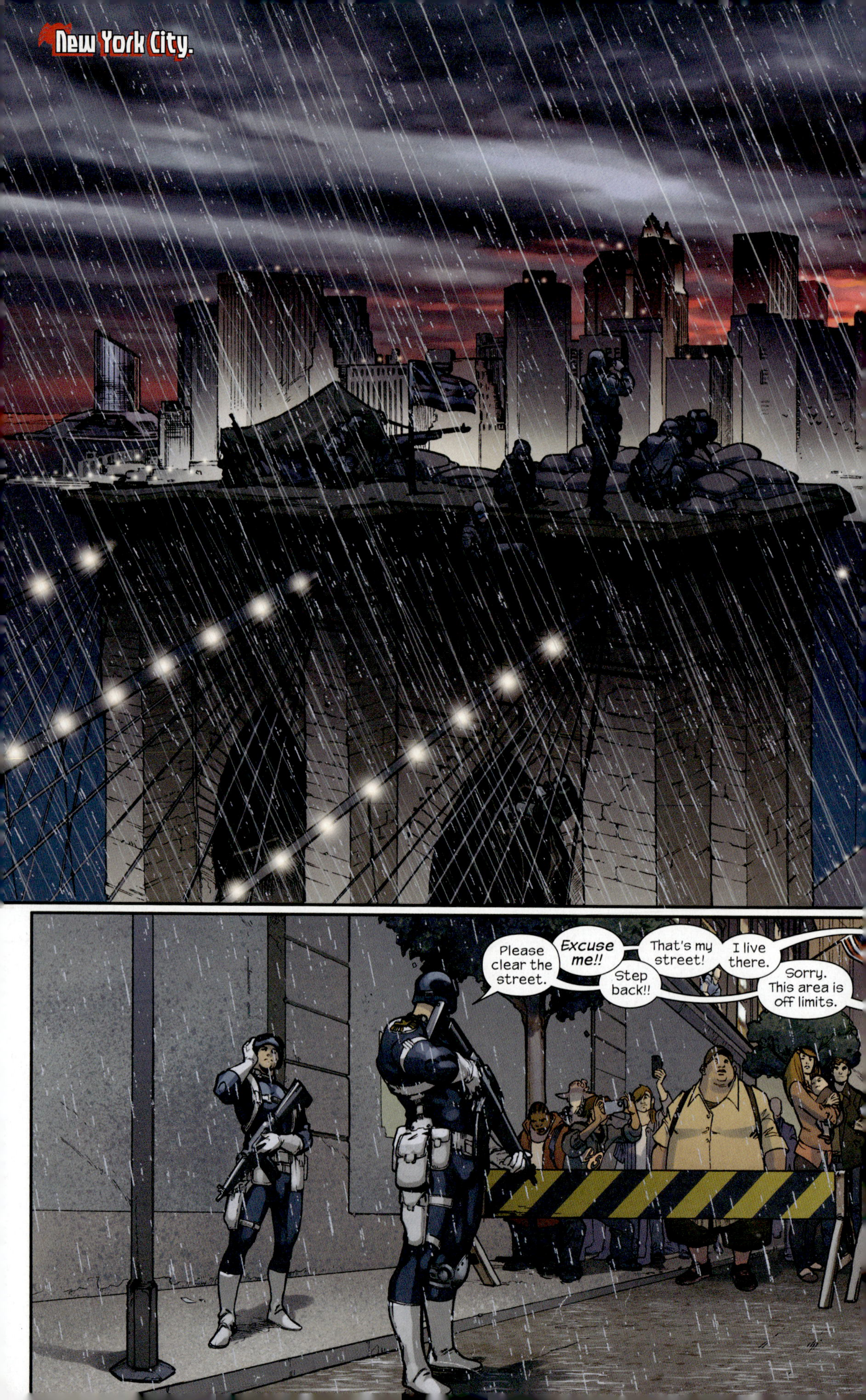
New York City.
Please clear the street.
Excuse me!!
Step back!!
That's my street!
I live there.
Sorry. This area is off limits.

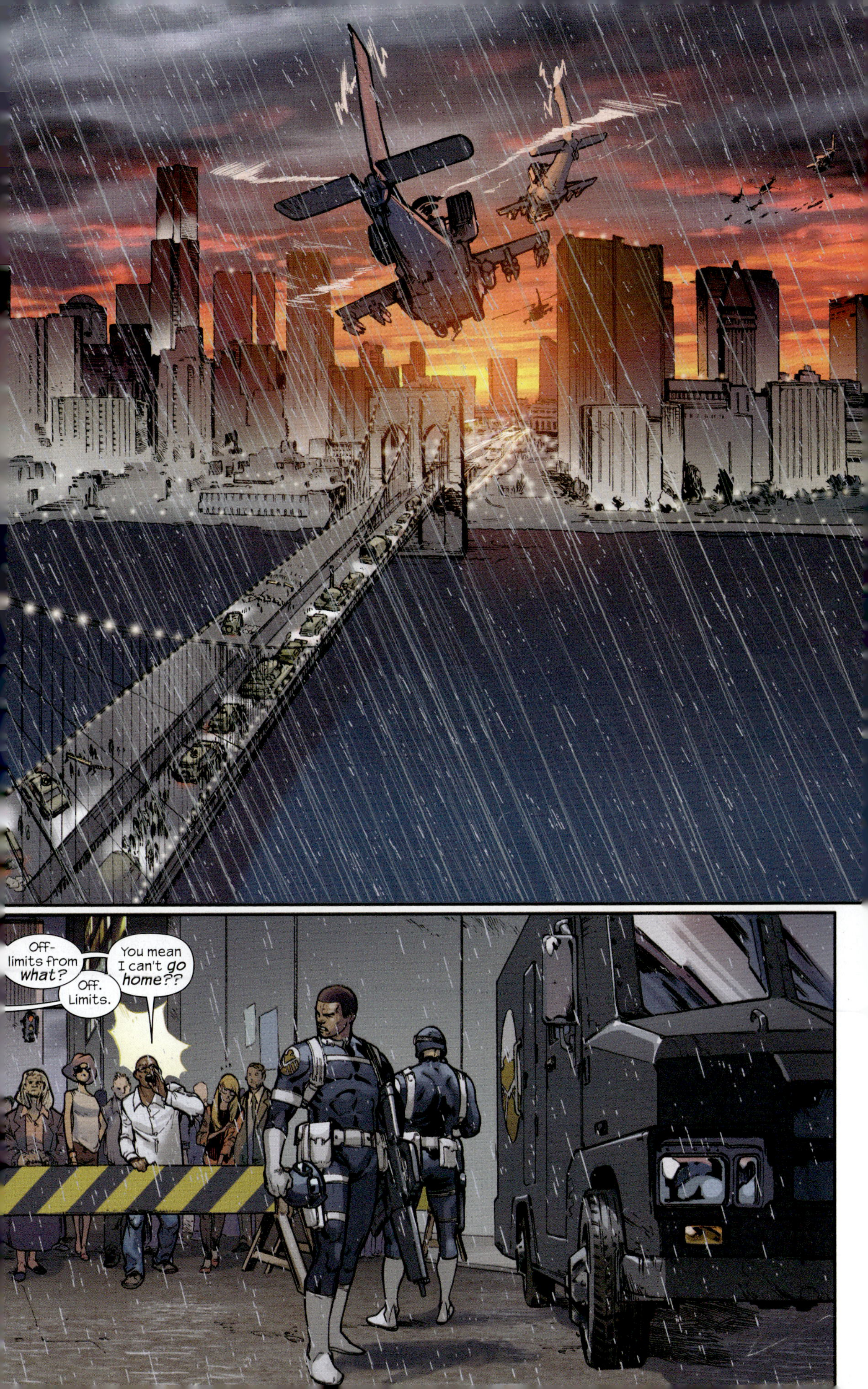
Off-limits from what?
Off. Limits.
You mean I can't go home??

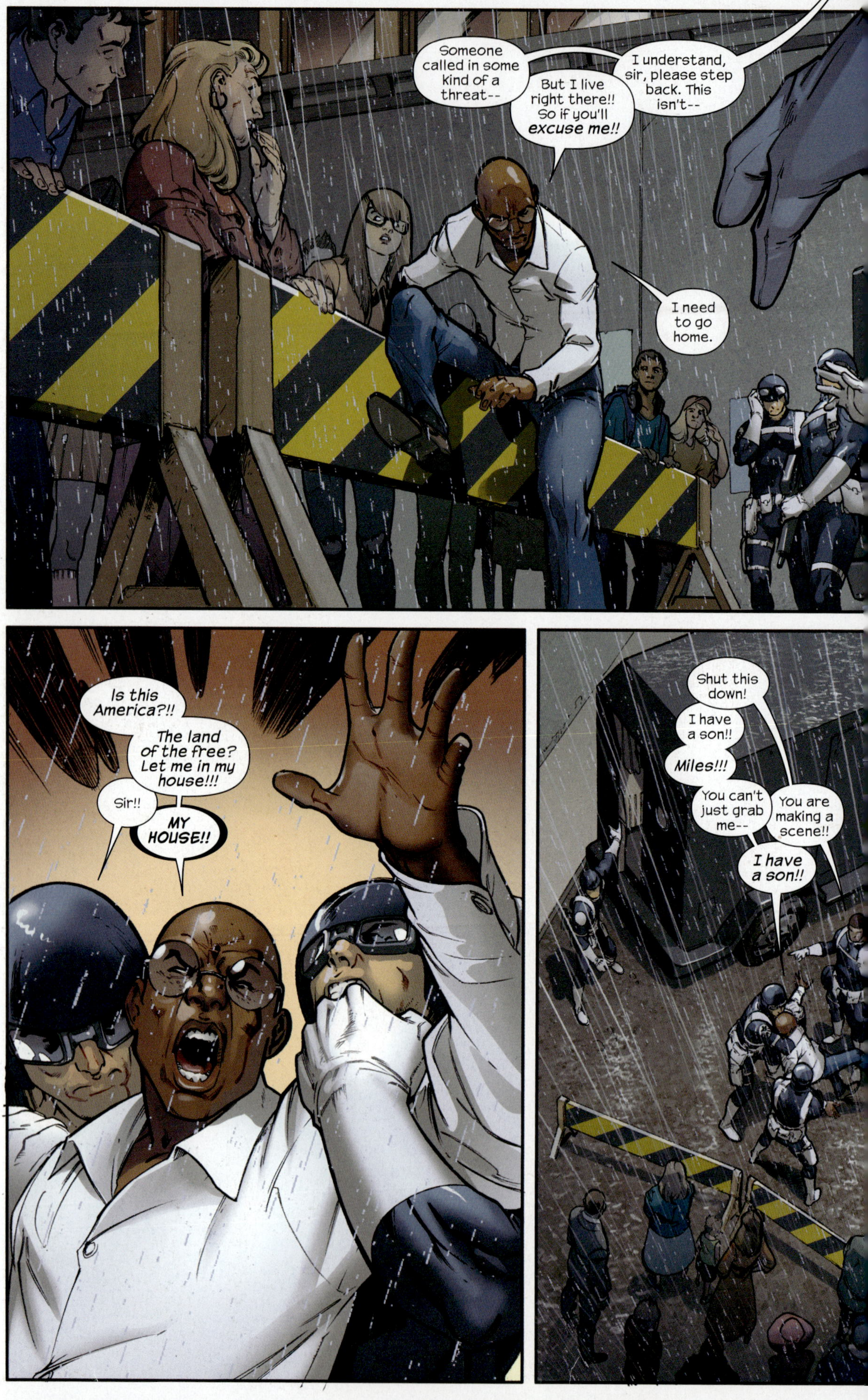
Someone called in some kind of a threat--
I understand, sir, please step back. This isn't--
But I live right there!! So if you'll *excuse me!!*
I need to go home.
Is this America?!!
The land of the free? Let me in my house!!!
Sir!!
MY HOUSE!!
Shut this down!
I have a son!!
Miles!!!
You can't just grab me--
You are making a scene!!
I have a son!!

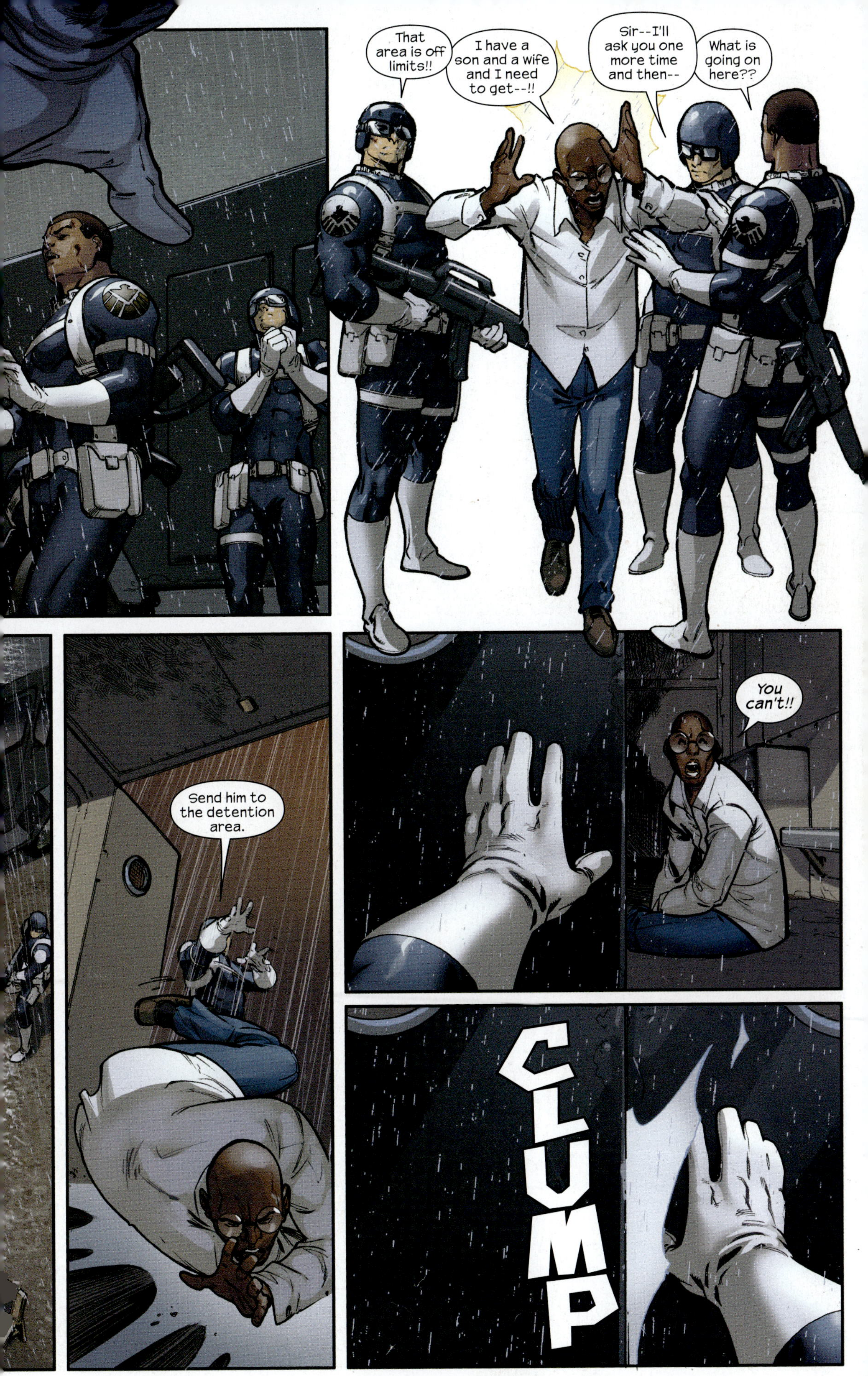
That area is off limits!!
I have a son and a wife and I need to get--!!
Sir--I'll ask you one more time and then--
What is going on here??
Send him to the detention area.
You can't!!
CLUMP

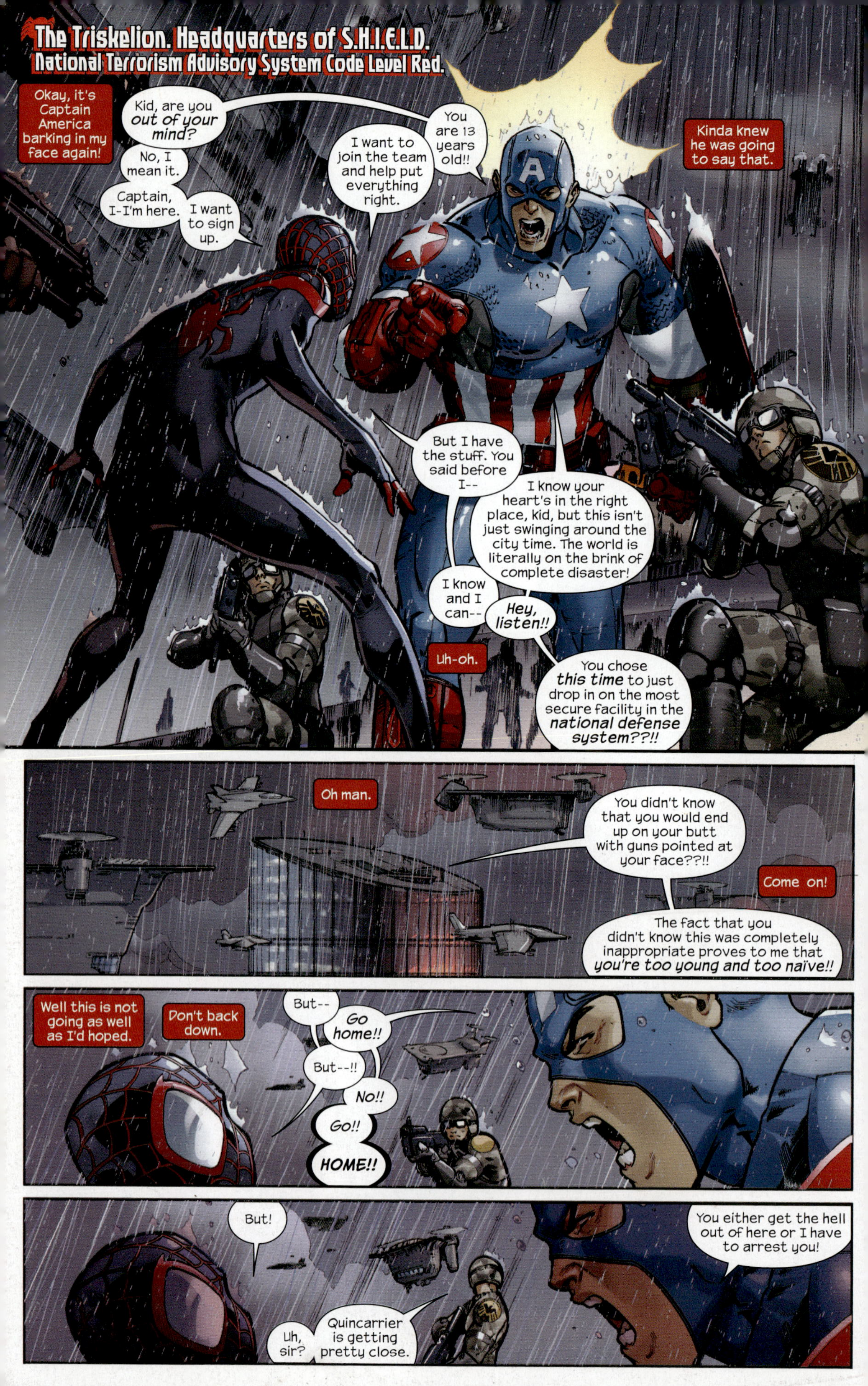
The Triskelion. Headquarters of S.H.I.E.L.D.
National Terrorism Advisory System Code Level Red.
Okay, it's Captain America barking in my face again!
Captain, I-I'm here.
I want to sign up.
Kid, are you *out of your mind?*
No, I mean it.
I want to join the team and help put everything right.
You are 13 years old!!
Kinda knew he was going to say that.
But I have the stuff. You said before I--
I know your heart's in the right place, kid, but this isn't just swinging around the city time. The world is literally on the brink of complete disaster!
I know and I can--
Hey, listen!!
Uh-oh.
You chose *this time* to just drop in on the most secure facility in the *national defense system??!!*
Oh man.
You didn't know that you would end up on your butt with guns pointed at your face??!!
Come on!
The fact that you didn't know this was completely inappropriate proves to me that *you're too young and too naïve!!*
Well this is not going as well as I'd hoped.
Don't back down.
But--
Go home!!
But--!!
No!!
Go!!
HOME!!
But!
You either get the hell out of here or I have to arrest you!
Uh, sir?
Quincarrier is getting pretty close.

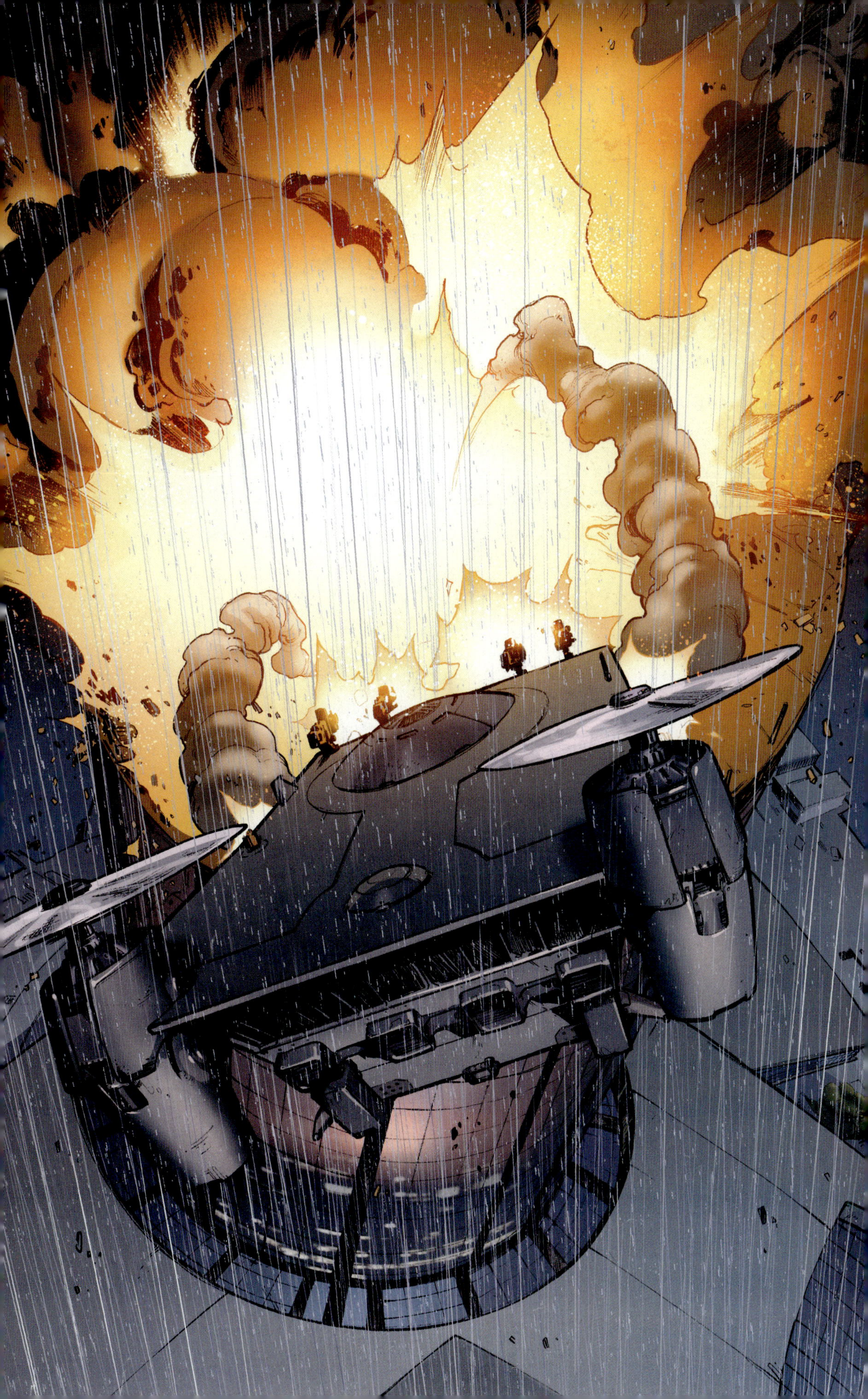

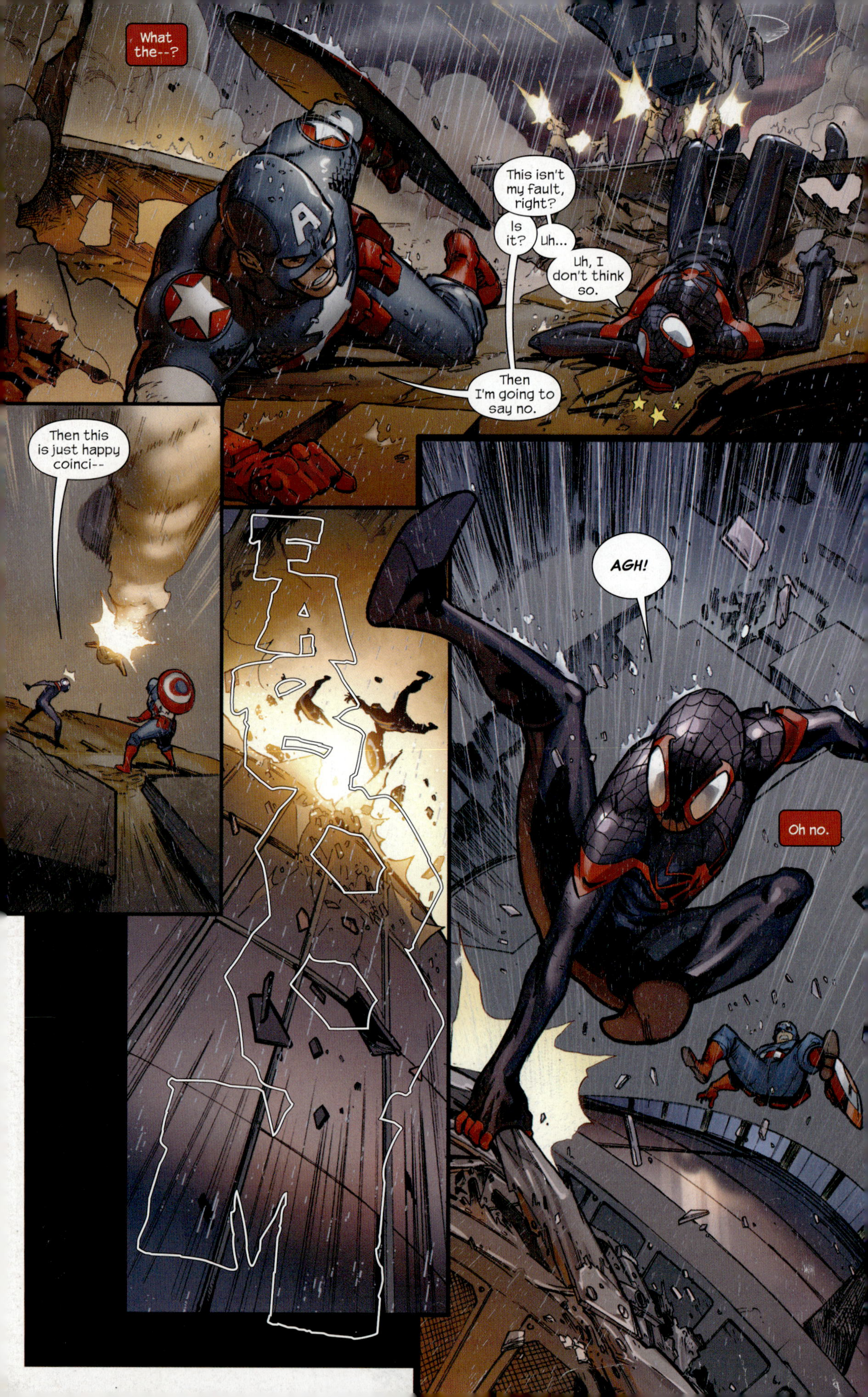
What the--?
This isn't my fault, right?
Uh...
Uh, I don't think so.
Is it?
Then I'm going to say no.
Then this is just happy coinci--
AGH!
Oh no.

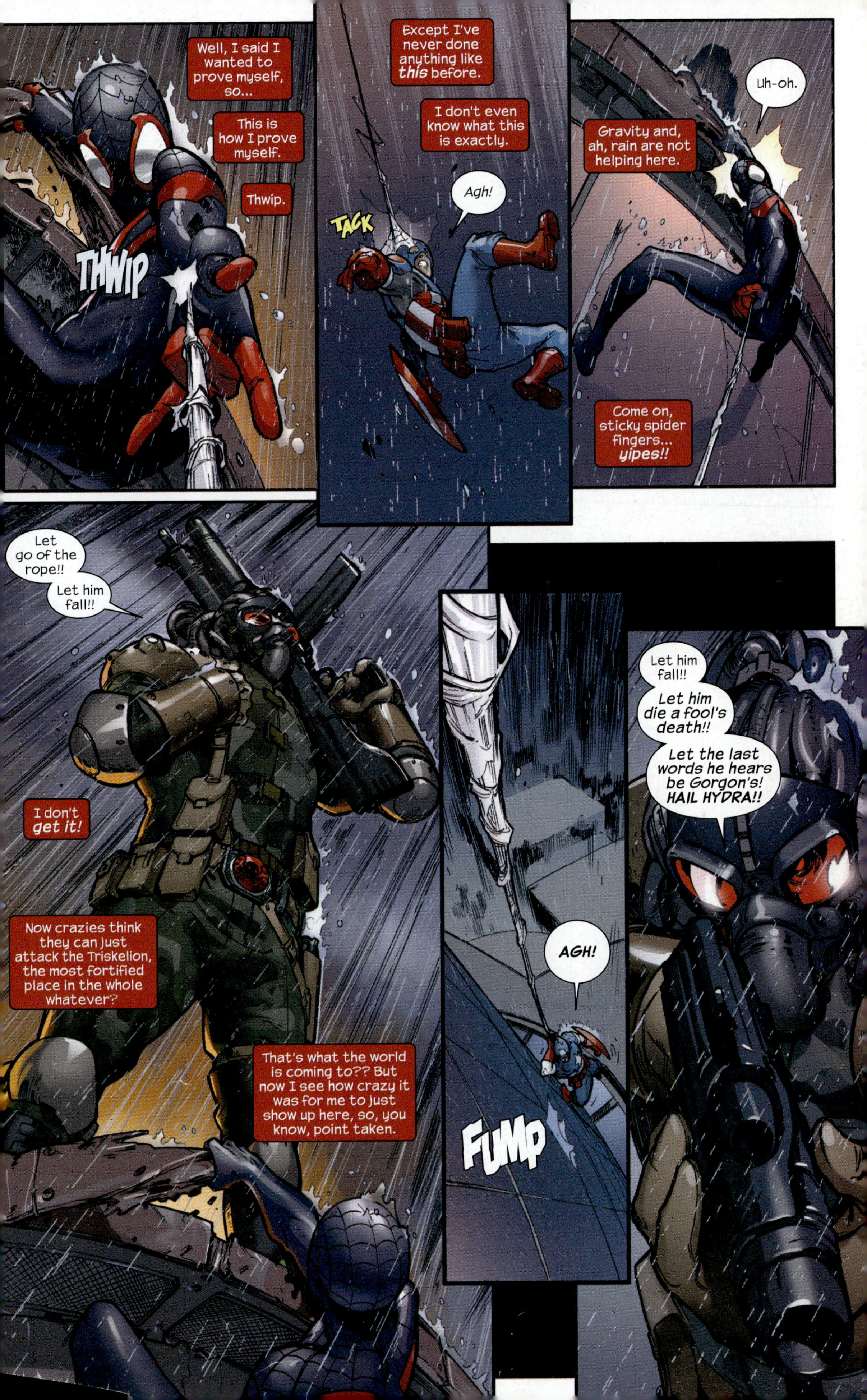
Well, I said I wanted to prove myself, so...
This is how I prove myself.
Thwip.
THWIP
Except I've never done anything like *this* before.
I don't even know what this is exactly.
TACK
Agh!
Uh-oh.
Gravity and, ah, rain are not helping here.
Come on, sticky spider fingers... *yipes!!*
Let go of the rope!!
Let him fall!!
I don't *get it!*
Now crazies think they can just attack the Triskelion, the most fortified place in the whole whatever?
That's what the world is coming to?? But now I see how crazy it was for me to just show up here, so, you know, point taken.
AGH!
FUMP
Let him fall!!
Let him die a fool's death!!
Let the last words he hears be Gorgon's! HAIL HYDRA!!

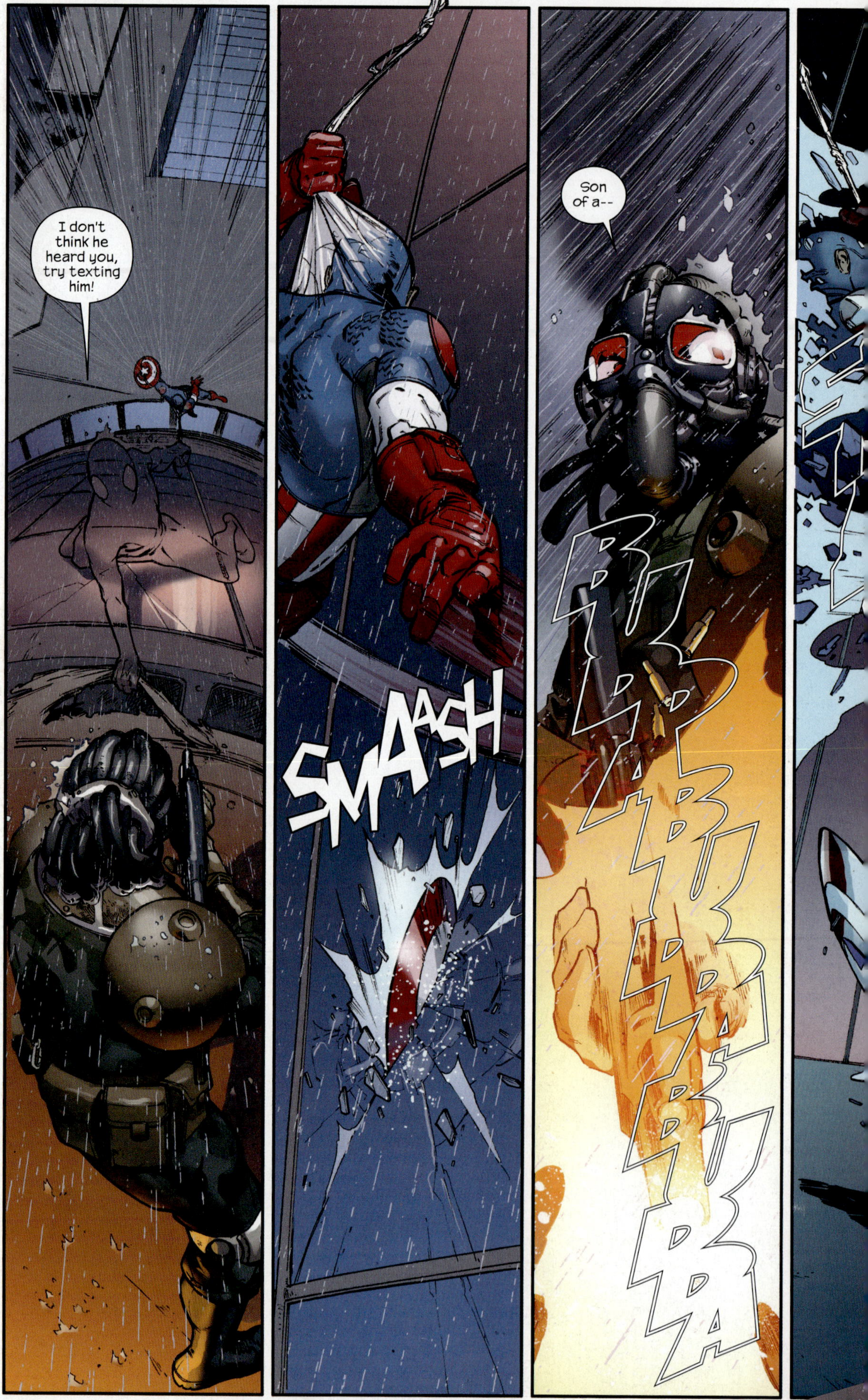

I don't think he heard you, try texting him!
SMAASH
Son of a--
BUDDABUDDABUDDA

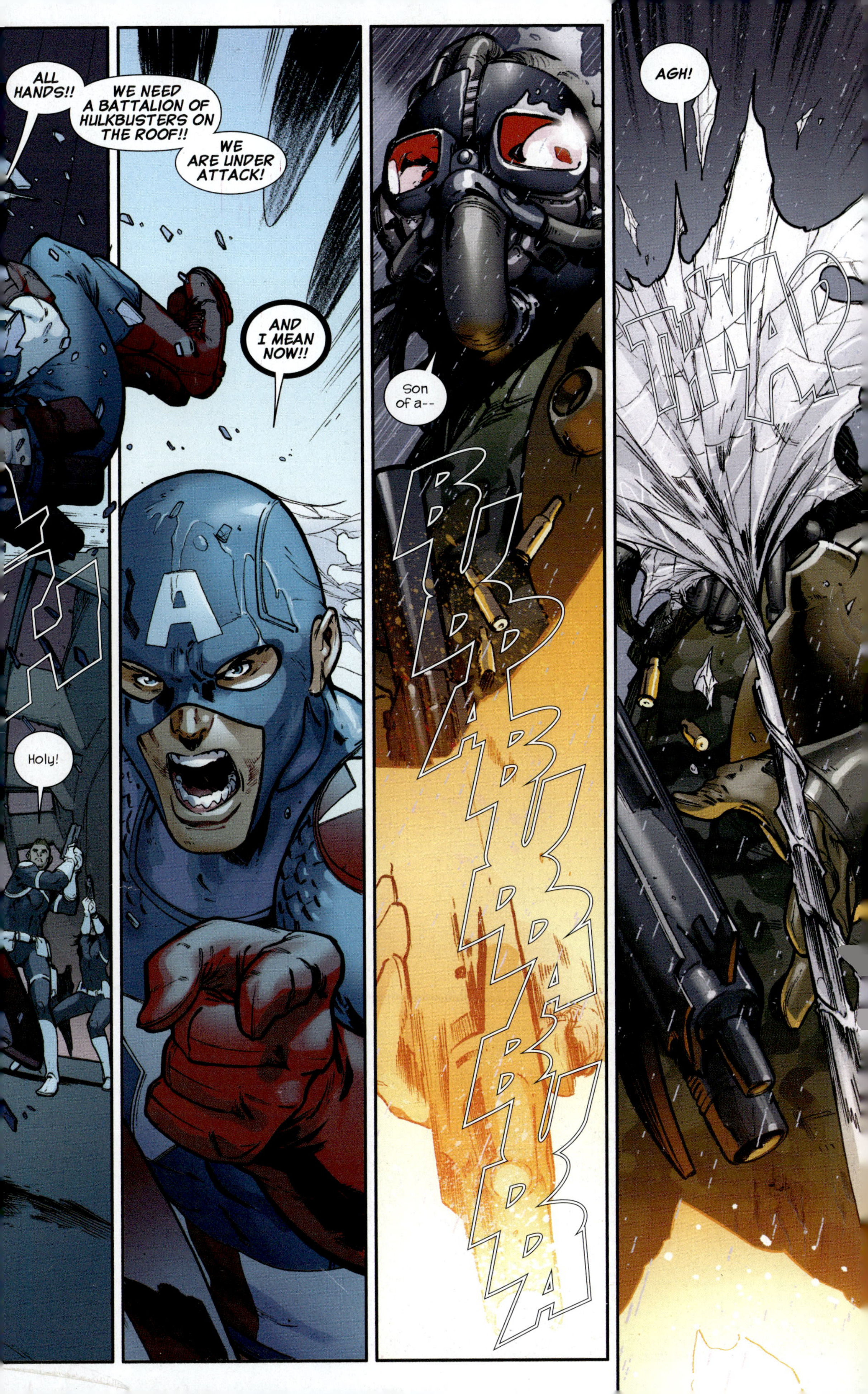
ALL HANDS!!
WE NEED A BATTALION OF HULKBUSTERS ON THE ROOF!!
WE ARE UNDER ATTACK!
AND I MEAN NOW!!
Holy!
Son of a--
AGH!

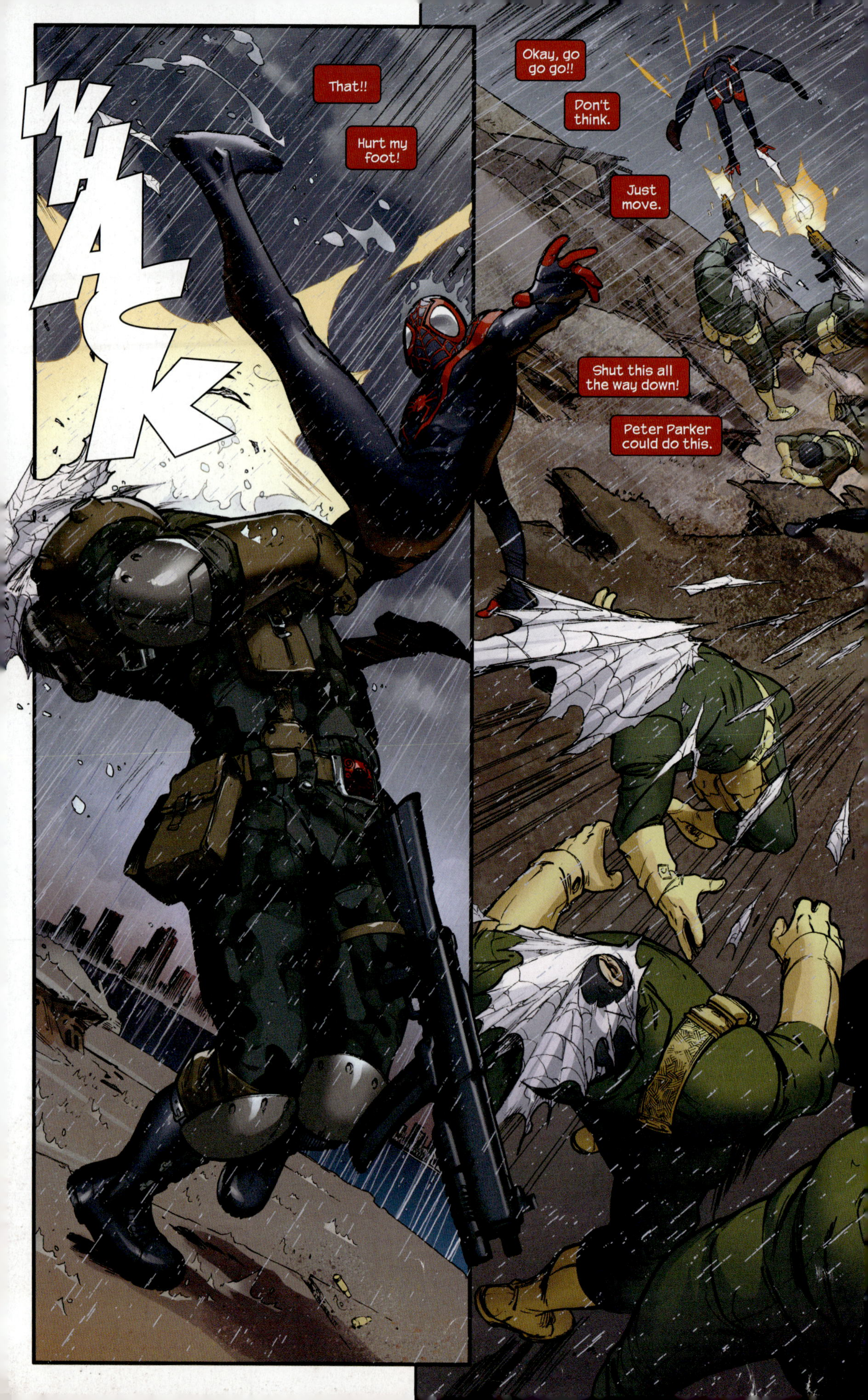
WHACK
That!!
Hurt my foot!
Okay, go go go!!
Don't think.
Just move.
Shut this all the way down!
Peter Parker could do this.

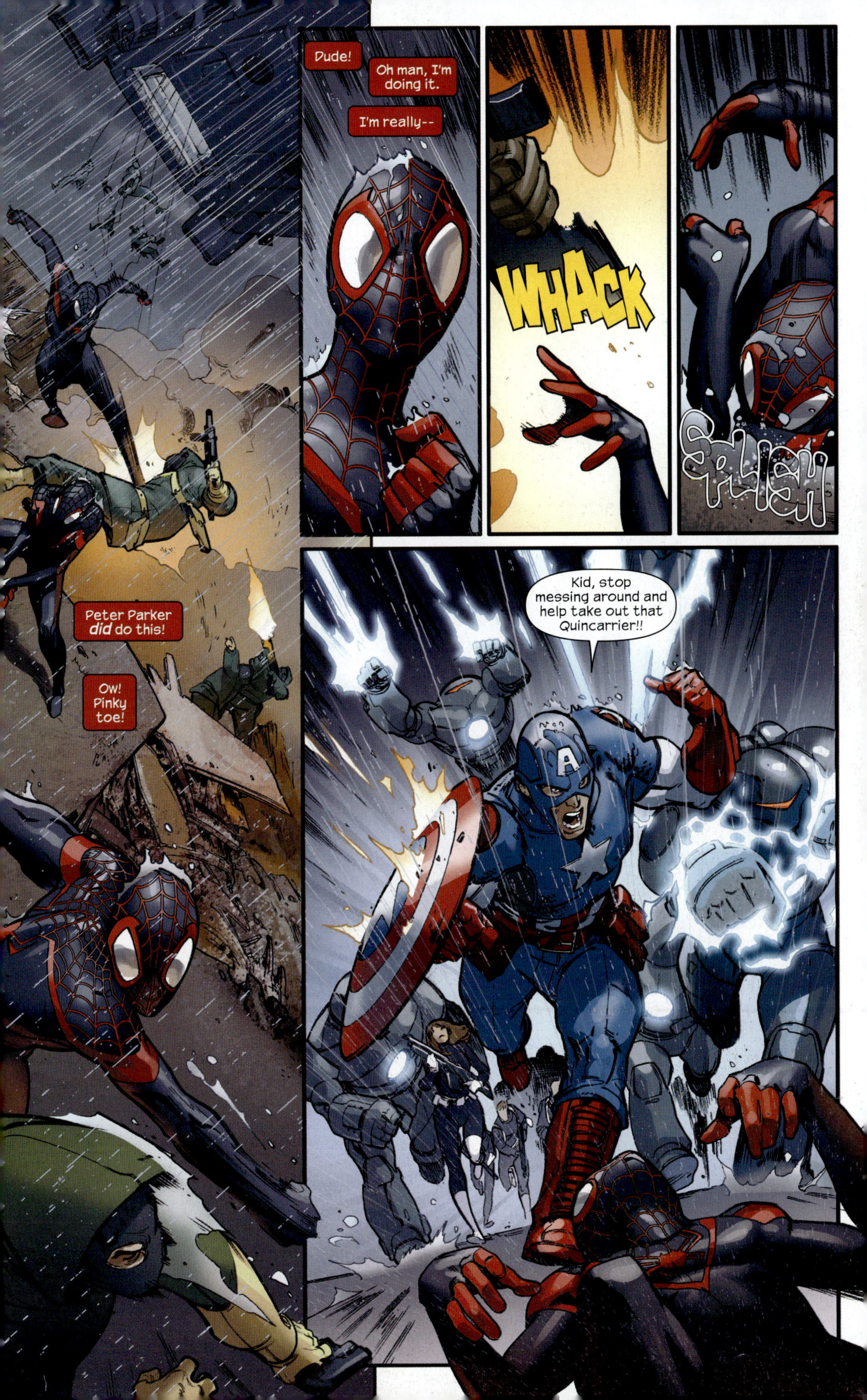
Dude!
Oh man, I'm doing it.
I'm really--
WHACK
SPLISH
Peter Parker did do this!
Ow! Pinky toe!
Kid, stop messing around and help take out that Quincarrier!!

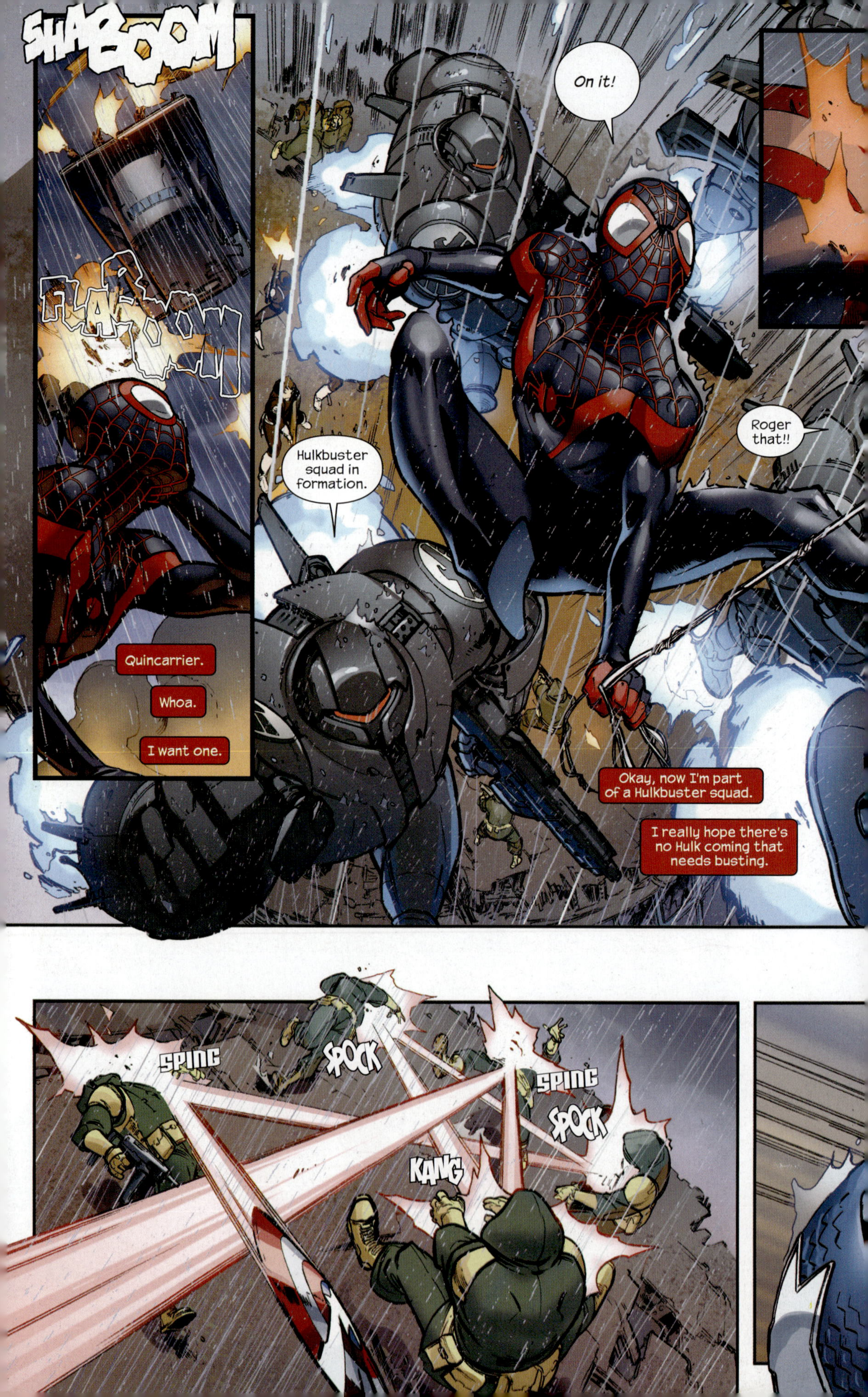

SHABOOM
FLABOOM
Quincarrier.
Whoa.
I want one.
On it!
Hulkbuster squad in formation.
Roger that!!
Okay, now I'm part of a Hulkbuster squad.
I really hope there's no Hulk coming that needs busting.
SPING
SPOCK
SPING
SPOCK
KANG

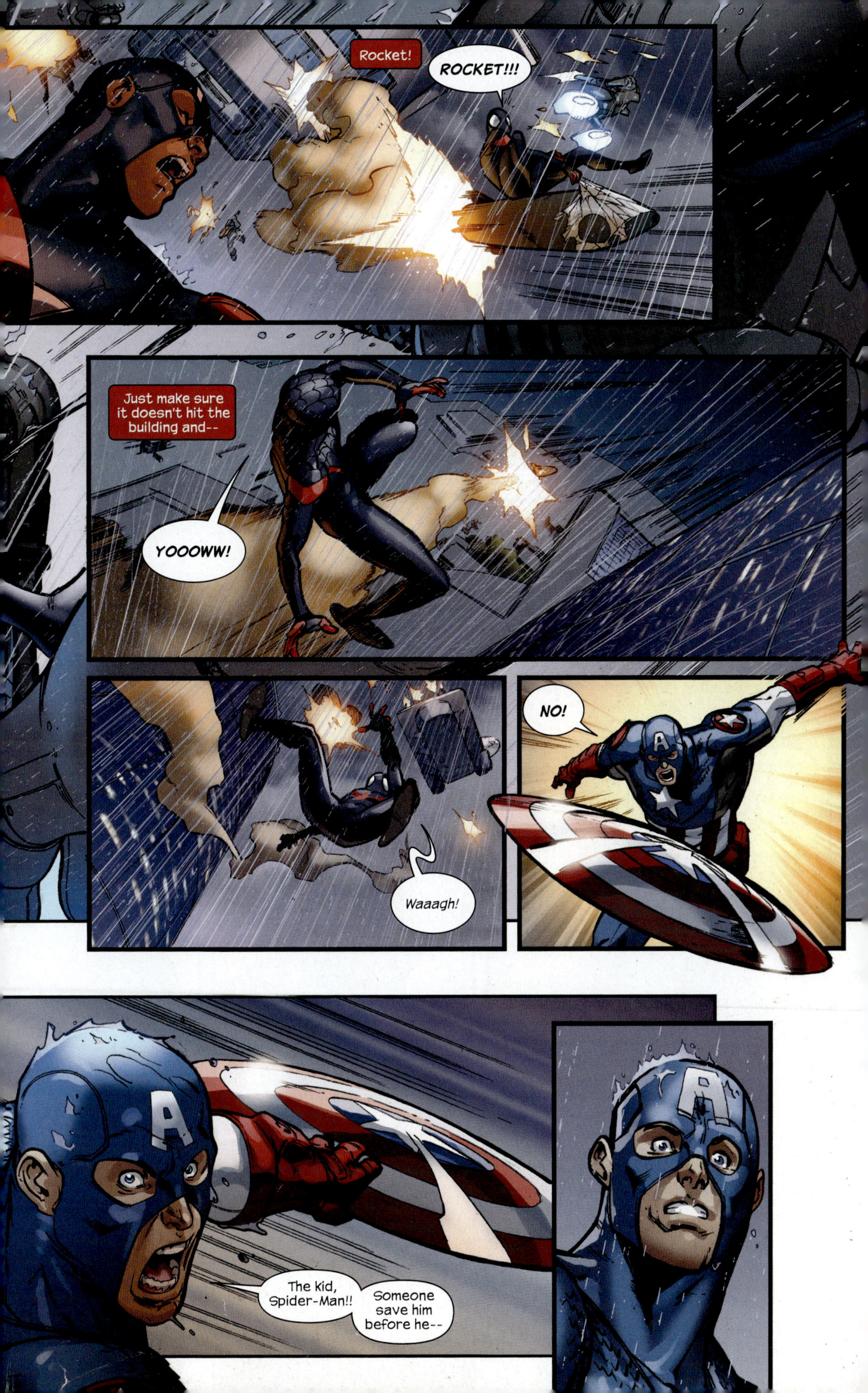
Rocket!
ROCKET!!!
Just make sure it doesn't hit the building and--
YOOOWW!
Waaagh!
NO!
The kid, Spider-Man!!
Someone save him before he--

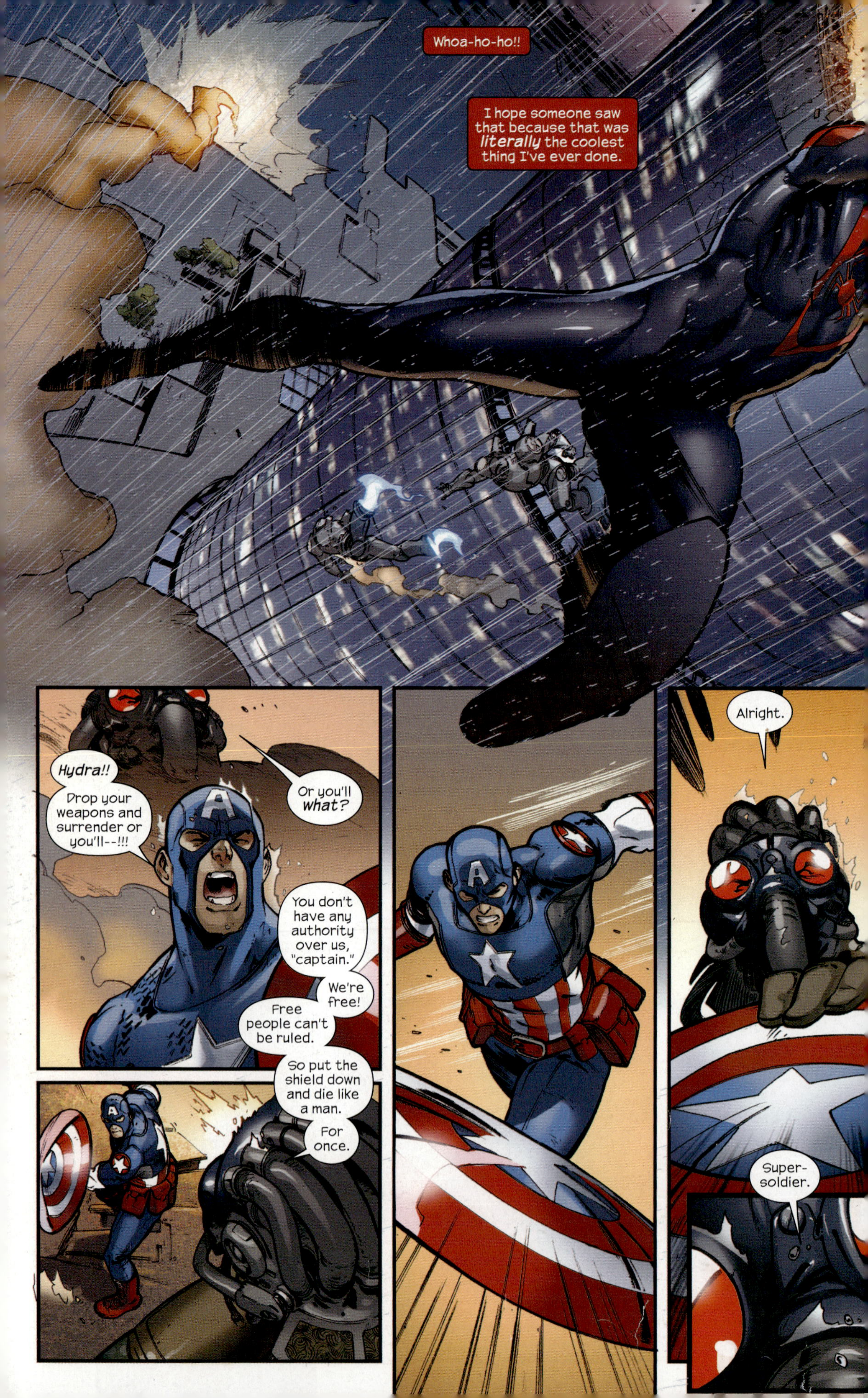
Whoa-ho-ho!!
I hope someone saw that because that was *literally* the coolest thing I've ever done.
Hydra!!
Drop your weapons and surrender or you'll--!!!
Or you'll *what?*
You don't have any authority over us, "captain."
We're free!
Free people can't be ruled.
So put the shield down and die like a man.
For once.
Alright.
Super-soldier.

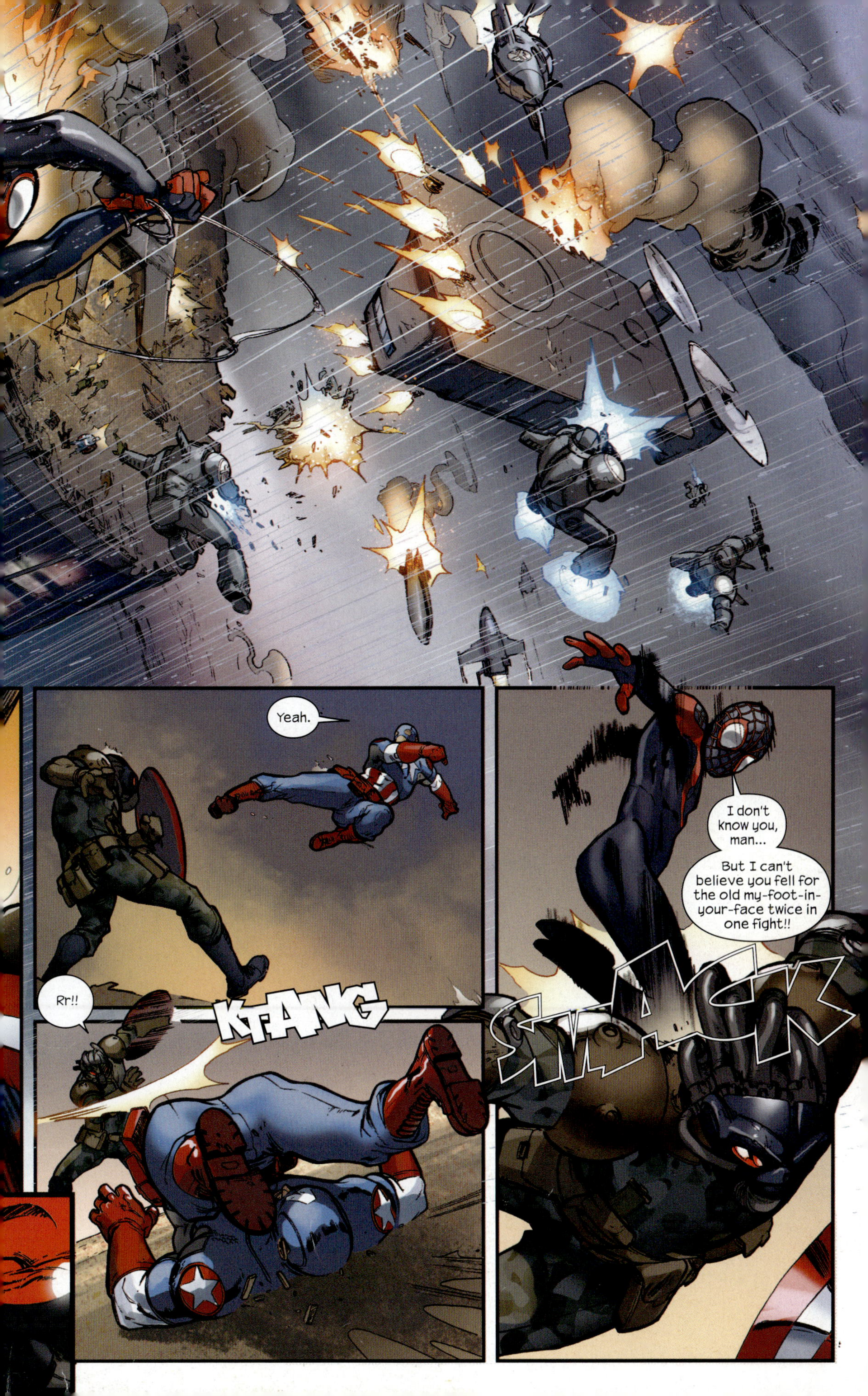
Yeah.
I don't know you, man...
But I can't believe you fell for the old my-foot-in-your-face twice in one fight!!
Rr!!
KTANG
SMACK

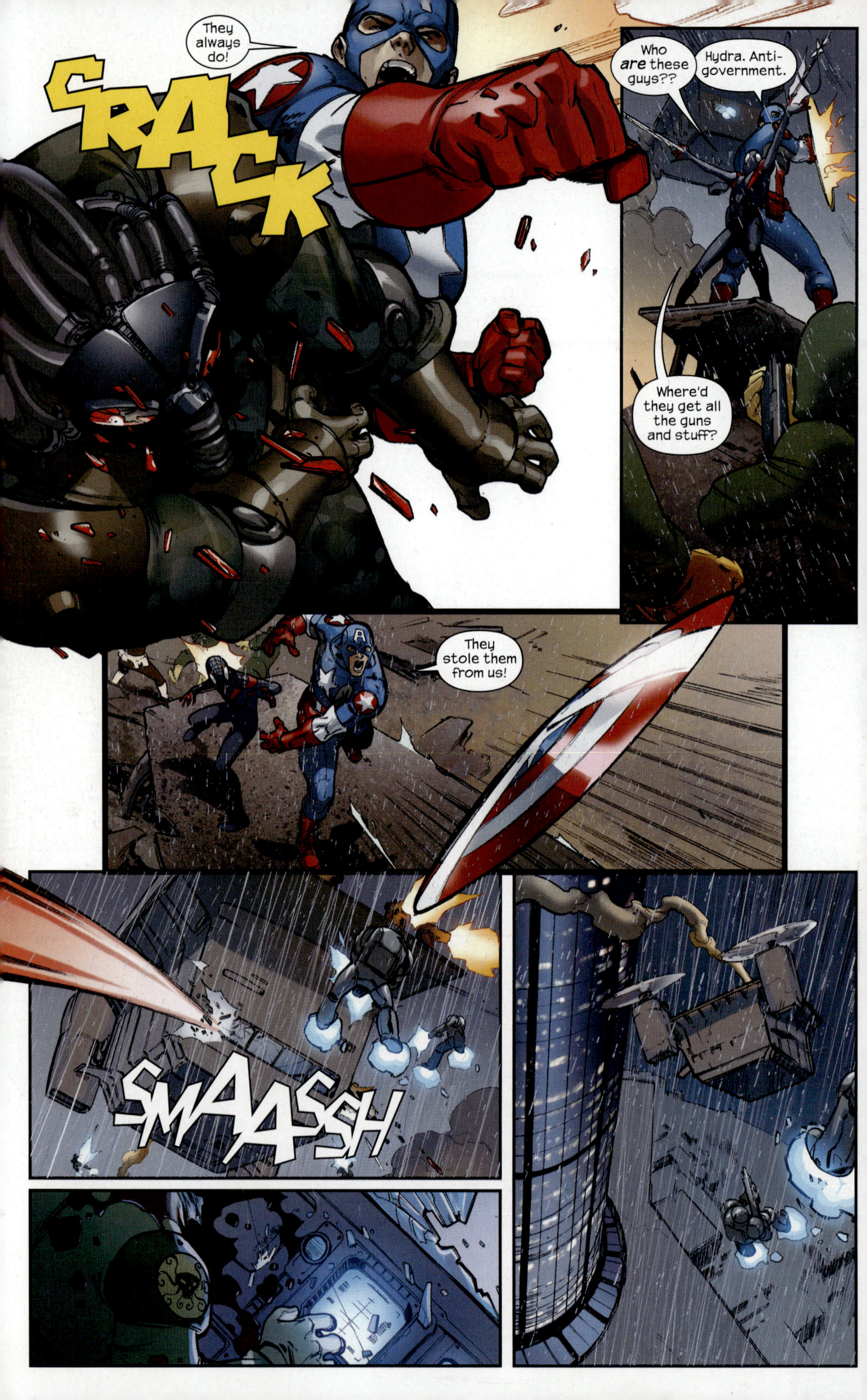
They always do!
CRACK
Who are these guys??
Hydra. Anti-government.
Where'd they get all the guns and stuff?
They stole them from us!
SMAASSH

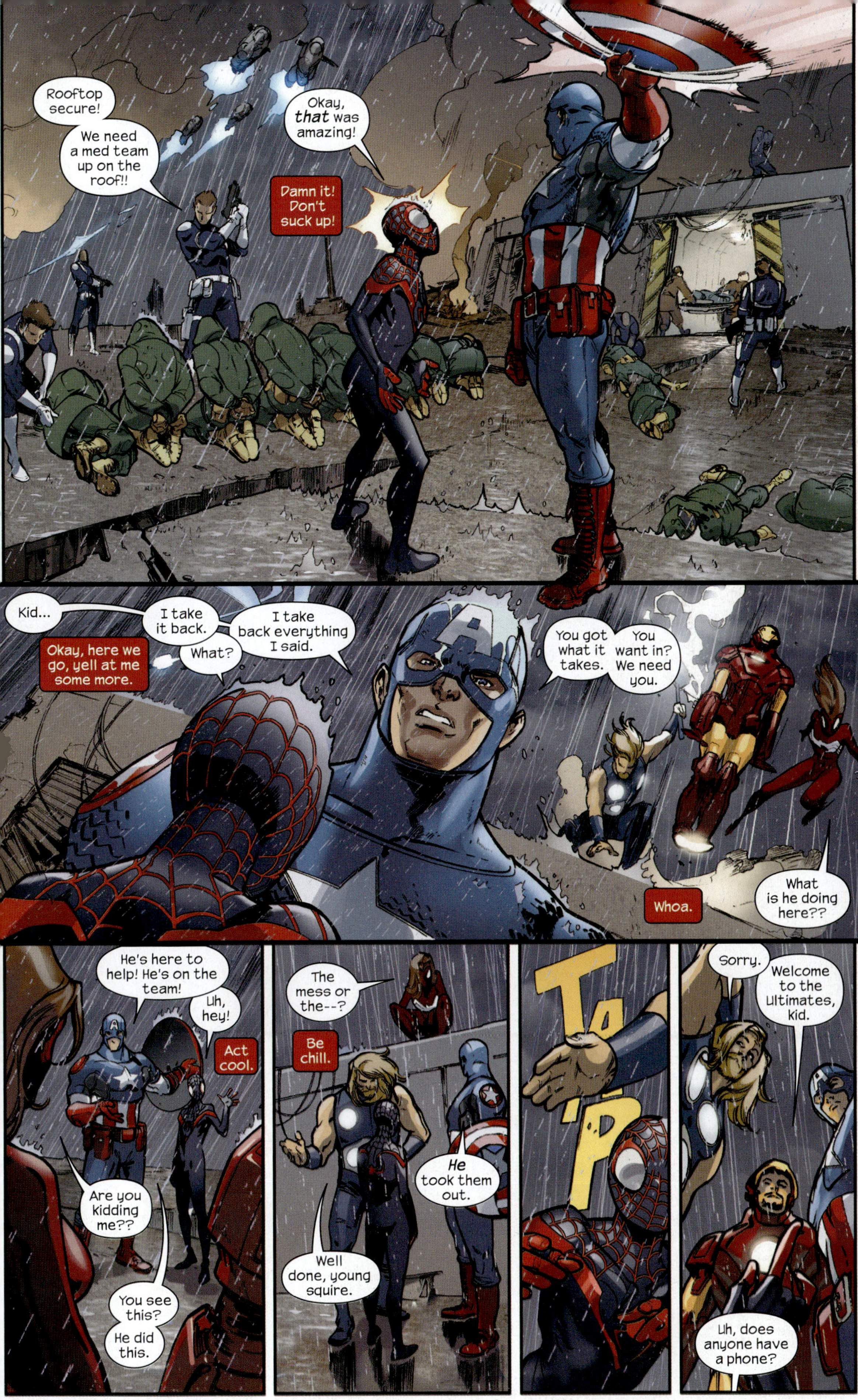

Rooftop secure!
We need a med team up on the roof!!
Okay, *that* was amazing!
Damn it! Don't suck up!
Kid...
I take it back.
Okay, here we go, yell at me some more.
What?
I take back everything I said.
You got what it takes.
You want in? We need you.
Whoa.
What is he doing here??
He's here to help! He's on the team!
Uh, hey!
Act cool.
Are you kidding me??
You see this?
He did this.
The mess or the--?
Be chill.
He took them out.
Well done, young squire.
TAP
Sorry.
Welcome to the Ultimates, kid.
Uh, does anyone have a phone?

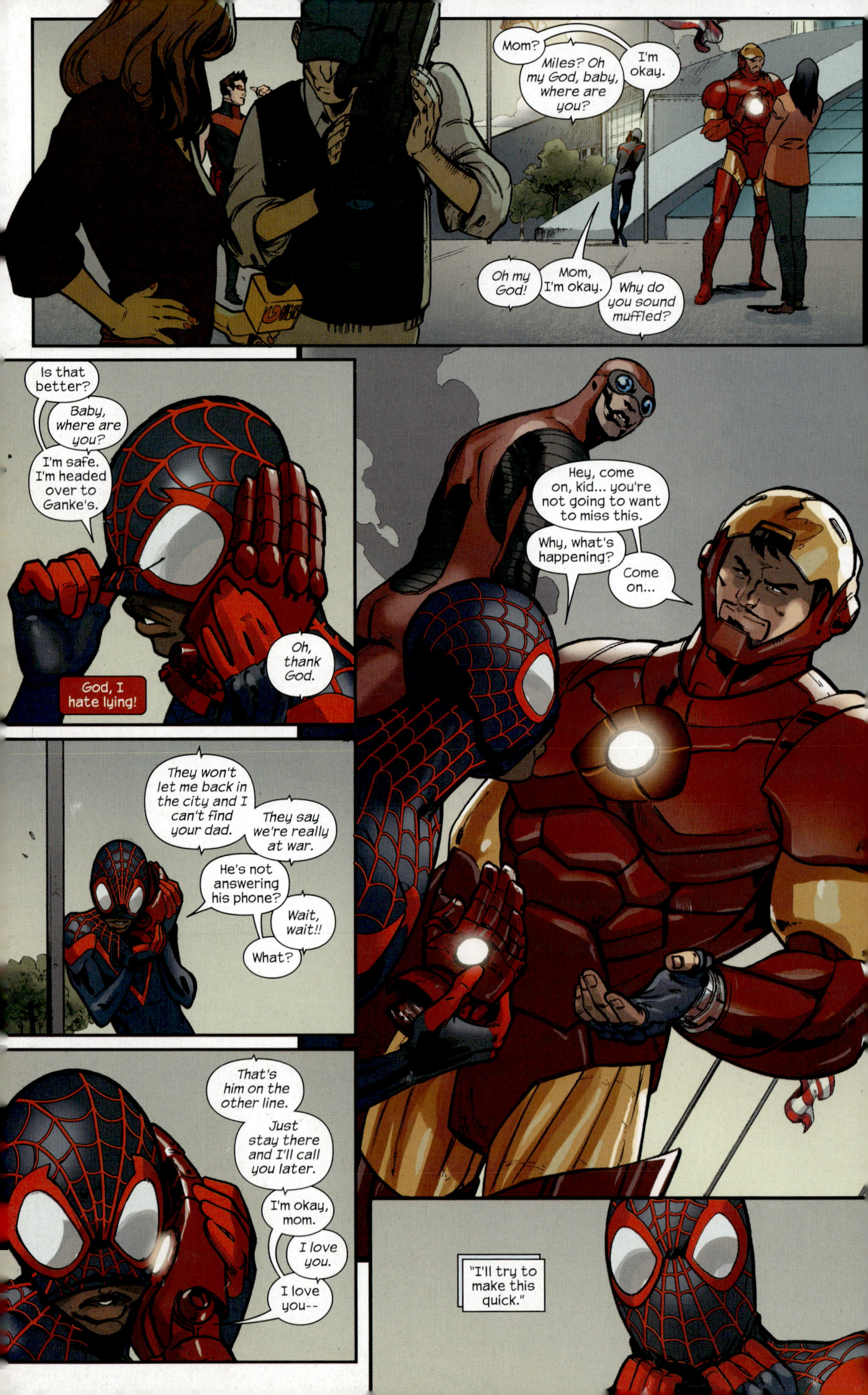
Mom?
Miles? Oh my God, baby, where are you?
I'm okay.
Oh my God!
Mom, I'm okay.
Why do you sound muffled?
Is that better?
Baby, where are you?
I'm safe. I'm headed over to Ganke's.
Oh, thank God.
God, I hate lying!
Hey, come on, kid... you're not going to want to miss this.
Why, what's happening?
Come on...
They won't let me back in the city and I can't find your dad.
They say we're really at war.
He's not answering his phone?
Wait, wait!!
What?
That's him on the other line.
Just stay there and I'll call you later.
I'm okay, mom.
I love you.
I love you--
"I'll try to make this quick."

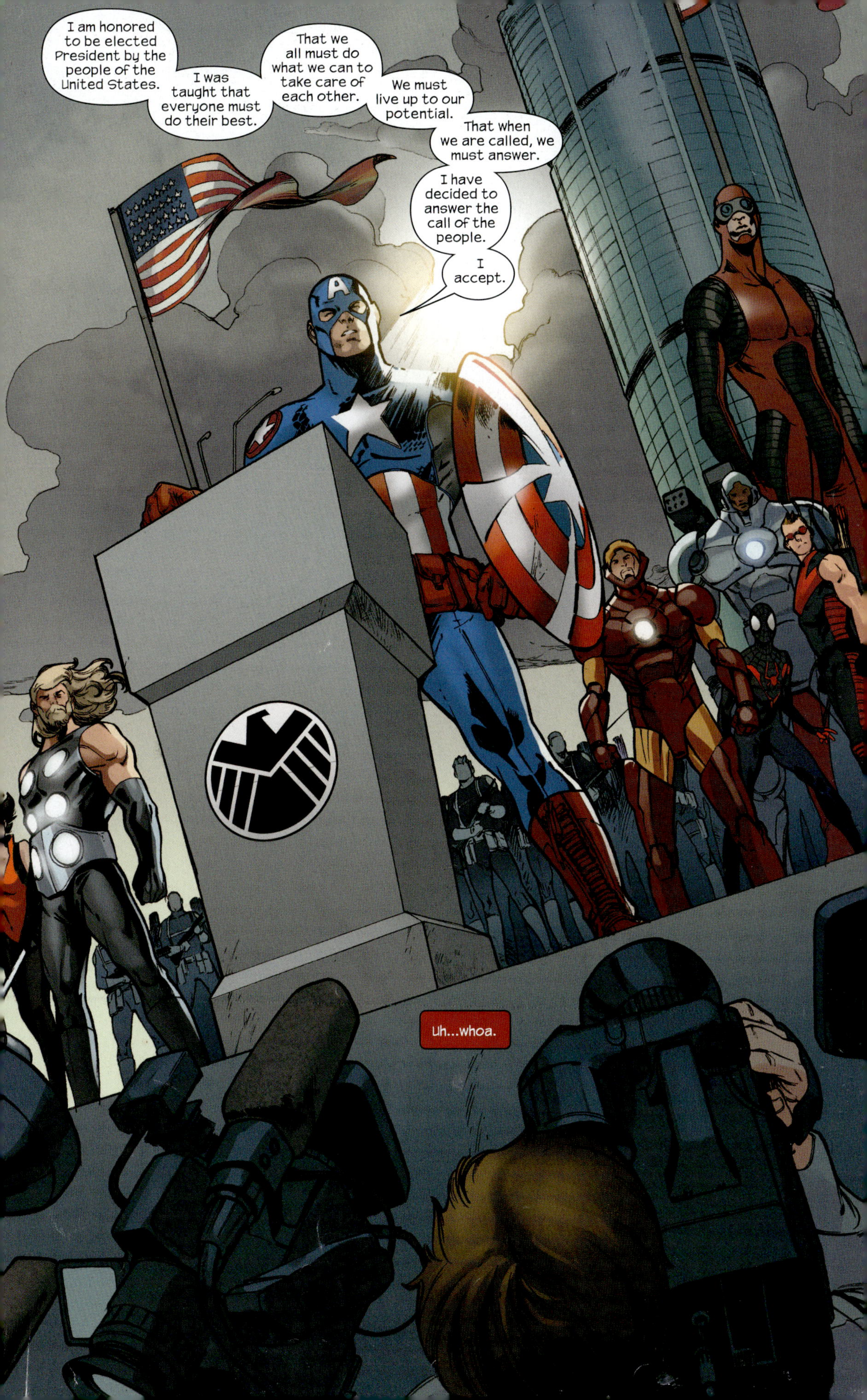
I am honored to be elected President by the people of the United States.
I was taught that everyone must do their best.
That we all must do what we can to take care of each other.
We must live up to our potential.
That when we are called, we must answer.
I have decided to answer the call of the people.
I accept.
Uh...whoa.

UNITED WE STAND

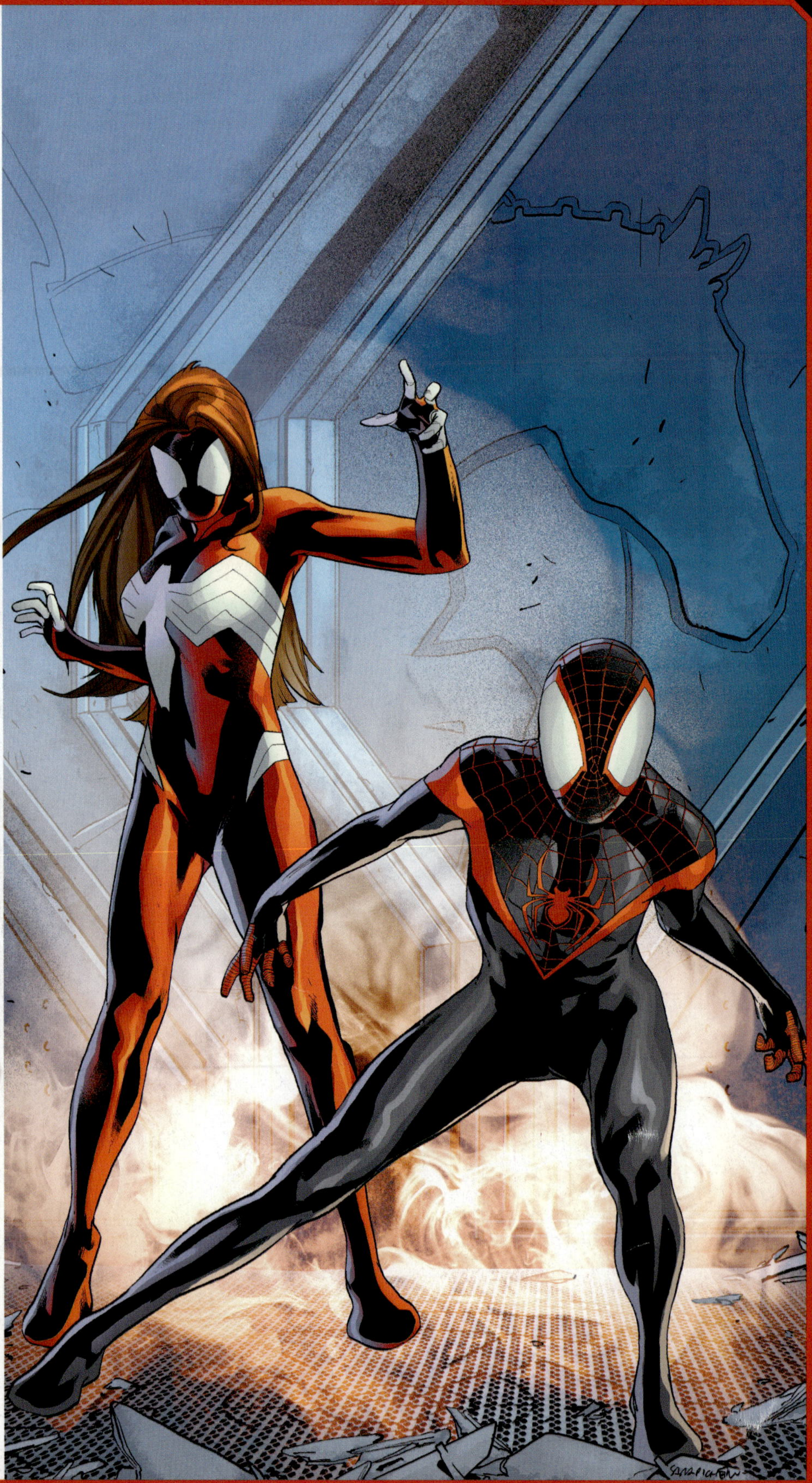

S.H.I.E.L.D. SITUATION MAP:

[Anti-government militia hot spots]

Idaho, Montana, N. Dakota, S. Dakota, Arizona, Wyoming

Wyoming

status unknown

[Eastern seaboard control zone]

New England, New York, New Jersey, Delaware, Washington, D.C., Maryland, Pennsylvania, Virginia

secured by National Guard under emergency powers committee

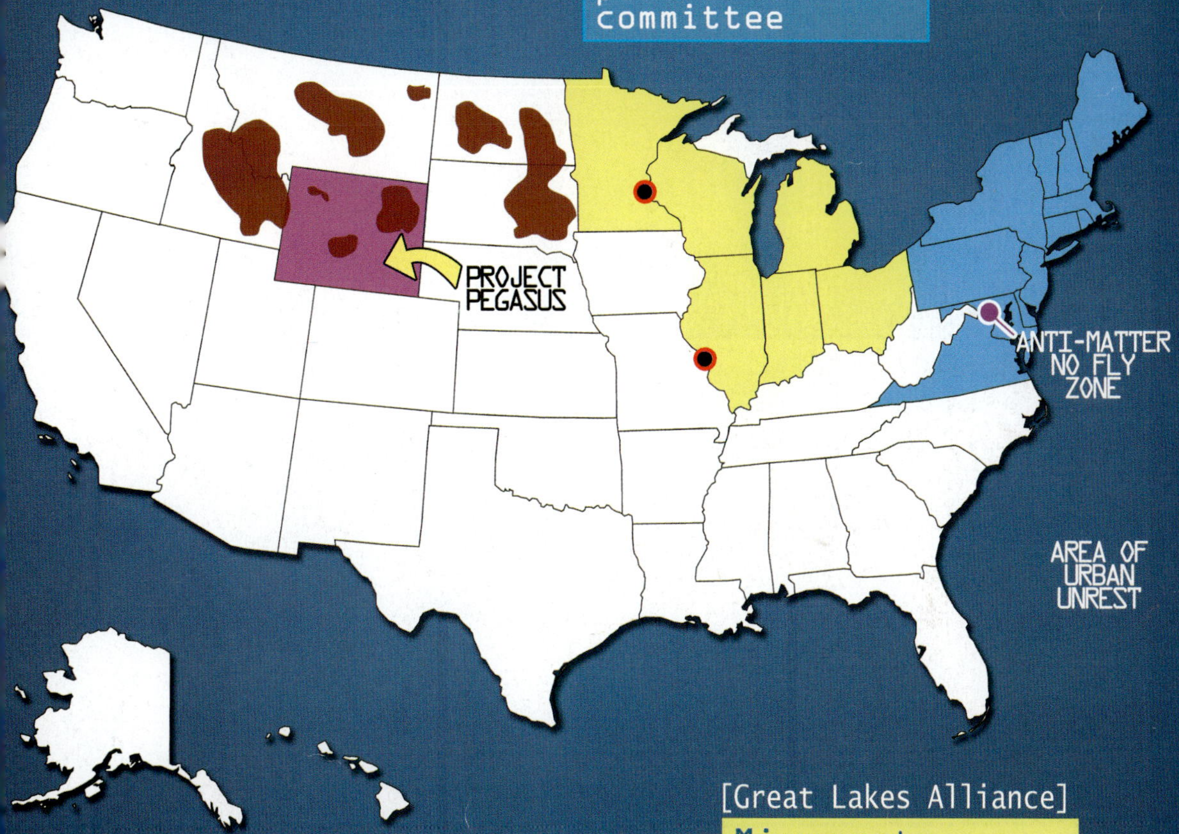
PROJECT PEGASUS
ANTI-MATTER NO FLY ZONE
AREA OF URBAN UNREST

[Great Lakes Alliance]

Minnesota, Wisconsin, Michigan, Illinois, Indiana, Ohio

Independent nation

ALL STATES SHOWN IN WHITE ARE U.S. GOVERNMENT-CONTROLLED ZONES

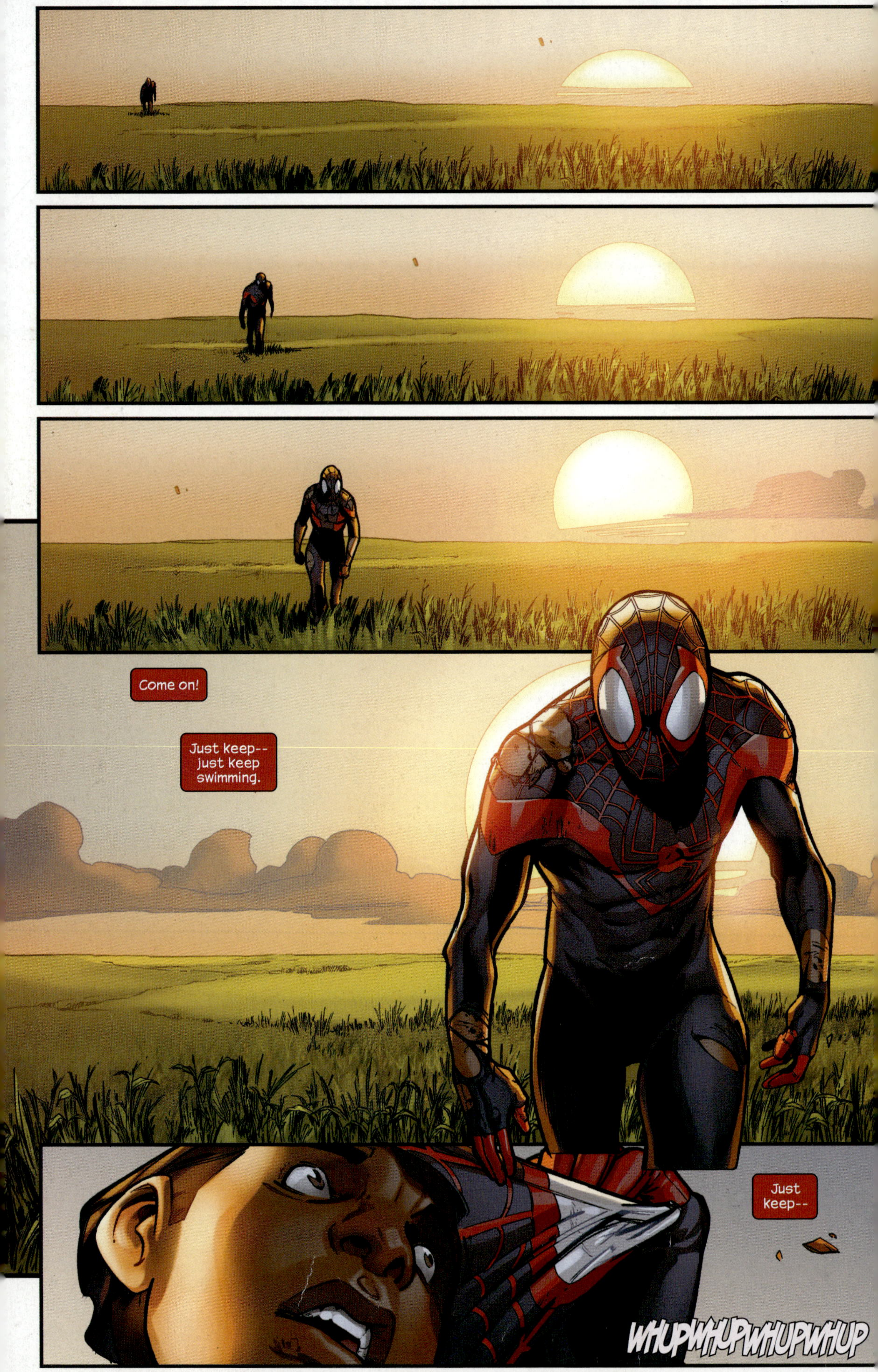
Come on!
Just keep-- just keep swimming.
Just keep--
WHUPWHUPWHUPWHUP

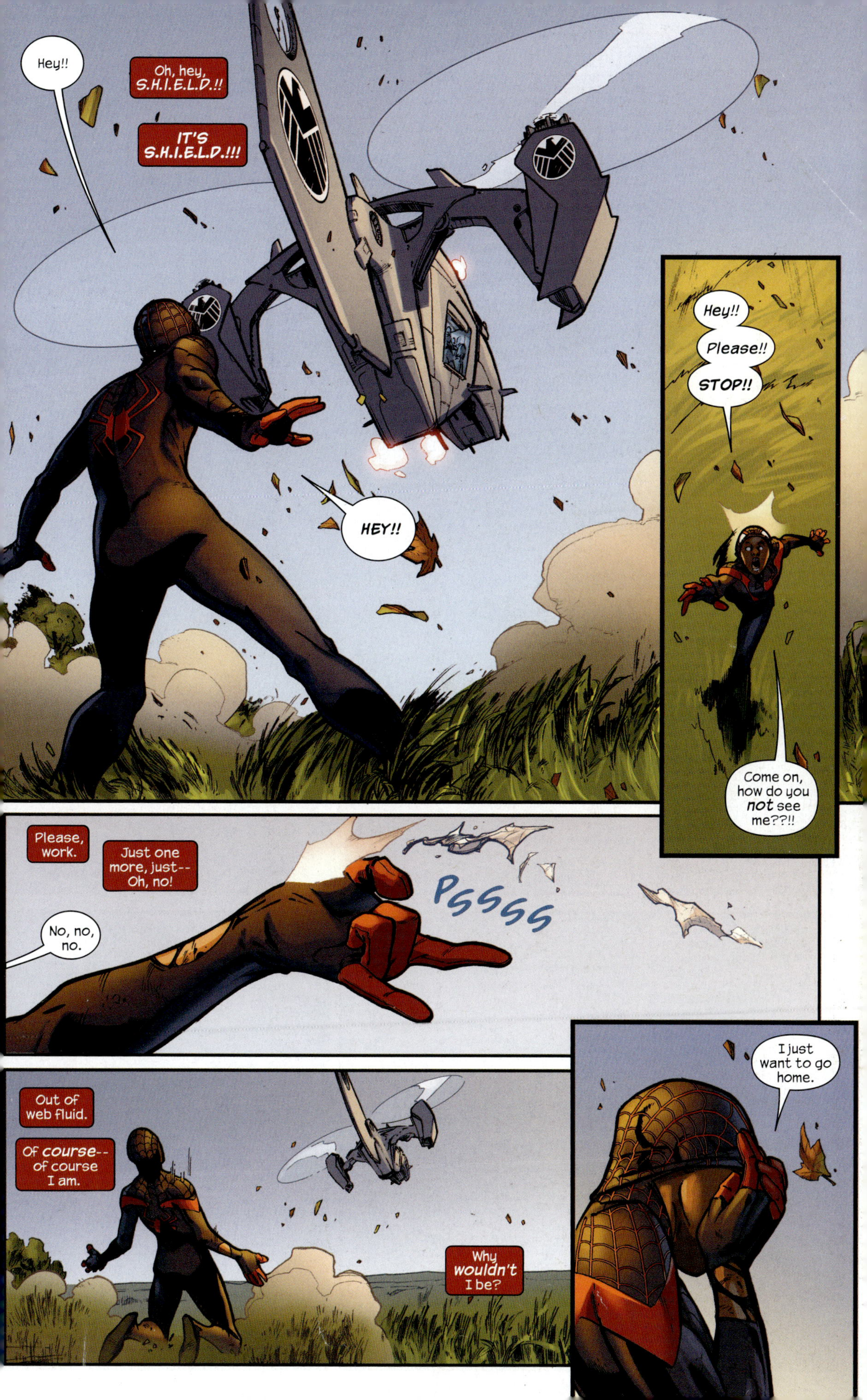

Hey!!
Oh, hey, S.H.I.E.L.D.!!
IT'S S.H.I.E.L.D.!!!
HEY!!
Hey!!
Please!!
STOP!!
Come on, how do you not see me??!!
Please, work.
Just one more, just-- Oh, no!
No, no, no.
PSSSS
Out of web fluid.
Of course-- of course I am.
Why wouldn't I be?
I just want to go home.

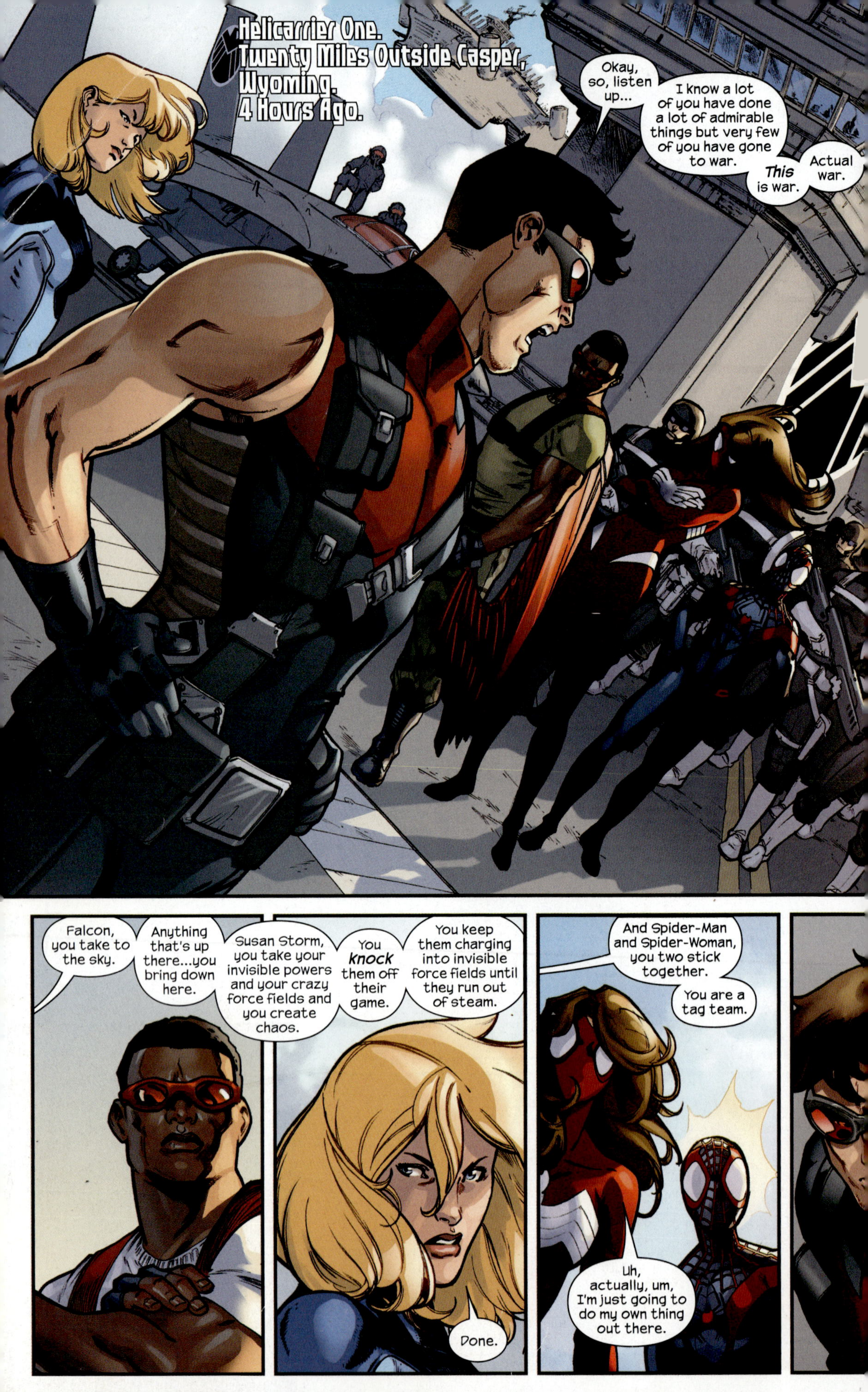
Helicarrier One.
Twenty Miles Outside Casper, Wyoming.
4 Hours Ago.
Okay, so, listen up...
I know a lot of you have done a lot of admirable things but very few of you have gone to war.
This is war.
Actual war.
Falcon, you take to the sky.
Anything that's up there...you bring down here.
Susan Storm, you take your invisible powers and your crazy force fields and you create chaos.
You ***knock*** them off their game.
You keep them charging into invisible force fields until they run out of steam.
Done.
And Spider-Man and Spider-Woman, you two stick together.
You are a tag team.
Uh, actually, um, I'm just going to do my own thing out there.

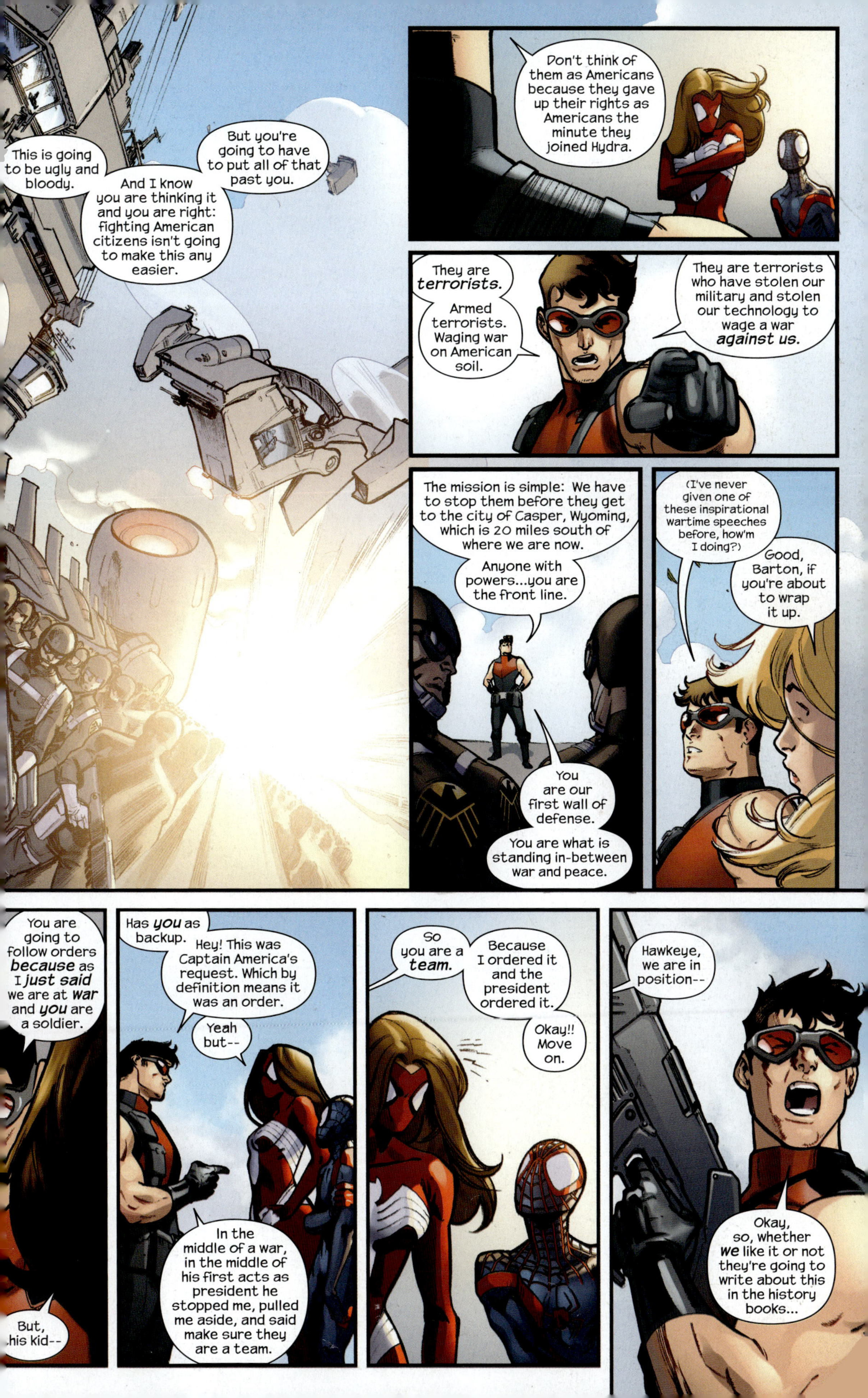

This is going to be ugly and bloody.
And I know you are thinking it and you are right: fighting American citizens isn't going to make this any easier.
But you're going to have to put all of that past you.
Don't think of them as Americans because they gave up their rights as Americans the minute they joined Hydra.
They are *terrorists.*
Armed terrorists. Waging war on American soil.
They are terrorists who have stolen our military and stolen our technology to wage a war *against us.*
The mission is simple: We have to stop them before they get to the city of Casper, Wyoming, which is 20 miles south of where we are now.
Anyone with powers...you are the front line.
You are our first wall of defense.
You are what is standing in-between war and peace.
(I've never given one of these inspirational wartime speeches before, how'm I doing?)
Good, Barton, if you're about to wrap it up.
You are going to follow orders *because* as I *just said* we are at *war* and *you* are a soldier.
But, his kid--
Has *you* as backup.
Hey! This was Captain America's request. Which by definition means it was an order.
Yeah but--
In the middle of a war, in the middle of his first acts as president he stopped me, pulled me aside, and said make sure they are a team.
So you are a *team.*
Because I ordered it and the president ordered it.
Okay!! Move on.
Hawkeye, we are in position--
Okay, so, whether *we* like it or not they're going to write about this in the history books...

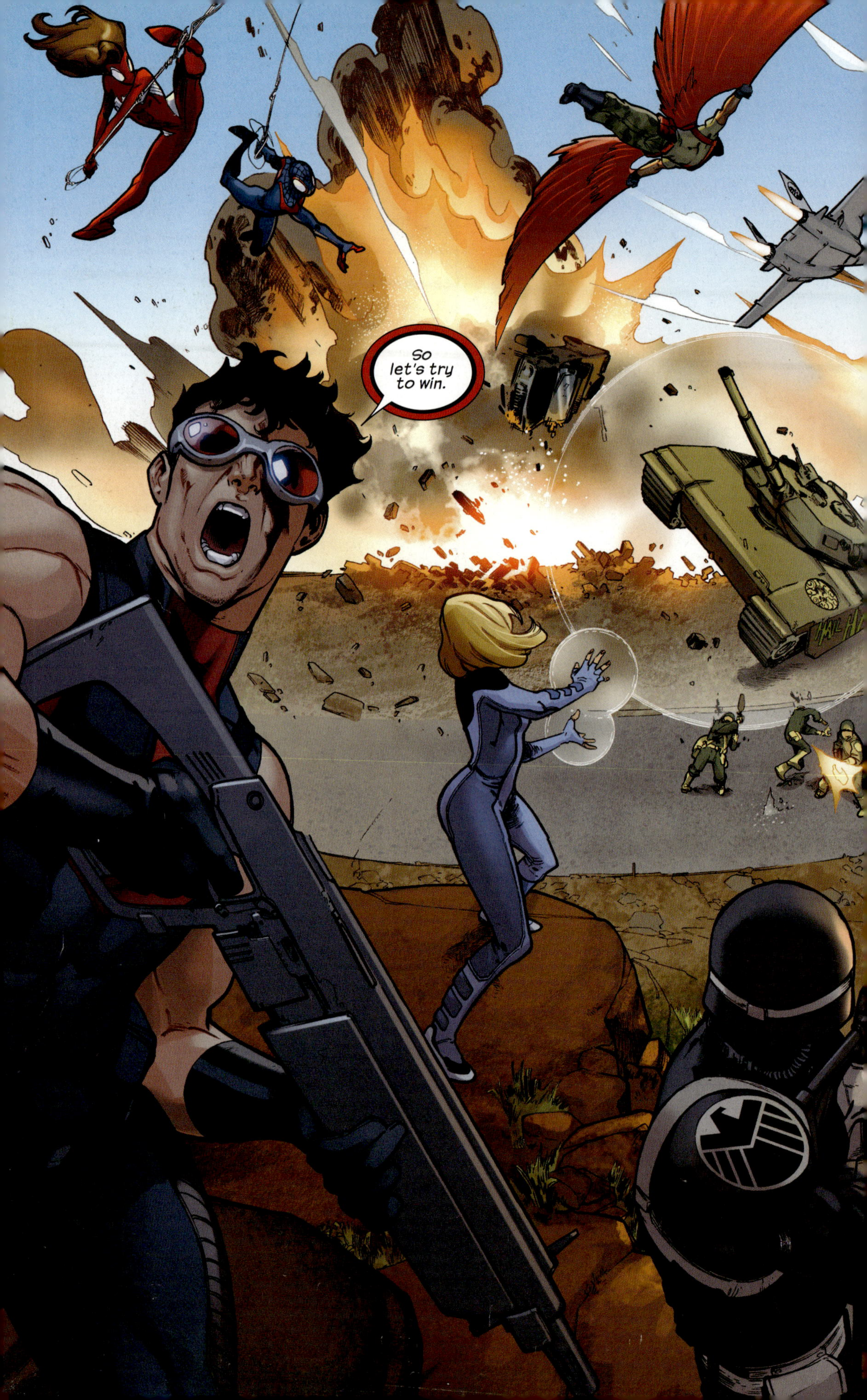
So let's try to win.

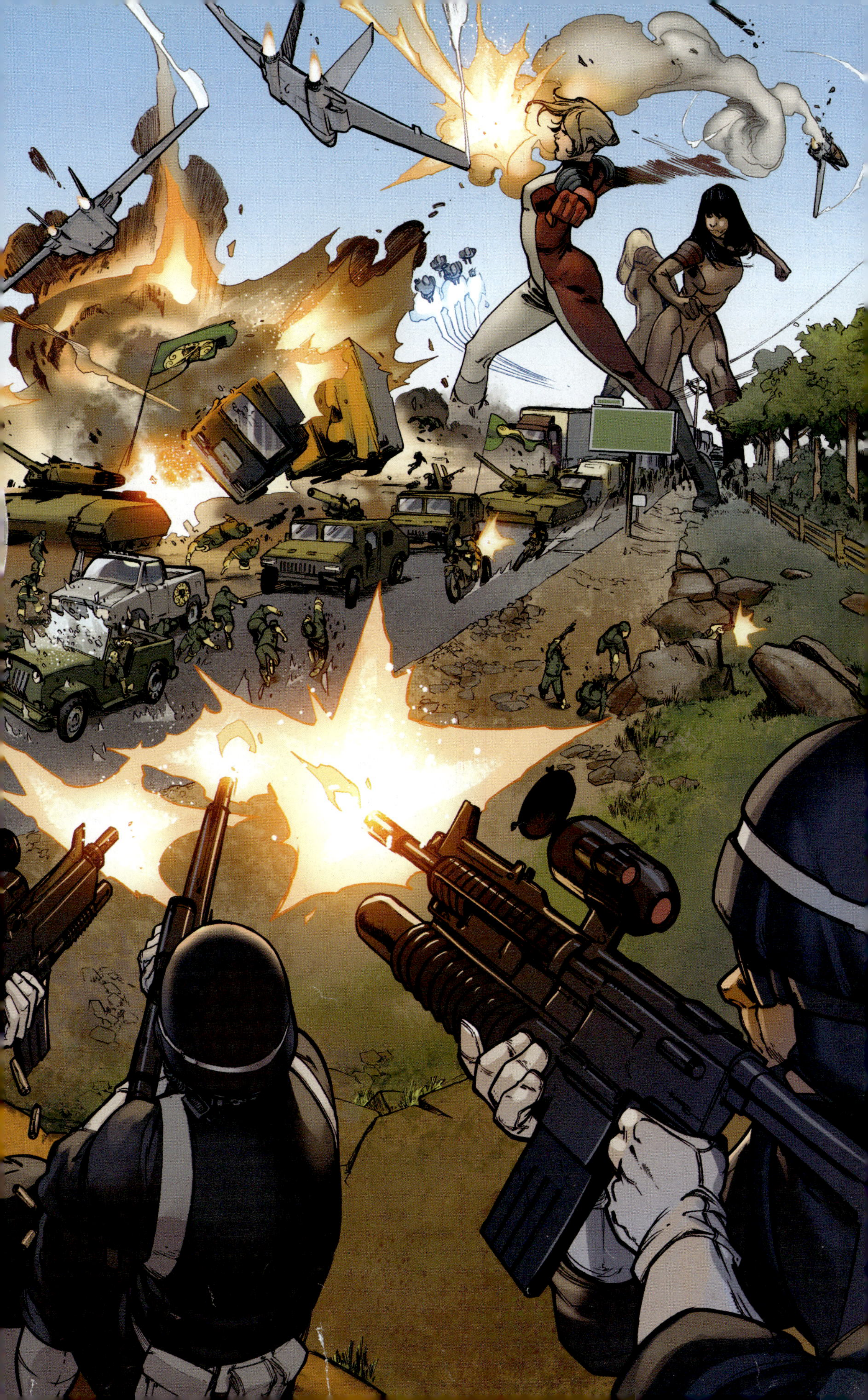

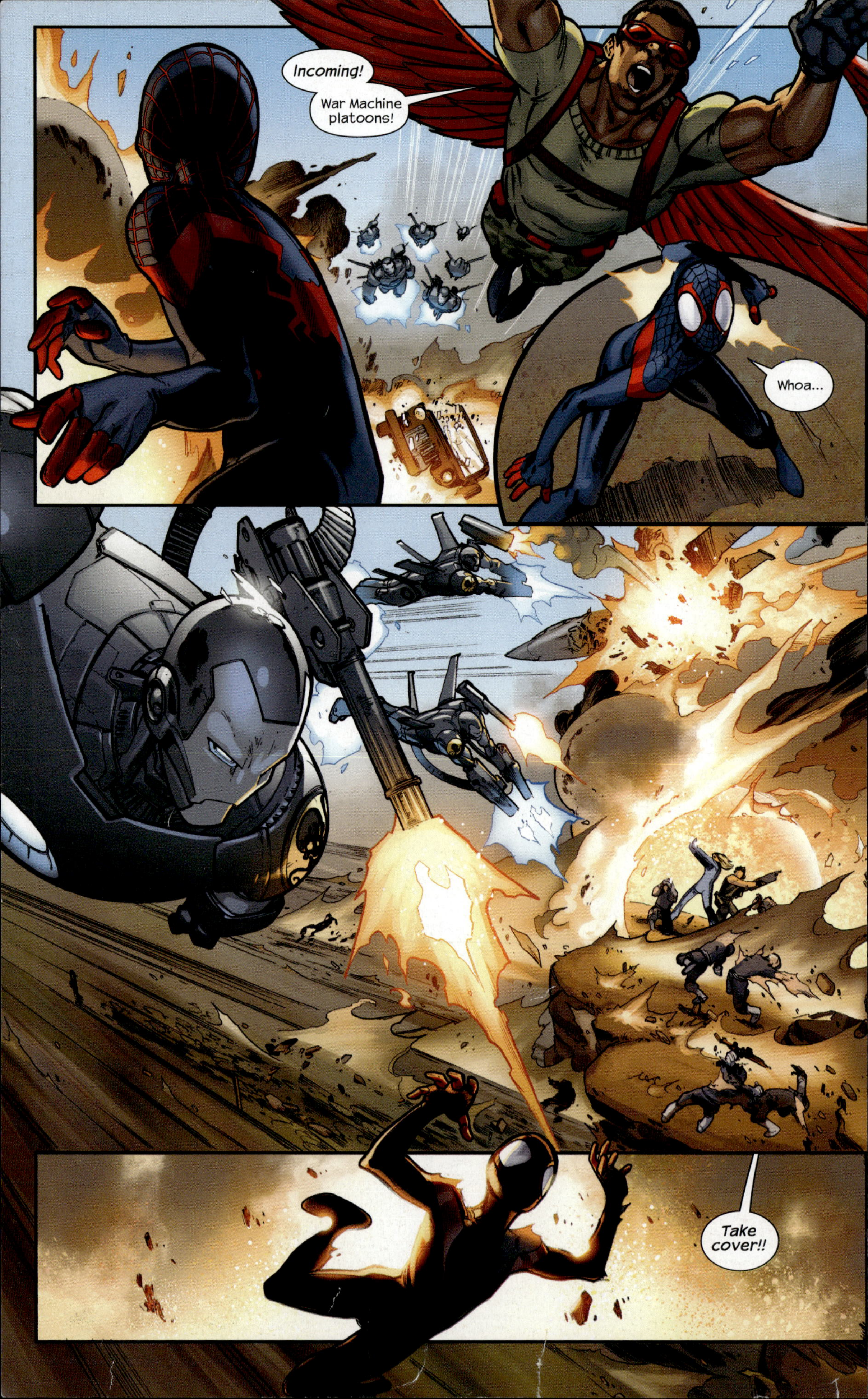

Incoming!
War Machine platoons!
Whoa...
Take cover!!

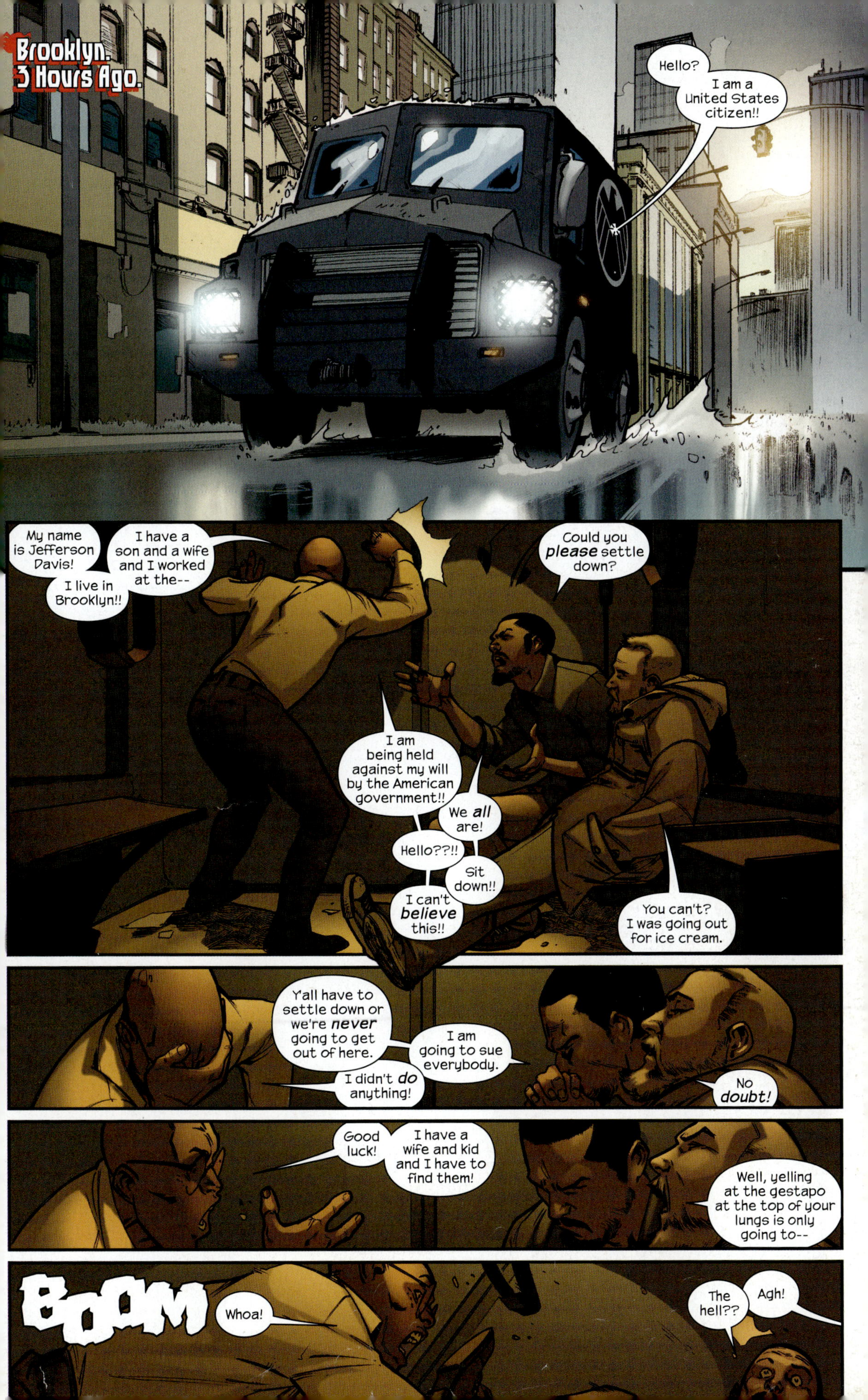
Brooklyn. 3 Hours Ago.
Hello?
I am a United States citizen!!
My name is Jefferson Davis!
I live in Brooklyn!!
I have a son and a wife and I worked at the--
Could you please settle down?
I am being held against my will by the American government!!
We all are!
Hello??!!
Sit down!!
I can't believe this!!
You can't? I was going out for ice cream.
Y'all have to settle down or we're never going to get out of here.
I am going to sue everybody.
I didn't do anything!
No doubt!
Good luck!
I have a wife and kid and I have to find them!
Well, yelling at the gestapo at the top of your lungs is only going to--
BOOM
Whoa!
The hell??
Agh!

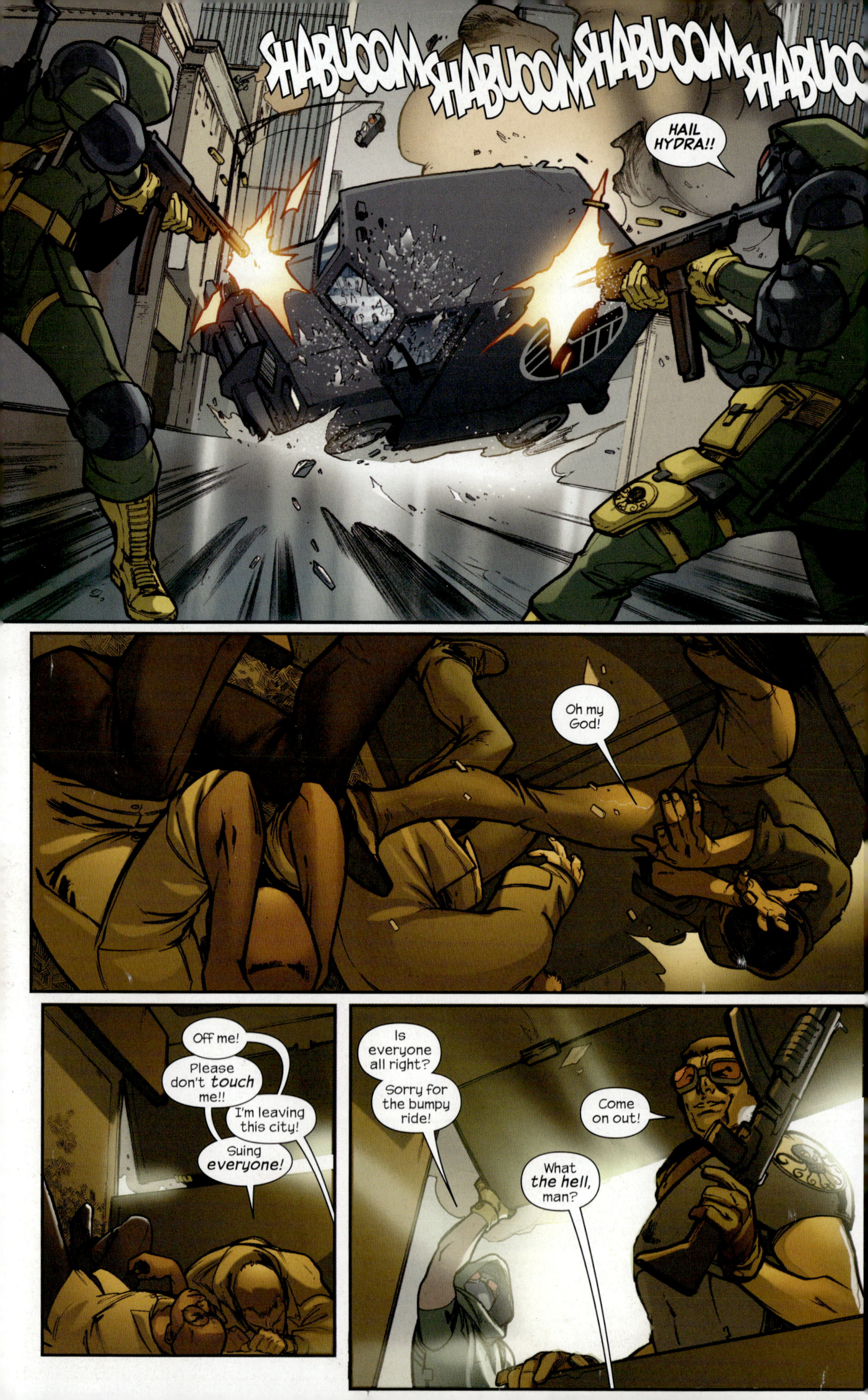
SHABUOOM SHABUOOM SHABUOOM SHABUOO
HAIL HYDRA!!
Oh my God!
Off me!
Please don't *touch* me!!
I'm leaving this city!
Suing *everyone!*
Is everyone all right?
Sorry for the bumpy ride!
Come on out!
What *the hell,* man?

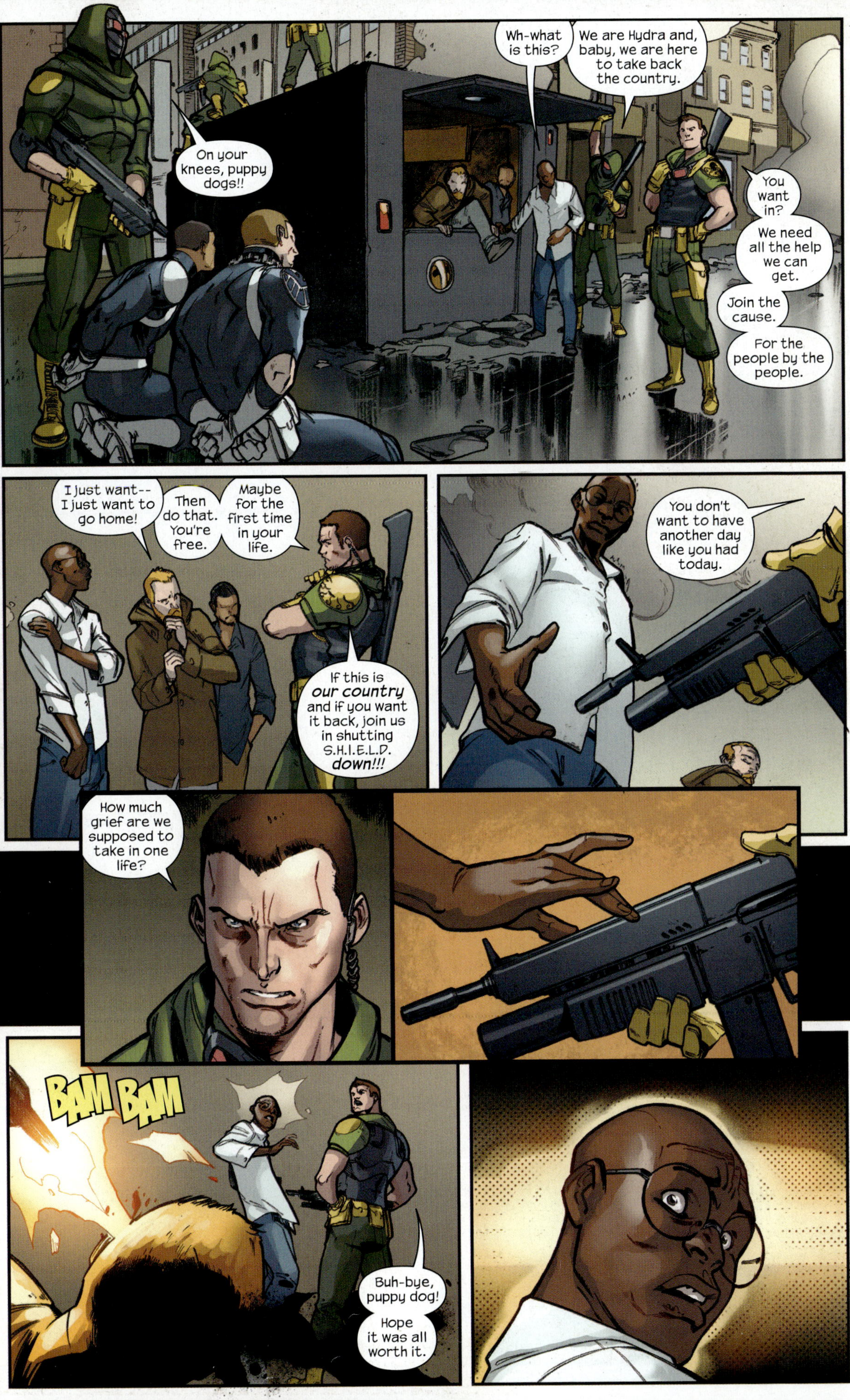
On your knees, puppy dogs!!
Wh-what is this?
We are Hydra and, baby, we are here to take back the country.
You want in?
We need all the help we can get.
Join the cause.
For the people by the people.
I just want-- I just want to go home!
Then do that. You're free.
Maybe for the first time in your life.
If this is our country and if you want it back, join us in shutting S.H.I.E.L.D. down!!!
You don't want to have another day like you had today.
How much grief are we supposed to take in one life?
BAM BAM
Buh-bye, puppy dog!
Hope it was all worth it.

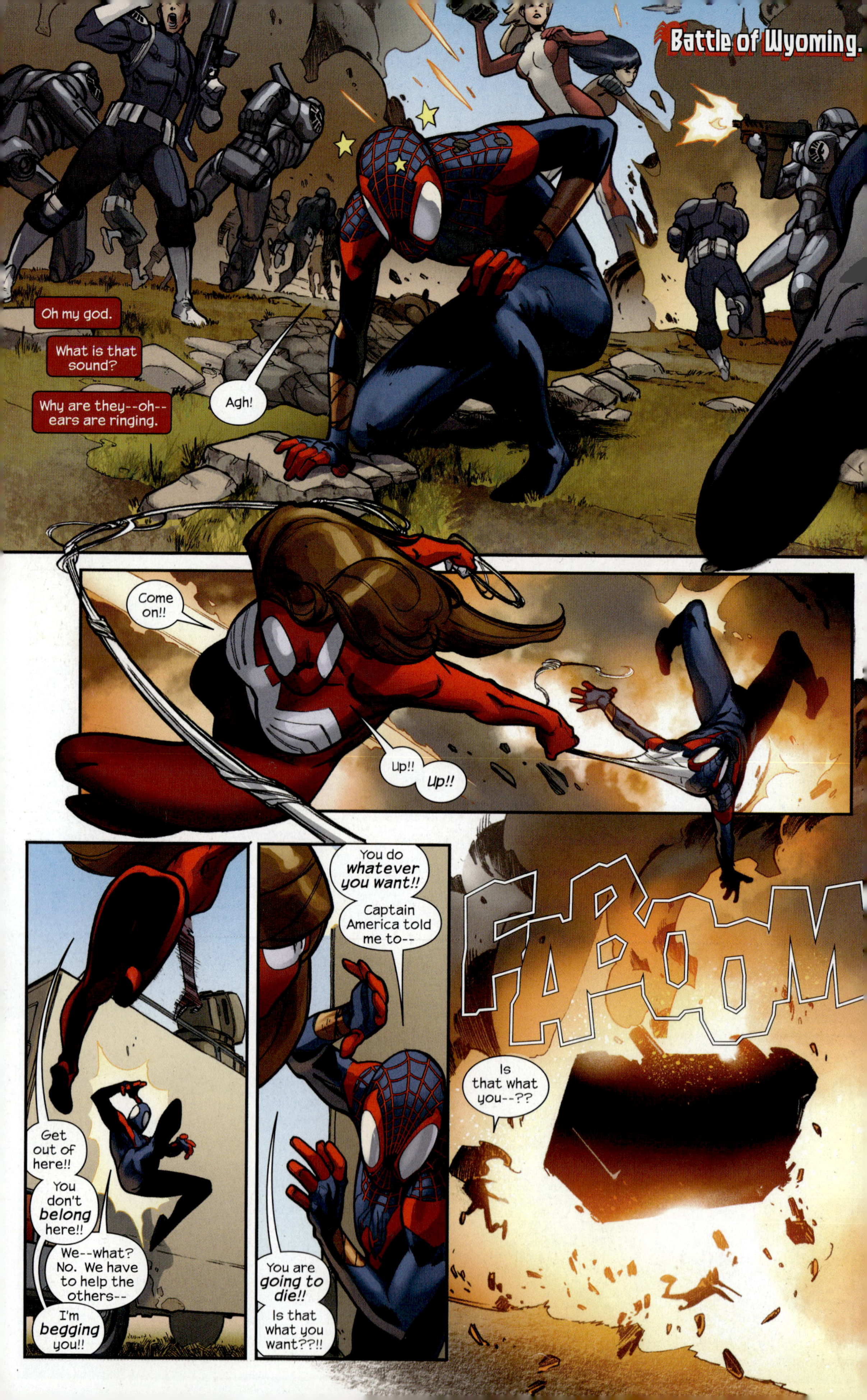
Battle of Wyoming.
Oh my god.
What is that sound?
Why are they--oh--ears are ringing.
Agh!
Come on!!
Up!!
Up!!
FABOOM
Get out of here!!
You don't belong here!!
We--what? No. We have to help the others--
I'm begging you!!
You do whatever you want!!
Captain America told me to--
You are going to die!!
Is that what you want??!!
Is that what you--??

Ow!

What is *her* problem?

Okay, forget it.

Forget her.

Fight.

THWAP

Webs. Hit.

Do it!!

You can do it!!

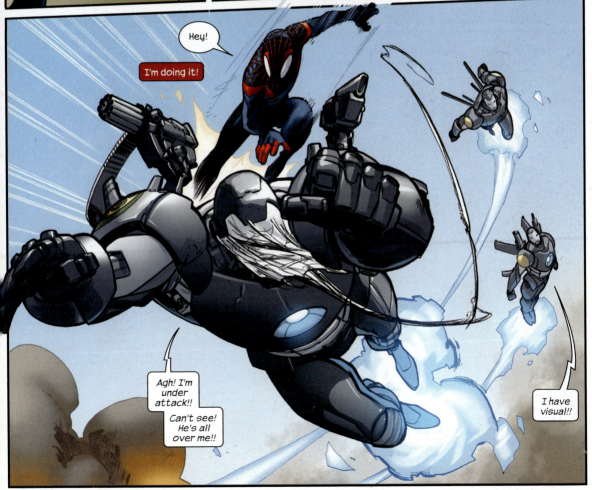

Hey!

I'm doing it!

Agh! I'm under attack!! Can't see! He's all over me!!

I have visual!!

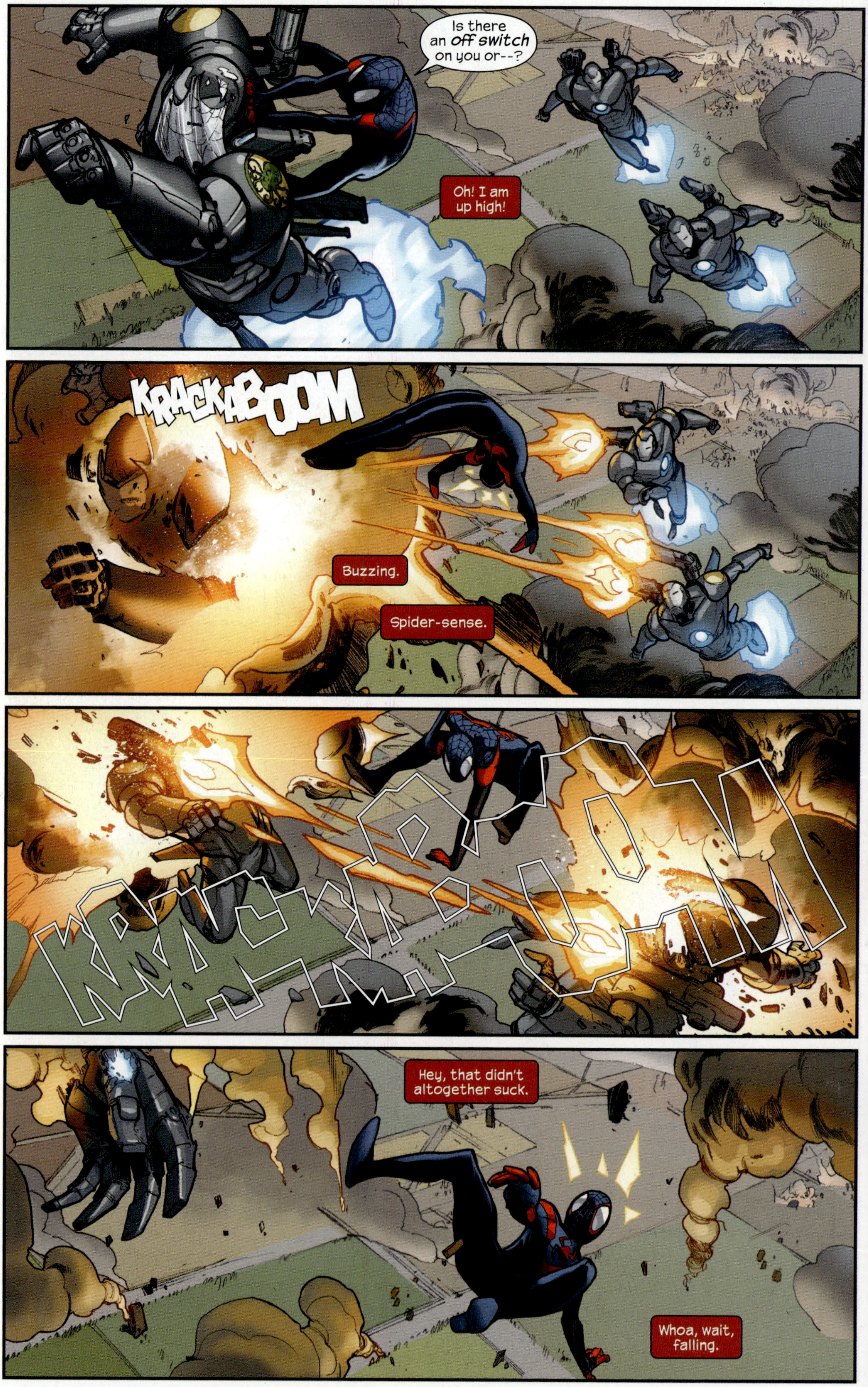
Is there an off switch on you or--?
Oh! I am up high!
KRACKABOOM
Buzzing.
Spider-sense.
KRACKABOOM
Hey, that didn't altogether suck.
Whoa, wait, falling.

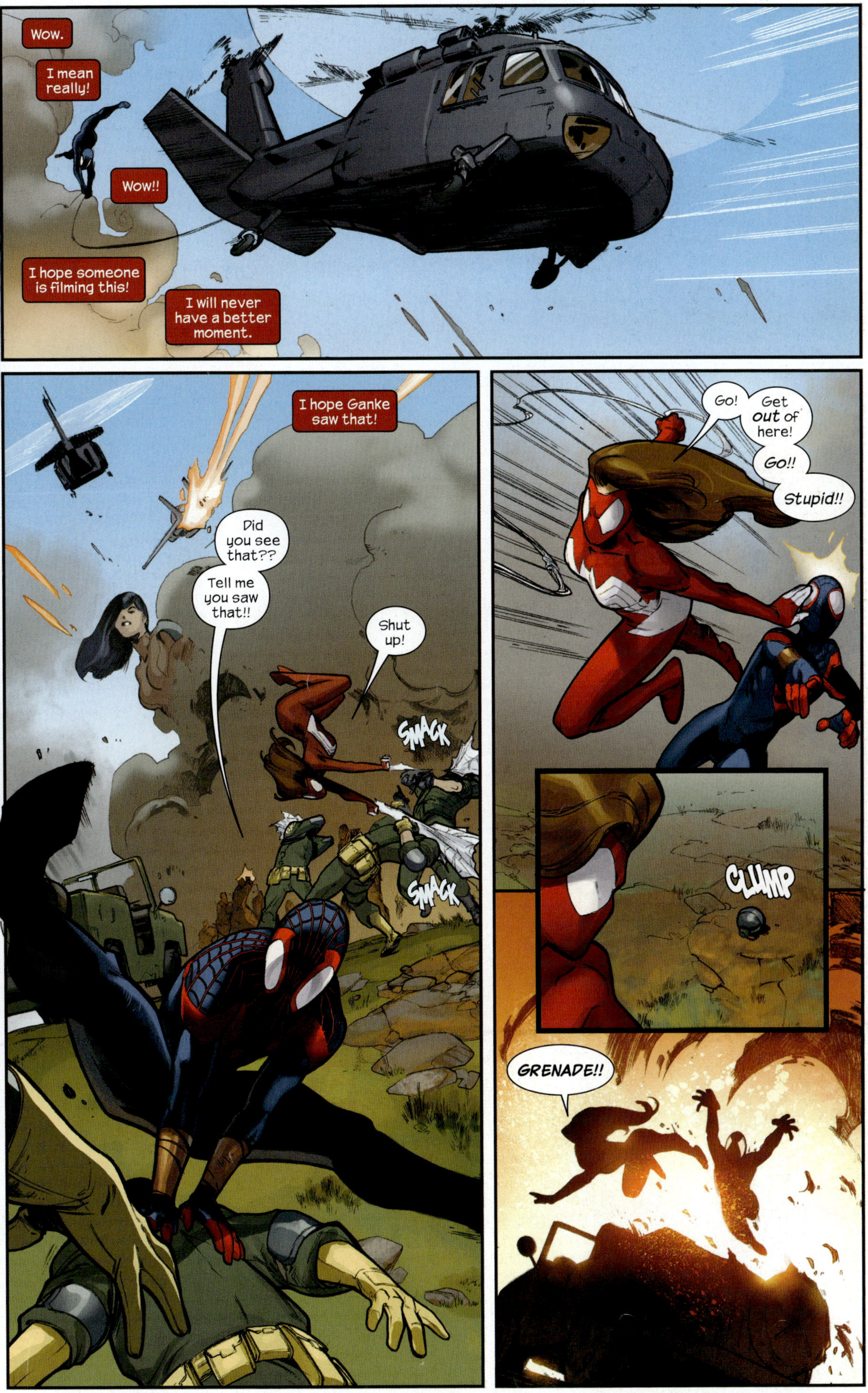
Wow.
I mean really!
Wow!!
I hope someone is filming this!
I will never have a better moment.
I hope Ganke saw that!
Did you see that??
Tell me you saw that!!
Shut up!
SMACK
SMACK
Go!
Get out of here!
Go!!
Stupid!!
CLUMP
GRENADE!!

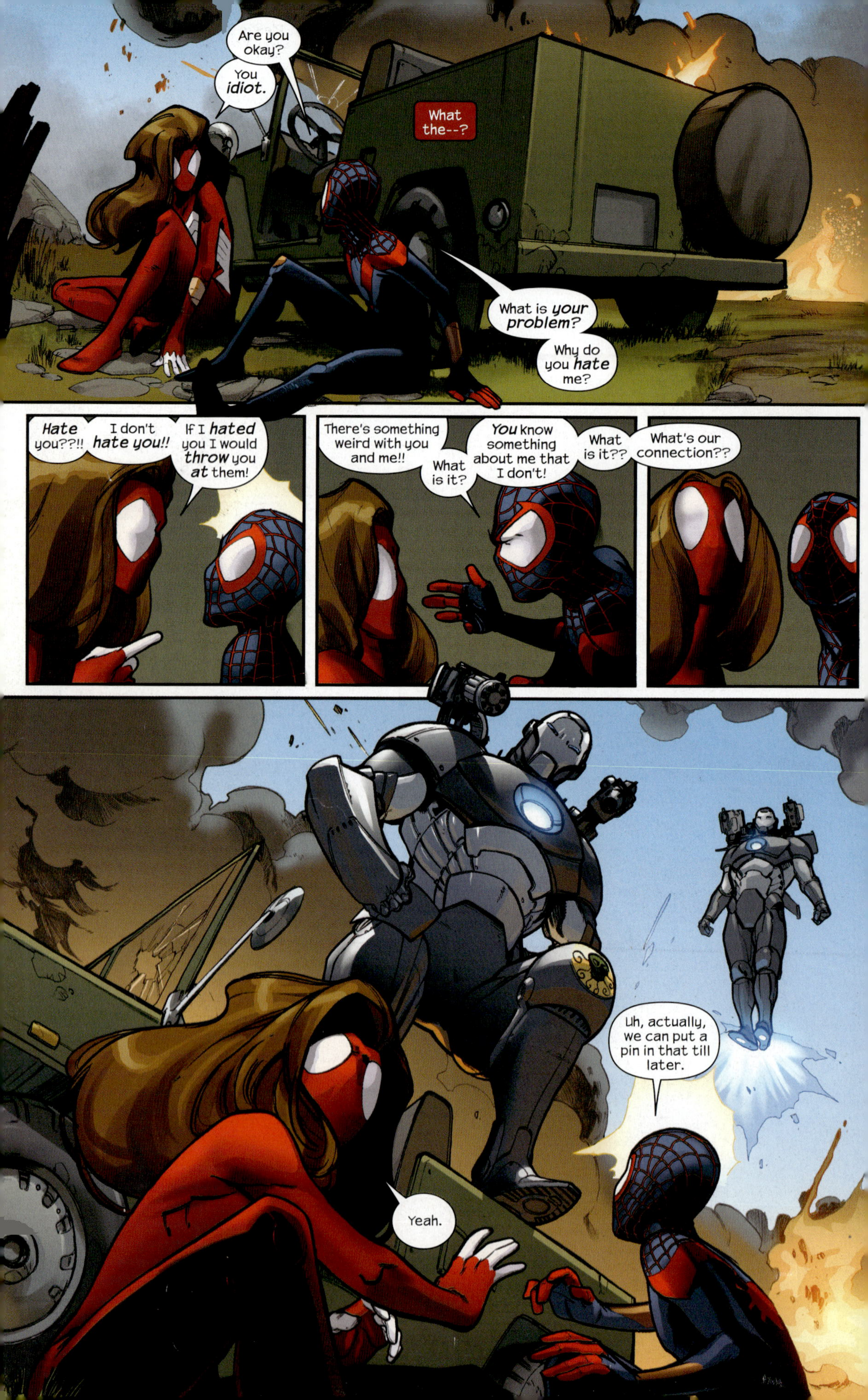
Are you okay?
You idiot.
What the--?
What is your problem?
Why do you hate me?
Hate you??!!
I don't hate you!!
If I hated you I would throw you at them!
There's something weird with you and me!!
What is it?
You know something about me that I don't!
What is it??
What's our connection??
Uh, actually, we can put a pin in that till later.
Yeah.

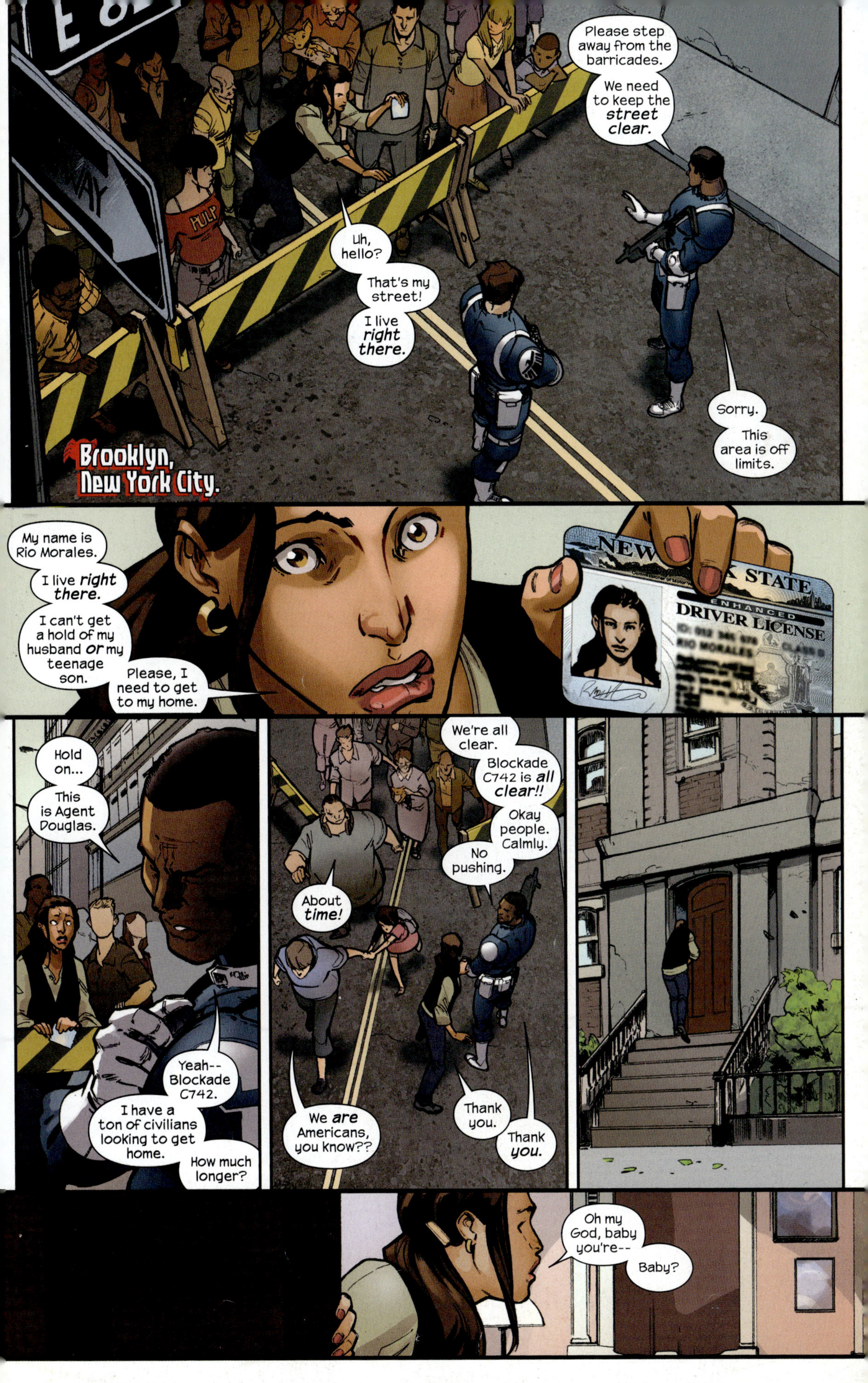
Please step away from the barricades.
We need to keep the *street clear.*
Uh, hello?
That's my street!
I live *right there.*
Sorry.
This area is off limits.
Brooklyn, New York City.
My name is Rio Morales.
I live *right there.*
I can't get a hold of my husband *or* my teenage son.
Please, I need to get to my home.
STATE
ENHANCED
DRIVER LICENSE
Hold on...
This is Agent Douglas.
Yeah-- Blockade C742.
I have a ton of civilians looking to get home.
How much longer?
We're all clear.
Blockade C742 is *all clear!!*
Okay people. Calmly.
No pushing.
About *time!*
We *are* Americans, you know??
Thank you.
Thank *you.*
Oh my God, baby you're--
Baby?

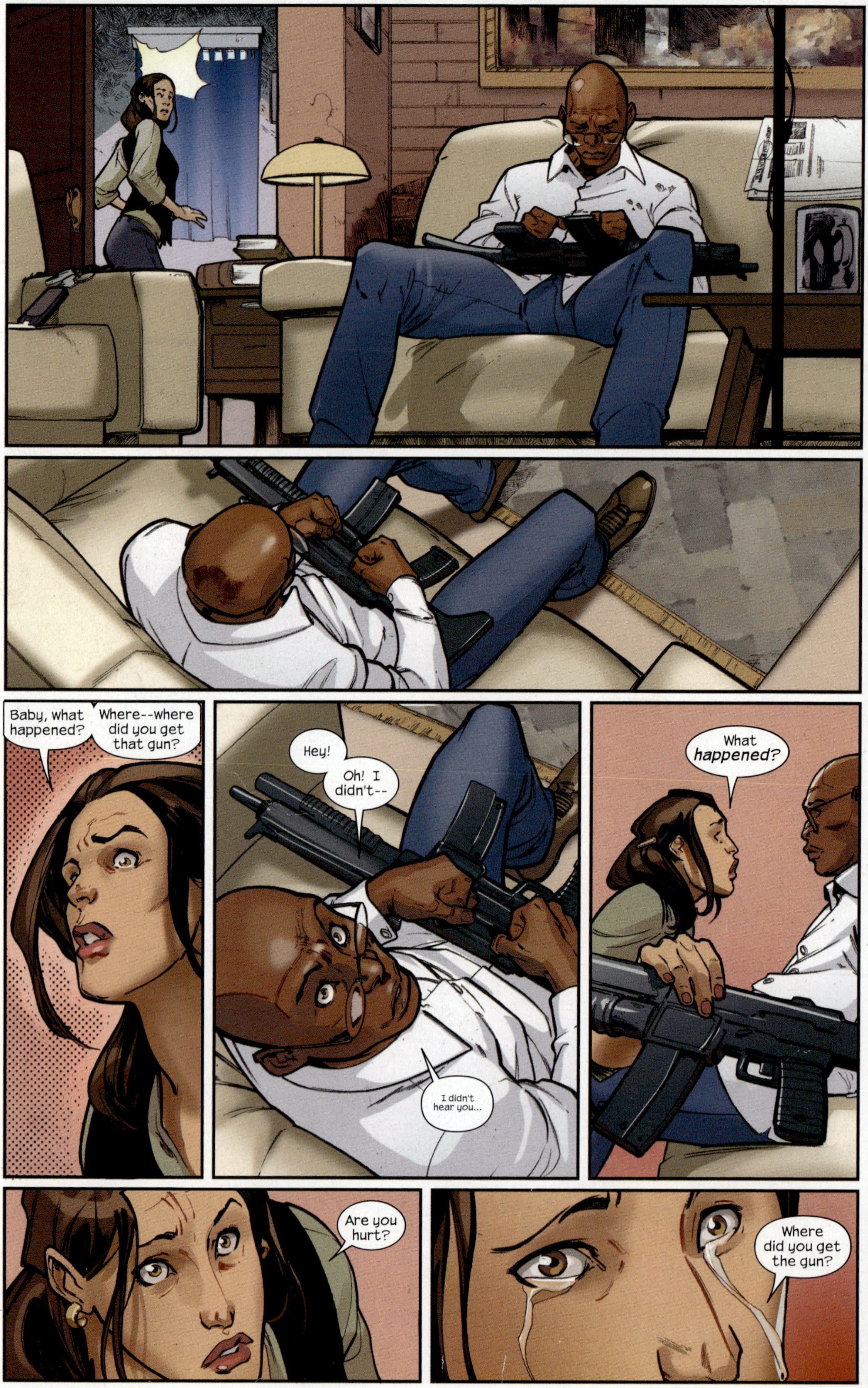
Baby, what happened?
Where--where did you get that gun?
Hey!
Oh! I didn't--
I didn't hear you...
What *happened?*
Are you hurt?
Where did you get the gun?

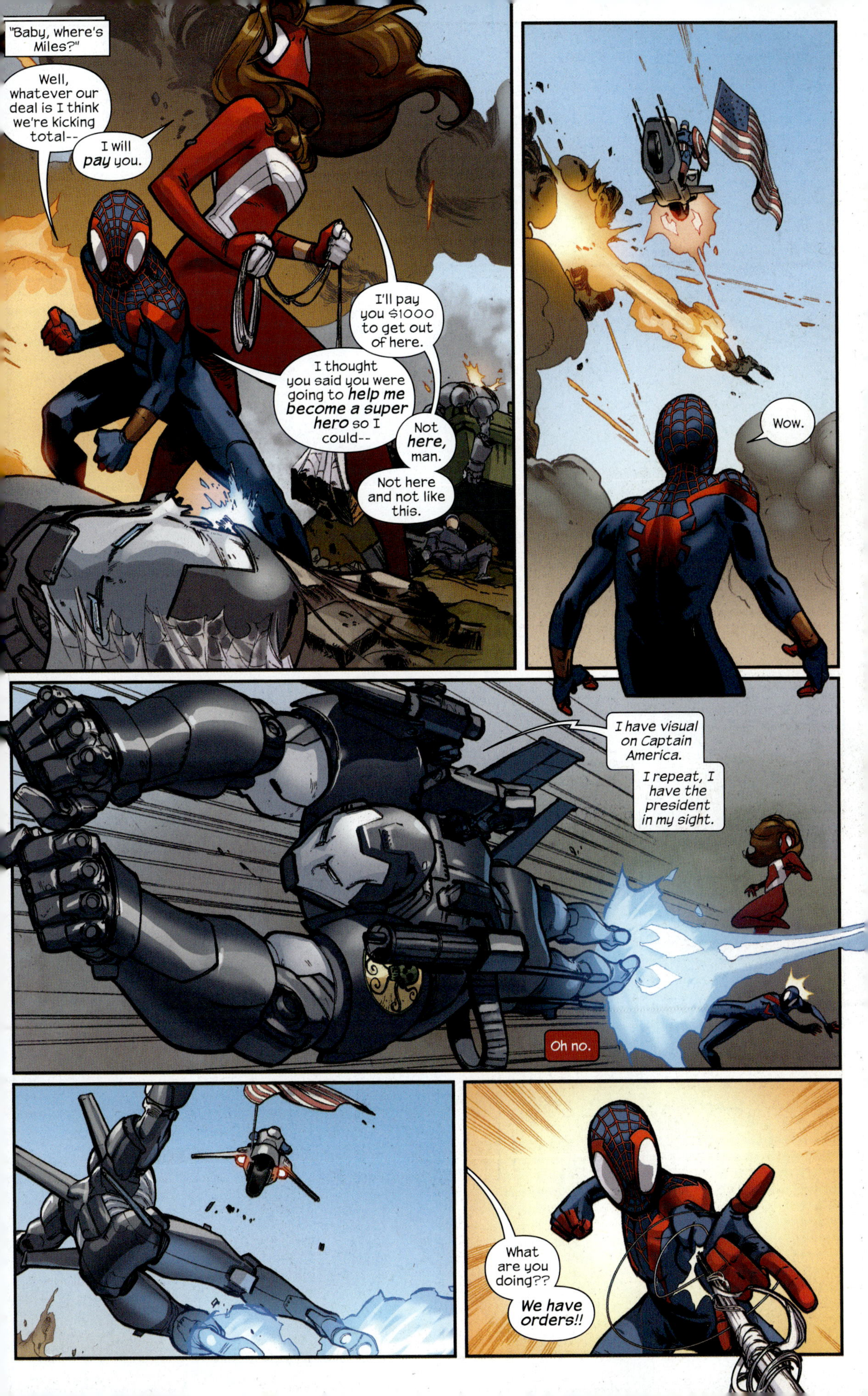
"Baby, where's Miles?"
Well, whatever our deal is I think we're kicking total--
I will pay you.
I'll pay you $1000 to get out of here.
I thought you said you were going to help me become a super hero so I could--
Not here, man.
Not here and not like this.
Wow.
I have visual on Captain America.
I repeat, I have the president in my sight.
Oh no.
What are you doing??
We have orders!!

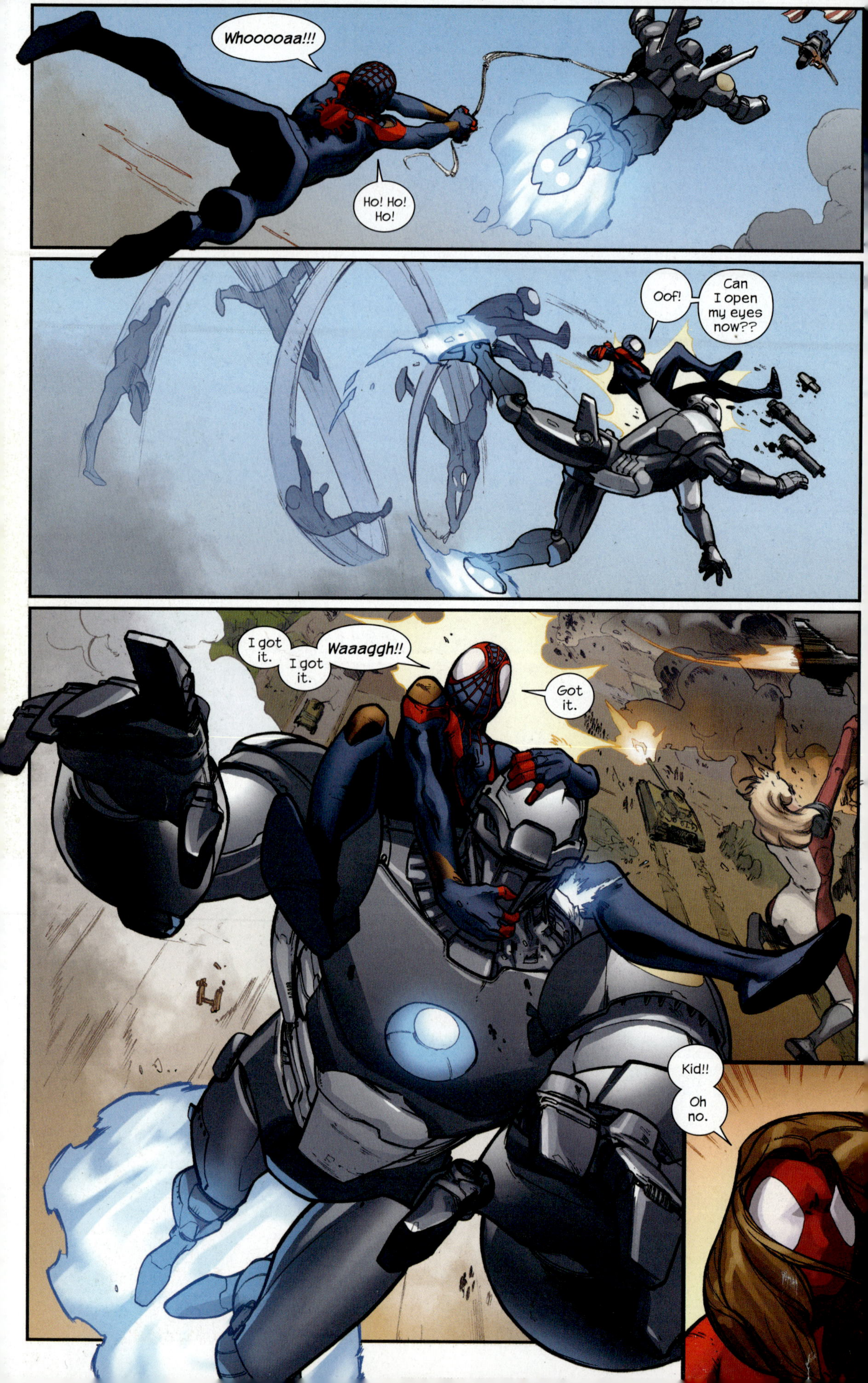

Whoooooaa!!!
Ho! Ho! Ho!
Oof!
Can I open my eyes now??
I got it.
I got it.
Waaaggh!!
Got it.
Kid!!
Oh no.

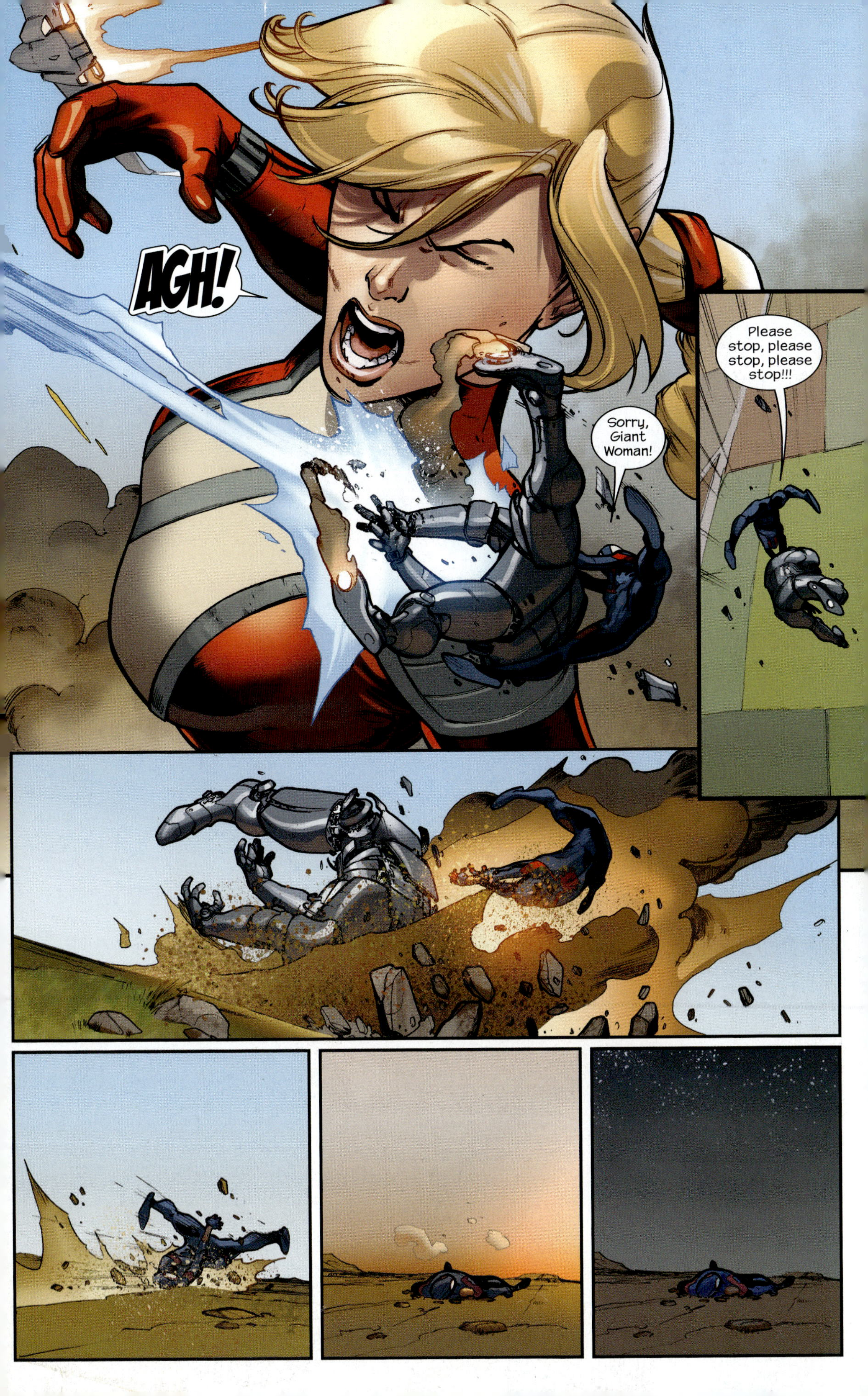
AGH!
Sorry, Giant Woman!
Please stop, please stop, please stop!!!

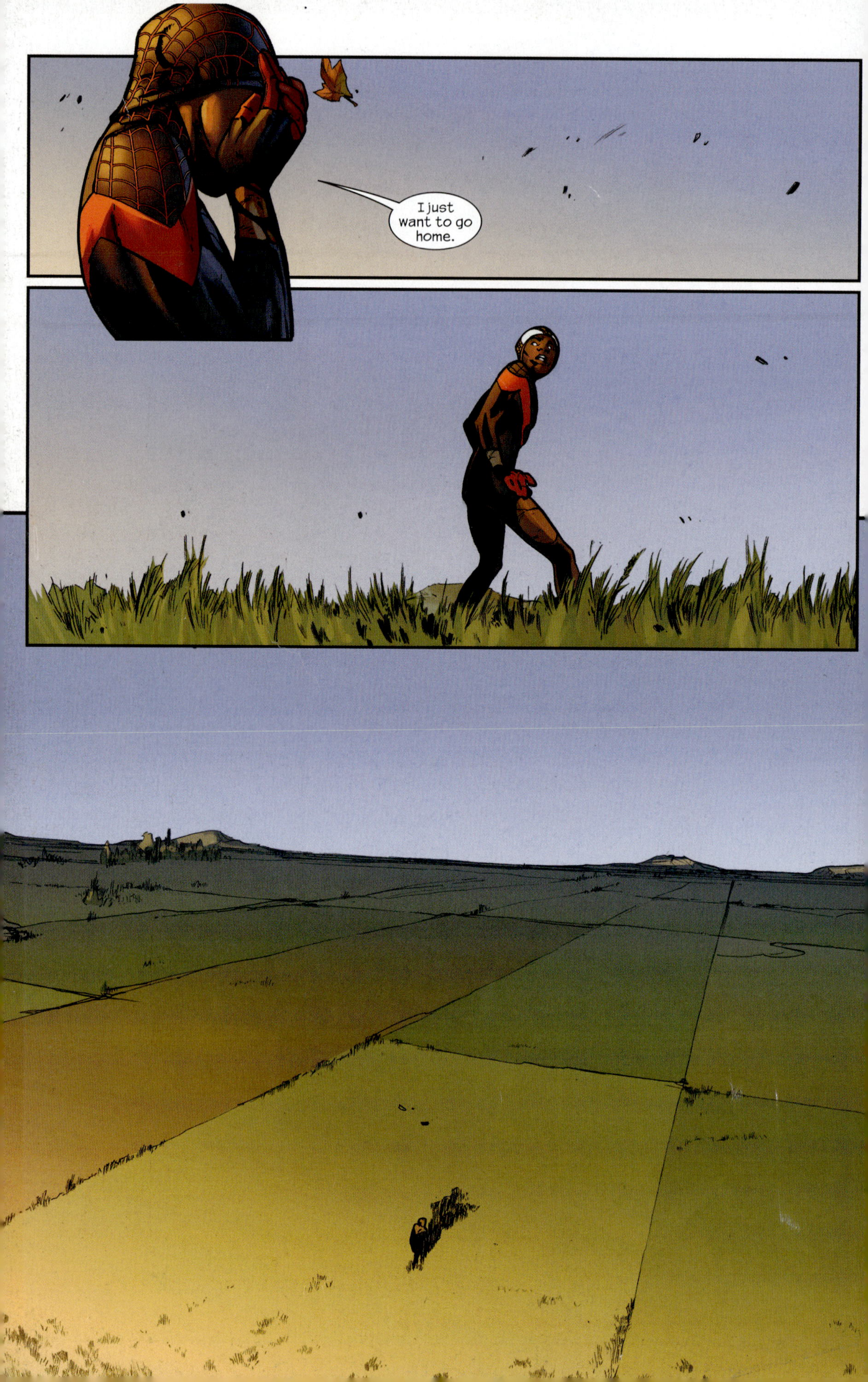
I just want to go home.

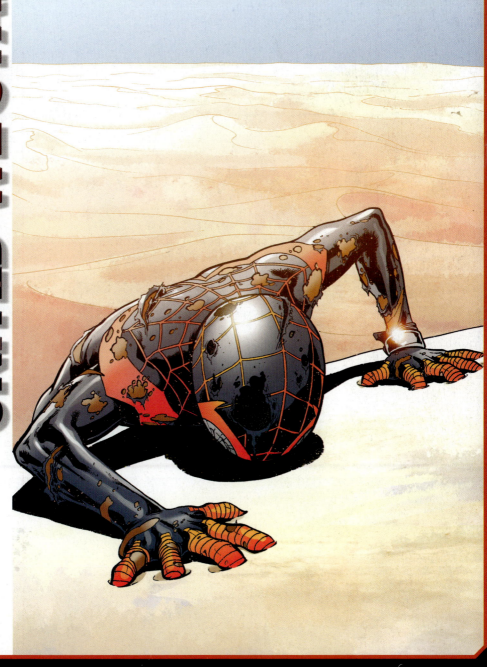

UNITED WE STAND

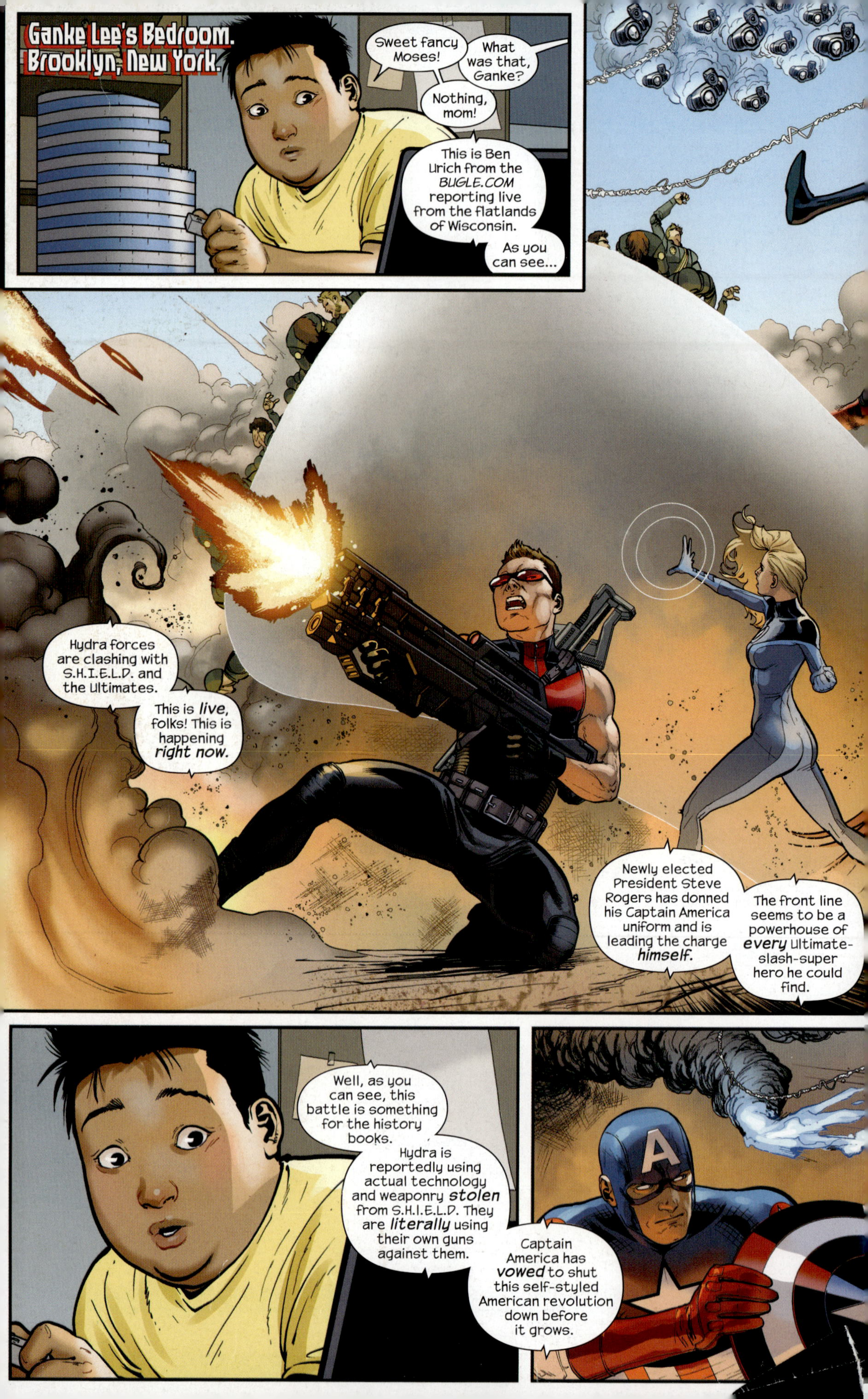
Ganke Lee's Bedroom. Brooklyn, New York.
Sweet fancy Moses!
What was that, Ganke?
Nothing, mom!
This is Ben Urich from the BUGLE.COM reporting live from the flatlands of Wisconsin.
As you can see...
Hydra forces are clashing with S.H.I.E.L.D. and the Ultimates.
This is *live*, folks! This is happening *right now.*
Newly elected President Steve Rogers has donned his Captain America uniform and is leading the charge *himself.*
The front line seems to be a powerhouse of *every* Ultimate-slash-super hero he could find.
Well, as you can see, this battle is something for the history books.
Hydra is reportedly using actual technology and weaponry *stolen* from S.H.I.E.L.D. They are *literally* using their own guns against them.
Captain America has *vowed* to shut this self-styled American revolution down before it grows.

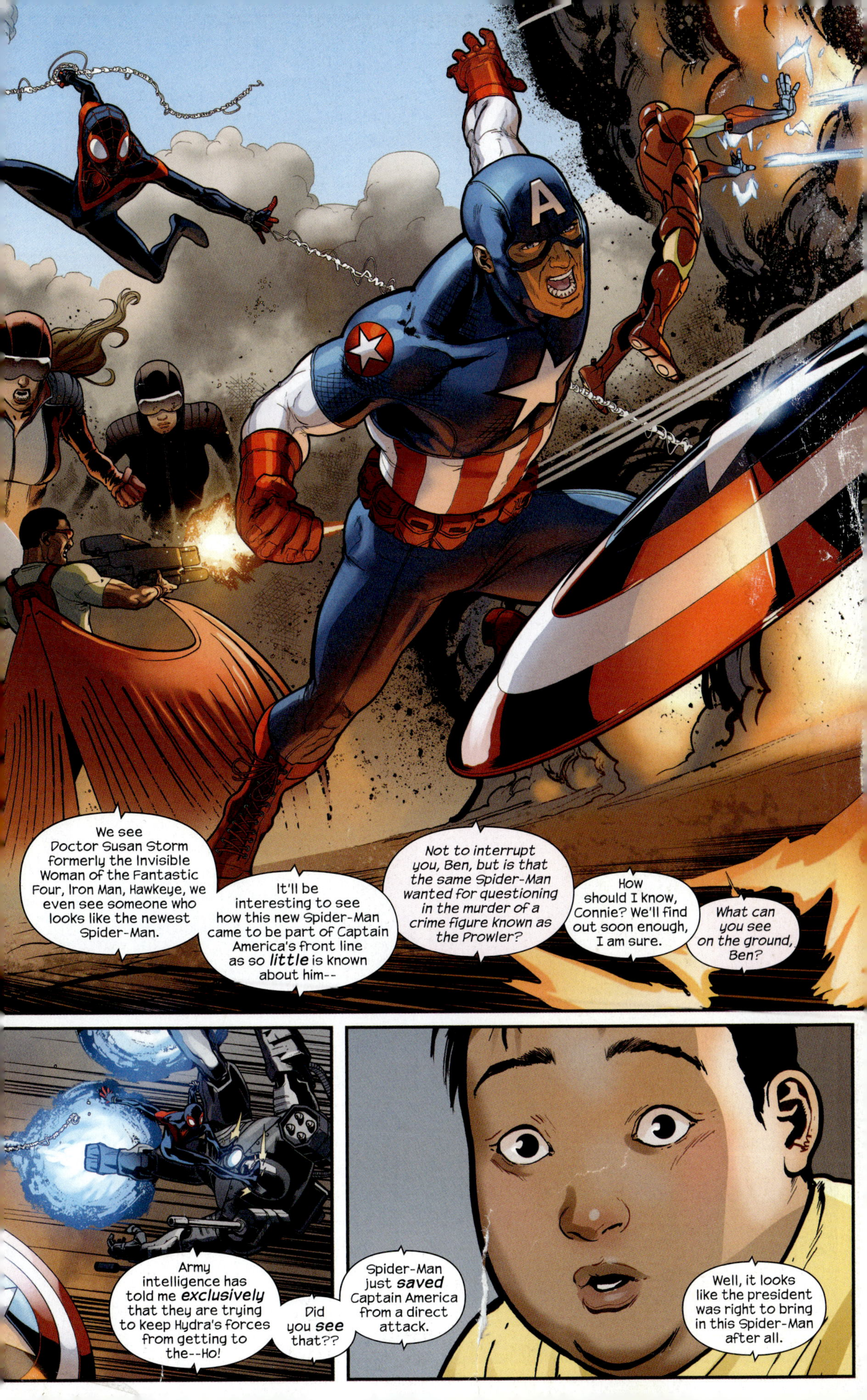

We see Doctor Susan Storm formerly the Invisible Woman of the Fantastic Four, Iron Man, Hawkeye, we even see someone who looks like the newest Spider-Man.
It'll be interesting to see how this new Spider-Man came to be part of Captain America's front line as so *little* is known about him--
Not to interrupt you, Ben, but is that the same Spider-Man wanted for questioning in the murder of a crime figure known as the Prowler?
How should I know, Connie? We'll find out soon enough, I am sure.
What can you see on the ground, Ben?
Army intelligence has told me *exclusively* that they are trying to keep Hydra's forces from getting to the--Ho!
Did you *see* that??
Spider-Man just *saved* Captain America from a direct attack.
Well, it looks like the president was right to bring in this Spider-Man after all.

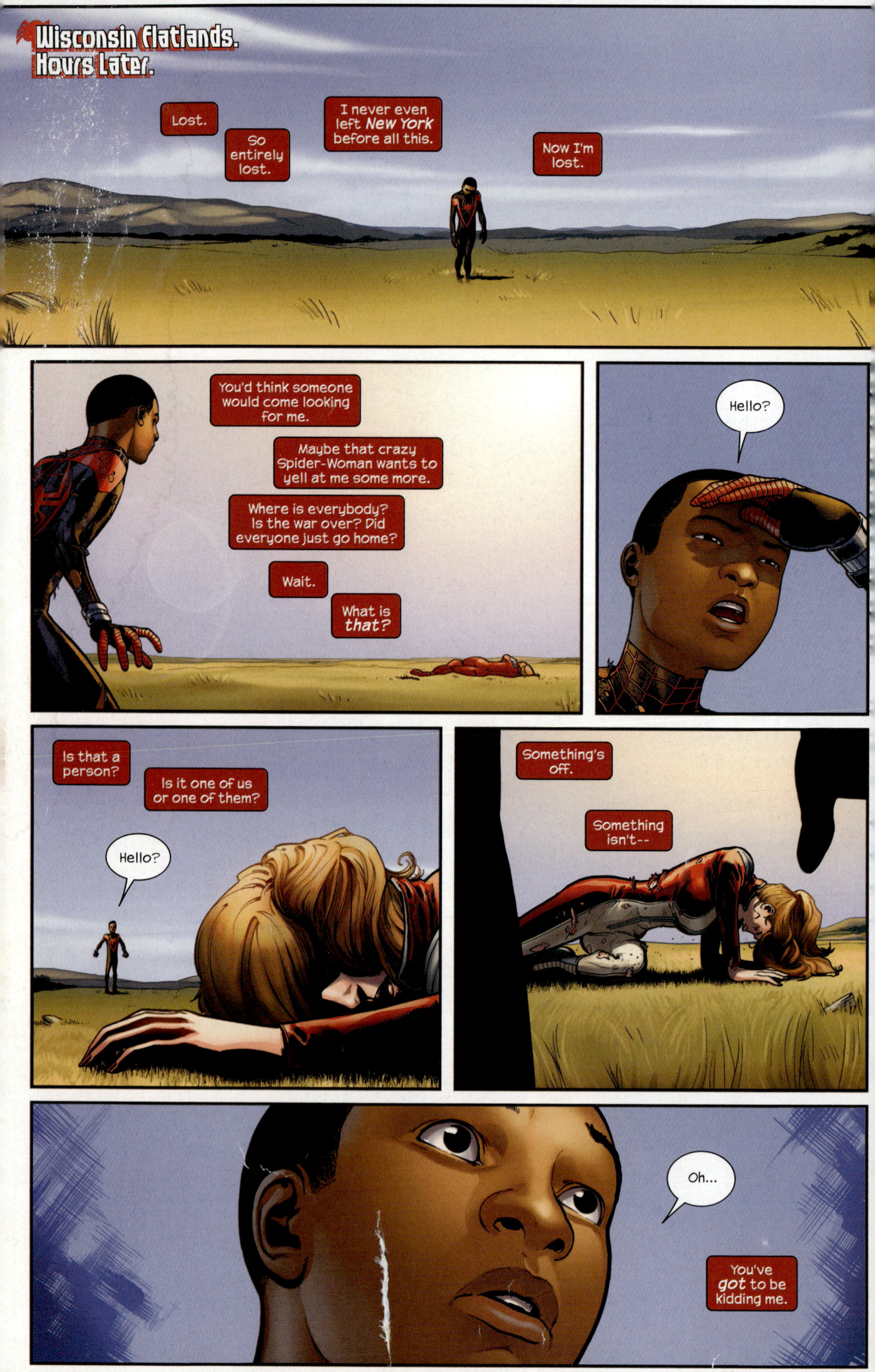
Wisconsin Flatlands.
Hours Later.
Lost.
So entirely lost.
I never even left New York before all this.
Now I'm lost.
You'd think someone would come looking for me.
Maybe that crazy Spider-Woman wants to yell at me some more.
Where is everybody? Is the war over? Did everyone just go home?
Wait.
What is that?
Hello?
Is that a person?
Is it one of us or one of them?
Hello?
Something's off.
Something isn't--
Oh...
You've got to be kidding me.

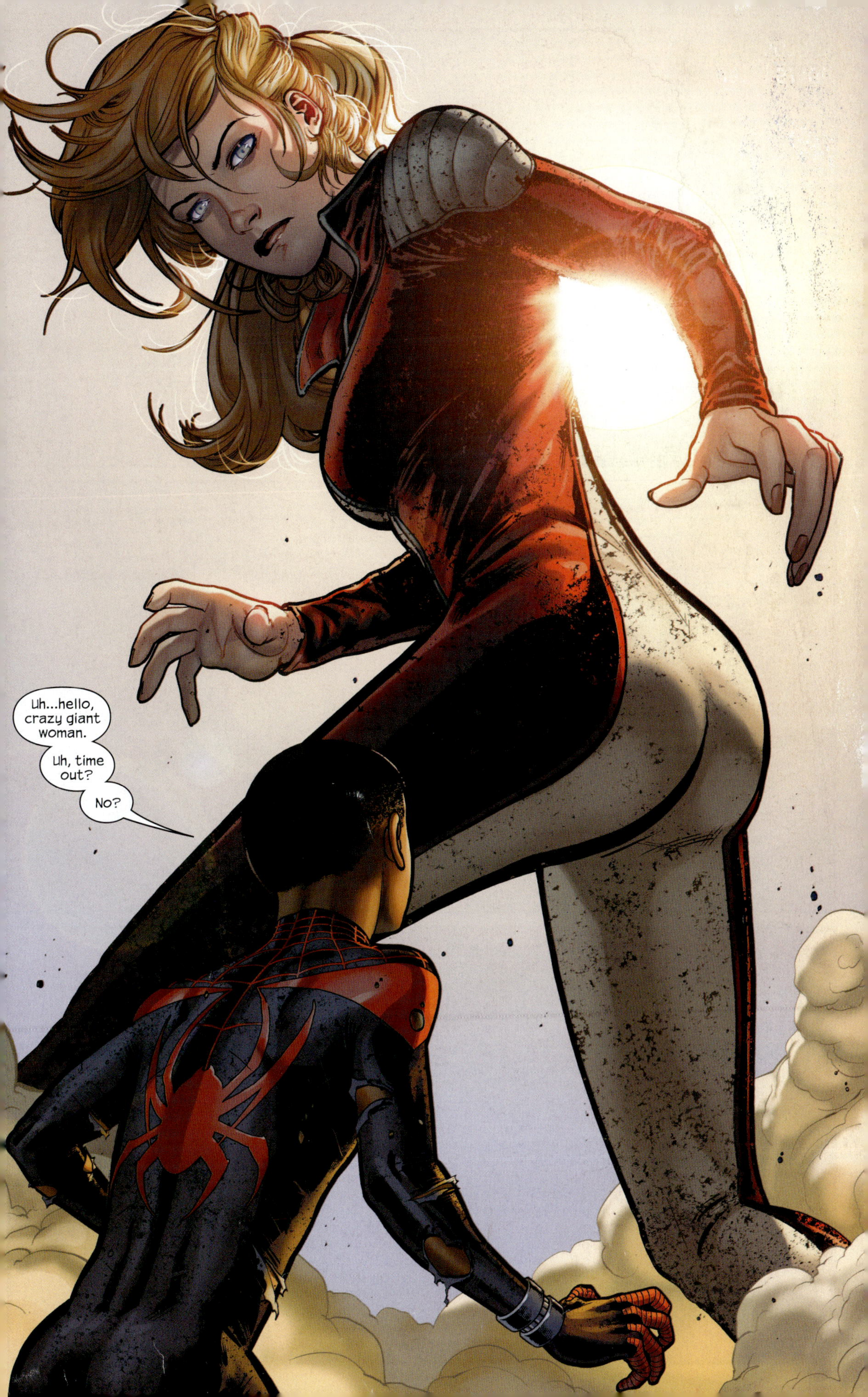
Uh...hello, crazy giant woman.
Uh, time out?
No?

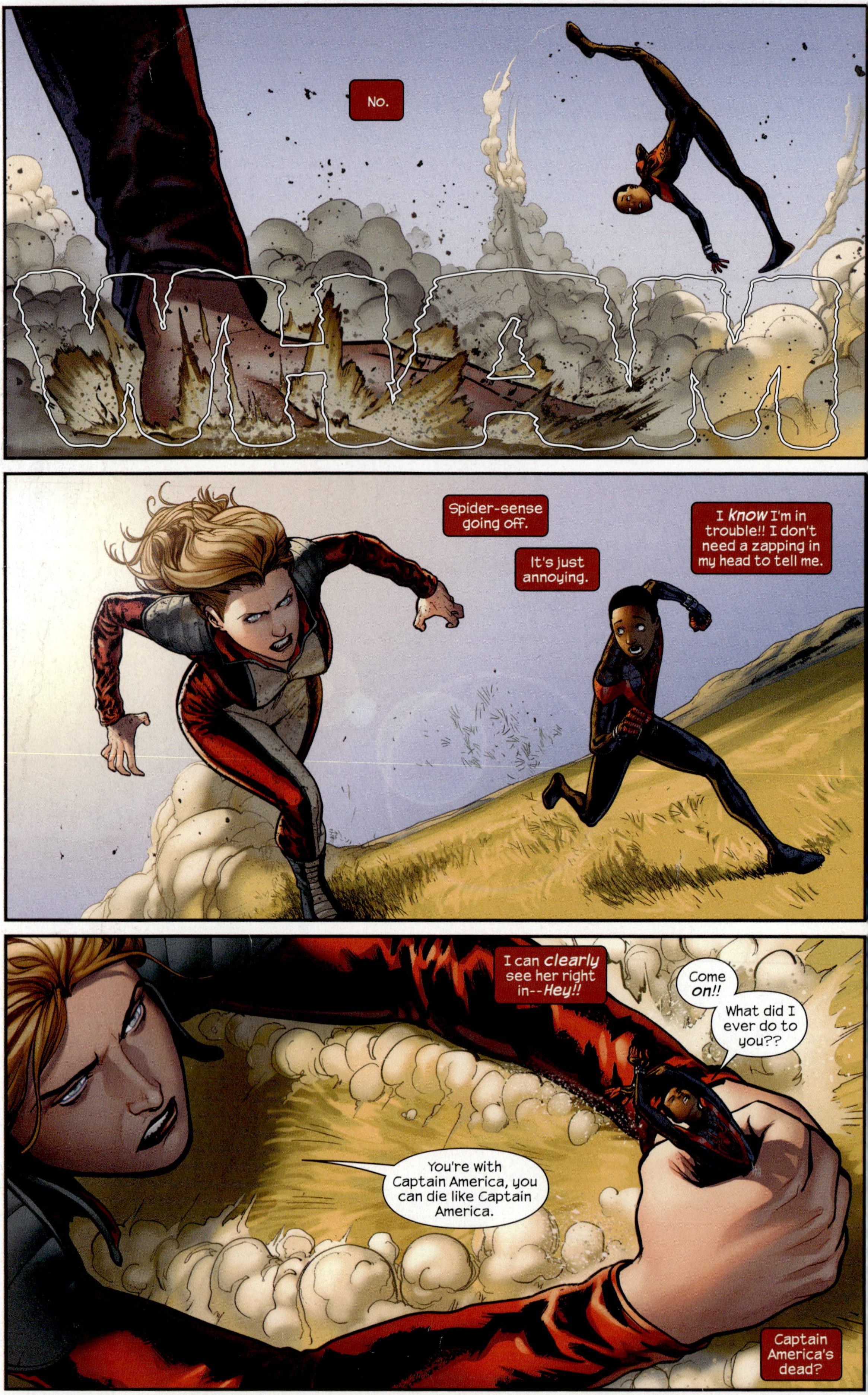
No.
WHAM
Spider-sense going off.
It's just annoying.
I *know* I'm in trouble!! I don't need a zapping in my head to tell me.
I can *clearly* see her right in--*Hey!!*
Come *on!!*
What did I ever do to you??
You're with Captain America, you can die like Captain America.
Captain America's dead?

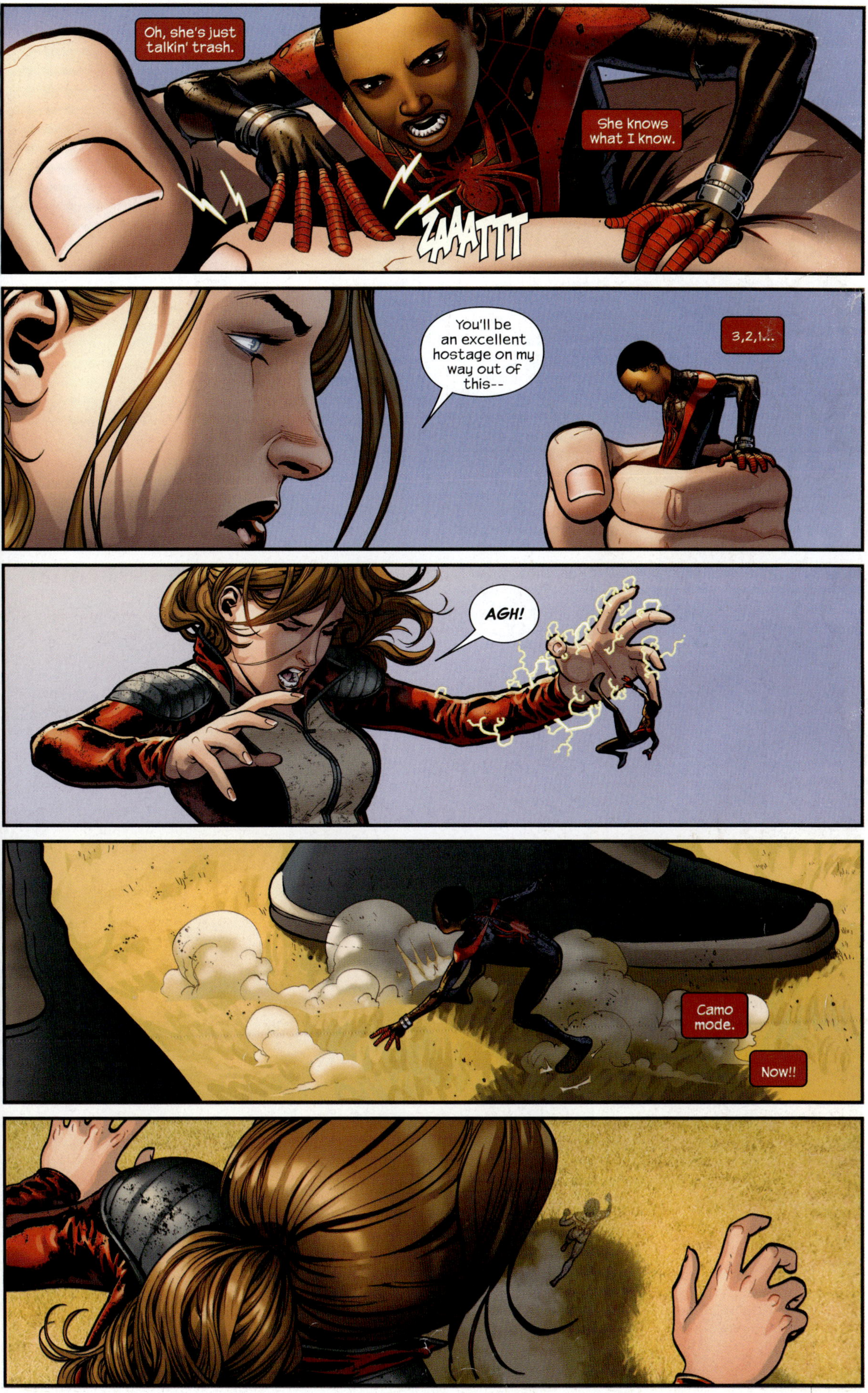
Oh, she's just talkin' trash.
She knows what I know.
ZAAATTT
You'll be an excellent hostage on my way out of this--
3,2,1...
AGH!
Camo mode.
Now!!

What the hell?

I'm embarrassed that I find her so hot.

Gotta tiptoe.

Can't let her see me.

Just get out of here and find the rest of the war that I seem to have misplaced.

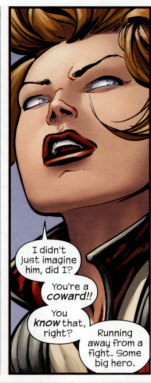

I didn't just imagine him, did I?

You're a *coward!!*

You *know* that, right?

Running away from a fight. Some big hero.

I'm a coward for not getting into it with a giant crazy terrorist girl?

I'm *not* going to hit a girl. Even a *giant* girl.

My mom would *kill* me.

Seriously,
how did
you--?

Gotcha.

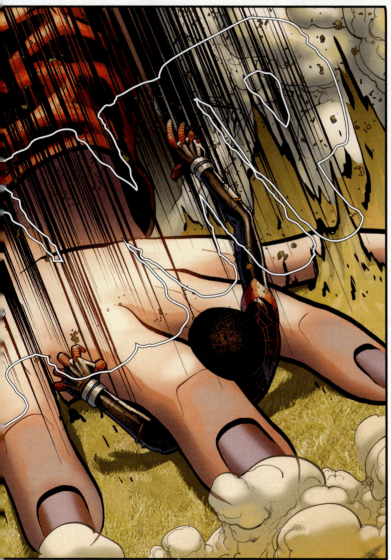

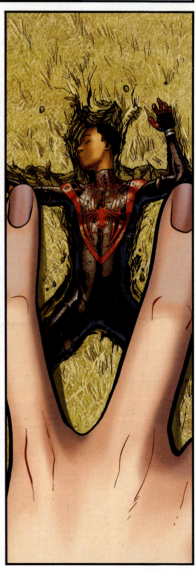

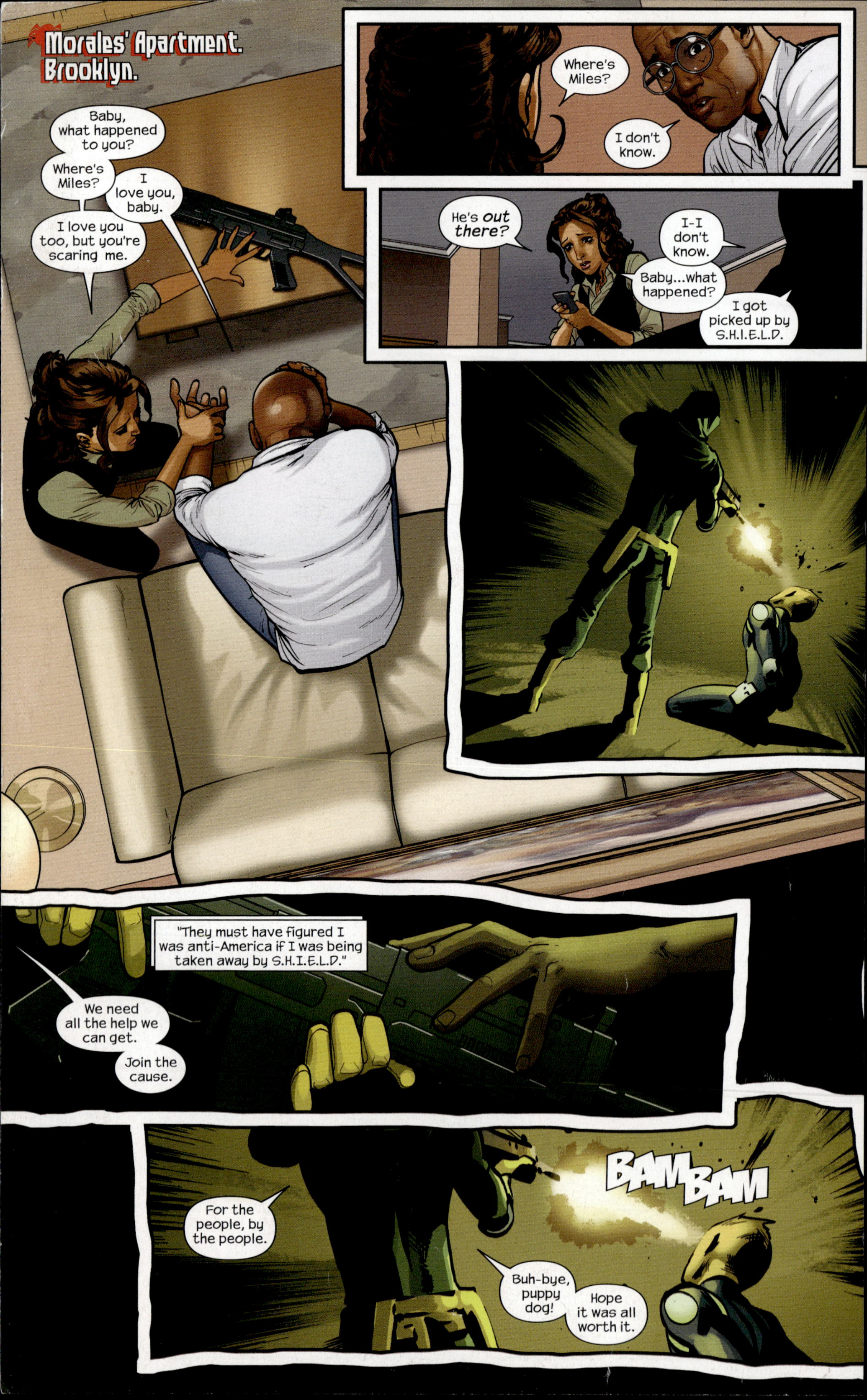
Morales' Apartment. Brooklyn.
Baby, what happened to you?
Where's Miles?
I love you, baby.
I love you too, but you're scaring me.
Where's Miles?
I don't know.
He's out there?
I-I don't know.
Baby...what happened?
I got picked up by S.H.I.E.L.D.
"They must have figured I was anti-America if I was being taken away by S.H.I.E.L.D."
We need all the help we can get.
Join the cause.
For the people, by the people.
BAM BAM
Buh-bye, puppy dog!
Hope it was all worth it.

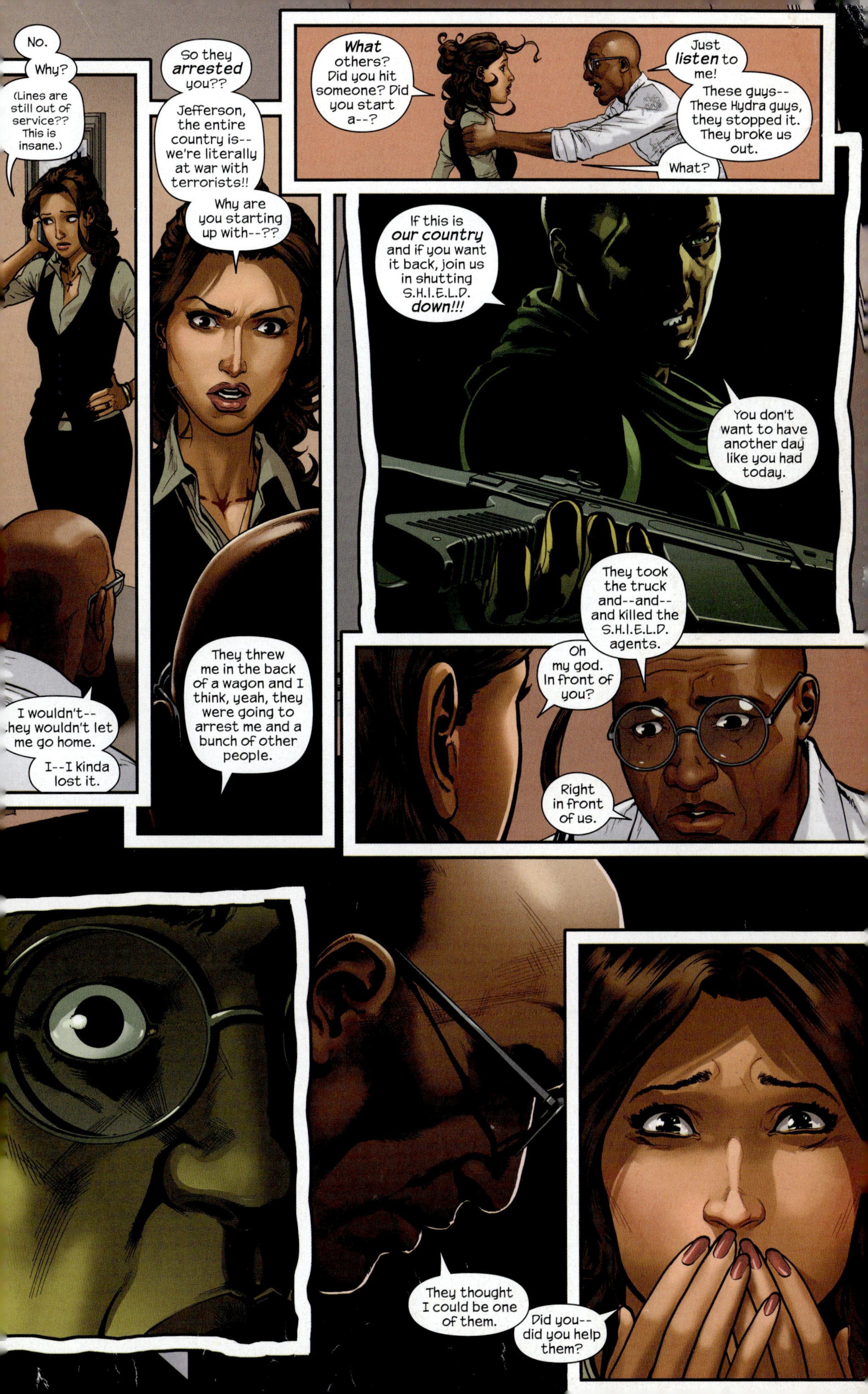
No.
Why?
(Lines are still out of service?? This is insane.)
So they *arrested* you??
Jefferson, the entire country is-- we're literally at war with terrorists!!
Why are you starting up with--??
What others? Did you hit someone? Did you start a--?
Just *listen* to me!
These guys-- These Hydra guys, they stopped it. They broke us out.
What?
If this is *our country* and if you want it back, join us in shutting S.H.I.E.L.D. *down!!!*
You don't want to have another day like you had today.
I wouldn't-- they wouldn't let me go home.
I--I kinda lost it.
They threw me in the back of a wagon and I think, yeah, they were going to arrest me and a bunch of other people.
They took the truck and--and--and killed the S.H.I.E.L.D. agents.
Oh my god. In front of you?
Right in front of us.
They thought I could be one of them.
Did you-- did you help them?

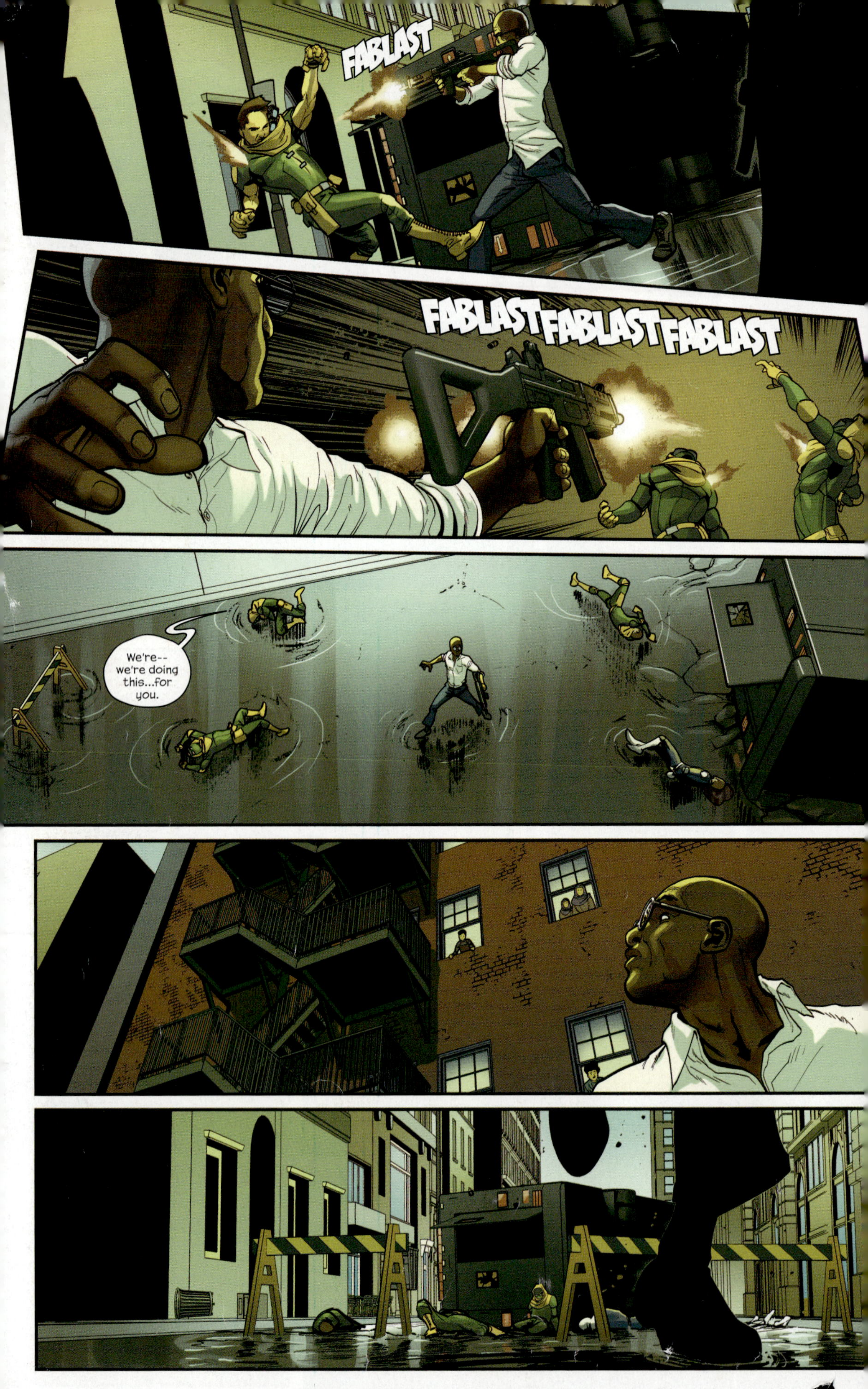
FABLAST
FABLAST FABLAST FABLAST
We're-- we're doing this...for you.

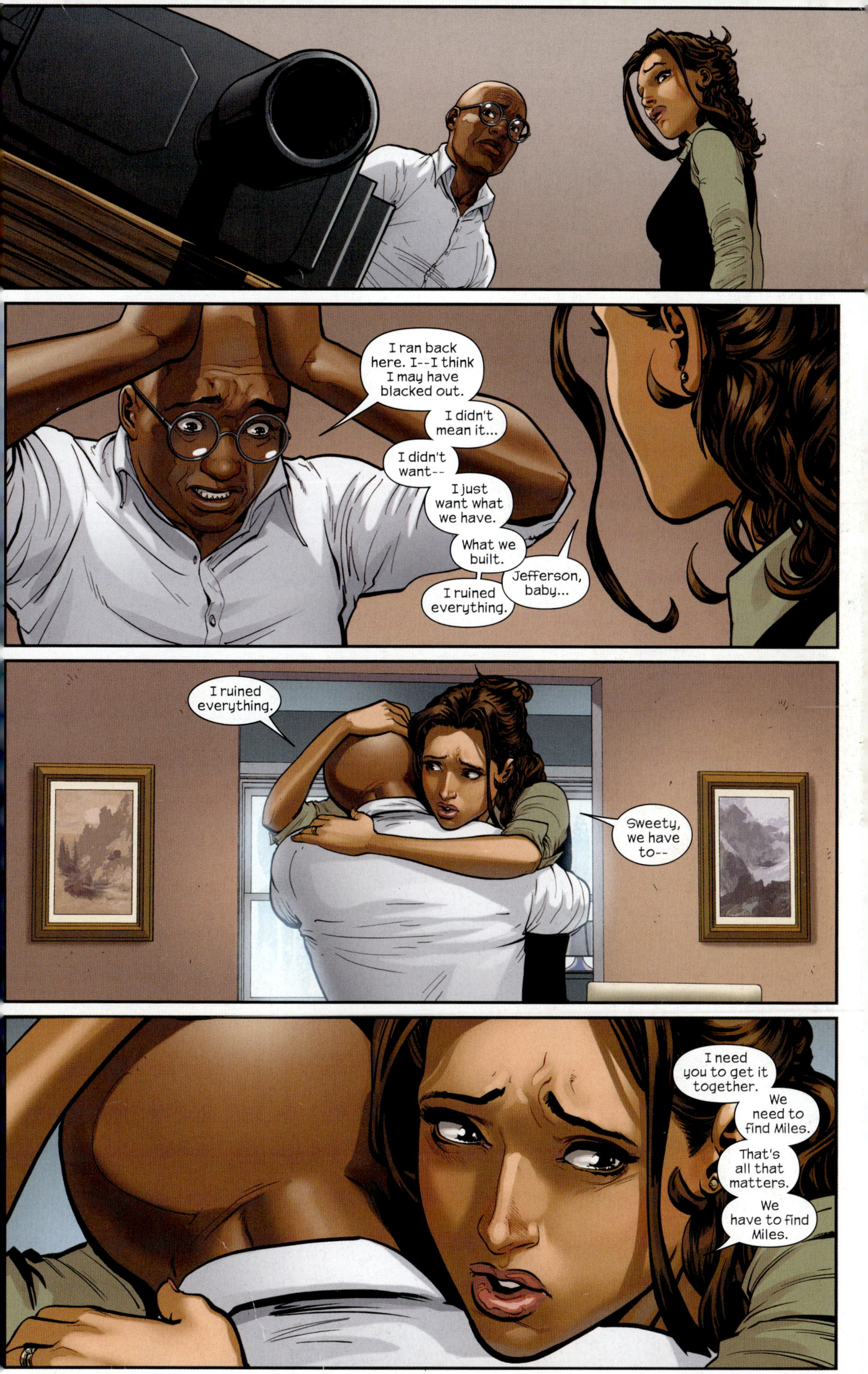
I ran back here. I--I think I may have blacked out.
I didn't mean it...
I didn't want--
I just want what we have.
What we built.
I ruined everything.
Jefferson, baby...
I ruined everything.
Sweety, we have to--
I need you to get it together.
We need to find Miles.
That's all that matters.
We have to find Miles.

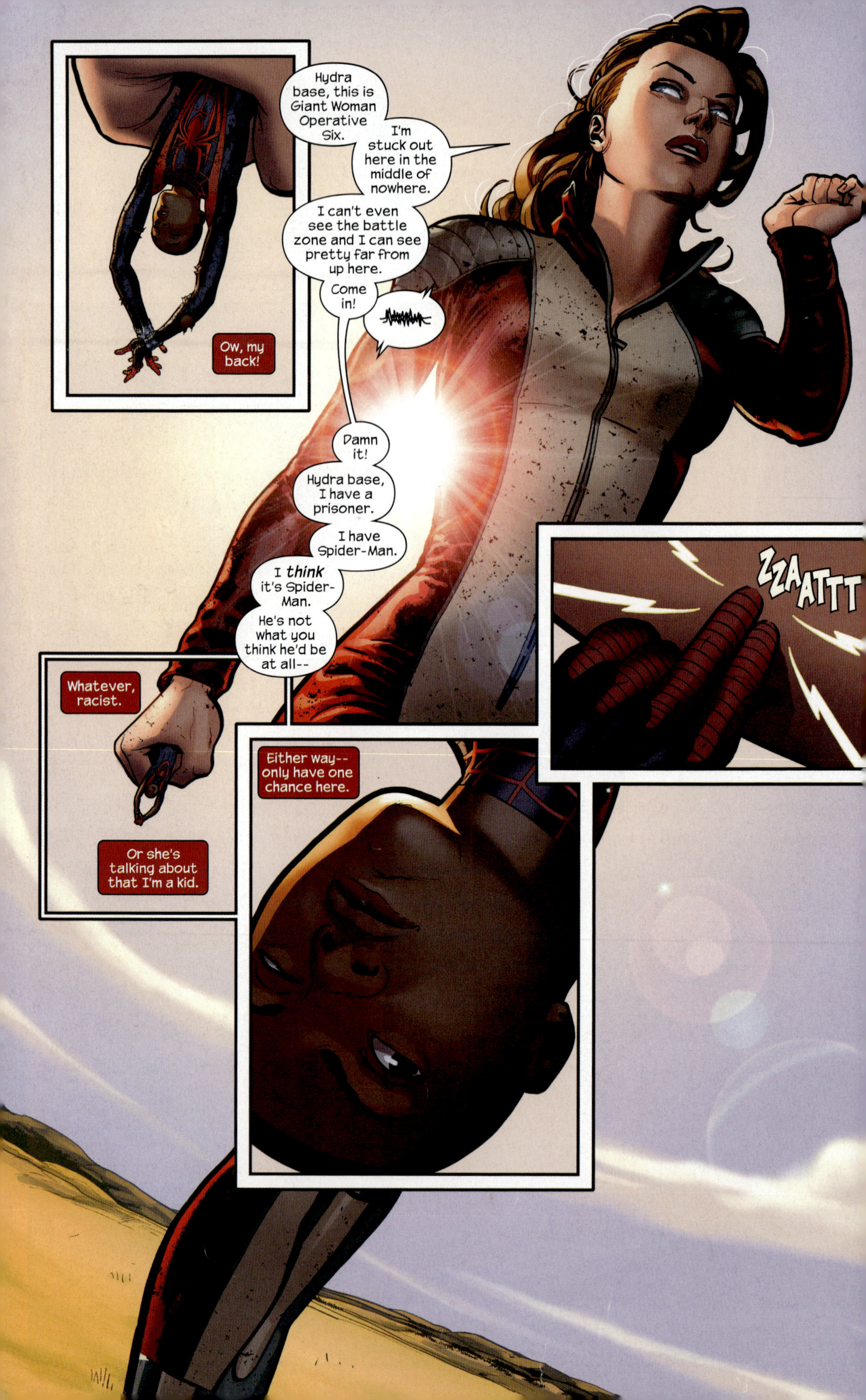
Hydra base, this is Giant Woman Operative Six.
I'm stuck out here in the middle of nowhere.
I can't even see the battle zone and I can see pretty far from up here.
Come in!
Ow, my back!
Damn it!
Hydra base, I have a prisoner.
I have Spider-Man.
I *think* it's Spider-Man.
He's not what you think he'd be at all--
Whatever, racist.
Or she's talking about that I'm a kid.
ZZAATTT
Either way-- only have one chance here.

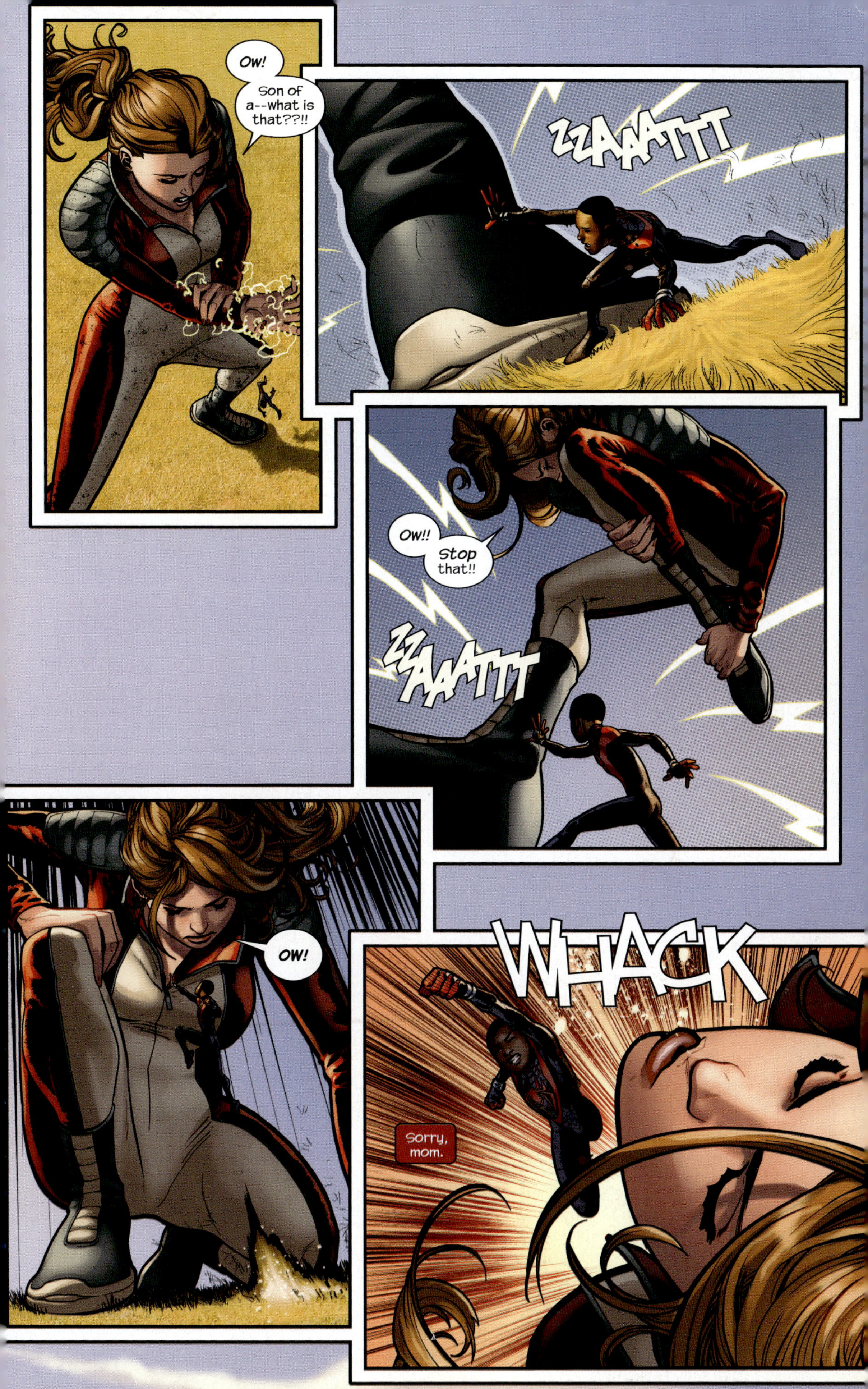
Ow!
Son of a--what is that??!!
ZZAAATTT
Ow!! Stop that!!
ZZAAATTT
Ow!
WHACK
Sorry, mom.

CRACK

Jackie Chan--Ow!

FALUMP

Oof!

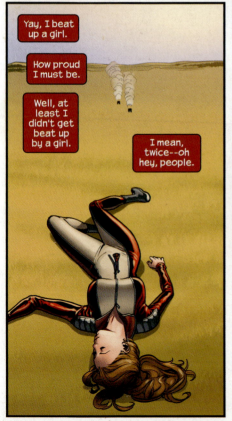

Yay, I beat up a girl.

How proud I must be.

Well, at least I didn't get beat up by a girl.

I mean, twice--oh hey, people.

Please don't be terrorist people.

Uh, please just be people.

Either way, damn, there goes my secret identity.

Here I am, no mask and a giant terrorist.

No pretending this is a cosplay thing or--

Oh my god!

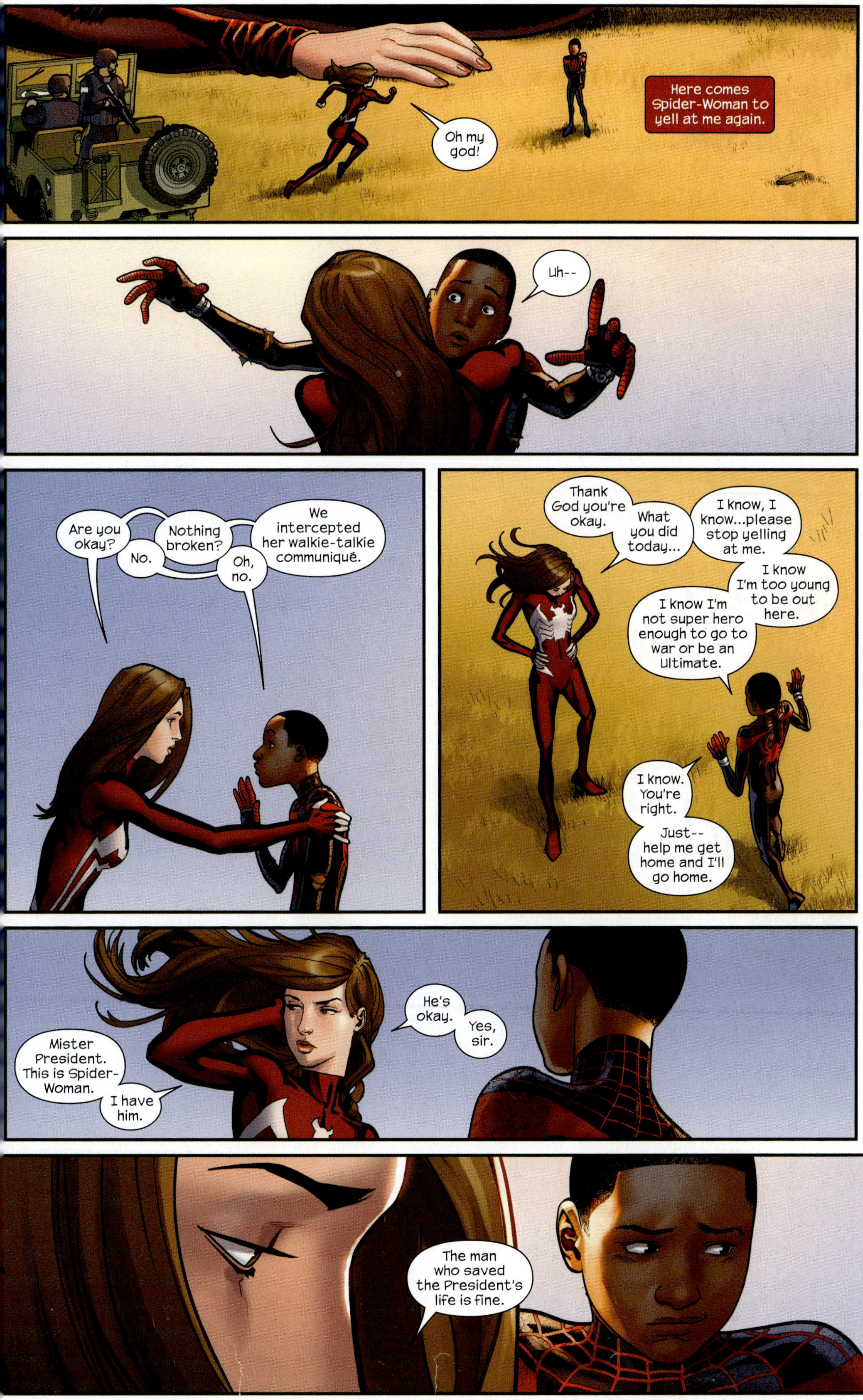

Oh my god!
Here comes Spider-Woman to yell at me again.
Uh--
Are you okay?
No.
Nothing broken?
Oh, no.
We intercepted her walkie-talkie communiqué.
Thank God you're okay.
What you did today...
I know, I know...please stop yelling at me.
I know I'm too young to be out here.
I know I'm not super hero enough to go to war or be an Ultimate.
I know. You're right.
Just-- help me get home and I'll go home.
Mister President. This is Spider-Woman.
I have him.
He's okay.
Yes, sir.
The man who saved the President's life is fine.

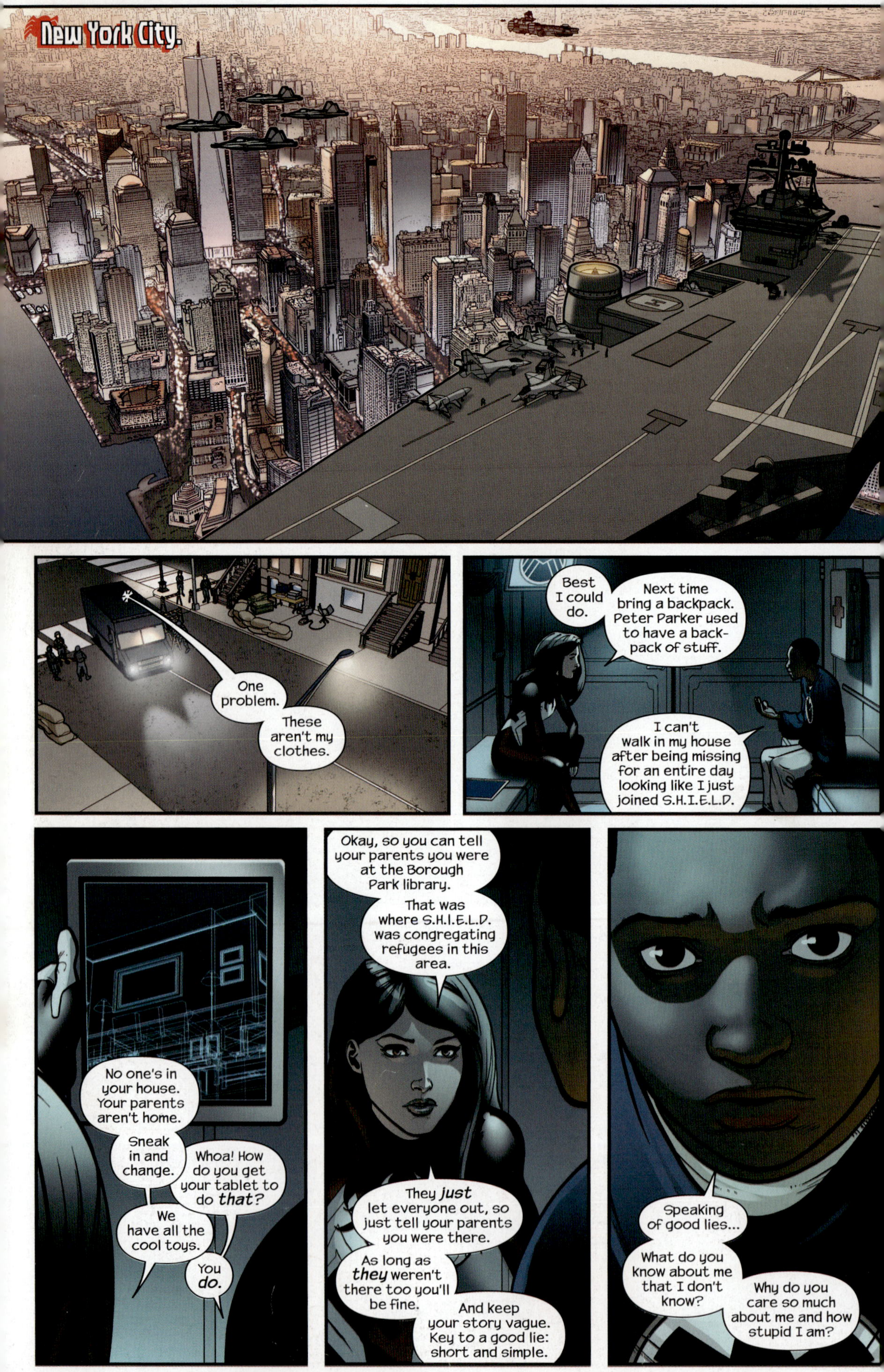
New York City.
One problem.
These aren't my clothes.
Best I could do.
Next time bring a backpack. Peter Parker used to have a back-pack of stuff.
I can't walk in my house after being missing for an entire day looking like I just joined S.H.I.E.L.D.
No one's in your house. Your parents aren't home.
Sneak in and change.
Whoa! How do you get your tablet to do *that?*
We have all the cool toys.
You *do.*
Okay, so you can tell your parents you were at the Borough Park library.
That was where S.H.I.E.L.D. was congregating refugees in this area.
They *just* let everyone out, so just tell your parents you were there.
As long as *they* weren't there too you'll be fine.
And keep your story vague. Key to a good lie: short and simple.
Speaking of good lies...
What do you know about me that I don't know?
Why do you care so much about me and how stupid I am?

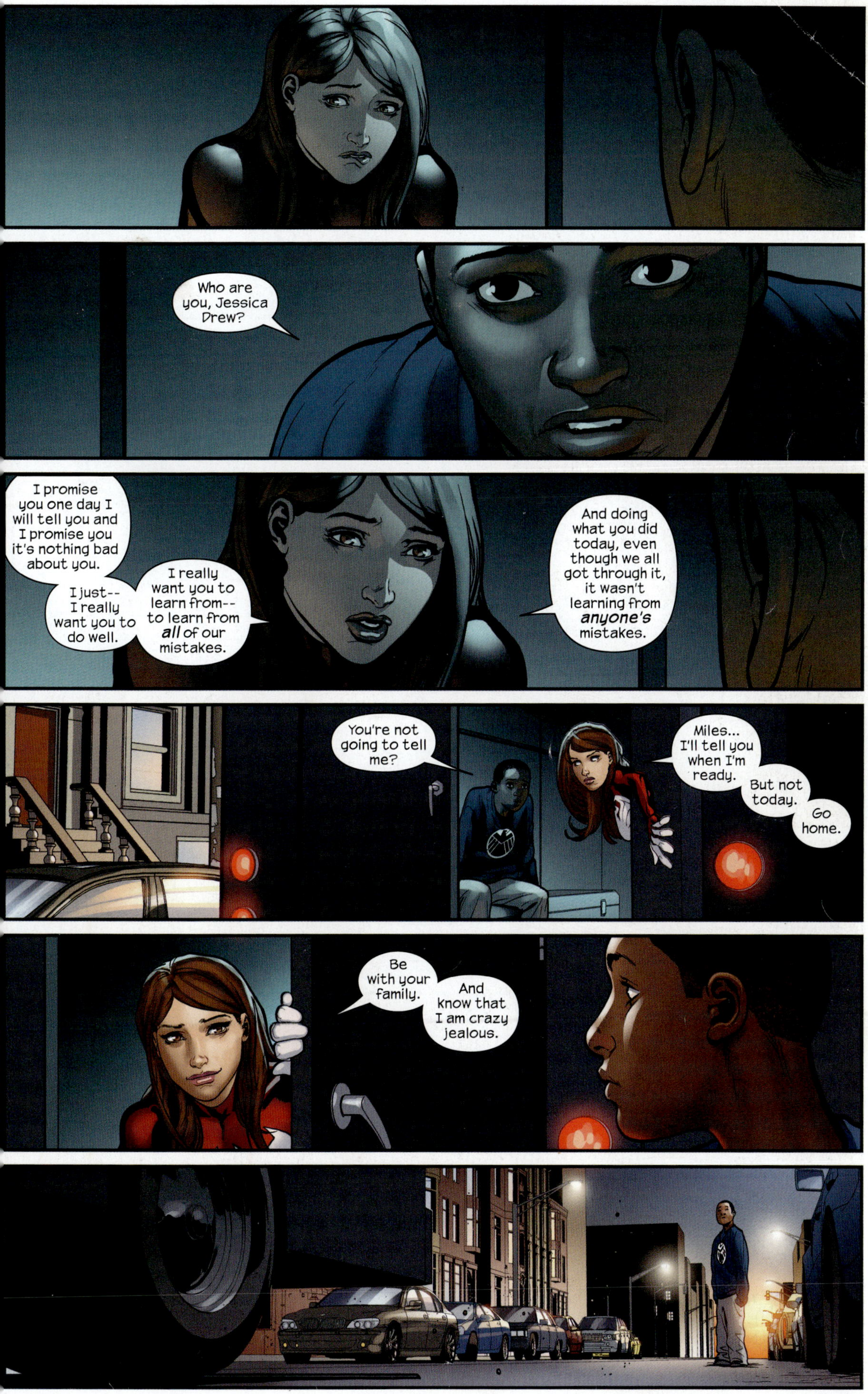
Who are you, Jessica Drew?
I promise you one day I will tell you and I promise you it's nothing bad about you.
I just-- I really want you to do well.
I really want you to learn from-- to learn from *all* of our mistakes.
And doing what you did today, even though we all got through it, it wasn't learning from *anyone's* mistakes.
You're not going to tell me?
Miles... I'll tell you when I'm ready.
But not today.
Go home.
Be with your family.
And know that I am crazy jealous.

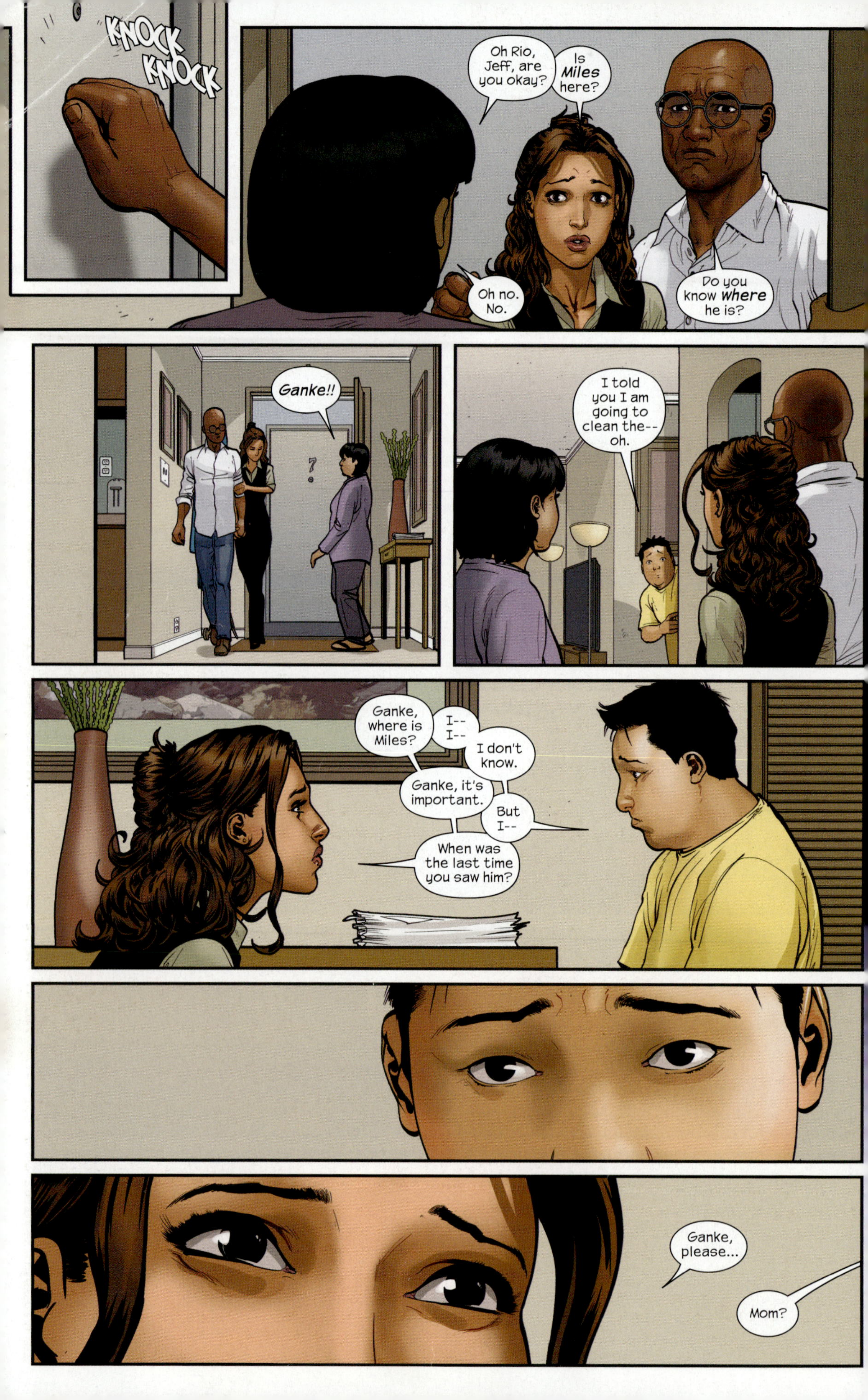
KNOCK KNOCK
Oh Rio, Jeff, are you okay?
Is *Miles* here?
Oh no. No.
Do you know **where** he is?
Ganke!!
?
I told you I am going to clean the-- oh.
Ganke, where is Miles?
I-- I--
I don't know.
Ganke, it's important.
But I--
When was the last time you saw him?
Ganke, please...
Mom?

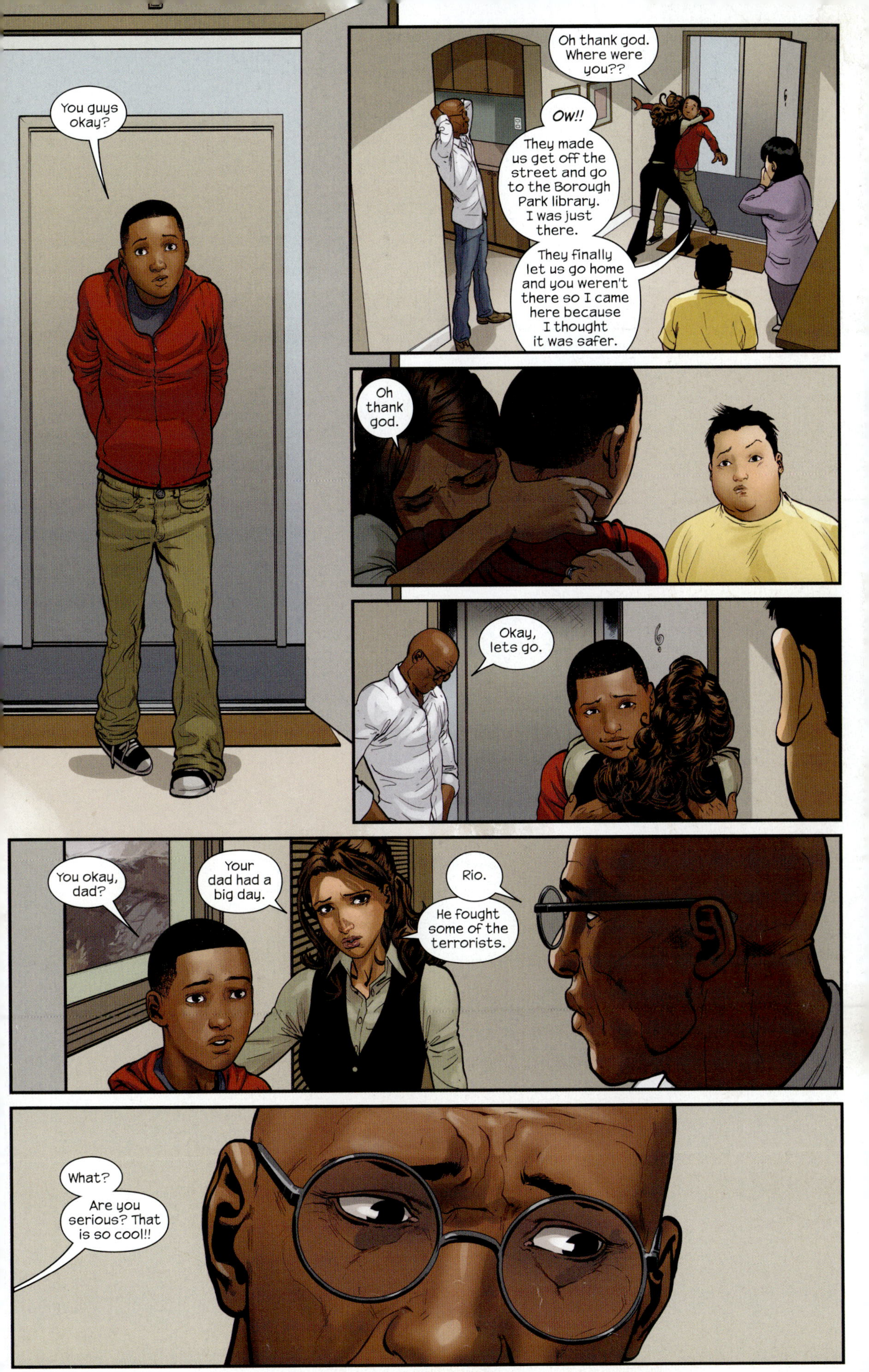
You guys okay?
Oh thank god. Where were you??
OW!!
They made us get off the street and go to the Borough Park library. I was just there.
They finally let us go home and you weren't there so I came here because I thought it was safer.
Oh thank god.
Okay, lets go.
You okay, dad?
Your dad had a big day.
Rio.
He fought some of the terrorists.
What?
Are you serious? That is so cool!!

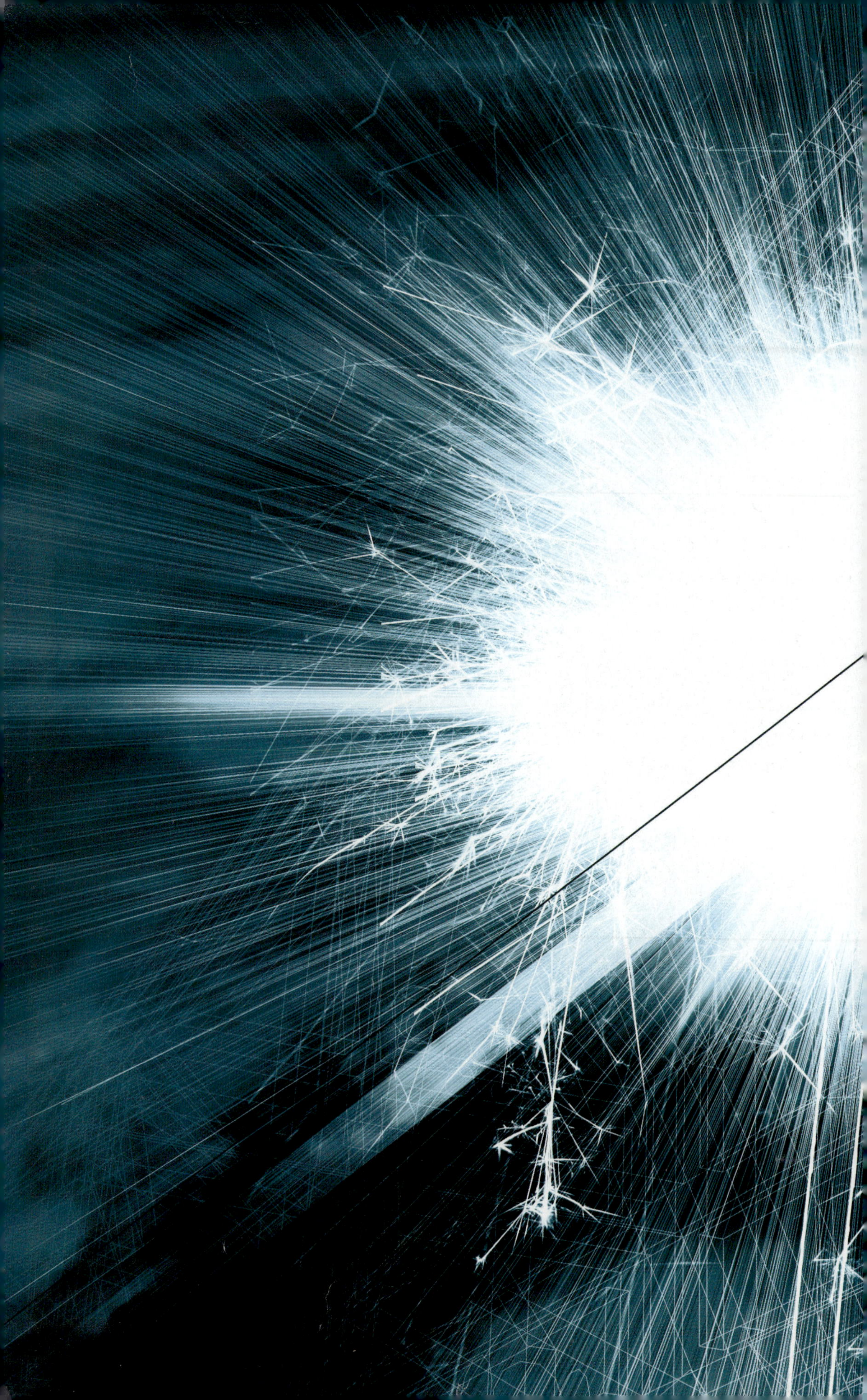

POINT·ONE

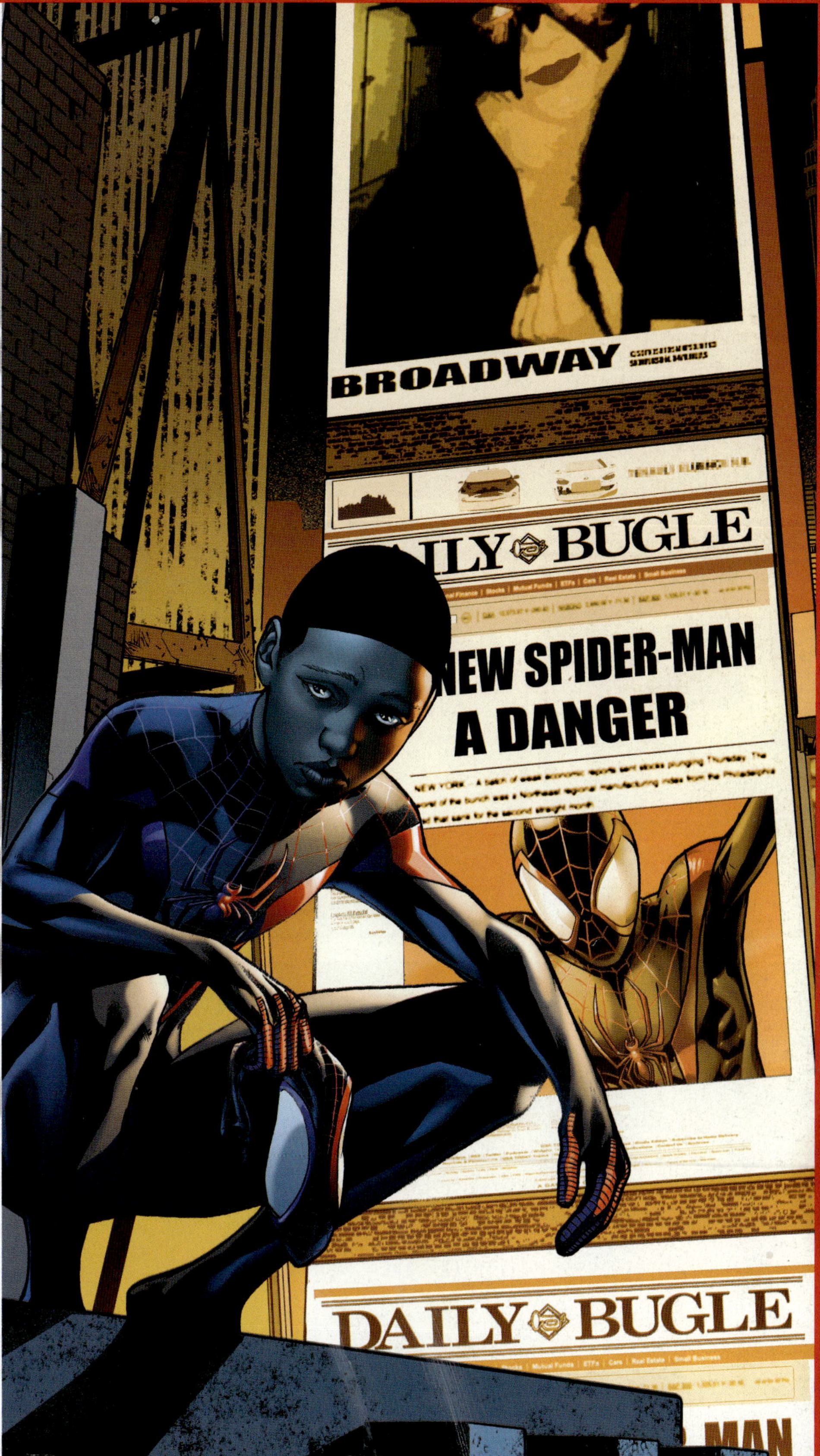
BROADWAY
DAILY BUGLE
NEW SPIDER-MAN
A DANGER
DAILY BUGLE
MAN

16.1

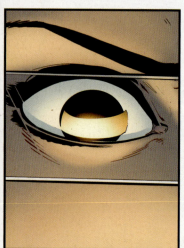

Oh my God!

You are...

just...

...like me.

What? **What** did you say?

They're calling someone. Hold on.

You are...

just...

...like me.

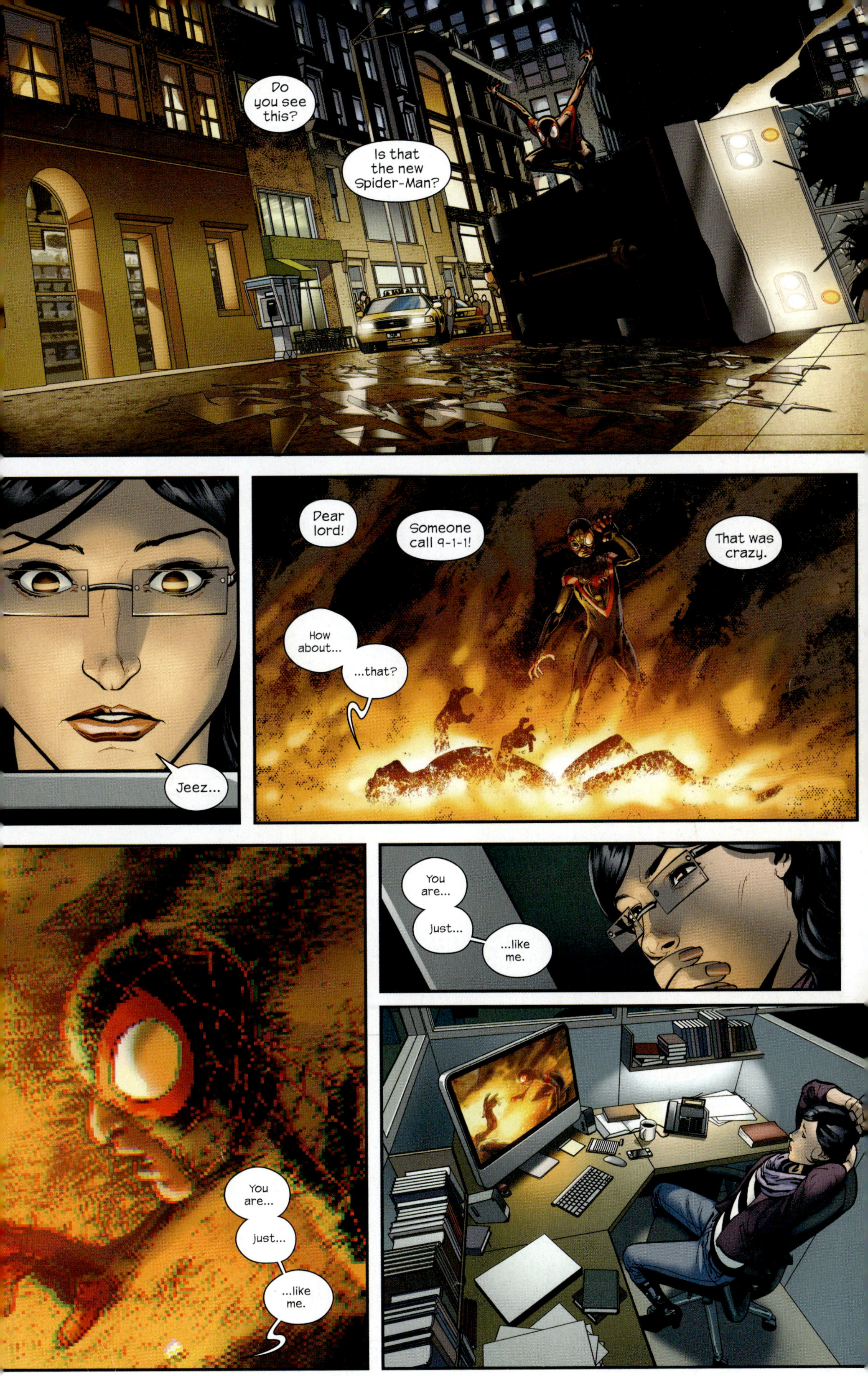
Do you see this?
Is that the new Spider-Man?
Jeez...
Dear lord!
Someone call 9-1-1!
That was crazy.
How about...
...that?
You are...
just...
...like me.
You are...
just...
...like me.

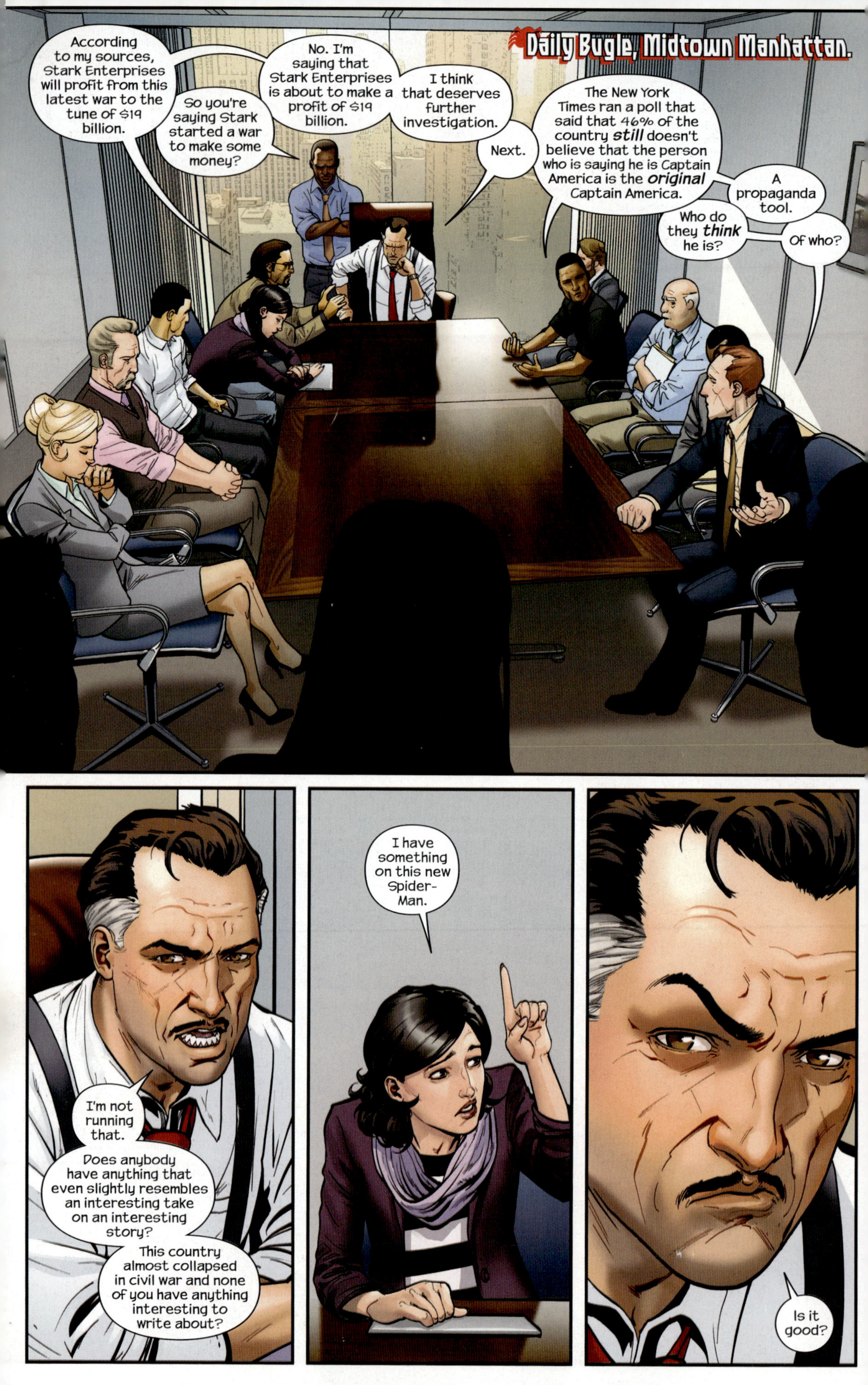
Daily Bugle, Midtown Manhattan.
According to my sources, Stark Enterprises will profit from this latest war to the tune of $19 billion.
So you're saying Stark started a war to make some money?
No. I'm saying that Stark Enterprises is about to make a profit of $19 billion.
I think that deserves further investigation.
Next.
The New York Times ran a poll that said that 46% of the country *still* doesn't believe that the person who is saying he is Captain America is the *original* Captain America.
Who do they *think* he is?
A propaganda tool.
Of who?
I'm not running that.
Does anybody have anything that even slightly resembles an interesting take on an interesting story?
This country almost collapsed in civil war and none of you have anything interesting to write about?
I have something on this new Spider-Man.
Is it good?

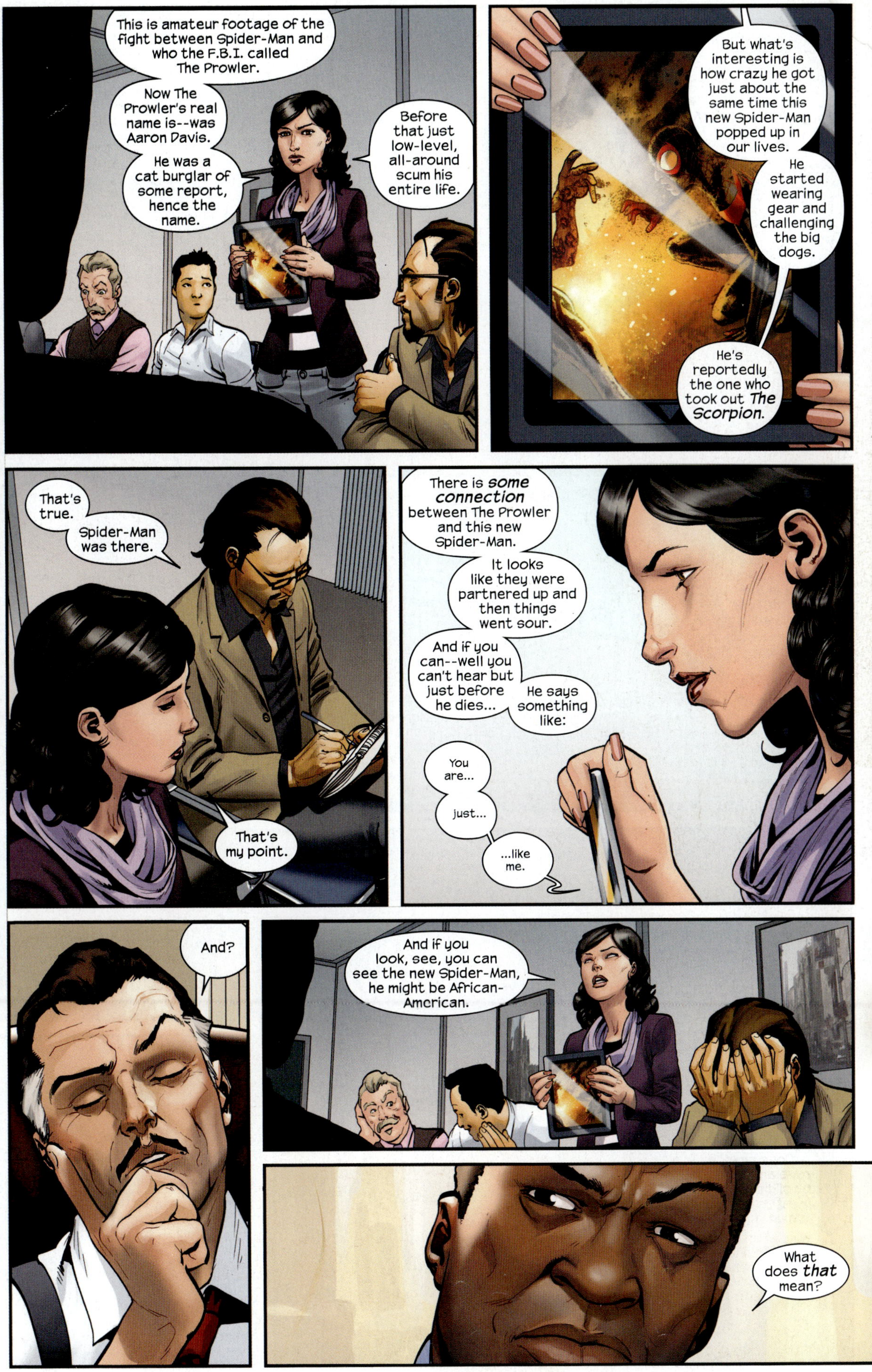

This is amateur footage of the fight between Spider-Man and who the F.B.I. called The Prowler.
Now The Prowler's real name is--was Aaron Davis.
He was a cat burglar of some report, hence the name.
Before that just low-level, all-around scum his entire life.
But what's interesting is how crazy he got just about the same time this new Spider-Man popped up in our lives.
He started wearing gear and challenging the big dogs.
He's reportedly the one who took out *The Scorpion*.
That's true.
Spider-Man was there.
That's my point.
There is *some connection* between The Prowler and this new Spider-Man.
It looks like they were partnered up and then things went sour.
And if you can--well you can't hear but just before he dies...
He says something like:
You are...
just...
...like me.
And?
And if you look, see, you can see the new Spider-Man, he might be African-American.
What does *that* mean?

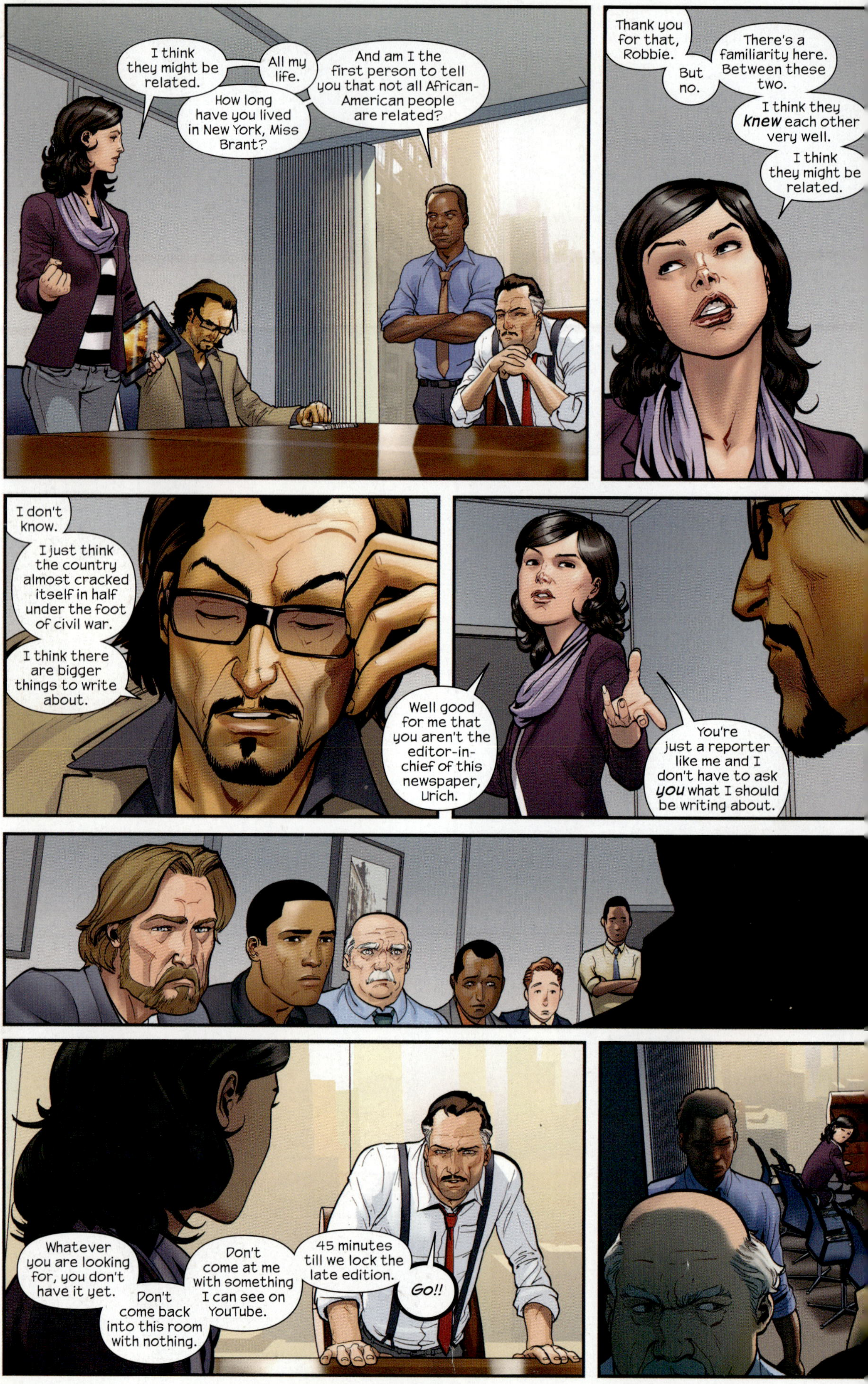
I think they might be related.
All my life.
How long have you lived in New York, Miss Brant?
And am I the first person to tell you that not all African-American people are related?
Thank you for that, Robbie.
But no.
There's a familiarity here. Between these two.
I think they *knew* each other very well.
I think they might be related.
I don't know.
I just think the country almost cracked itself in half under the foot of civil war.
I think there are bigger things to write about.
Well good for me that you aren't the editor-in-chief of this newspaper, Urich.
You're just a reporter like me and I don't have to ask *you* what I should be writing about.
Whatever you are looking for, you don't have it yet.
Don't come back into this room with nothing.
Don't come at me with something I can see on YouTube.
45 minutes till we lock the late edition.
Go!!

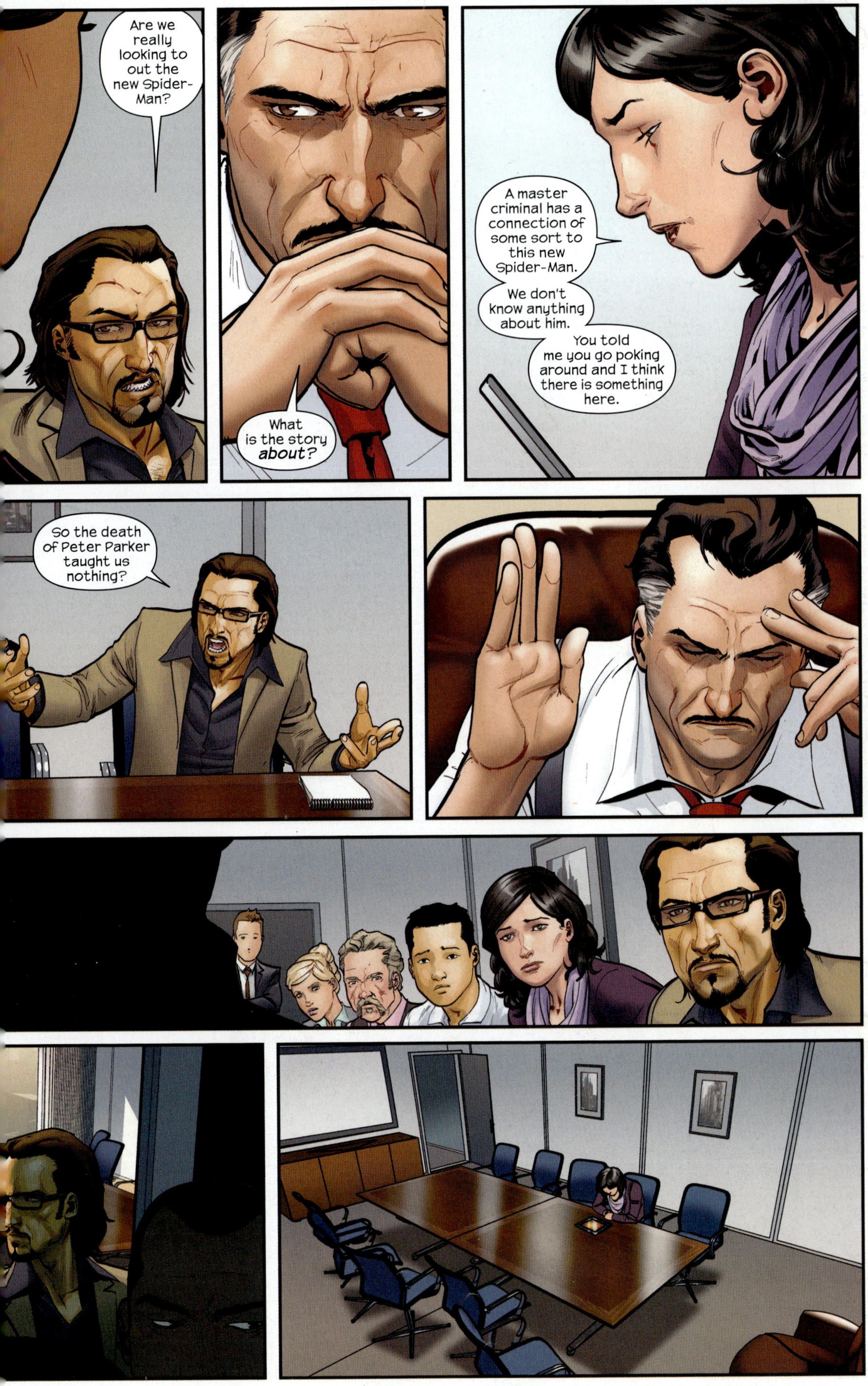

Are we really looking to out the new Spider-Man?
What is the story *about?*
A master criminal has a connection of some sort to this new Spider-Man.
We don't know anything about him.
You told me you go poking around and I think there is something here.
So the death of Peter Parker taught us nothing?

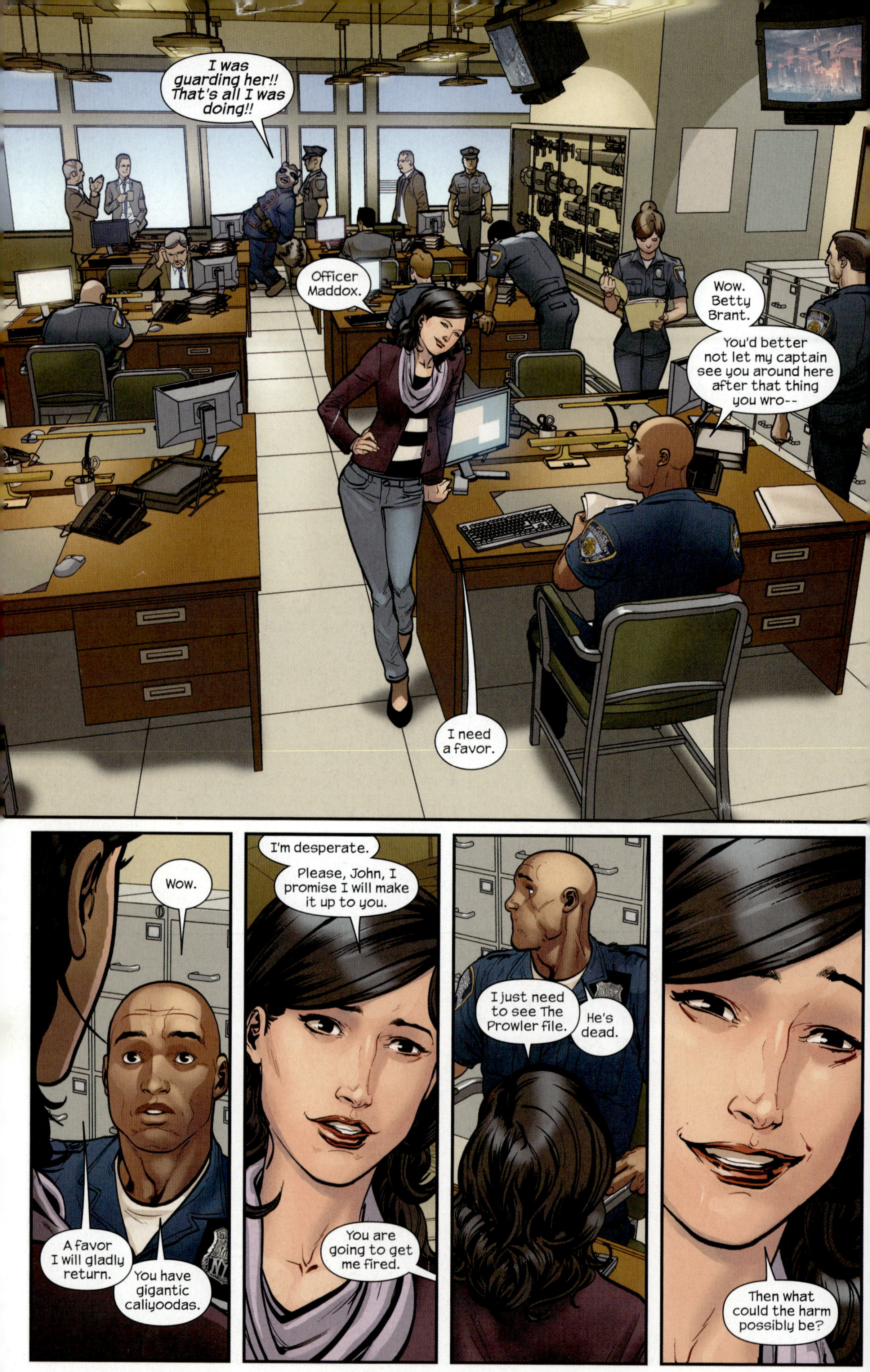
I was guarding her!! That's all I was doing!!
Officer Maddox.
Wow. Betty Brant.
You'd better not let my captain see you around here after that thing you wro--
I need a favor.
Wow.
A favor I will gladly return.
You have gigantic caliyoodas.
I'm desperate.
Please, John, I promise I will make it up to you.
You are going to get me fired.
I just need to see The Prowler file.
He's dead.
Then what could the harm possibly be?

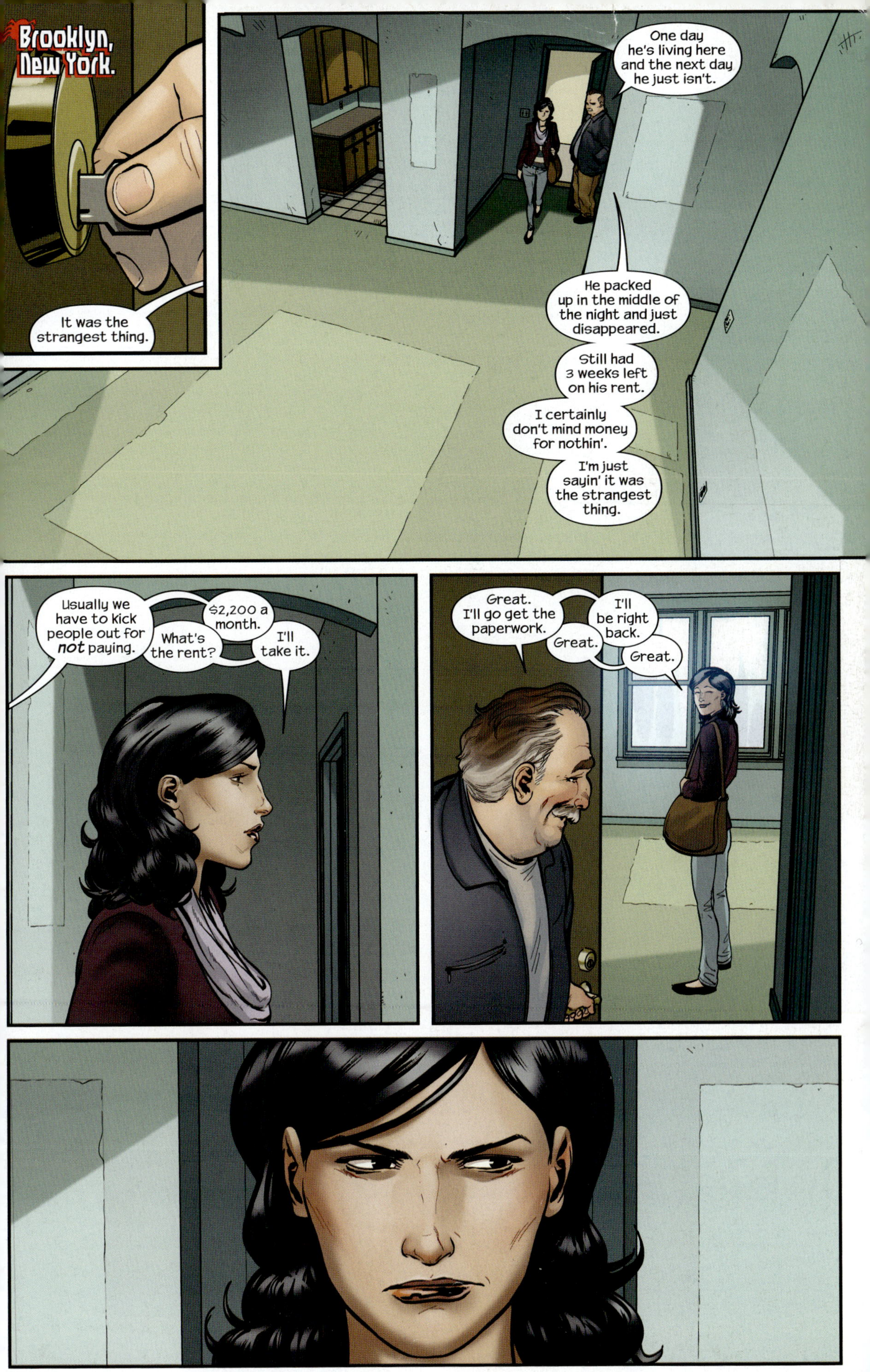
Brooklyn, New York.
It was the strangest thing.
One day he's living here and the next day he just isn't.
He packed up in the middle of the night and just disappeared.
Still had 3 weeks left on his rent.
I certainly don't mind money for nothin'.
I'm just sayin' it was the strangest thing.
Usually we have to kick people out for **not** paying.
What's the rent?
$2,200 a month.
I'll take it.
Great. I'll go get the paperwork.
Great.
I'll be right back.
Great.

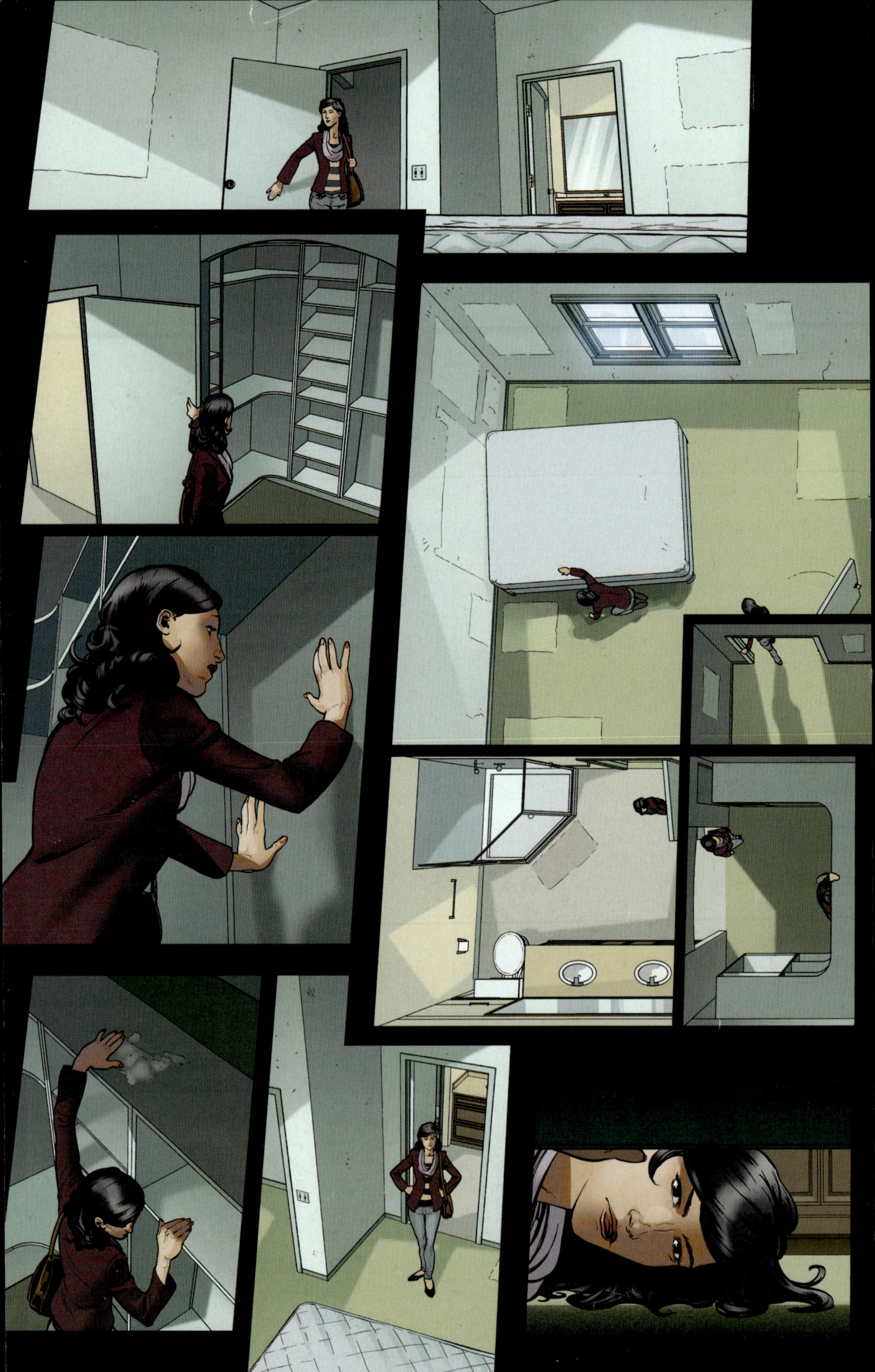

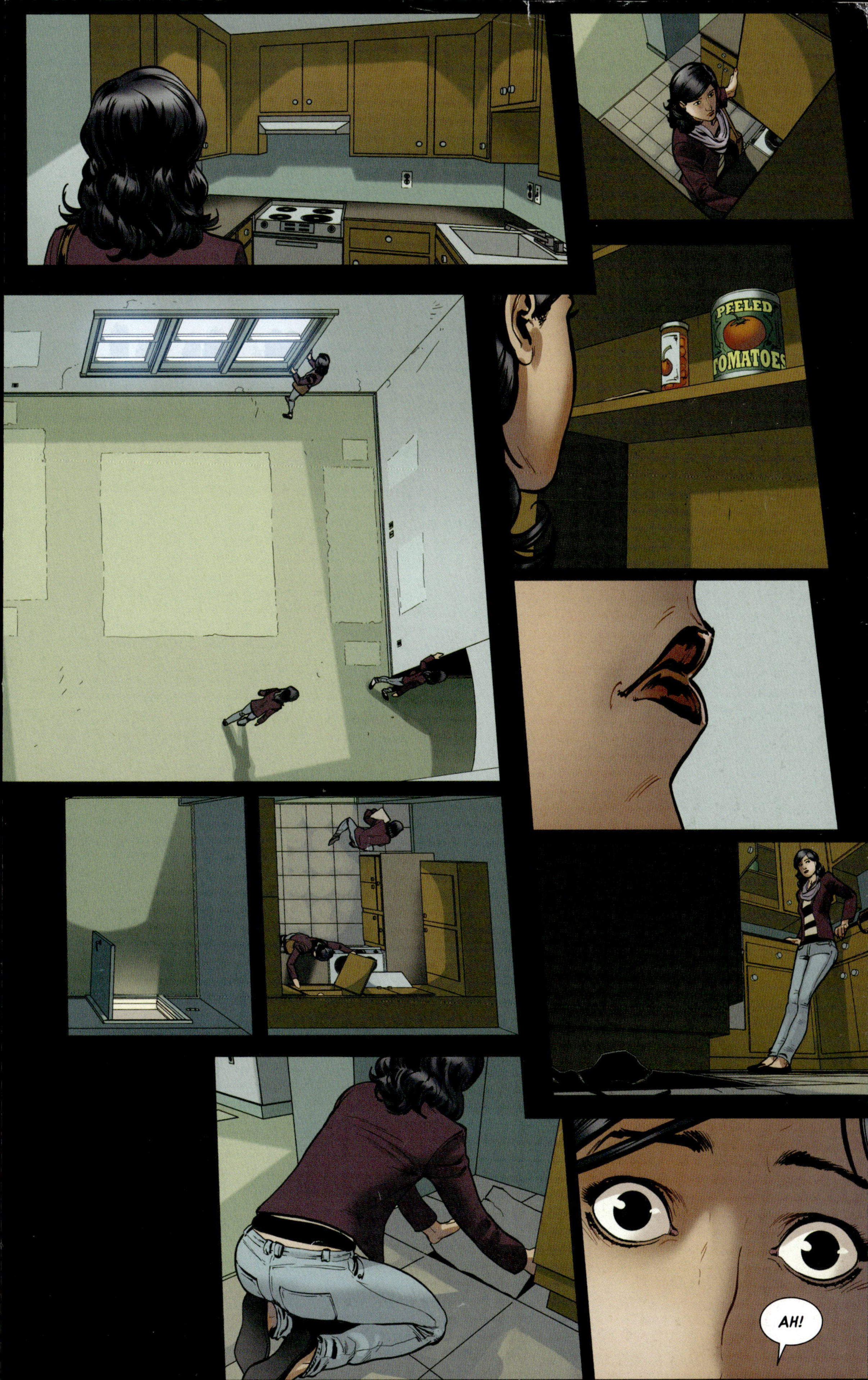
PEELED
TOMATOES
AH!

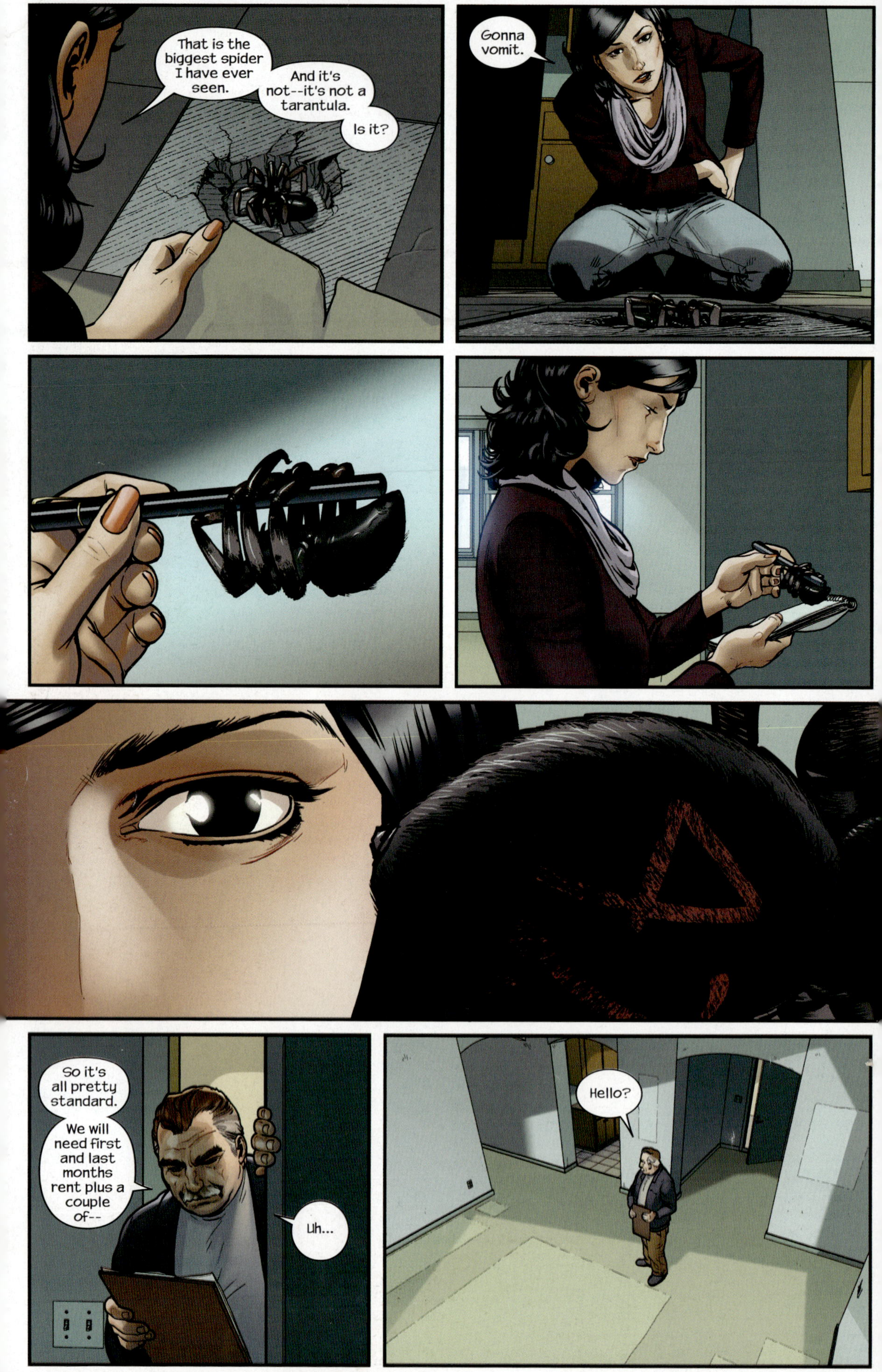
That is the biggest spider I have ever seen.
And it's not--it's not a tarantula.
Is it?
Gonna vomit.
So it's all pretty standard.
We will need first and last months rent plus a couple of--
Uh...
Hello?

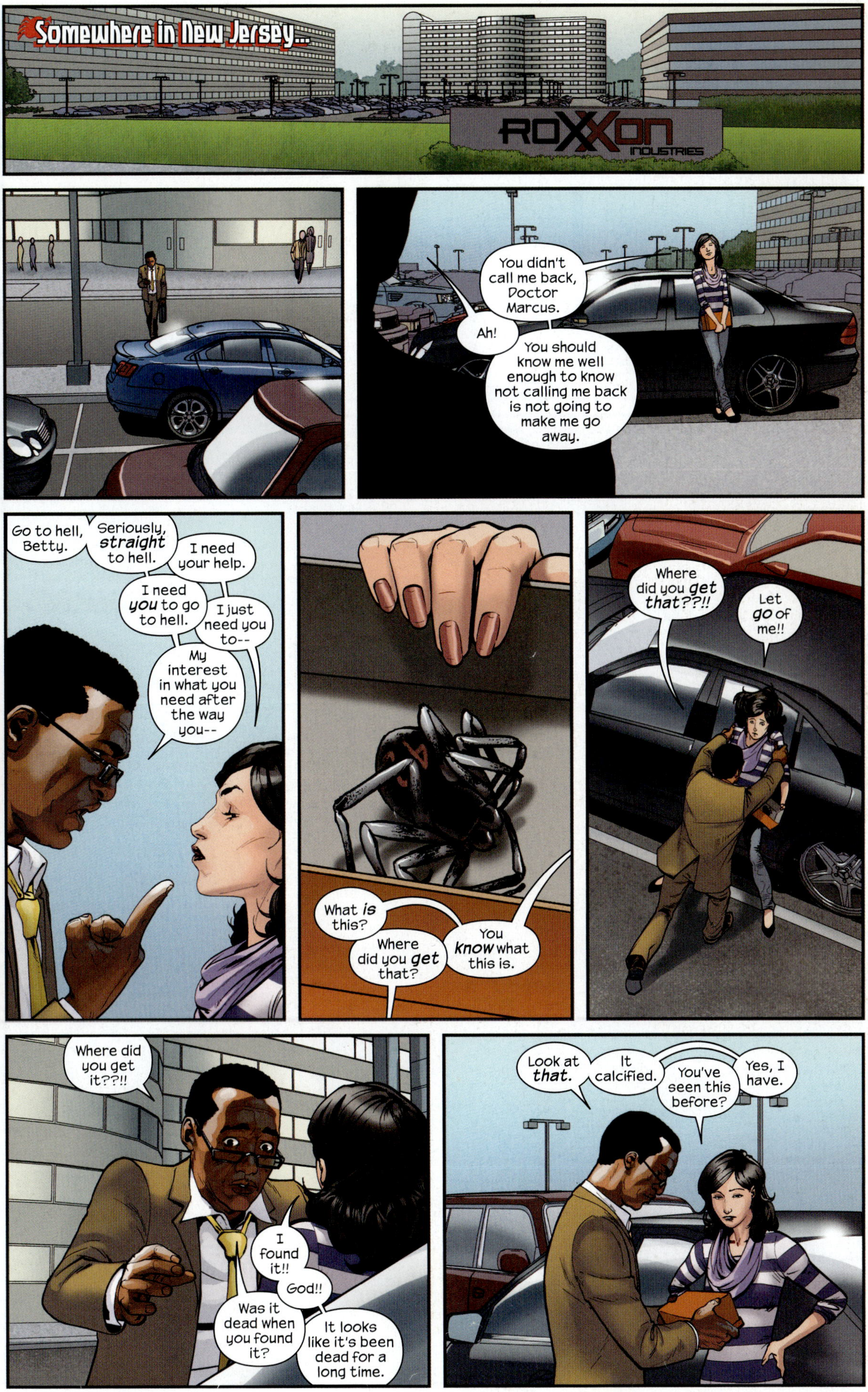
Somewhere in New Jersey...
ROXXON INDUSTRIES
You didn't call me back, Doctor Marcus.
Ah!
You should know me well enough to know not calling me back is not going to make me go away.
Go to hell, Betty.
Seriously, *straight* to hell.
I need your help.
I need *you* to go to hell.
I just need you to--
My interest in what you need after the way you--
What *is* this?
Where did you *get* that?
You *know* what this is.
Where did you *get that??!!*
Let *go* of me!!
Where did you get it??!!
I found it!!
God!!
Was it dead when you found it?
It looks like it's been dead for a long time.
Look at *that.*
It calcified.
You've seen this before?
Yes, I have.

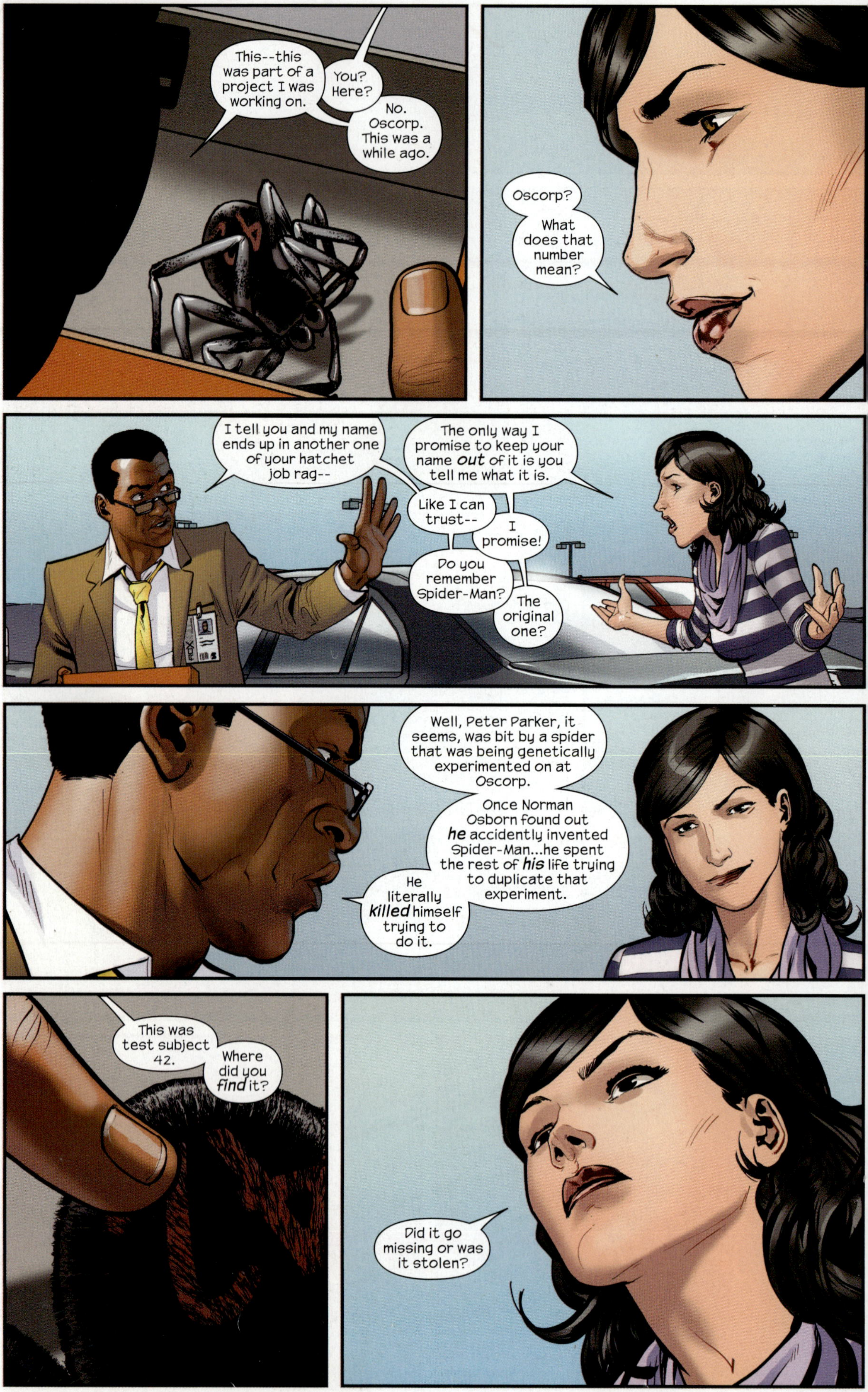
This--this was part of a project I was working on.
You? Here?
No. Oscorp. This was a while ago.
Oscorp?
What does that number mean?
I tell you and my name ends up in another one of your hatchet job rag--
The only way I promise to keep your name *out* of it is you tell me what it is.
Like I can trust--
I promise!
Do you remember Spider-Man?
The original one?
Well, Peter Parker, it seems, was bit by a spider that was being genetically experimented on at Oscorp.
Once Norman Osborn found out *he* accidently invented Spider-Man...he spent the rest of *his* life trying to duplicate that experiment.
He literally *killed* himself trying to do it.
This was test subject 42.
Where did you *find* it?
Did it go missing or was it stolen?

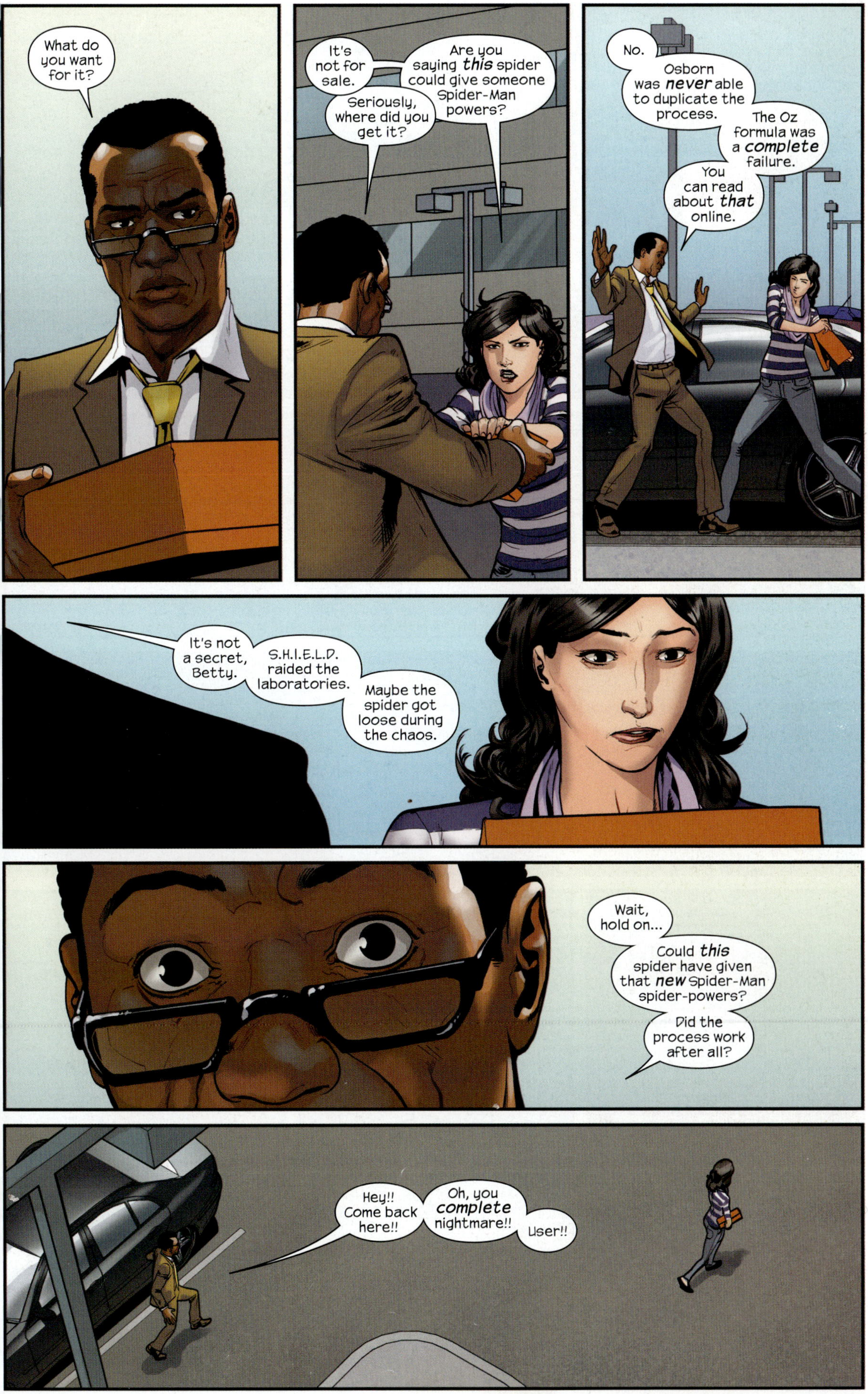
What do you want for it?
It's not for sale.
Are you saying *this* spider could give someone Spider-Man powers?
Seriously, where did you get it?
No.
Osborn was *never* able to duplicate the process.
The Oz formula was a *complete* failure.
You can read about *that* online.
It's not a secret, Betty.
S.H.I.E.L.D. raided the laboratories.
Maybe the spider got loose during the chaos.
Wait, hold on...
Could *this* spider have given that *new* Spider-Man spider-powers?
Did the process work after all?
Hey!! Come back here!!
Oh, you *complete* nightmare!!
User!!

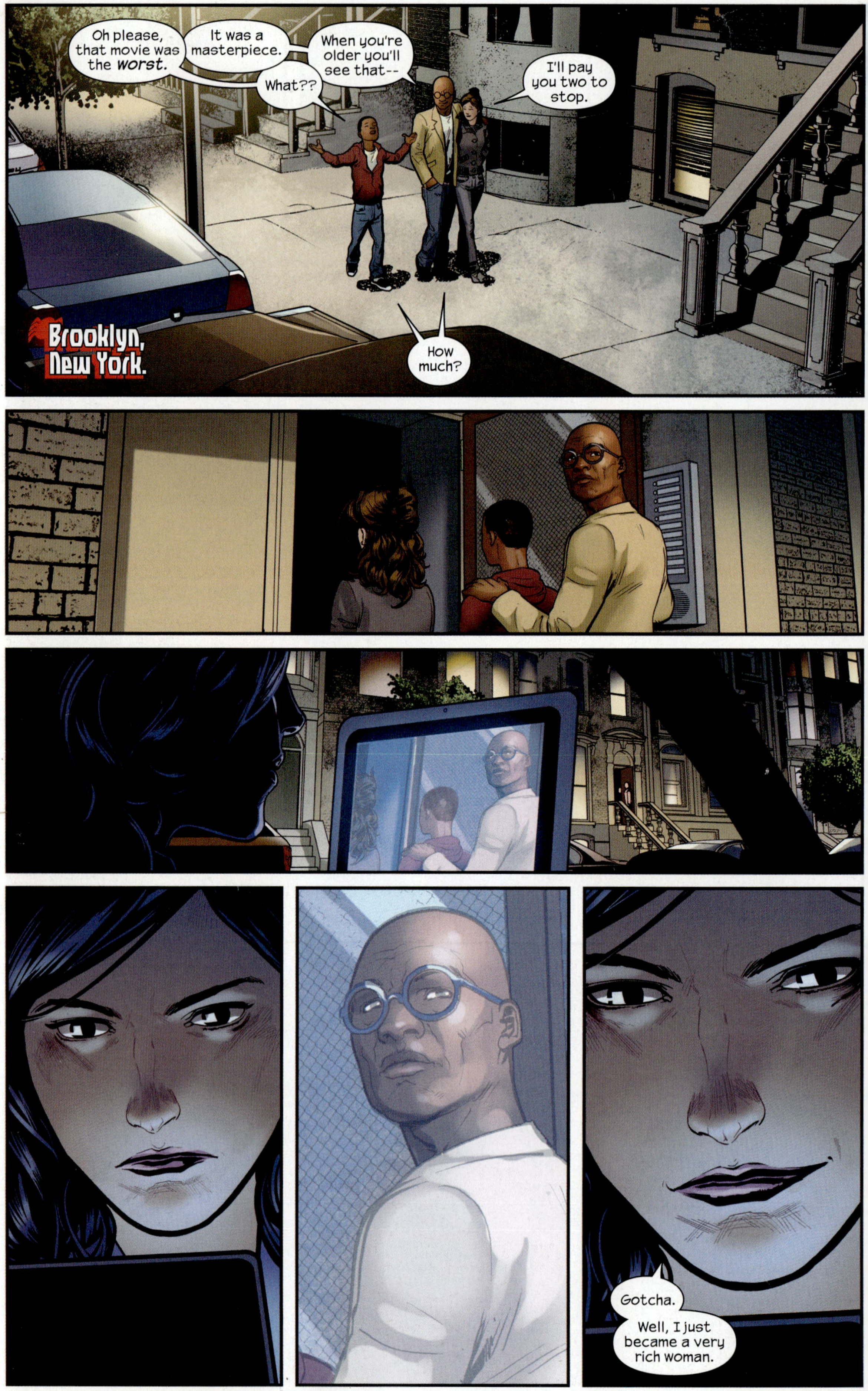
Oh please, that movie was the *worst.*
It was a masterpiece.
When you're older you'll see that--
What??
I'll pay you two to stop.
Brooklyn, New York.
How much?
Gotcha.
Well, I just became a very rich woman.

You don't say.

I know who the new Spider-Man is.

I have physical evidence.

I have proof.

It's a great story.

And I want you and I, right now, to work out our financial differences.

We have financial differences?

I don't like how much I make.

I don't like that I'm treated like a lesser reporter because of past indiscretions.

And I would like to rectify all of this in exchange for this world-wide exclusive.

Let me see it.

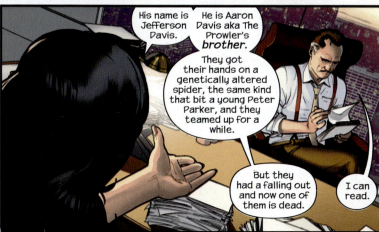

His name is Jefferson Davis.

He is Aaron Davis aka The Prowler's *brother*.

They got their hands on a genetically altered spider, the same kind that bit a young Peter Parker, and they teamed up for a while.

But they had a falling out and now one of them is dead.

I can read.

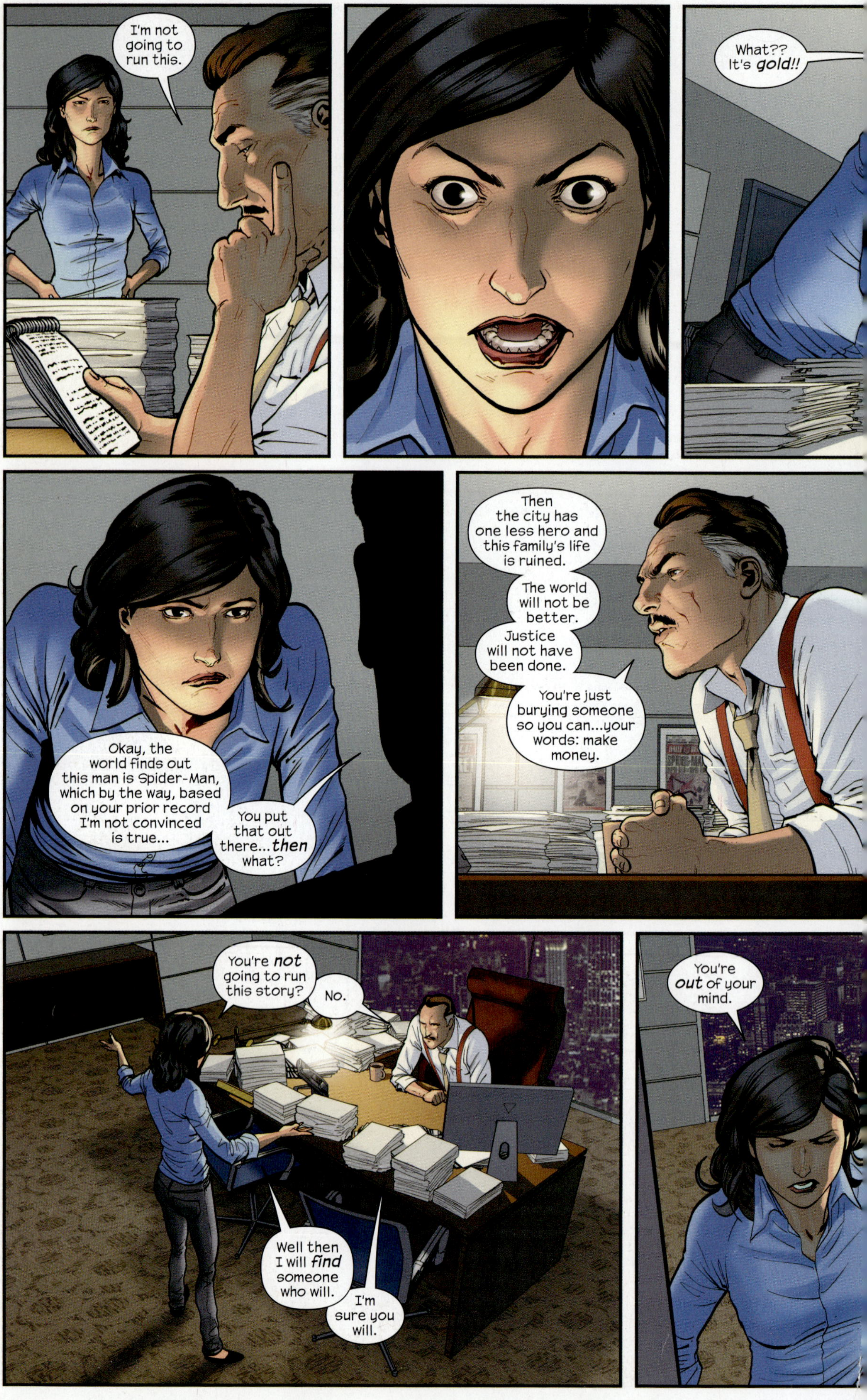

I'm not going to run this.
What?? It's *gold!!*
Okay, the world finds out this man is Spider-Man, which by the way, based on your prior record I'm not convinced is true...
You put that out there...*then* what?
Then the city has one less hero and this family's life is ruined.
The world will not be better.
Justice will not have been done.
You're just burying someone so you can...your words: make money.
You're *not* going to run this story?
No.
Well then I will *find* someone who will.
I'm sure you will.
You're *out* of your mind.

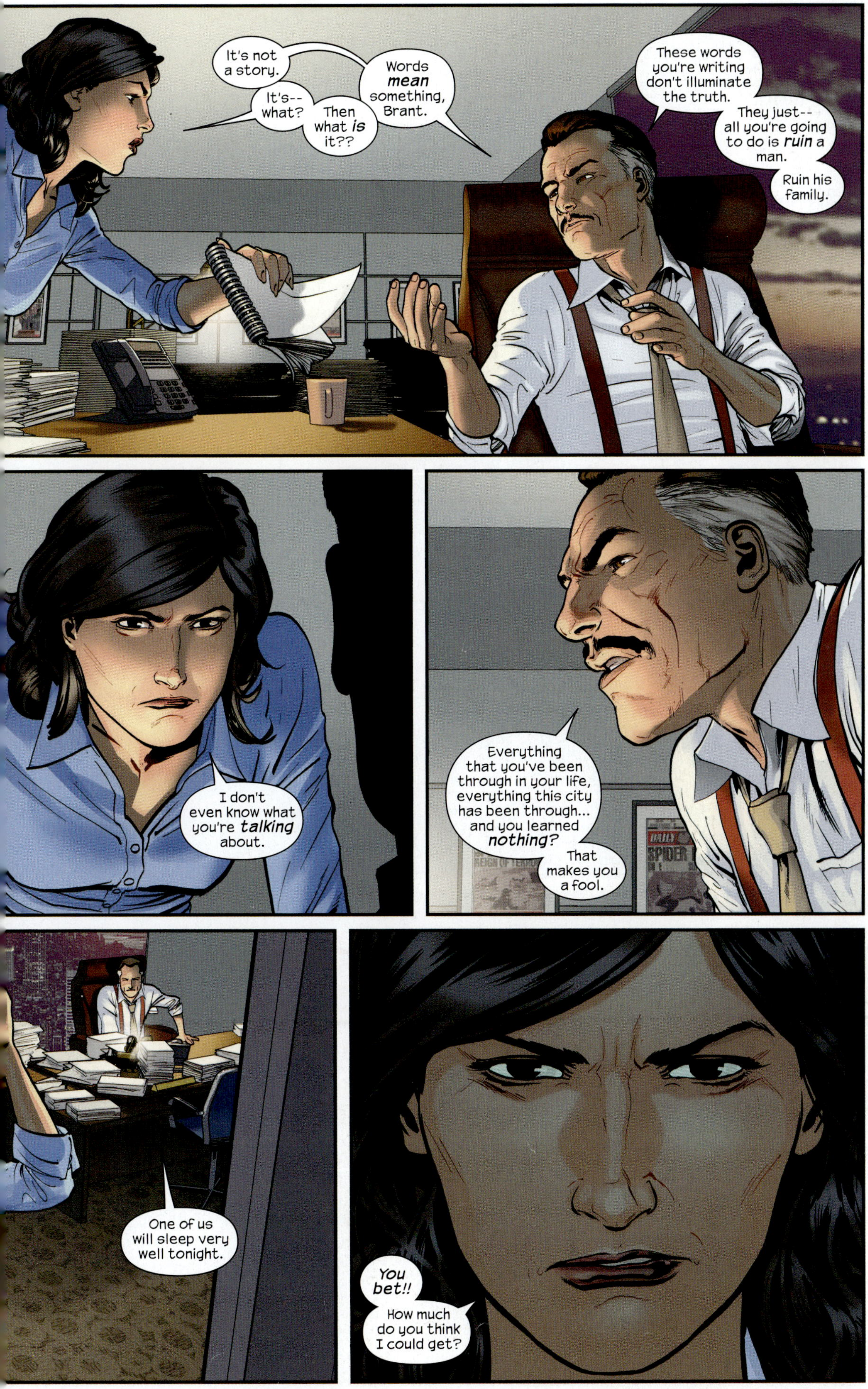
It's not a story.
Words *mean* something, Brant.
These words you're writing don't illuminate the truth.
They just-- all you're going to do is *ruin* a man.
Ruin his family.
It's-- what?
Then what *is* it??
I don't even know what you're *talking* about.
Everything that you've been through in your life, everything this city has been through... and you learned *nothing?*
That makes you a fool.
One of us will sleep very well tonight.
You bet!!
How much do you think I could get?

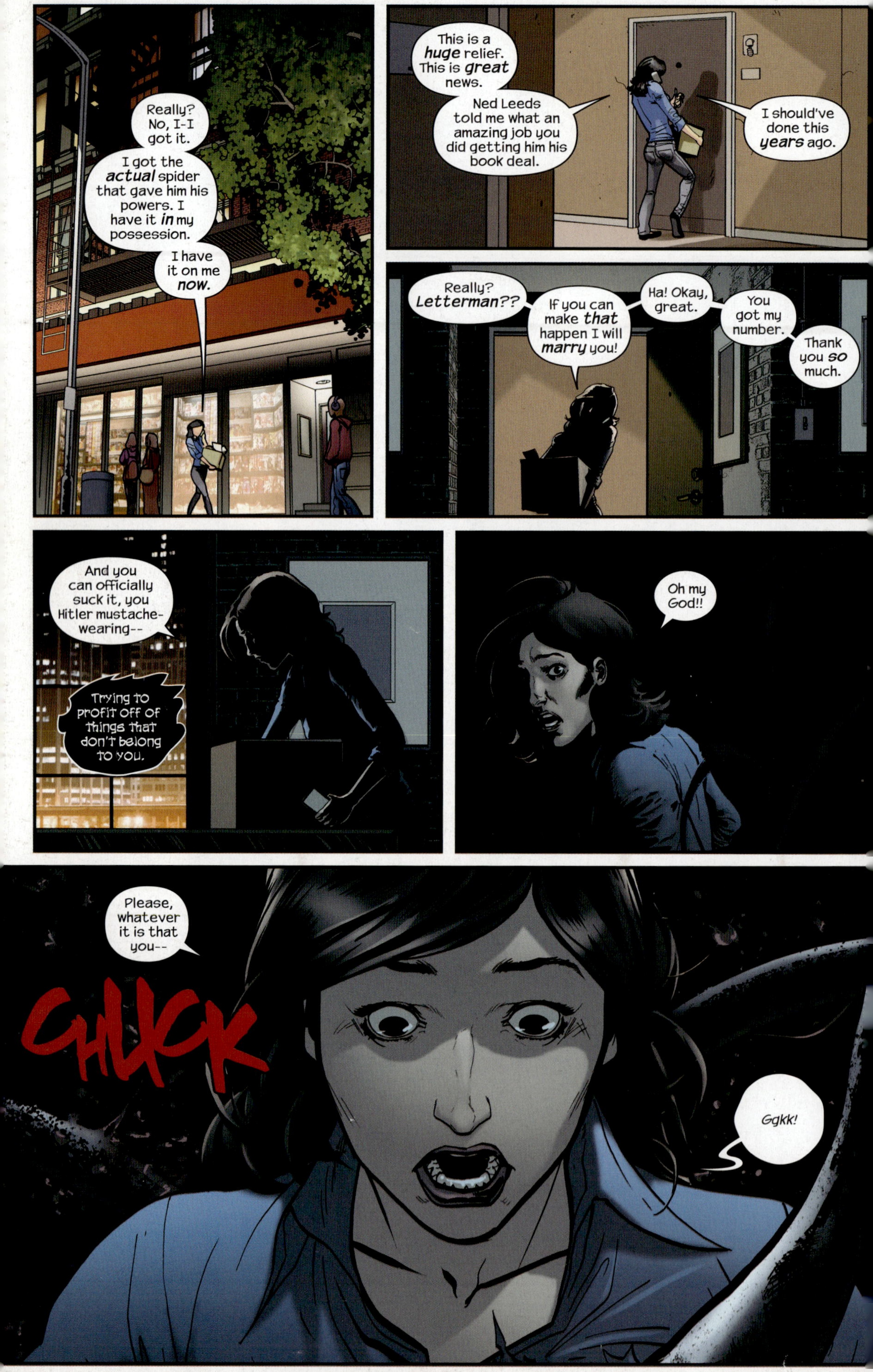

Really? No, I-I got it.
I got the actual spider that gave him his powers. I have it in my possession.
I have it on me now.
This is a huge relief. This is great news.
Ned Leeds told me what an amazing job you did getting him his book deal.
I should've done this years ago.
Really? Letterman??
If you can make that happen I will marry you!
Ha! Okay, great.
You got my number.
Thank you so much.
And you can officially suck it, you Hitler mustache-wearing--
Trying to profit off of things that don't belong to you.
Oh my God!!
Please, whatever it is that you--
CHUCK
Ggkk!

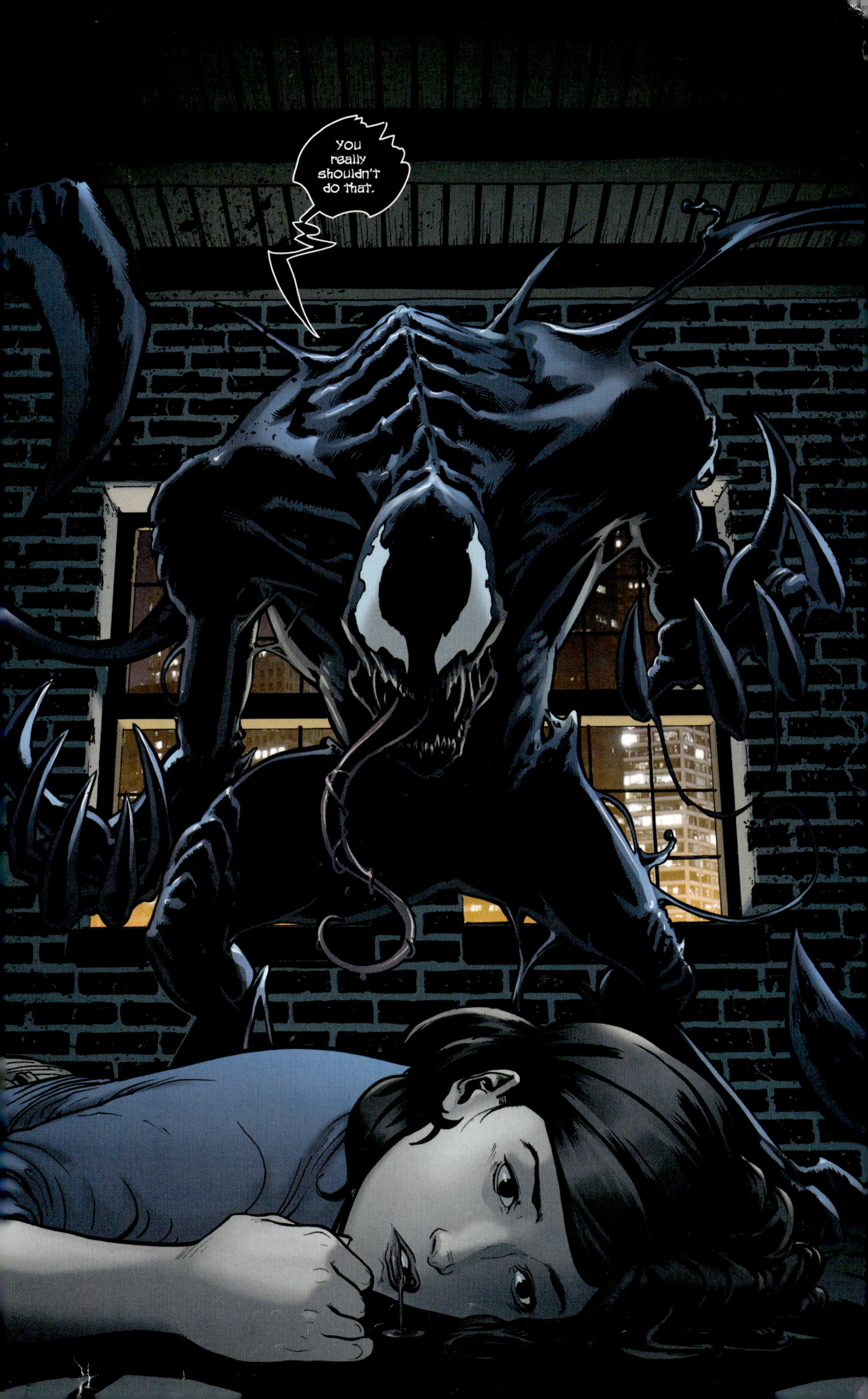
you really shouldn't do that.

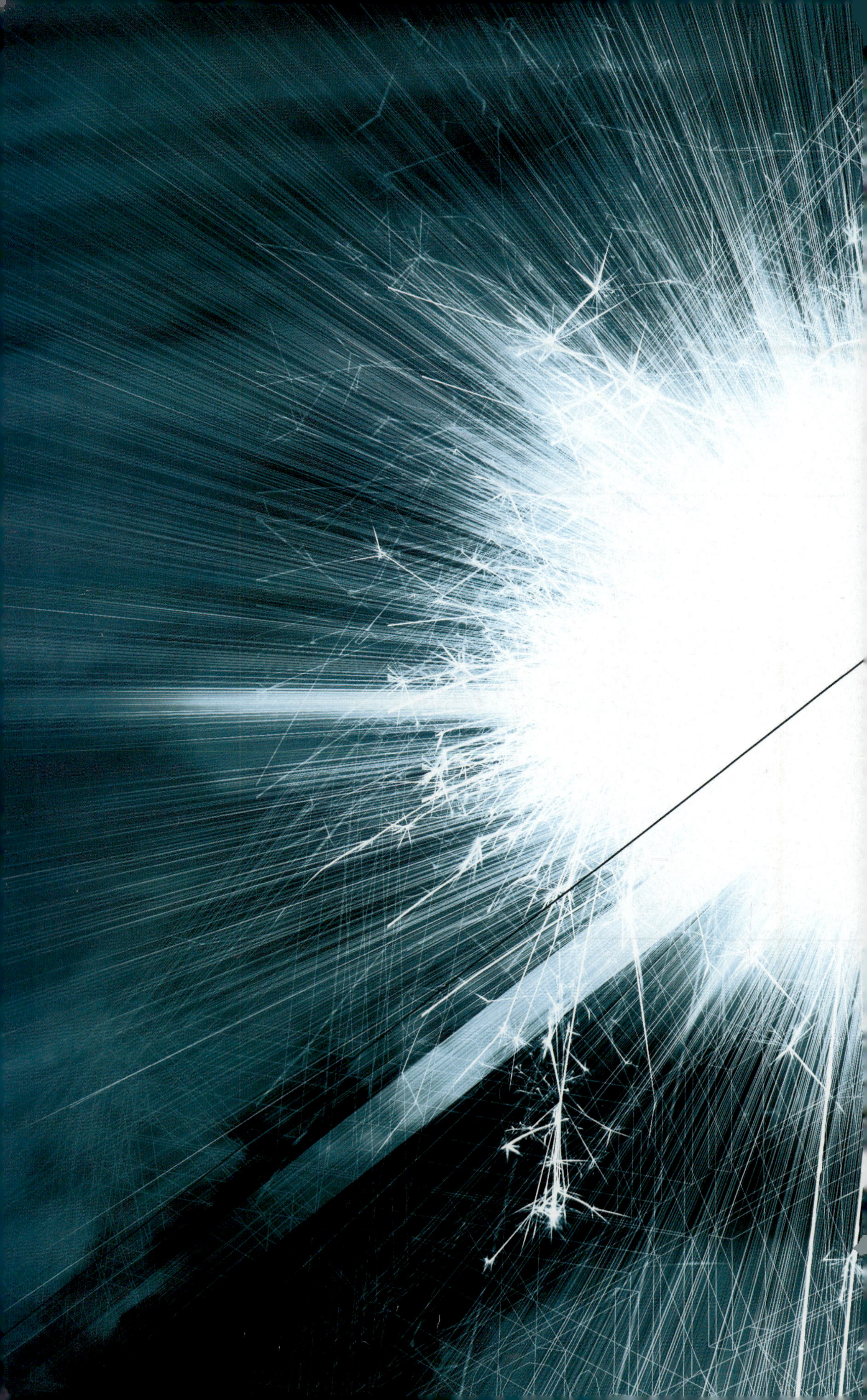

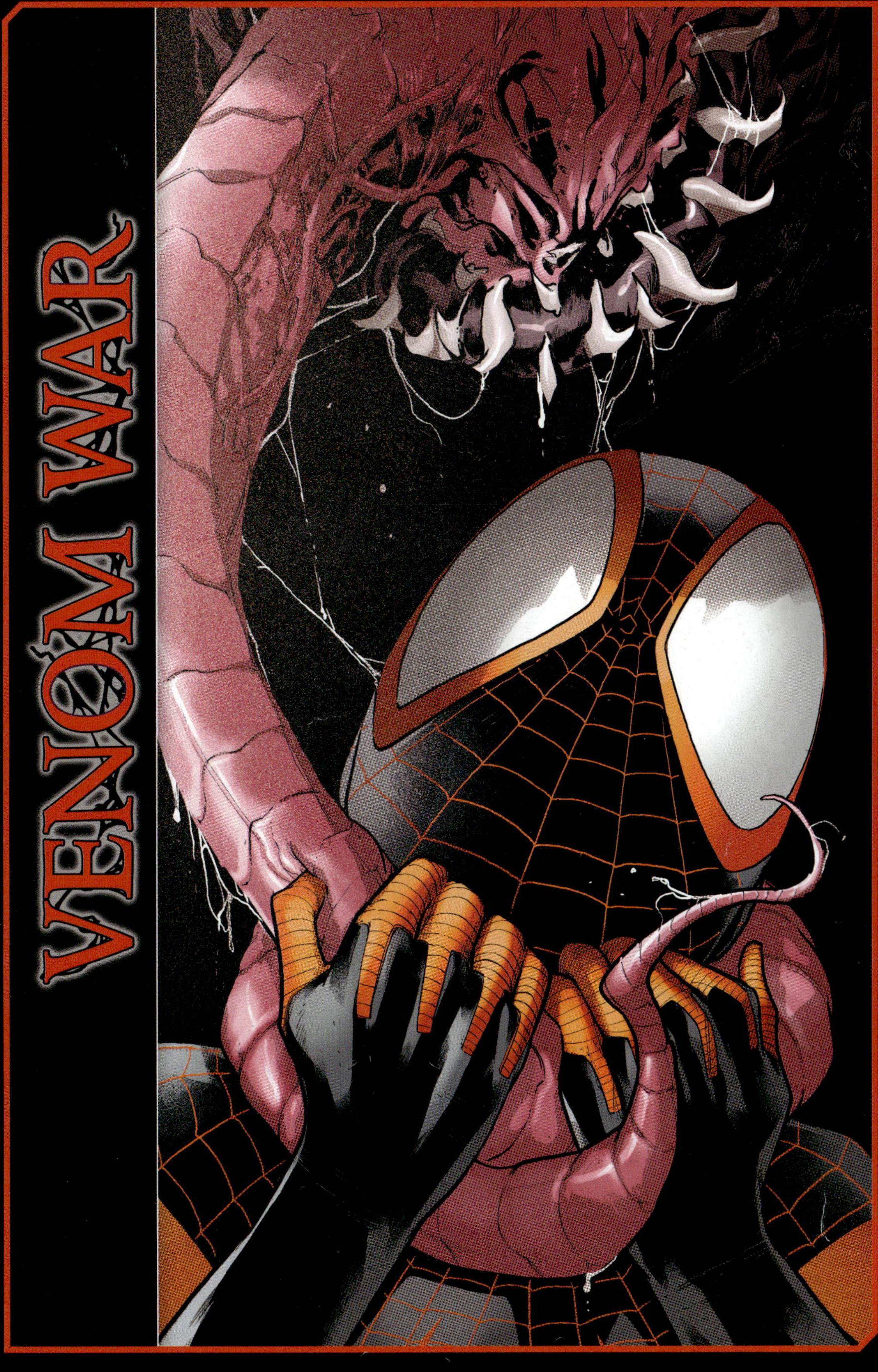
VENOM WAR

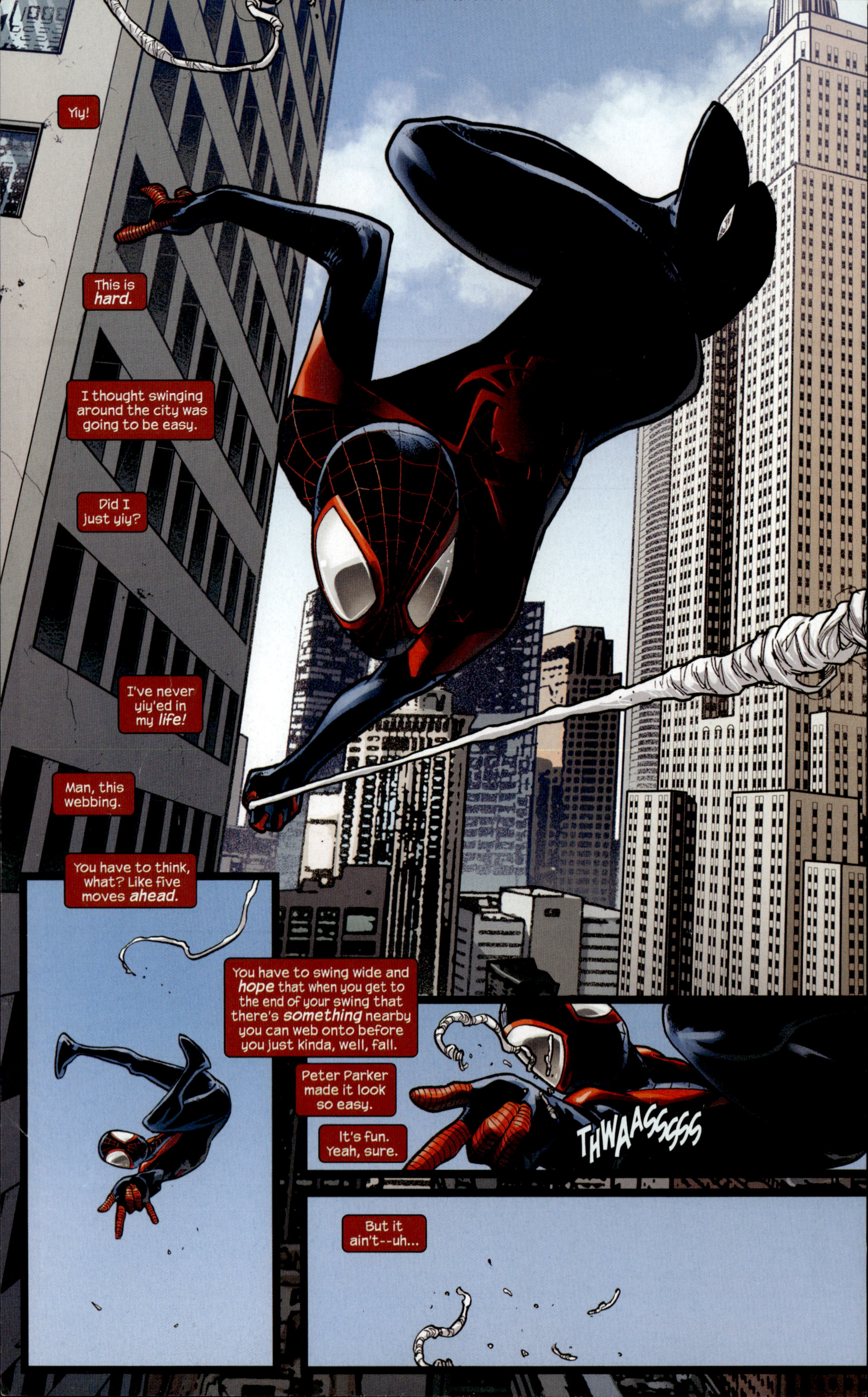
Yiy!
This is *hard.*
I thought swinging around the city was going to be easy.
Did I just yiy?
I've never yiy'ed in my *life!*
Man, this webbing.
You have to think, what? Like five moves *ahead.*
You have to swing wide and *hope* that when you get to the end of your swing that there's *something* nearby you can web onto before you just kinda, well, fall.
Peter Parker made it look so easy.
It's fun. Yeah, sure.
THWAASSSSS
But it ain't--uh...

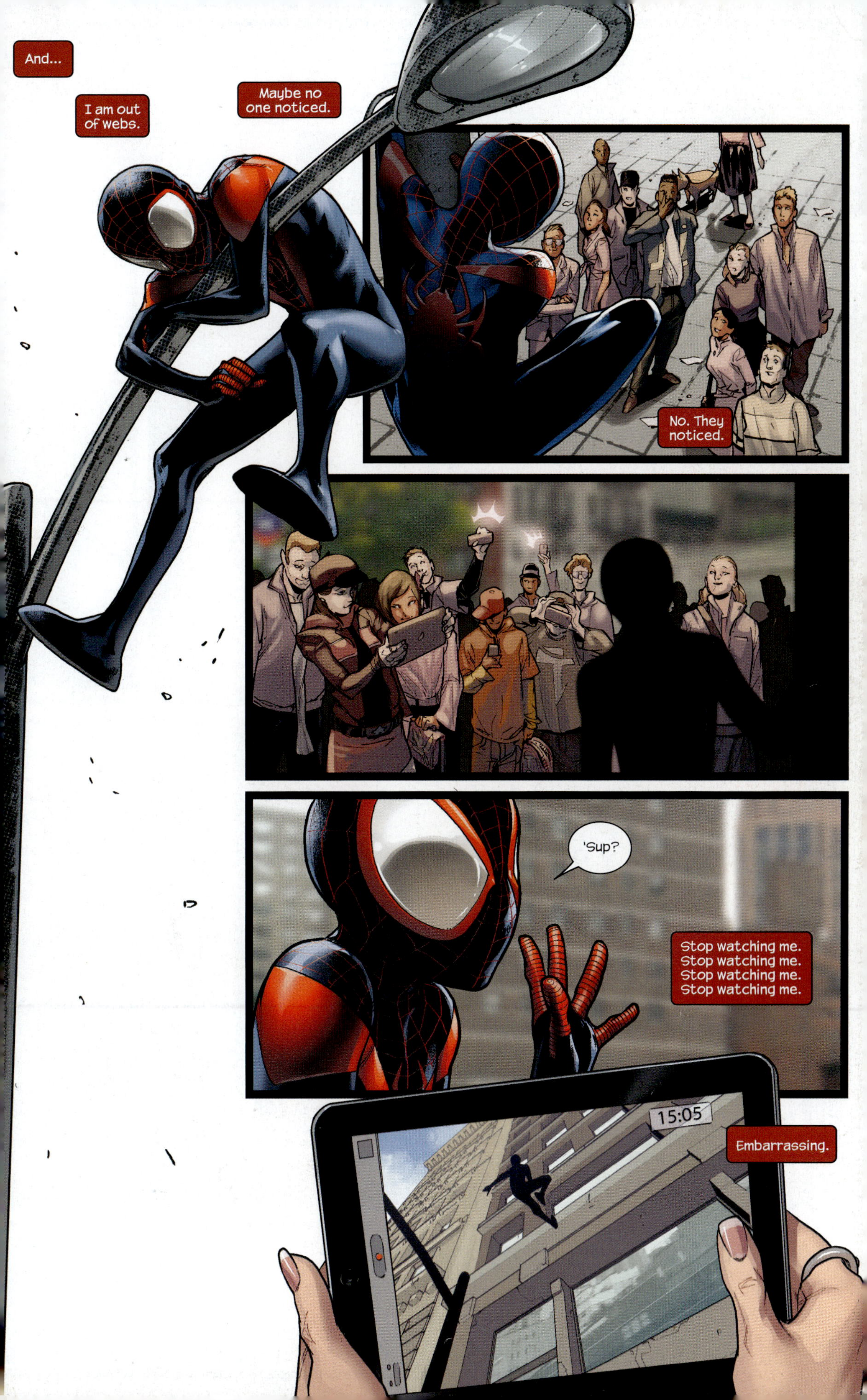

And...
I am out of webs.
Maybe no one noticed.
No. They noticed.
'Sup?
Stop watching me. Stop watching me. Stop watching me. Stop watching me.
15:05
Embarrassing.

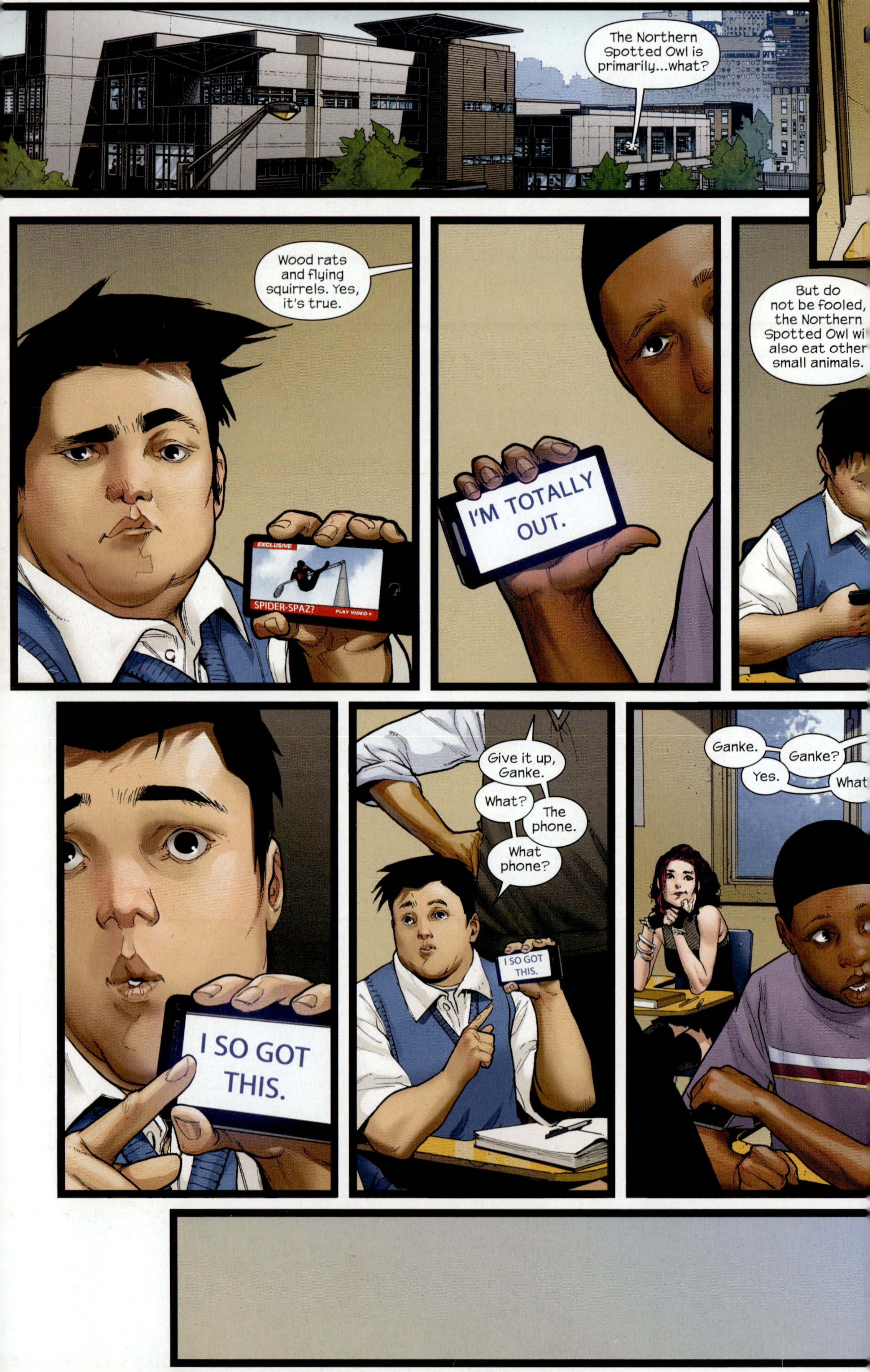
The Northern Spotted Owl is primarily...what?
Wood rats and flying squirrels. Yes, it's true.
EXCLUSIVE
SPIDER-SPAZ?
PLAY VIDEO
I'M TOTALLY OUT.
But do not be fooled, the Northern Spotted Owl wi
also eat other small animals.
I SO GOT THIS.
Give it up, Ganke.
What?
The phone.
What phone?
I SO GOT THIS.
Ganke.
Ganke?
Yes.
What

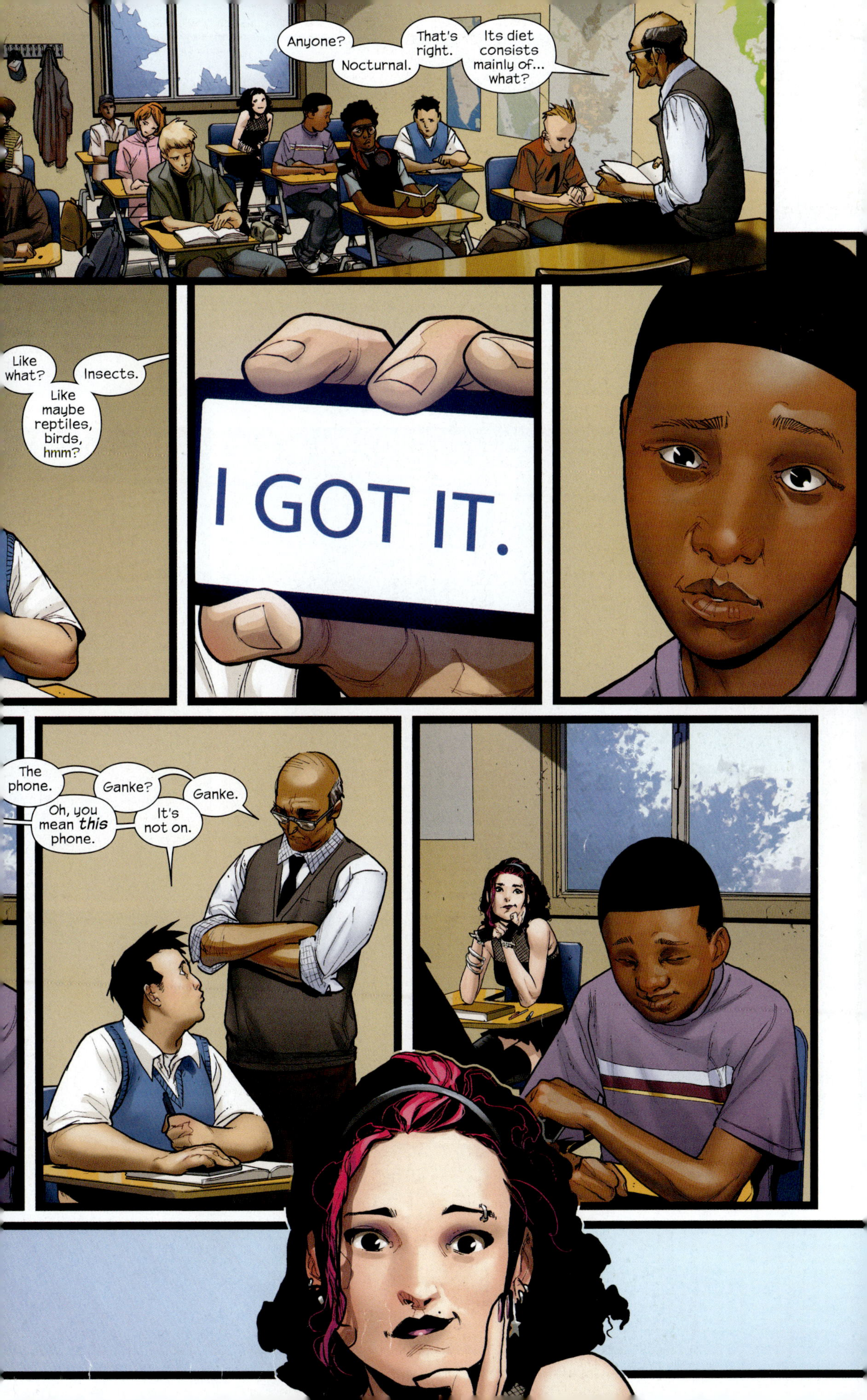
Anyone?
Nocturnal.
That's right.
Its diet consists mainly of... what?
Like what?
Insects.
Like maybe reptiles, birds, hmm?
I GOT IT.
The phone.
Ganke?
Ganke.
Oh, you mean *this* phone.
It's not on.

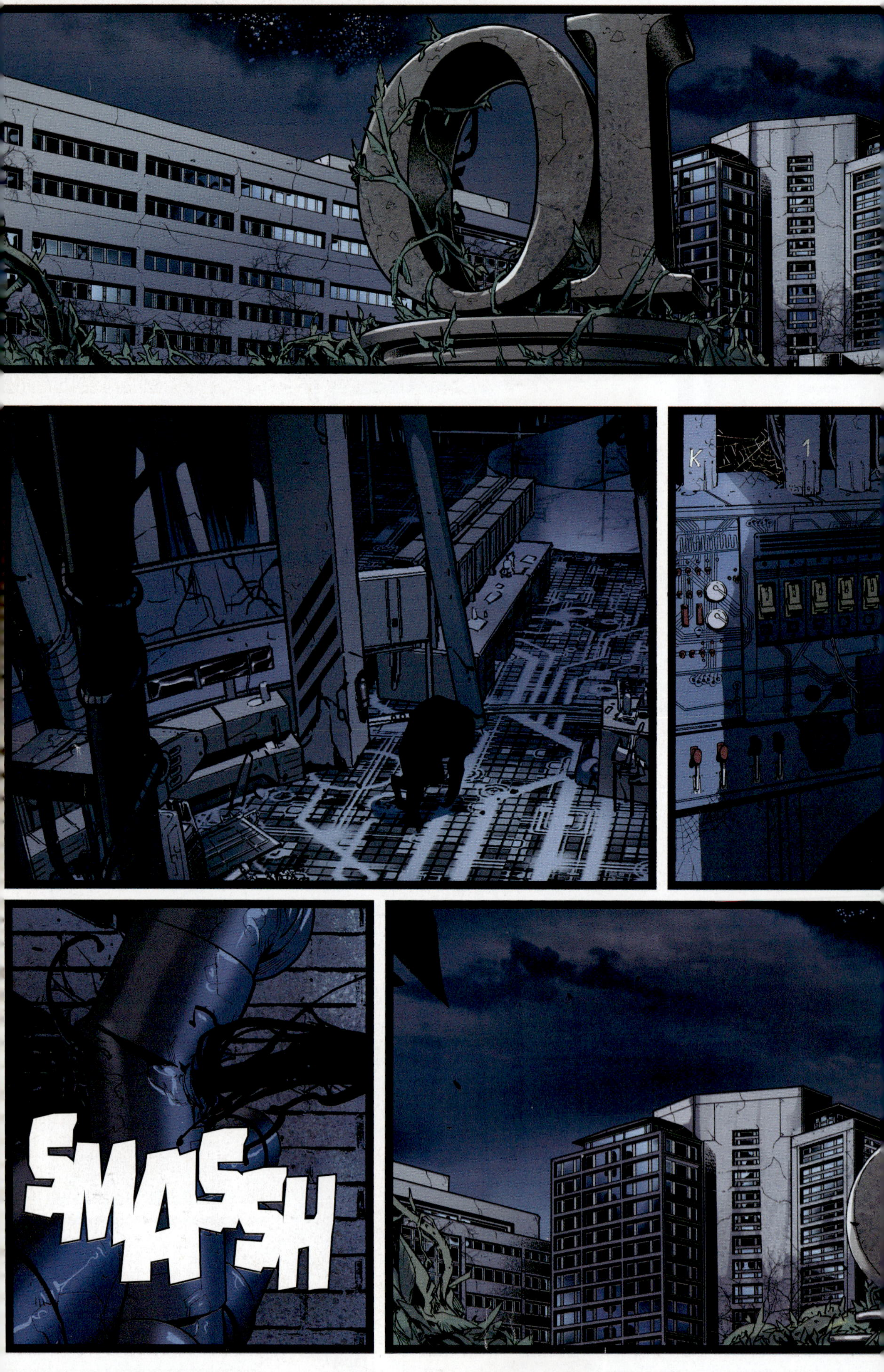
K
1
SMASSH

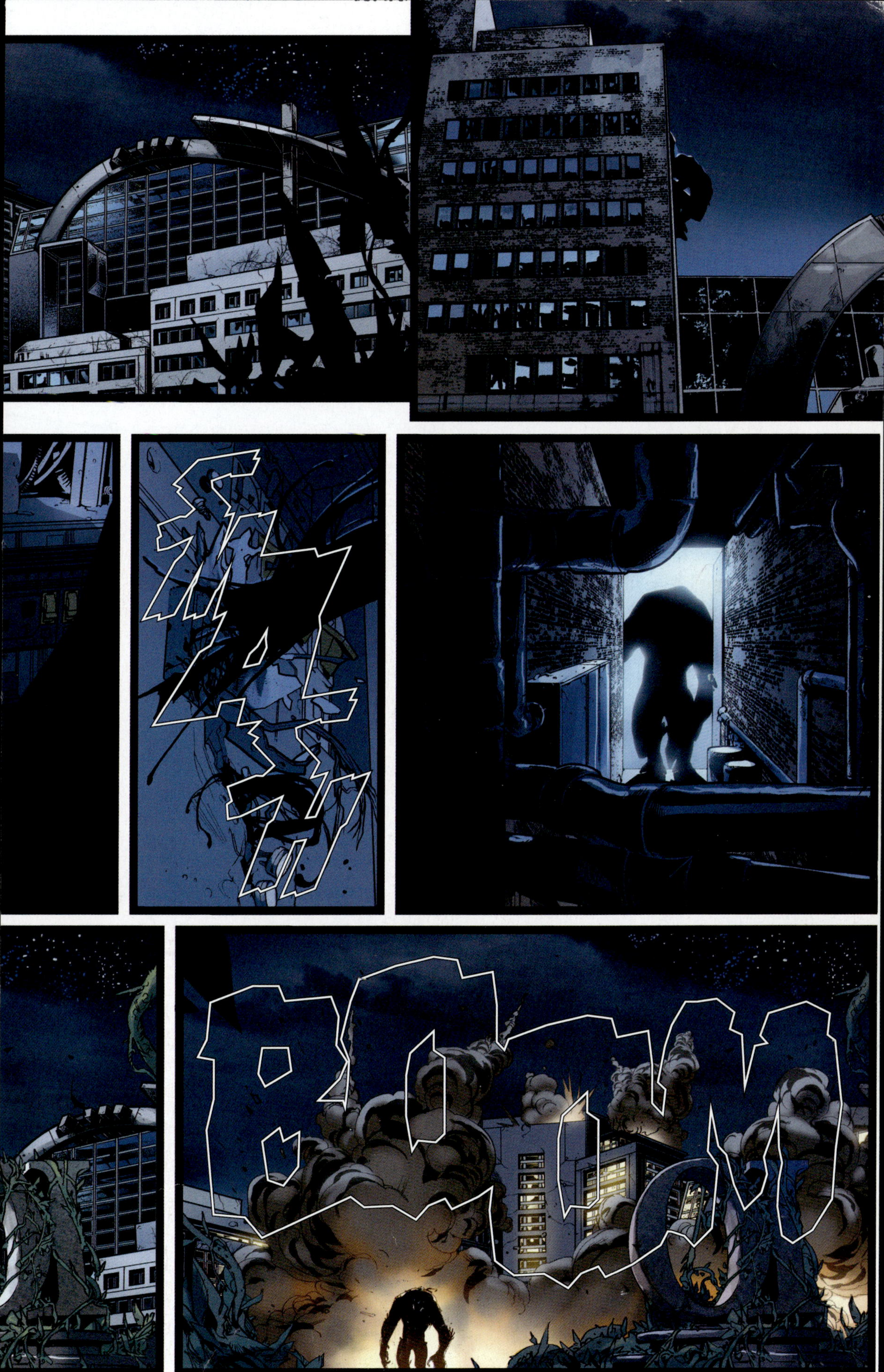
BOOM

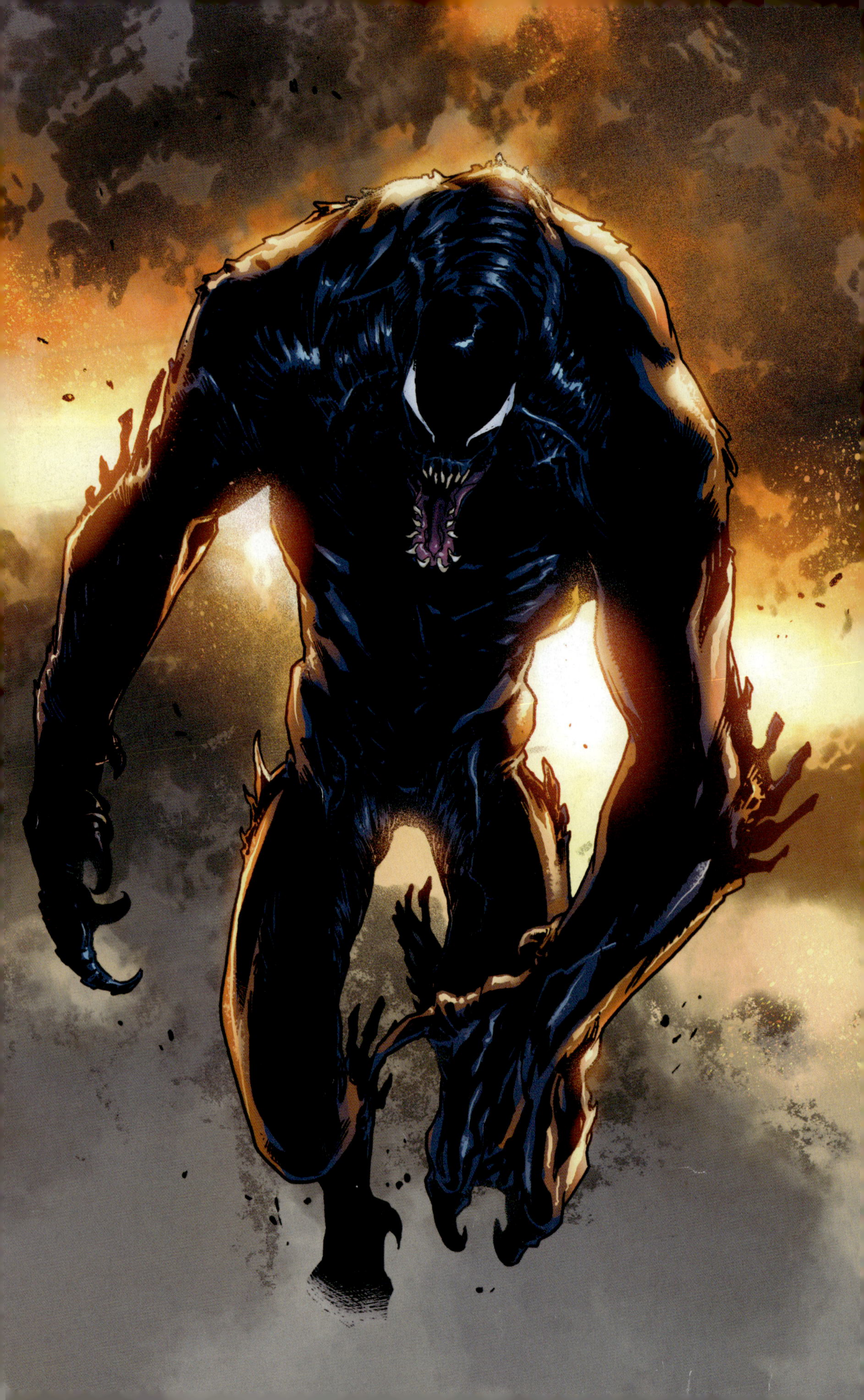

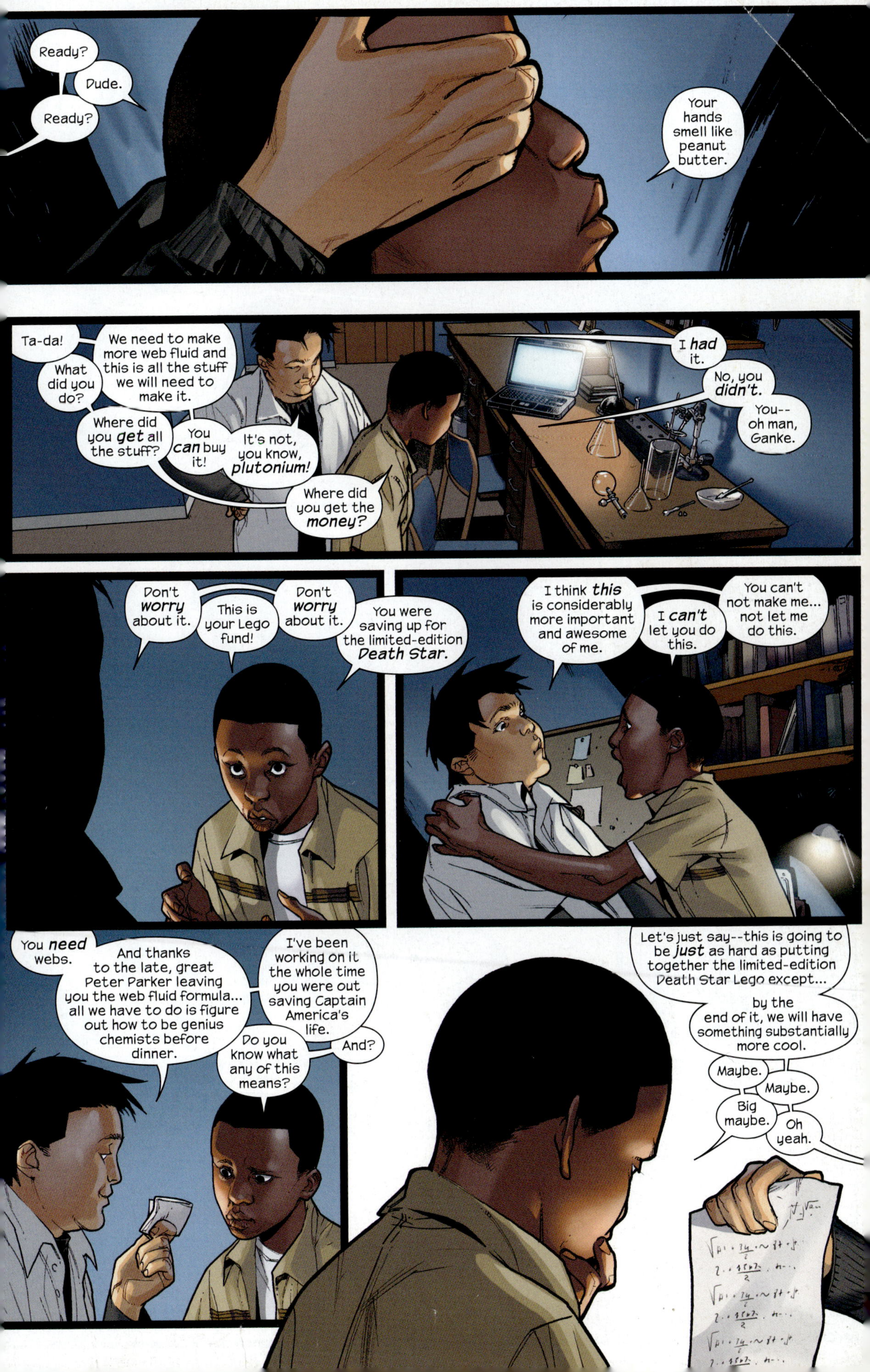

Ready?
Dude.
Ready?
Your hands smell like peanut butter.
Ta-da!
We need to make more web fluid and this is all the stuff we will need to make it.
What did you do?
Where did you **get** all the stuff?
You **can** buy it!
It's not, you know, ***plutonium!***
Where did you get the ***money?***
I ***had*** it.
No, you ***didn't.***
You-- oh man, Ganke.
Don't ***worry*** about it.
This is your Lego fund!
Don't ***worry*** about it.
You were saving up for the limited-edition ***Death Star.***
I think ***this*** is considerably more important and awesome of me.
I ***can't*** let you do this.
You can't not make me... not let me do this.
You ***need*** webs.
And thanks to the late, great Peter Parker leaving you the web fluid formula... all we have to do is figure out how to be genius chemists before dinner.
I've been working on it the whole time you were out saving Captain America's life.
Do you know what any of this means?
And?
Let's just say--this is going to be ***just*** as hard as putting together the limited-edition Death Star Lego except...
by the end of it, we will have something substantially more cool.
Maybe.
Maybe.
Big maybe.
Oh yeah.

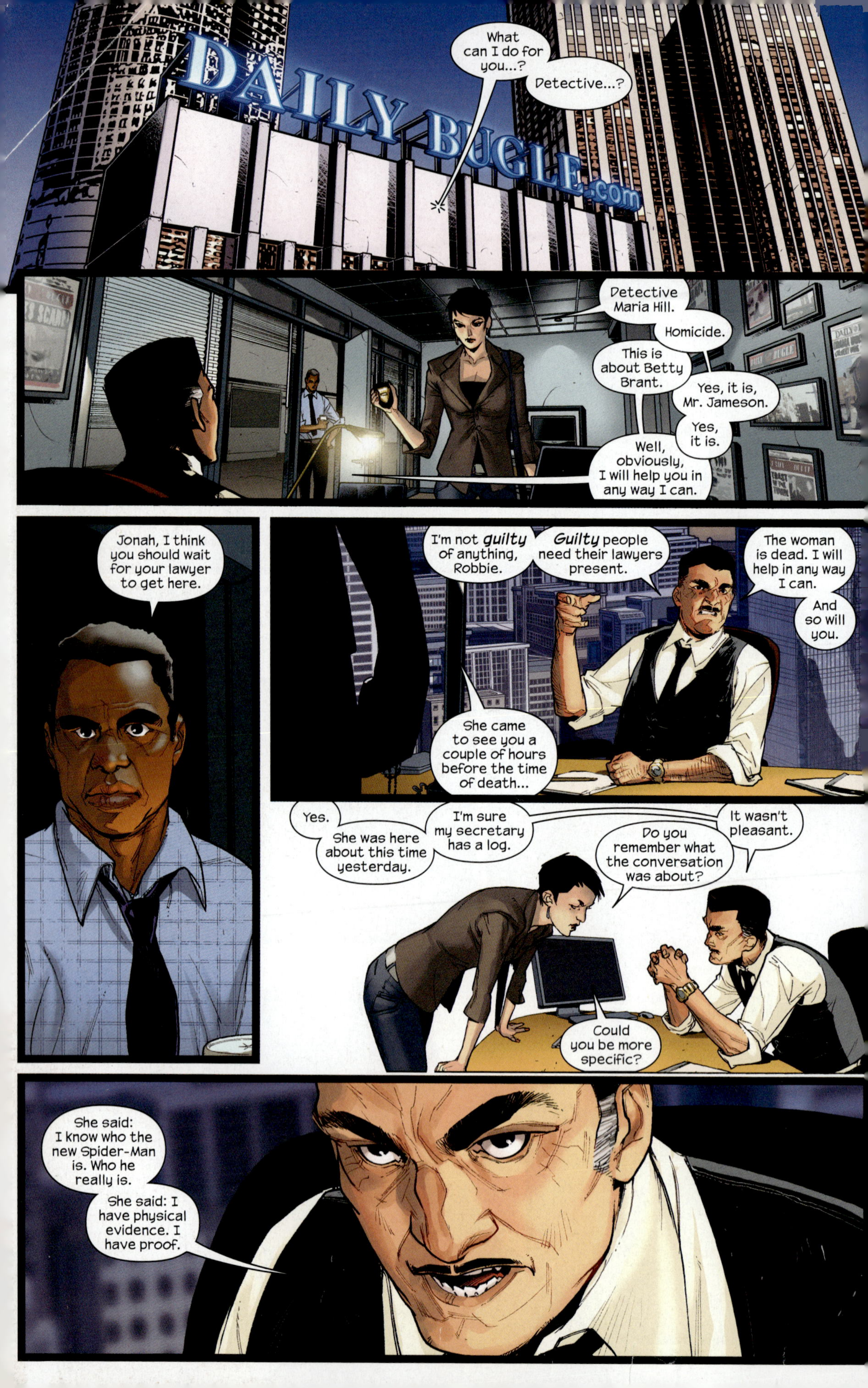
DAILY BUGLE.com
What can I do for you...?
Detective...?
Detective Maria Hill.
Homicide.
This is about Betty Brant.
Yes, it is, Mr. Jameson.
Yes, it is.
Well, obviously, I will help you in any way I can.
Jonah, I think you should wait for your lawyer to get here.
I'm not *guilty* of anything, Robbie.
Guilty people need their lawyers present.
The woman is dead. I will help in any way I can.
And so will you.
She came to see you a couple of hours before the time of death...
Yes.
She was here about this time yesterday.
I'm sure my secretary has a log.
It wasn't pleasant.
Do you remember what the conversation was about?
Could you be more specific?
She said: I know who the new Spider-Man is. Who he really is.
She said: I have physical evidence. I have proof.

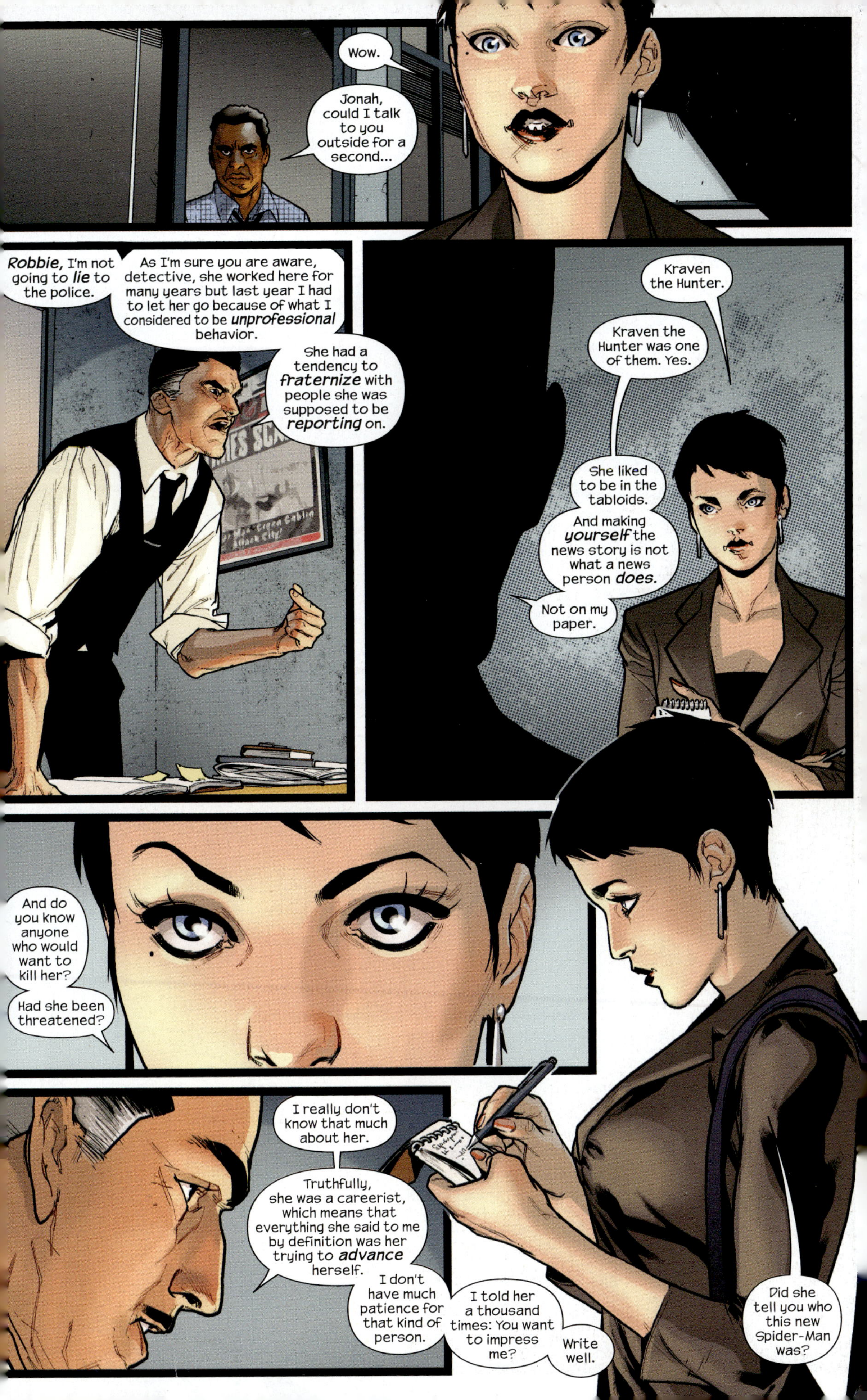
Wow.
Jonah, could I talk to you outside for a second...
Robbie, I'm not going to lie to the police.
As I'm sure you are aware, detective, she worked here for many years but last year I had to let her go because of what I considered to be unprofessional behavior.
She had a tendency to fraternize with people she was supposed to be reporting on.
Kraven the Hunter.
Kraven the Hunter was one of them. Yes.
She liked to be in the tabloids.
And making yourself the news story is not what a news person does.
Not on my paper.
And do you know anyone who would want to kill her?
Had she been threatened?
I really don't know that much about her.
Truthfully, she was a careerist, which means that everything she said to me by definition was her trying to advance herself.
I don't have much patience for that kind of person.
I told her a thousand times: You want to impress me?
Write well.
Did she tell you who this new Spider-Man was?

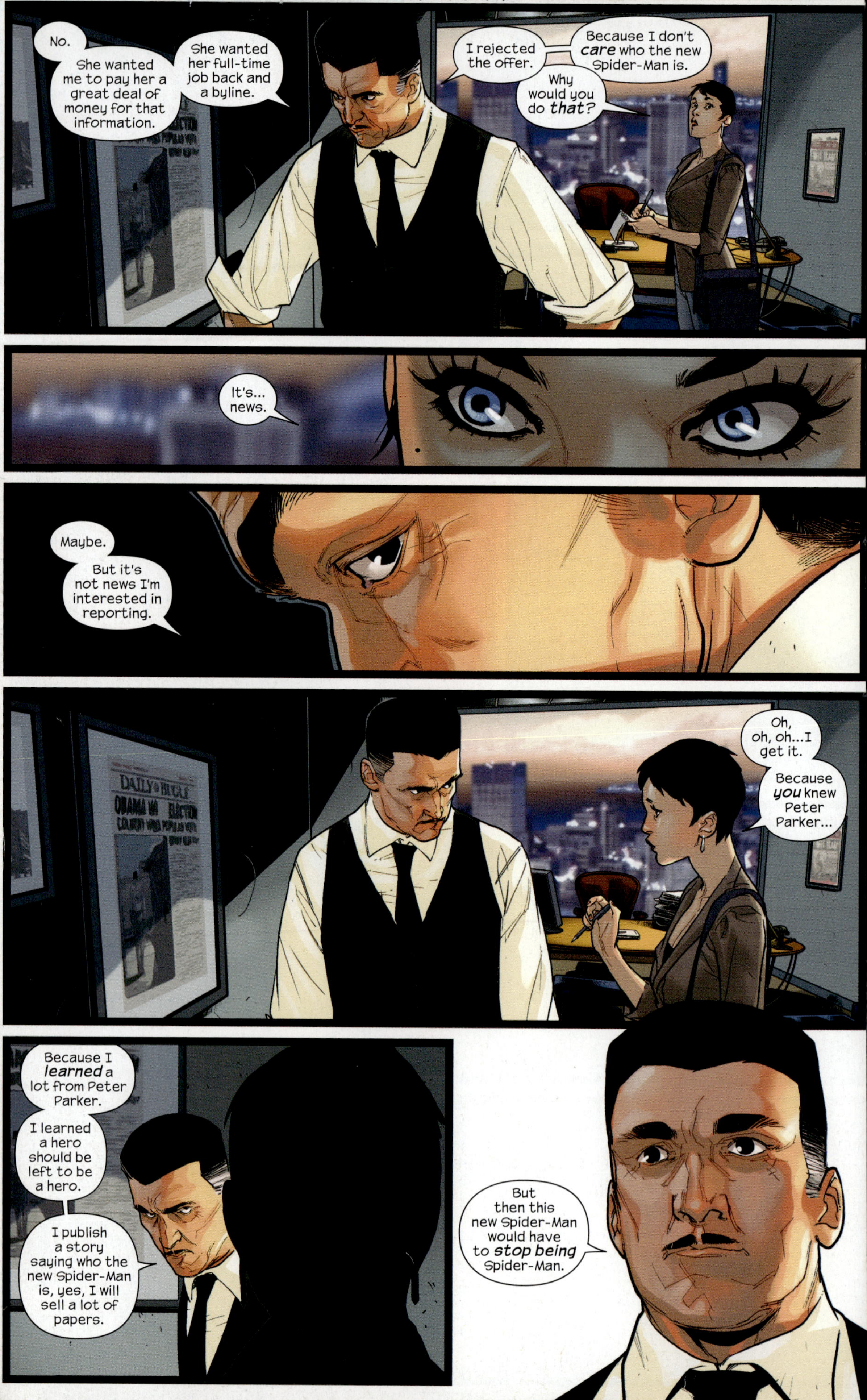
No.
She wanted me to pay her a great deal of money for that information.
She wanted her full-time job back and a byline.
I rejected the offer.
Because I don't *care* who the new Spider-Man is.
Why would you do *that?*
It's... news.
Maybe.
But it's not news I'm interested in reporting.
DAILY BUGLE
OBAMA WI ELECTION
Oh, oh, oh...I get it.
Because *you* knew Peter Parker...
Because I *learned* a lot from Peter Parker.
I learned a hero should be left to be a hero.
I publish a story saying who the new Spider-Man is, yes, I will sell a lot of papers.
But then this new Spider-Man would have to *stop being* Spider-Man.

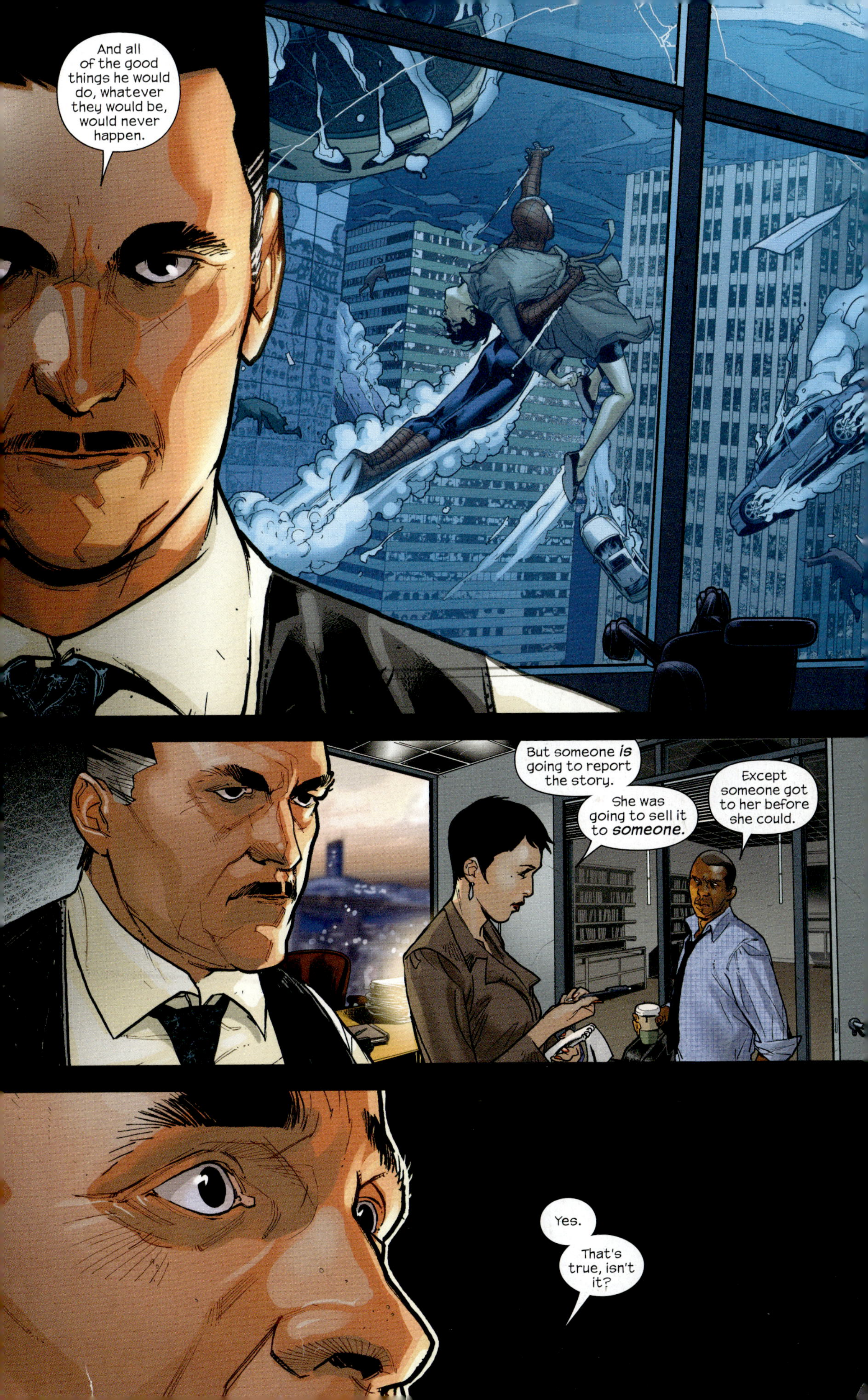
And all of the good things he would do, whatever they would be, would never happen.
But someone *is* going to report the story.
She was going to sell it to ***someone.***
Except someone got to her before she could.
Yes.
That's true, isn't it?

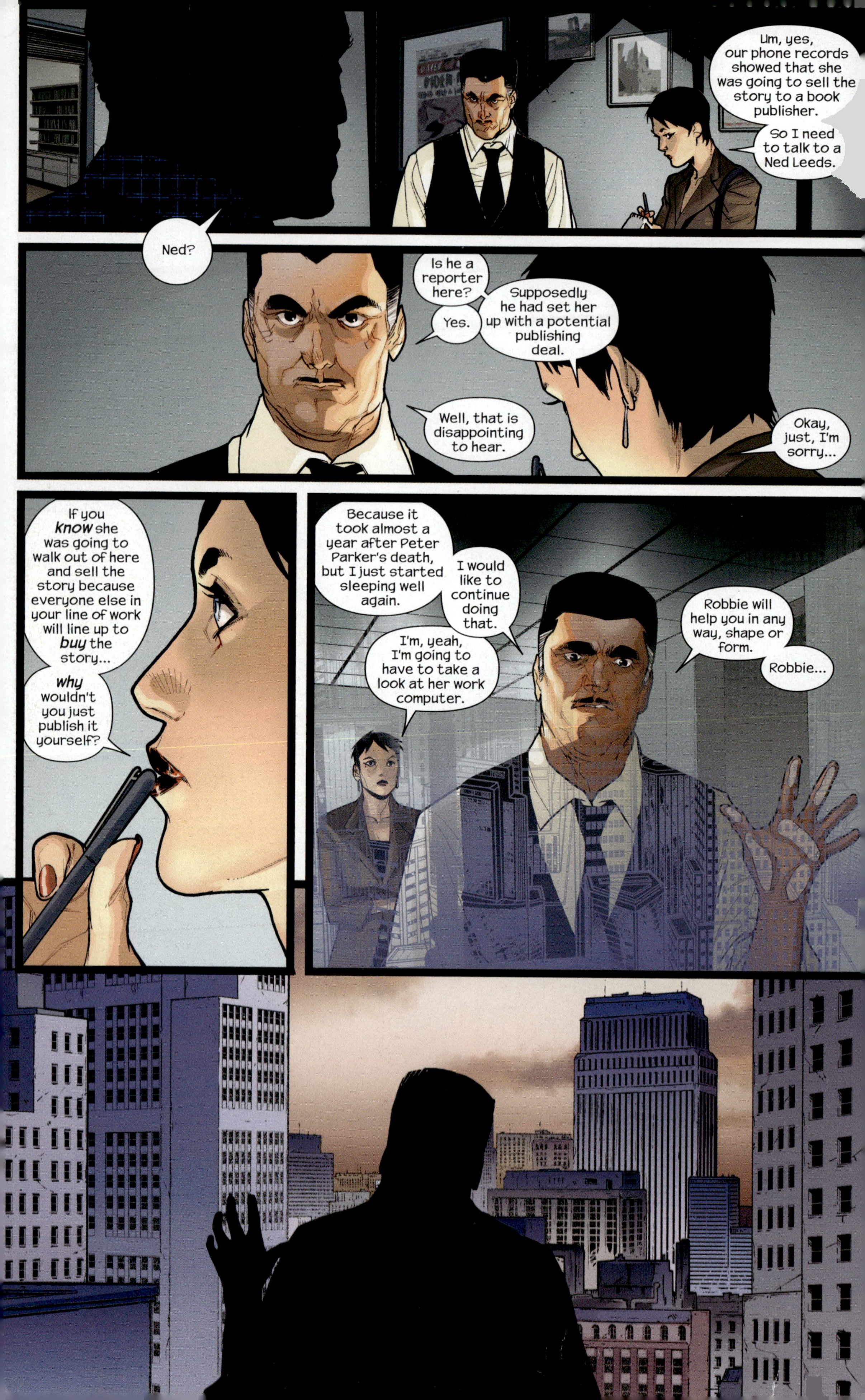
Um, yes, our phone records showed that she was going to sell the story to a book publisher.
So I need to talk to a Ned Leeds.
Ned?
Is he a reporter here?
Yes.
Supposedly he had set her up with a potential publishing deal.
Well, that is disappointing to hear.
Okay, just, I'm sorry...
If you *know* she was going to walk out of here and sell the story because everyone else in your line of work will line up to *buy* the story...
why wouldn't you just publish it yourself?
Because it took almost a year after Peter Parker's death, but I just started sleeping well again.
I would like to continue doing that.
I'm, yeah, I'm going to have to take a look at her work computer.
Robbie will help you in any way, shape or form.
Robbie...

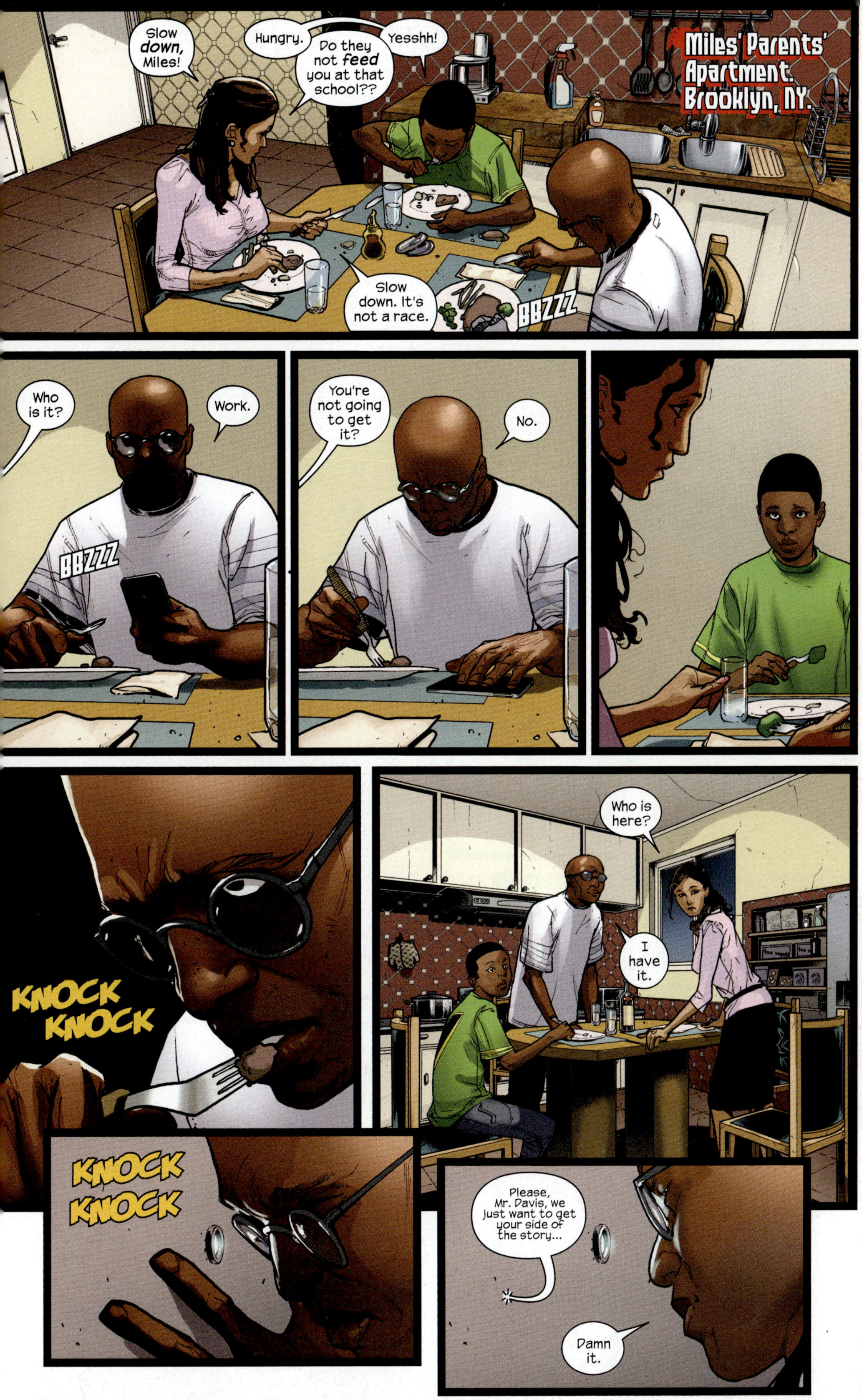
Miles' Parents' Apartment. Brooklyn, NY.
Slow down, Miles!
Hungry.
Do they not feed you at that school??
Yesshh!
Slow down. It's not a race.
BBZZZ
Who is it?
Work.
BBZZZ
You're not going to get it?
No.
KNOCK KNOCK
Who is here?
I have it.
KNOCK KNOCK
Please, Mr. Davis, we just want to get your side of the story...
Damn it.

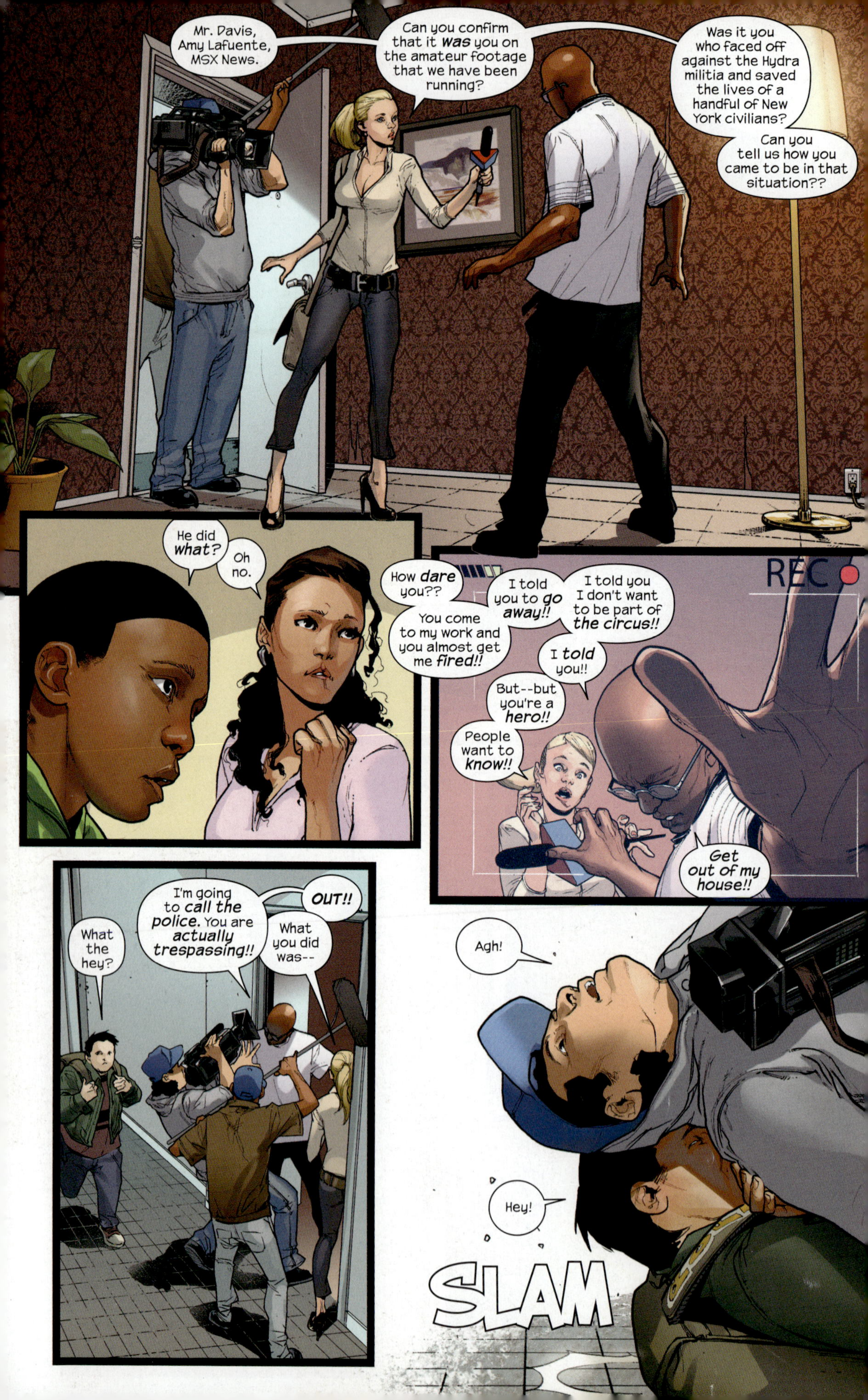
Mr. Davis, Amy Lafuente, MSX News.
Can you confirm that it *was* you on the amateur footage that we have been running?
Was it you who faced off against the Hydra militia and saved the lives of a handful of New York civilians?
Can you tell us how you came to be in that situation??
He did *what?*
Oh no.
REC
How *dare* you??
You come to my work and you almost get me *fired!!*
I told you to *go away!!*
I told you I don't want to be part of *the circus!!*
I *told* you!!
But--but you're a *hero!!*
People want to *know!!*
Get out of my house!!
What the hey?
I'm going to *call the police.* You are *actually trespassing!!*
OUT!!
What you did was--
Agh!
Hey!
SLAM

Ow! My **back**!!

You're on a **kid**!

Yeah, uh, **could you** get off me, please!?

Why didn't you tell me this was **happening**?

24-hour news cycle.

It's a 24-hour news cycle.

It'll go away in 24 hours.

Why won't you **talk** to them and be done with it?

Come on...

Wait, what did you do?

I'm sorry, boy.

Sorry you had to see that.

You fought **HYDRA??!!**

I did too.

We--we have that in common.

Kind of.

Did you **get** that?

Wasn't much.

It was enough.

I--yeah, I know this--this was...weird.

Uh, **yeah!!**

Hydra??!! Dad??!!

So, okay, during all the craziness last week your dad got into it with some of those Hydra people.

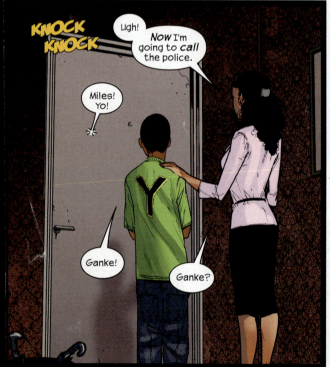

KNOCK KNOCK

Ugh!

Now I'm going to **call** the police.

Miles! Yo!

Ganke!

Ganke?

Let me in.

Are they still **out** there?

No.

SLAM

Jefferson?

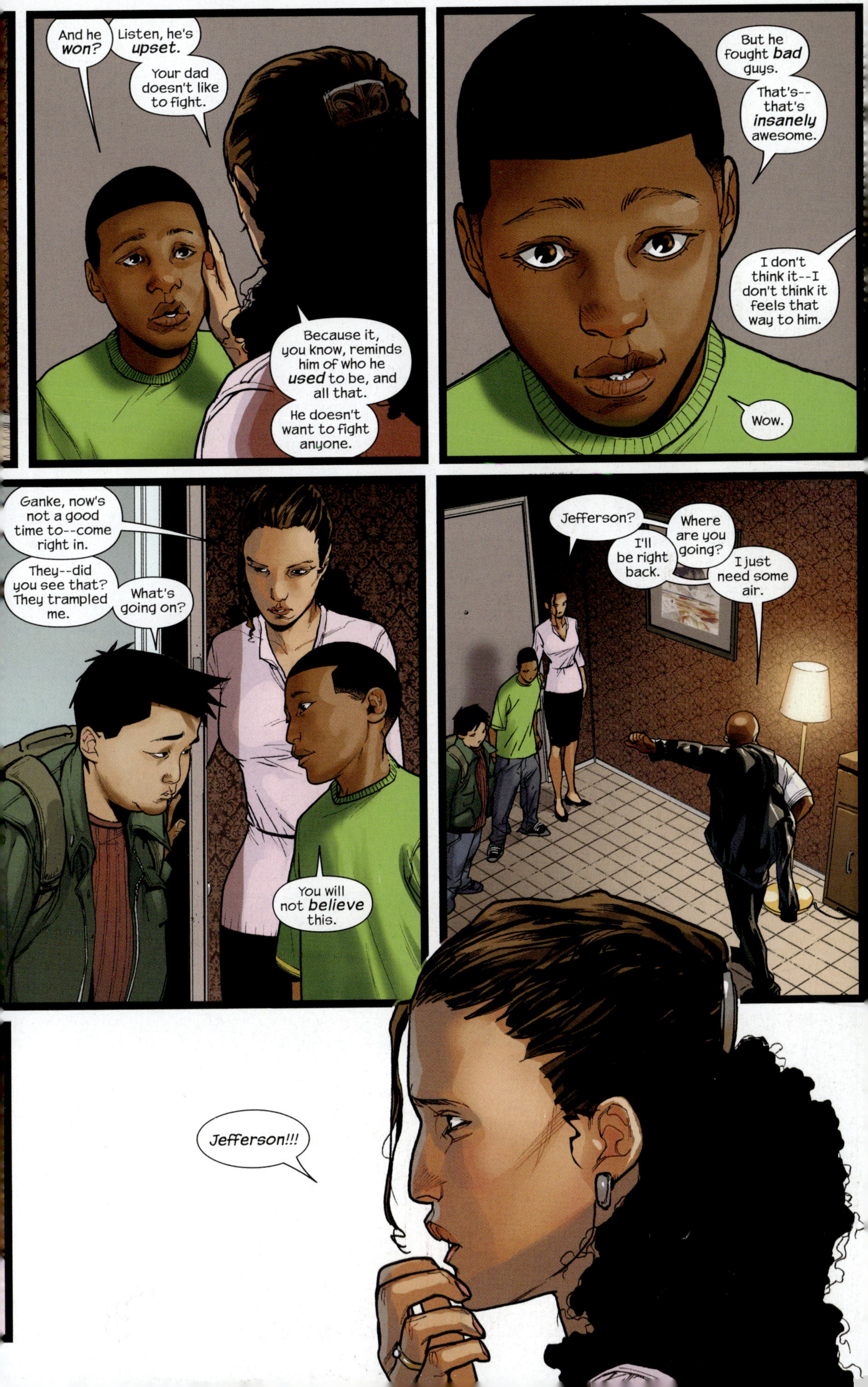
And he won?
Listen, he's upset.
Your dad doesn't like to fight.
Because it, you know, reminds him of who he used to be, and all that.
He doesn't want to fight anyone.
But he fought bad guys.
That's-- that's insanely awesome.
I don't think it--I don't think it feels that way to him.
Wow.
Ganke, now's not a good time to--come right in.
They--did you see that? They trampled me.
What's going on?
You will not believe this.
Jefferson?
Where are you going?
I'll be right back.
I just need some air.
Jefferson!!!

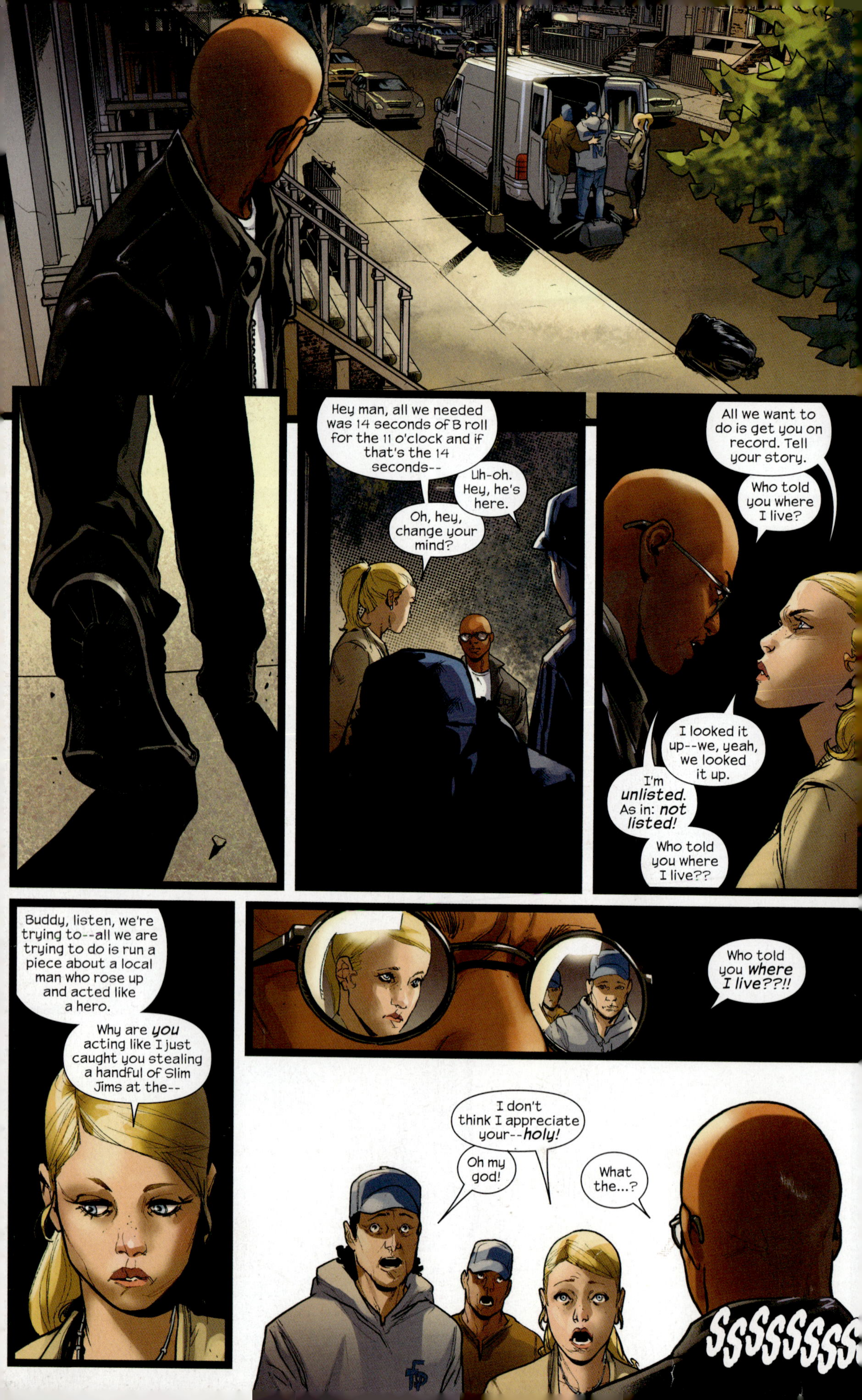
Hey man, all we needed was 14 seconds of B roll for the 11 o'clock and if that's the 14 seconds--
Uh-oh. Hey, he's here.
Oh, hey, change your mind?
All we want to do is get you on record. Tell your story.
Who told you where I live?
I looked it up--we, yeah, we looked it up.
I'm *unlisted*. As in: *not listed!*
Who told you where I live??
Buddy, listen, we're trying to--all we are trying to do is run a piece about a local man who rose up and acted like a hero.
Why are *you* acting like I just caught you stealing a handful of Slim Jims at the--
Who told you *where I live??!!*
I don't think I appreciate your--*holy!*
Oh my god!
What the...?
SSSSSSSSS

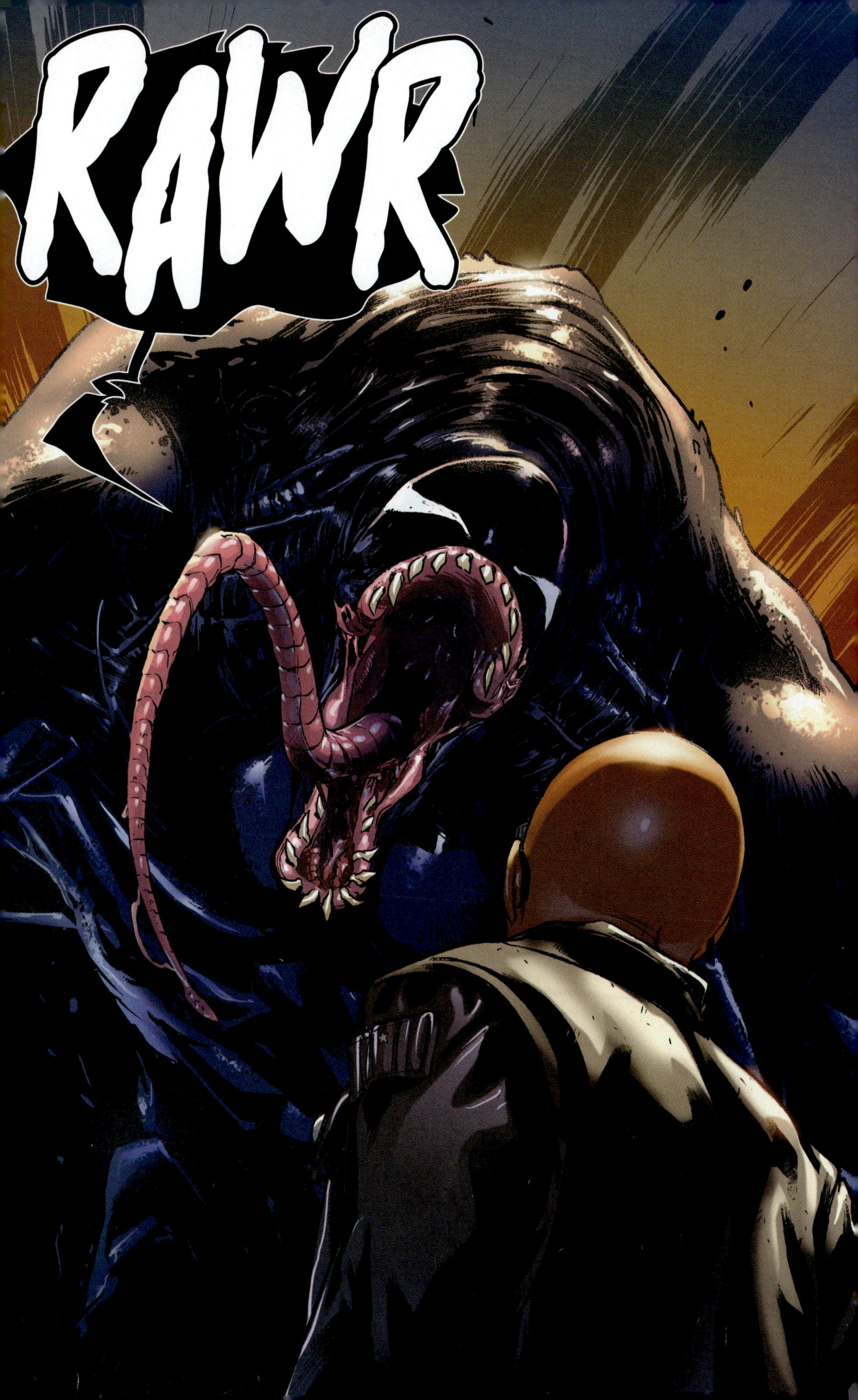
RAWR

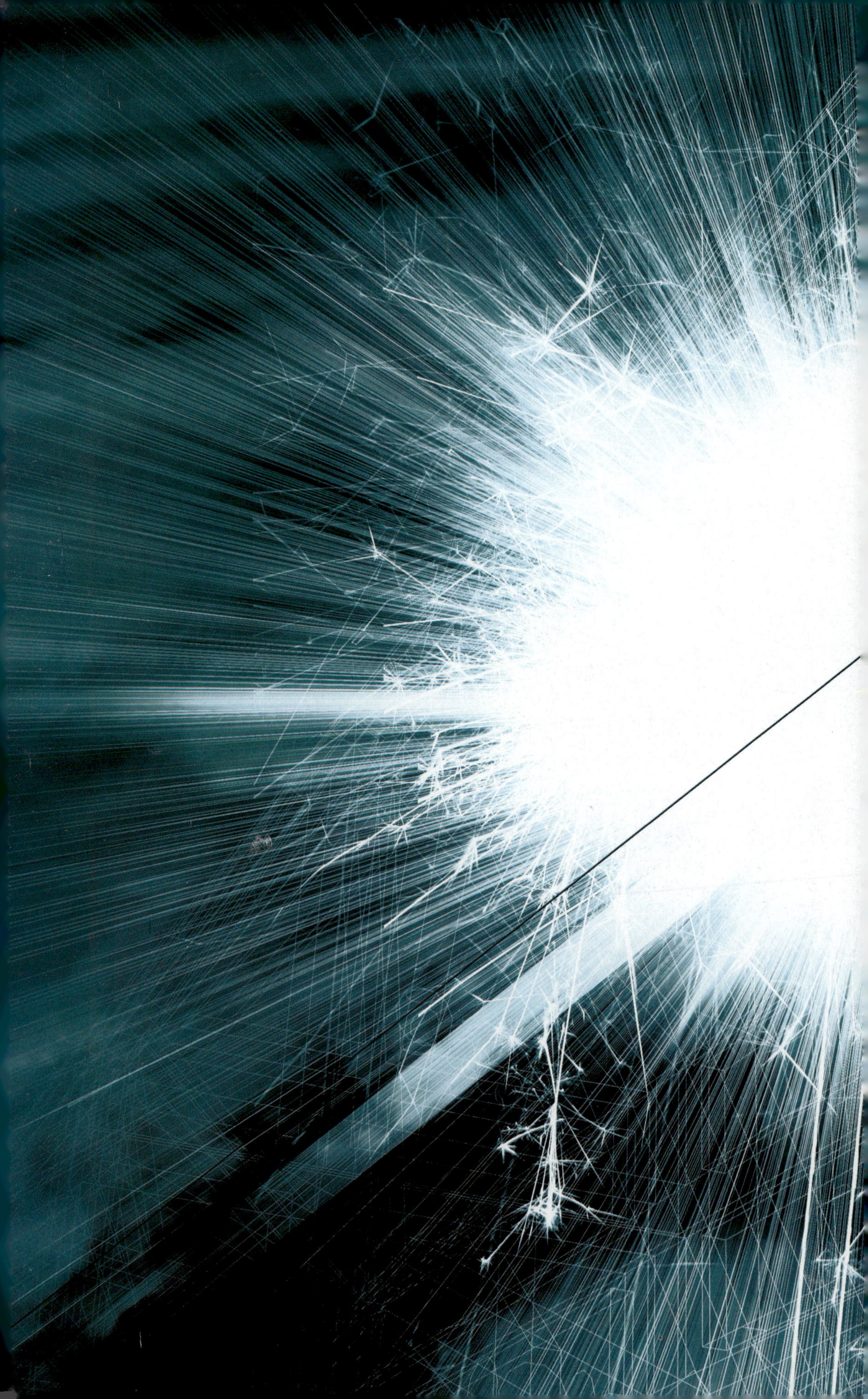

VENOM WAR

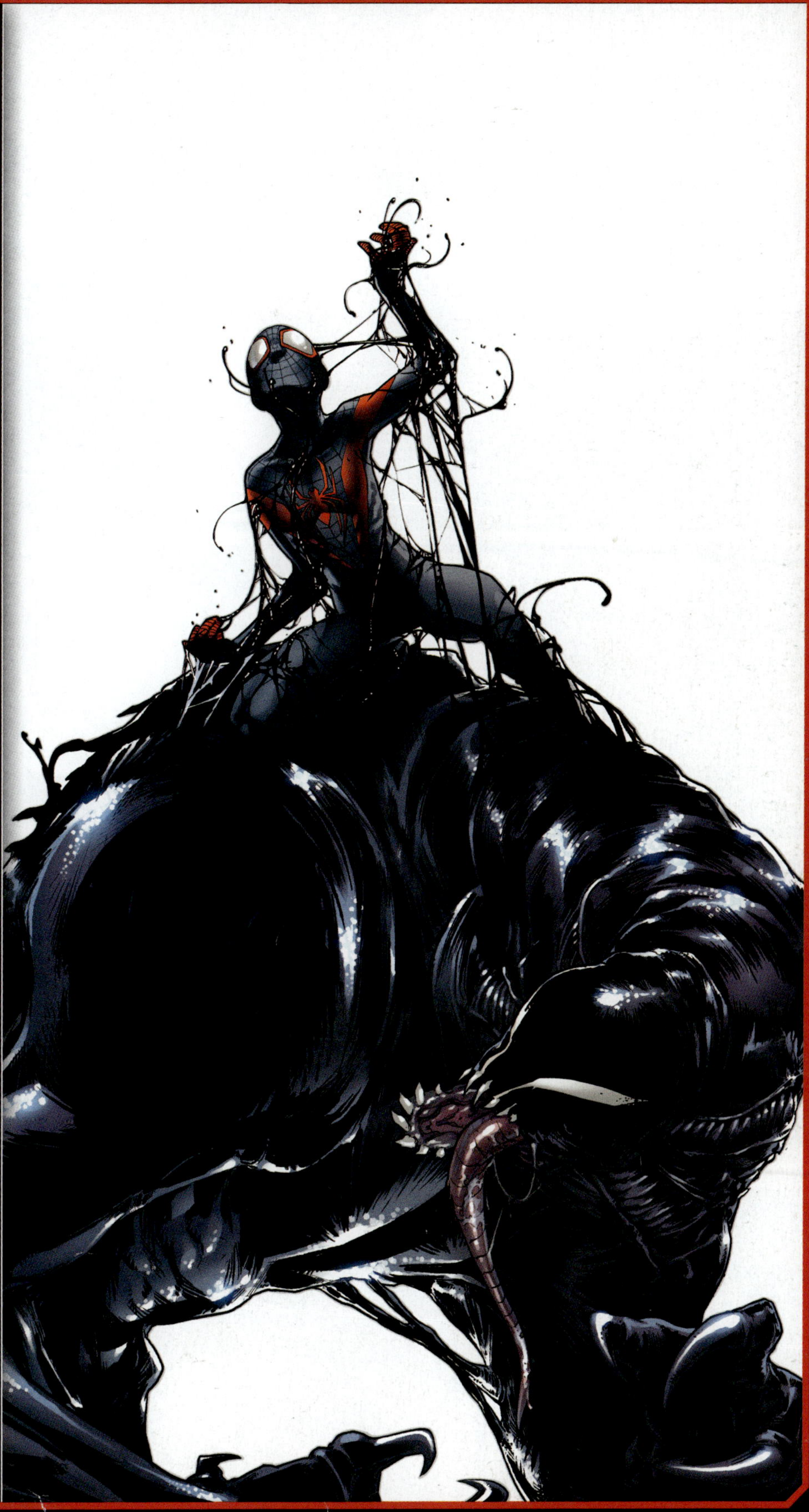

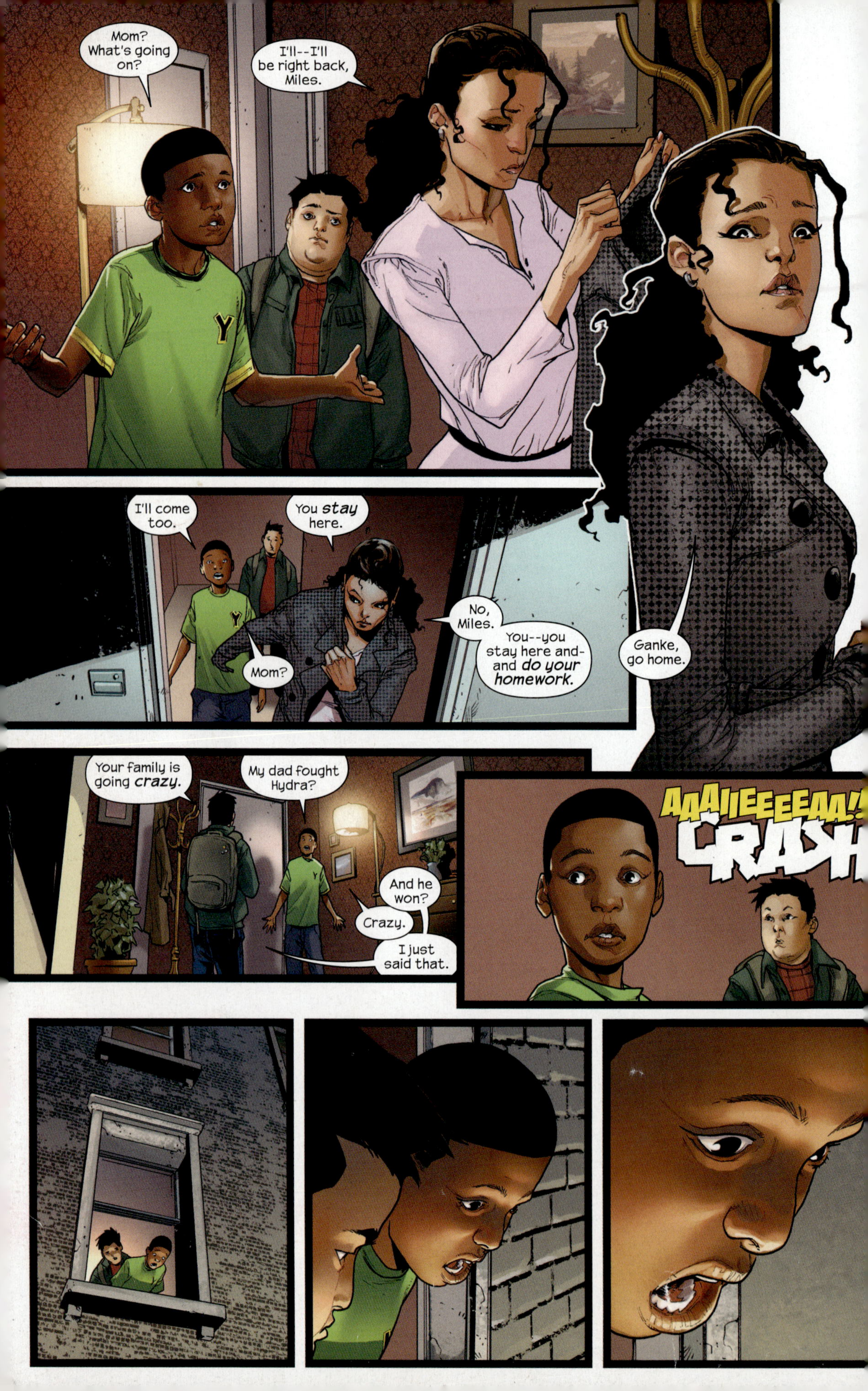
Mom? What's going on?
I'll--I'll be right back, Miles.
I'll come too.
You stay here.
Mom?
No, Miles.
You--you stay here and--and do your homework.
Ganke, go home.
Your family is going crazy.
My dad fought Hydra?
And he won?
Crazy.
I just said that.
AAAIIEEEEAA!!
CRASH

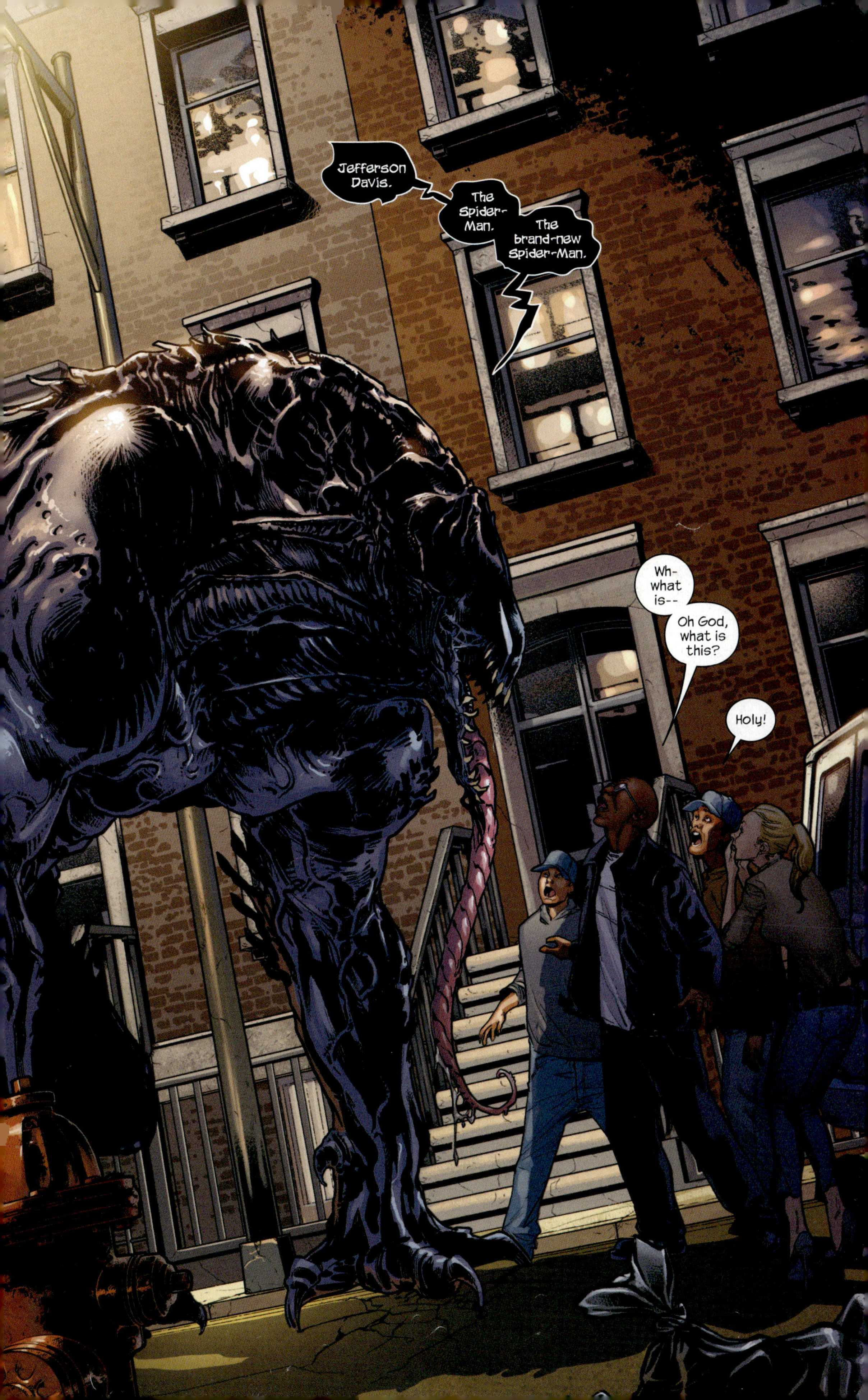
Jefferson Davis.
The Spider-Man.
The brand-new Spider-Man.
Wh-what is--
Oh God, what is this?
Holy!

Oh!! What *is* that?

Whoa!!

Your dad-- he's--

Being attacked *by a monster??!!*

Go!!

What *is* that??

Talk *later!!* Go!

Throw your mask on and go!!

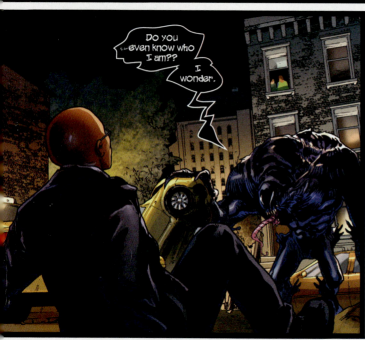

Do you even know who I am??

I wonder.

Here, hey, wait, I did it.

This is why I came over.

I have more web fluid for you!!

I made it!

Call the police!!

What *is* that monster thing? It looks familiar!

I'm calling *The Hulk!*

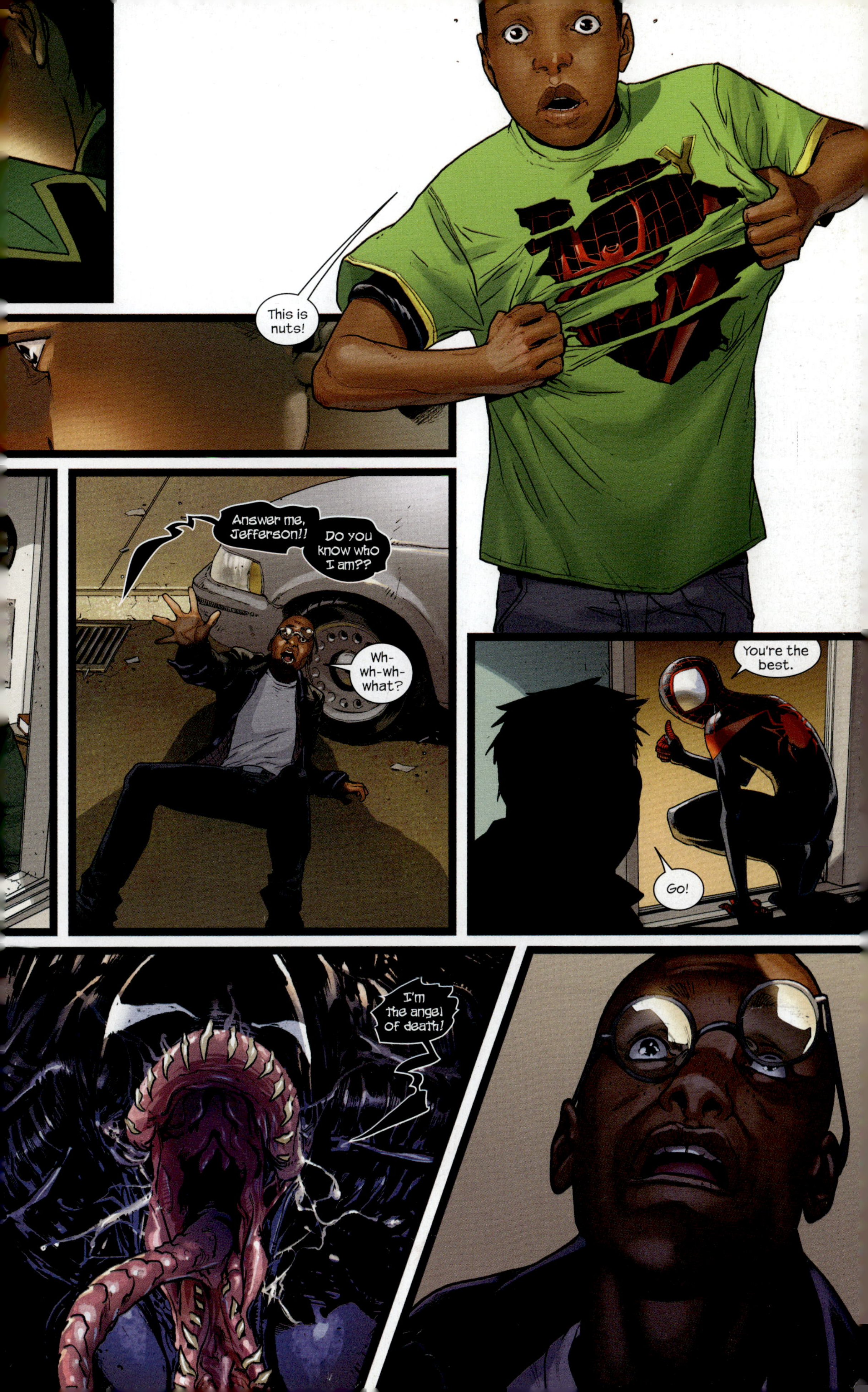
This is nuts!
Answer me, Jefferson!!
Do you know who I am??
Wh-wh-wh-what?
You're the best.
Go!
I'm the angel of death!

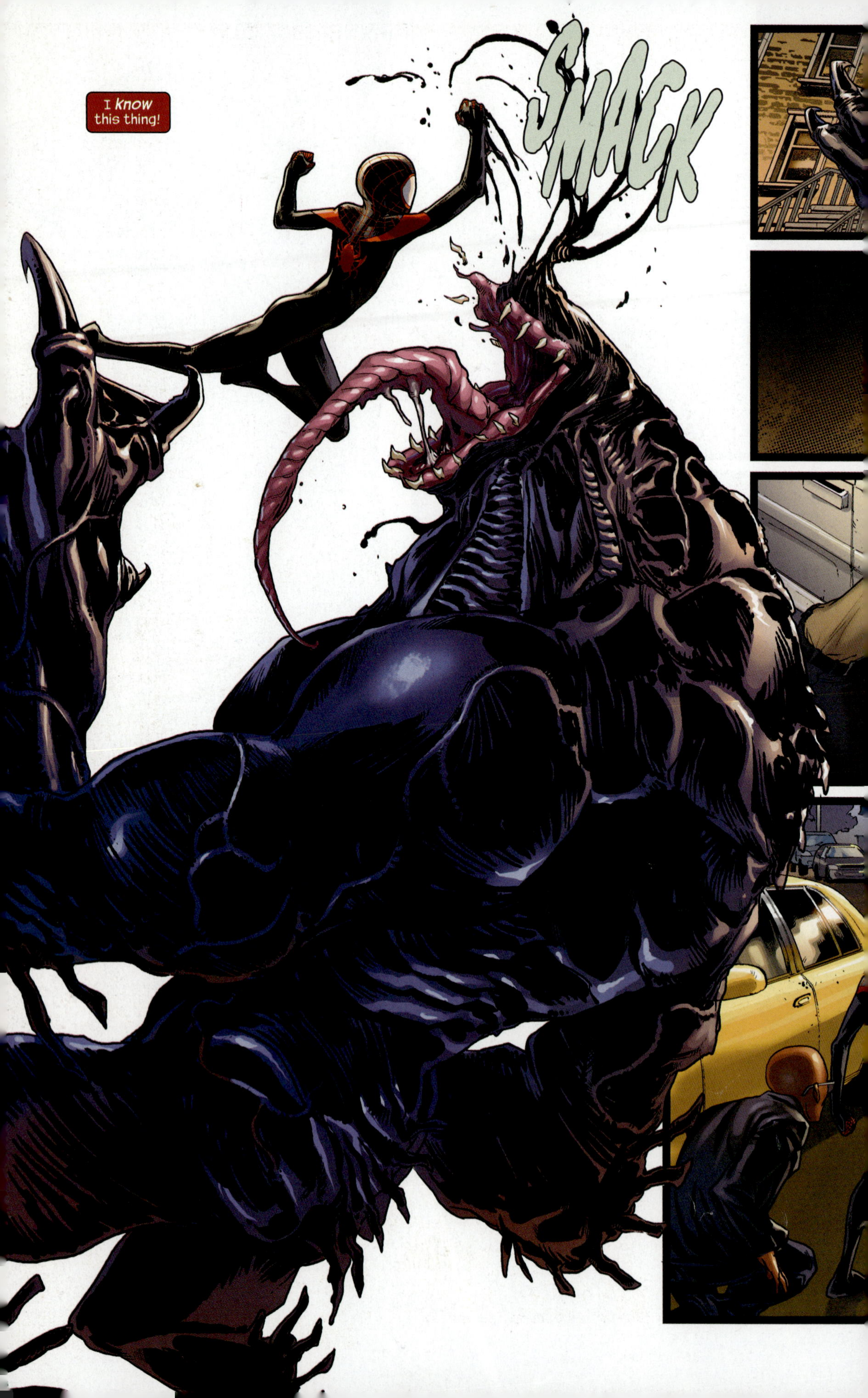
I *know* this thing!
SMACK

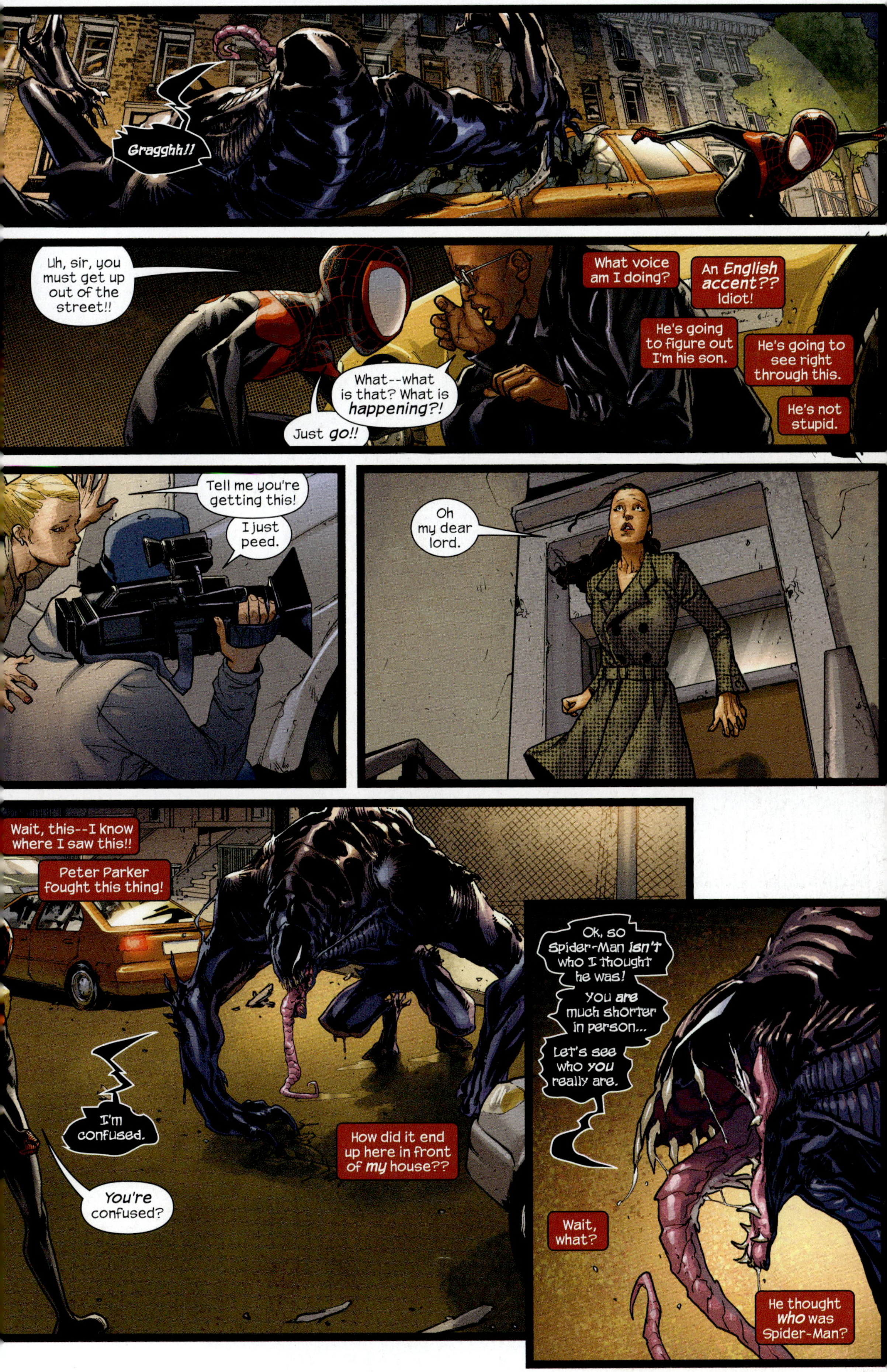
Gragghh!!
Uh, sir, you must get up out of the street!!
What--what is that? What is happening?!
Just go!!
What voice am I doing?
An English accent?? Idiot!
He's going to figure out I'm his son.
He's going to see right through this.
He's not stupid.
Tell me you're getting this!
I just peed.
Oh my dear lord.
Wait, this--I know where I saw this!!
Peter Parker fought this thing!
I'm confused.
You're confused?
How did it end up here in front of my house??
Ok, so Spider-Man isn't who I thought he was!
You are much shorter in person...
Let's see who you really are.
Wait, what?
He thought who was Spider-Man?

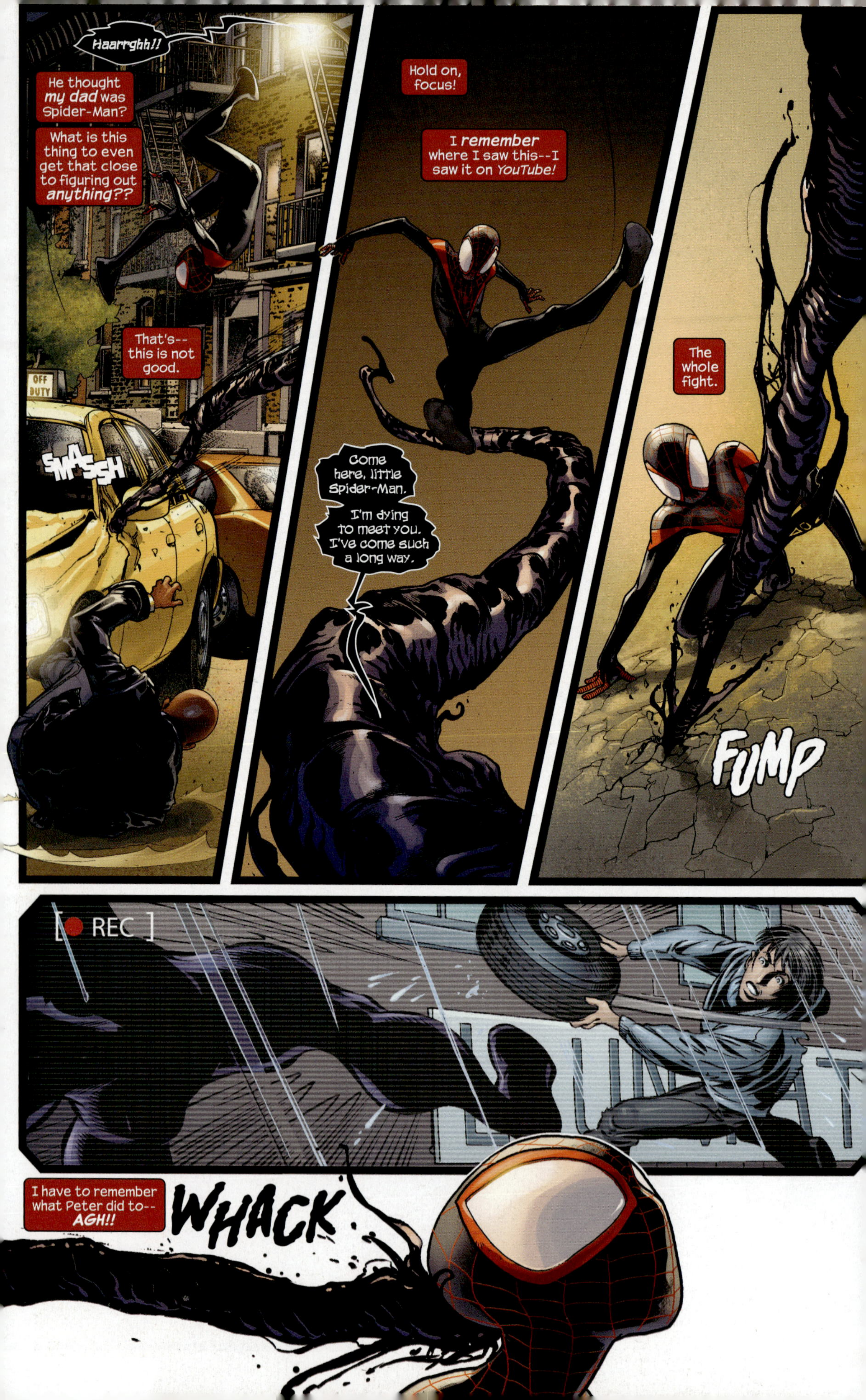
Haarrghh!!
He thought my dad was Spider-Man?
What is this thing to even get that close to figuring out anything??
That's-- this is not good.
OFF DUTY
SMASSH
Hold on, focus!
I remember where I saw this--I saw it on YouTube!
Come here, little Spider-Man.
I'm dying to meet you. I've come such a long way.
The whole fight.
FUMP
REC
I have to remember what Peter did to-- AGH!!
WHACK

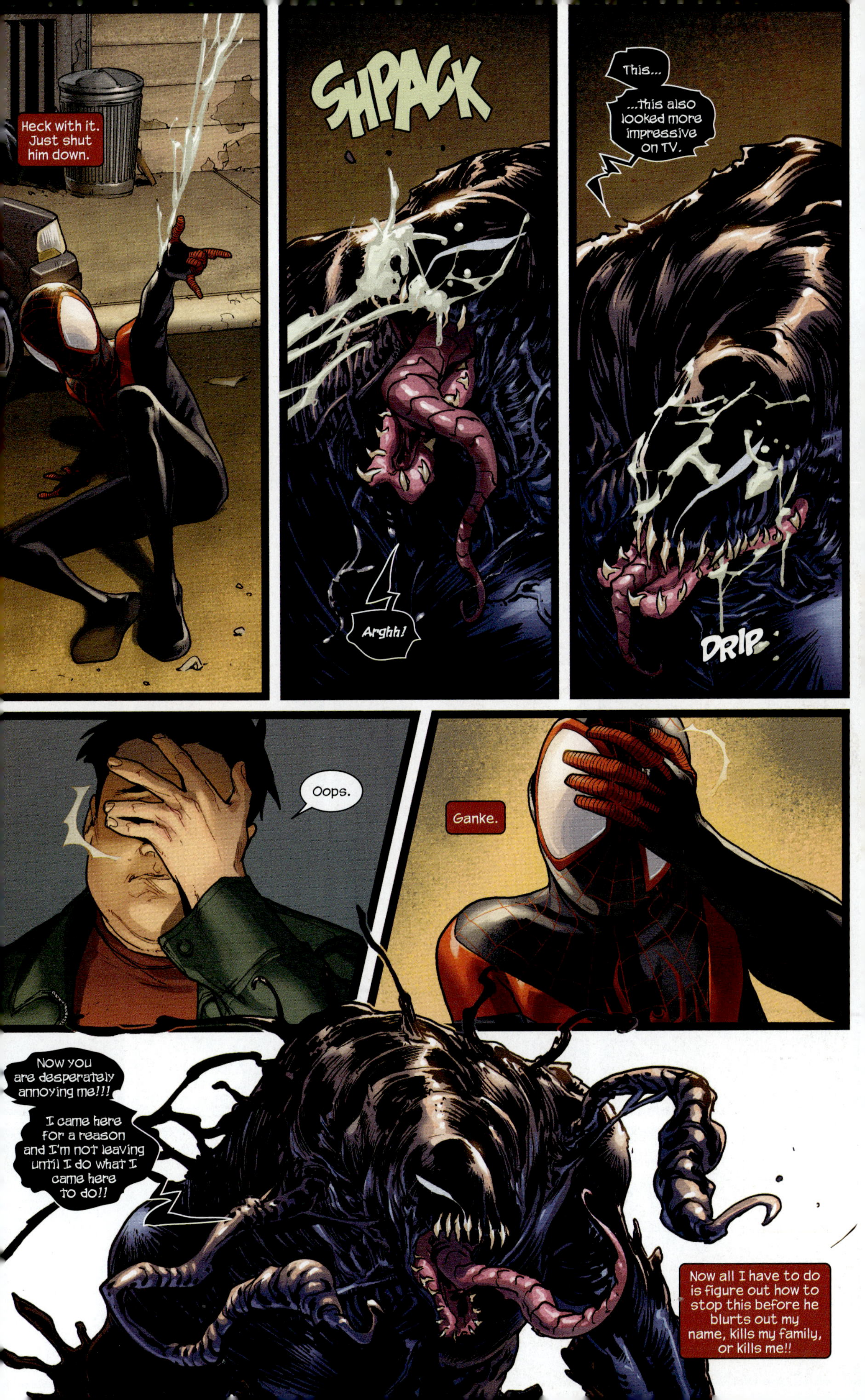
Heck with it. Just shut him down.
SHPACK
Arghh!
This...
...this also looked more impressive on TV.
DRIP
Oops.
Ganke.
Now you are desperately annoying me!!!
I came here for a reason and I'm not leaving until I do what I came here to do!!
Now all I have to do is figure out how to stop this before he blurts out my name, kills my family, or kills me!!

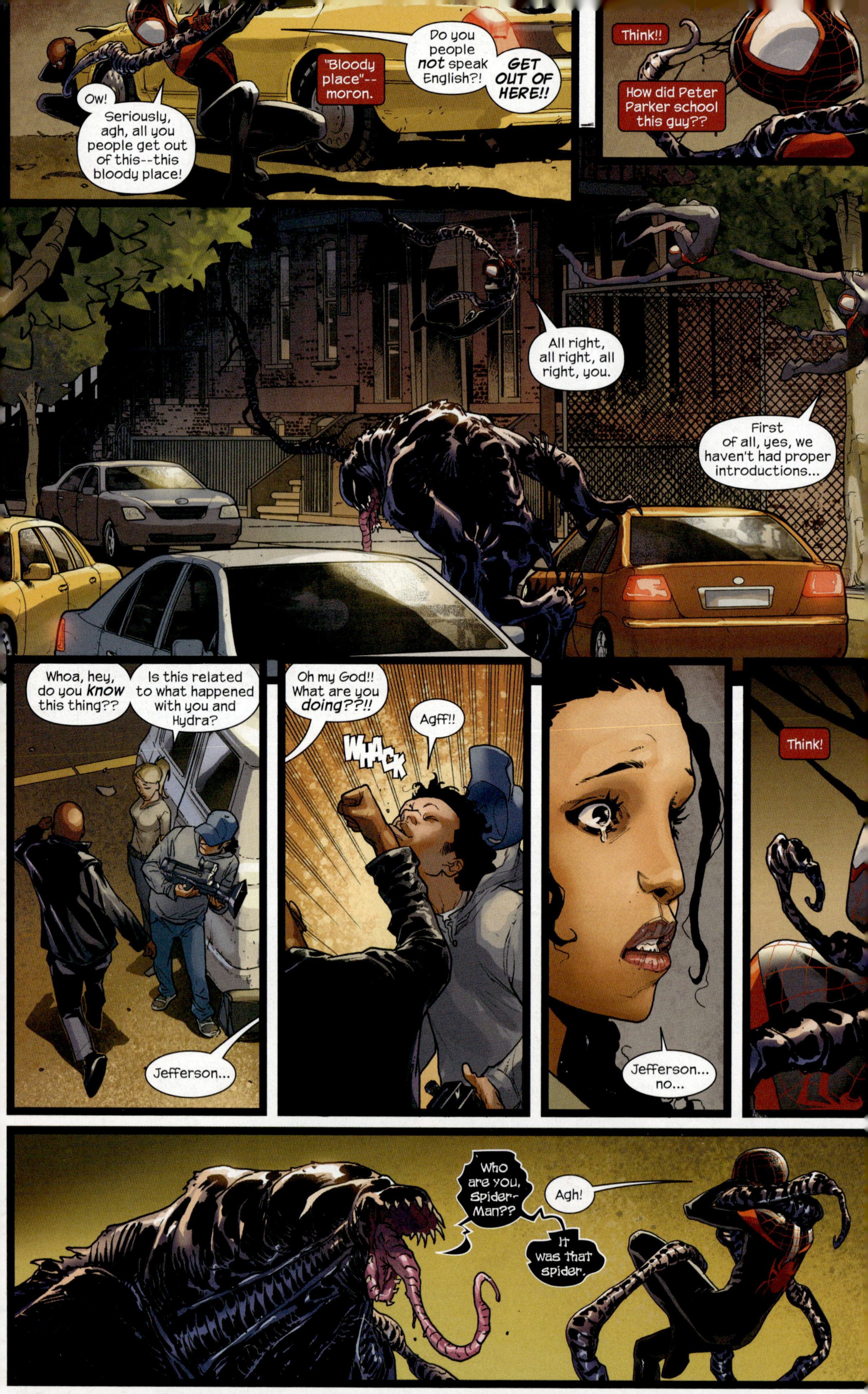
Ow!
Seriously, agh, all you people get out of this--this bloody place!
"Bloody place"-- moron.
Do you people not speak English?!
GET OUT OF HERE!!
Think!!
How did Peter Parker school this guy??
All right, all right, all right, you.
First of all, yes, we haven't had proper introductions...
Whoa, hey, do you know this thing??
Is this related to what happened with you and Hydra?
Jefferson...
Oh my God!! What are you doing??!!
WHACK
Agff!!
Jefferson... no...
Think!
Who are you, Spider-Man??
Agh!
It was that spider.

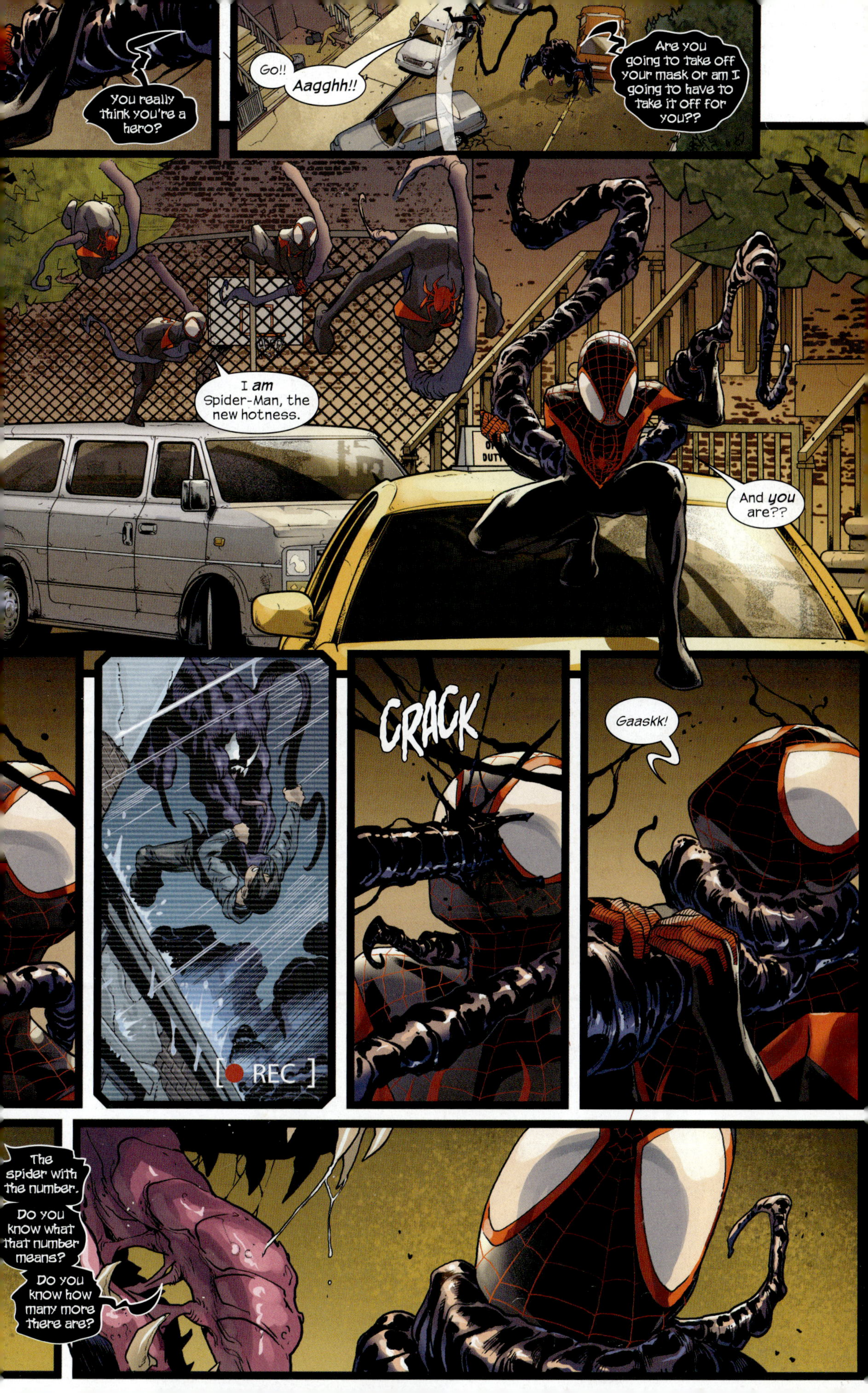
You really think you're a hero?
Go!!
Aagghh!!
Are you going to take off your mask or am I going to have to take it off for you??
I *am* Spider-Man, the new hotness.
And *you* are??
REC
CRACK
Gaaskk!
The spider with the number.
Do you know what that number means?
Do you know how many more there are?

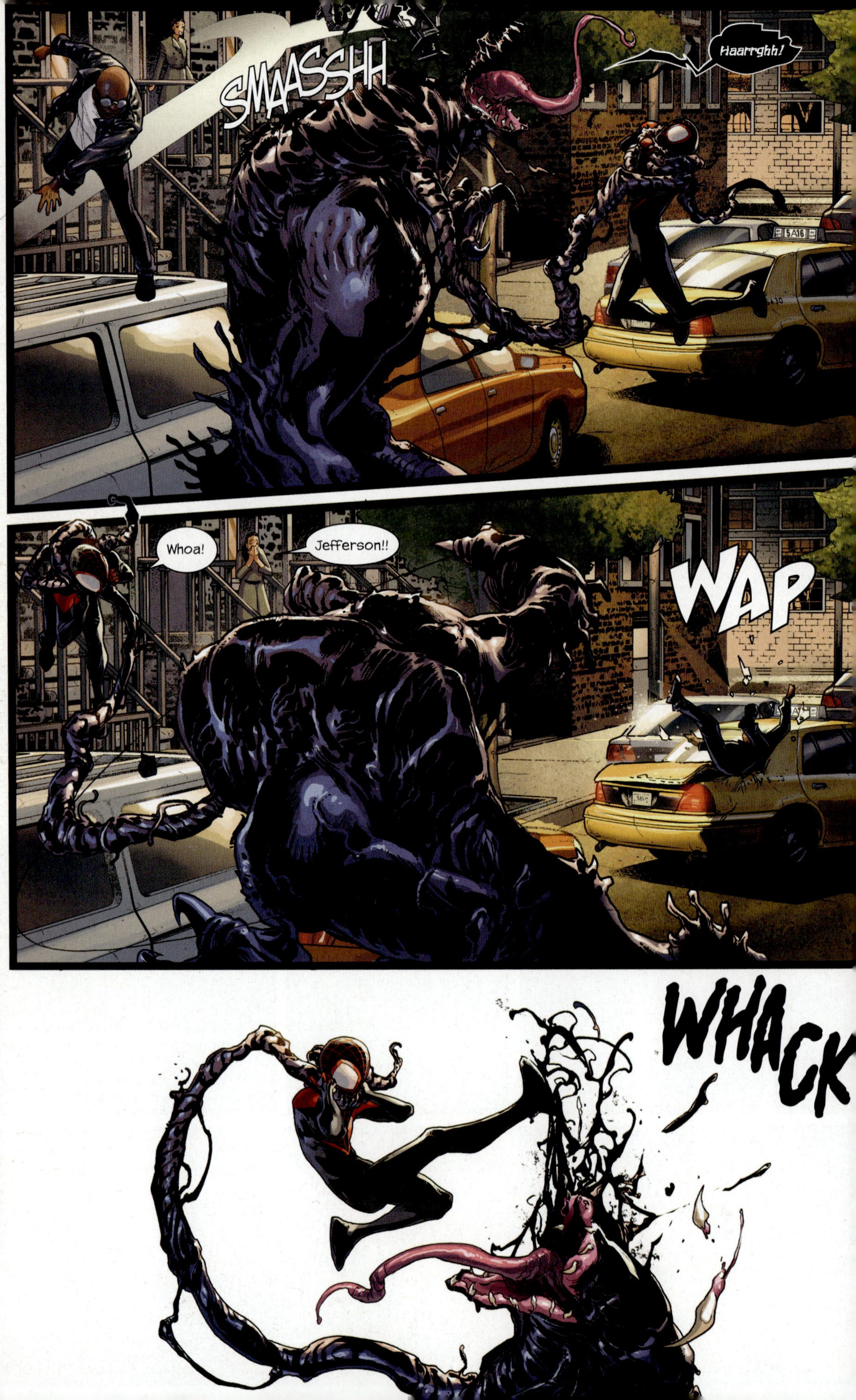
SMAASSHH
Haarrghh!
Whoa!
Jefferson!!
WAP
WHACK

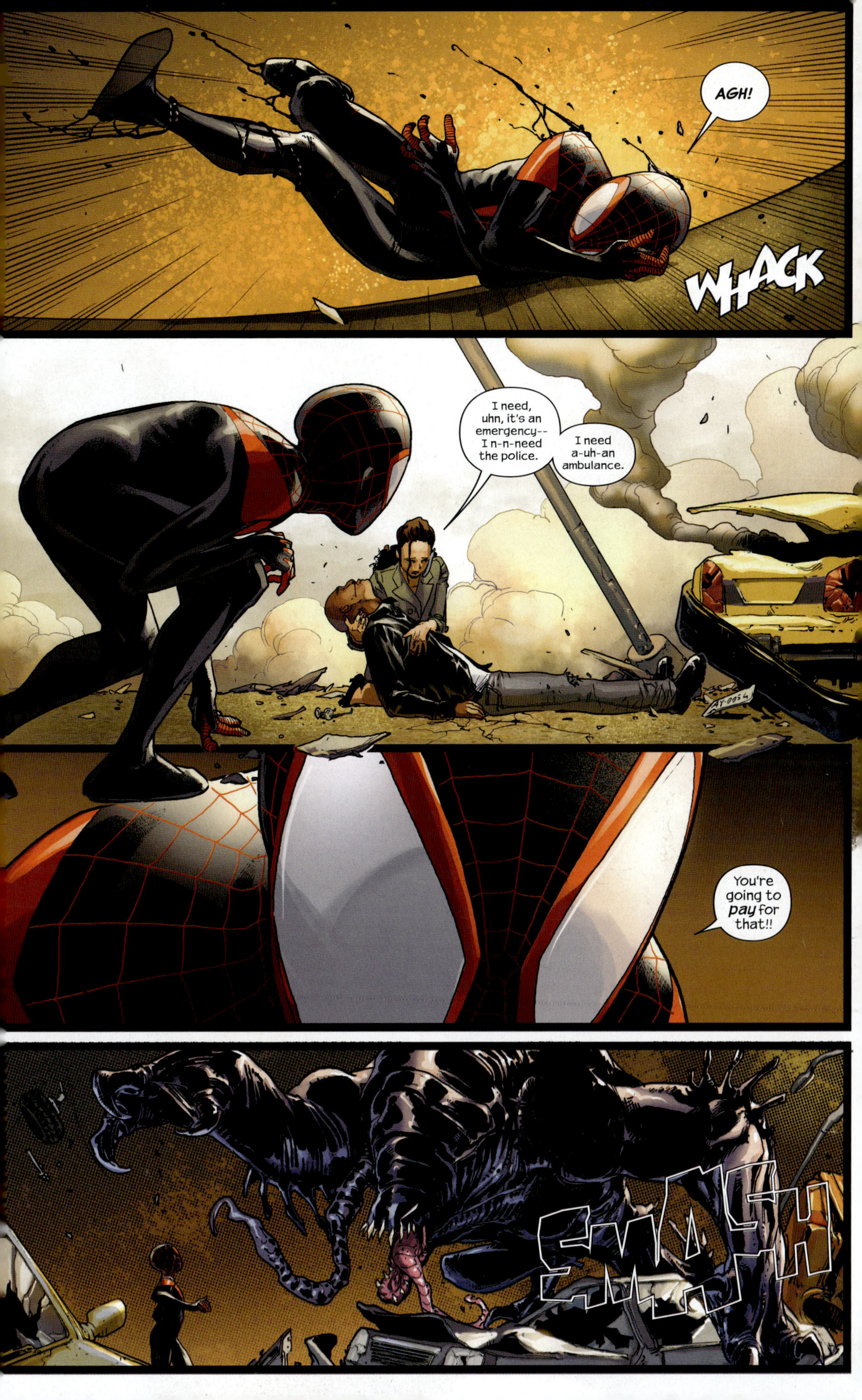
AGH!
WHACK
I need, uhn, it's an emergency-- I n-n-need the police.
I need a-uh-an ambulance.
You're going to pay for that!!
SMASH

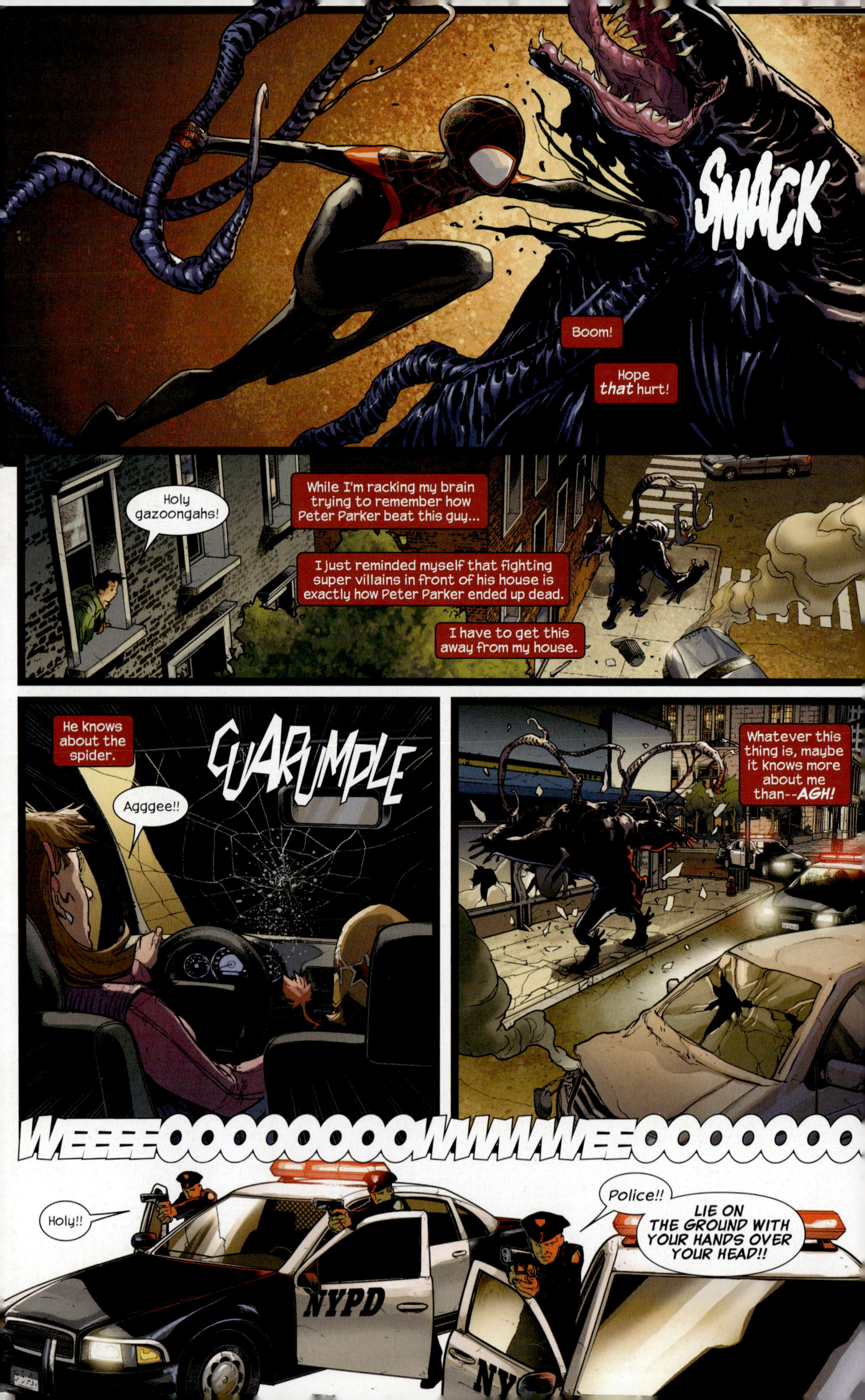
SMACK
Boom!
Hope *that* hurt!
Holy gazoongahs!
While I'm racking my brain trying to remember how Peter Parker beat this guy...
I just reminded myself that fighting super villains in front of his house is exactly how Peter Parker ended up dead.
I have to get this away from my house.
He knows about the spider.
GUARUMPLE
Agggee!!
Whatever this thing is, maybe it knows more about me than--*AGH!*
WEEEEOOOOOOOOOWWWWEEOOOOOOOO
Holy!!
Police!!
LIE ON THE GROUND WITH YOUR HANDS OVER YOUR HEAD!!
NYPD

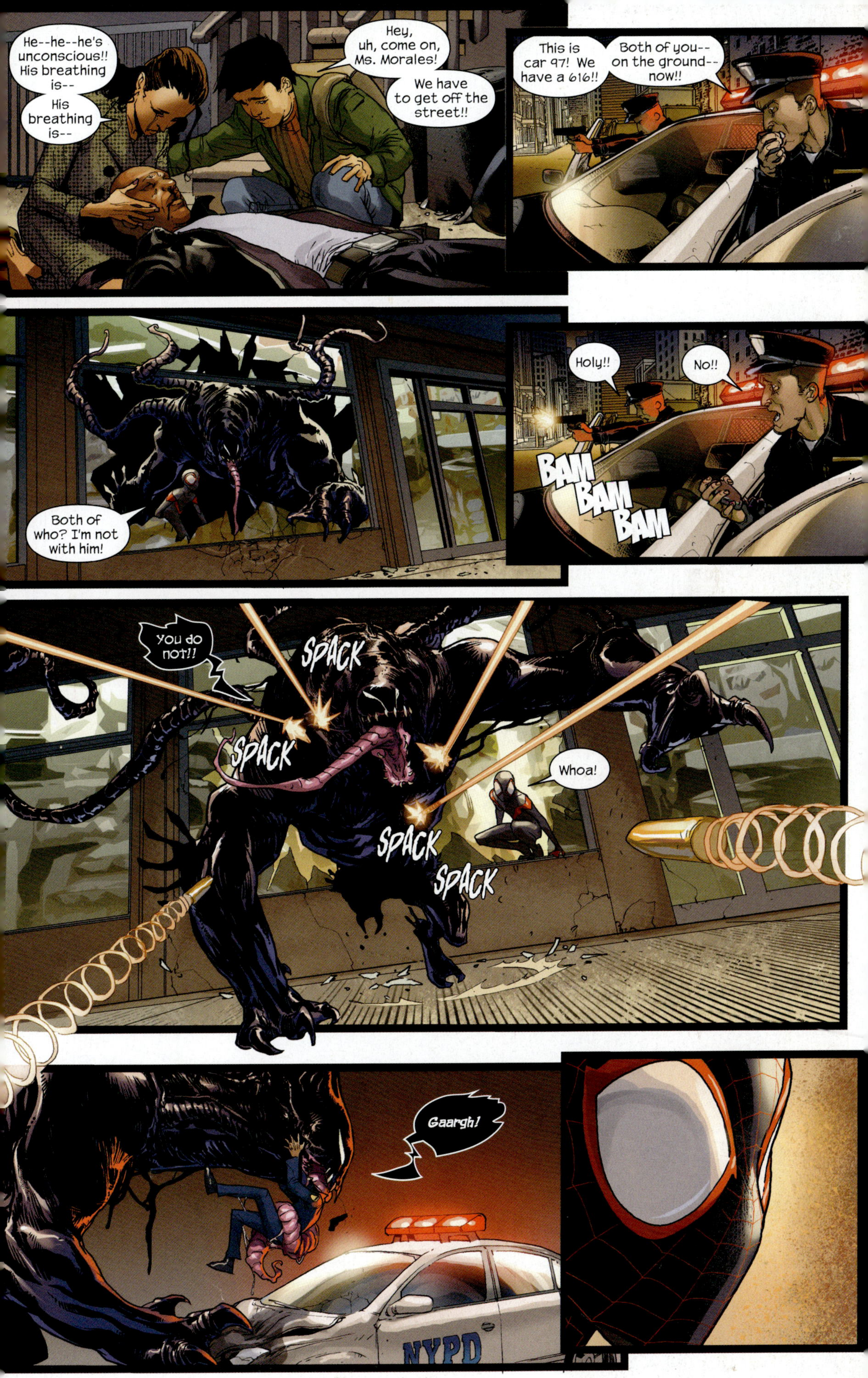

He--he--he's unconscious!! His breathing is--
His breathing is--
Hey, uh, come on, Ms. Morales!
We have to get off the street!!
This is car 97! We have a 616!!
Both of you-- on the ground-- now!!
Both of who? I'm not with him!
Holy!!
No!!
BAM
BAM
BAM
You do not!!
SPACK
SPACK
Whoa!
SPACK
SPACK
Gaargh!
NYPD

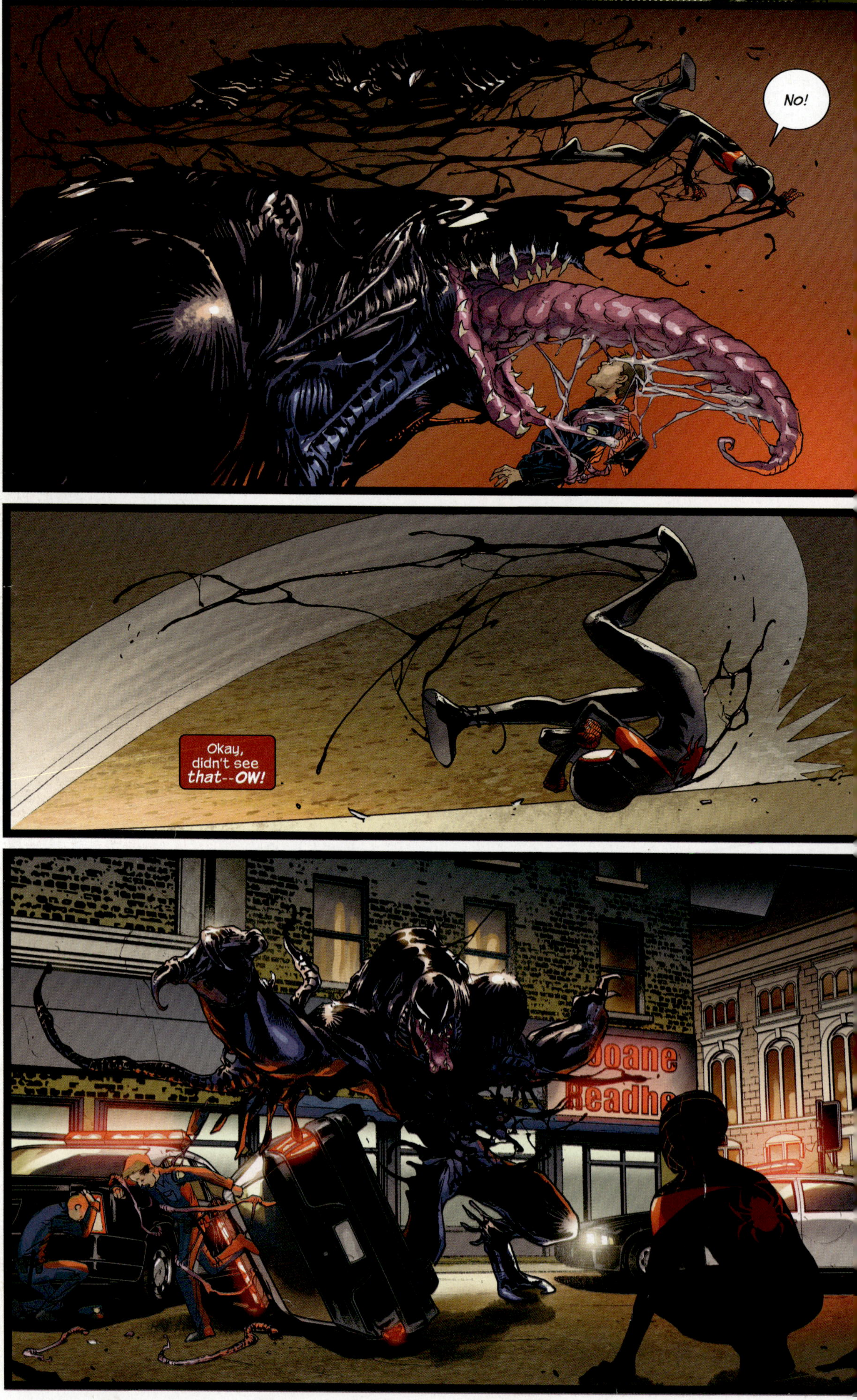
No!
Okay, didn't see that--OW!

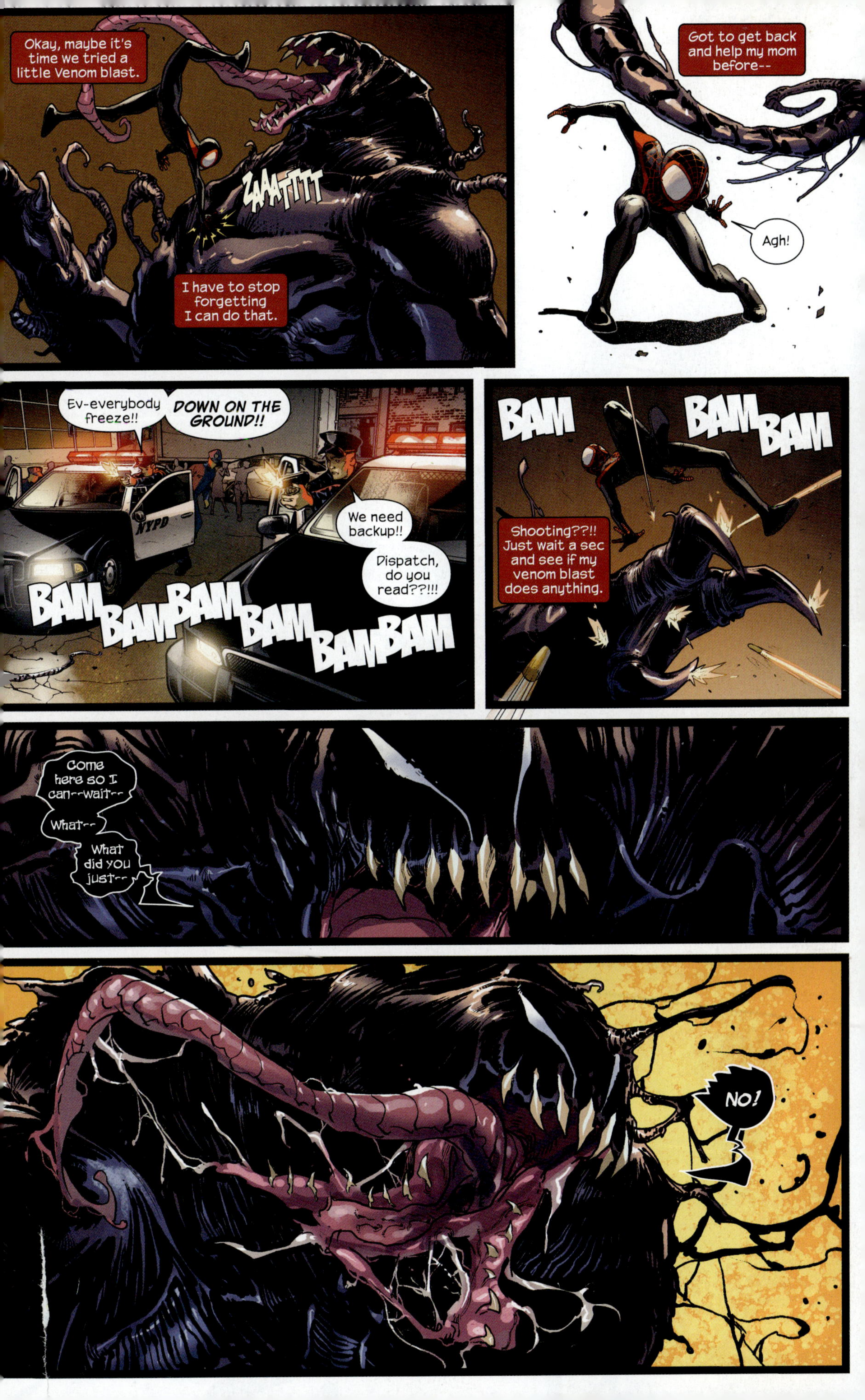
Okay, maybe it's time we tried a little Venom blast.
ZAAATTTT
I have to stop forgetting I can do that.
Got to get back and help my mom before--
Agh!
Ev-everybody freeze!!
DOWN ON THE GROUND!!
NYPD
We need backup!!
Dispatch, do you read??!!!
BAM BAM BAM BAM BAM BAM
BAM
BAM BAM
Shooting??!! Just wait a sec and see if my venom blast does anything.
Come here so I can--wait--
What--
What did you just--
NO!

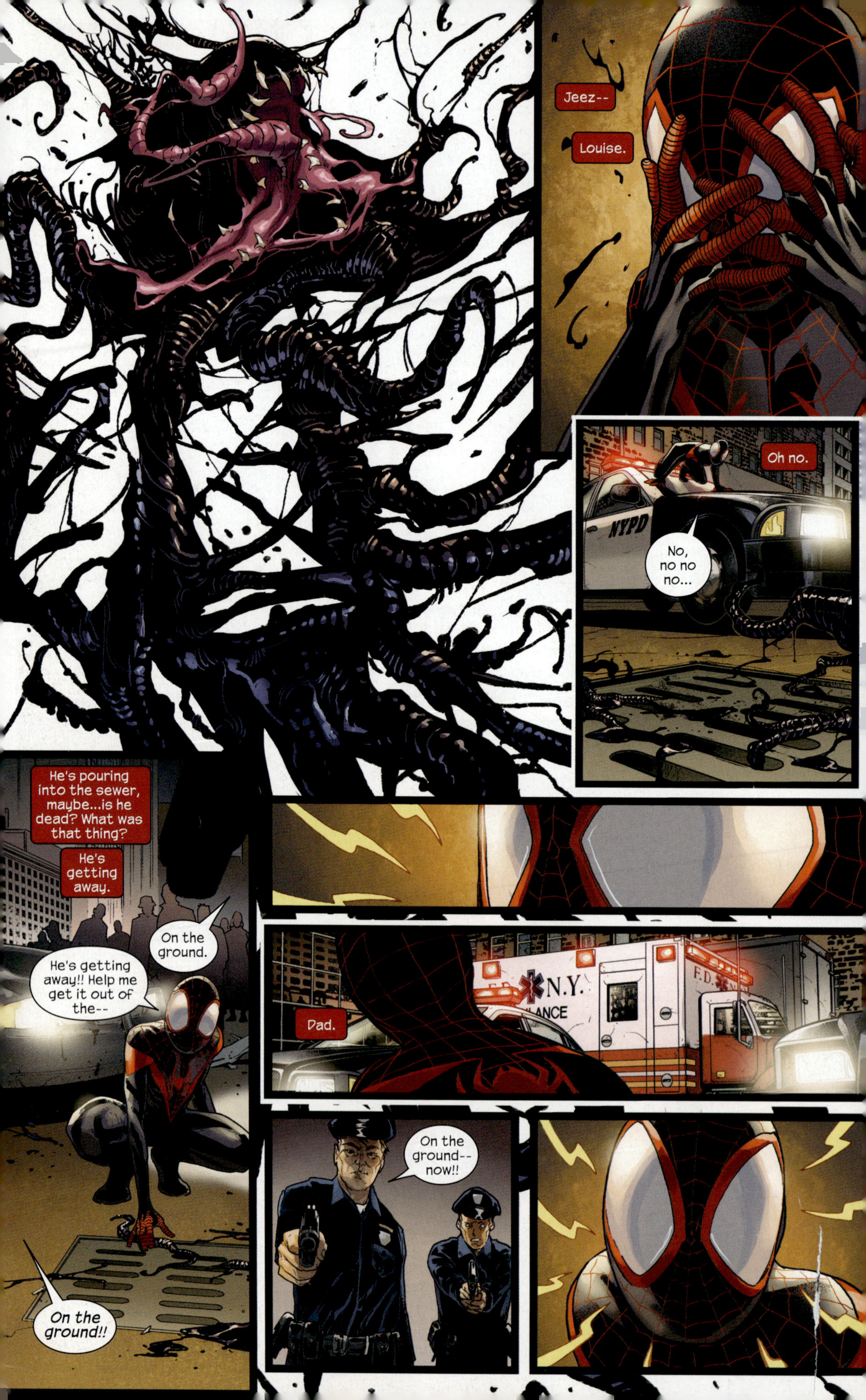
Jeez--
Louise.
Oh no.
No, no no no...
He's pouring into the sewer, maybe...is he dead? What was that thing?
He's getting away.
On the ground.
He's getting away!! Help me get it out of the--
On the ground!!
Dad.
On the ground-- now!!

SPSSSHOOO

SPSSSHOOO

You **lost** him!

I lost him!

I think I see him!

Do **not** fire!!

You are **not** firing at a civilian apartment building!!

I think I **see** him!!

I'm going to need you to step away from the body, ma'am.

What's his name? Do you know his name?

He--he--his breathing--

Je-je-je-Jefferson.

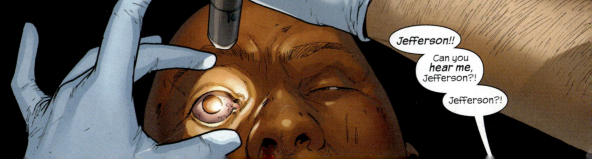

Jefferson!!

Can you **hear** me, Jefferson?!

Jefferson?!

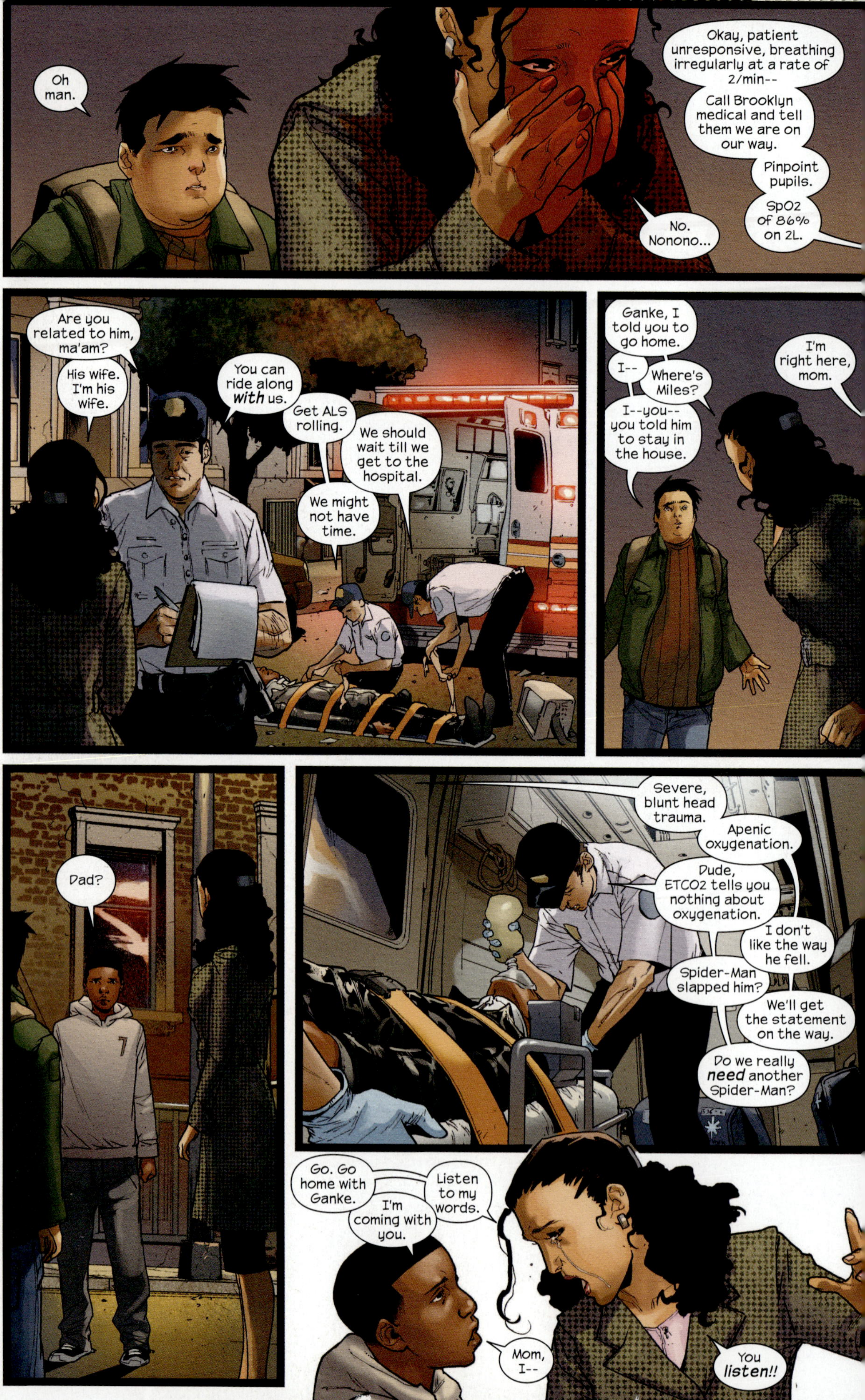
Oh man.
Okay, patient unresponsive, breathing irregularly at a rate of 2/min--
Call Brooklyn medical and tell them we are on our way.
Pinpoint pupils.
SpO2 of 86% on 2L.
No. Nonono...
Are you related to him, ma'am?
His wife. I'm his wife.
You can ride along *with* us.
Get ALS rolling.
We should wait till we get to the hospital.
We might not have time.
Ganke, I told you to go home.
I--
Where's Miles?
I--you--you told him to stay in the house.
I'm right here, mom.
Dad?
Severe, blunt head trauma.
Apenic oxygenation.
Dude, ETCO2 tells you nothing about oxygenation.
I don't like the way he fell.
Spider-Man slapped him?
We'll get the statement on the way.
Do we really *need* another Spider-Man?
Go. Go home with Ganke.
I'm coming with you.
Listen to my words.
Mom, I--
You *listen!!*

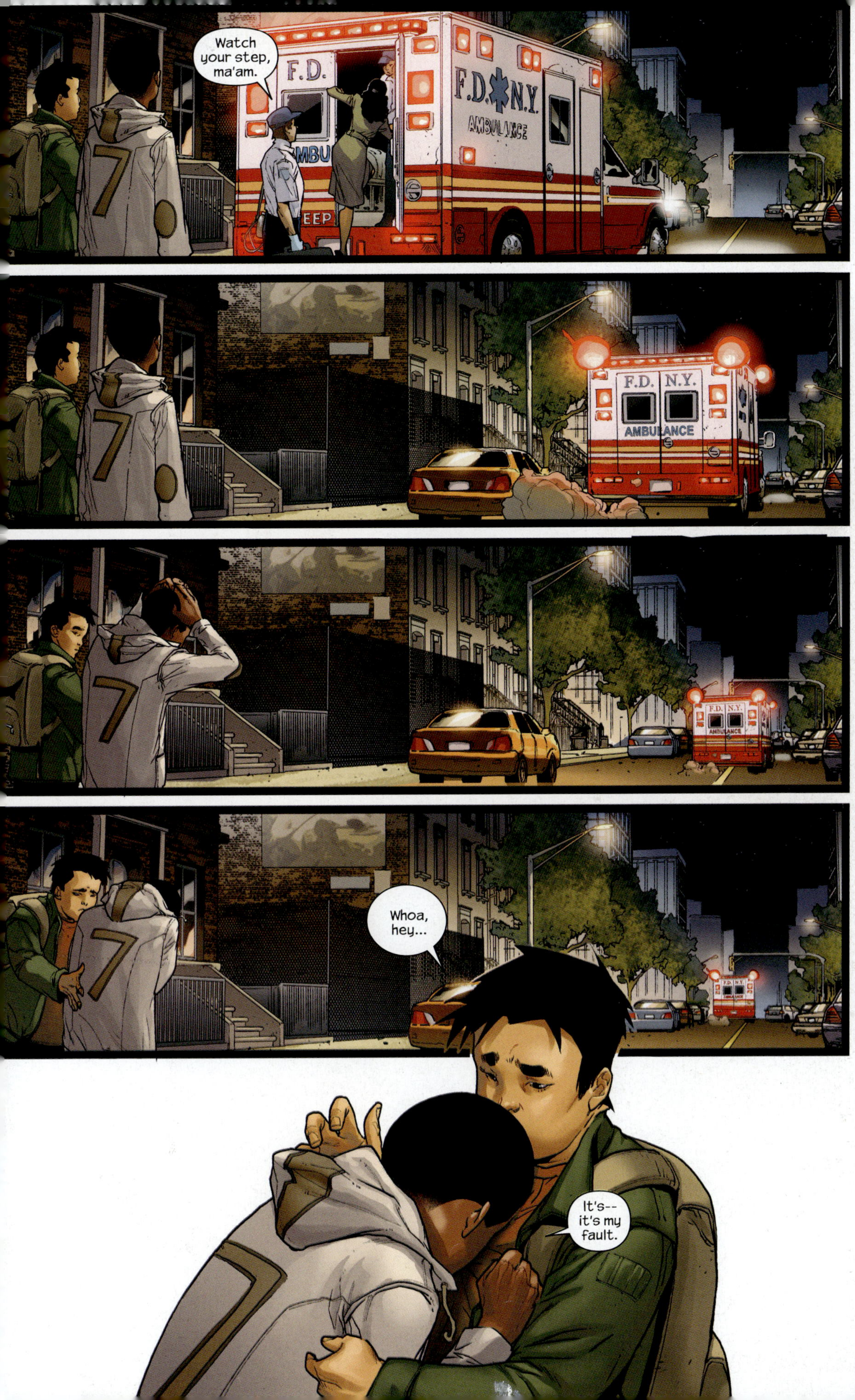
Watch your step, ma'am.
F.D.
F.D.N.Y.
AMBULANCE
F.D. N.Y.
AMBULANCE
Whoa, hey...
It's-- it's my fault.

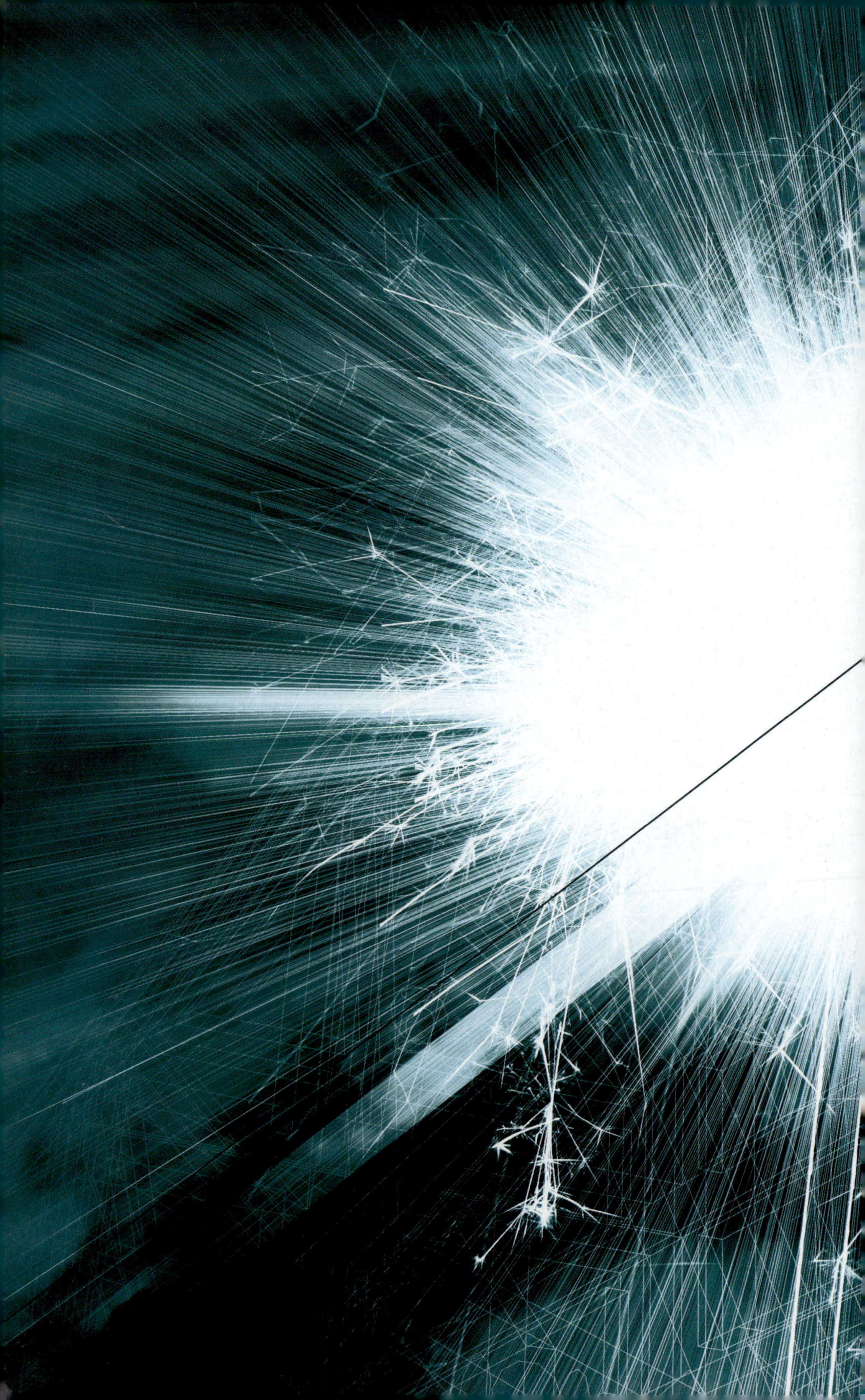

VENOM WAR

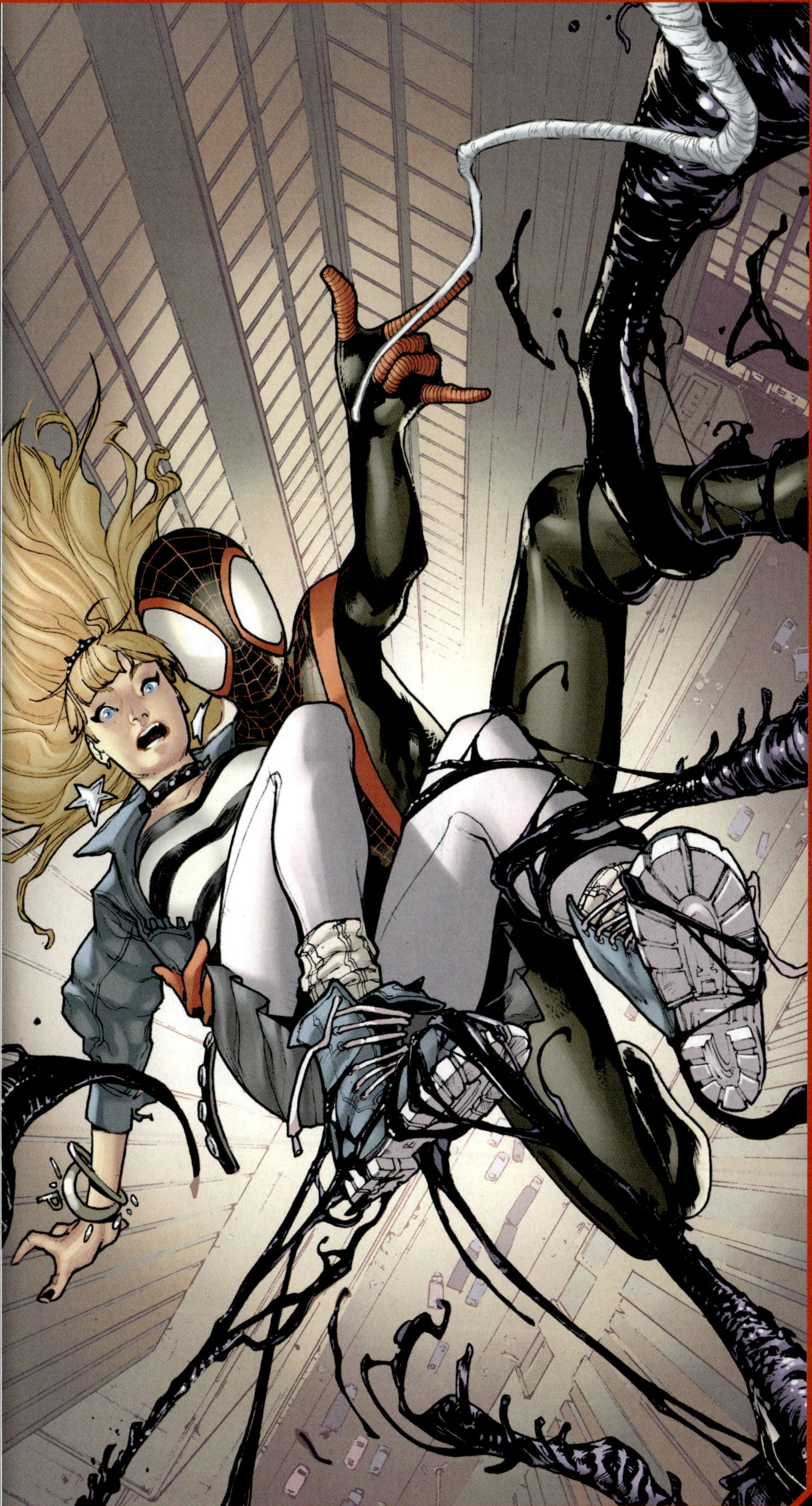

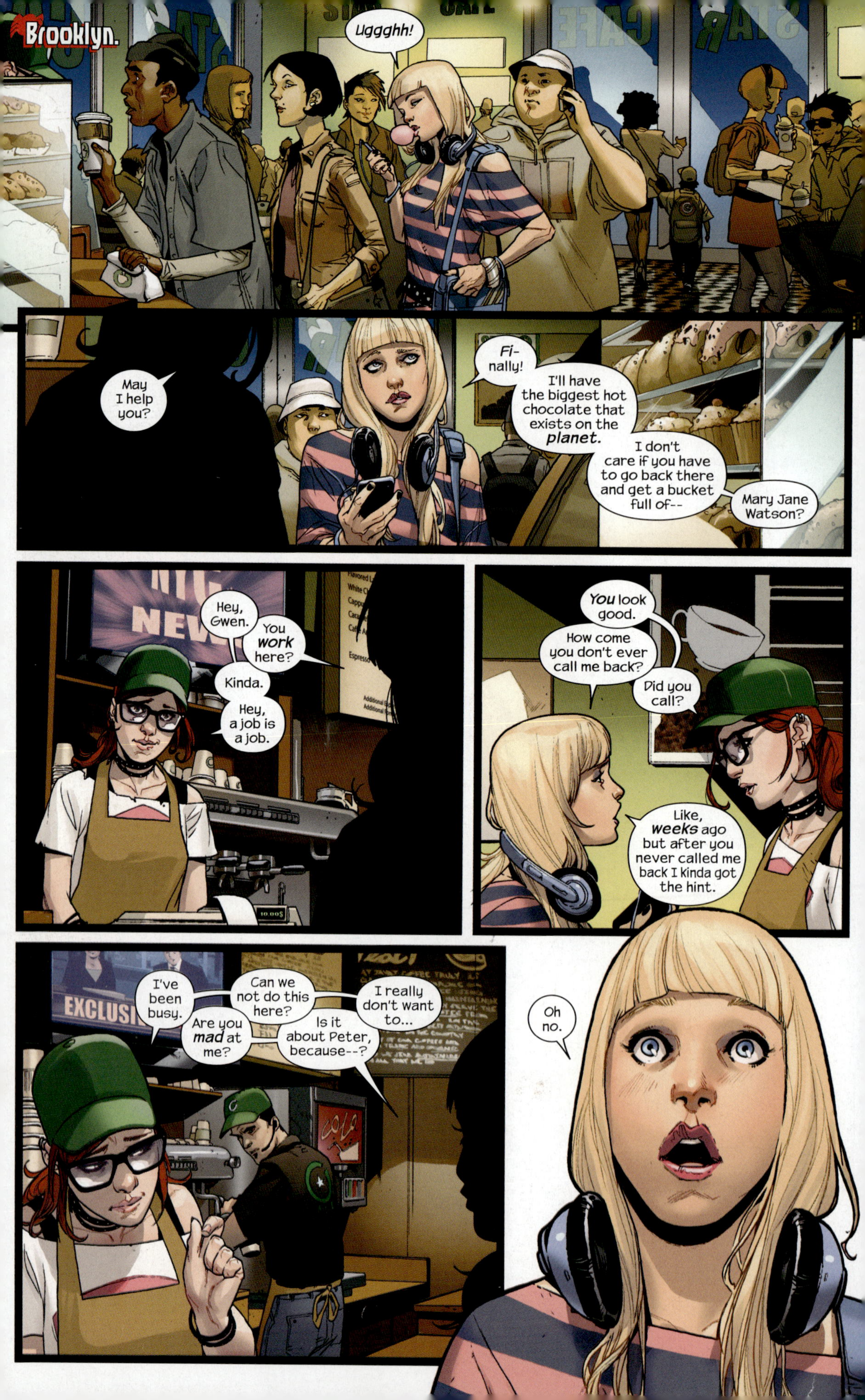
Brooklyn.
Uggghh!
May I help you?
Fi-nally!
I'll have the biggest hot chocolate that exists on the planet.
I don't care if you have to go back there and get a bucket full of--
Mary Jane Watson?
Hey, Gwen.
You work here?
Kinda.
Hey, a job is a job.
You look good.
How come you don't ever call me back?
Did you call?
Like, weeks ago but after you never called me back I kinda got the hint.
I've been busy.
Can we not do this here?
I really don't want to...
Are you mad at me?
Is it about Peter, because--?
Oh no.

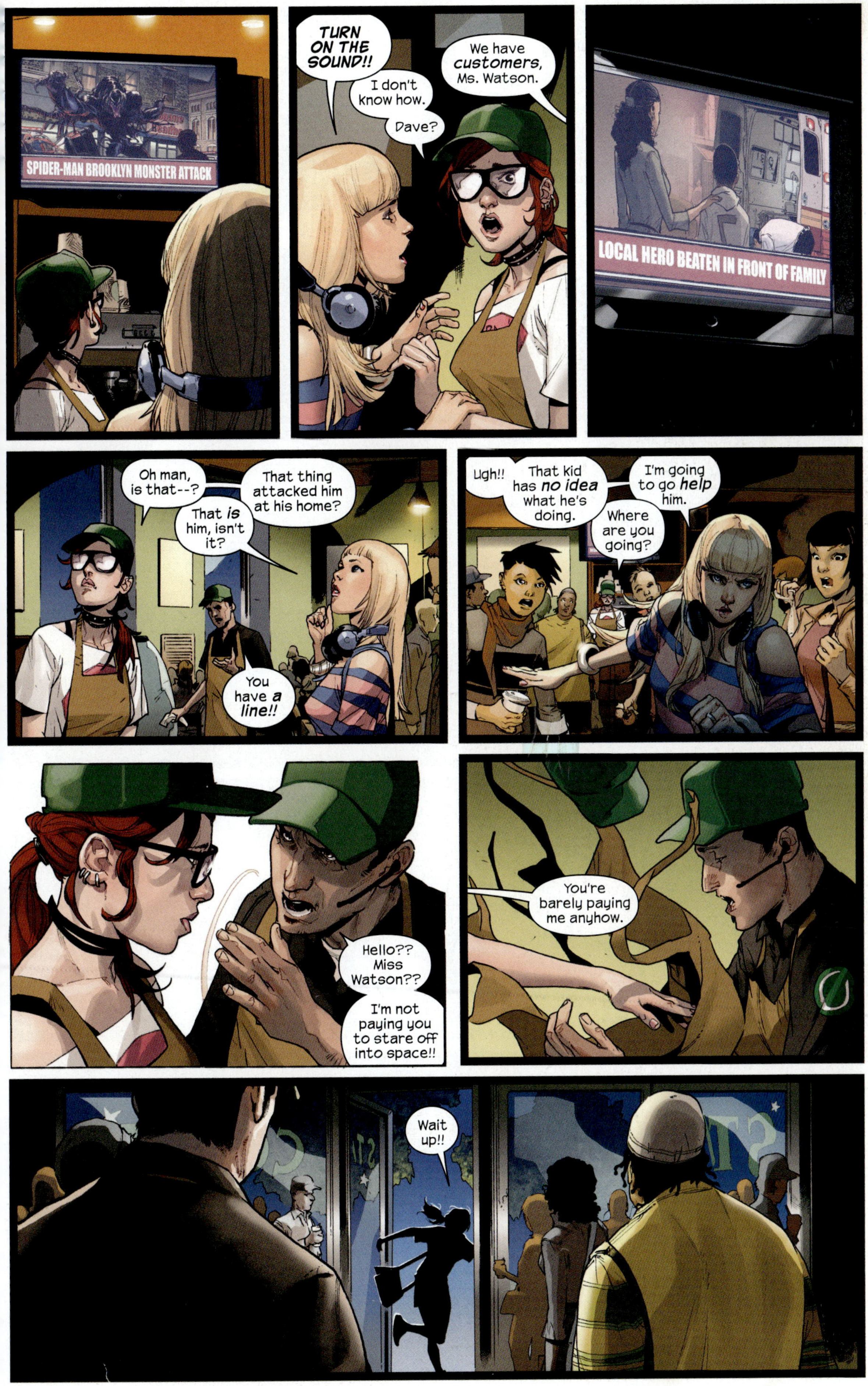
SPIDER-MAN BROOKLYN MONSTER ATTACK
TURN ON THE SOUND!!
I don't know how.
Dave?
We have customers, Ms. Watson.
LOCAL HERO BEATEN IN FRONT OF FAMILY
Oh man, is that--?
That is him, isn't it?
That thing attacked him at his home?
You have a line!!
Ugh!!
That kid has no idea what he's doing.
I'm going to go help him.
Where are you going?
Hello?? Miss Watson??
I'm not paying you to stare off into space!!
You're barely paying me anyhow.
Wait up!!

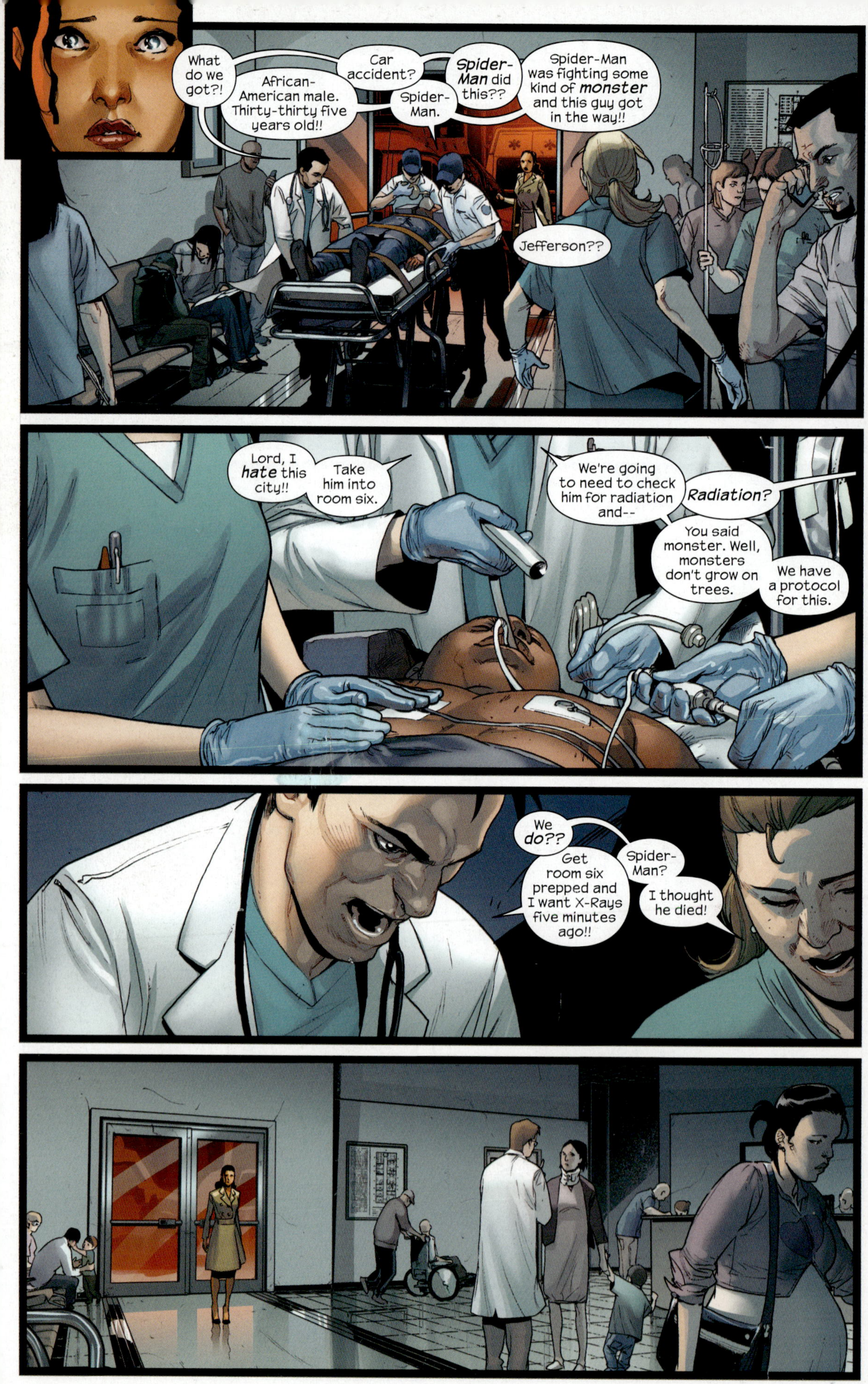
What do we got?!
African-American male. Thirty-thirty five years old!!
Car accident?
Spider-Man.
Spider-Man did this??
Spider-Man was fighting some kind of monster and this guy got in the way!!
Jefferson??
Lord, I hate this city!!
Take him into room six.
We're going to need to check him for radiation and--
Radiation?
You said monster. Well, monsters don't grow on trees.
We have a protocol for this.
We do??
Get room six prepped and I want X-Rays five minutes ago!!
Spider-Man?
I thought he died!

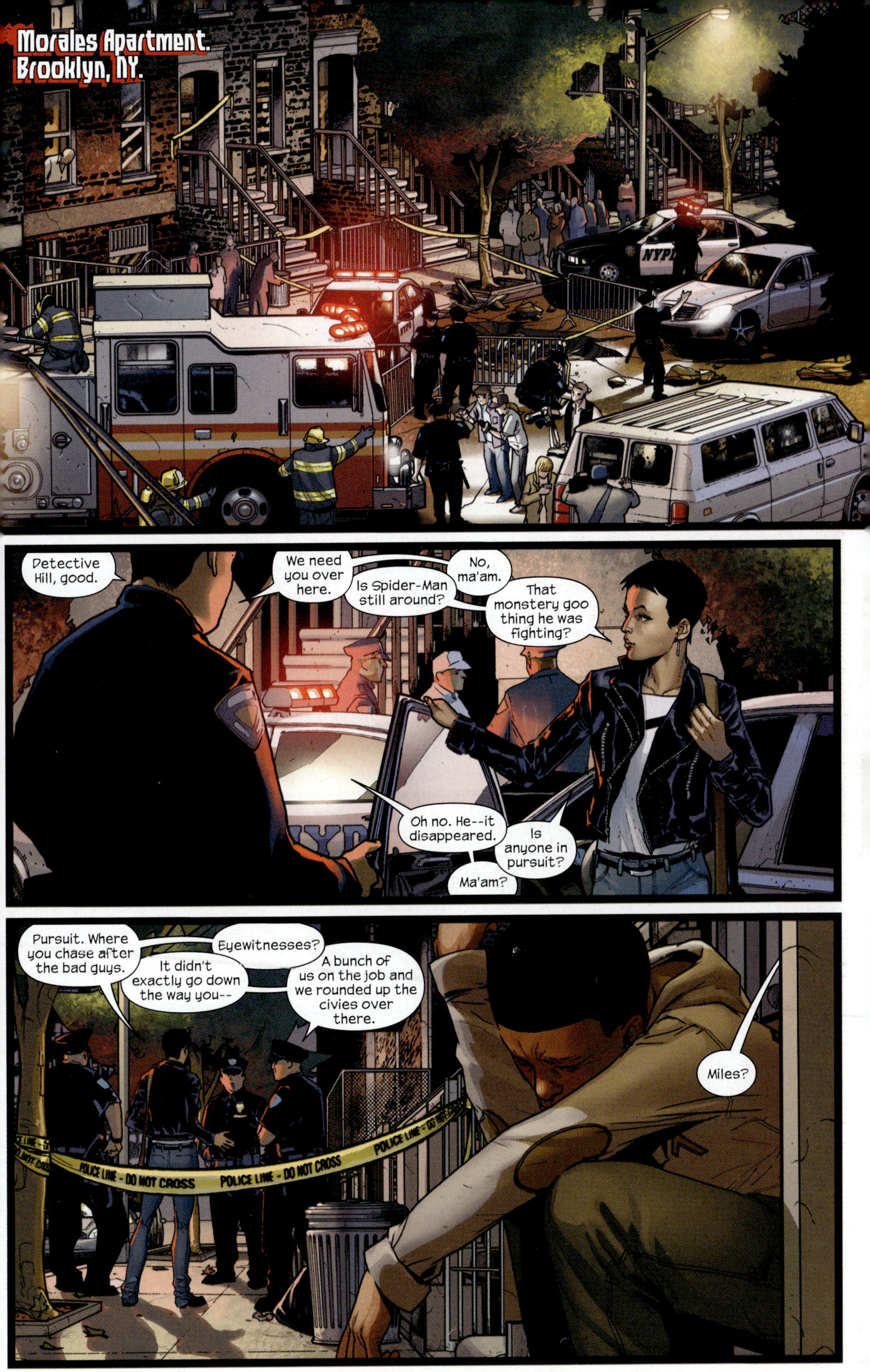
Morales Apartment. Brooklyn, NY.
Detective Hill, good.
We need you over here.
No, ma'am.
Is Spider-Man still around?
That monstery goo thing he was fighting?
Oh no. He--it disappeared.
Is anyone in pursuit?
Ma'am?
Pursuit. Where you chase after the bad guys.
Eyewitnesses?
It didn't exactly go down the way you--
A bunch of us on the job and we rounded up the civies over there.
Miles?
POLICE LINE - DO NOT CROSS
POLICE LINE - DO NOT CROSS

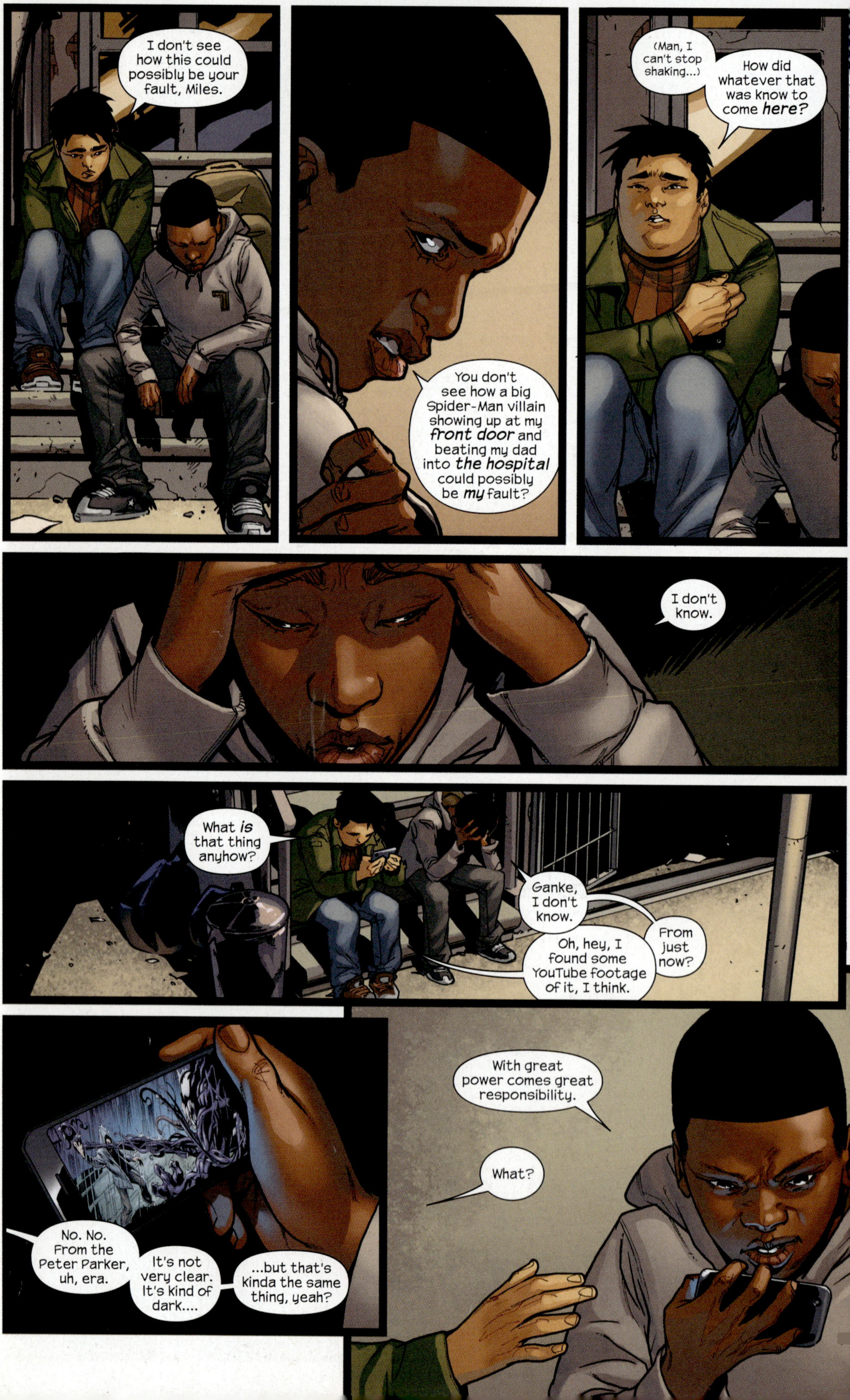
I don't see how this could possibly be your fault, Miles.
You don't see how a big Spider-Man villain showing up at my *front door* and beating my dad into *the hospital* could possibly be *my* fault?
(Man, I can't stop shaking...)
How did whatever that was know to come *here?*
I don't know.
What *is* that thing anyhow?
Ganke, I don't know.
From just now?
Oh, hey, I found some YouTube footage of it, I think.
No. No. From the Peter Parker, uh, era.
It's not very clear. It's kind of dark....
...but that's kinda the same thing, yeah?
With great power comes great responsibility.
What?

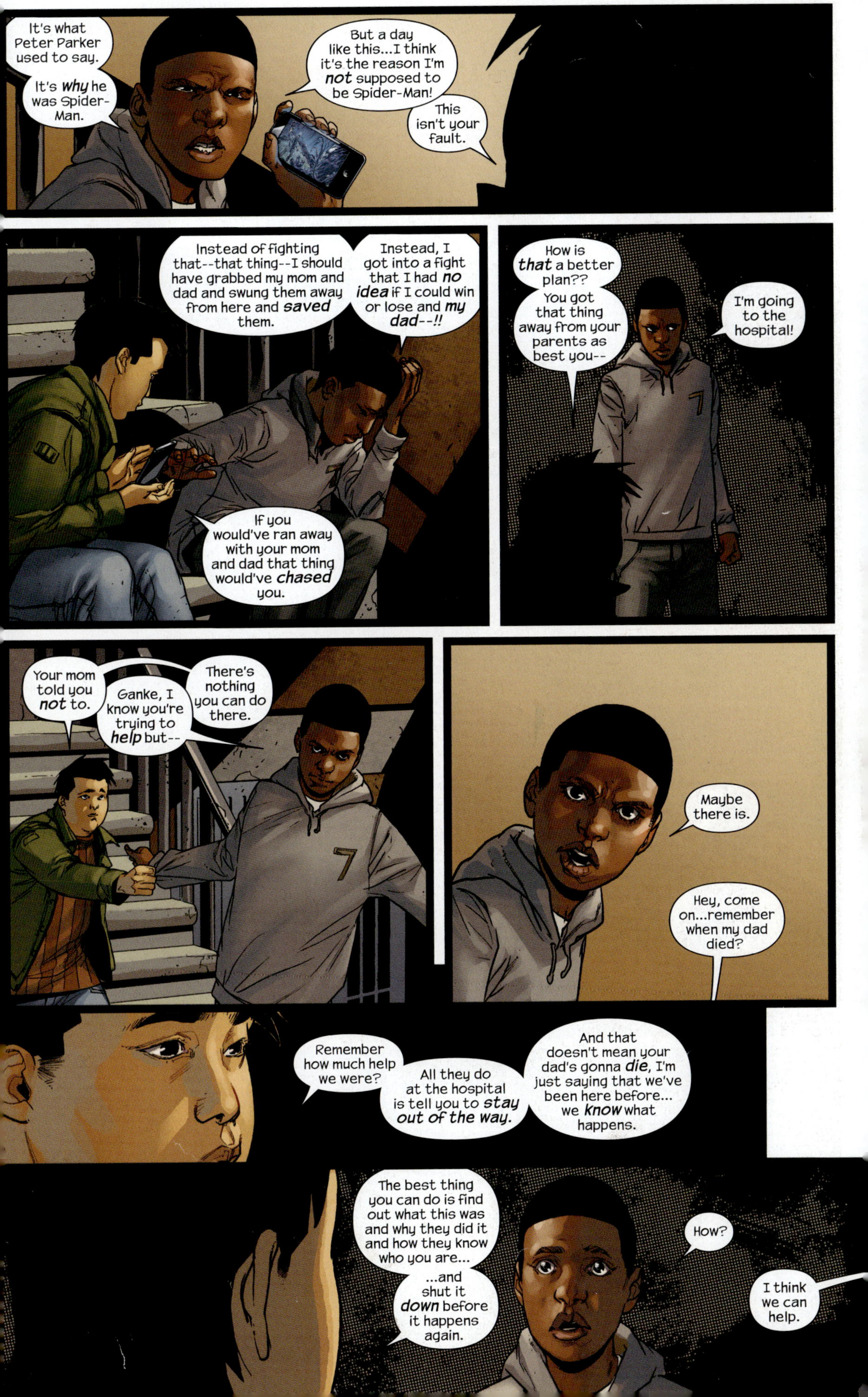

It's what Peter Parker used to say.
It's why he was Spider-Man.
But a day like this...I think it's the reason I'm not supposed to be Spider-Man!
This isn't your fault.
Instead of fighting that--that thing--I should have grabbed my mom and dad and swung them away from here and saved them.
Instead, I got into a fight that I had no idea if I could win or lose and my dad--!!
If you would've ran away with your mom and dad that thing would've chased you.
How is that a better plan??
You got that thing away from your parents as best you--
I'm going to the hospital!
Your mom told you not to.
There's nothing you can do there.
Ganke, I know you're trying to help but--
Maybe there is.
Hey, come on...remember when my dad died?
Remember how much help we were?
All they do at the hospital is tell you to stay out of the way.
And that doesn't mean your dad's gonna die, I'm just saying that we've been here before... we know what happens.
The best thing you can do is find out what this was and why they did it and how they know who you are...
...and shut it down before it happens again.
How?
I think we can help.

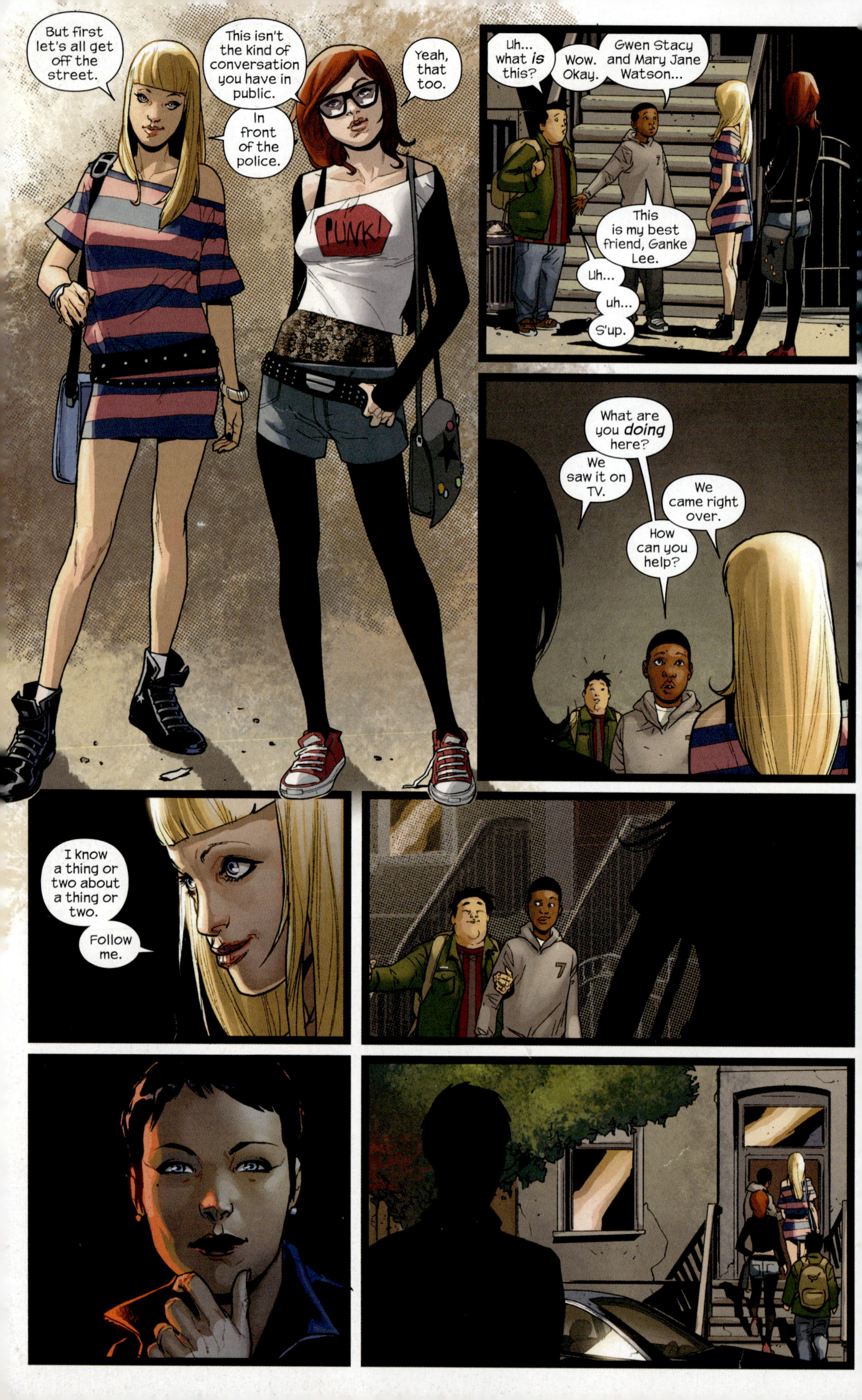
But first let's all get off the street.
This isn't the kind of conversation you have in public.
In front of the police.
Yeah, that too.
PUNK!
Uh... what *is* this?
Wow. Okay.
Gwen Stacy and Mary Jane Watson...
This is my best friend, Ganke Lee.
Uh...
uh...
S'up.
What are you *doing* here?
We saw it on TV.
We came right over.
How can you help?
I know a thing or two about a thing or two.
Follow me.

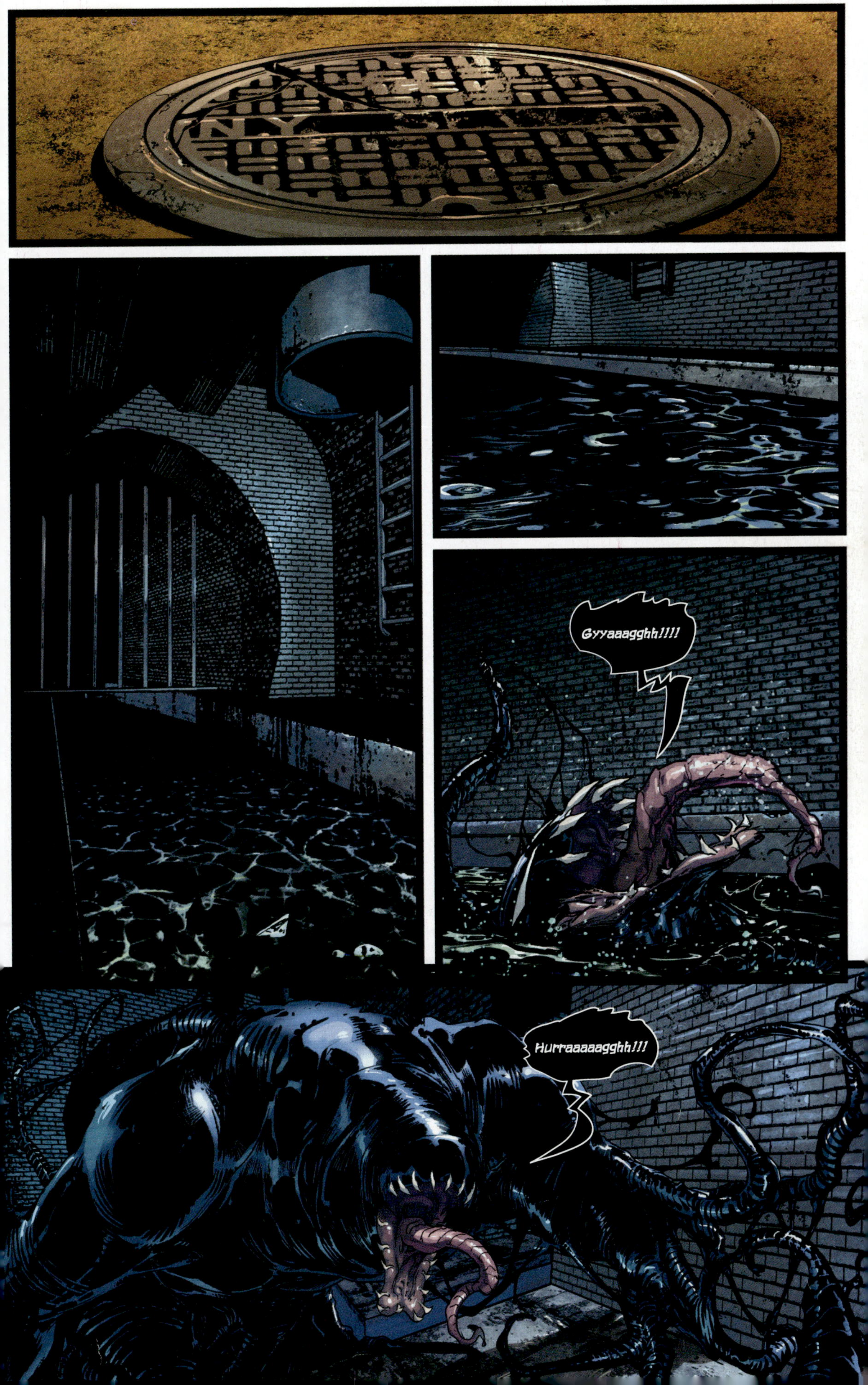
Gyyaaagghh!!!!
Hurraaaaagghh!!!

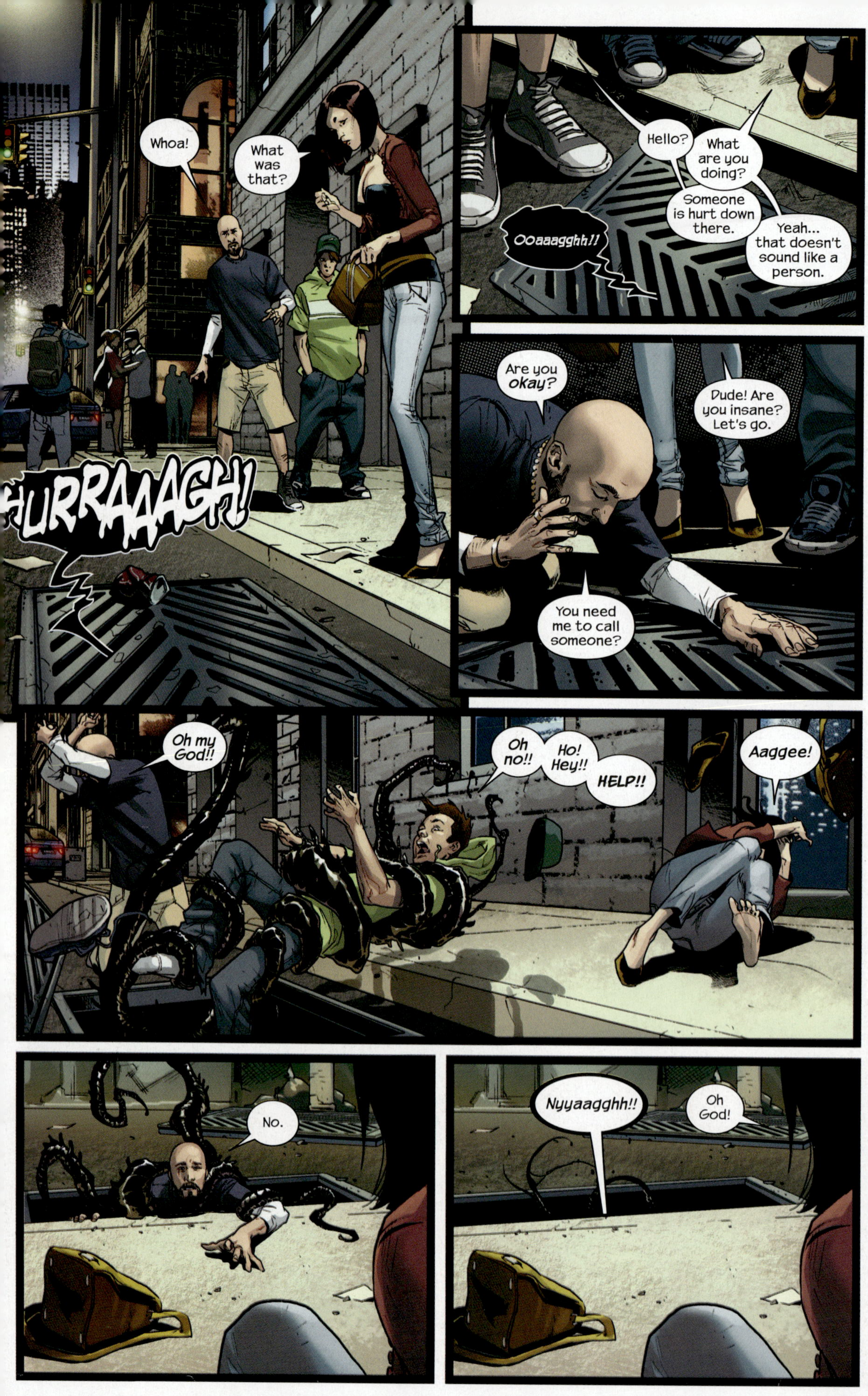

Whoa!
What was that?
HURRAAAGH!
Hello?
What are you doing?
Someone is hurt down there.
Yeah... that doesn't sound like a person.
Ooaaagghh!!
Are you okay?
Dude! Are you insane? Let's go.
You need me to call someone?
Oh my God!!
Oh no!!
Ho! Hey!!
HELP!!
Aaggee!
No.
Nyyaagghh!!
Oh God!

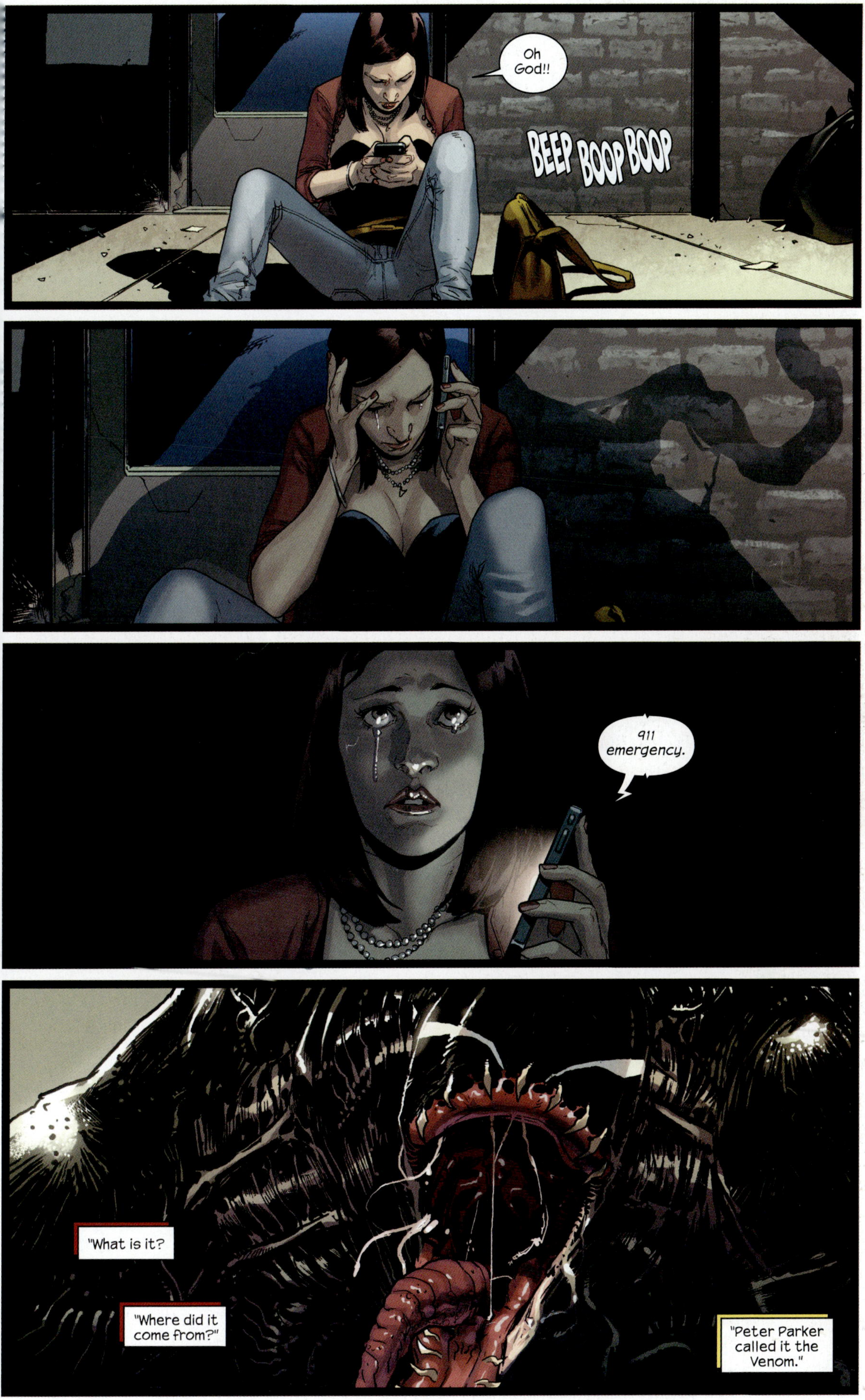

Oh God!!
BEEP BOOP BOOP
911 emergency.
"What is it?
"Where did it come from?"
"Peter Parker called it the Venom."

Peter Parker's father was working on a cure for cancer and he accidentally created it.

What?

Wow.

Yes.

Peter Parker has a father?

No.

That's what *that* thing is. It's a parasite.

It needs a host--a body to become what it is.

No host. No monster.

But with a host...

Well, you saw it.

Obviously it thinks this is where Spider-Man lives.

And obviously it's right.

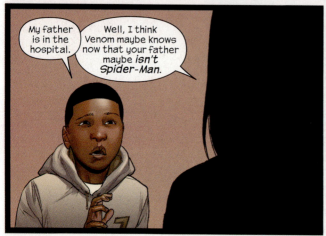

My father is in the hospital.

Well, I think Venom maybe knows now that your father maybe *isn't* Spider-Man.

How do *you* know so much about all this?

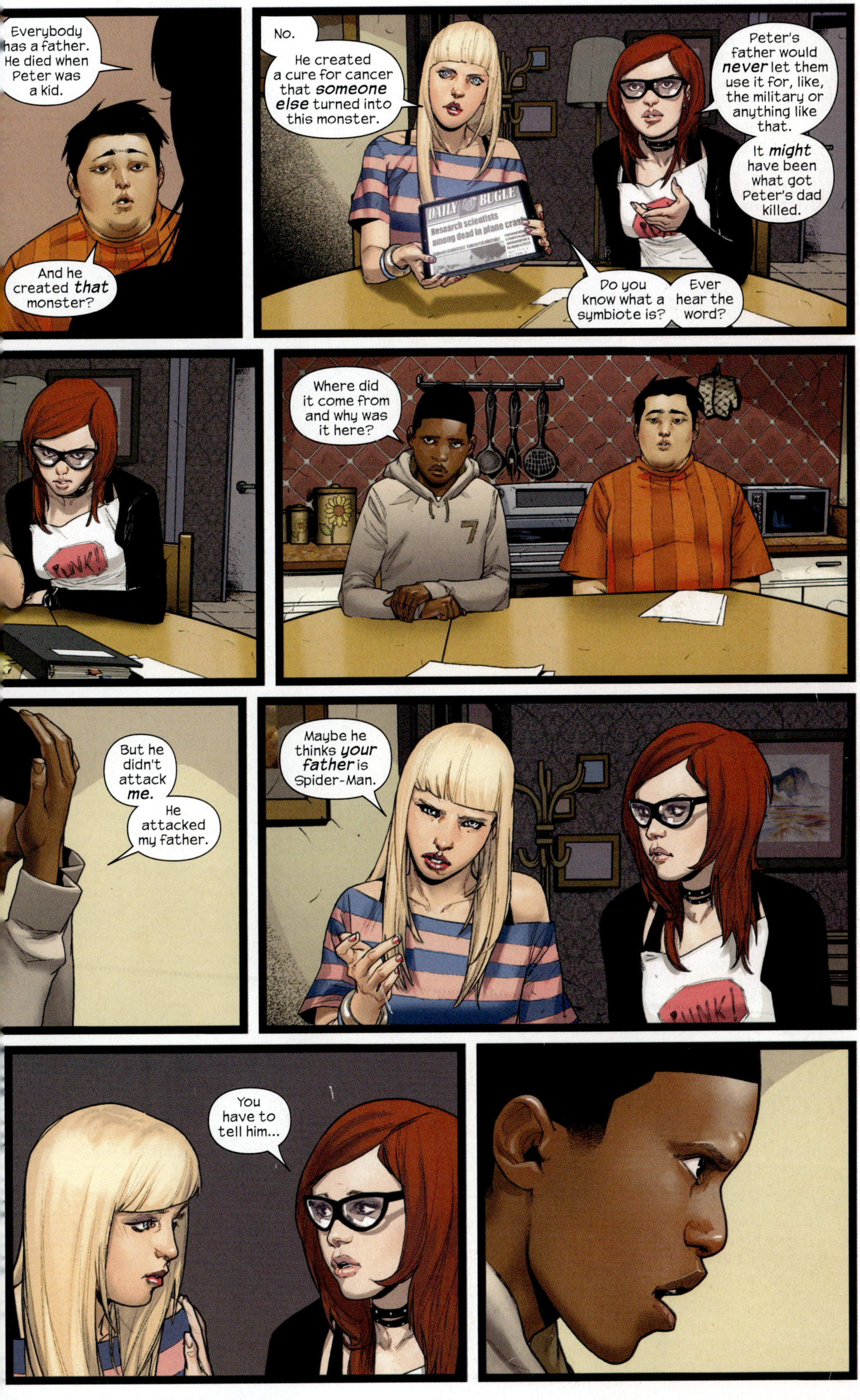
Everybody has a father. He died when Peter was a kid.
And he created *that* monster?
No.
He created a cure for cancer that *someone else* turned into this monster.
DAILY BUGLE
Research scientists among dead in plane cras
Peter's father would *never* let them use it for, like, the military or anything like that.
It *might* have been what got Peter's dad killed.
Do you know what a symbiote is?
Ever hear the word?
Where did it come from and why was it here?
But he didn't attack *me.*
He attacked my father.
Maybe he thinks *your father* is Spider-Man.
You have to tell him...

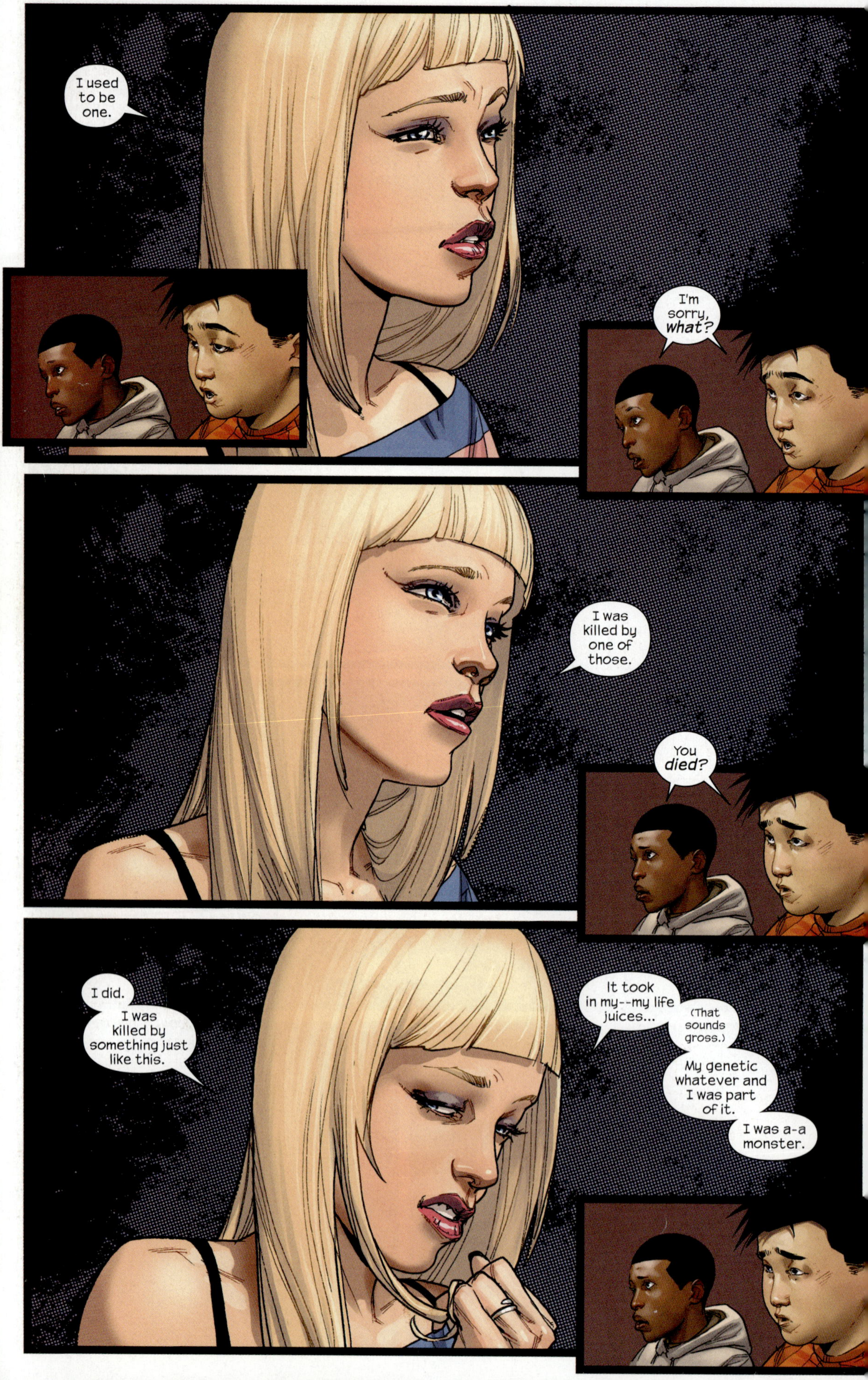

I used to be one.
I'm sorry, *what?*
I was killed by one of those.
You *died?*
I did.
I was killed by something just like this.
It took in my--my life juices...
(That sounds gross.)
My genetic whatever and I was part of it.
I was a-a monster.

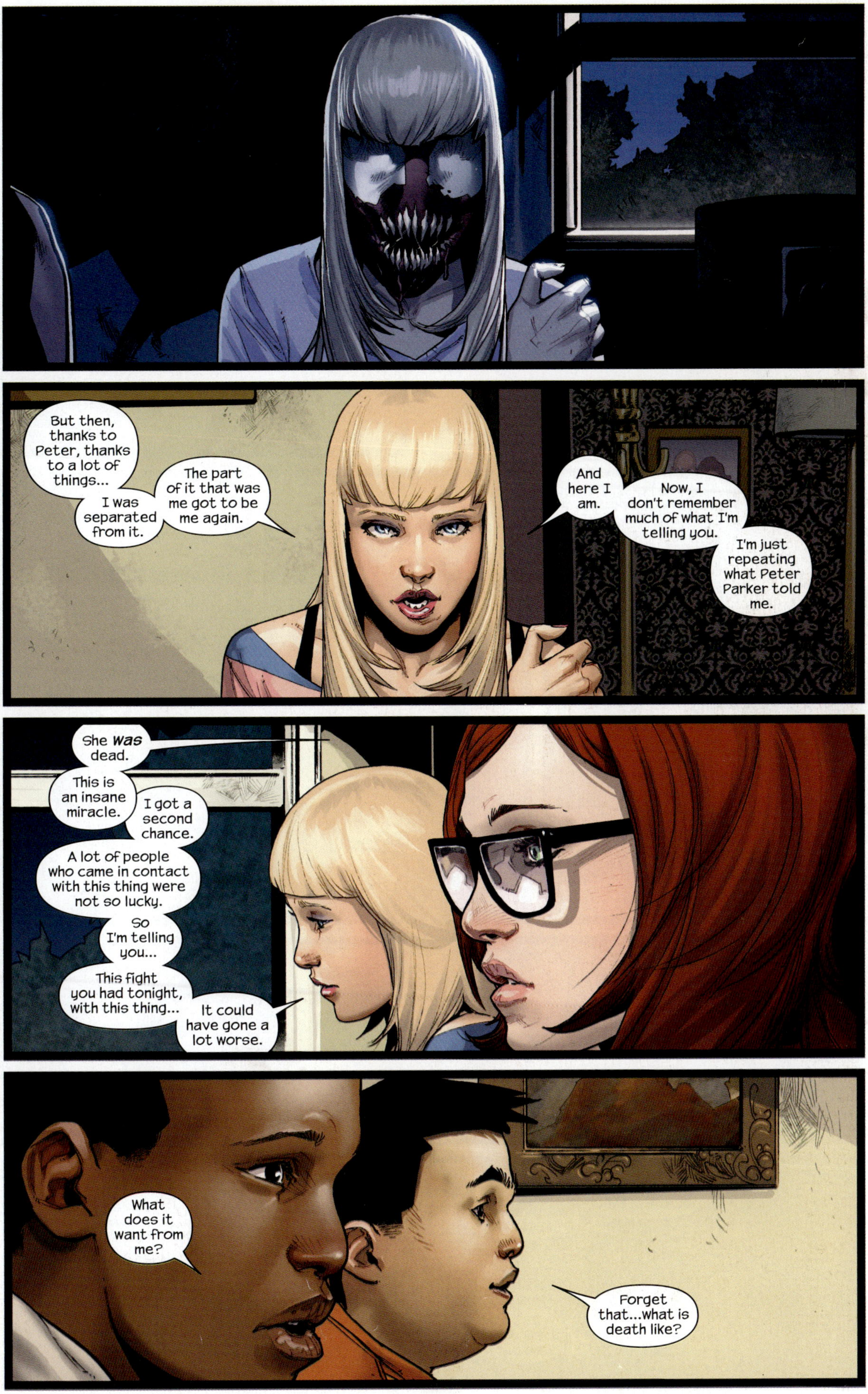
But then, thanks to Peter, thanks to a lot of things...
I was separated from it.
The part of it that was me got to be me again.
And here I am.
Now, I don't remember much of what I'm telling you.
I'm just repeating what Peter Parker told me.
She *was* dead.
This is an insane miracle.
I got a second chance.
A lot of people who came in contact with this thing were not so lucky.
So I'm telling you...
This fight you had tonight, with this thing...
It could have gone a lot worse.
What does it want from me?
Forget that...what is death like?

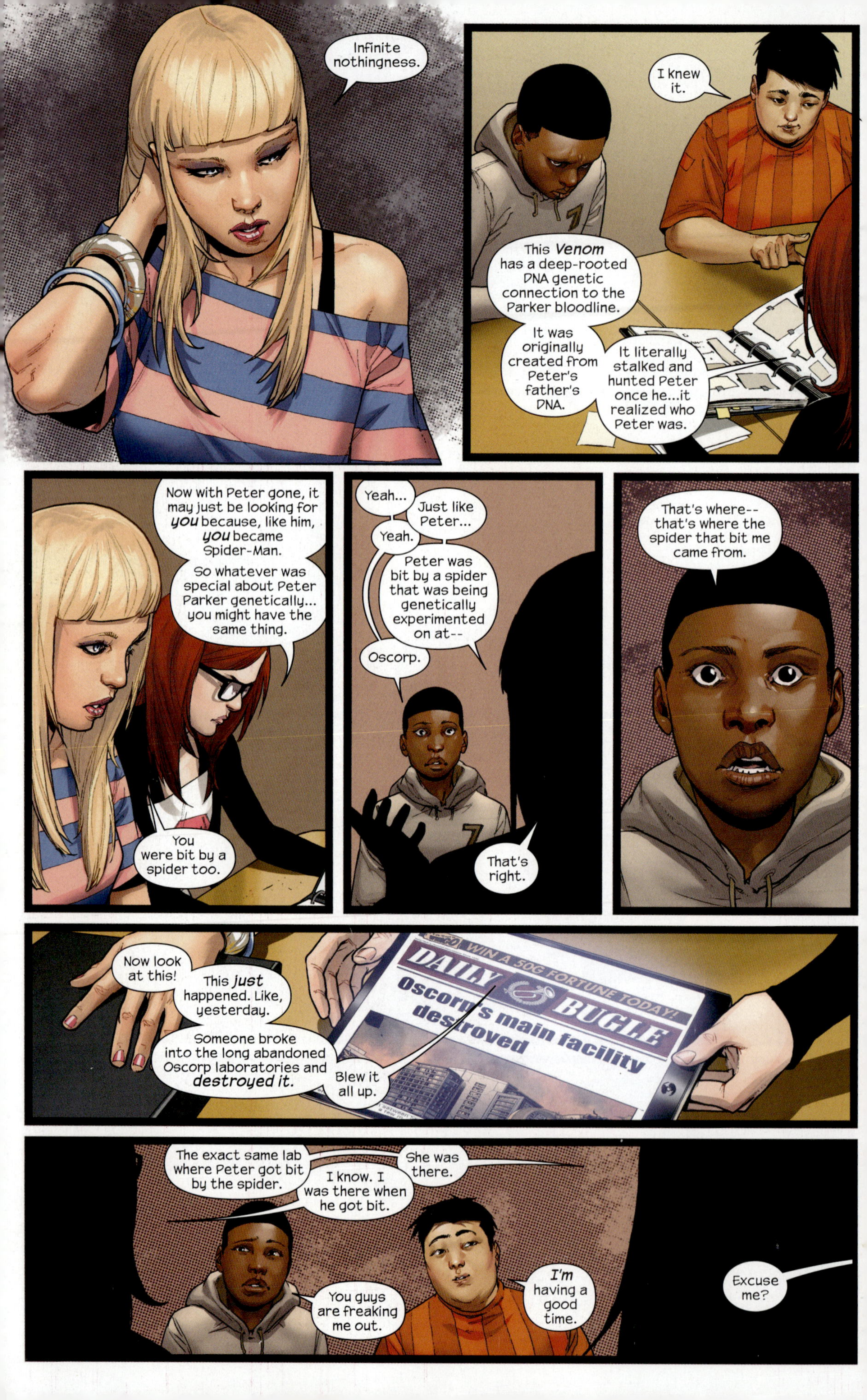
Infinite nothingness.
I knew it.
This *Venom* has a deep-rooted DNA genetic connection to the Parker bloodline.
It was originally created from Peter's father's DNA.
It literally stalked and hunted Peter once he...it realized who Peter was.
Now with Peter gone, it may just be looking for *you* because, like him, *you* became Spider-Man.
So whatever was special about Peter Parker genetically... you might have the same thing.
You were bit by a spider too.
Yeah...
Just like Peter...
Yeah.
Peter was bit by a spider that was being genetically experimented on at--
Oscorp.
That's right.
That's where-- that's where the spider that bit me came from.
Now look at this!
This *just* happened. Like, yesterday.
Someone broke into the long abandoned Oscorp laboratories and *destroyed it.*
Blew it all up.
WIN A 50G FORTUNE TODAY!
DAILY BUGLE
Oscorp's main facility destroyed
The exact same lab where Peter got bit by the spider.
She was there.
I know. I was there when he got bit.
You guys are freaking me out.
I'm having a good time.
Excuse me?

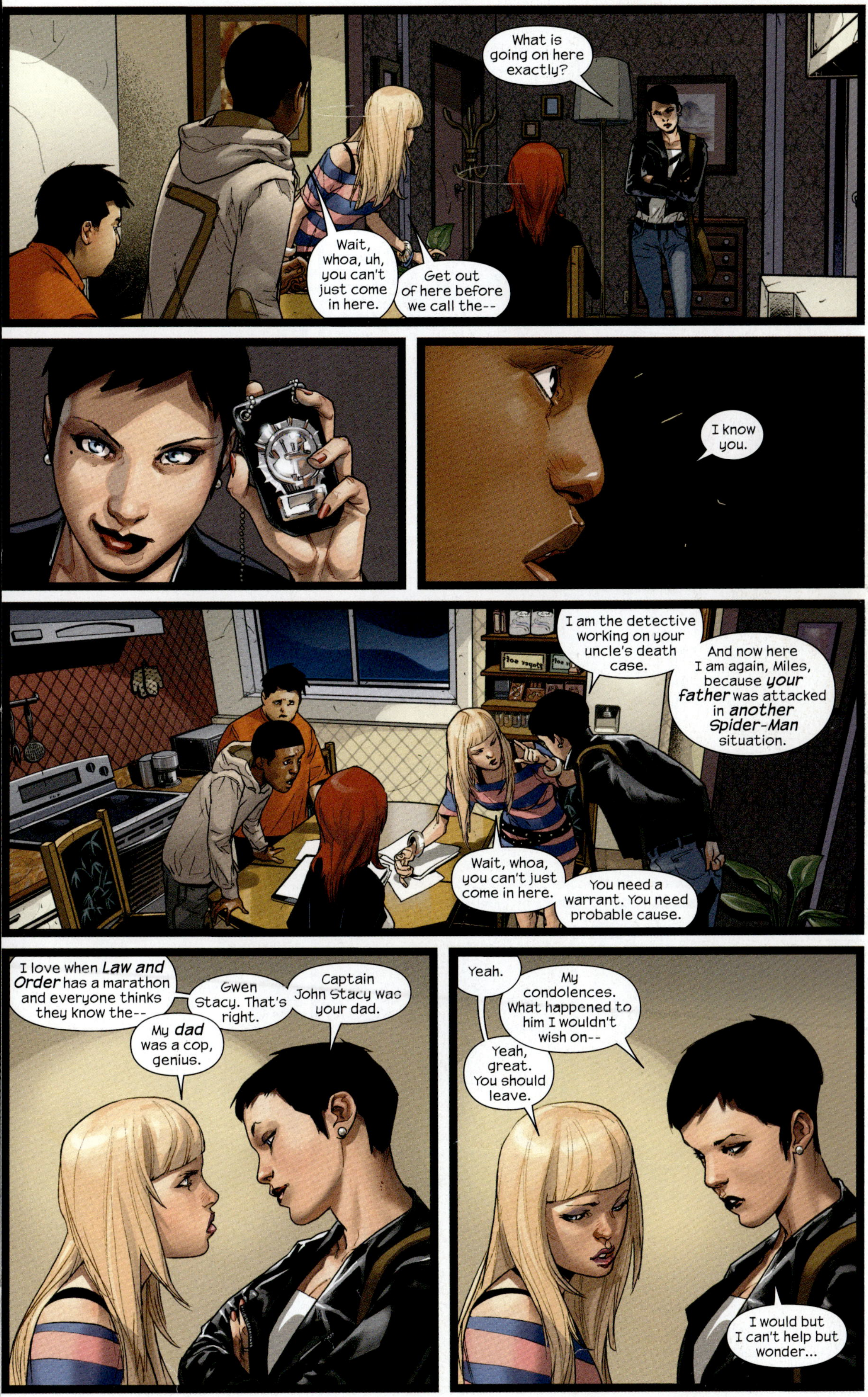
What is going on here exactly?
Wait, whoa, uh, you can't just come in here.
Get out of here before we call the--
I know you.
I am the detective working on your uncle's death case.
And now here I am again, Miles, because *your father* was attacked in *another Spider-Man* situation.
Wait, whoa, you can't just come in here.
You need a warrant. You need probable cause.
I love when *Law and Order* has a marathon and everyone thinks they know the--
My *dad* was a cop, genius.
Gwen Stacy. That's right.
Captain John Stacy was your dad.
Yeah.
My condolences. What happened to him I wouldn't wish on--
Yeah, great. You should leave.
I would but I can't help but wonder...

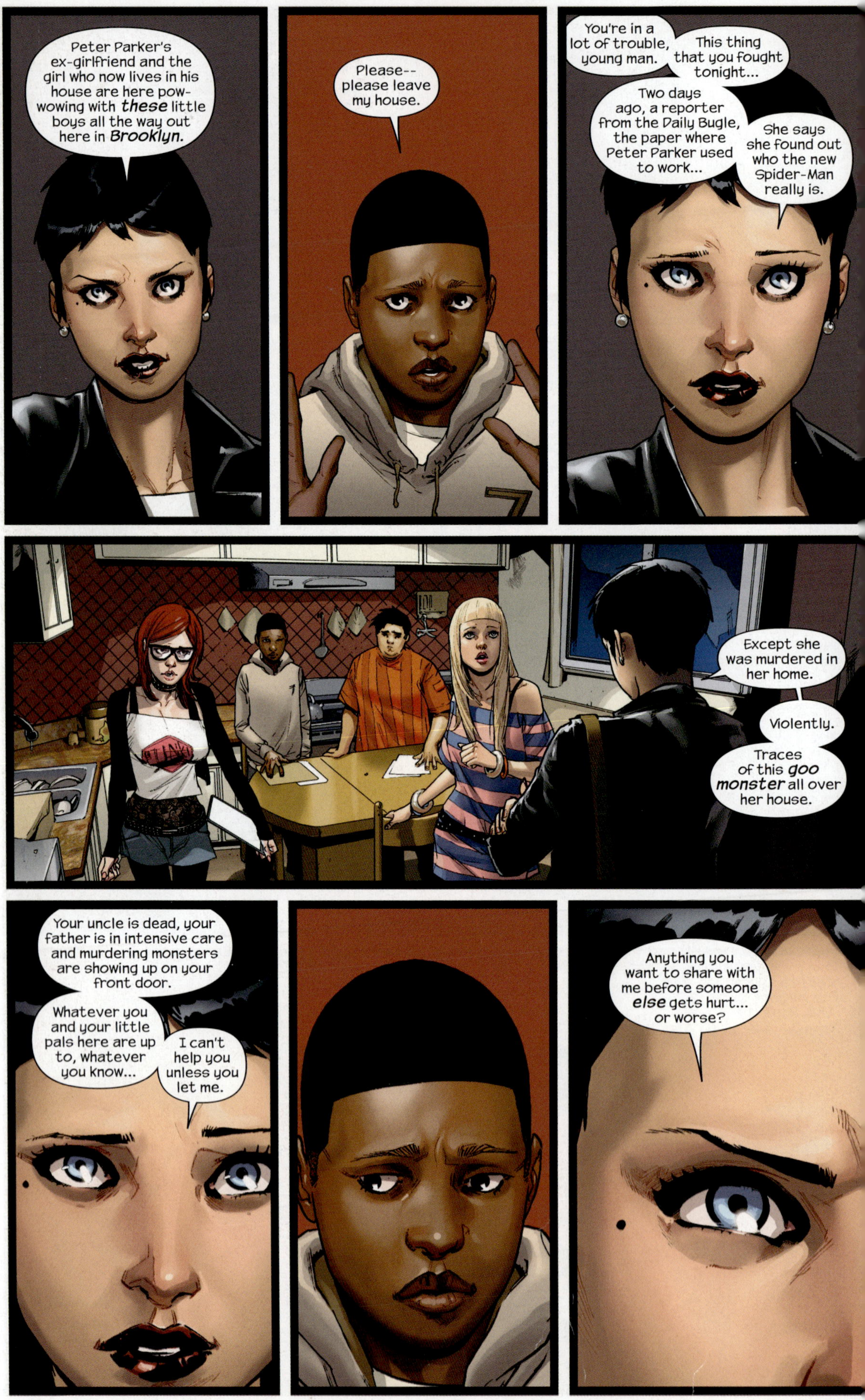
Peter Parker's ex-girlfriend and the girl who now lives in his house are here pow-wowing with *these* little boys all the way out here in *Brooklyn.*
Please-- please leave my house.
You're in a lot of trouble, young man.
This thing that you fought tonight...
Two days ago, a reporter from the Daily Bugle, the paper where Peter Parker used to work...
She says she found out who the new Spider-Man really is.
Except she was murdered in her home.
Violently.
Traces of this *goo monster* all over her house.
Your uncle is dead, your father is in intensive care and murdering monsters are showing up on your front door.
Whatever you and your little pals here are up to, whatever you know...
I can't help you unless you let me.
Anything you want to share with me before someone *else* gets hurt... or worse?

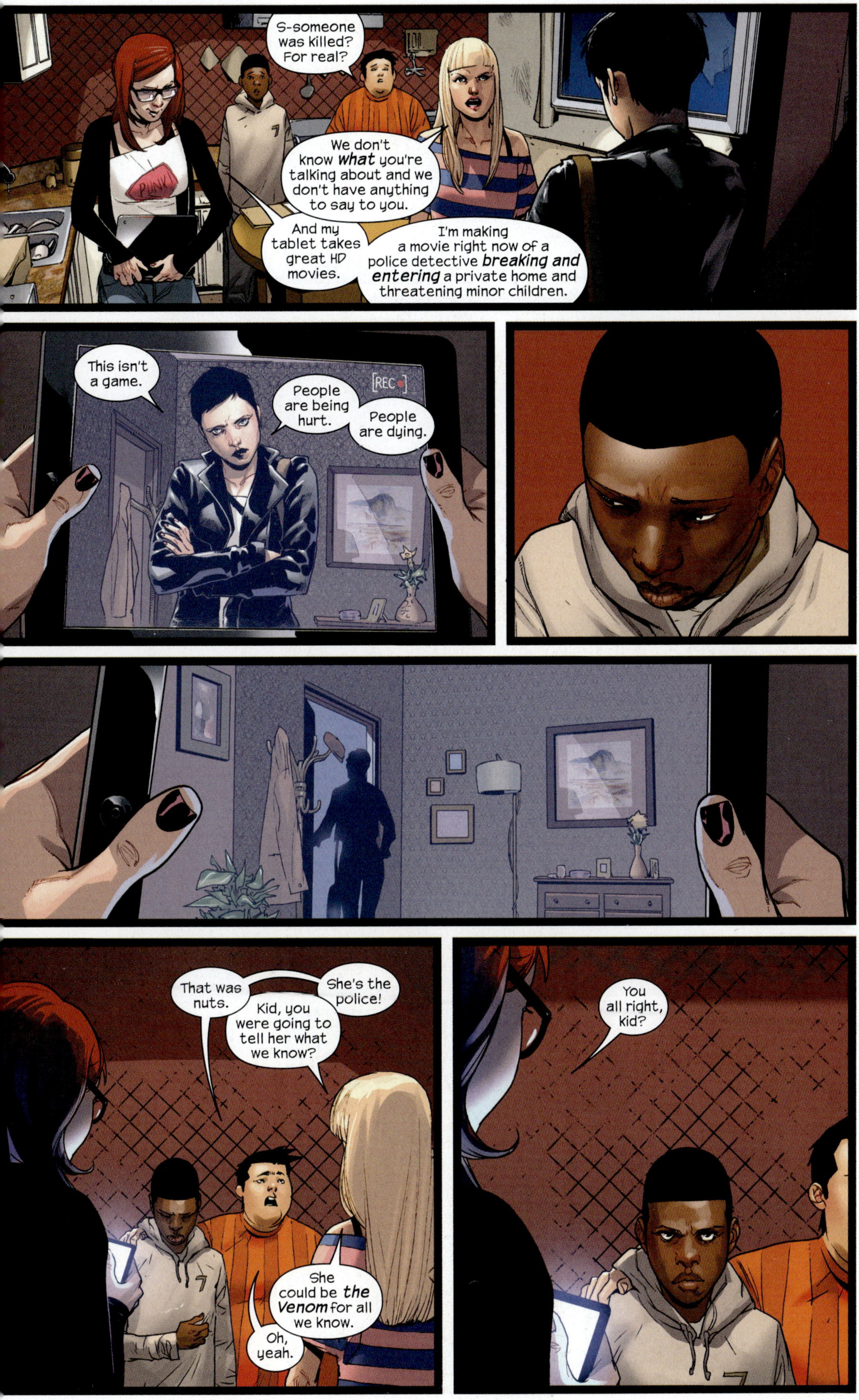
S-someone was killed? For real?
We don't know *what* you're talking about and we don't have anything to say to you.
And my tablet takes great HD movies.
I'm making a movie right now of a police detective *breaking and entering* a private home and threatening minor children.
This isn't a game.
REC
People are being hurt.
People are dying.
That was nuts.
She's the police!
Kid, you were going to tell her what we know?
She could be *the Venom* for all we know.
Oh, yeah.
You all right, kid?

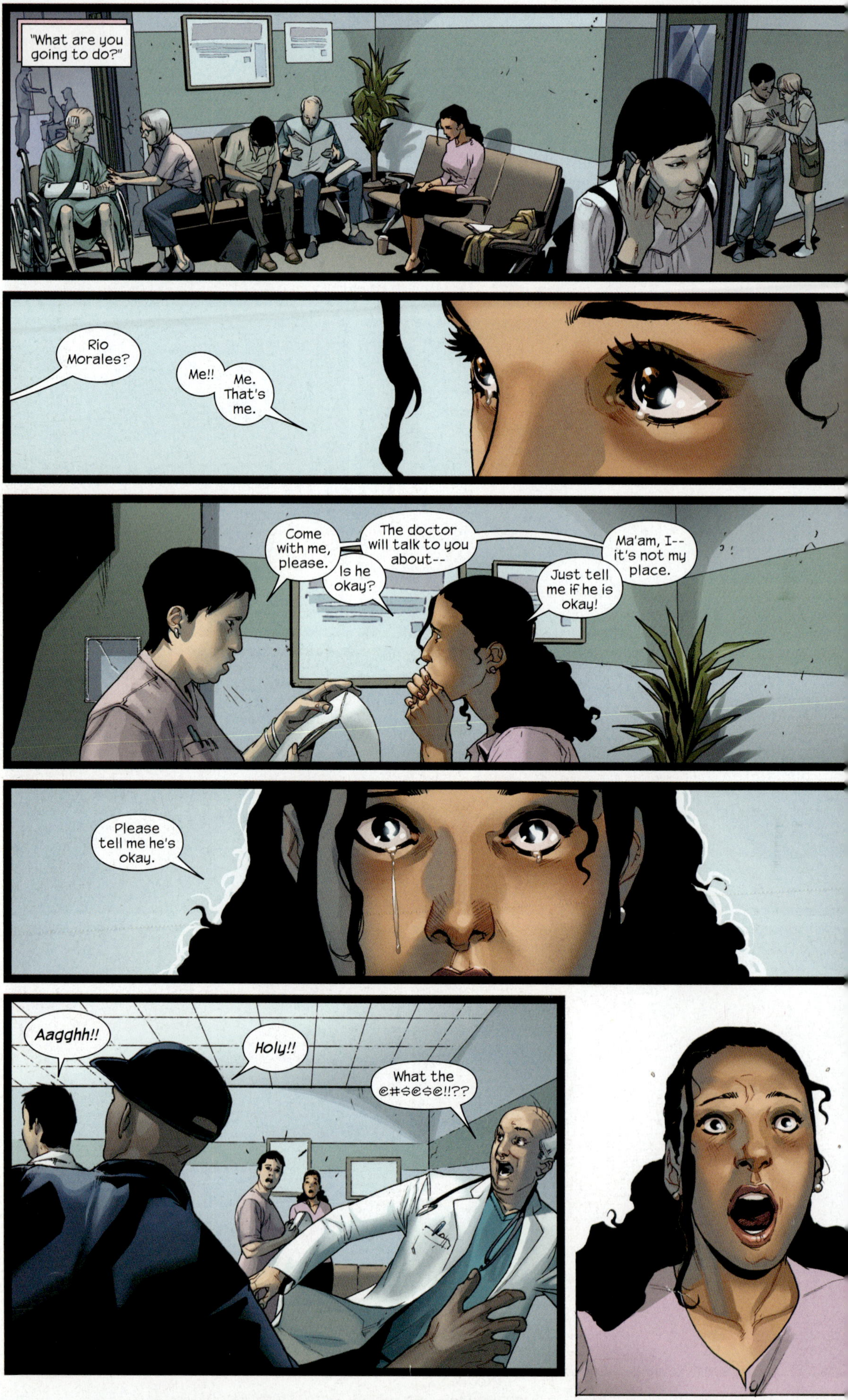
"What are you going to do?"
Rio Morales?
Me!!
Me. That's me.
Come with me, please.
The doctor will talk to you about--
Is he okay?
Ma'am, I-- it's not my place.
Just tell me if he is okay!
Please tell me he's okay.
Aagghh!!
Holy!!
What the @#$@$@!!??

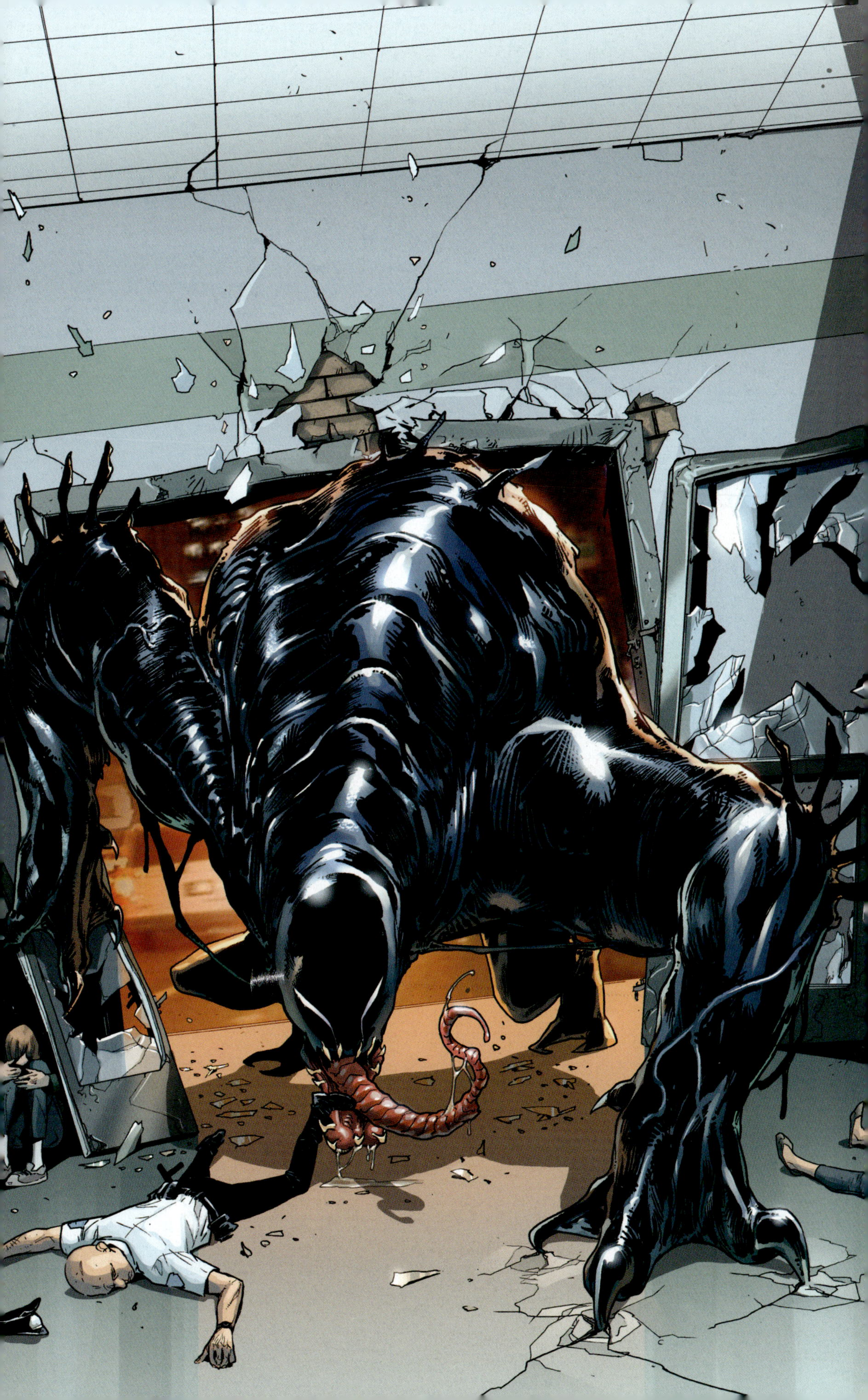

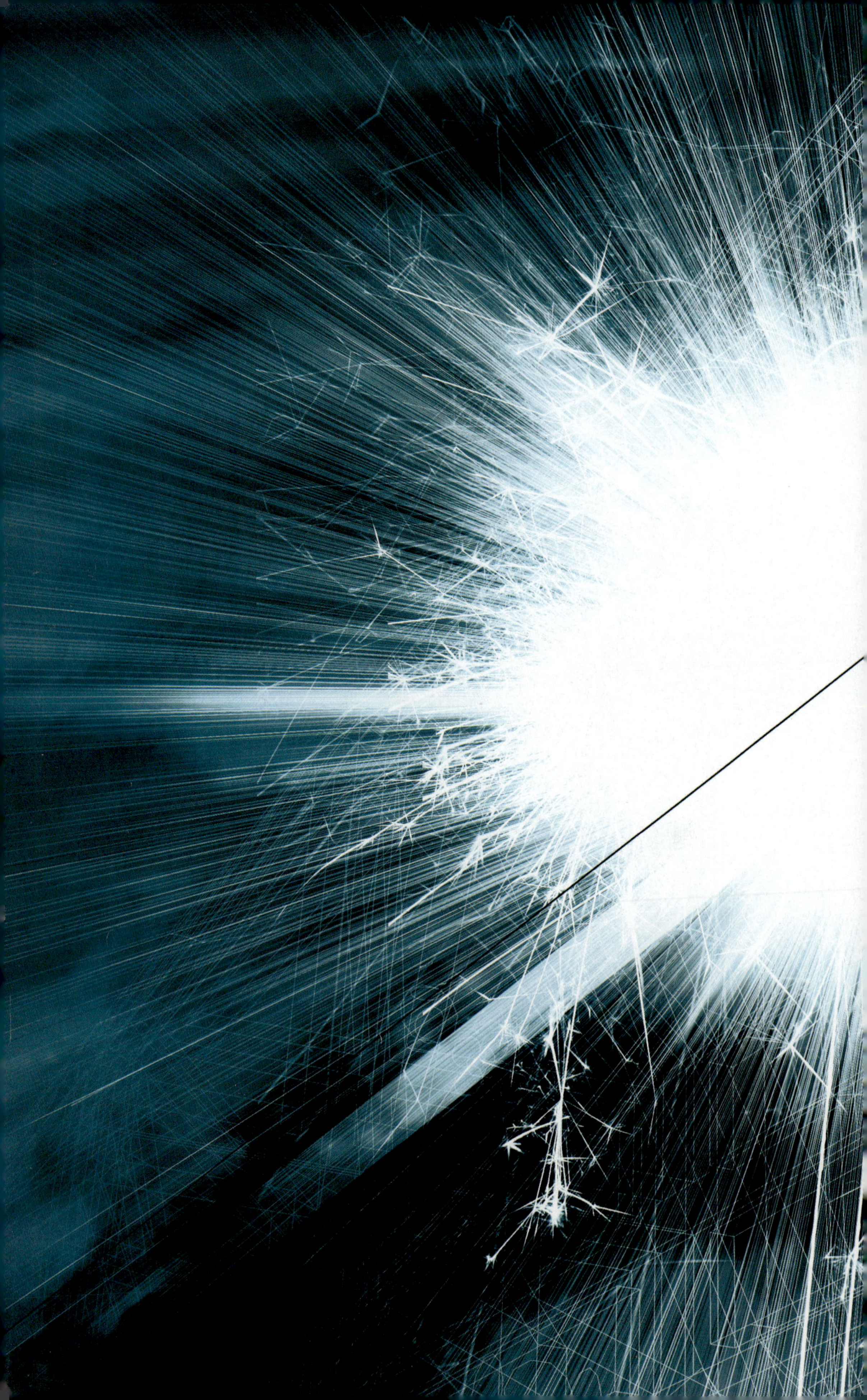

VENOM WAR

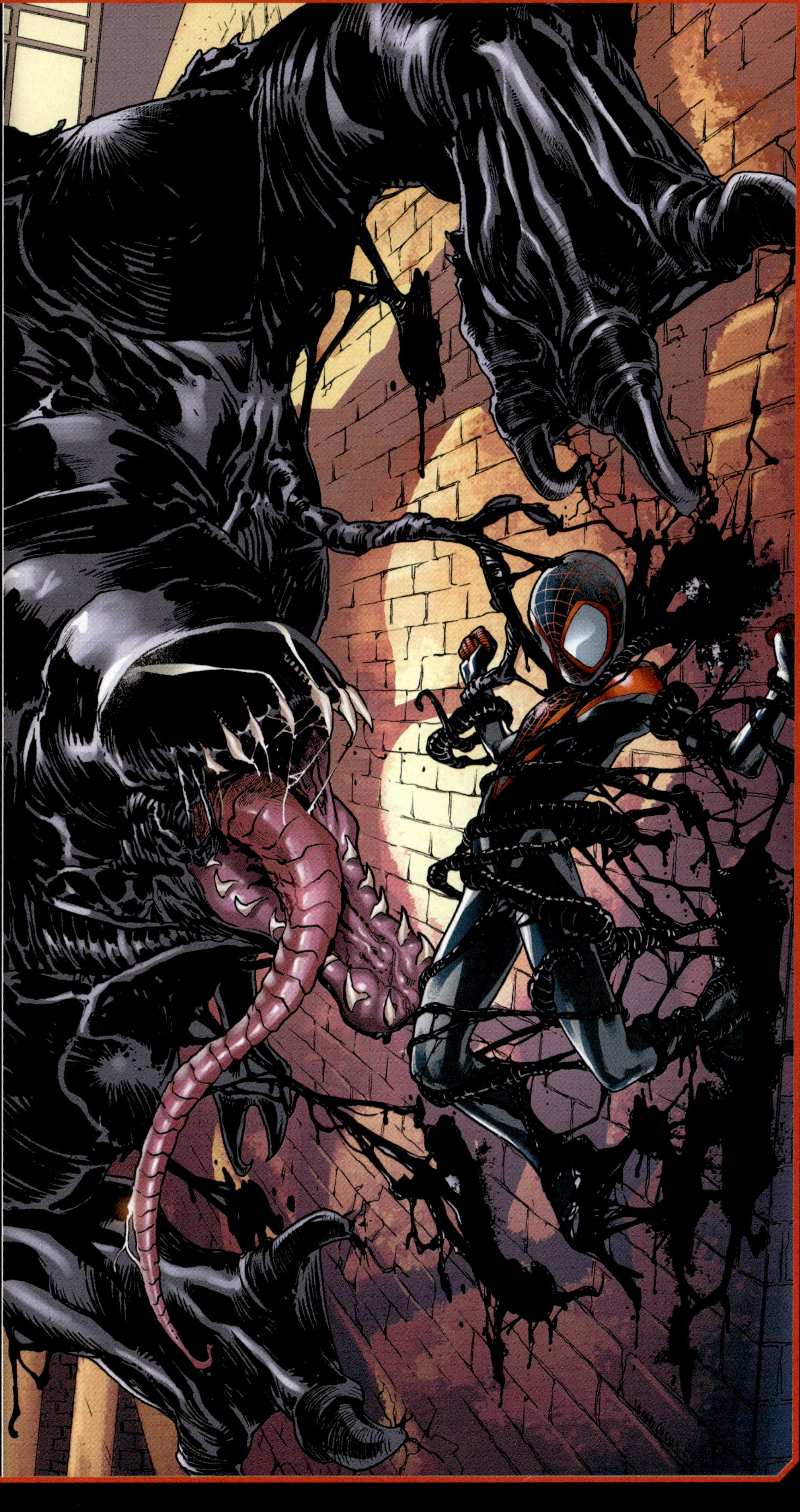

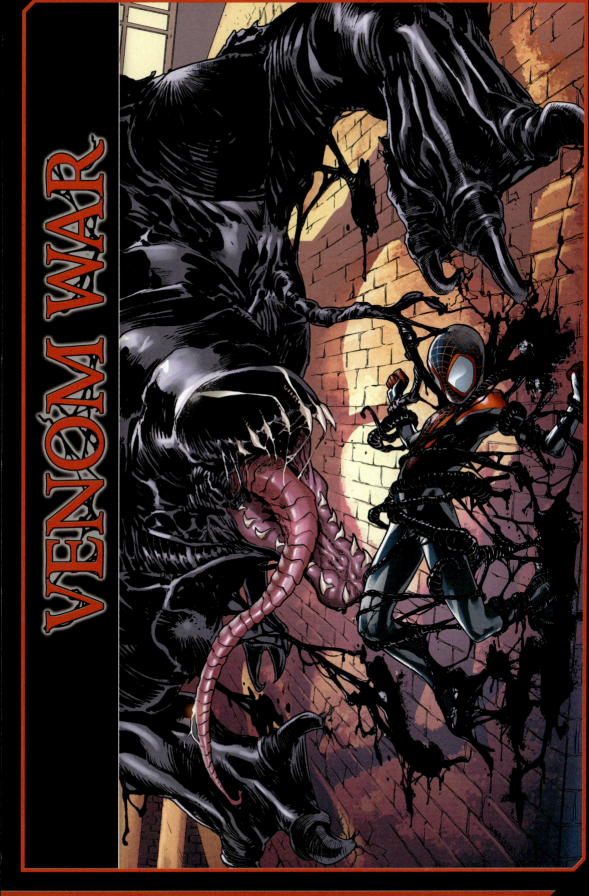

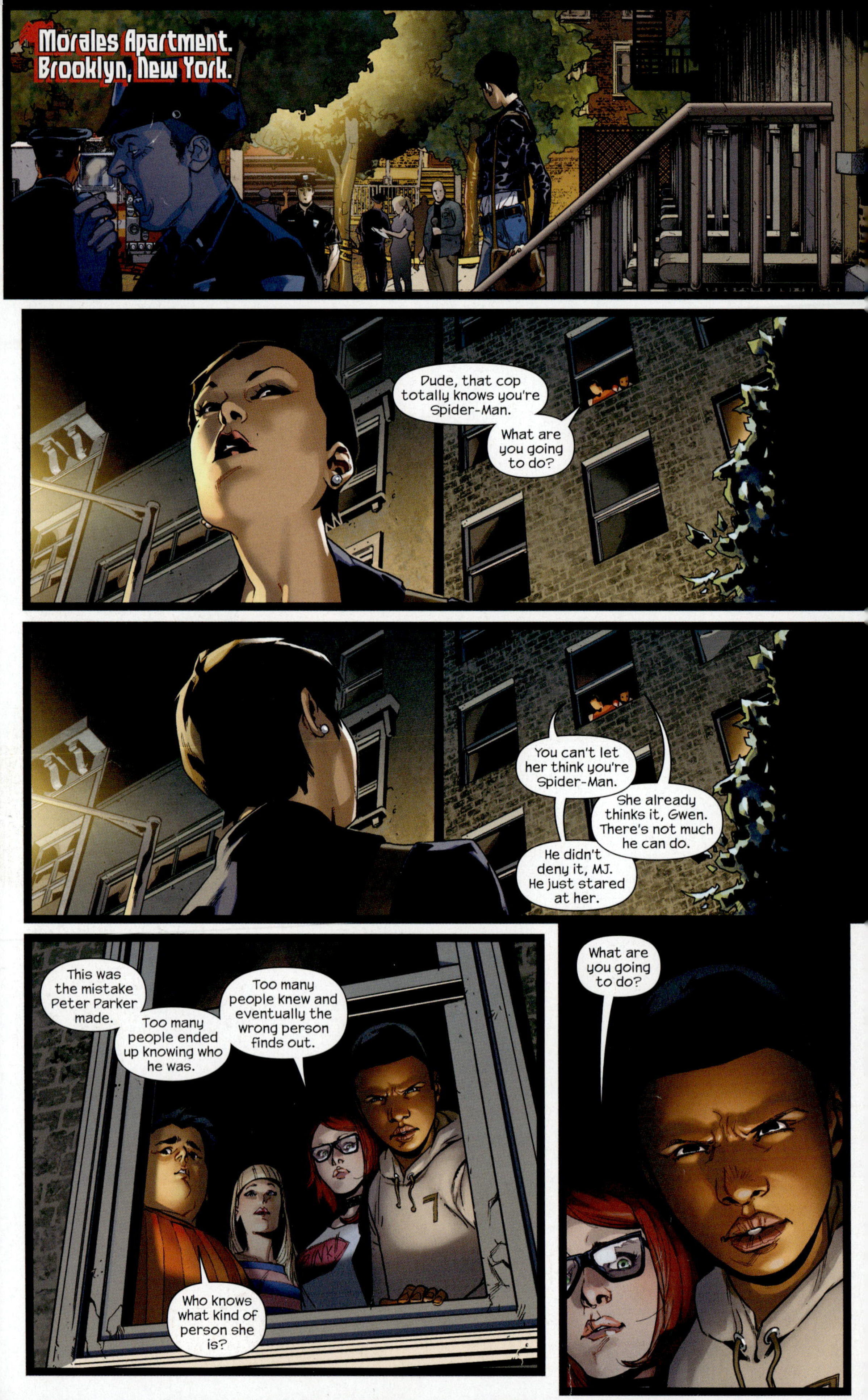
Morales Apartment.
Brooklyn, New York.
Dude, that cop totally knows you're Spider-Man.
What are you going to do?
You can't let her think you're Spider-Man.
She already thinks it, Gwen. There's not much he can do.
He didn't deny it, MJ. He just stared at her.
This was the mistake Peter Parker made.
Too many people ended up knowing who he was.
Too many people knew and eventually the wrong person finds out.
Who knows what kind of person she is?
What are you going to do?

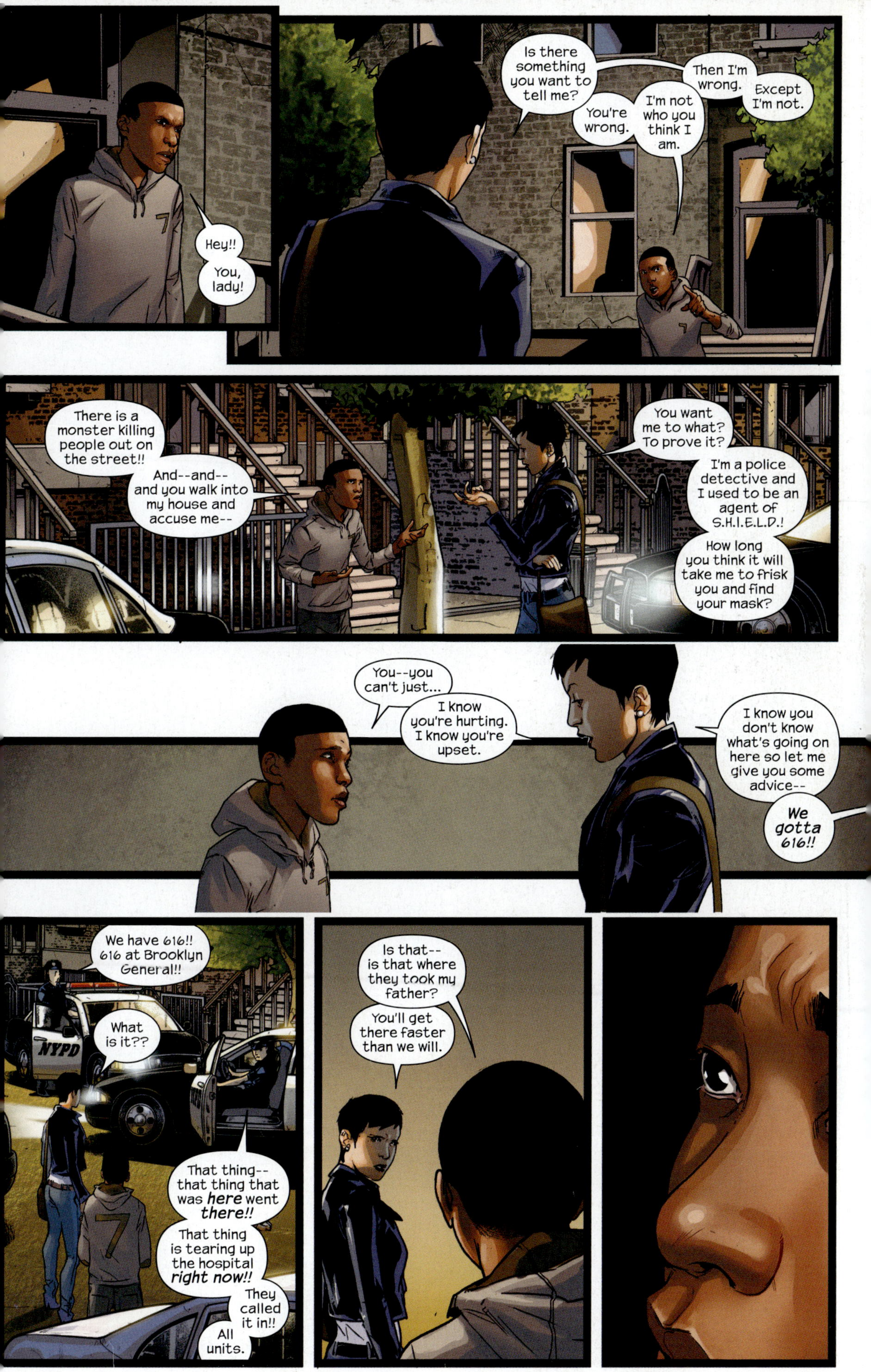
Hey!!
You, lady!
Is there something you want to tell me?
You're wrong.
I'm not who you think I am.
Then I'm wrong.
Except I'm not.
There is a monster killing people out on the street!!
And--and--and you walk into my house and accuse me--
You want me to what? To prove it?
I'm a police detective and I used to be an agent of S.H.I.E.L.D.!
How long you think it will take me to frisk you and find your mask?
You--you can't just...
I know you're hurting. I know you're upset.
I know you don't know what's going on here so let me give you some advice--
We gotta 616!!
We have 616!! 616 at Brooklyn General!!
What is it??
That thing--that thing that was here went there!!
That thing is tearing up the hospital right now!!
They called it in!!
All units.
Is that--is that where they took my father?
You'll get there faster than we will.

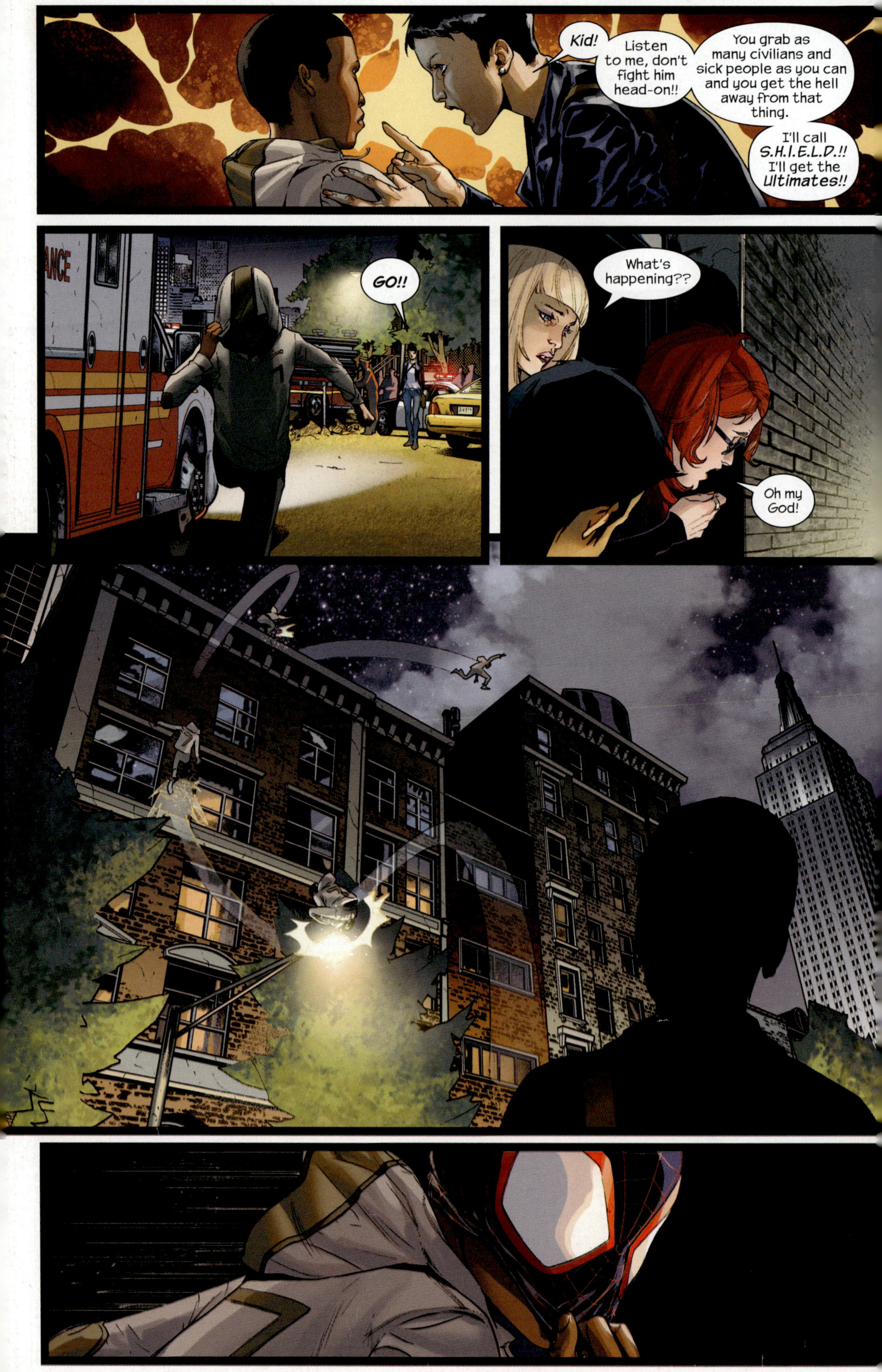
Kid!
Listen to me, don't fight him head-on!!
You grab as many civilians and sick people as you can and you get the hell away from that thing.
I'll call S.H.I.E.L.D.!! I'll get the Ultimates!!
ANCE
GO!!
What's happening??
Oh my God!

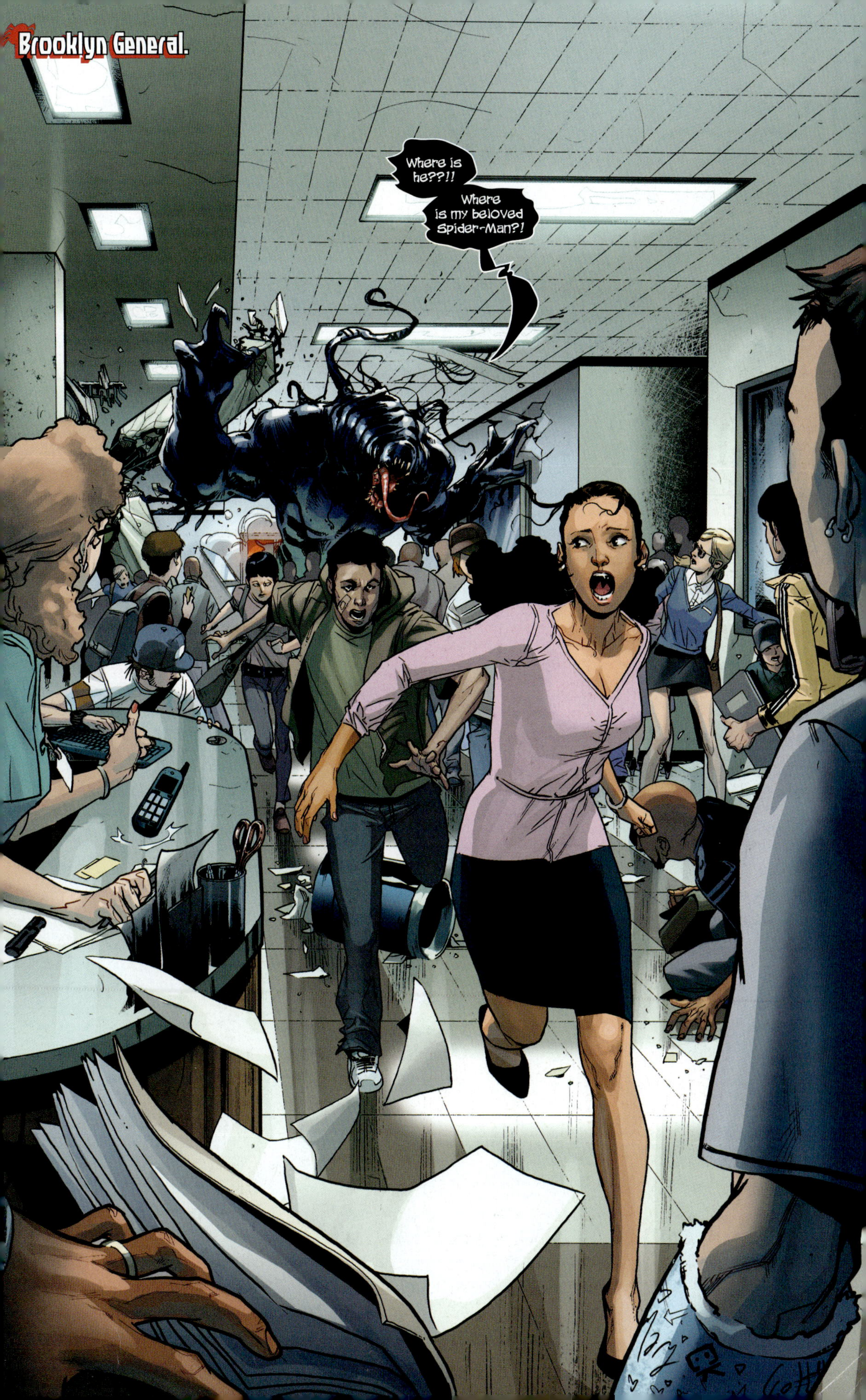
Brooklyn General.
Where is he??!!
Where is my beloved Spider-Man?!

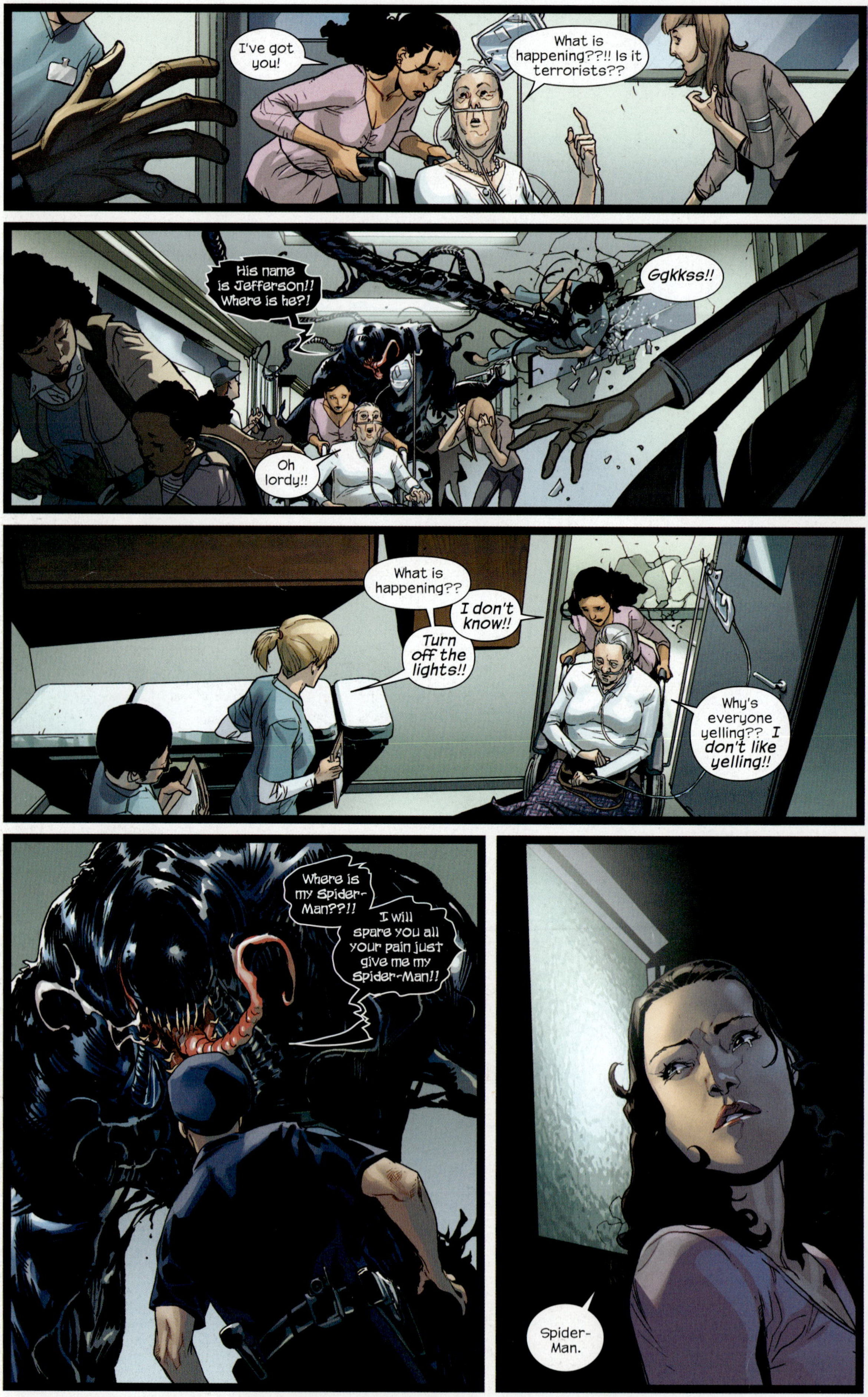
I've got you!
What is happening??!! Is it terrorists??
His name is Jefferson!! Where is he?!
Ggkkss!!
Oh lordy!!
What is happening??
I don't know!!
Turn off the lights!!
Why's everyone yelling?? I don't like yelling!!
Where is my Spider-Man??!!
I will spare you all your pain just give me my Spider-Man!!
Spider-Man.

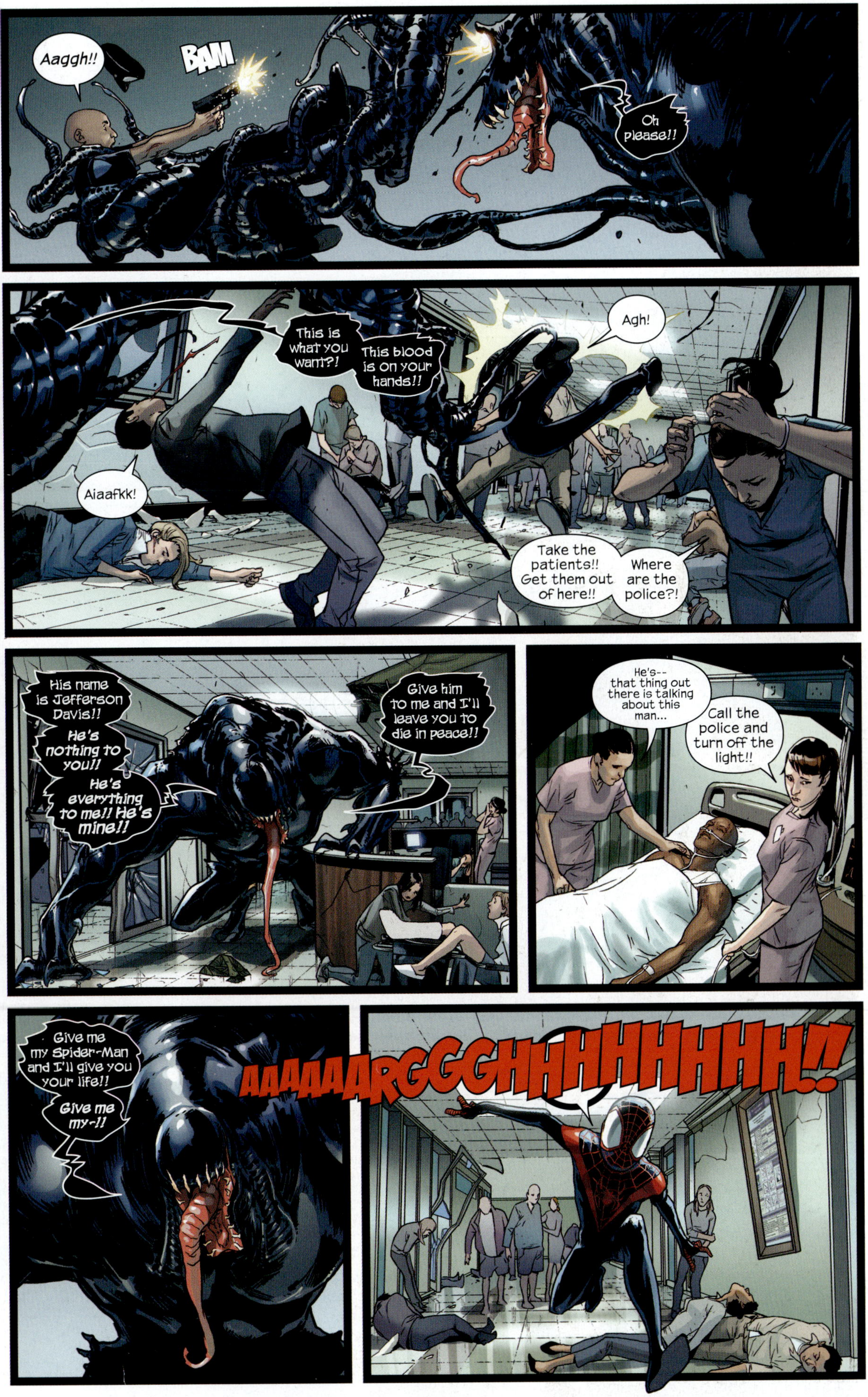
Aaggh!!
BAM
Oh please!!
This is what you want?!
This blood is on your hands!!
Agh!
Aiaafkk!
Take the patients!! Get them out of here!!
Where are the police?!
His name is Jefferson Davis!!
He's nothing to you!!
He's everything to me!! He's mine!!
Give him to me and I'll leave you to die in peace!!
He's-- that thing out there is talking about this man...
Call the police and turn off the light!!
Give me my Spider-Man and I'll give you your life!!
Give me my--!!
AAAAAARGGGHHHHHHHH!!

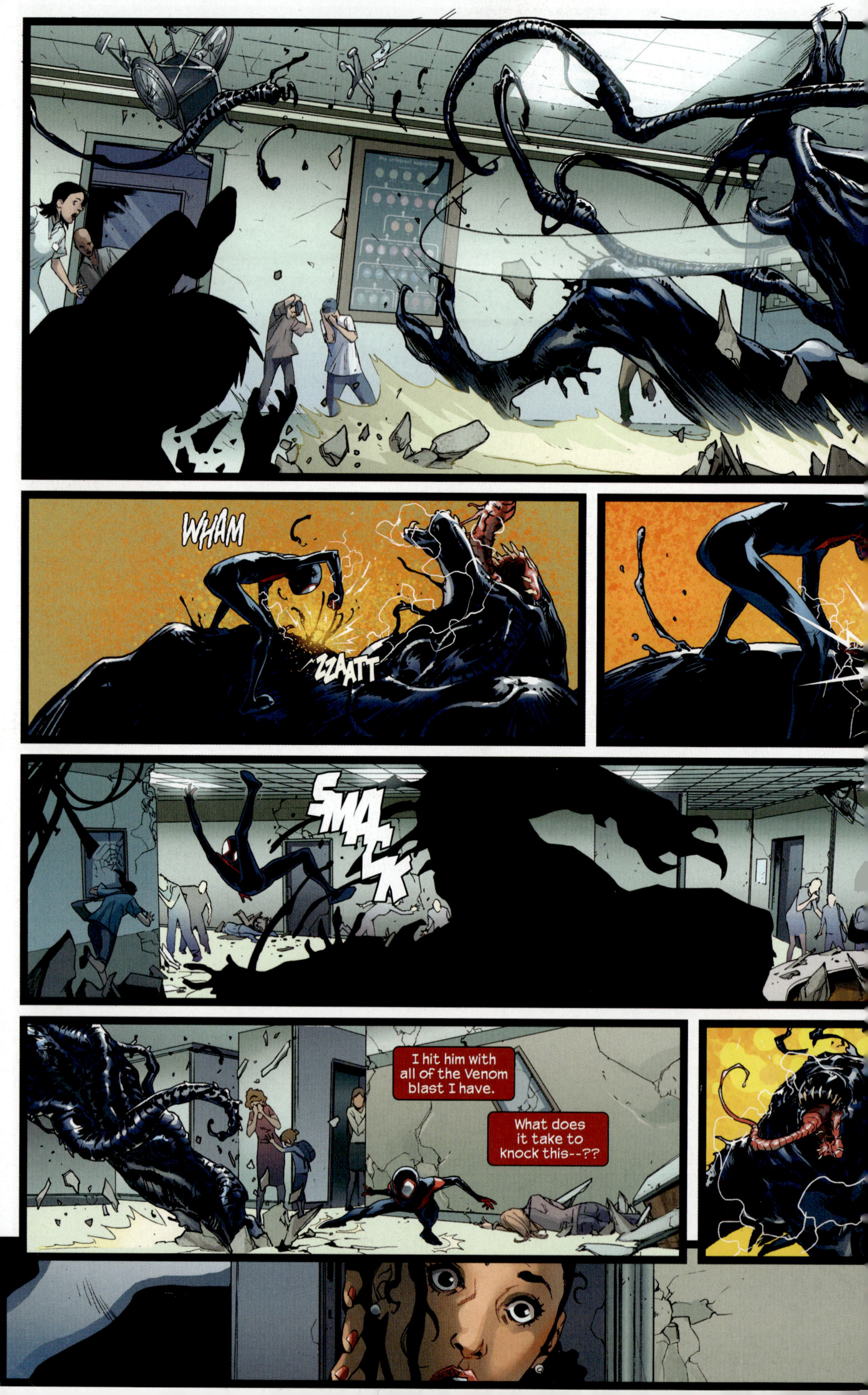
WHAM
ZZAATT
SMACK
I hit him with all of the Venom blast I have.
What does it take to knock this--??

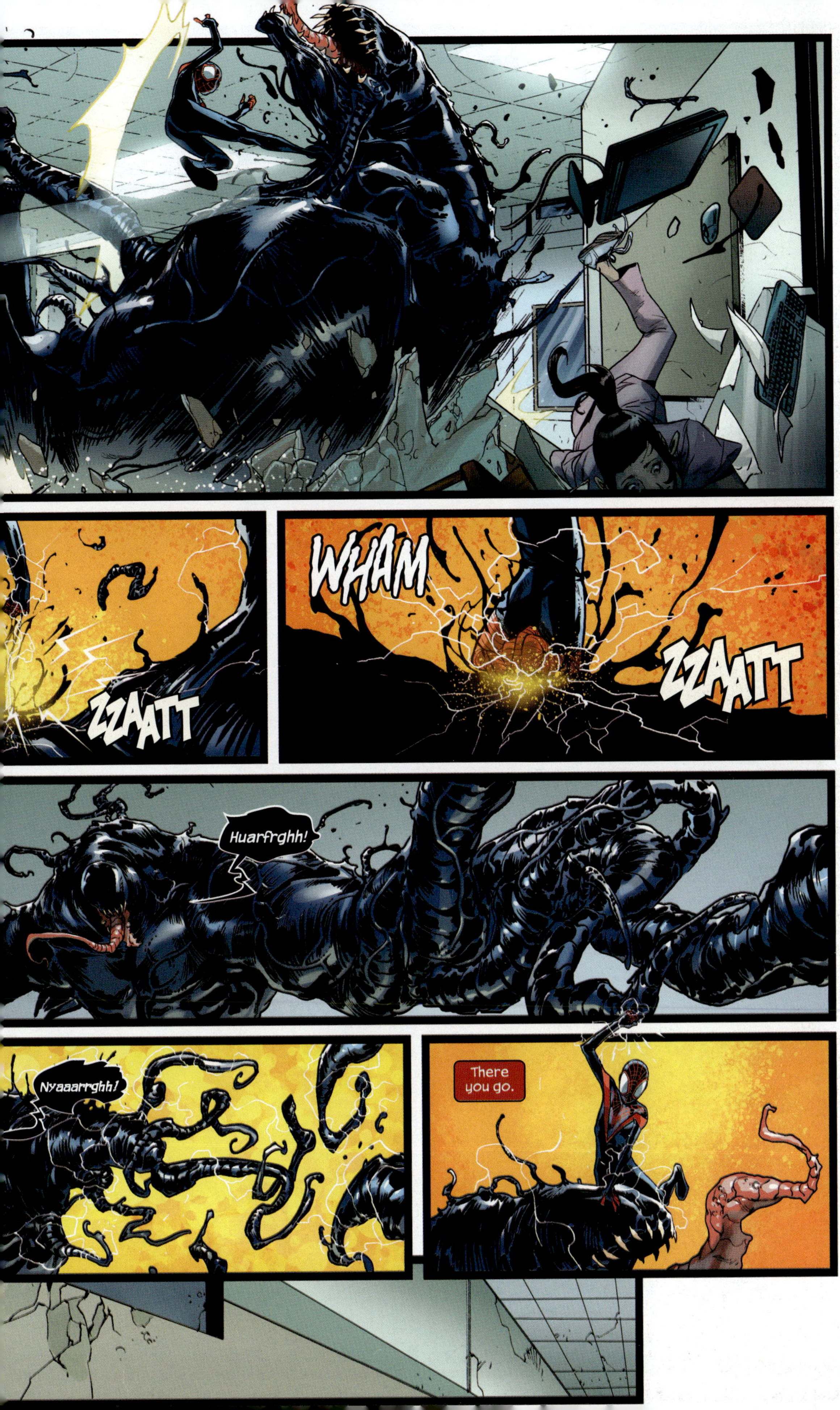
ZZAATT
WHAM
ZZAATT
Huarfrghh!
Nyaaarrghh!
There you go.

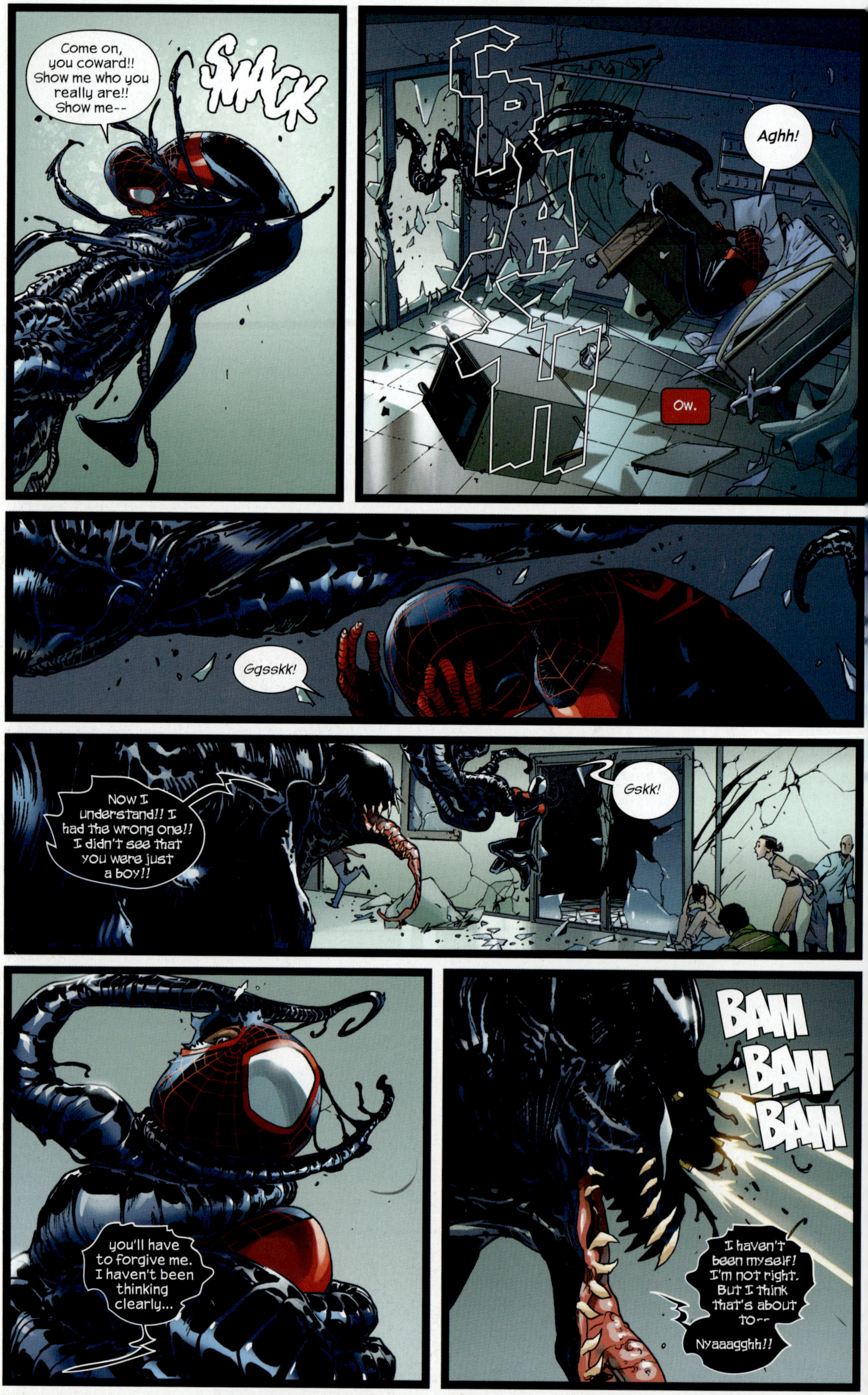
Come on, you coward!! Show me who you really are!! Show me--
SMACK
CRASH
Aghh!
Ow.
Ggsskk!
Now I understand!! I had the wrong one!! I didn't see that you were just a boy!!
Gskk!
you'll have to forgive me. I haven't been thinking clearly...
BAM BAM BAM
I haven't been myself! I'm not right. But I think that's about to--
Nyaaagghh!!

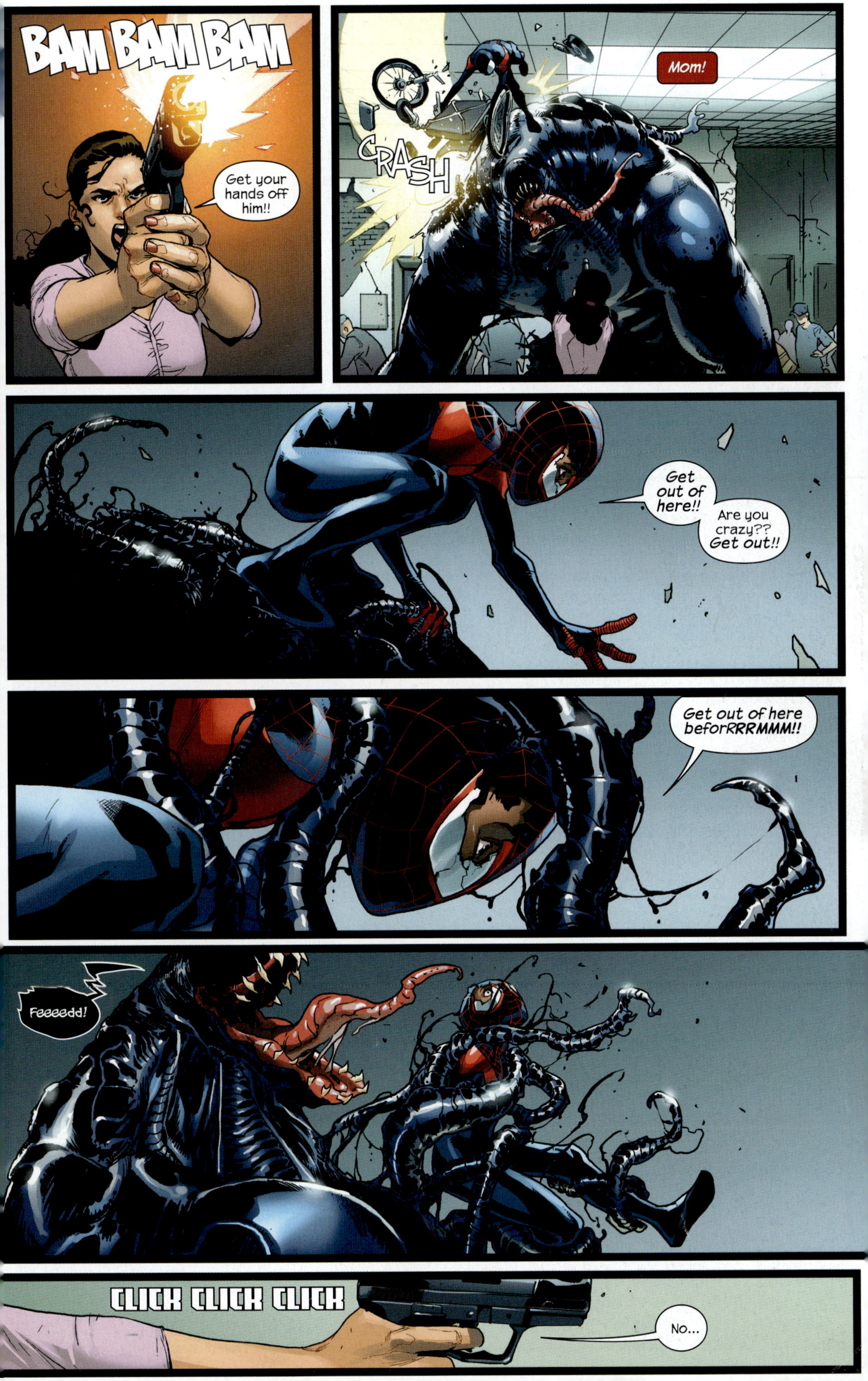
BAM BAM BAM
Get your hands off him!!
CRASH
Mom!
Get out of here!!
Are you crazy?? Get out!!
Get out of here beforRRRMMM!!
Feeeedd!
CLICK CLICK CLICK
No...

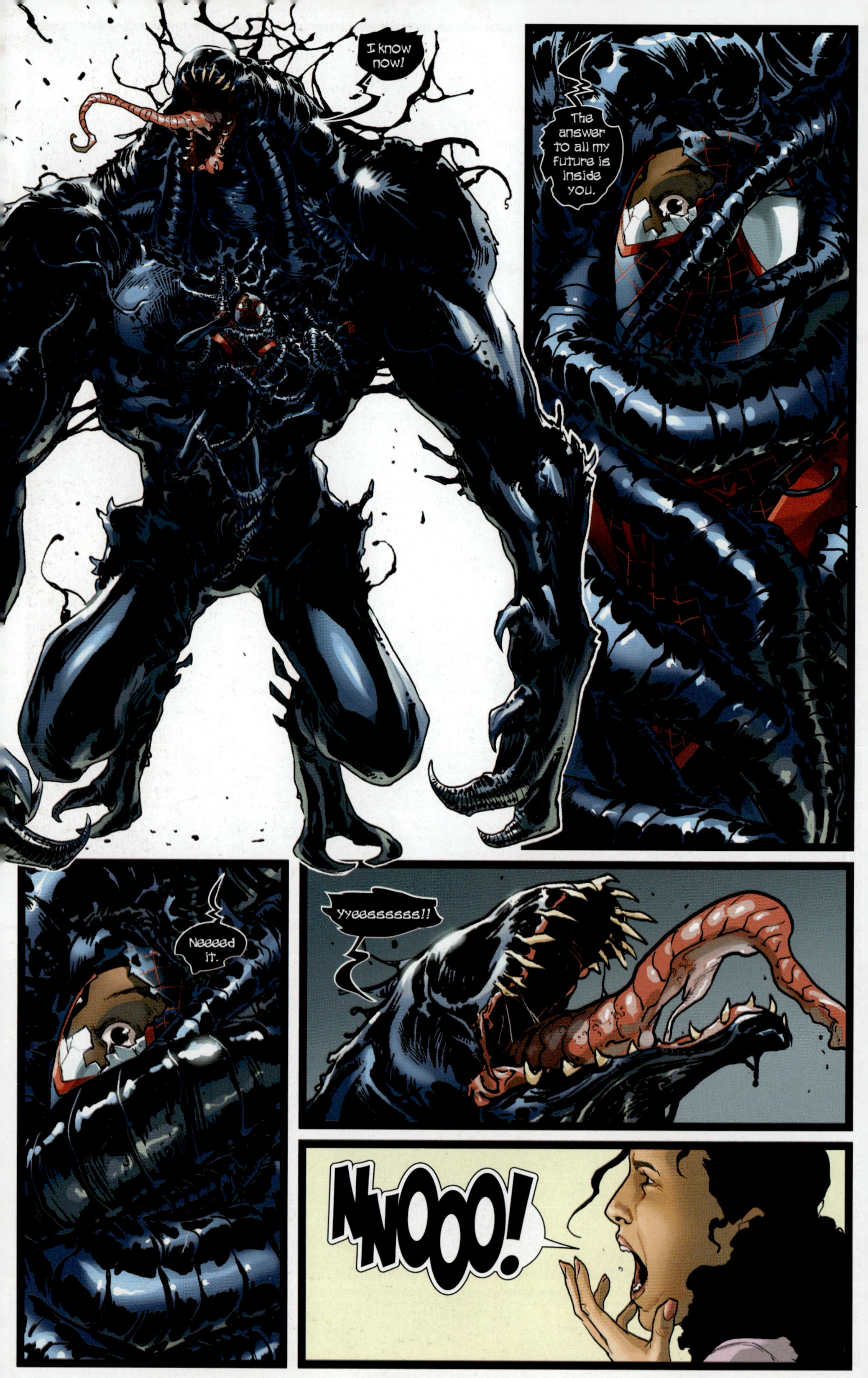
I know now!
The answer to all my future is inside you.
Neeeed it.
yyeesssssss!!
NNOOO!

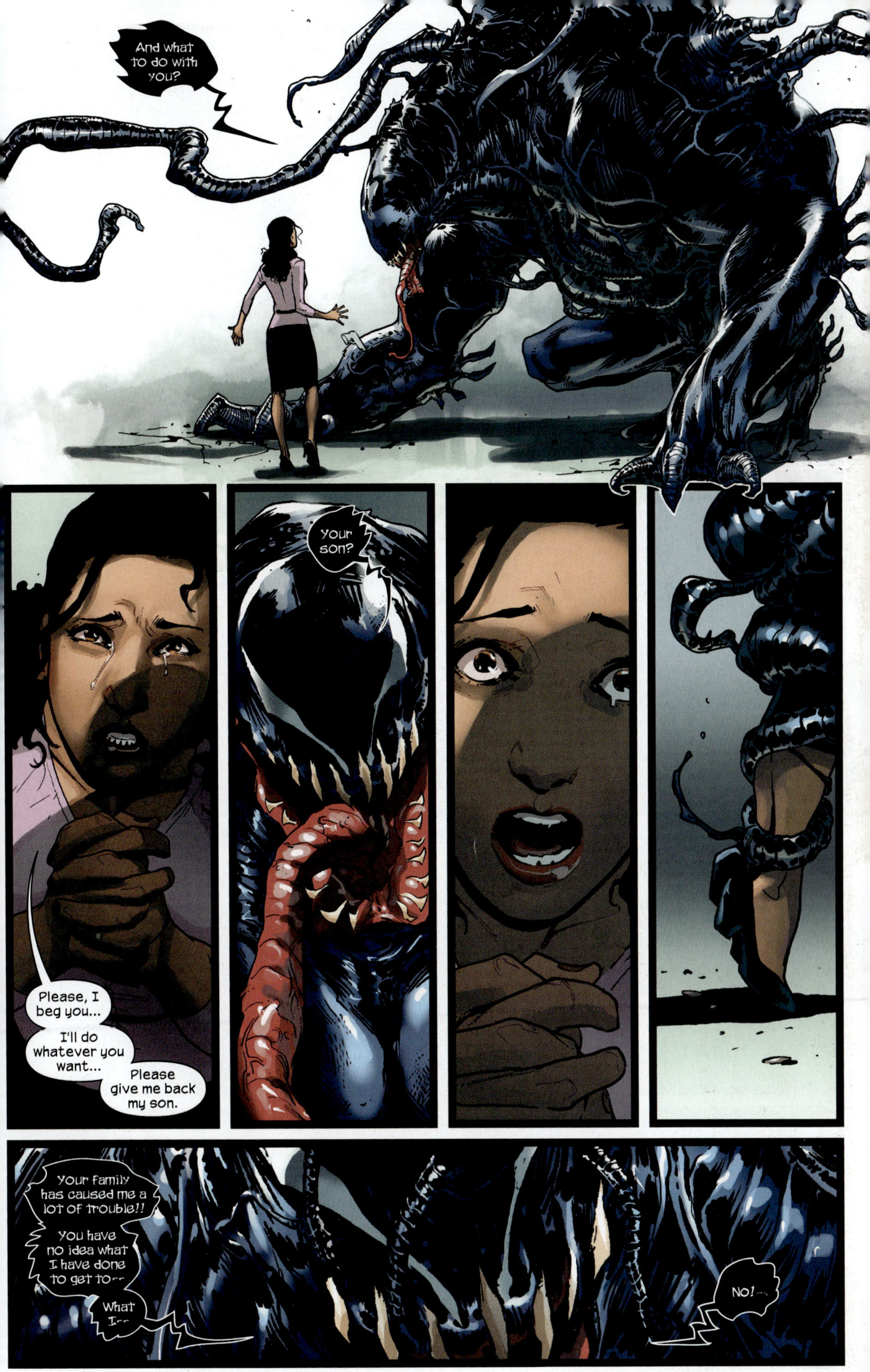

And what to do with you?
Please, I beg you...
I'll do whatever you want...
Please give me back my son.
Your son?
Your family has caused me a lot of trouble!!
You have no idea what I have done to get to--
What I--
No!

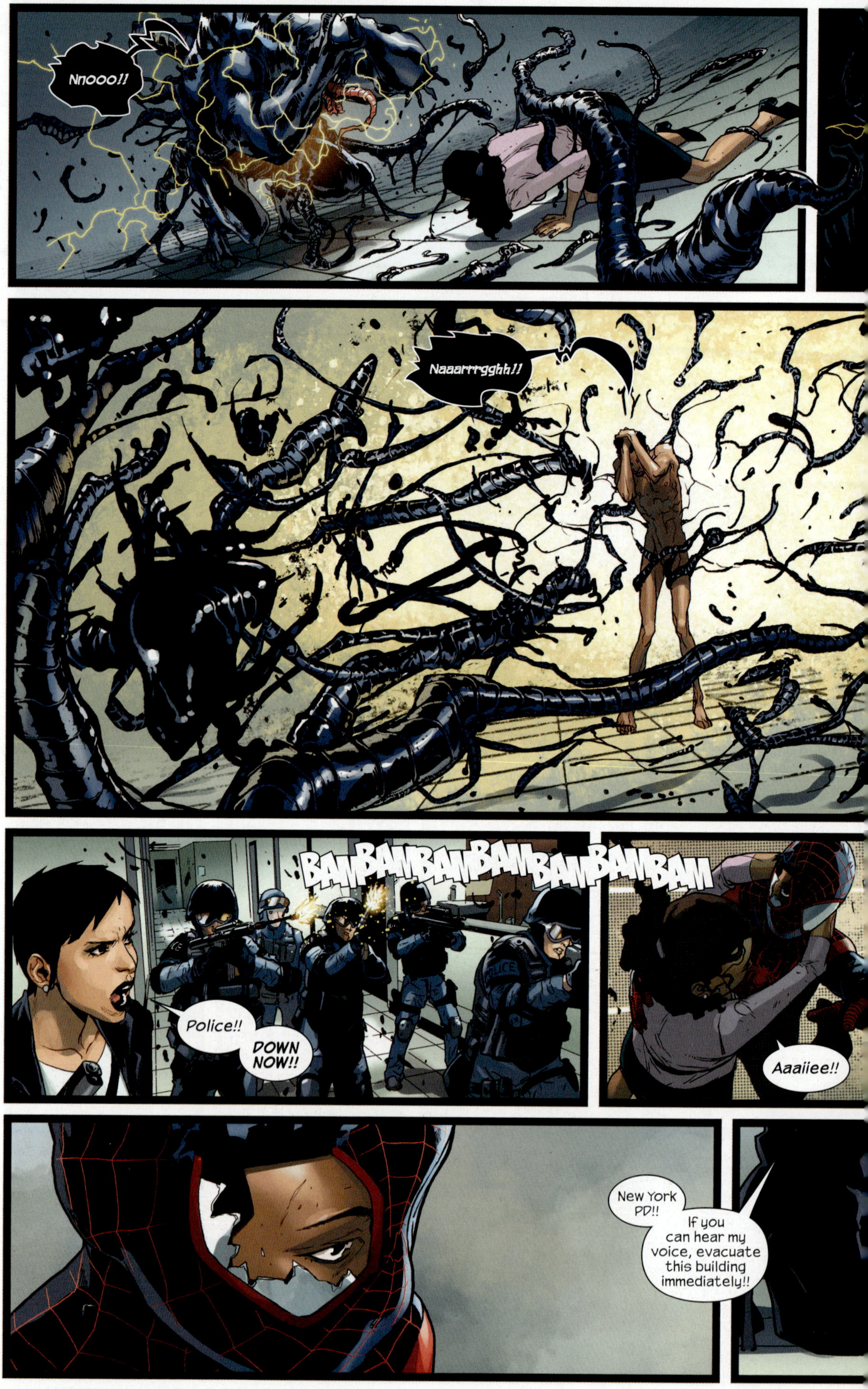
Nnooo!!
Naaarrrgghh!!
BAMBAMBAMBAMBAMBAMBAM
Police!!
DOWN NOW!!
Aaaiiee!!
New York PD!!
If you can hear my voice, evacuate this building immediately!!

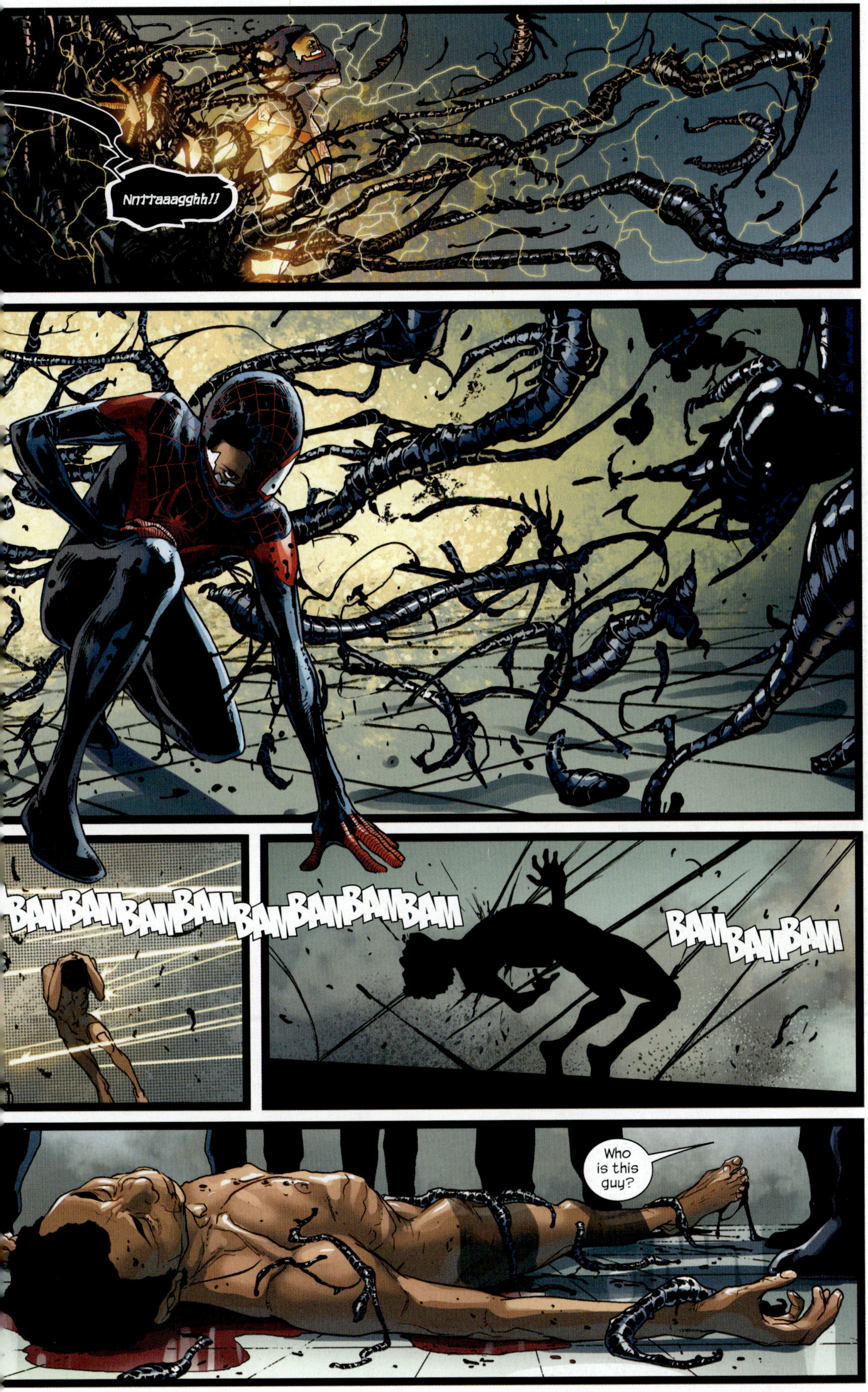
Nnttaaagghh!!
BAMBAMBAMBAMBAMBAMBAMBAM
BAMBAMBAM
Who is this guy?

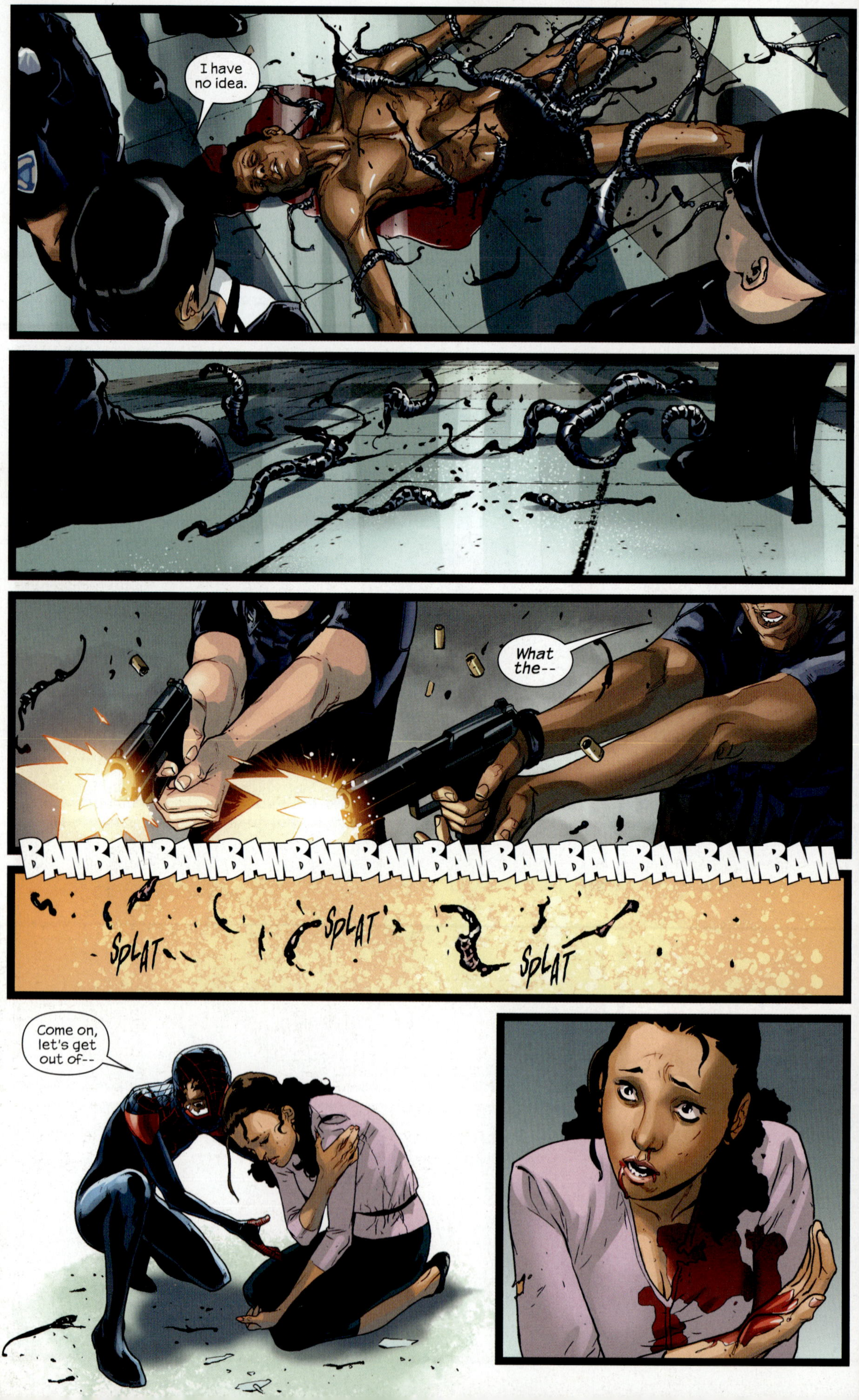
I have no idea.
What the--
BAMBAMBAMBAMBAMBAMBAMBAMBAMBAMBAMBAM
SPLAT
SPLAT
SPLAT
Come on, let's get out of--

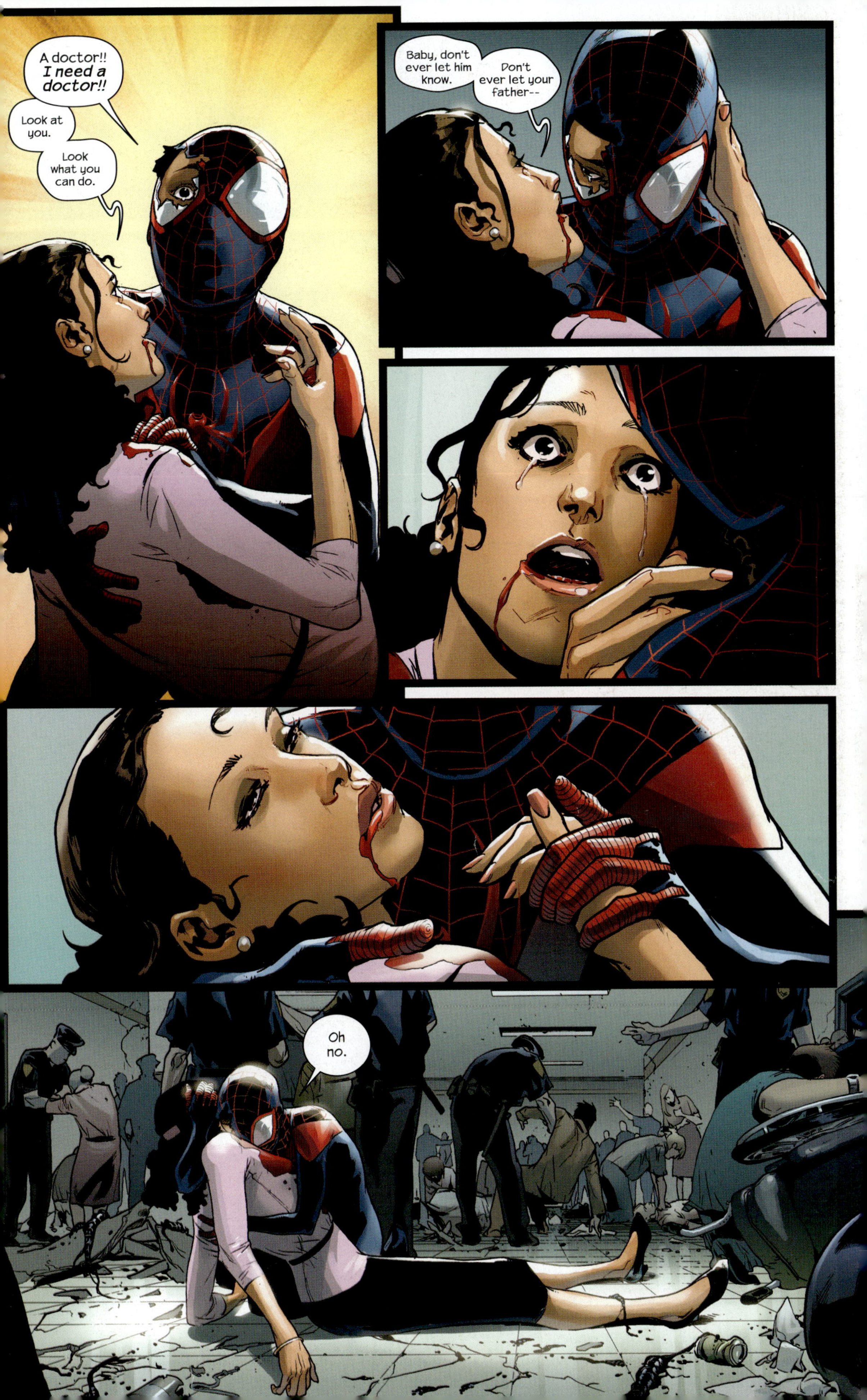
A doctor!! *I need a doctor!!*
Look at you.
Look what you can do.
Baby, don't ever let him know.
Don't ever let your father--
Oh no.

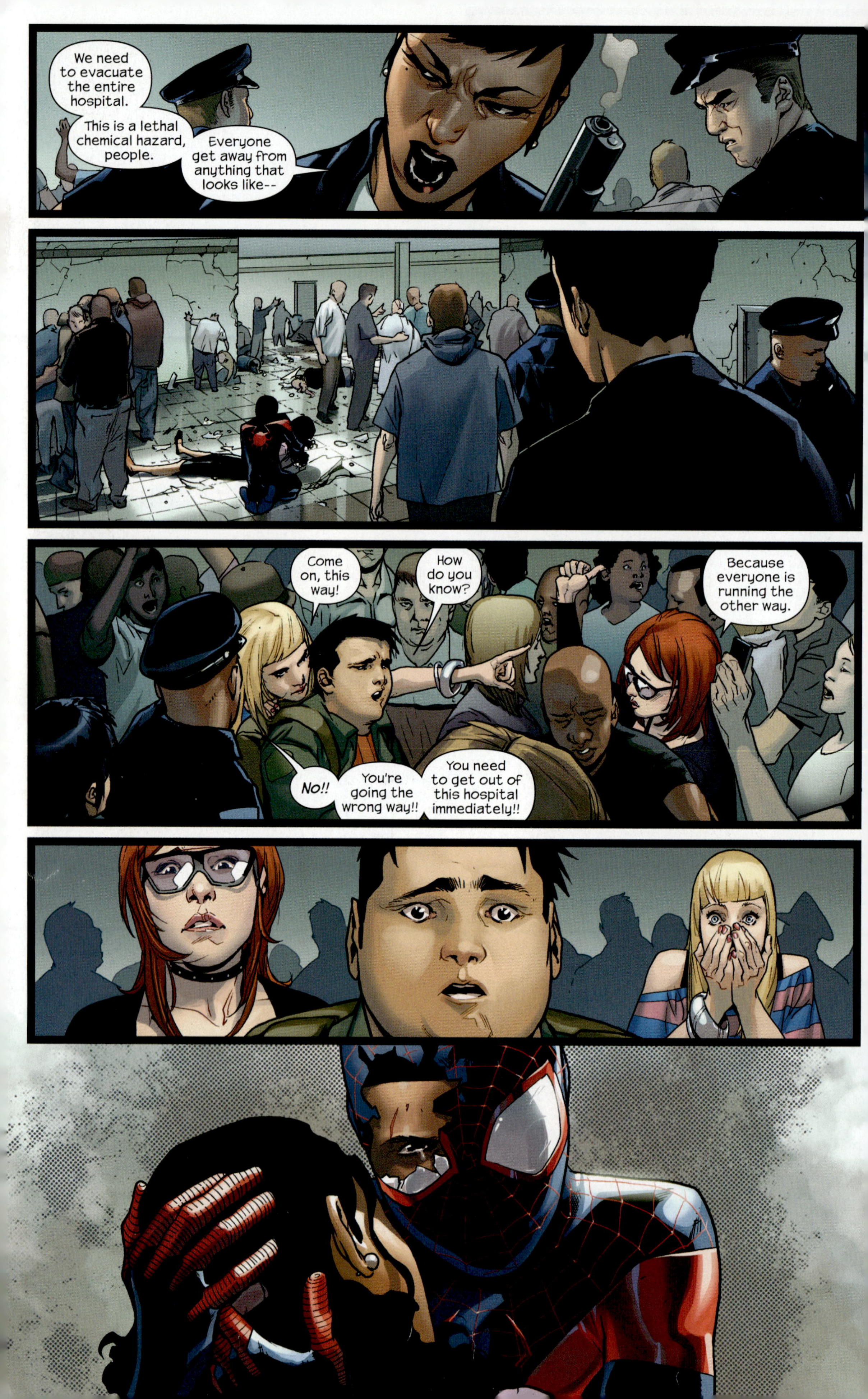
We need to evacuate the entire hospital.
This is a lethal chemical hazard, people.
Everyone get away from anything that looks like--
Come on, this way!
How do you know?
Because everyone is running the other way.
No!!
You're going the wrong way!!
You need to get out of this hospital immediately!!

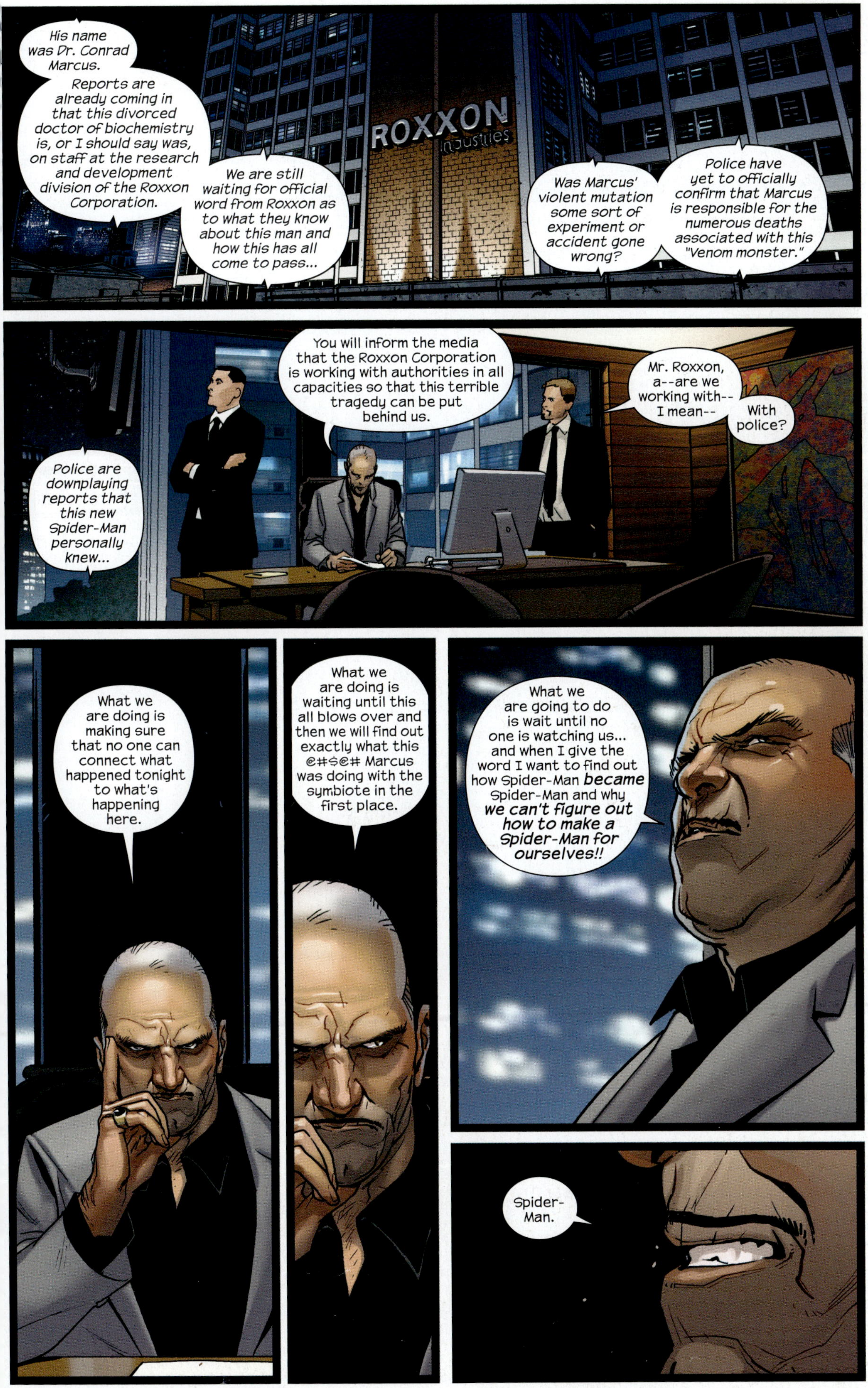
His name was Dr. Conrad Marcus.
Reports are already coming in that this divorced doctor of biochemistry is, or I should say was, on staff at the research and development division of the Roxxon Corporation.
We are still waiting for official word from Roxxon as to what they know about this man and how this has all come to pass...
ROXXON Industries
Was Marcus' violent mutation some sort of experiment or accident gone wrong?
Police have yet to officially confirm that Marcus is responsible for the numerous deaths associated with this "Venom monster."
You will inform the media that the Roxxon Corporation is working with authorities in all capacities so that this terrible tragedy can be put behind us.
Mr. Roxxon, a--are we working with-- I mean--
With police?
Police are downplaying reports that this new Spider-Man personally knew...
What we are doing is making sure that no one can connect what happened tonight to what's happening here.
What we are doing is waiting until this all blows over and then we will find out exactly what this @#$@# Marcus was doing with the symbiote in the first place.
What we are going to do is wait until no one is watching us... and when I give the word I want to find out how Spider-Man *became* Spider-Man and why ***we can't figure out how to make a Spider-Man for ourselves!!***
Spider-Man.

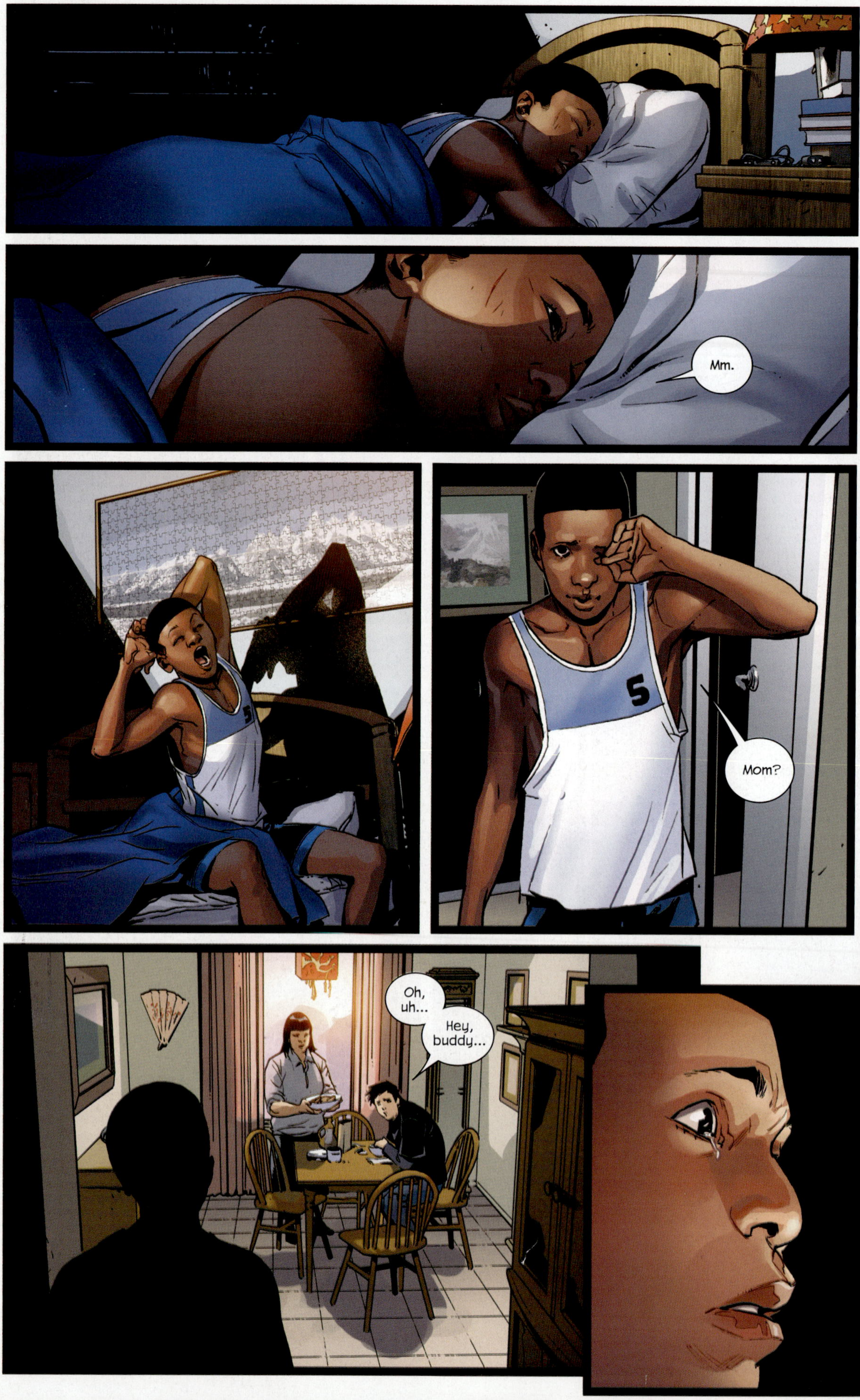
Mm.
Mom?
Oh, uh...
Hey, buddy...

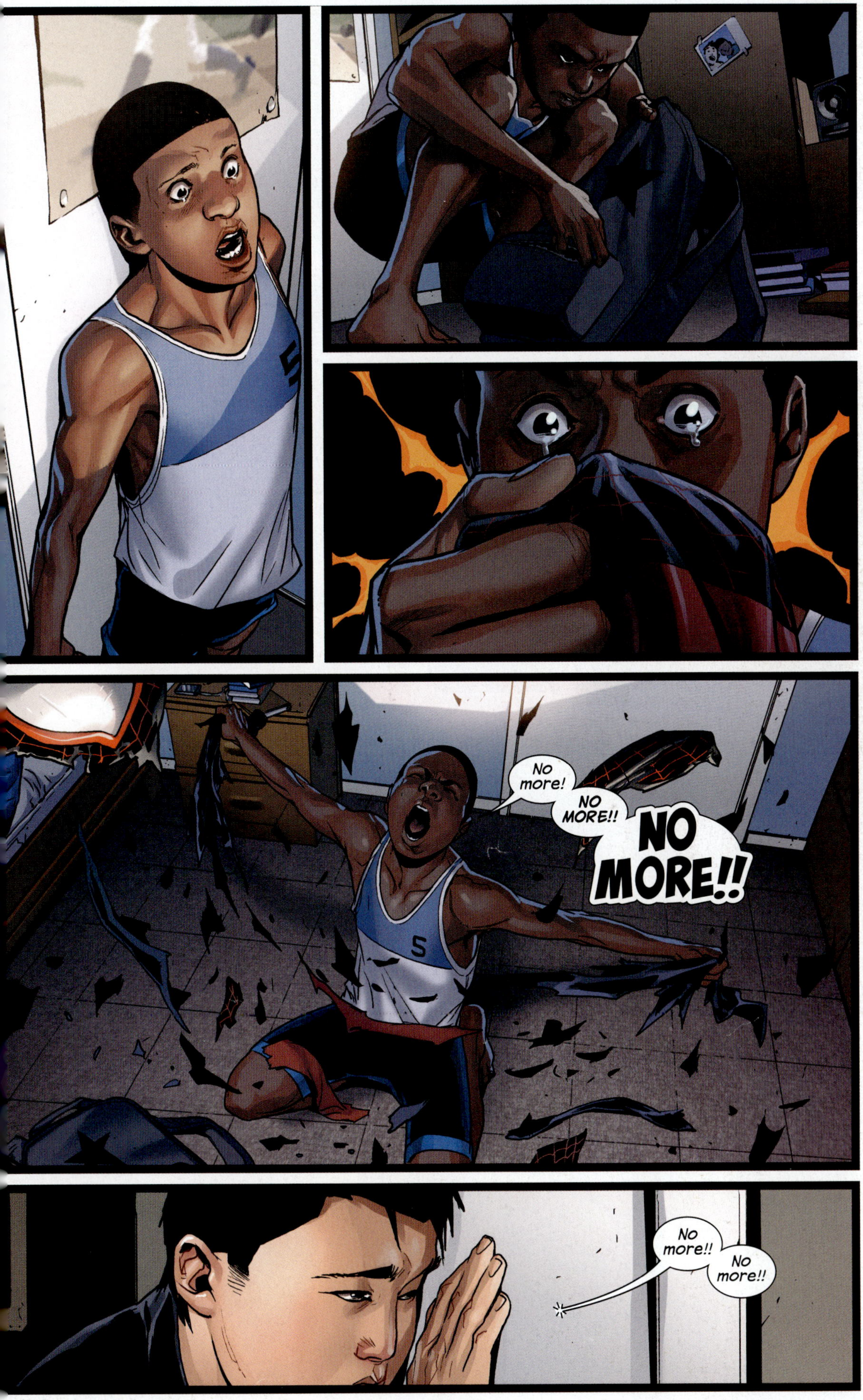
No more!
NO MORE!!
NO MORE!!
No more!!
No more!!

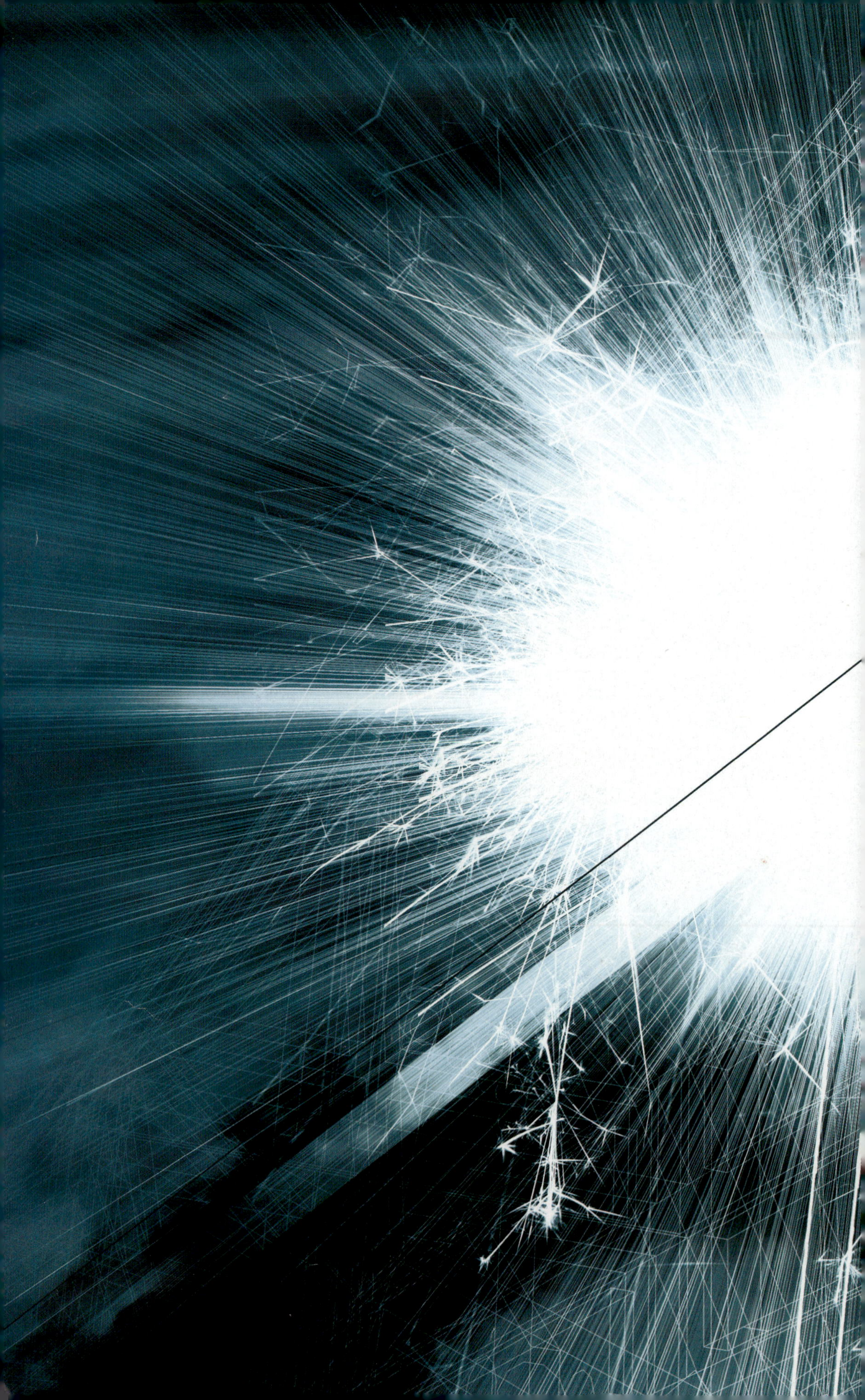

SPIDER-MAN NO MORE

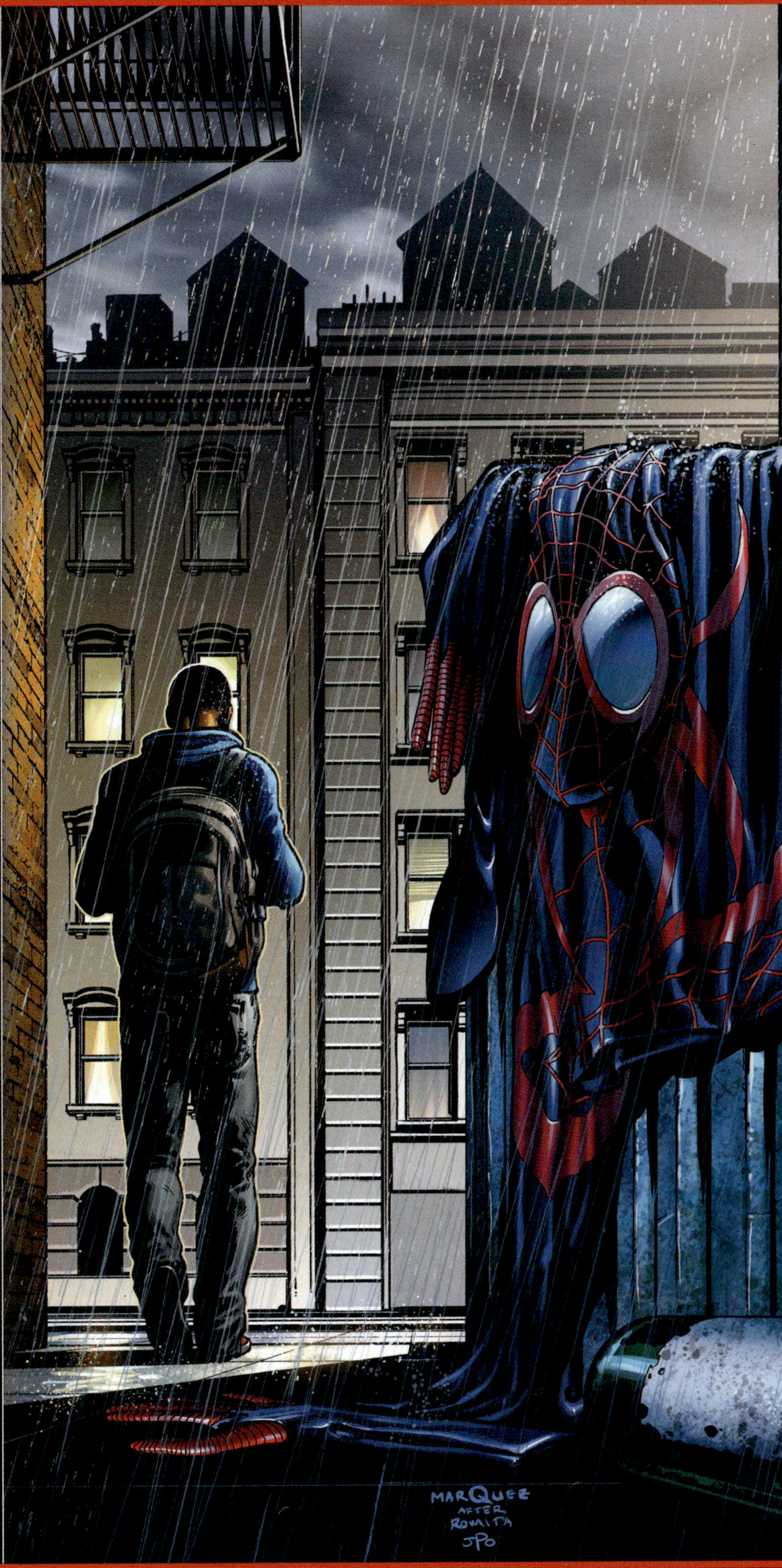
MARQUEZ
AFTER
ROMITA
JPO

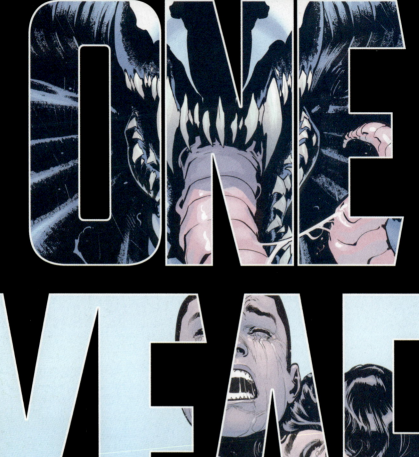

ONE YEAR LATER

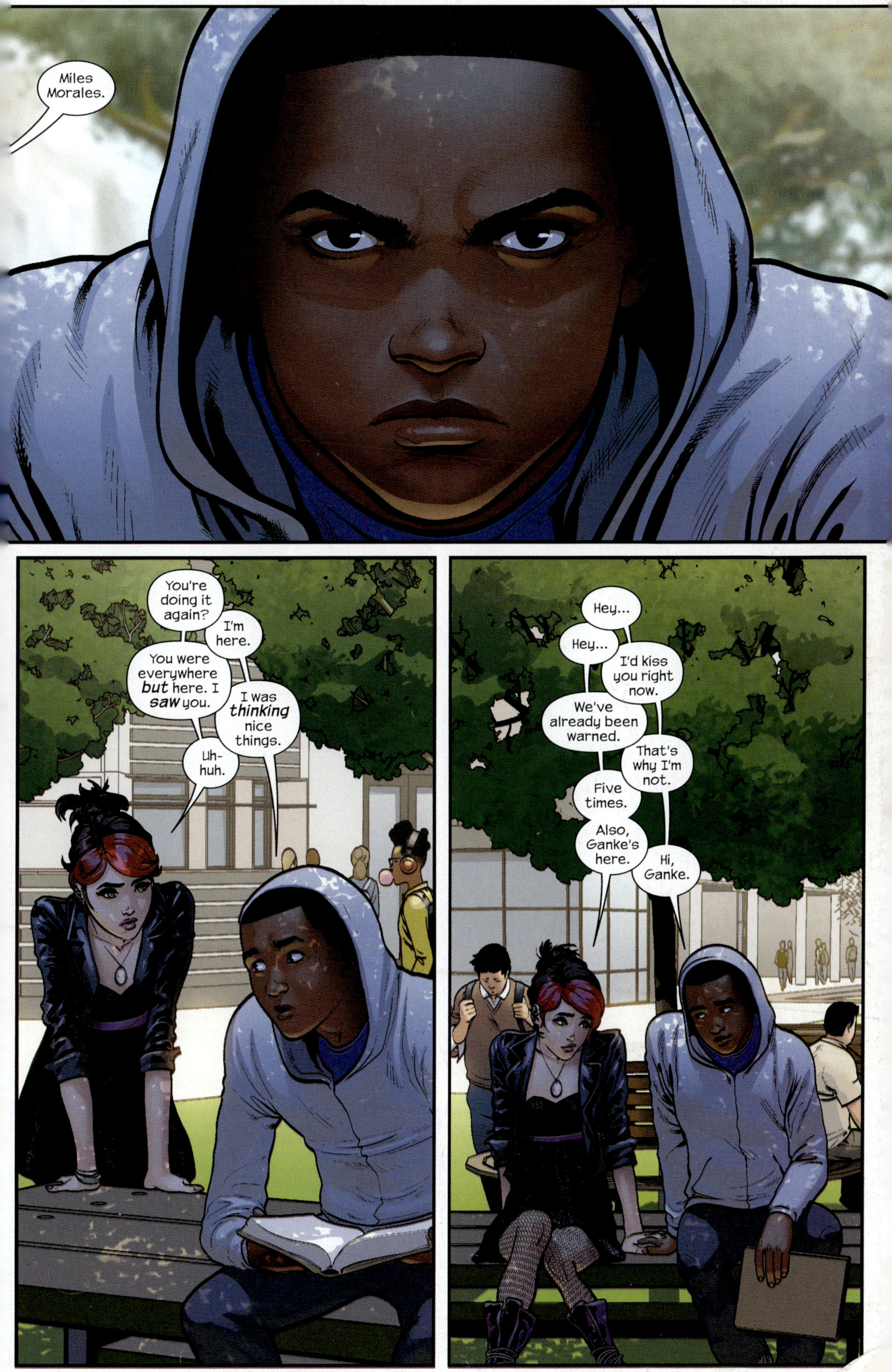
Miles Morales.
You're doing it again?
I'm here.
You were everywhere **but** here. I **saw** you.
I was ***thinking*** nice things.
Uh-huh.
Hey...
Hey...
I'd kiss you right now.
We've already been warned.
That's why I'm not.
Five times.
Also, Ganke's here.
Hi, Ganke.

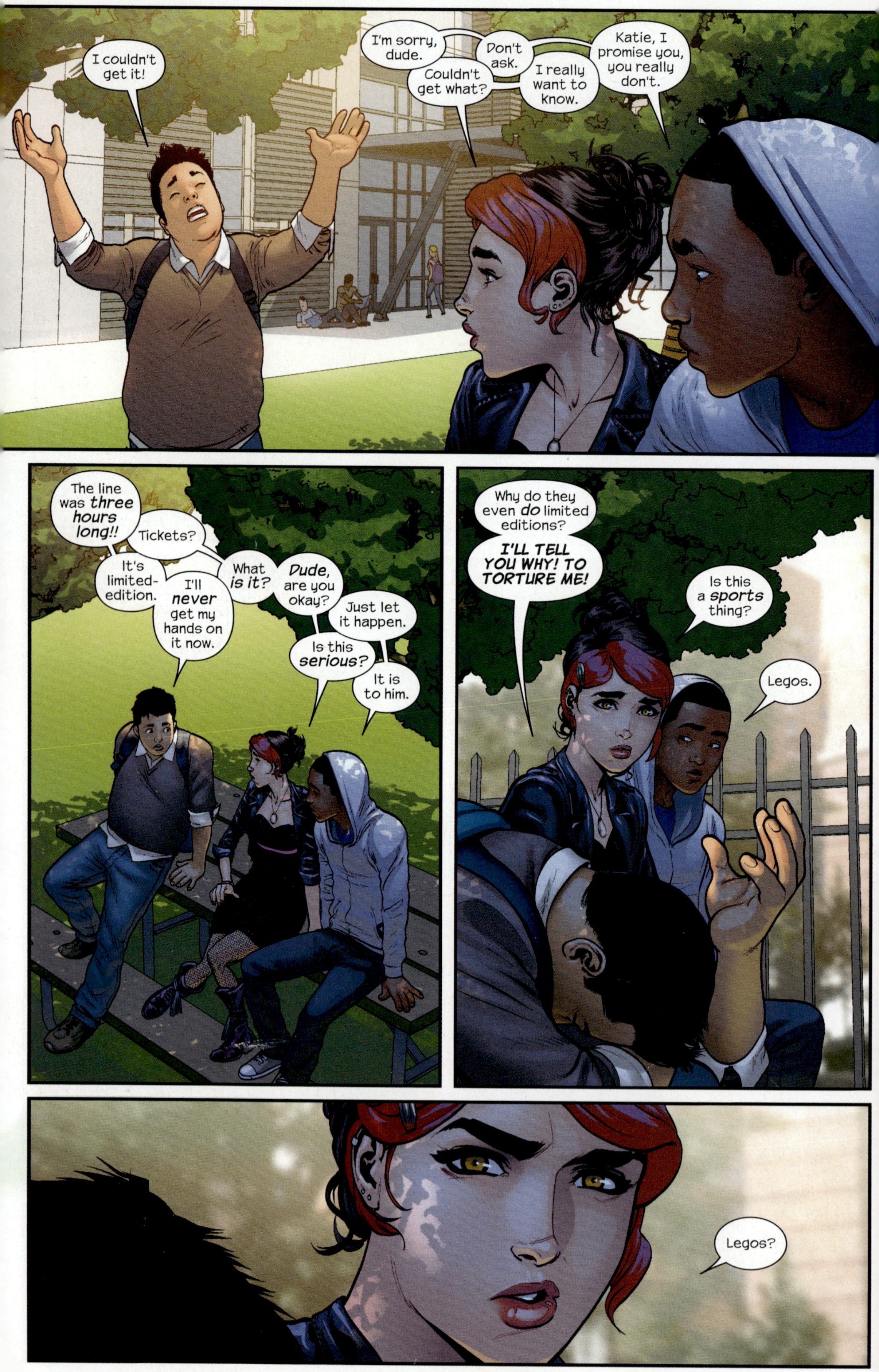

I couldn't get it!
I'm sorry, dude.
Couldn't get what?
Don't ask.
I really want to know.
Katie, I promise you, you really don't.
The line was **three hours long!!**
Tickets?
It's limited-edition.
What *is it?*
I'll **never** get my hands on it now.
Dude, are you okay?
Just let it happen.
Is this **serious?**
It is to him.
Why do they even **do** limited editions?
I'LL TELL YOU WHY! TO TORTURE ME!
Is this a **sports** thing?
Legos.
Legos?

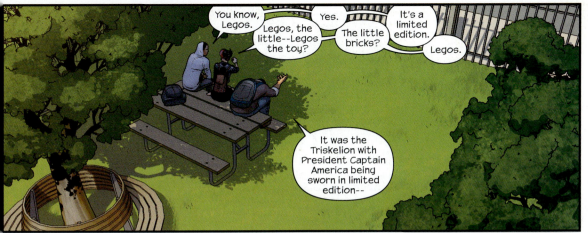

You know, Legos.

Legos, the little--Legos the toy?

Yes.

The little bricks?

It's a limited edition.

Legos.

It was the Triskelion with President Captain America being sworn in limited edition--

Edition. Yeah.

YES!!

I'm sorry.

Thank you!

So, uh, I'm going to go to my room and, let's say, e-mail my parents.

Yeah, okay.

See you after dinner.

Sure.

I ask for so little.

I think I'm going to tell her.

Tell her you love her?

What? No.

You haven't told Katie Bishop you love her yet?

No.

Girls like when you tell them.

Oh yeah?

She would.

You know what girls like to hear all of a sudden?

Sure.

This from the man who just chased another girl from our table crying over Legos.

That's not why she left. She had to e-mail--

Dude.

She had to go--

I promise you I don't know what girls want from us but I know they don't want to hear about you and the Legos.

The right girl will.

Wait, what were you going to tell her?

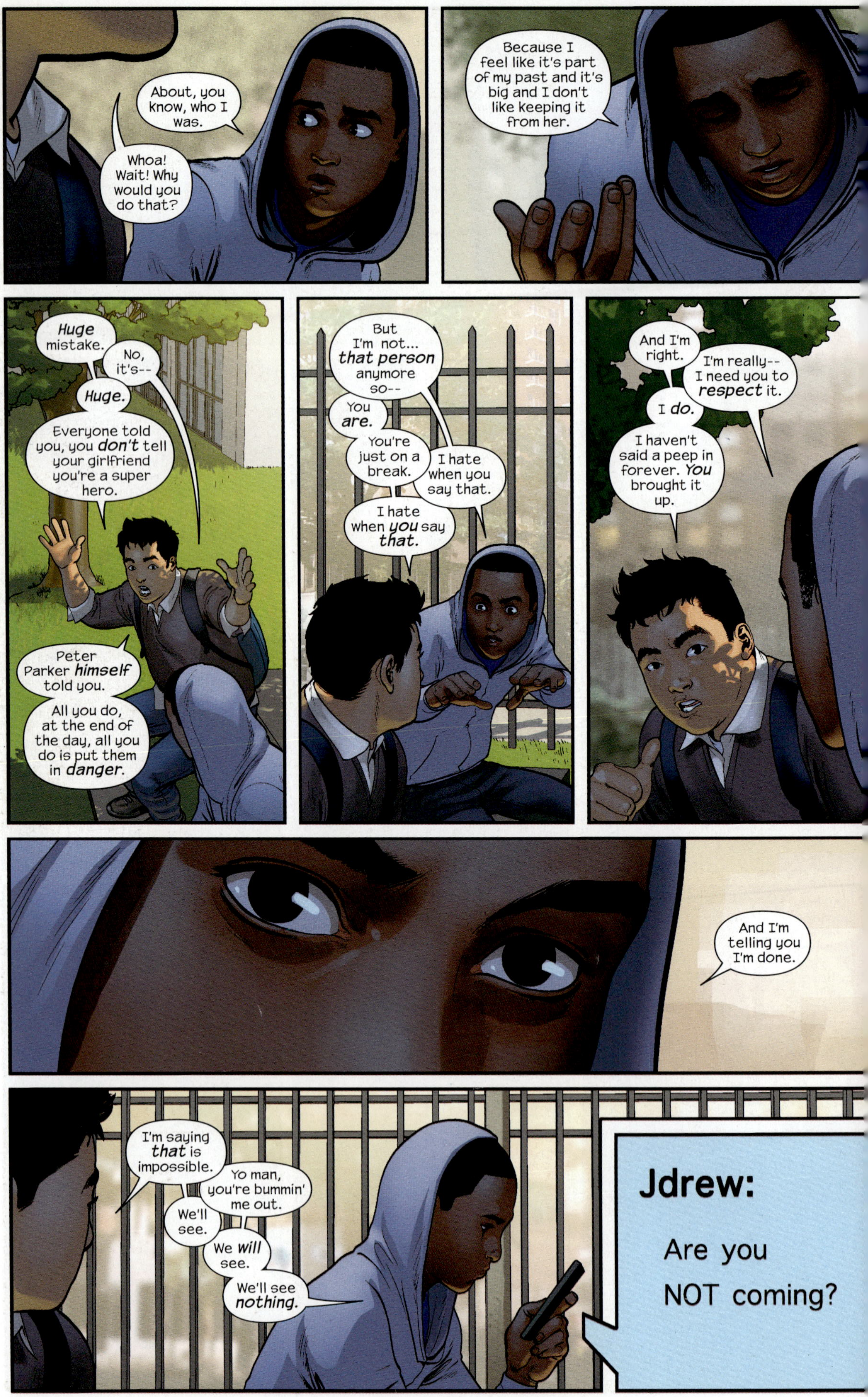
About, you know, who I was.
Whoa! Wait! Why would you do that?
Because I feel like it's part of my past and it's big and I don't like keeping it from her.
Huge mistake.
No, it's--
Huge.
Everyone told you, you don't tell your girlfriend you're a super hero.
Peter Parker himself told you.
All you do, at the end of the day, all you do is put them in danger.
But I'm not... that person anymore so--
You are.
You're just on a break.
I hate when you say that.
I hate when you say that.
And I'm right.
I'm really-- I need you to respect it.
I do.
I haven't said a peep in forever. You brought it up.
And I'm telling you I'm done.
I'm saying that is impossible.
Yo man, you're bummin' me out.
We'll see.
We will see.
We'll see nothing.
Jdrew:
Are you NOT coming?

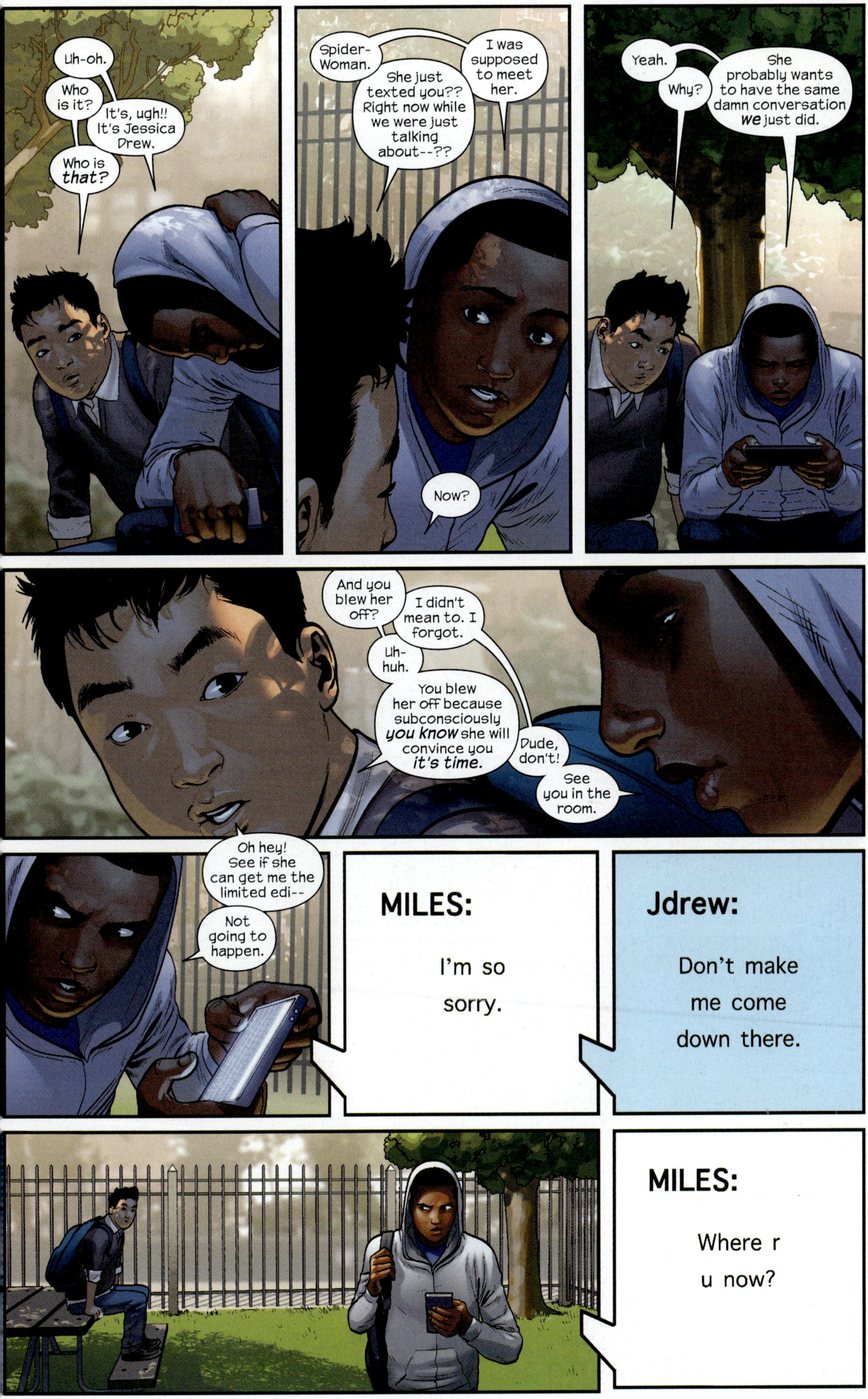

Uh-oh.
Who is it?
It's, ugh!! It's Jessica Drew.
Who is *that?*
Spider-Woman.
I was supposed to meet her.
She just texted you?? Right now while we were just talking about--??
Now?
Yeah.
Why?
She probably wants to have the same damn conversation *we* just did.
And you blew her off?
I didn't mean to. I forgot.
Uh-huh.
You blew her off because subconsciously *you know* she will convince you *it's time.*
Dude, don't!
See you in the room.
Oh hey! See if she can get me the limited edi--
Not going to happen.
MILES:
I'm so sorry.
Jdrew:
Don't make me come down there.
MILES:
Where r u now?

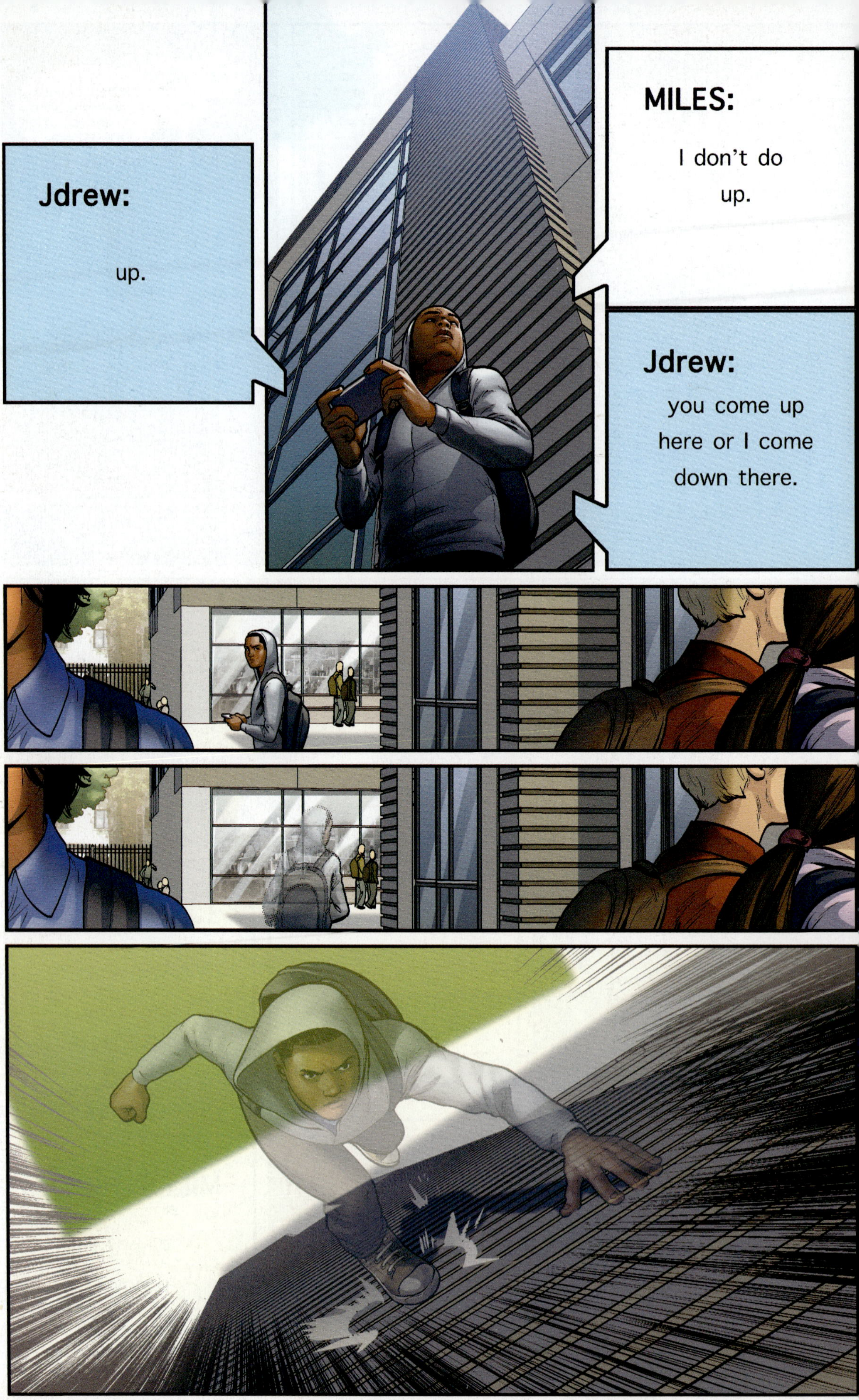
Jdrew:
up.
MILES:
I don't do
up.
Jdrew:
you come up
here or I come
down there.

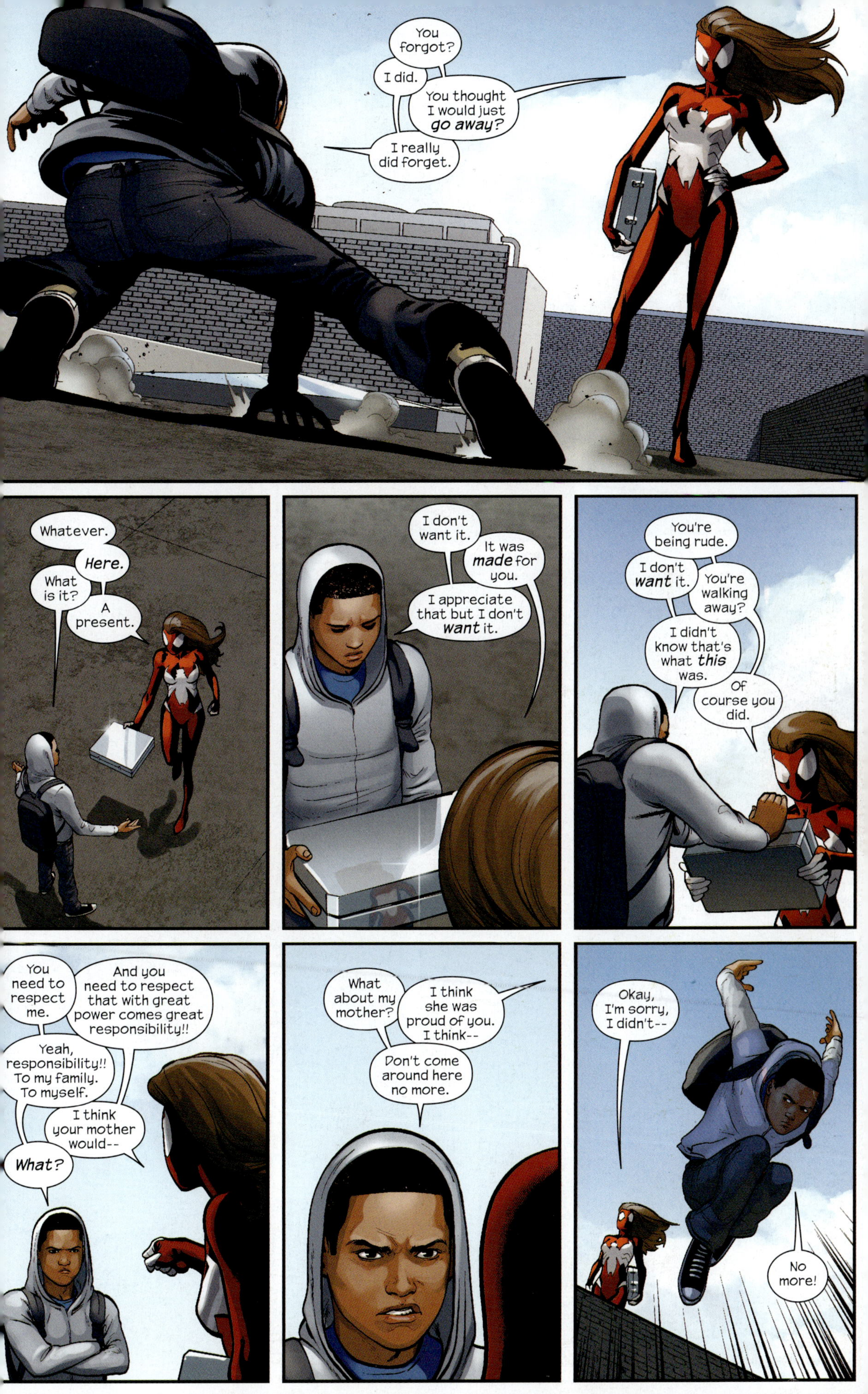
You forgot?
I did.
You thought I would just *go away?*
I really did forget.
Whatever.
Here.
What is it?
A present.
I don't want it.
It was *made* for you.
I appreciate that but I don't *want* it.
You're being rude.
I don't *want* it.
You're walking away?
I didn't know that's what *this* was.
Of course you did.
You need to respect me.
And you need to respect that with great power comes great responsibility!!
Yeah, responsibility!! To my family. To myself.
I think your mother would--
What?
What about my mother?
I think she was proud of you. I think--
Don't come around here no more.
Okay, I'm sorry, I didn't--
No more!

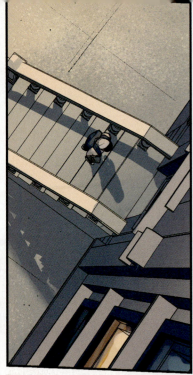

Dad?

There he is.

How's work?

It was work? You home for dinner?

Sure.

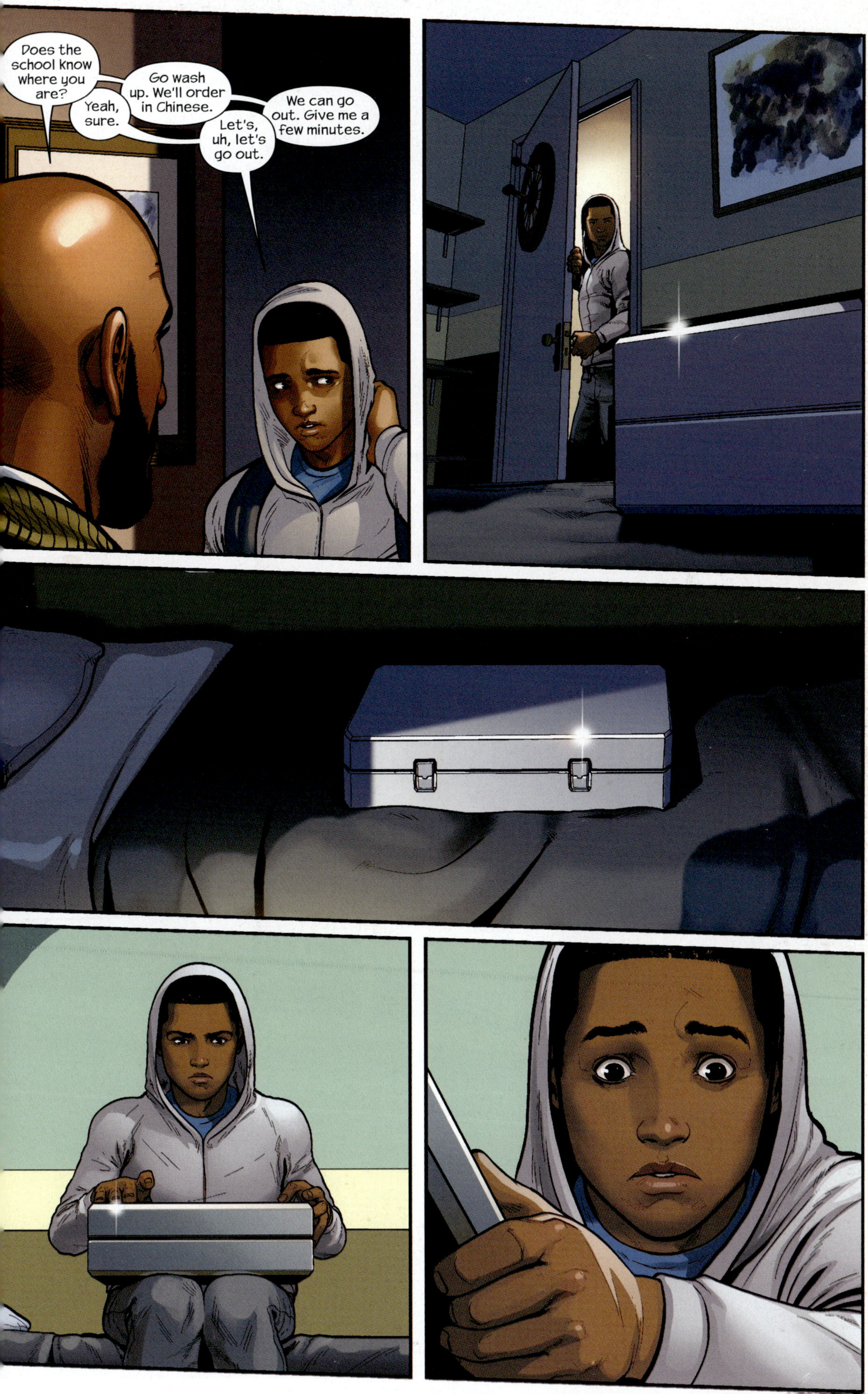
Does the school know where you are?
Yeah, sure.
Go wash up. We'll order in Chinese.
Let's, uh, let's go out.
We can go out. Give me a few minutes.

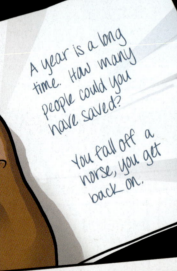
A year is a long time. How many people could you have saved?

You fall off a horse, you get back on.

You ready?

Almost.

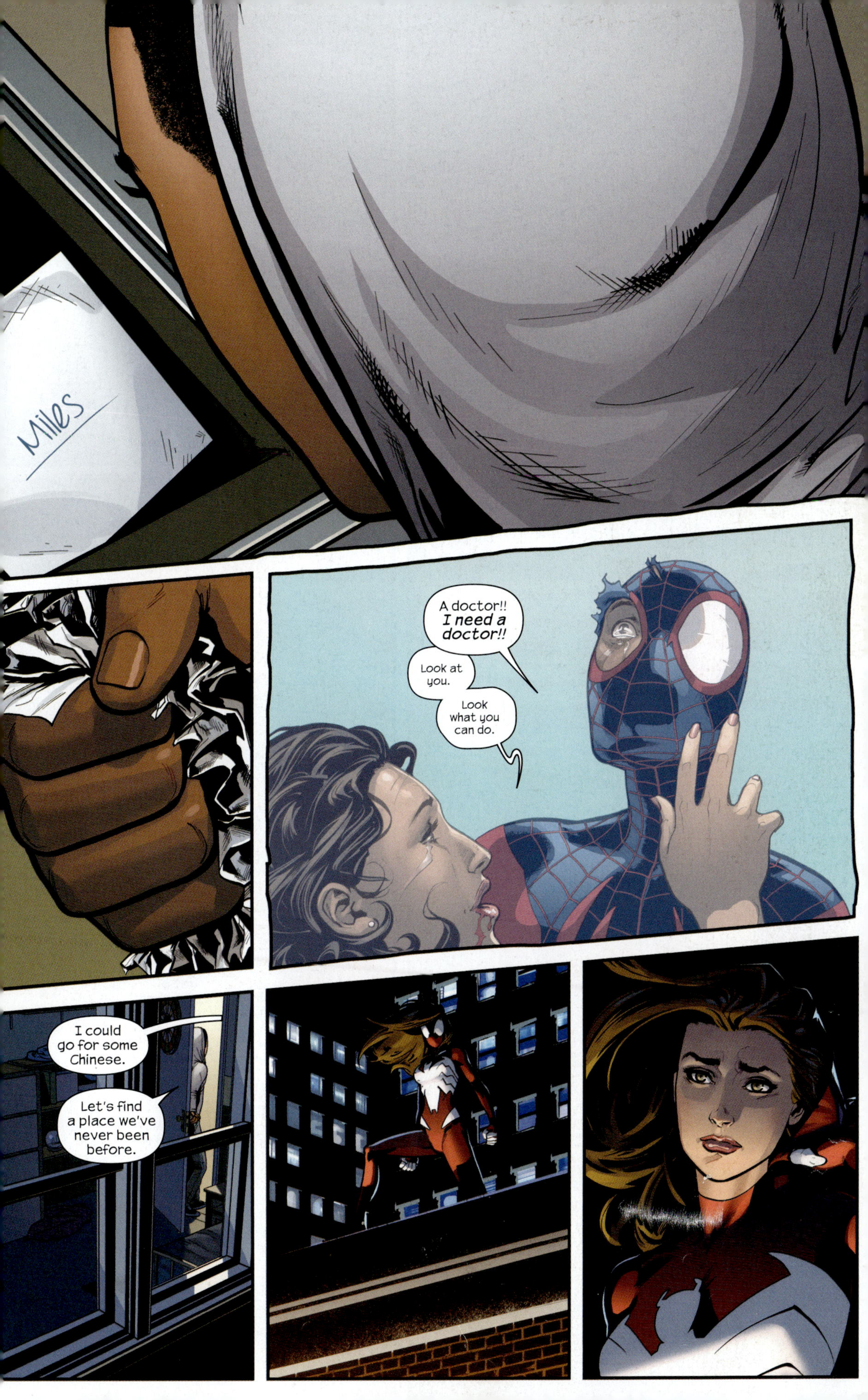

Miles
A doctor!! I need a doctor!!
Look at you.
Look what you can do.
I could go for some Chinese.
Let's find a place we've never been before.

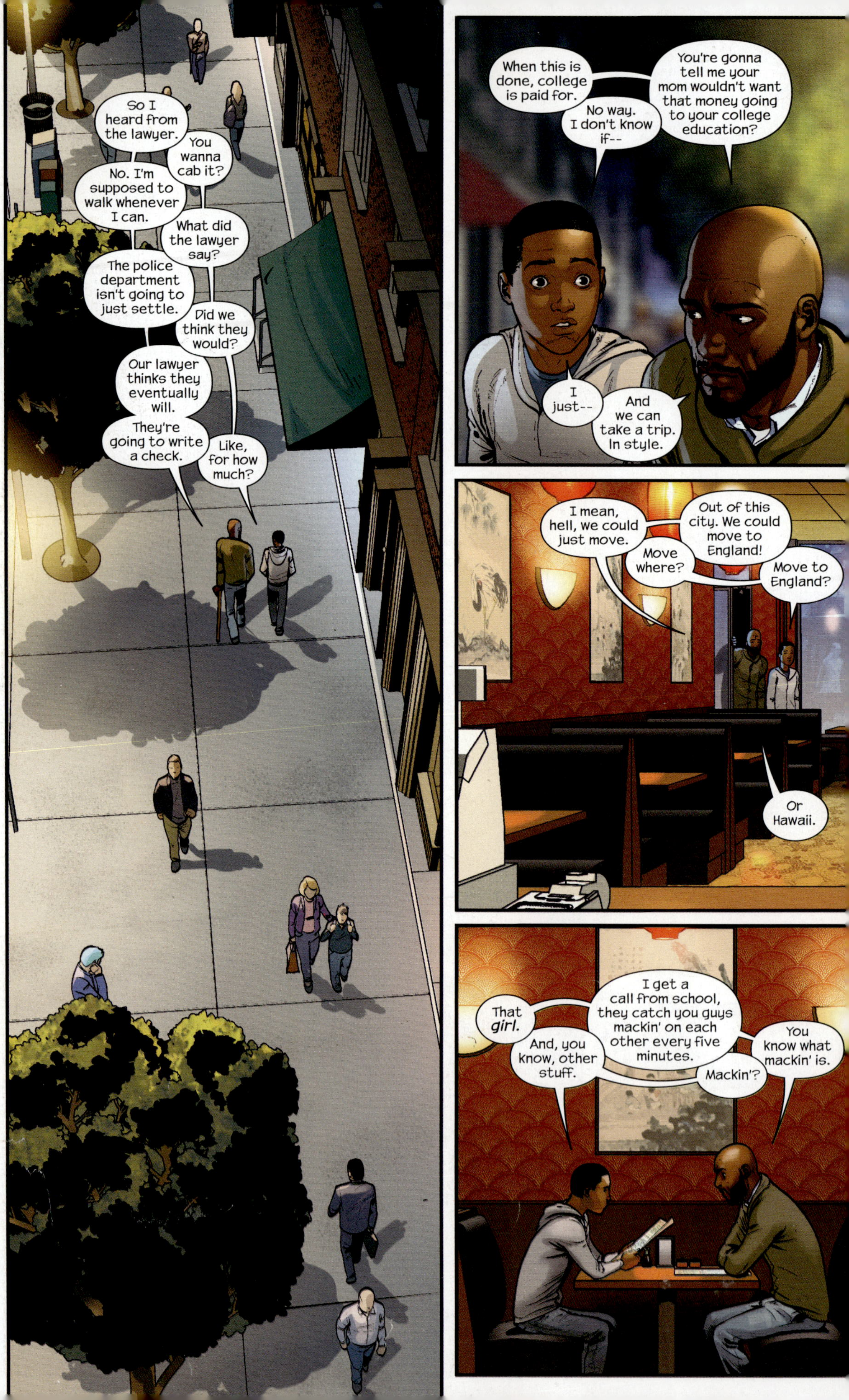

So I heard from the lawyer.
You wanna cab it?
No. I'm supposed to walk whenever I can.
What did the lawyer say?
The police department isn't going to just settle.
Did we think they would?
Our lawyer thinks they eventually will.
They're going to write a check.
Like, for how much?
When this is done, college is paid for.
You're gonna tell me your mom wouldn't want that money going to your college education?
No way. I don't know if--
I just--
And we can take a trip. In style.
I mean, hell, we could just move.
Out of this city. We could move to England!
Move where?
Move to England?
Or Hawaii.
That *girl*.
I get a call from school, they catch you guys mackin' on each other every five minutes.
And, you know, other stuff.
Mackin'?
You know what mackin' is.

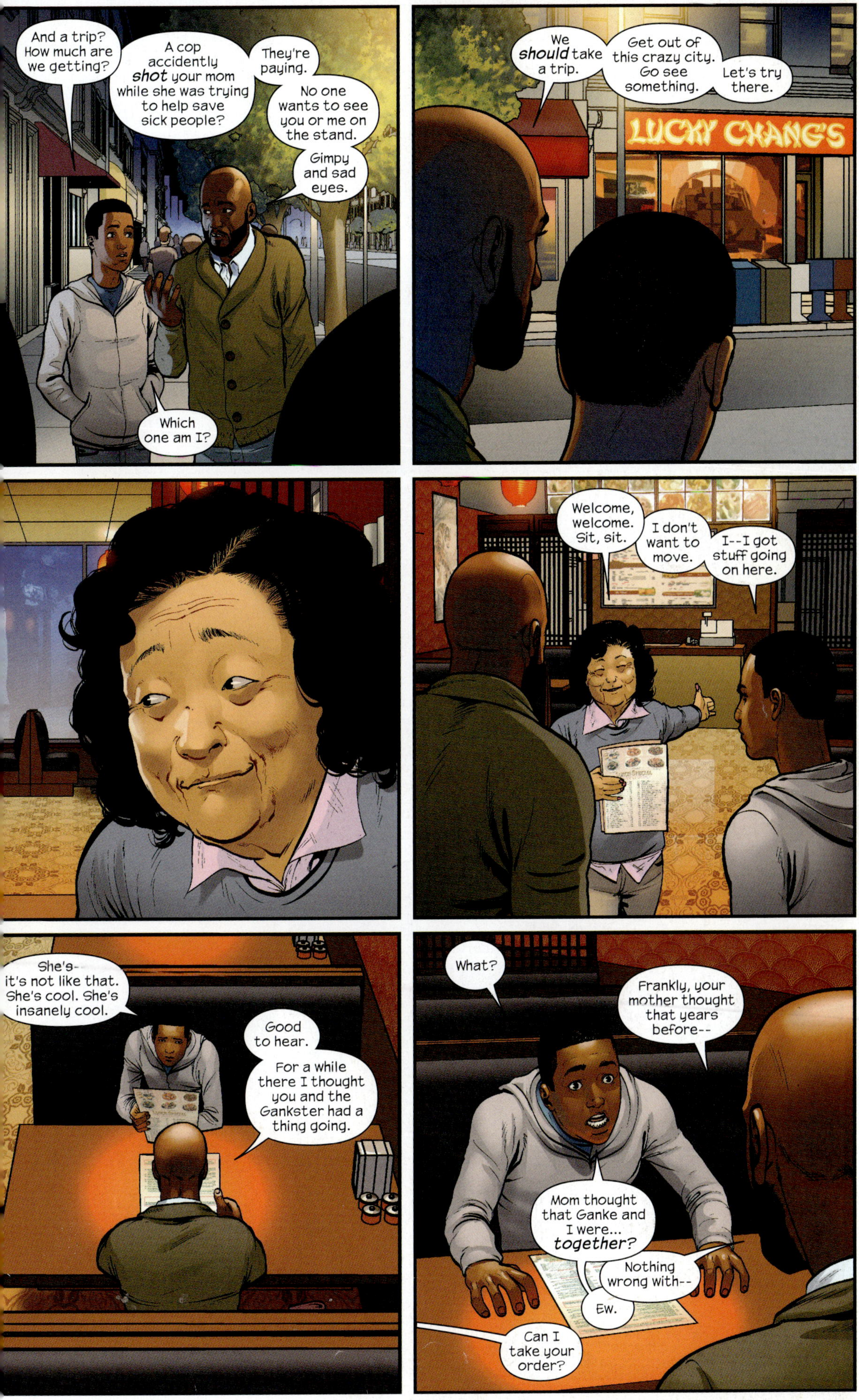
And a trip? How much are we getting?
A cop accidently *shot* your mom while she was trying to help save sick people?
They're paying.
No one wants to see you or me on the stand.
Gimpy and sad eyes.
Which one am I?
We *should* take a trip.
Get out of this crazy city. Go see something.
Let's try there.
LUCKY CHANG'S
Welcome, welcome. Sit, sit.
I don't want to move.
I--I got stuff going on here.
She's-- it's not like that. She's cool. She's insanely cool.
Good to hear.
For a while there I thought you and the Gankster had a thing going.
What?
Frankly, your mother thought that years before--
Mom thought that Ganke and I were... *together?*
Nothing wrong with--
Ew.
Can I take your order?

Oh, uh... um... hey.

Hi.

You know each other?

Yeah, uh, where do we know each other from?

School.

Oh, yeah. Yeah, you're the kid that-- uh, can I take your order?

I'm Jefferson.

Gwen.

What's good?

Uh, the duck.

Okay, duck for me.

He wants pot stickers and shrimp fried rice.

Something to drink?

Water.

You got Rolson?

I'll see.

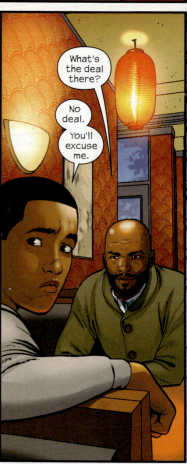

What's the deal there?

No deal.

You'll excuse me.

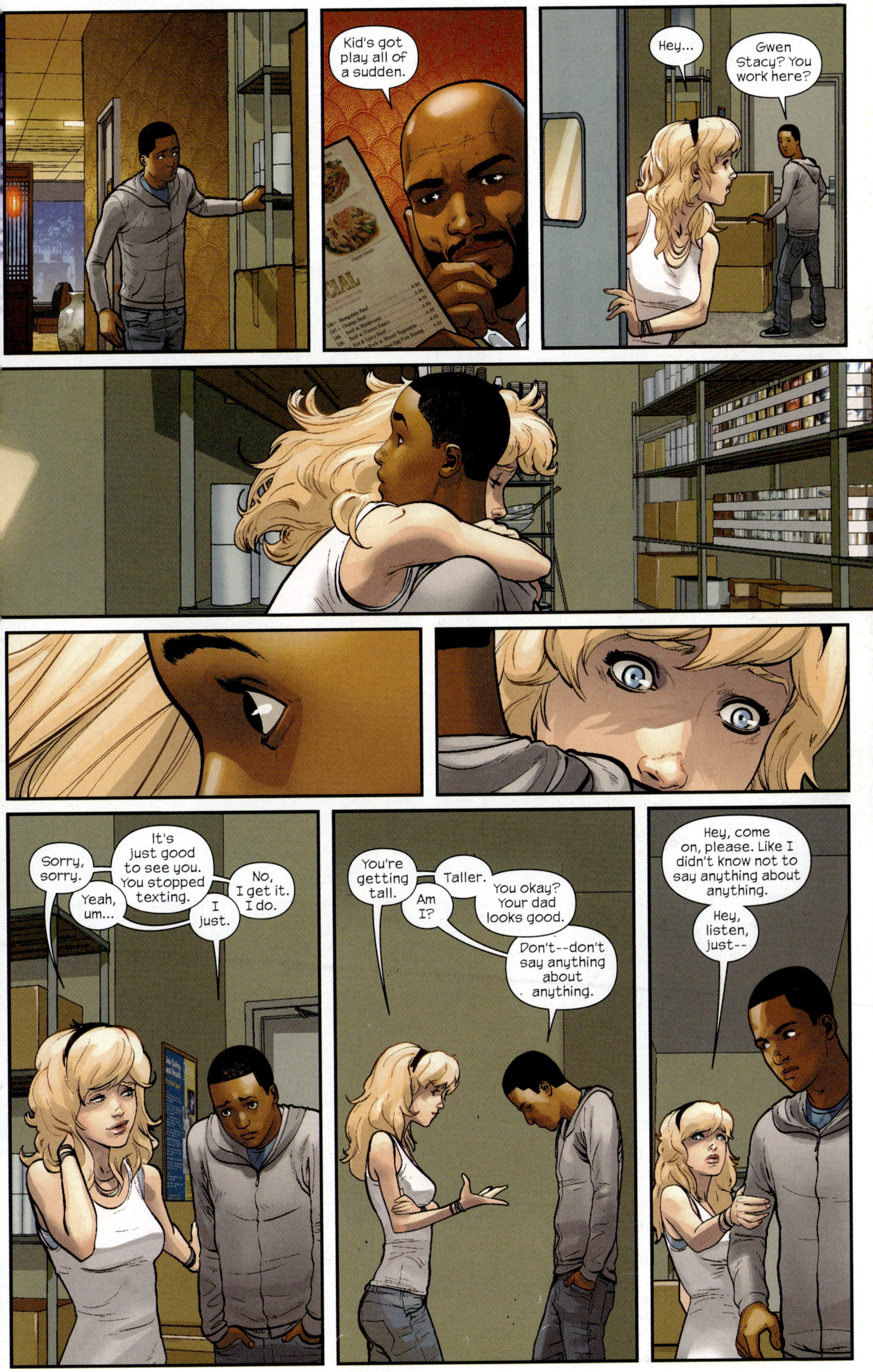
Kid's got play all of a sudden.
Hey...
Gwen Stacy? You work here?
Sorry, sorry.
It's just good to see you. You stopped texting.
Yeah, um...
No, I get it. I do.
I just.
You're getting tall.
Taller.
Am I?
You okay? Your dad looks good.
Don't--don't say anything about anything.
Hey, come on, please. Like I didn't know not to say anything about anything.
Hey, listen, just--

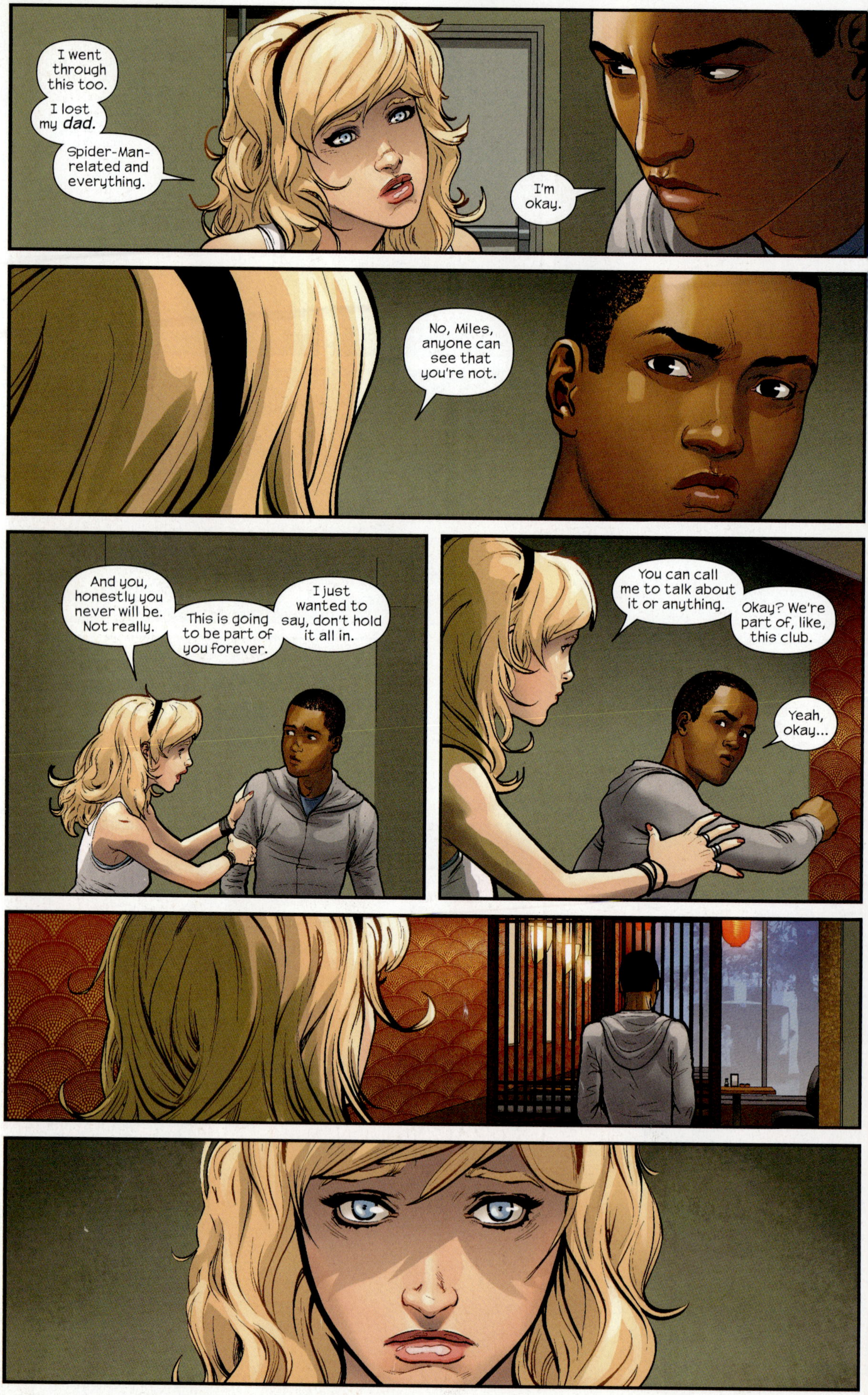

I went through this too.
I lost my *dad.*
Spider-Man-related and everything.
I'm okay.
No, Miles, anyone can see that you're not.
And you, honestly you never will be. Not really.
This is going to be part of you forever.
I just wanted to say, don't hold it all in.
You can call me to talk about it or anything.
Okay? We're part of, like, this club.
Yeah, okay...

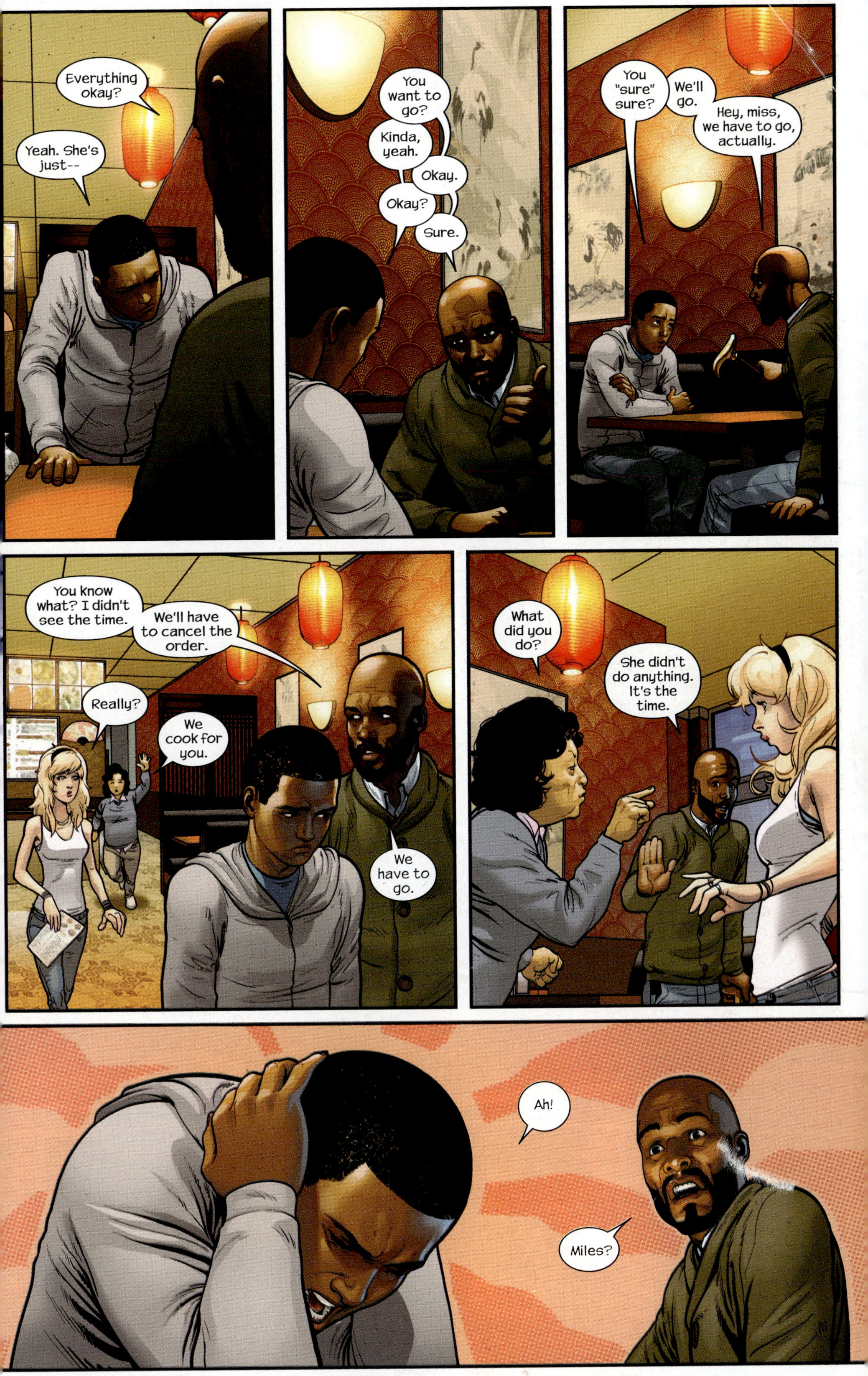
Everything okay?
Yeah. She's just--
You want to go?
Kinda, yeah.
Okay.
Okay?
Sure.
You "sure" sure?
We'll go.
Hey, miss, we have to go, actually.
You know what? I didn't see the time.
We'll have to cancel the order.
Really?
We cook for you.
We have to go.
What did you do?
She didn't do anything. It's the time.
Ah!
Miles?

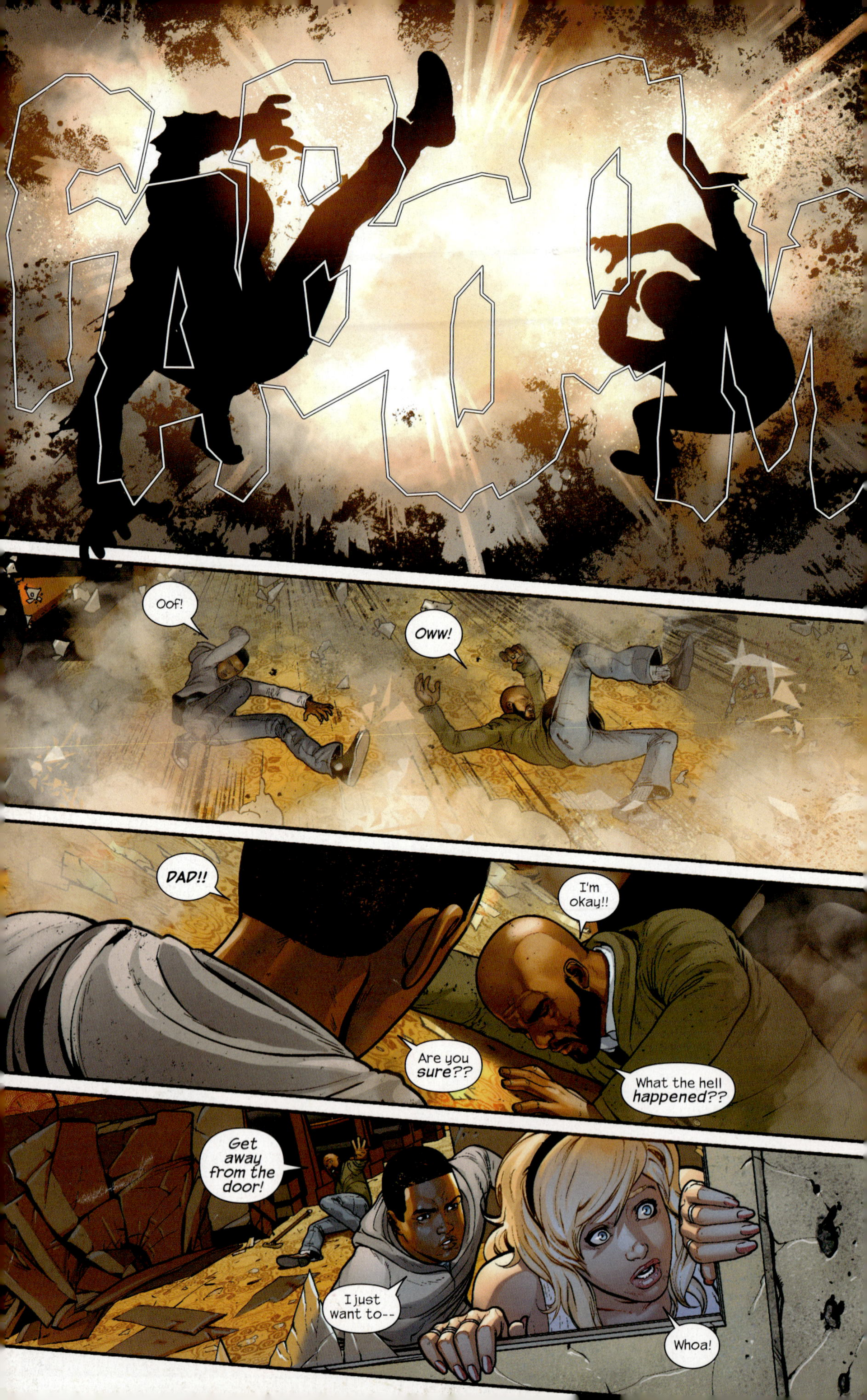
Oof!
Oww!
DAD!!
I'm okay!!
Are you sure??
What the hell happened??
Get away from the door!
I just want to--
Whoa!

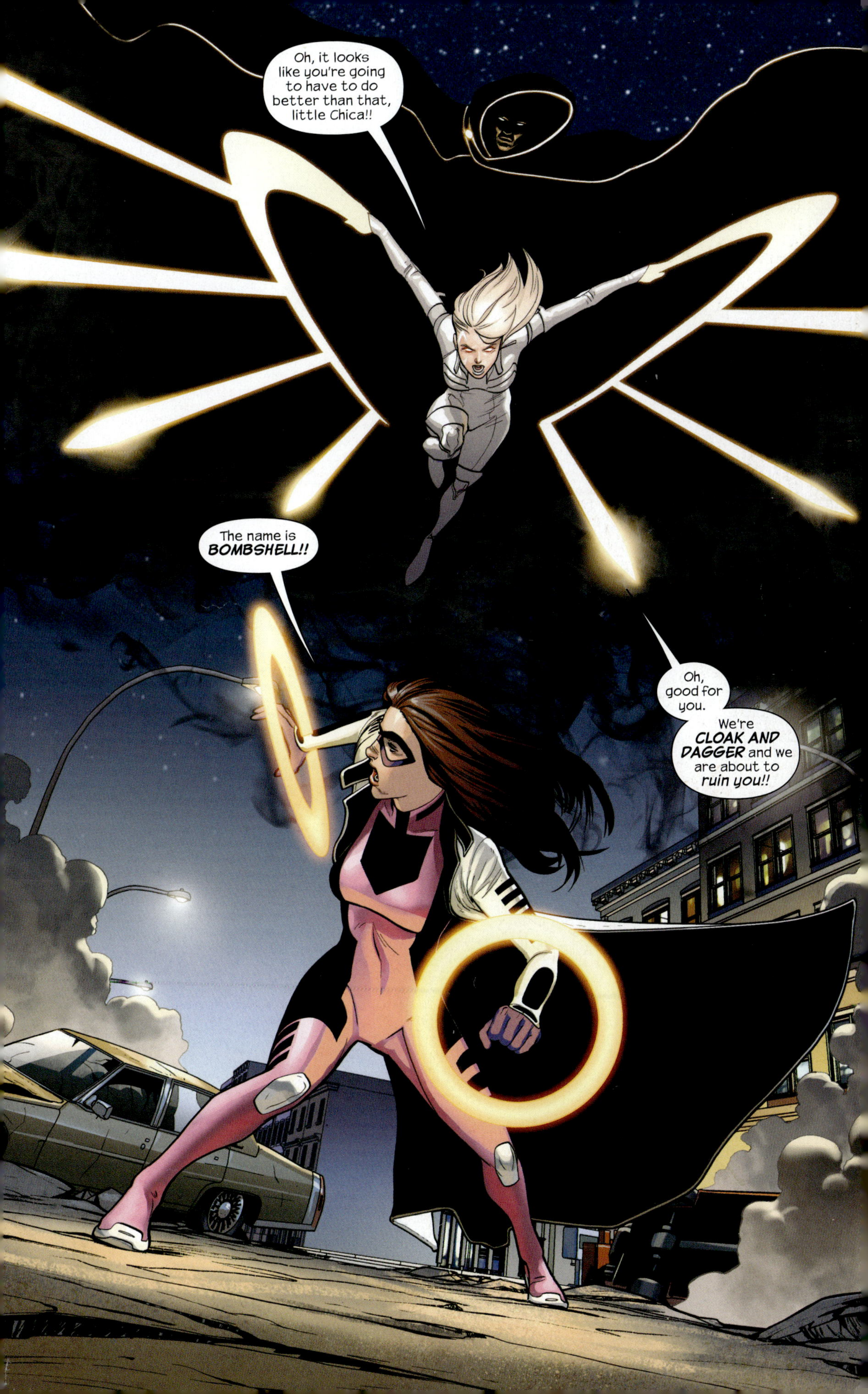
Oh, it looks like you're going to have to do better than that, little Chica!!
The name is BOMBSHELL!!
Oh, good for you.
We're CLOAK AND DAGGER and we are about to ruin you!!

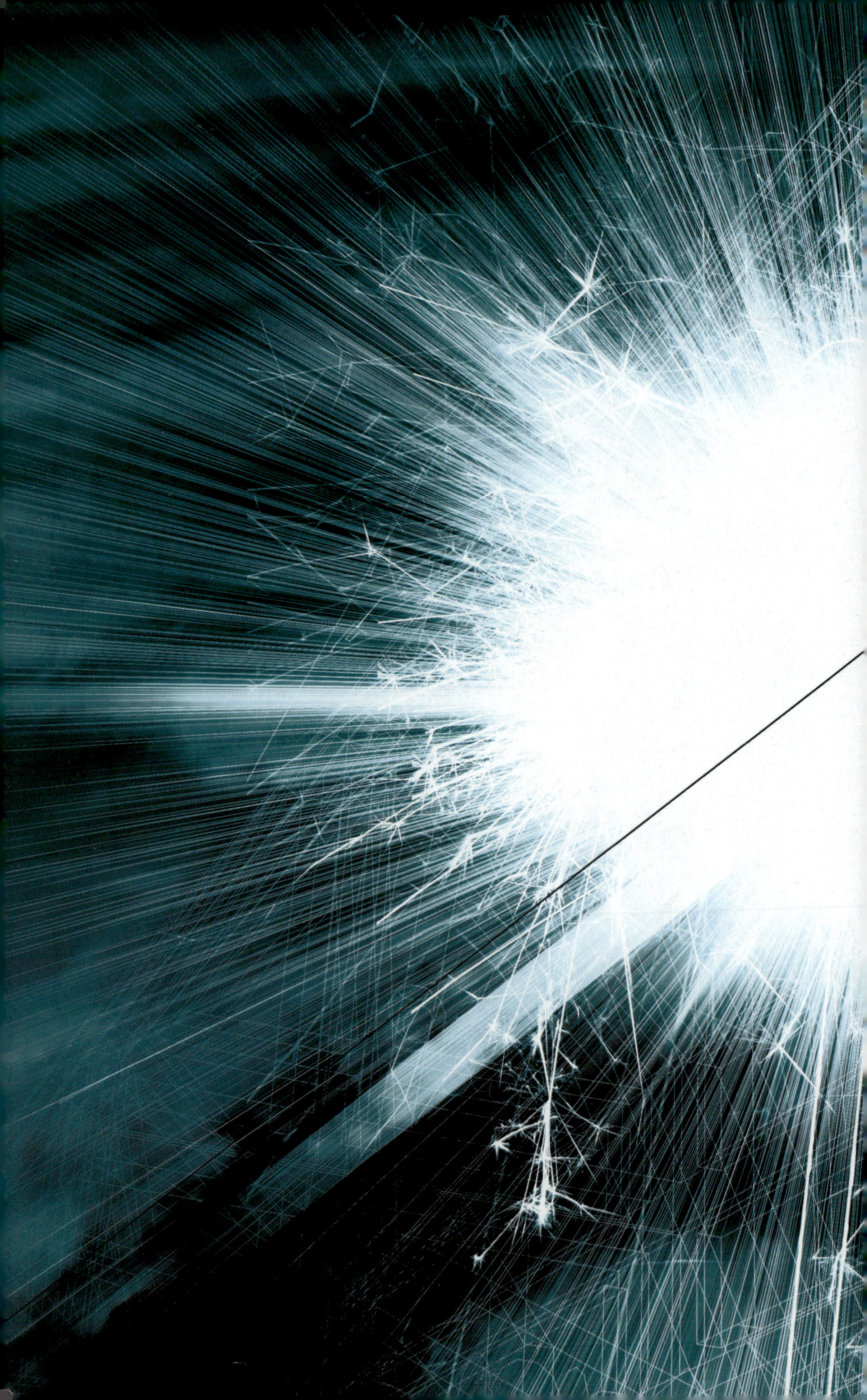

SPIDER-MAN NO MORE

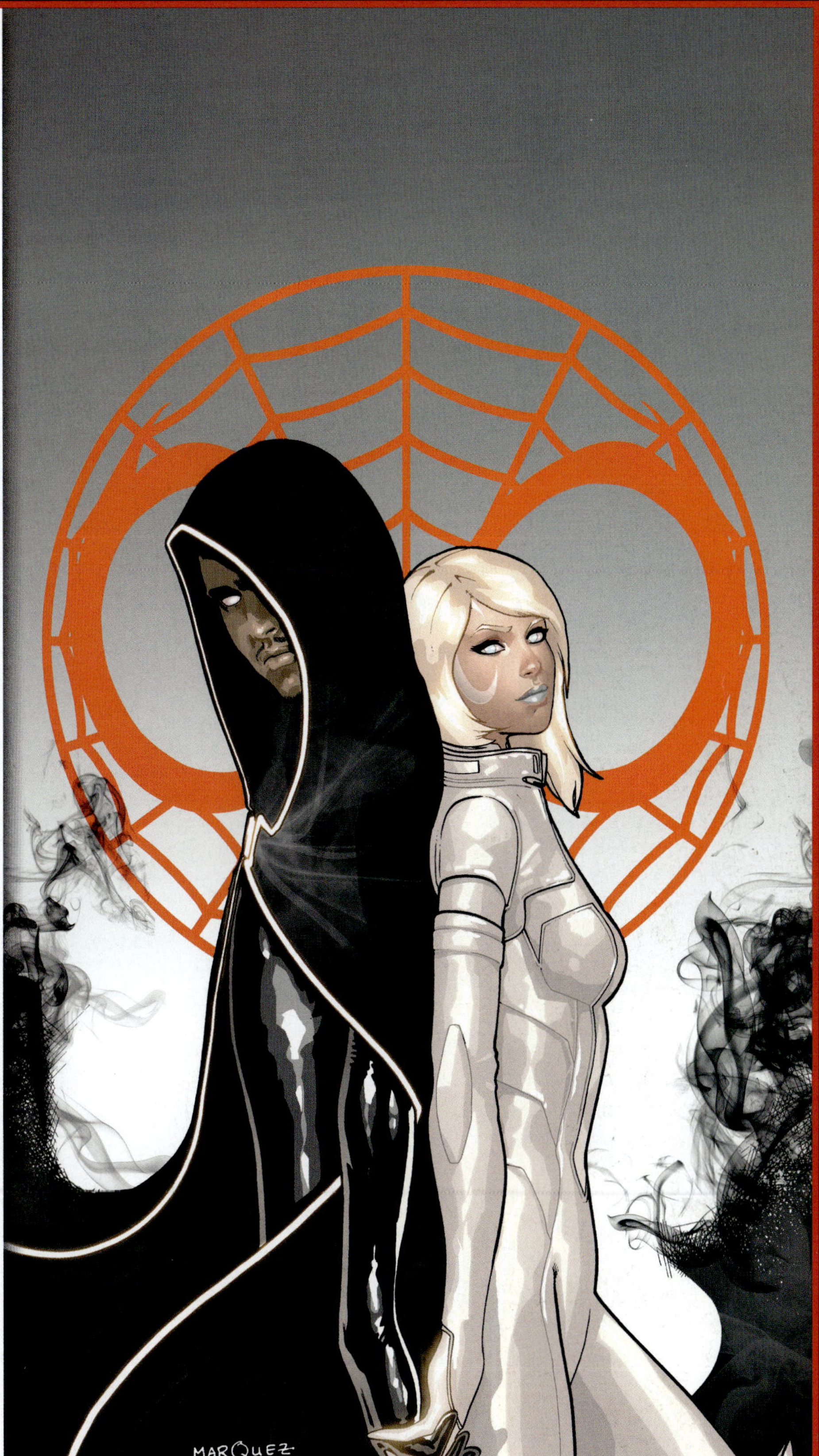
MARQUEZ
13

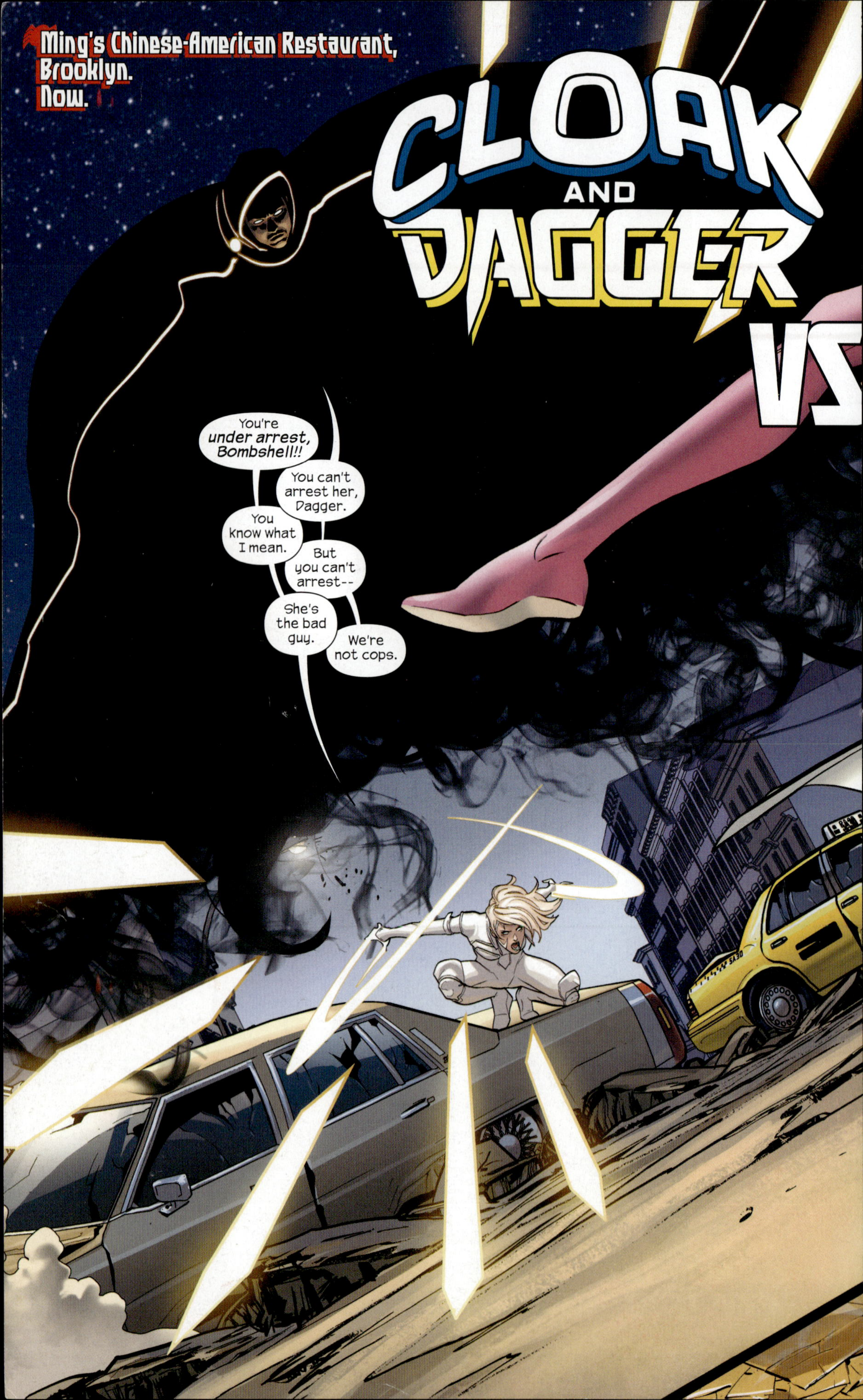
Ming's Chinese-American Restaurant, Brooklyn. Now.
CLOAK AND DAGGER VS
You're under arrest, Bombshell!!
You can't arrest her, Dagger.
You know what I mean.
But you can't arrest--
She's the bad guy.
We're not cops.

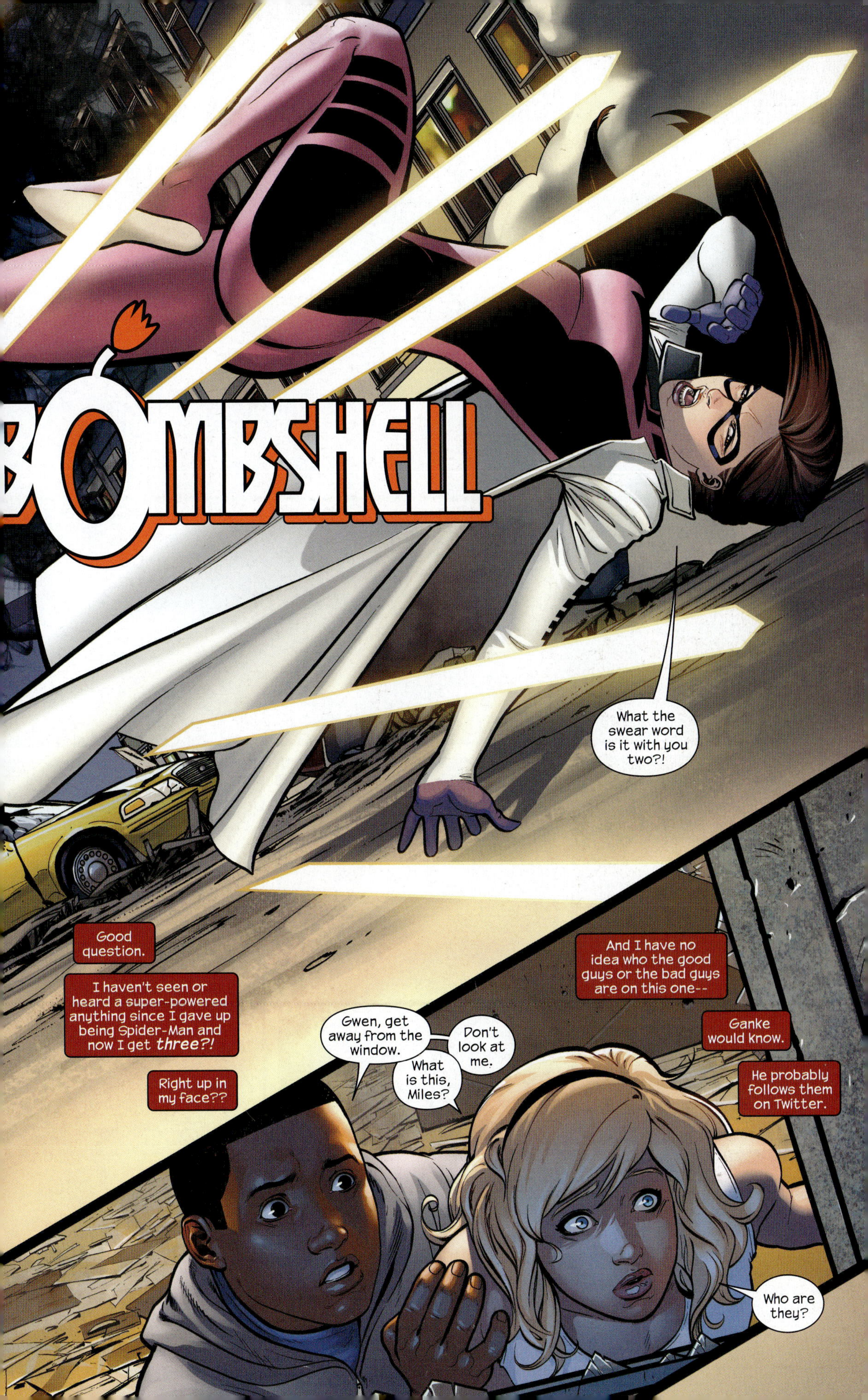
BOMBSHELL
What the swear word is it with you two?!
Good question.
I haven't seen or heard a super-powered anything since I gave up being Spider-Man and now I get *three?!*
Right up in my face??
And I have no idea who the good guys or the bad guys are on this one--
Ganke would know.
He probably follows them on Twitter.
Gwen, get away from the window.
Don't look at me.
What is this, Miles?
Who are they?

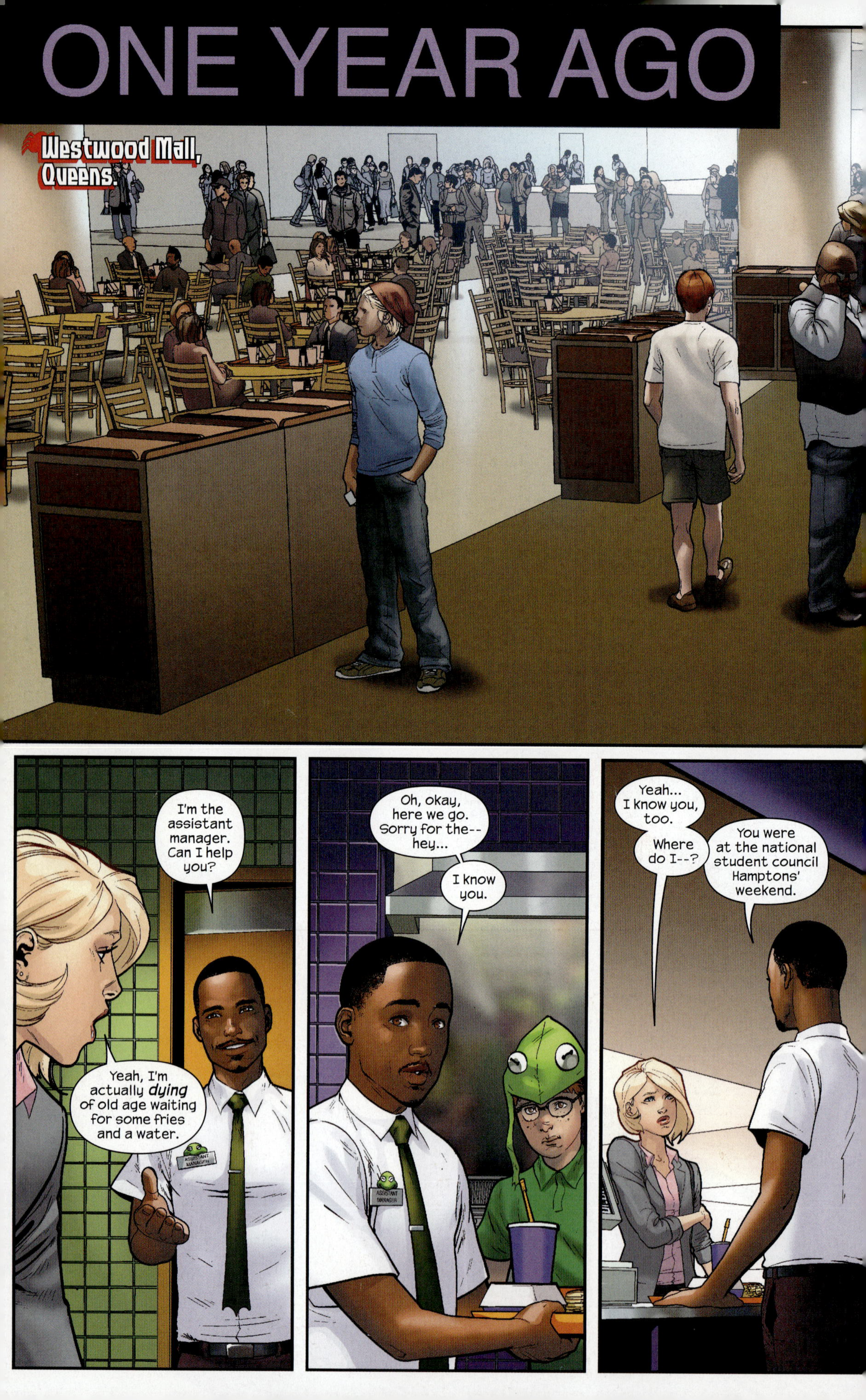
ONE YEAR AGO
Westwood Mall, Queens.
I'm the assistant manager. Can I help you?
Yeah, I'm actually *dying* of old age waiting for some fries and a water.
Oh, okay, here we go. Sorry for the-- hey...
I know you.
Yeah... I know you, too.
Where do I--?
You were at the national student council Hamptons' weekend.

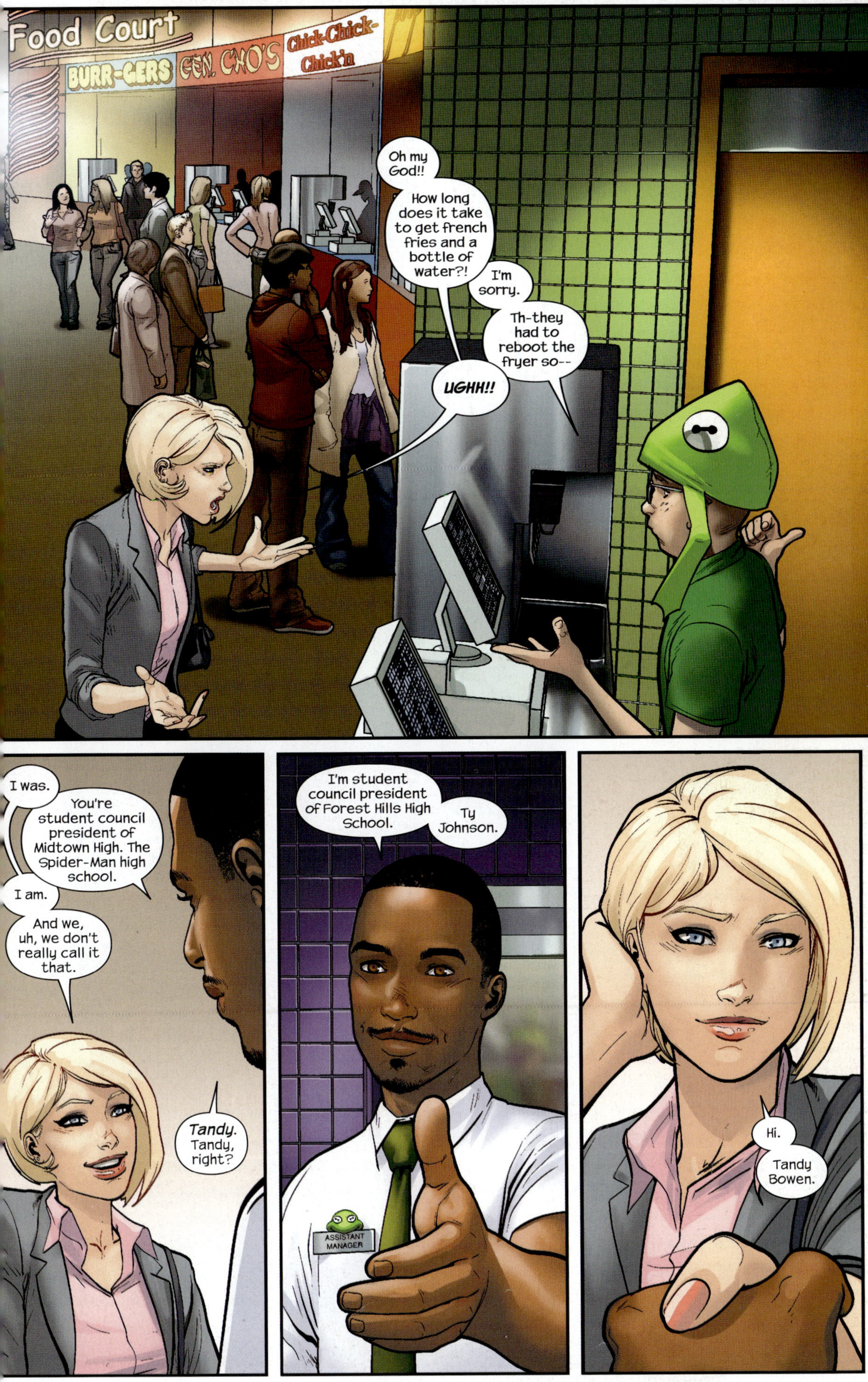
Food Court
BURR-GERS
GEN. CHO'S
Chick-Chick-Chick'n
Oh my God!!
How long does it take to get french fries and a bottle of water?!
I'm sorry.
Th-they had to reboot the fryer so--
UGHH!!
I was.
You're student council president of Midtown High. The Spider-Man high school.
I am.
And we, uh, we don't really call it that.
Tandy. Tandy, right?
I'm student council president of Forest Hills High School.
Ty Johnson.
ASSISTANT MANAGER
Hi.
Tandy Bowen.

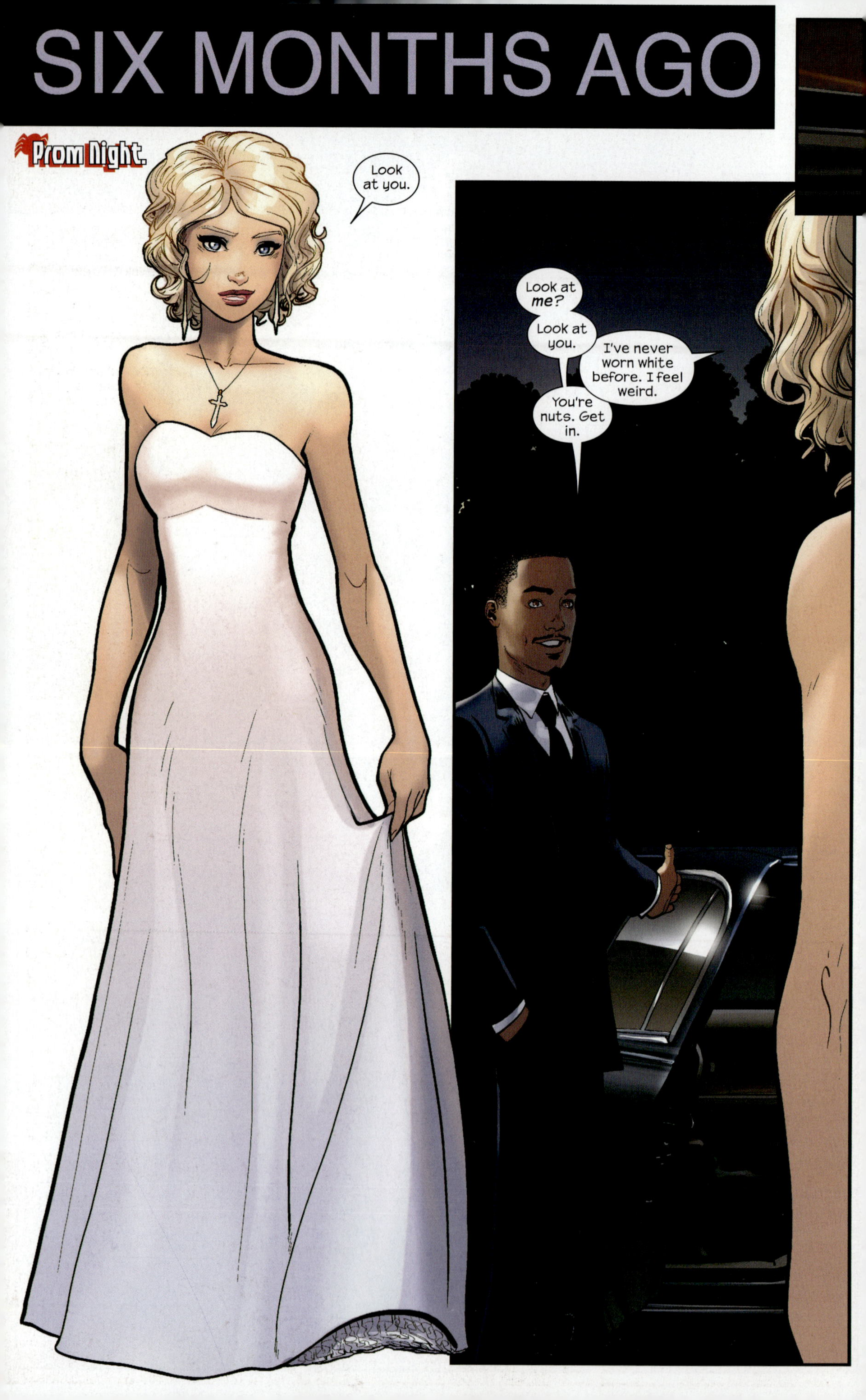
SIX MONTHS AGO
Prom Night.
Look at you.
Look at me?
Look at you.
I've never worn white before. I feel weird.
You're nuts. Get in.

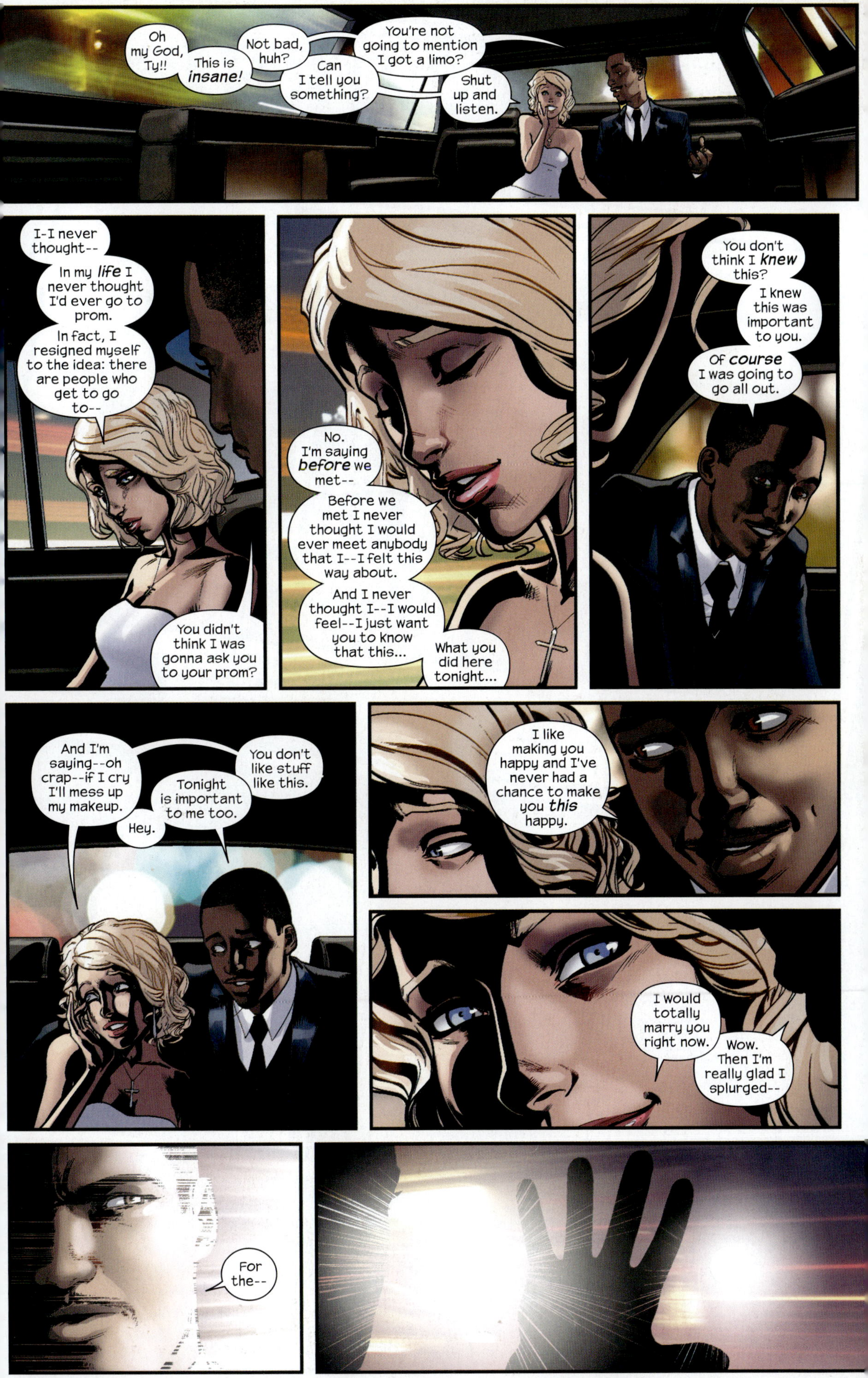
Oh my God, Ty!!
This is *insane!*
Not bad, huh?
You're not going to mention I got a limo?
Can I tell you something?
Shut up and listen.
I-I never thought--
In my *life* I never thought I'd ever go to prom.
In fact, I resigned myself to the idea: there are people who get to go to--
You didn't think I was gonna ask you to your prom?
No. I'm saying *before* we met--
Before we met I never thought I would ever meet anybody that I--I felt this way about.
And I never thought I--I would feel--I just want you to know that this...
What you did here tonight...
You don't think I *knew* this?
I knew this was important to you.
Of *course* I was going to go all out.
And I'm saying--oh crap--if I cry I'll mess up my makeup.
You don't like stuff like this.
Hey.
Tonight is important to me too.
I like making you happy and I've never had a chance to make you *this* happy.
I would totally marry you right now.
Wow. Then I'm really glad I splurged--
For the--

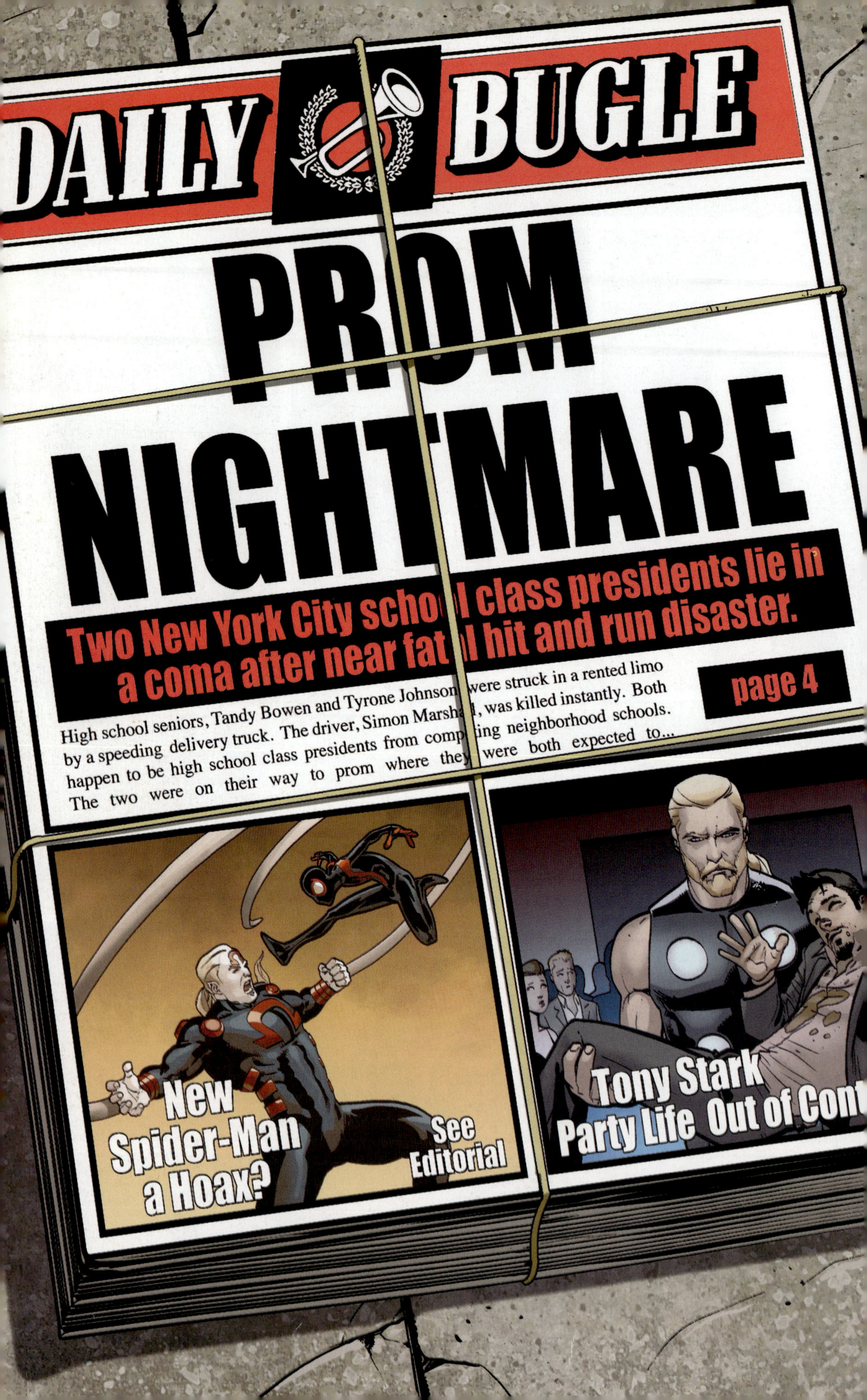

DAILY BUGLE
PROM NIGHTMARE
Two New York City school class presidents lie in a coma after near fatal hit and run disaster.
page 4
High school seniors, Tandy Bowen and Tyrone Johnson were struck in a rented limo by a speeding delivery truck. The driver, Simon Marshall, was killed instantly. Both happen to be high school class presidents from competing neighborhood schools. The two were on their way to prom where they were both expected to...
New Spider-Man a Hoax?
See Editorial
Tony Stark Party Life Out of Con

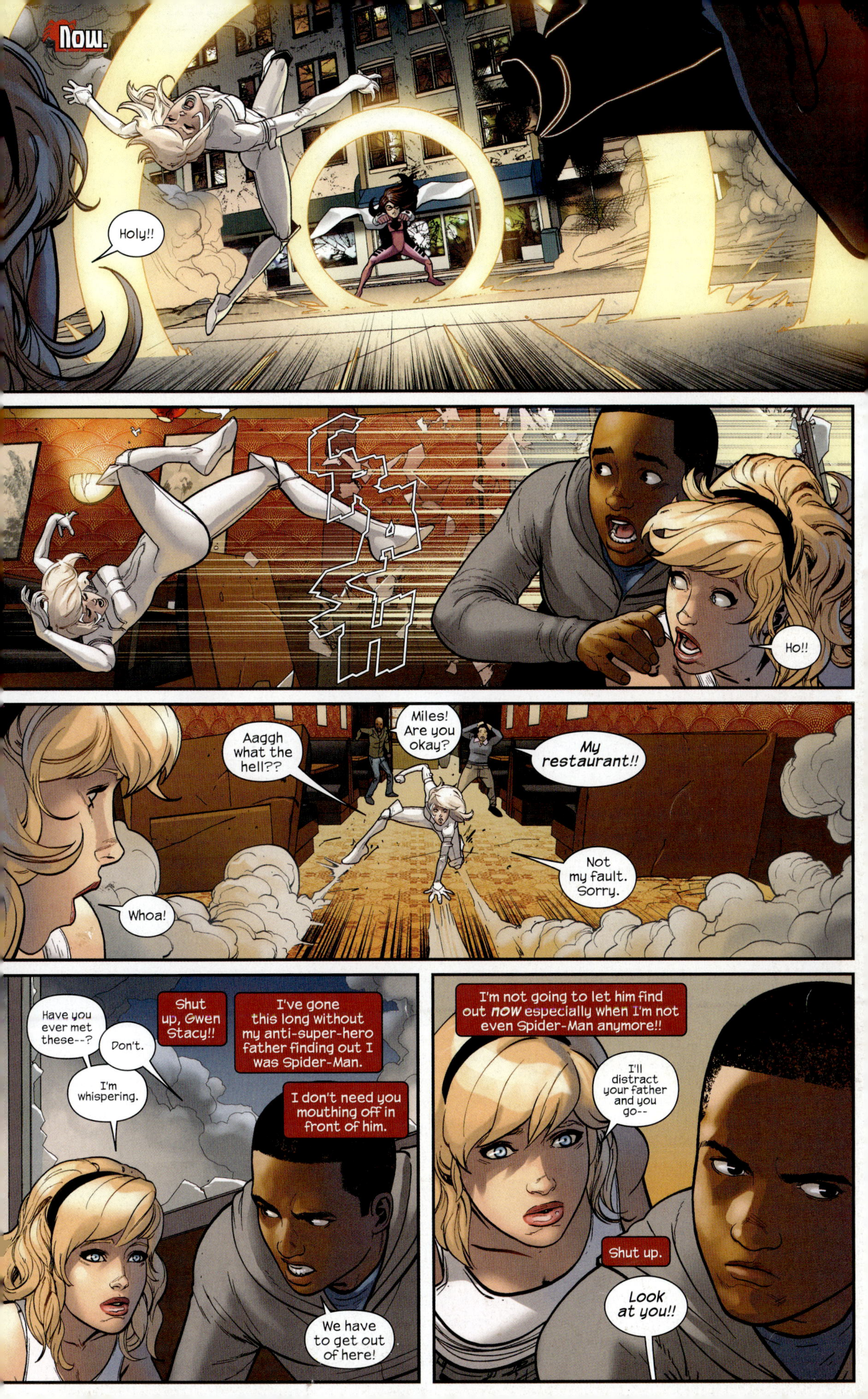
Now.
Holy!!
Ho!!
Aaggh what the hell??
Miles! Are you okay?
My restaurant!!
Whoa!
Not my fault. Sorry.
Have you ever met these--?
Don't.
I'm whispering.
Shut up, Gwen Stacy!!
I've gone this long without my anti-super-hero father finding out I was Spider-Man.
I don't need you mouthing off in front of him.
We have to get out of here!
I'm not going to let him find out *now* especially when I'm not even Spider-Man anymore!!
I'll distract your father and you go--
Shut up.
Look at you!!

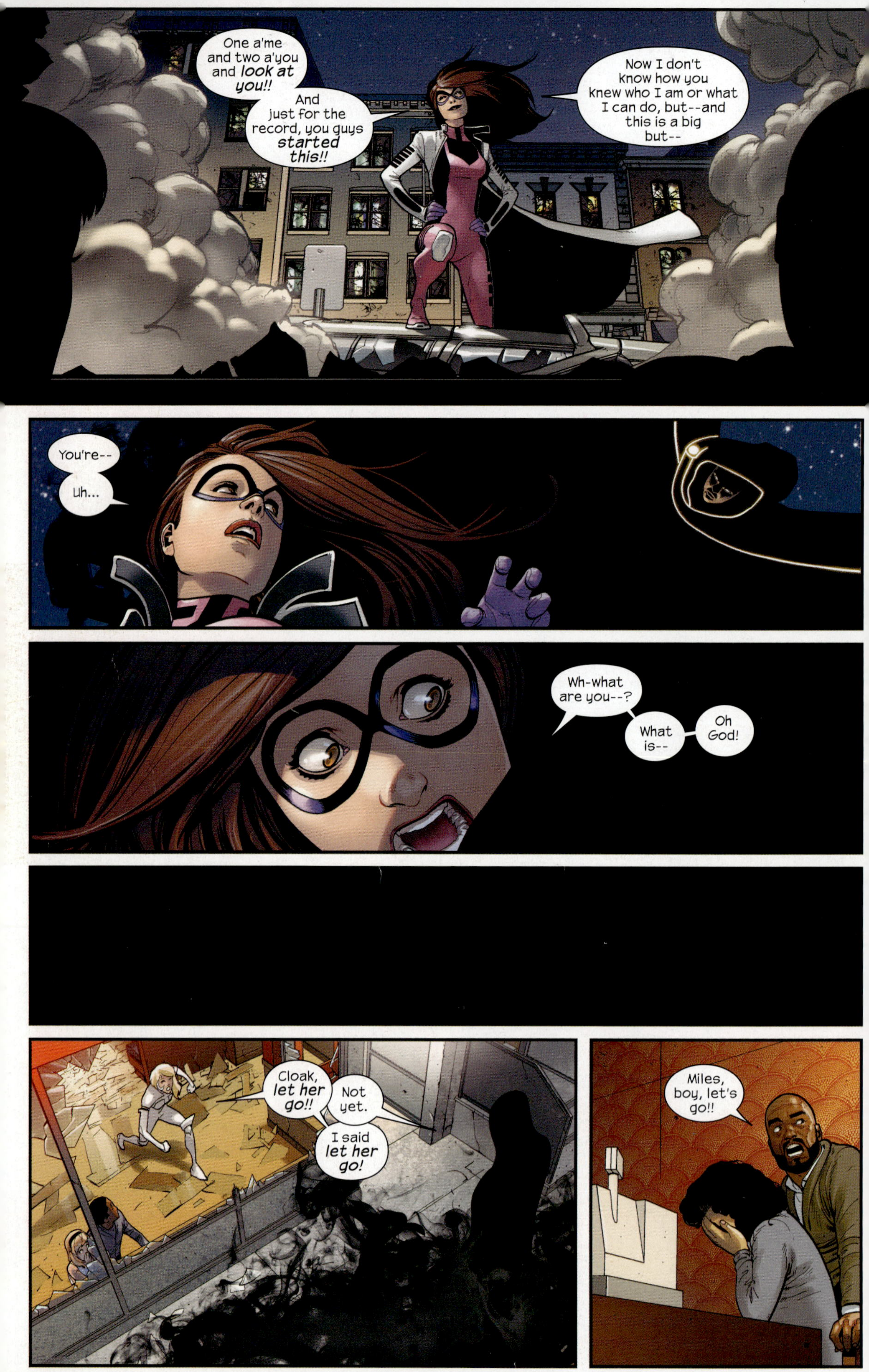

One a'me and two a'you and *look at you!!*
And just for the record, you guys *started this!!*
Now I don't know how you knew who I am or what I can do, but--and this is a big but--
You're--
uh...
Wh-what are you--?
What is--
Oh God!
Cloak, *let her go!!*
Not yet.
I said *let her go!*
Miles, boy, let's go!!

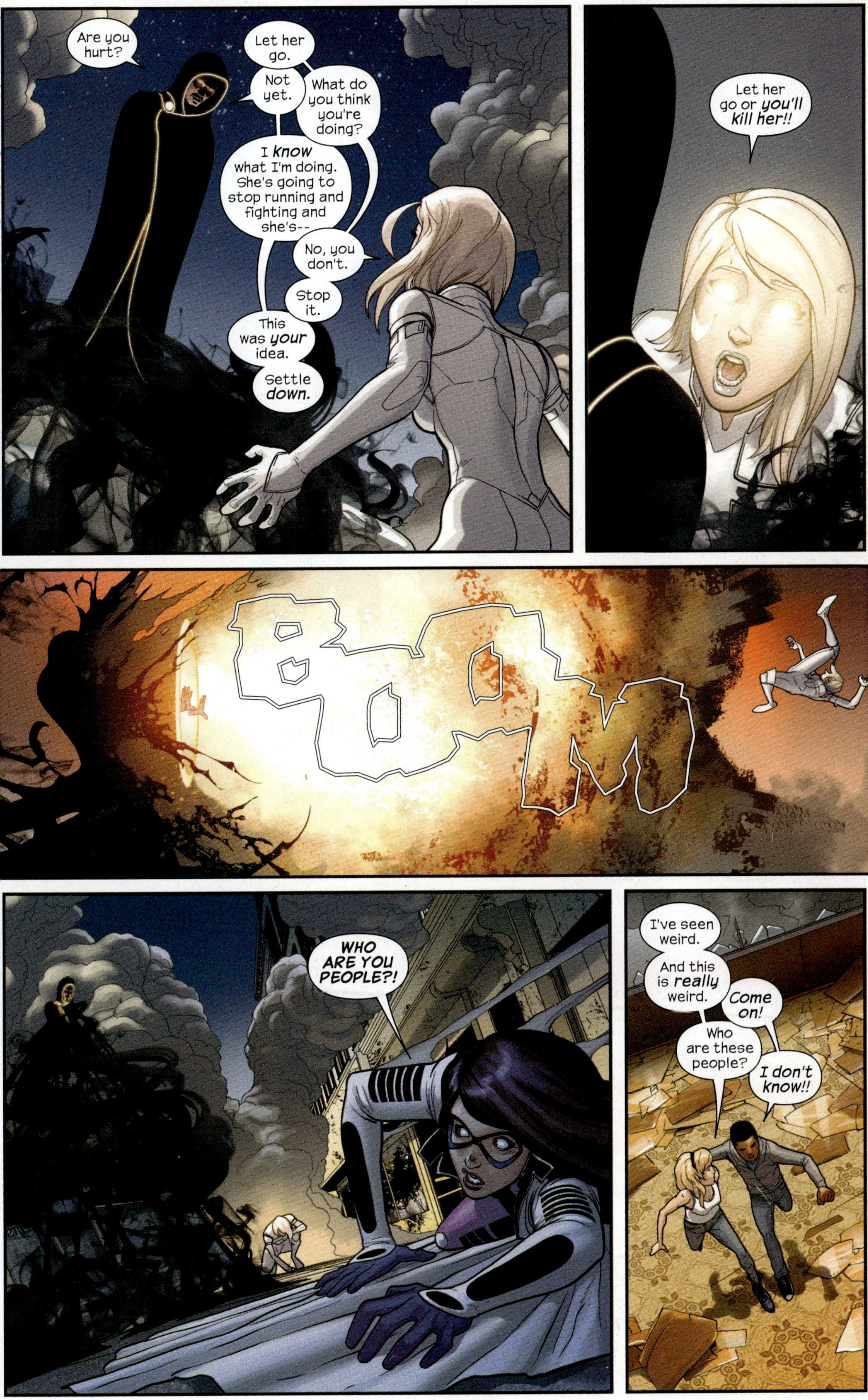
Are you hurt?
Let her go.
Not yet.
What do you think you're doing?
I *know* what I'm doing. She's going to stop running and fighting and she's--
No, you don't.
Stop it.
This was *your* idea.
Settle *down.*
Let her go or *you'll kill her!!*
BOOM
WHO ARE YOU PEOPLE?!
I've seen weird.
And this is *really* weird.
Come on!
Who are these people?
I don't know!!

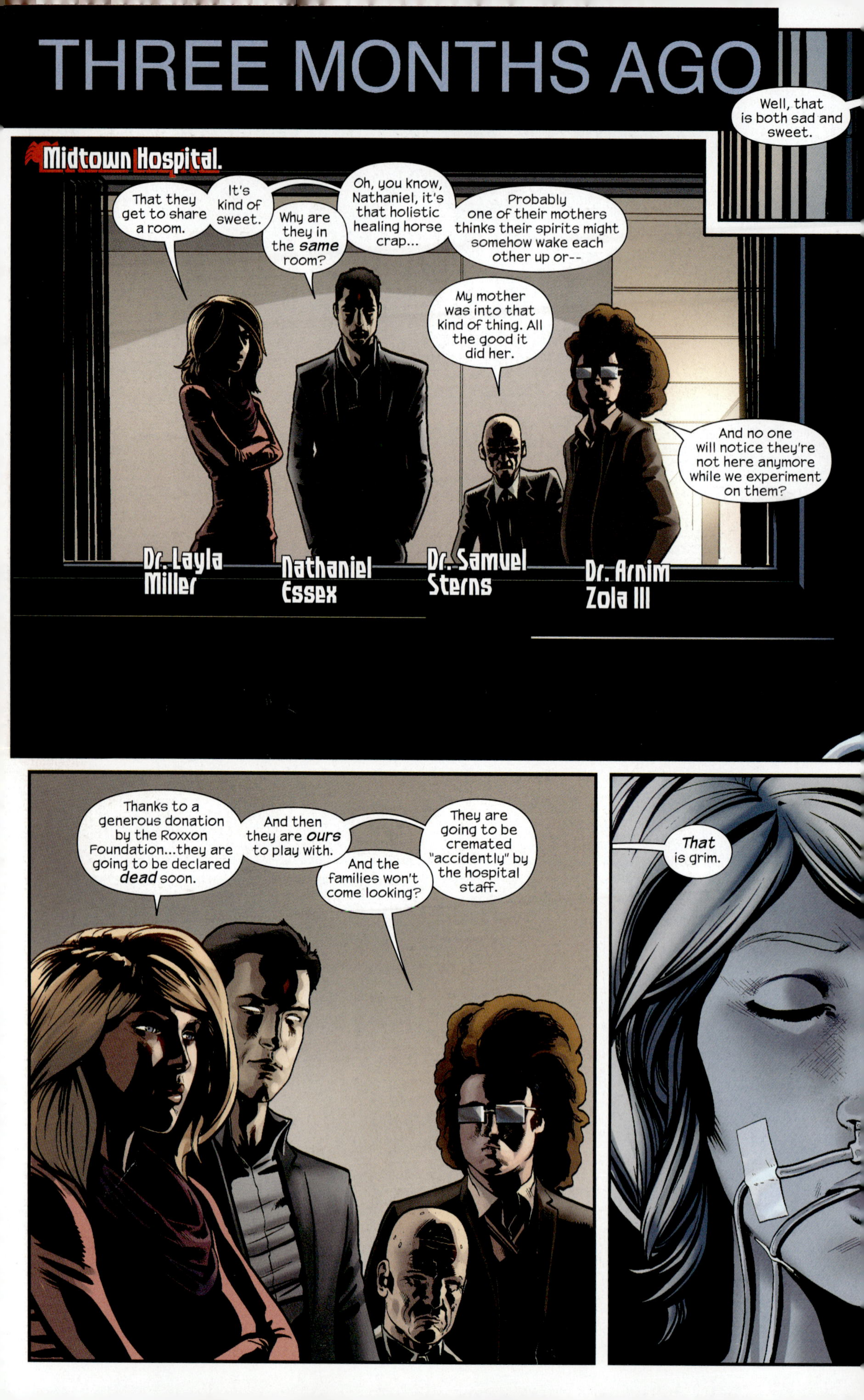
THREE MONTHS AGO
Well, that is both sad and sweet.
Midtown Hospital.
That they get to share a room.
It's kind of sweet.
Why are they in the *same* room?
Oh, you know, Nathaniel, it's that holistic healing horse crap...
Probably one of their mothers thinks their spirits might somehow wake each other up or--
My mother was into that kind of thing. All the good it did her.
And no one will notice they're not here anymore while we experiment on them?
Dr. Layla Miller
Nathaniel Essex
Dr. Samuel Sterns
Dr. Arnim Zola III
Thanks to a generous donation by the Roxxon Foundation...they are going to be declared *dead* soon.
And then they are *ours* to play with.
And the families won't come looking?
They are going to be cremated "accidently" by the hospital staff.
That is grim.

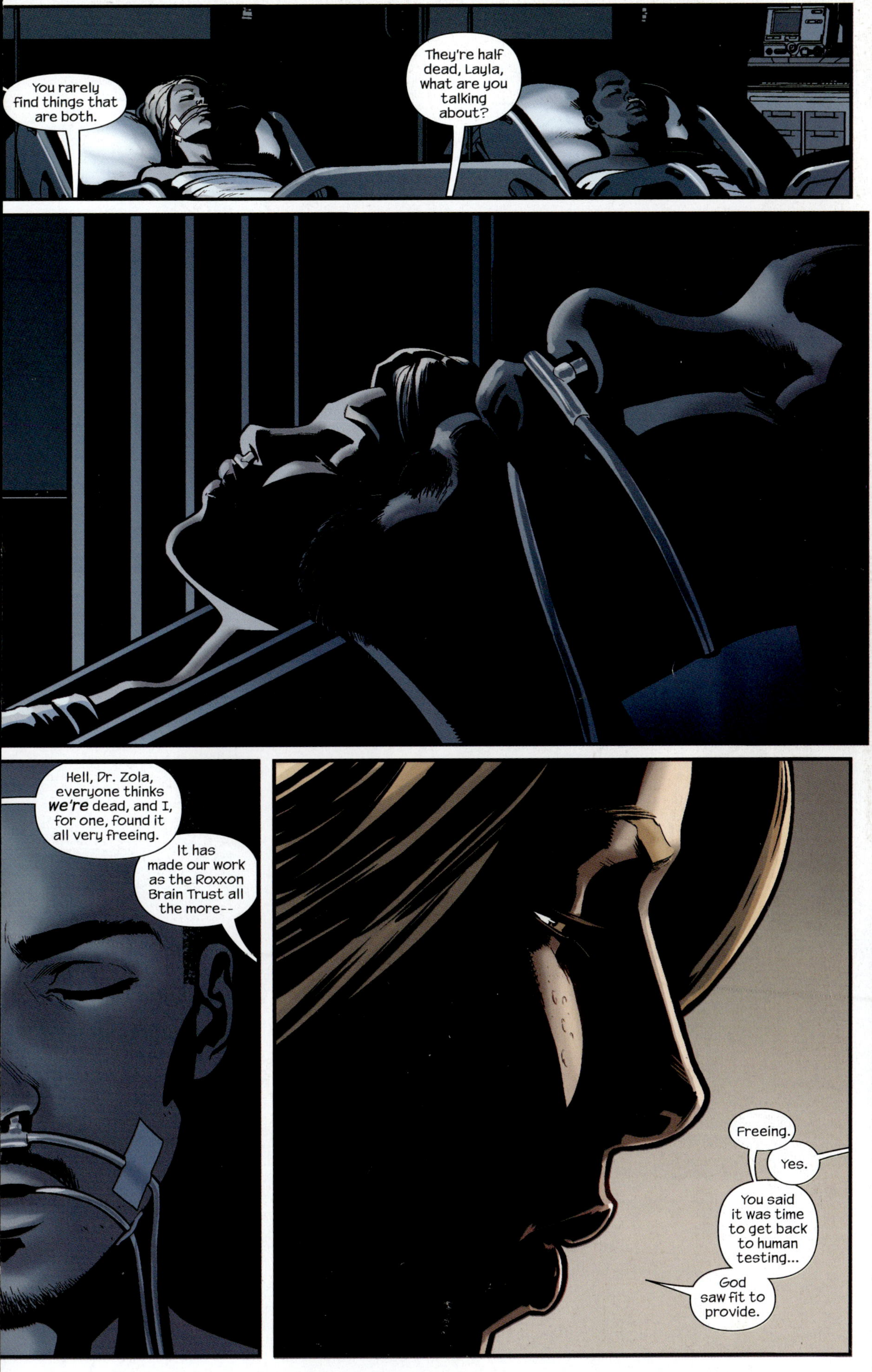
You rarely find things that are both.
They're half dead, Layla, what are you talking about?
Hell, Dr. Zola, everyone thinks *we're* dead, and I, for one, found it all very freeing.
It has made our work as the Roxxon Brain Trust all the more--
Freeing.
Yes.
You said it was time to get back to human testing...
God saw fit to provide.

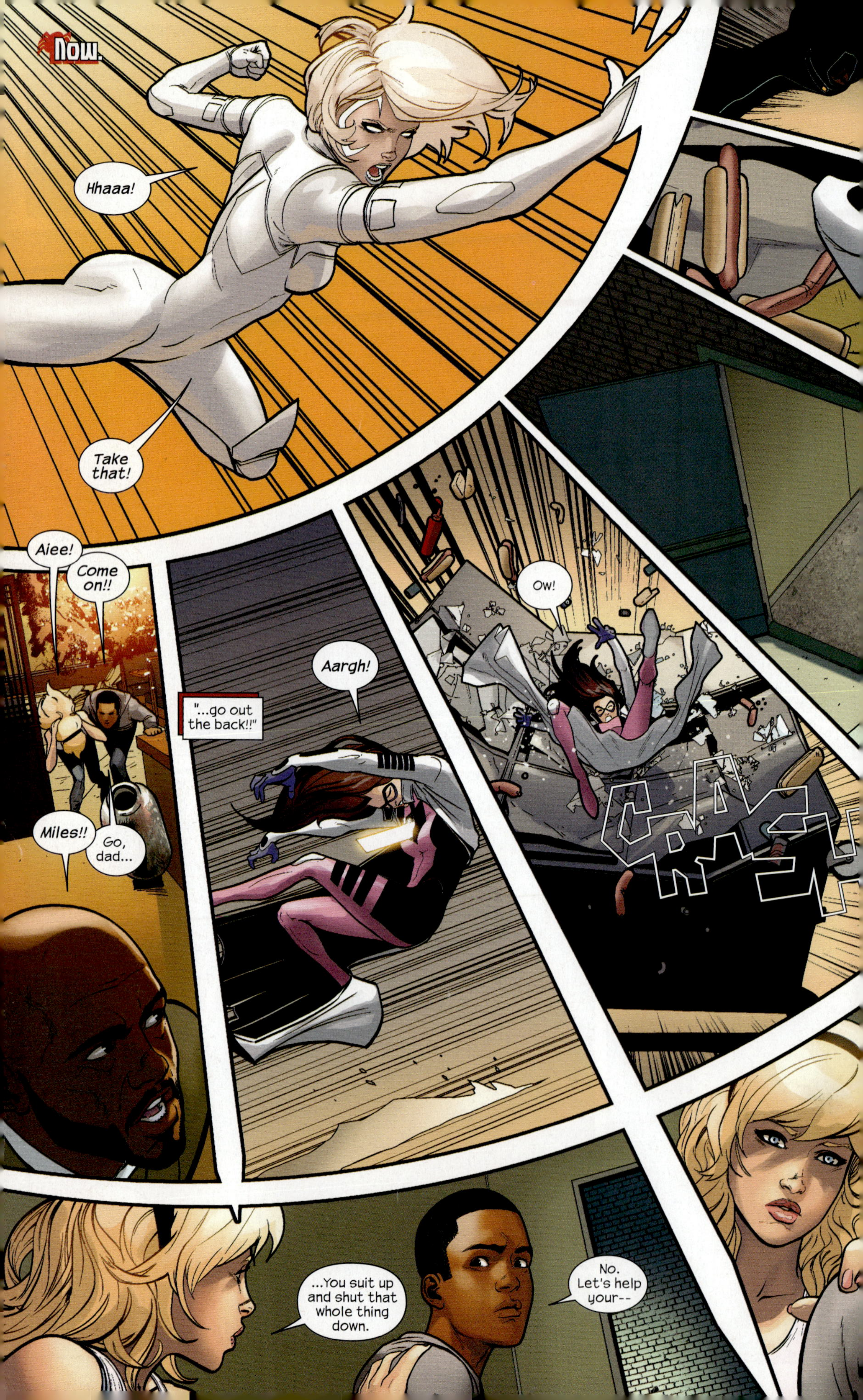
Now.
Hhaaa!
Take that!
Aiee!
Come on!!
Miles!!
Go, dad...
"...go out the back!!"
Aargh!
Ow!
...You suit up and shut that whole thing down.
No. Let's help your--

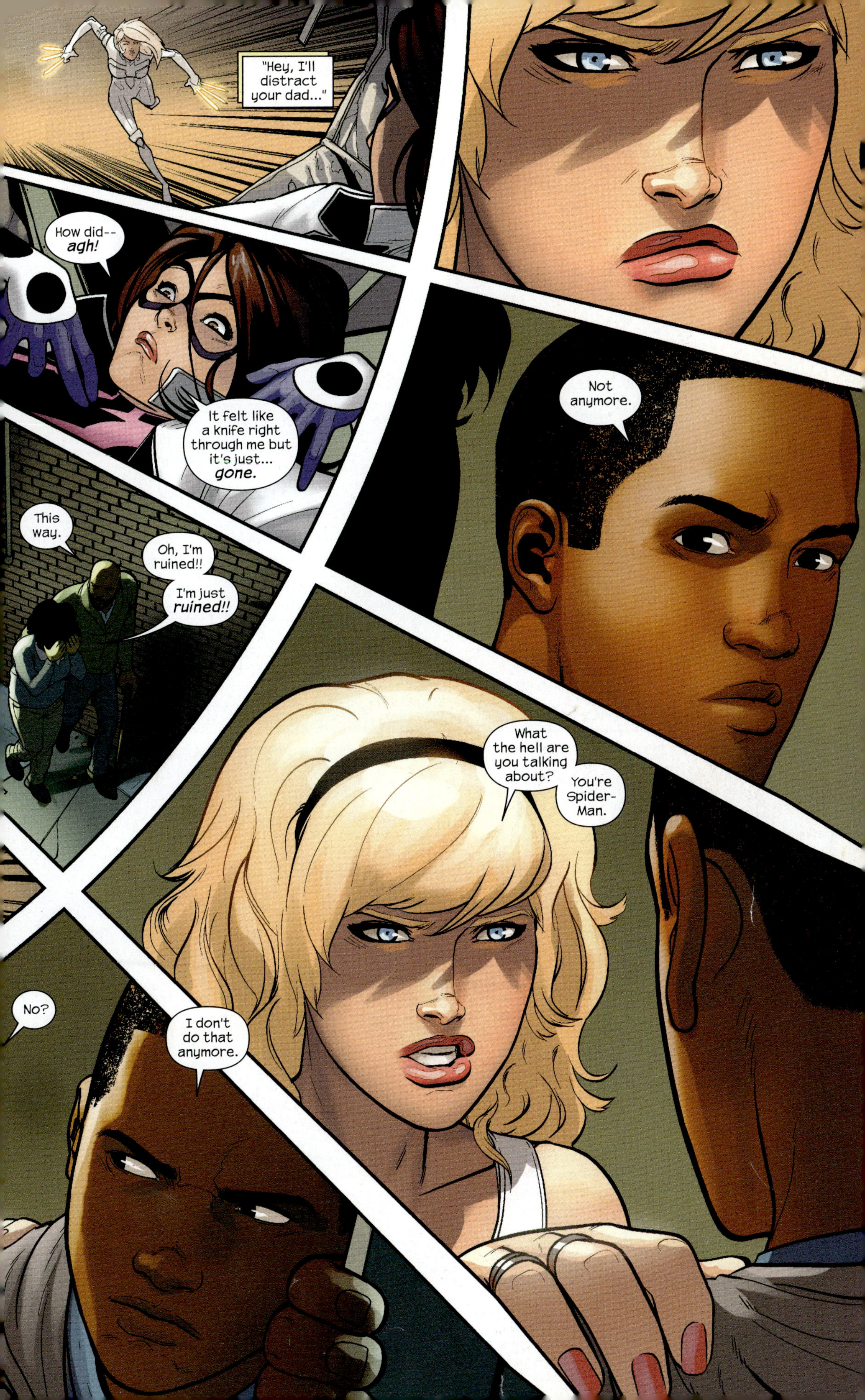
"Hey, I'll distract your dad..."
How did-- agh!
It felt like a knife right through me but it's just... gone.
This way.
Oh, I'm ruined!!
I'm just ruined!!
Not anymore.
What the hell are you talking about?
You're Spider-Man.
No?
I don't do that anymore.

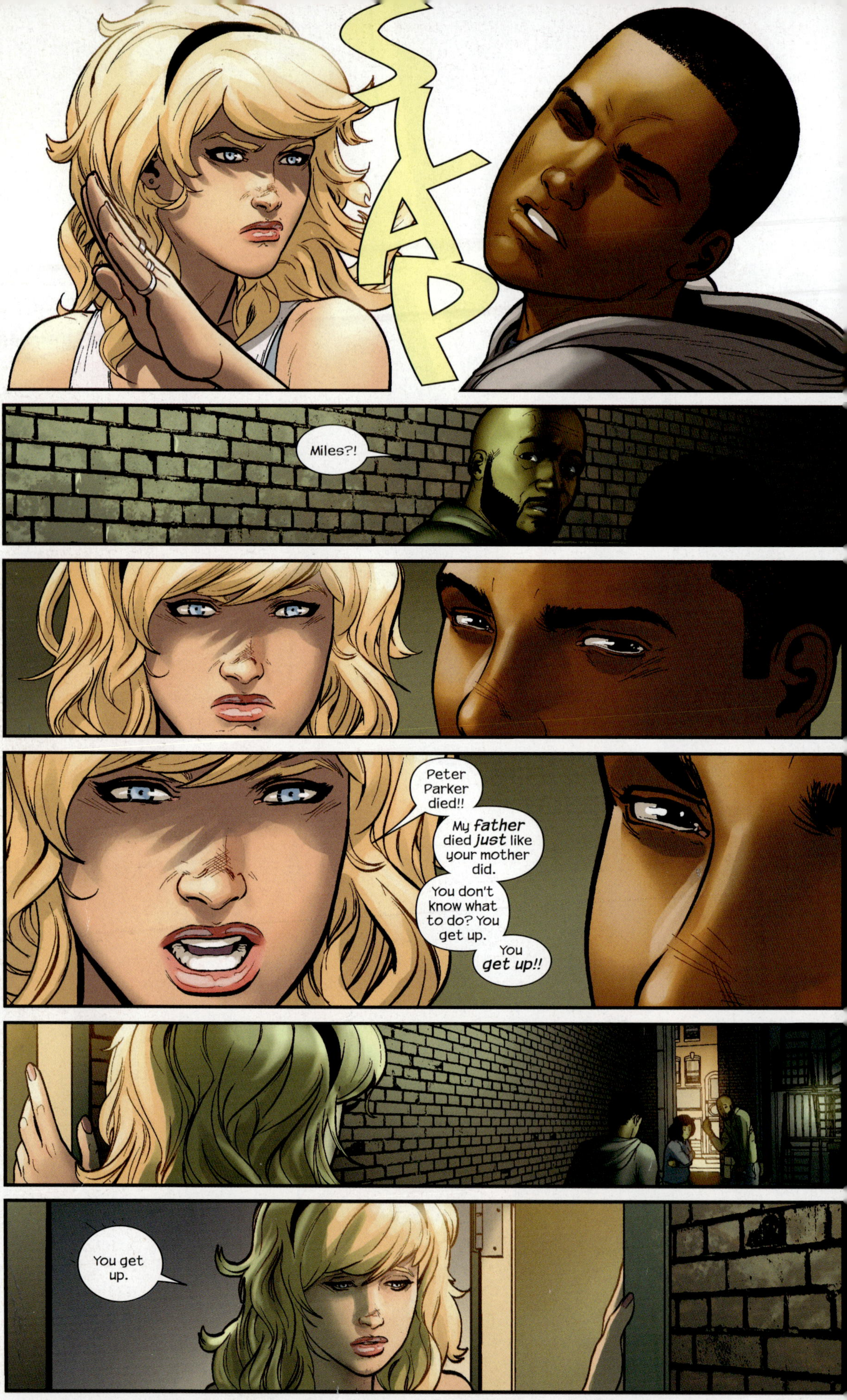
SLAP
Miles?!
Peter Parker died!!
My father died just like your mother did.
You don't know what to do? You get up.
You get up!!
You get up.

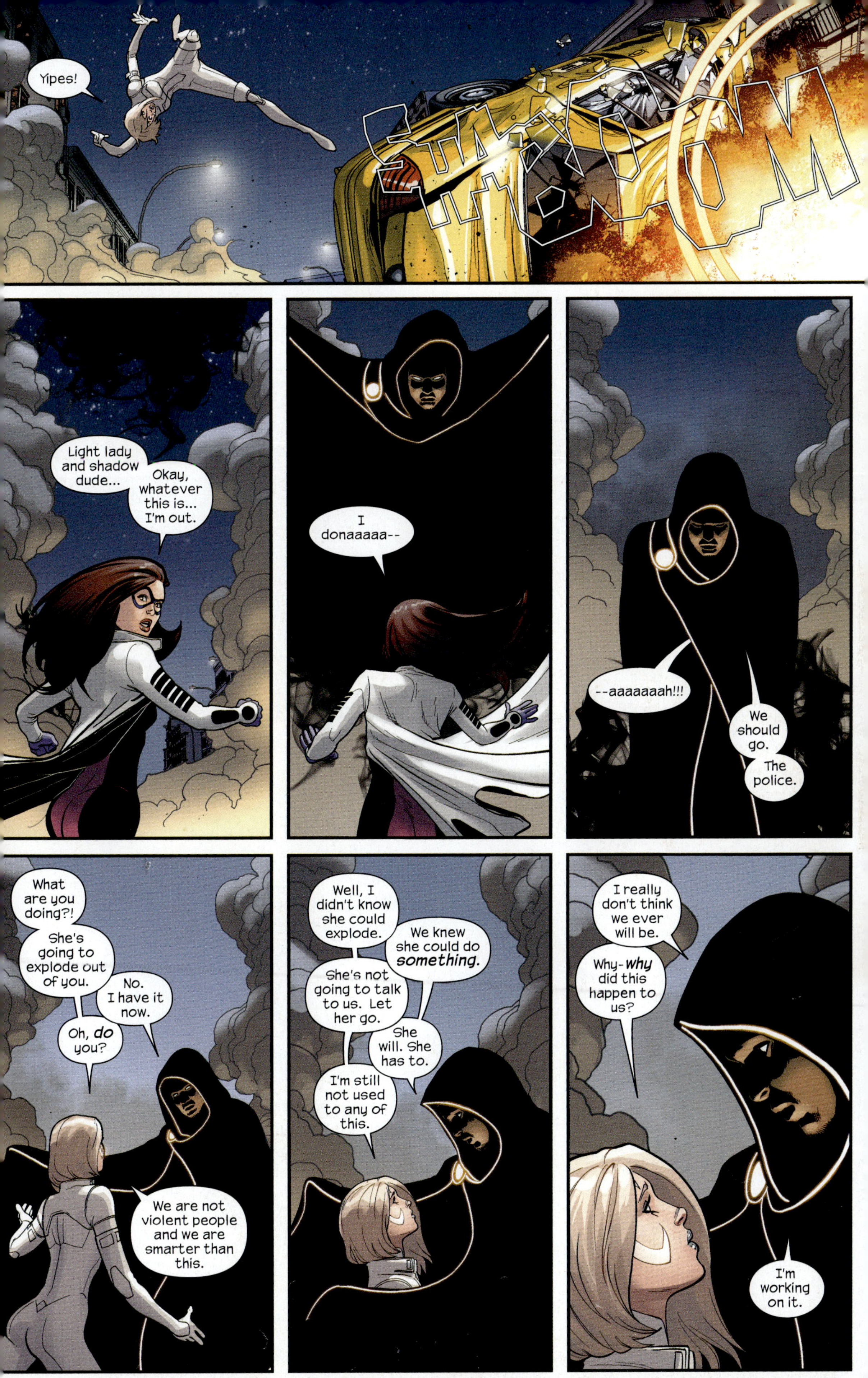
Yipes!
SHAKOOOM
Light lady and shadow dude...
Okay, whatever this is... I'm out.
I donaaaaa--
--aaaaaaah!!!
We should go.
The police.
What are you doing?!
She's going to explode out of you.
No. I have it now.
Oh, *do* you?
We are not violent people and we are smarter than this.
Well, I didn't know she could explode.
We knew she could do *something*.
She's not going to talk to us. Let her go.
She will. She has to.
I'm still not used to any of this.
I really don't think we ever will be.
Why-*why* did this happen to us?
I'm working on it.

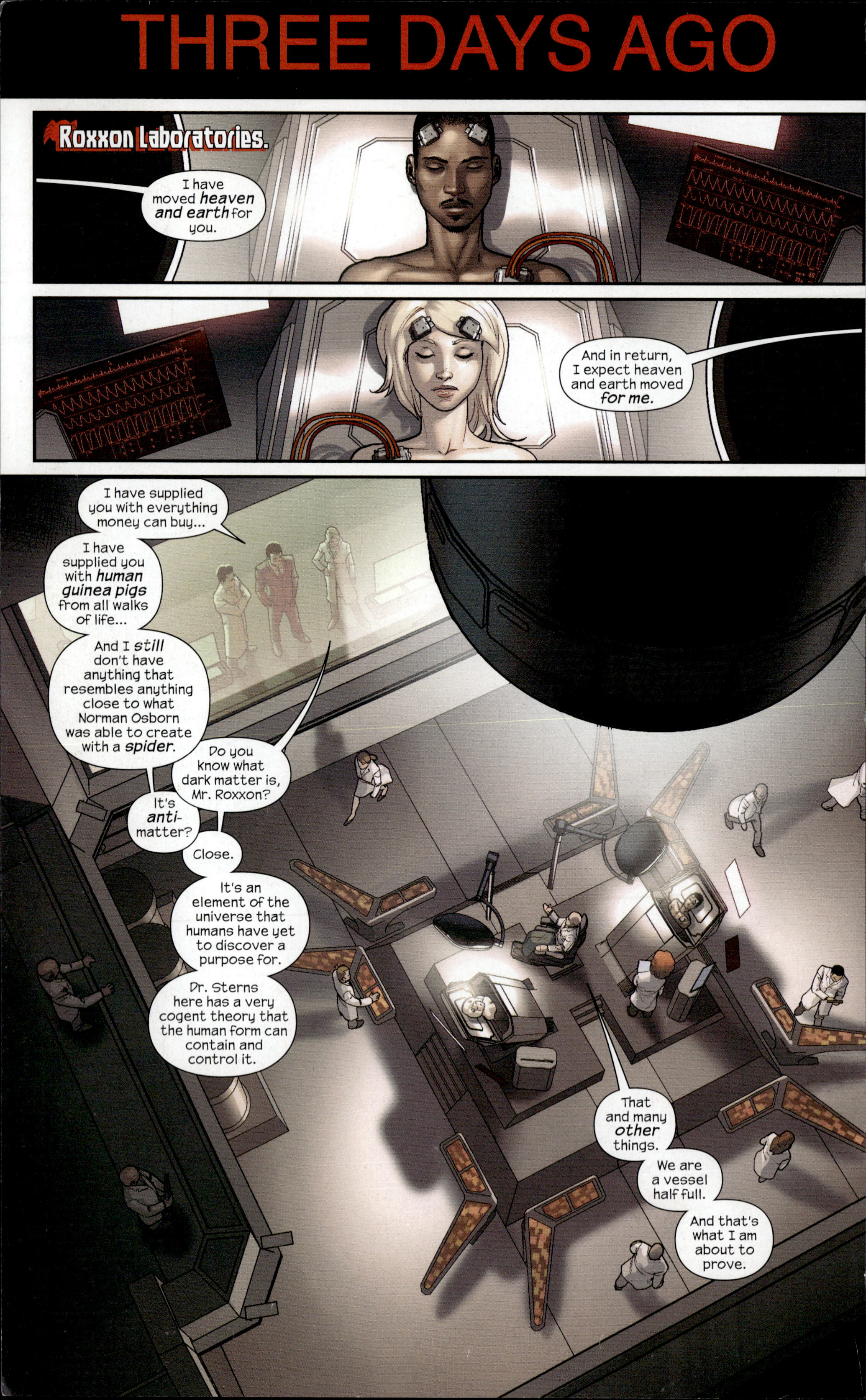
THREE DAYS AGO
Roxxon Laboratories.
I have moved heaven and earth for you.
And in return, I expect heaven and earth moved for me.
I have supplied you with everything money can buy...
I have supplied you with human guinea pigs from all walks of life...
And I still don't have anything that resembles anything close to what Norman Osborn was able to create with a spider.
Do you know what dark matter is, Mr. Roxxon?
It's anti-matter?
Close.
It's an element of the universe that humans have yet to discover a purpose for.
Dr. Sterns here has a very cogent theory that the human form can contain and control it.
That and many other things.
We are a vessel half full.
And that's what I am about to prove.

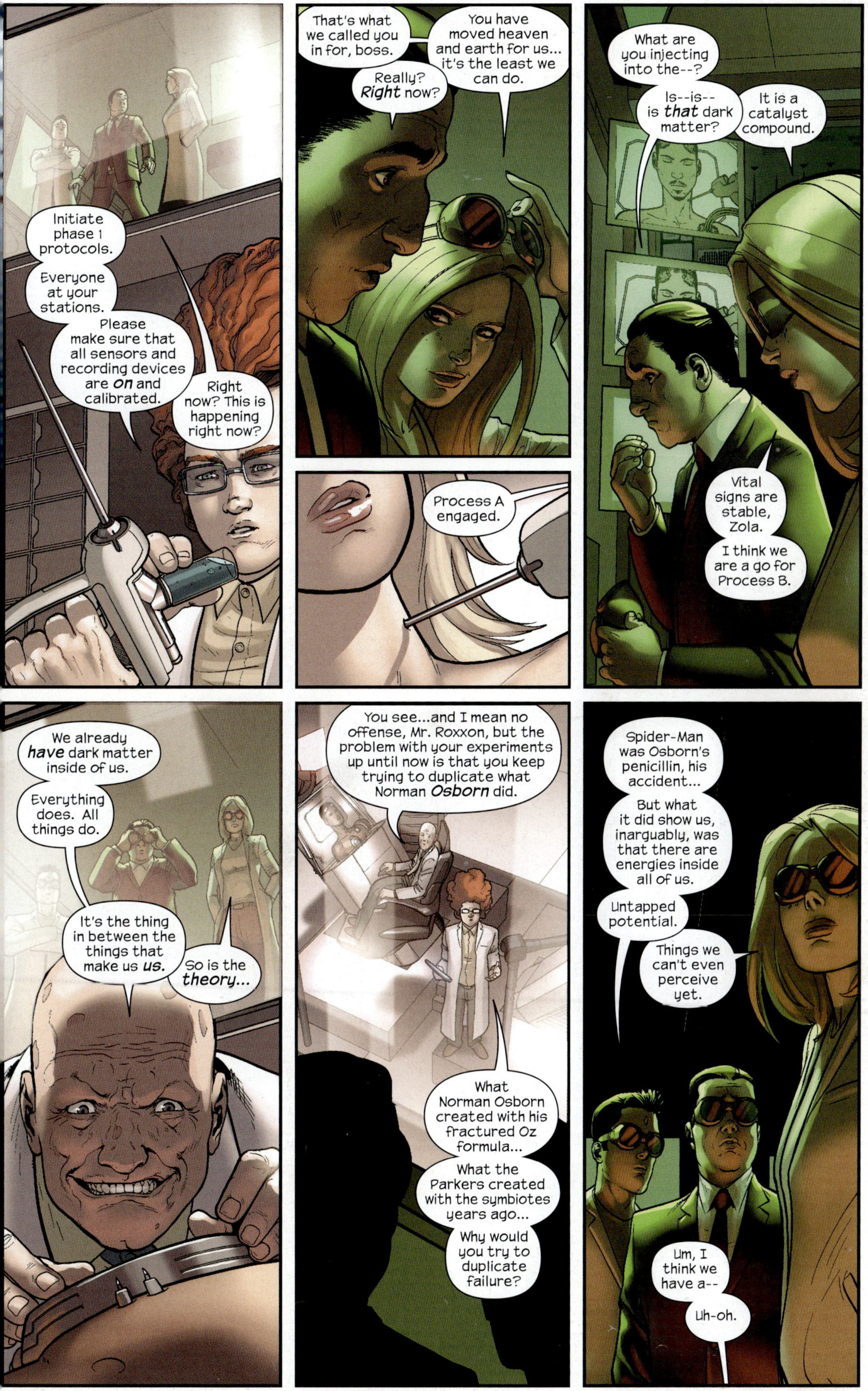

Initiate phase 1 protocols.
Everyone at your stations.
Please make sure that all sensors and recording devices are *on* and calibrated.
Right now? This is happening right now?
That's what we called you in for, boss.
You have moved heaven and earth for us... it's the least we can do.
Really? *Right* now?
Process A engaged.
What are you injecting into the--?
Is--is--is *that* dark matter?
It is a catalyst compound.
Vital signs are stable, Zola.
I think we are a go for Process B.
We already *have* dark matter inside of us.
Everything does. All things do.
It's the thing in between the things that make us *us.*
So is the *theory...*
You see...and I mean no offense, Mr. Roxxon, but the problem with your experiments up until now is that you keep trying to duplicate what Norman *Osborn* did.
What Norman Osborn created with his fractured Oz formula...
What the Parkers created with the symbiotes years ago...
Why would you try to duplicate failure?
Spider-Man was Osborn's penicillin, his accident...
But what it did show us, inarguably, was that there are energies inside all of us.
Untapped potential.
Things we can't even perceive yet.
Um, I think we have a--
Uh-oh.

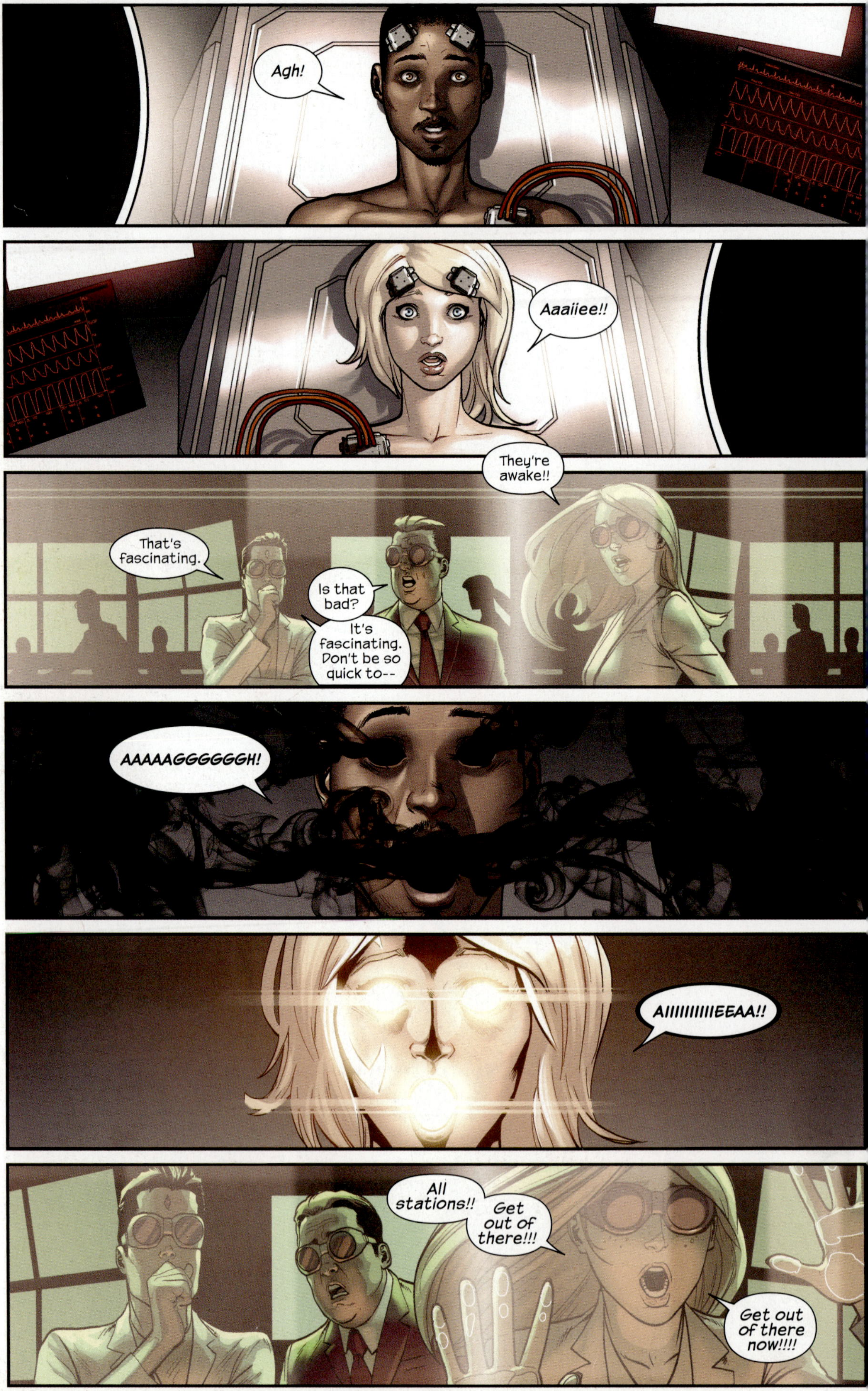
Agh!
Aaaiiee!!
They're awake!!
That's fascinating.
Is that bad?
It's fascinating. Don't be so quick to--
AAAAAGGGGGGH!
AIIIIIIIIIEEAA!!
All stations!!
Get out of there!!!
Get out of there now!!!!

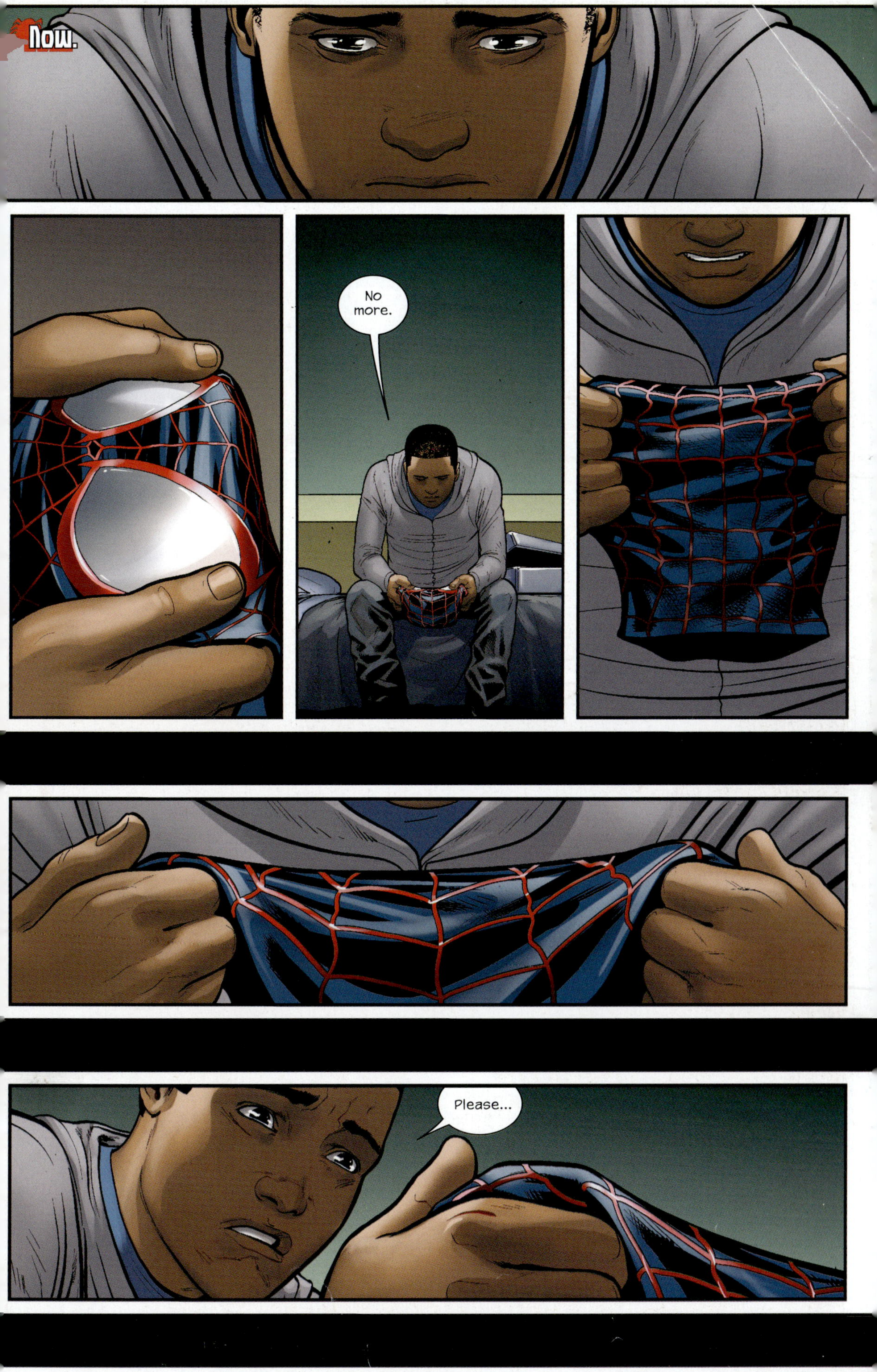
Now.
No more.
Please...

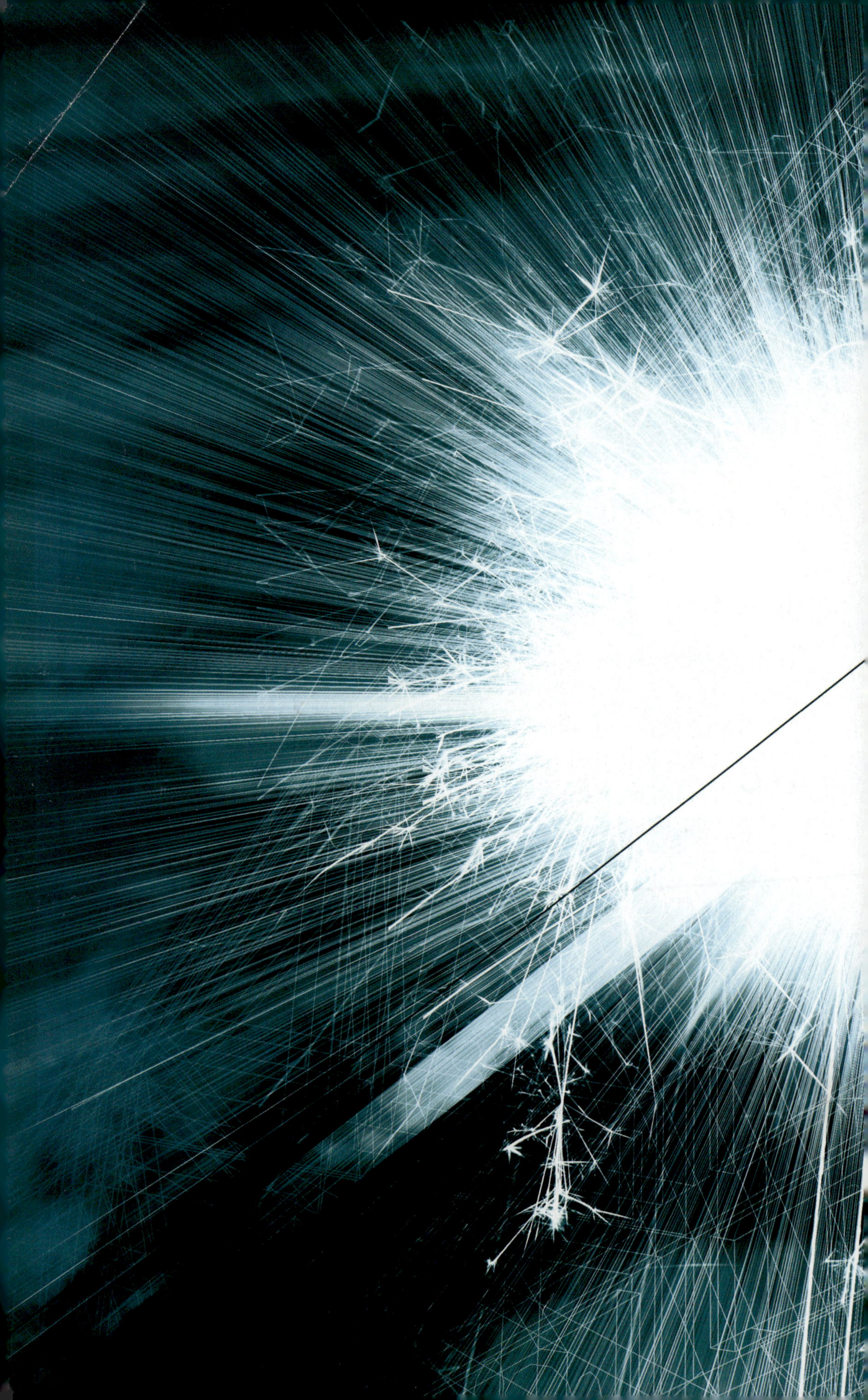

SPIDER-MAN NO MORE

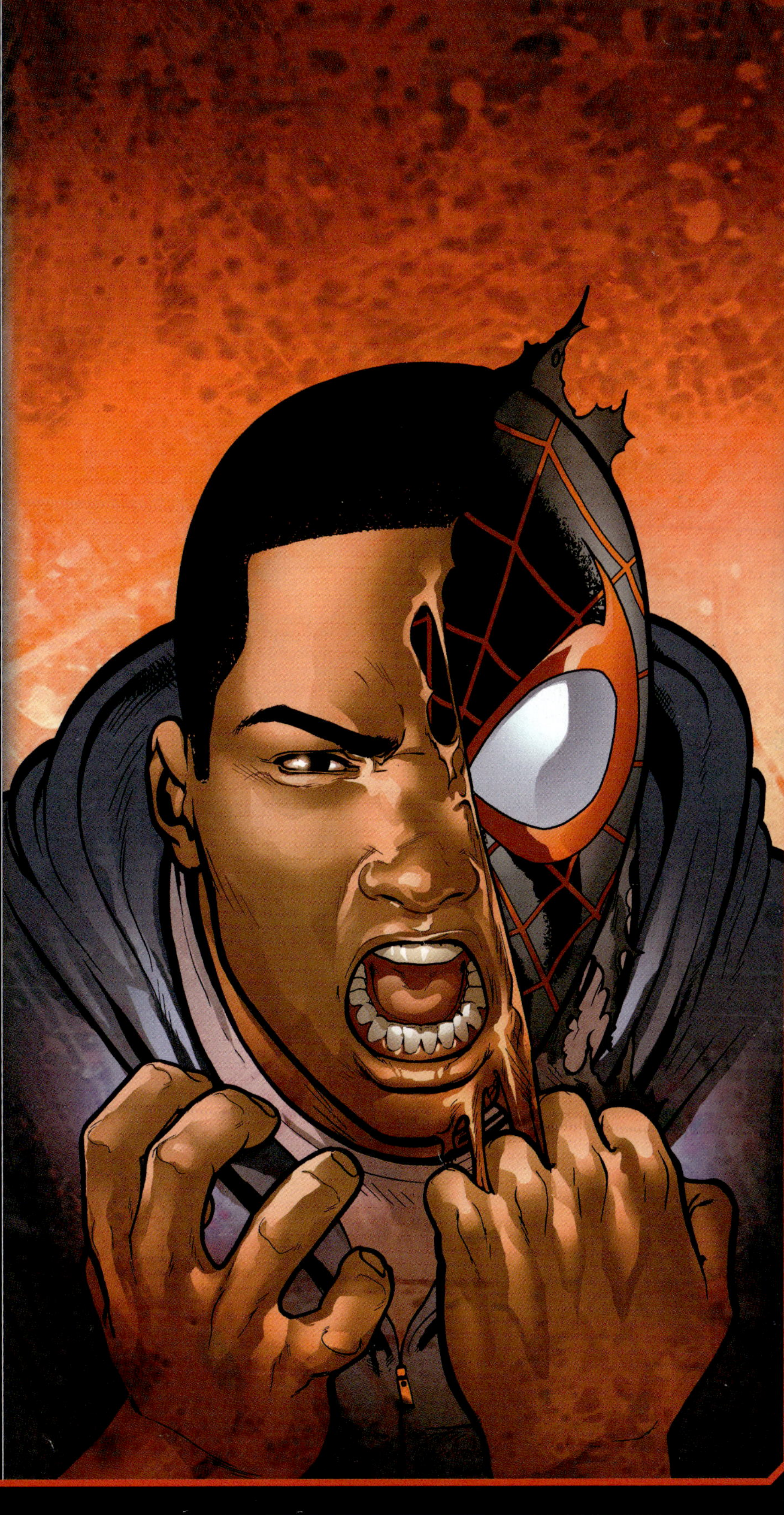

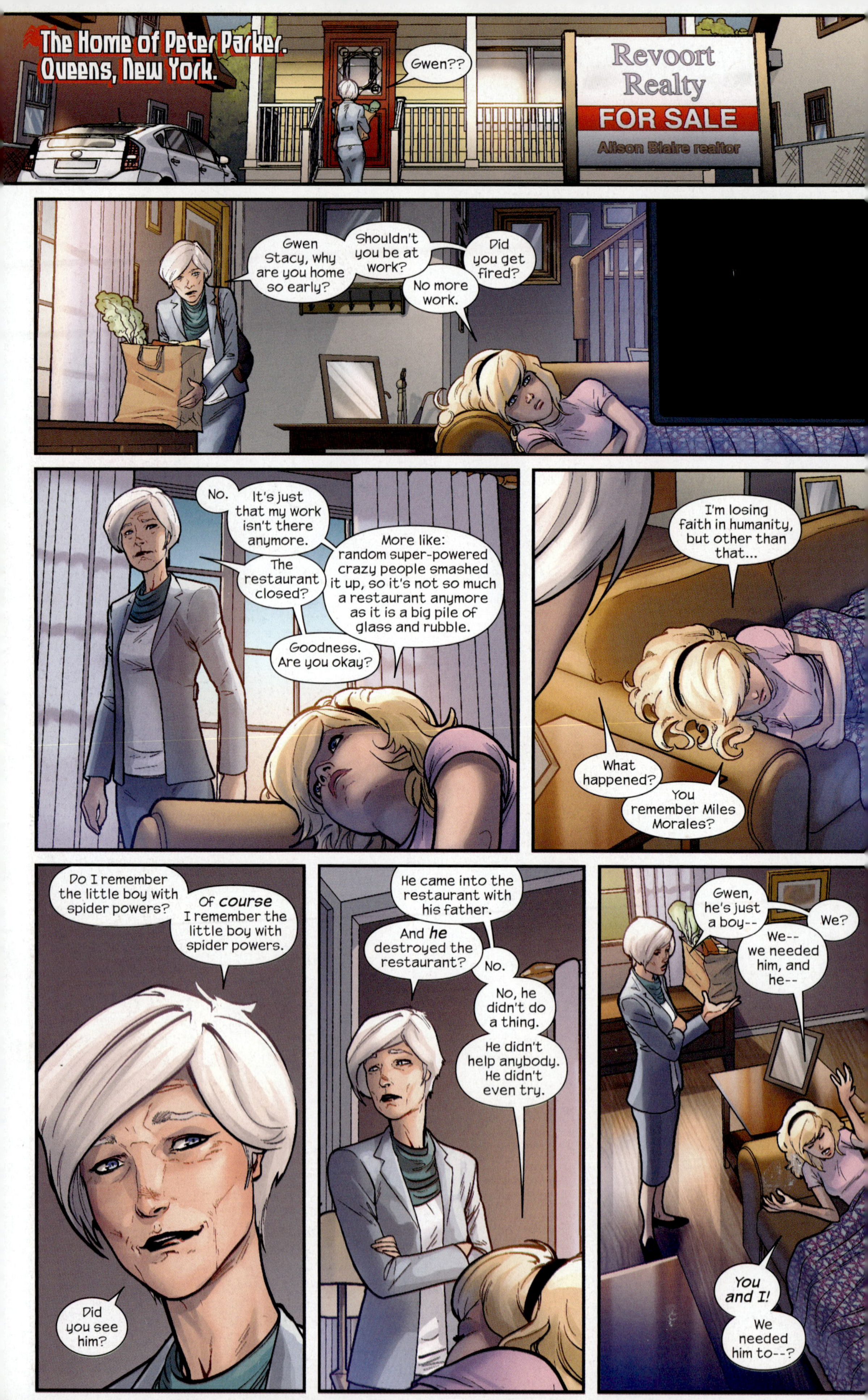

The Home of Peter Parker.
Queens, New York.
Gwen??
Revoort Realty
FOR SALE
Alison Blaire realtor
Gwen Stacy, why are you home so early?
Shouldn't you be at work?
Did you get fired?
No more work.
No.
It's just that my work isn't there anymore.
The restaurant closed?
More like: random super-powered crazy people smashed it up, so it's not so much a restaurant anymore as it is a big pile of glass and rubble.
Goodness. Are you okay?
I'm losing faith in humanity, but other than that...
What happened?
You remember Miles Morales?
Do I remember the little boy with spider powers?
Of *course* I remember the little boy with spider powers.
Did you see him?
He came into the restaurant with his father.
And *he* destroyed the restaurant?
No.
No, he didn't do a thing.
He didn't help anybody. He didn't even try.
Gwen, he's just a boy--
We?
We-- we needed him, and he--
You and I!
We needed him to--?

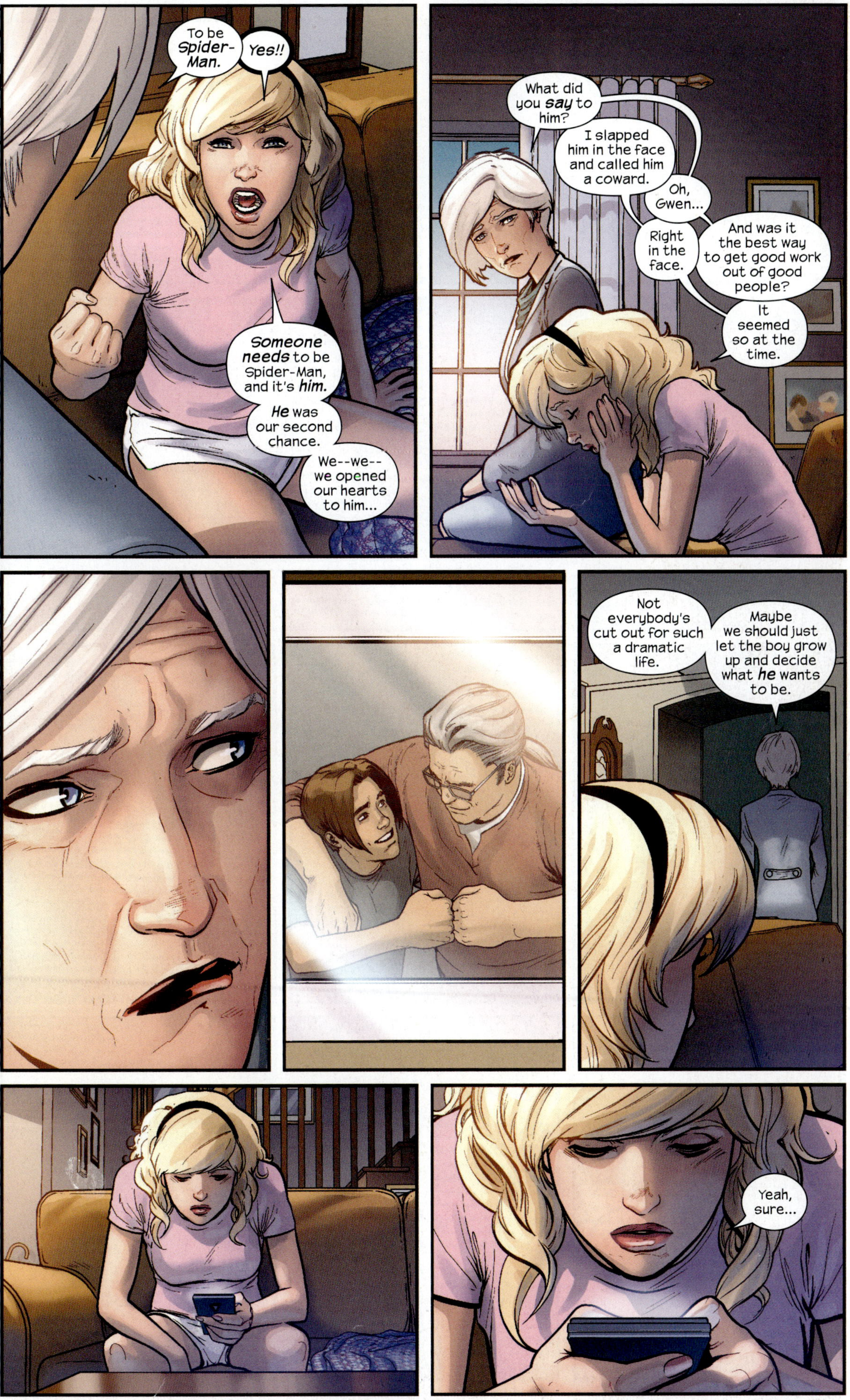
To be Spider-Man.
Yes!!
Someone needs to be Spider-Man, and it's him.
He was our second chance.
We--we--we opened our hearts to him...
What did you say to him?
I slapped him in the face and called him a coward.
Oh, Gwen...
Right in the face.
And was it the best way to get good work out of good people?
It seemed so at the time.
Not everybody's cut out for such a dramatic life.
Maybe we should just let the boy grow up and decide what he wants to be.
Yeah, sure...

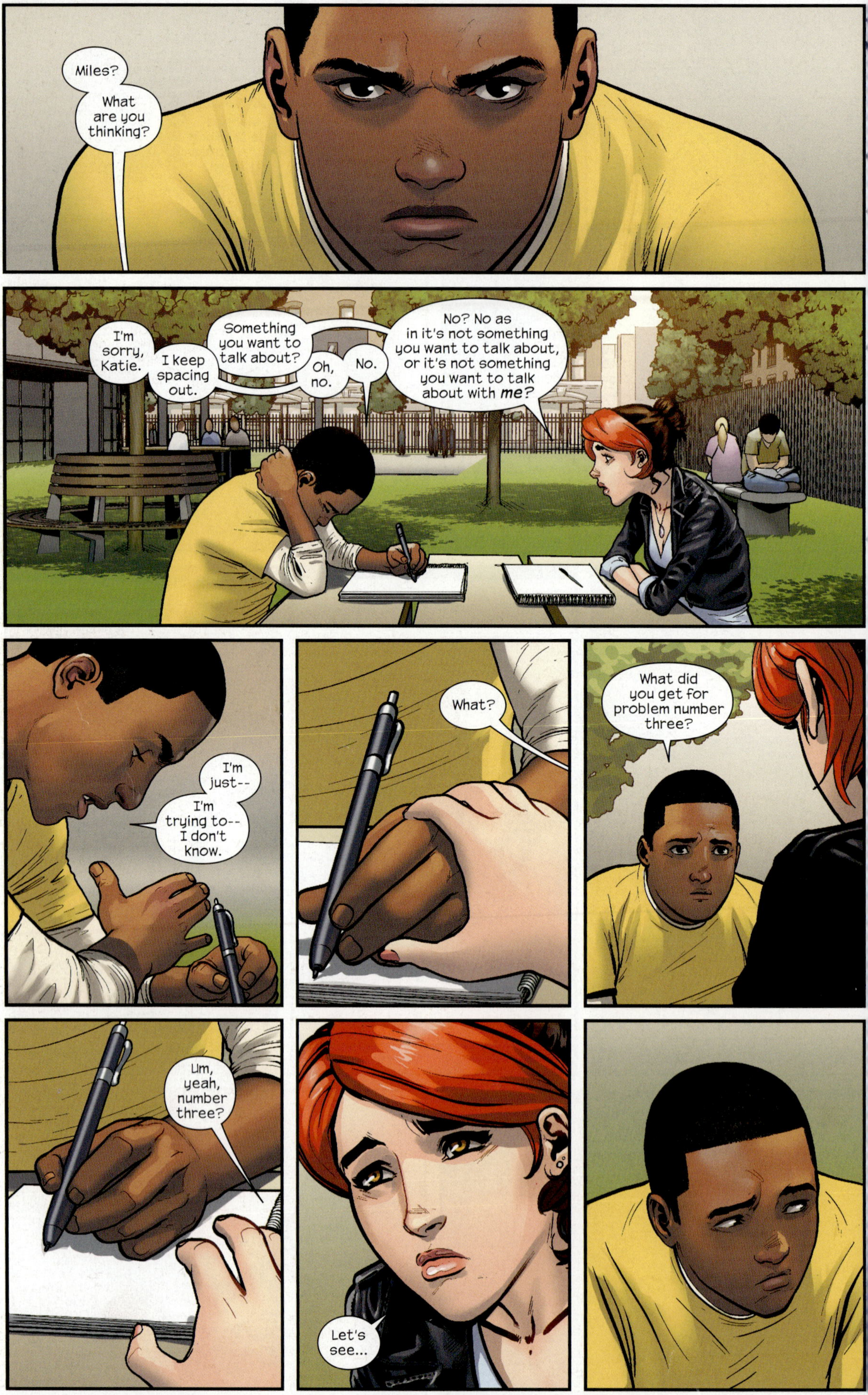

Miles?
What are you thinking?
I'm sorry, Katie.
I keep spacing out.
Something you want to talk about?
Oh, no.
No.
No? No as in it's not something you want to talk about, or it's not something you want to talk about with *me*?
I'm just--
I'm trying to-- I don't know.
What?
What did you get for problem number three?
Um, yeah, number three?
Let's see...

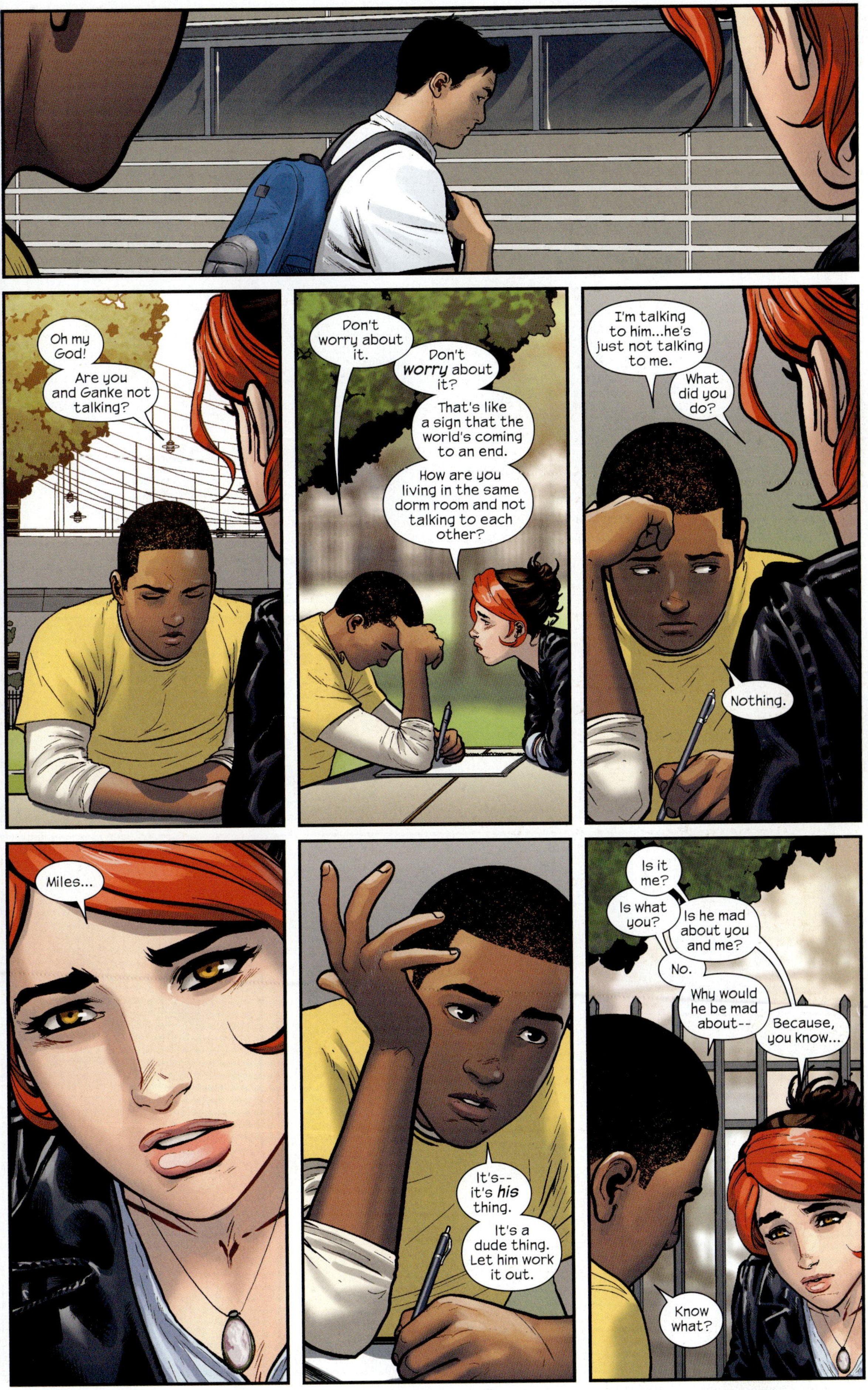
Oh my God!
Are you and Ganke not talking?
Don't worry about it.
Don't *worry* about it?
That's like a sign that the world's coming to an end.
How are you living in the same dorm room and not talking to each other?
I'm talking to him...he's just not talking to me.
What did you do?
Nothing.
Miles...
It's-- it's *his* thing.
It's a dude thing. Let him work it out.
Is it me?
Is what you?
Is he mad about you and me?
No.
Why would he be mad about--
Because, you know...
Know what?

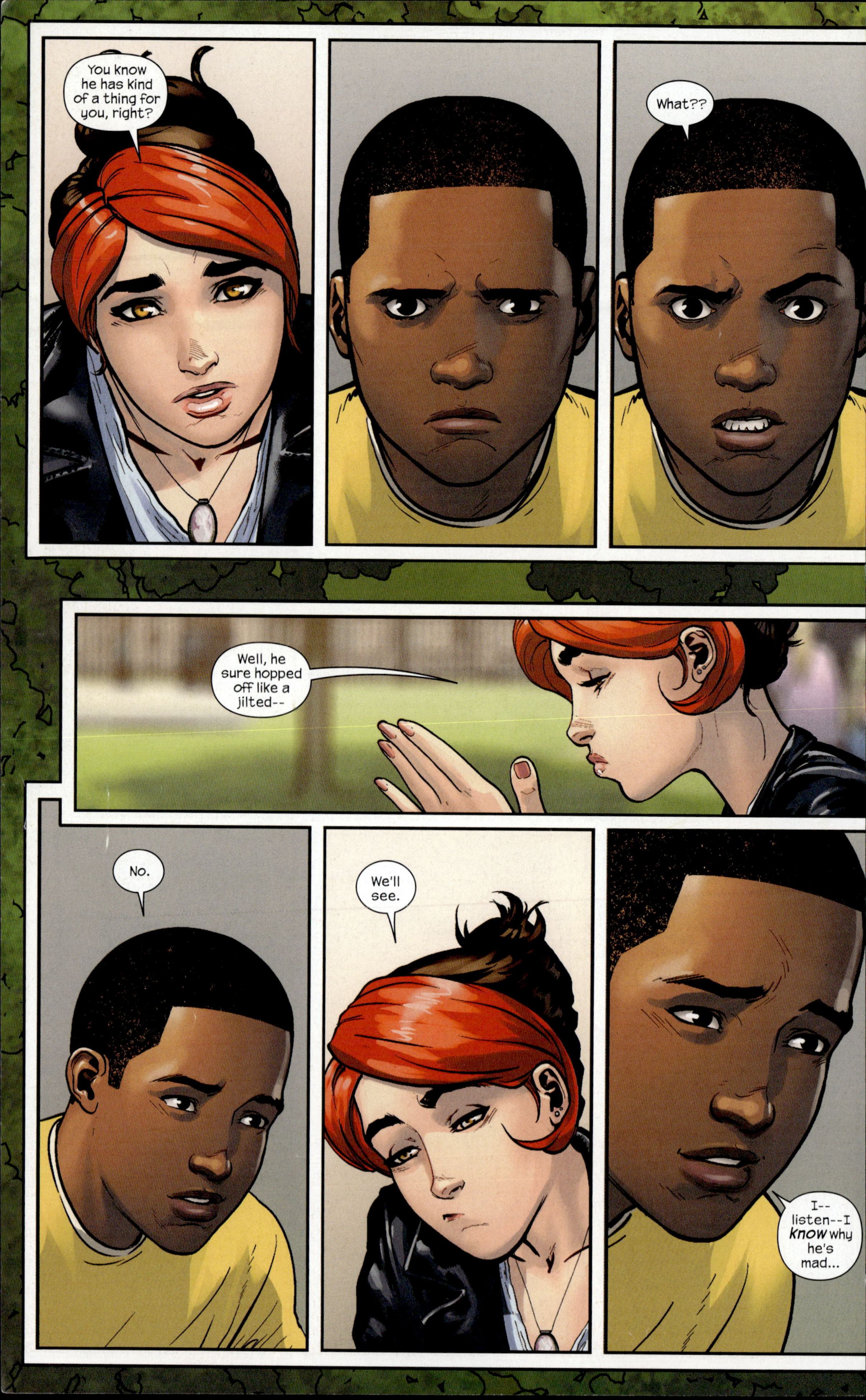
You know he has kind of a thing for you, right?
What??
Well, he sure hopped off like a jilted--
No.
We'll see.
I-- listen--I *know* why he's mad...

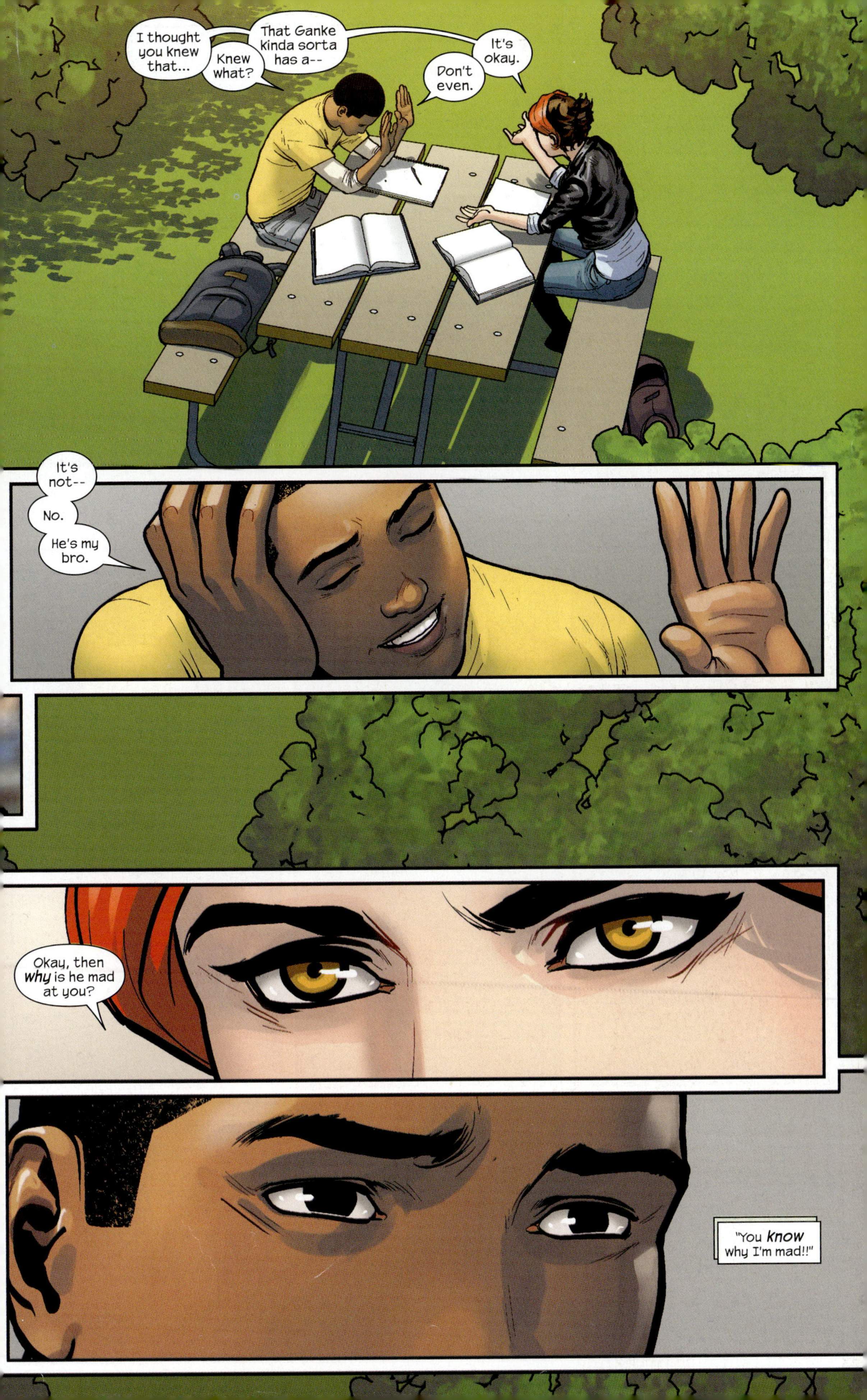
I thought you knew that...
That Ganke kinda sorta has a--
Knew what?
It's okay.
Don't even.
It's not--
No.
He's my bro.
Okay, then *why* is he mad at you?
"You **know** why I'm mad!!"

Because you're being selfish and--and a coward, and I've had it!!

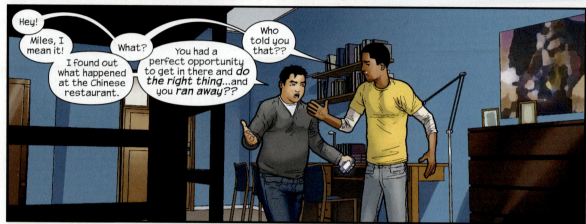

Hey!

Miles, I mean it!

What?

I found out what happened at the Chinese restaurant.

You had a perfect opportunity to get in there and *do the right thing*...and you *ran away??*

Who told you that??

Gwen Stacy *texted* me.

Yeah...

You ran away.

To *help* my *father!*

The way she tells it, your father was already safe.

You *really* don't understand what's going *on* here?

You really don't get that I *lost my mother!!*

Okay??!!

SHE'S DEAD!!

And what was the last thing she said to you?
Was it: Don't be Spider-Man anymore?
No.
You told me she was *proud* of you.
Lots of people die, Miles.
And *you* are Spider-Man.
You need to help the ones that aren't dead.
You needed some time to shake it off, sure, but that time has *waaaaay* passed.
It's been *a year!!*
Think of all the good you could have done!
She died *because* of Spider-Man. My father will *never* be the--
You didn't kill her.
It wasn't even that big, giant, scary monster Spider-Man villain you were fighting...
It was a bullet.
A stray *police bullet* killed her.
I'm saying when you remember that day... maybe focus on all of the people whose lives *you saved* that night.
Including the life of your father.
You don't understand how this feels.
It must feel like an insanely big burden.
Yes!
Like a giant responsibility.
It is.
That comes with the great power...
I know what you're doing.
I *know* you know what *I'm* doing.
What are *you* doing?
Everyone's *pushing me!!*
Because everyone *believes* in you.
Pushing me and *pushing* me!!
Miles!
YOU DON'T UNDERSTAND!!
YSTERY POWER TEENAGERS
RANSACK BOROUGH
I understand everything.
Except I don't get how-- how--don't you even *care* where these new super-powered kids *came* from?

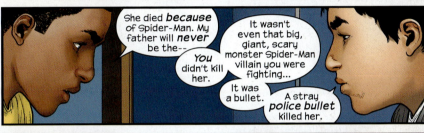

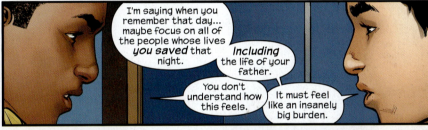

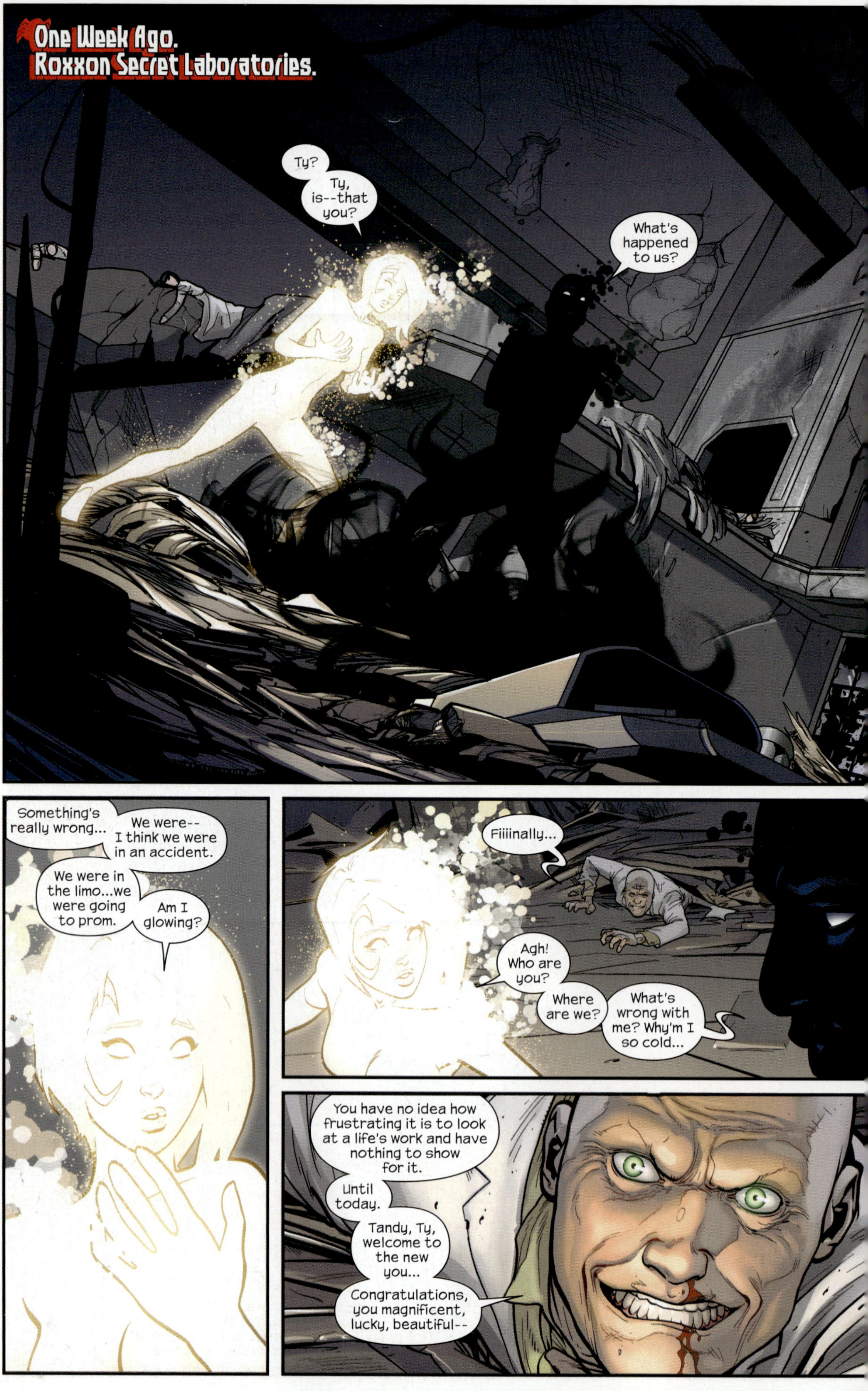
One Week Ago.
Roxxon Secret Laboratories.
Ty?
Ty, is--that you?
What's happened to us?
Something's really wrong...
We were-- I think we were in an accident.
We were in the limo...we were going to prom.
Am I glowing?
Fiiiinally...
Agh! Who are you?
Where are we?
What's wrong with me? Why'm I so cold...
You have no idea how frustrating it is to look at a life's work and have nothing to show for it.
Until today.
Tandy, Ty, welcome to the new you...
Congratulations, you magnificent, lucky, beautiful--

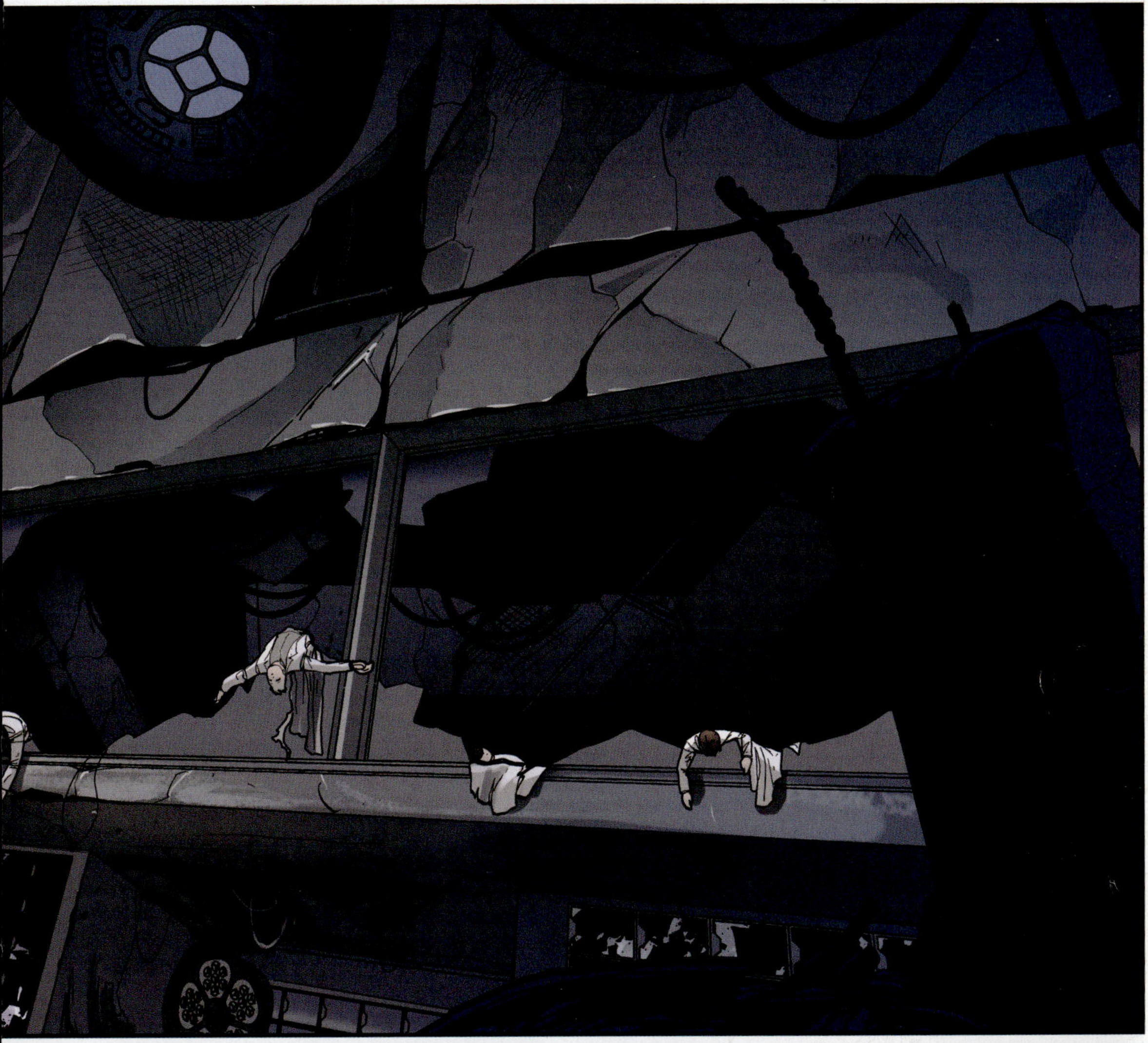

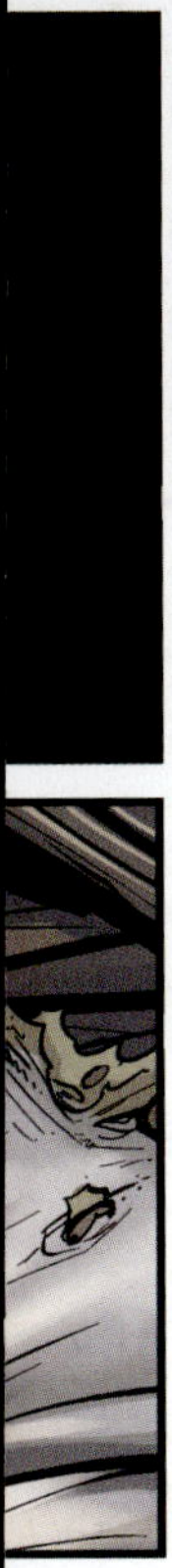

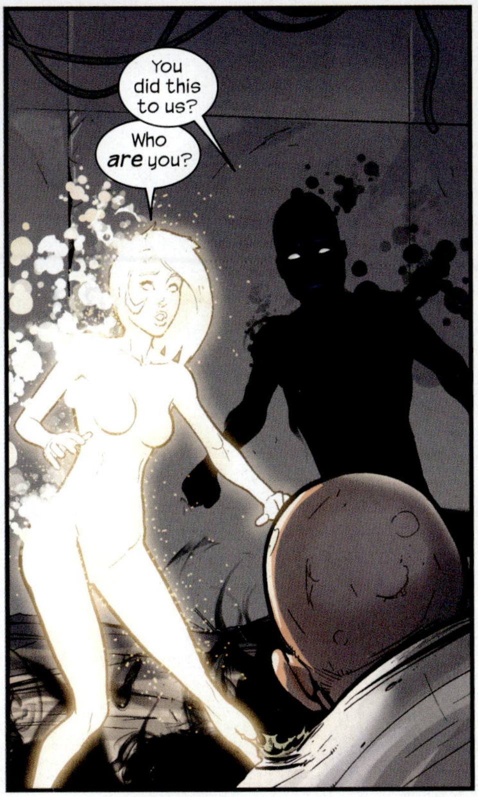
You did this to us?
Who **are** you?

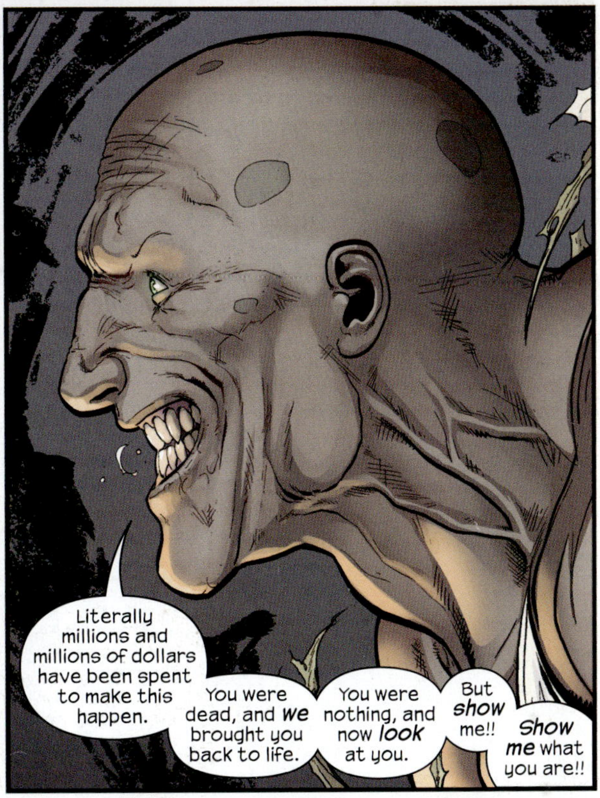
Literally millions and millions of dollars have been spent to make this happen.
You were dead, and **we** brought you back to life.
You were nothing, and now **look** at you.
But **show** me!!
Show me what you are!!

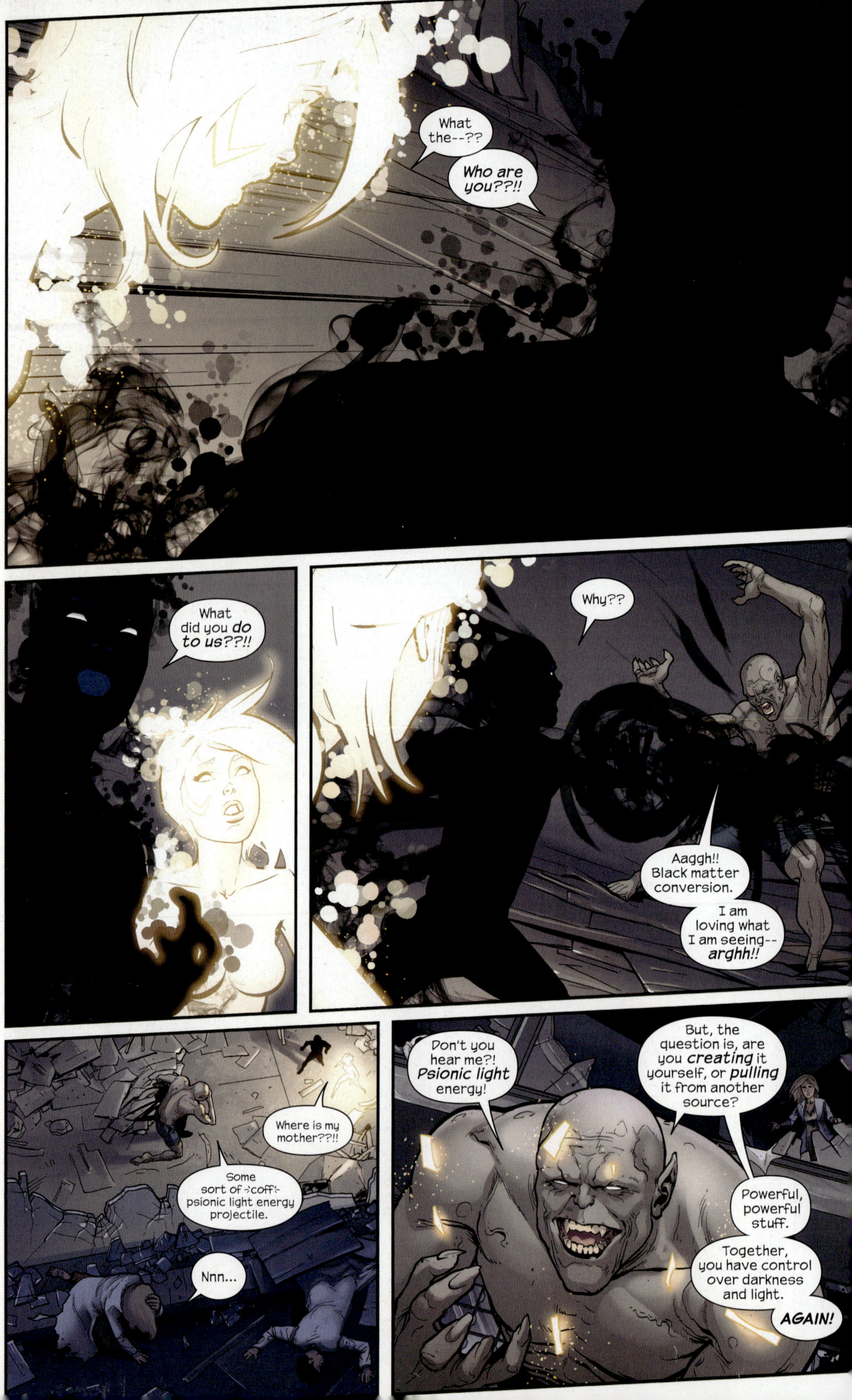

What the--??
Who are you??!!
What did you do to us??!!
Why??
Aaggh!! Black matter conversion.
I am loving what I am seeing-- arghh!!
Where is my mother??!!
Some sort of *coff* psionic light energy projectile.
Nnn...
Don't you hear me?! Psionic light energy!
But, the question is, are you creating it yourself, or pulling it from another source?
Powerful, powerful stuff.
Together, you have control over darkness and light.
AGAIN!

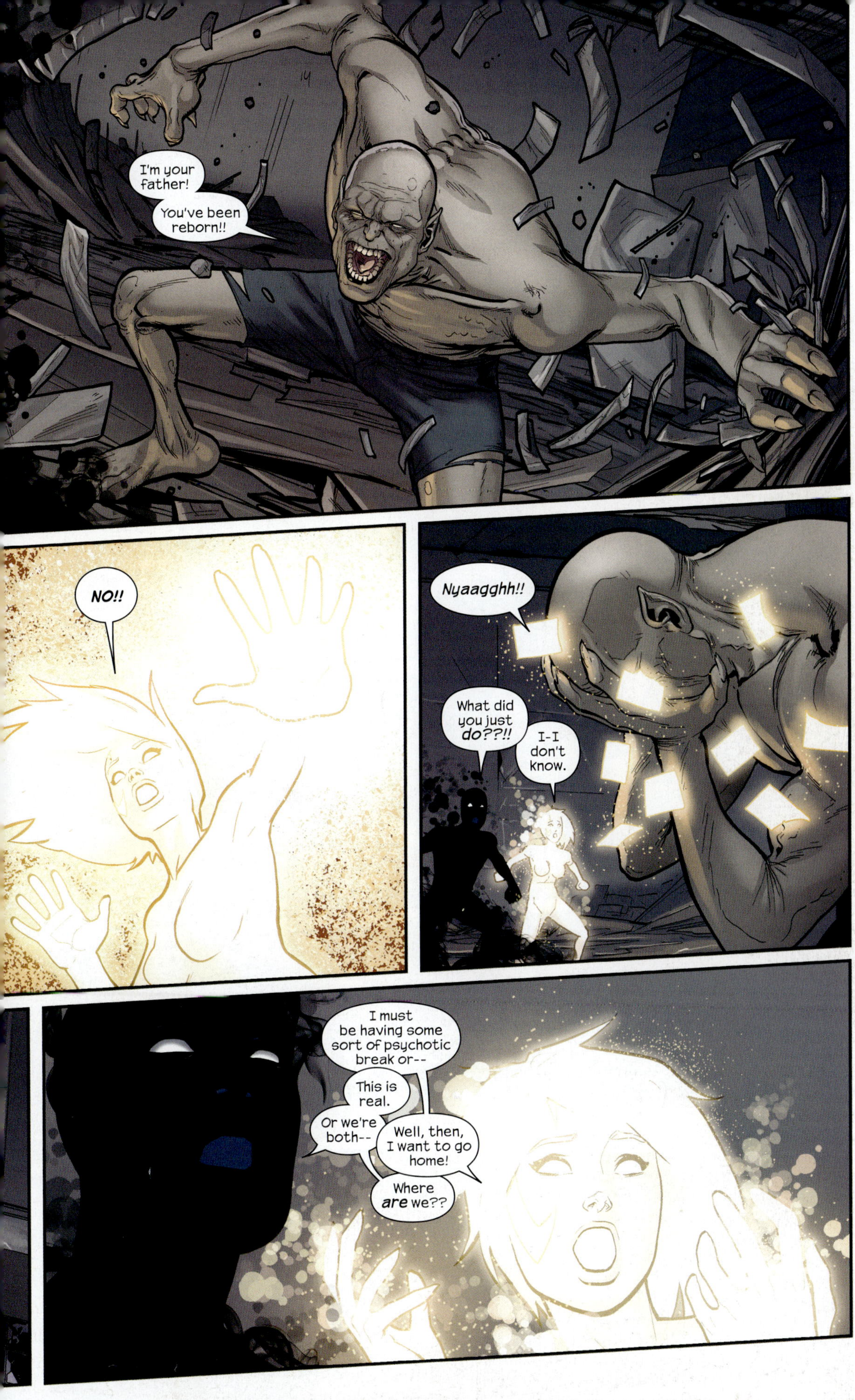
I'm your father!
You've been reborn!!
NO!!
Nyaagghh!!
What did you just *do??!!*
I-I don't know.
I must be having some sort of psychotic break or--
This is real.
Or we're both--
Well, then, I want to go home!
Where *are* we??

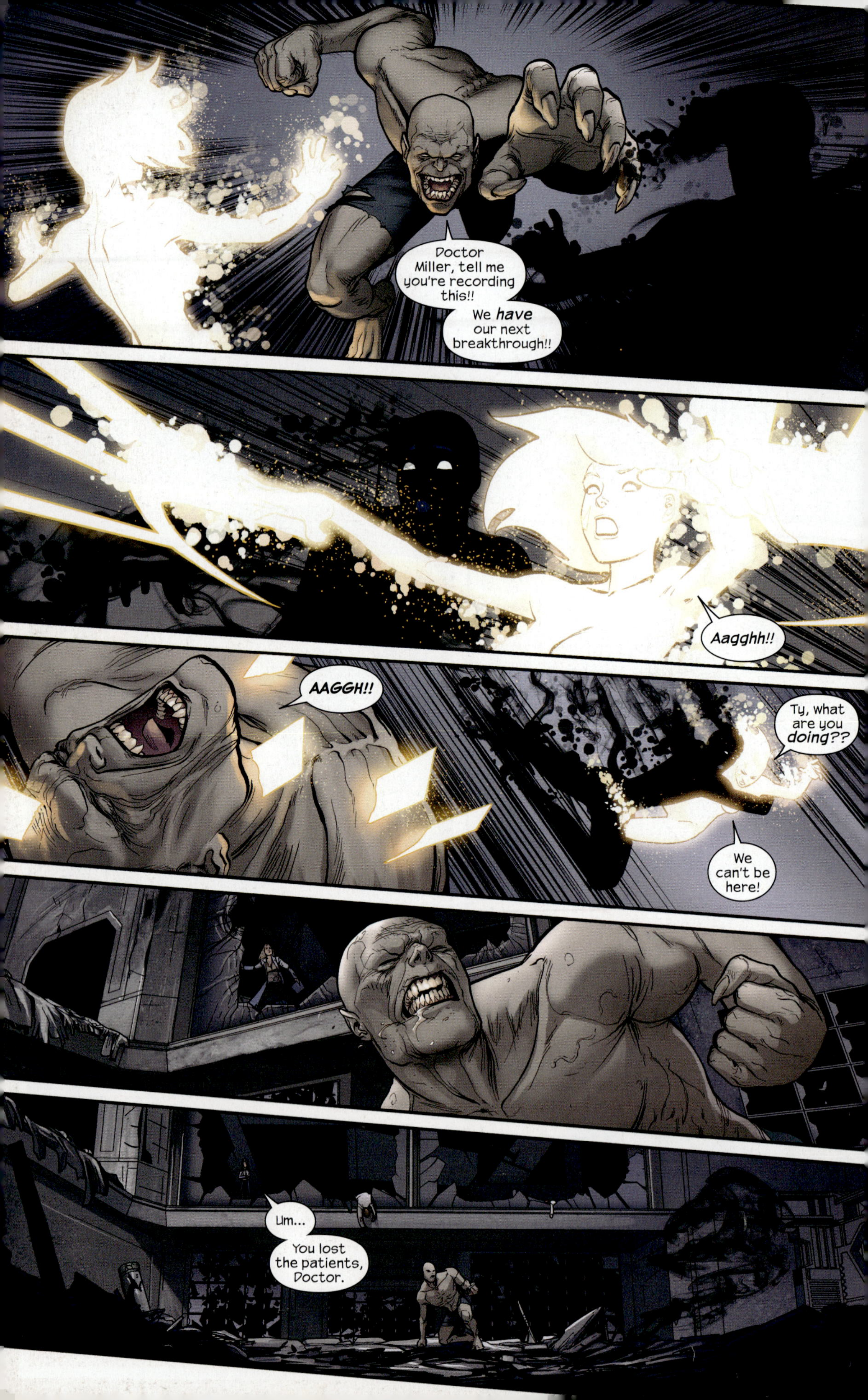
Doctor Miller, tell me you're recording this!!
We *have* our next breakthrough!!
Aagghh!!
AAGGH!!
Ty, what are you *doing*??
We can't be here!
Um...
You lost the patients, Doctor.

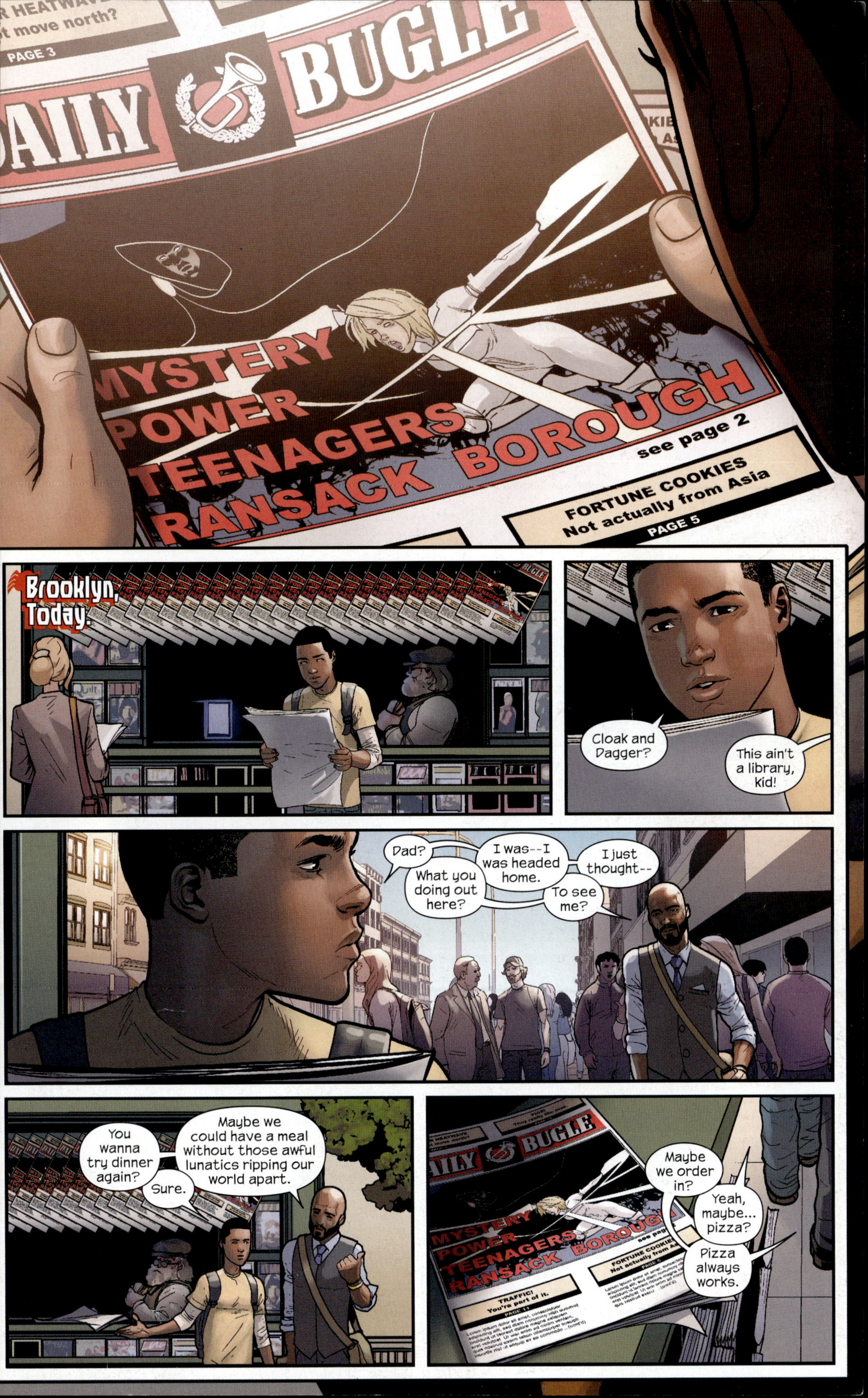

t move north?
PAGE 3
AILY
BUGLE
MYSTERY POWER TEENAGERS RANSACK BOROUGH
see page 2
FORTUNE COOKIES
Not actually from Asia
PAGE 5
Brooklyn, Today.
Cloak and Dagger?
This ain't a library, kid!
Dad?
What you doing out here?
I was--I was headed home.
To see me?
I just thought--
You wanna try dinner again?
Sure.
Maybe we could have a meal without those awful lunatics ripping our world apart.
BUGLE
MYSTERY POWER TEENAGERS RANSACK BOROUGH
TRAFFIC!
You're part of it.
Maybe we order in?
Yeah, maybe... pizza?
Pizza always works.

Give me like a half an hour! I just need to rest my eyes.

Yeah, no problem.

Jesus!!

You--you can't just *sneak in* here.

Of course I can. I just did.

How did you know I was going to be here?

I didn't even know I was coming here until--

You know who I work for, right? You know what I can do.

But!

You might want to keep it to a whisper--

Your dad's been through enough for one week, don't you think?

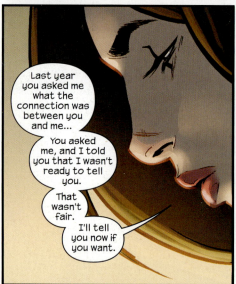

Last year you asked me what the connection was between you and me...

You asked me, and I told you that I wasn't ready to tell you.

That wasn't fair.

I'll tell you now if you want.

Okay...

A couple of years ago, some scientists with absolutely no moral center took DNA samples from Peter Parker and attempted to clone him.

And then they poked around at the DNA, just, you know, to see what they'd get...

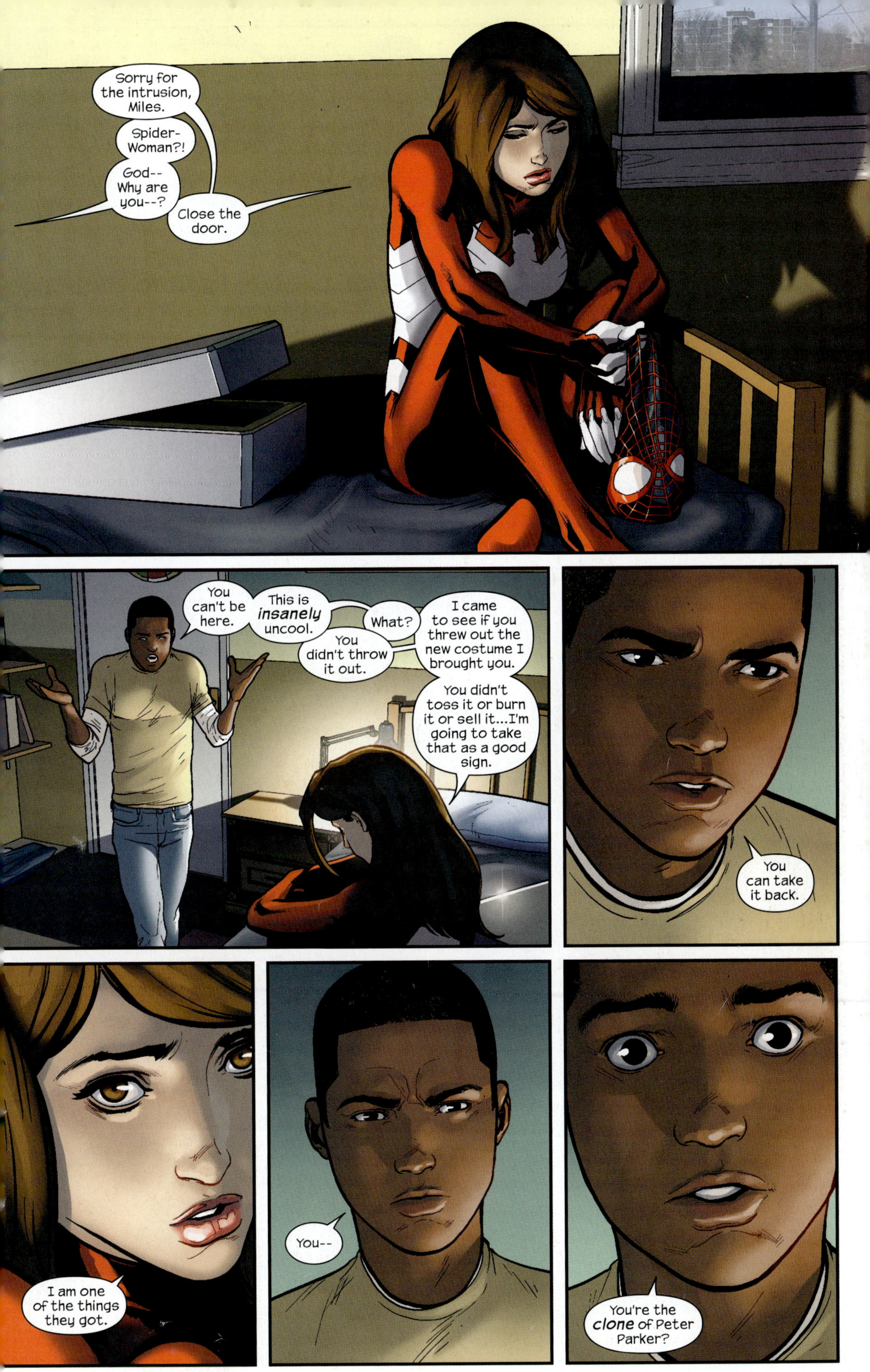

Sorry for the intrusion, Miles.
Spider-Woman?!
God-- Why are you--?
Close the door.
You can't be here.
This is *insanely* uncool.
What?
You didn't throw it out.
I came to see if you threw out the new costume I brought you.
You didn't toss it or burn it or sell it...I'm going to take that as a good sign.
You can take it back.
I am one of the things they got.
You--
You're the *clone* of Peter Parker?

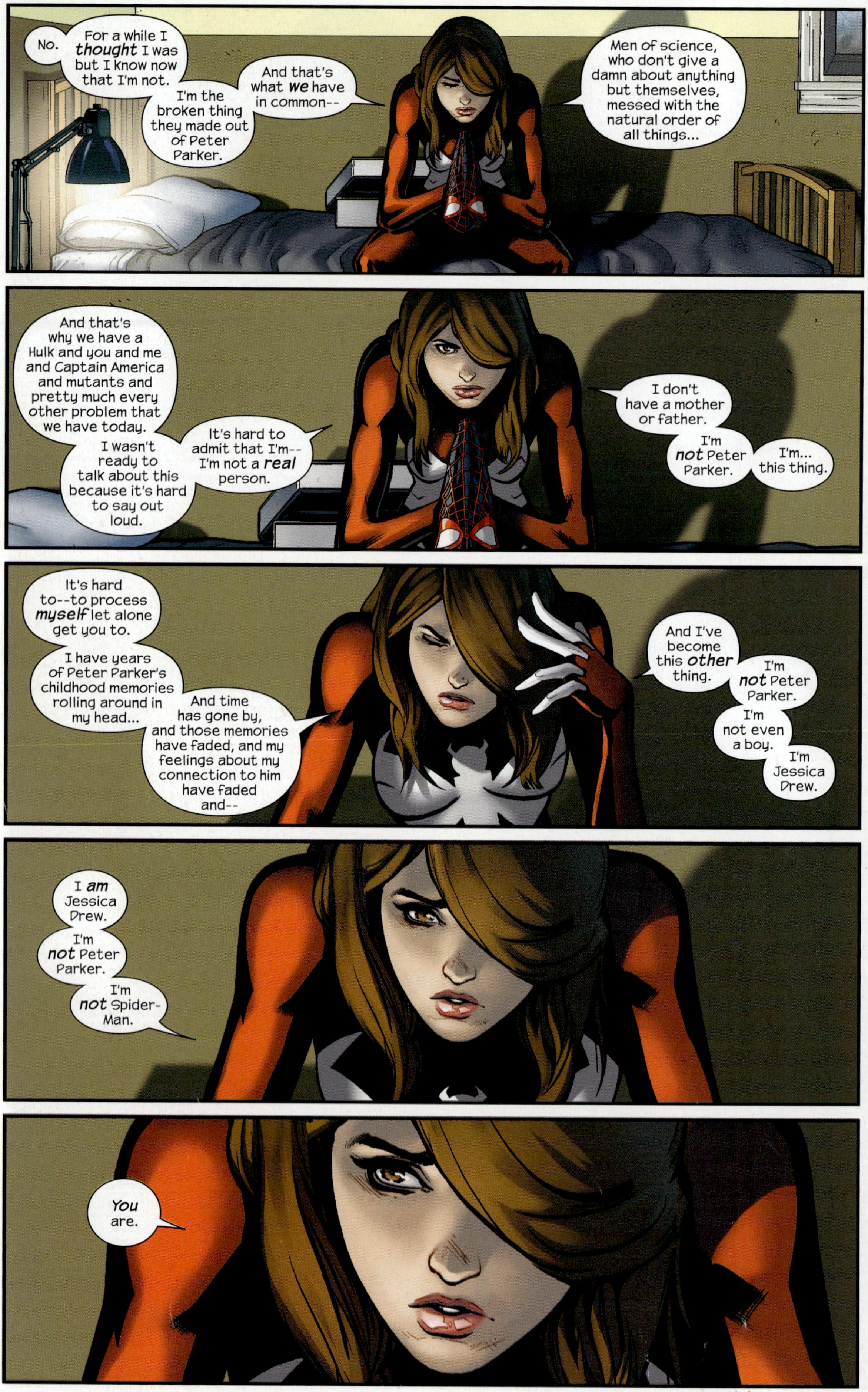
No.
For a while I *thought* I was but I know now that I'm not.
I'm the broken thing they made out of Peter Parker.
And that's what *we* have in common--
Men of science, who don't give a damn about anything but themselves, messed with the natural order of all things...
And that's why we have a Hulk and you and me and Captain America and mutants and pretty much every other problem that we have today.
I wasn't ready to talk about this because it's hard to say out loud.
It's hard to admit that I'm-- I'm not a *real* person.
I don't have a mother or father.
I'm *not* Peter Parker.
I'm... this thing.
It's hard to--to process *myself* let alone get you to.
I have years of Peter Parker's childhood memories rolling around in my head...
And time has gone by, and those memories have faded, and my feelings about my connection to him have faded and--
And I've become this *other* thing.
I'm *not* Peter Parker.
I'm not even a boy.
I'm Jessica Drew.
I *am* Jessica Drew.
I'm *not* Peter Parker.
I'm *not* Spider-Man.
You are.

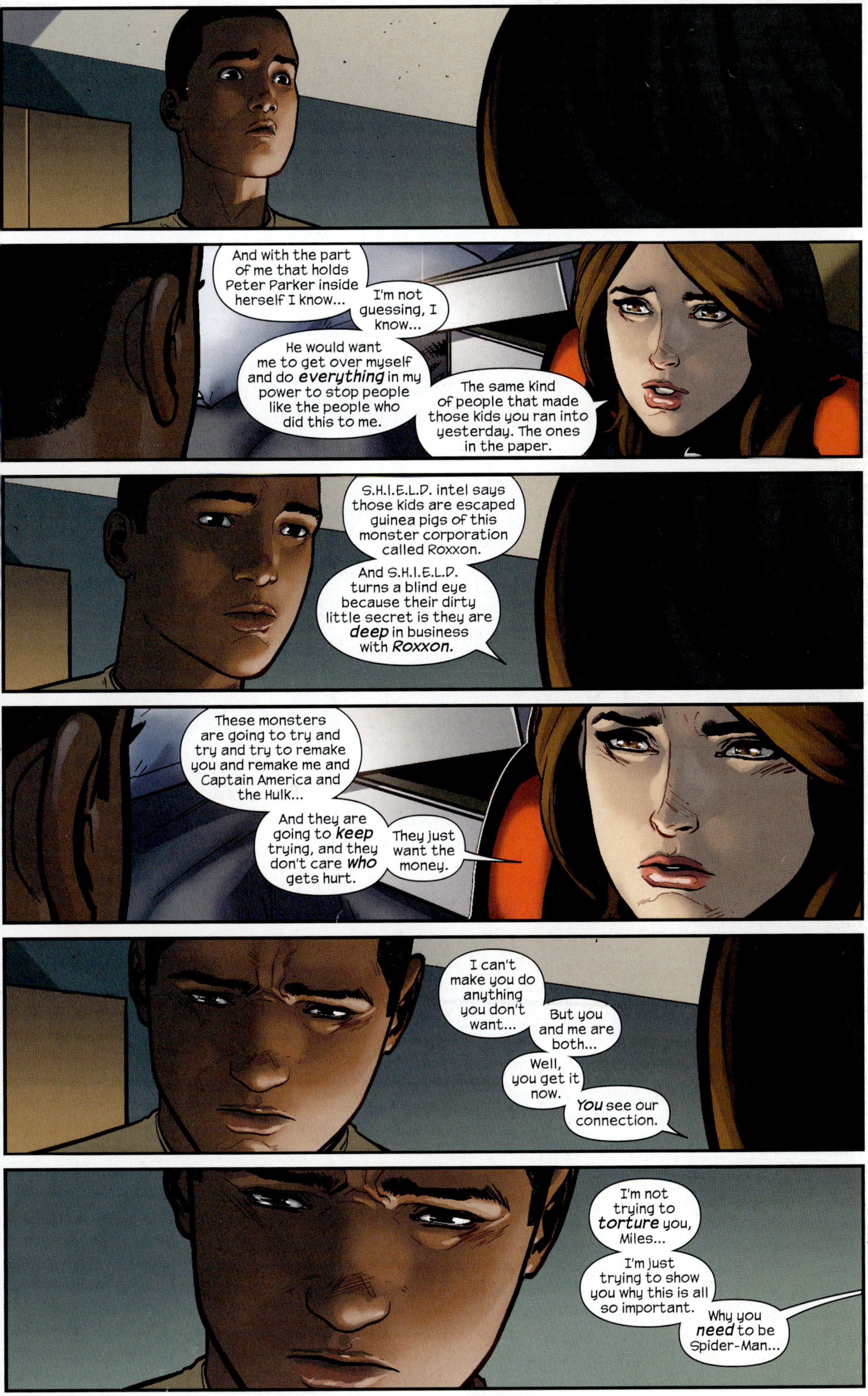
And with the part of me that holds Peter Parker inside herself I know...
I'm not guessing, I know...
He would want me to get over myself and do *everything* in my power to stop people like the people who did this to me.
The same kind of people that made those kids you ran into yesterday. The ones in the paper.
S.H.I.E.L.D. intel says those kids are escaped guinea pigs of this monster corporation called Roxxon.
And S.H.I.E.L.D. turns a blind eye because their dirty little secret is they are *deep* in business with *Roxxon.*
These monsters are going to try and try and try to remake you and remake me and Captain America and the Hulk...
And they are going to *keep* trying, and they don't care *who* gets hurt.
They just want the money.
I can't make you do anything you don't want...
But you and me are both...
Well, you get it now.
You see our connection.
I'm not trying to *torture* you, Miles...
I'm just trying to show you why this is all so important.
Why you *need* to be Spider-Man...

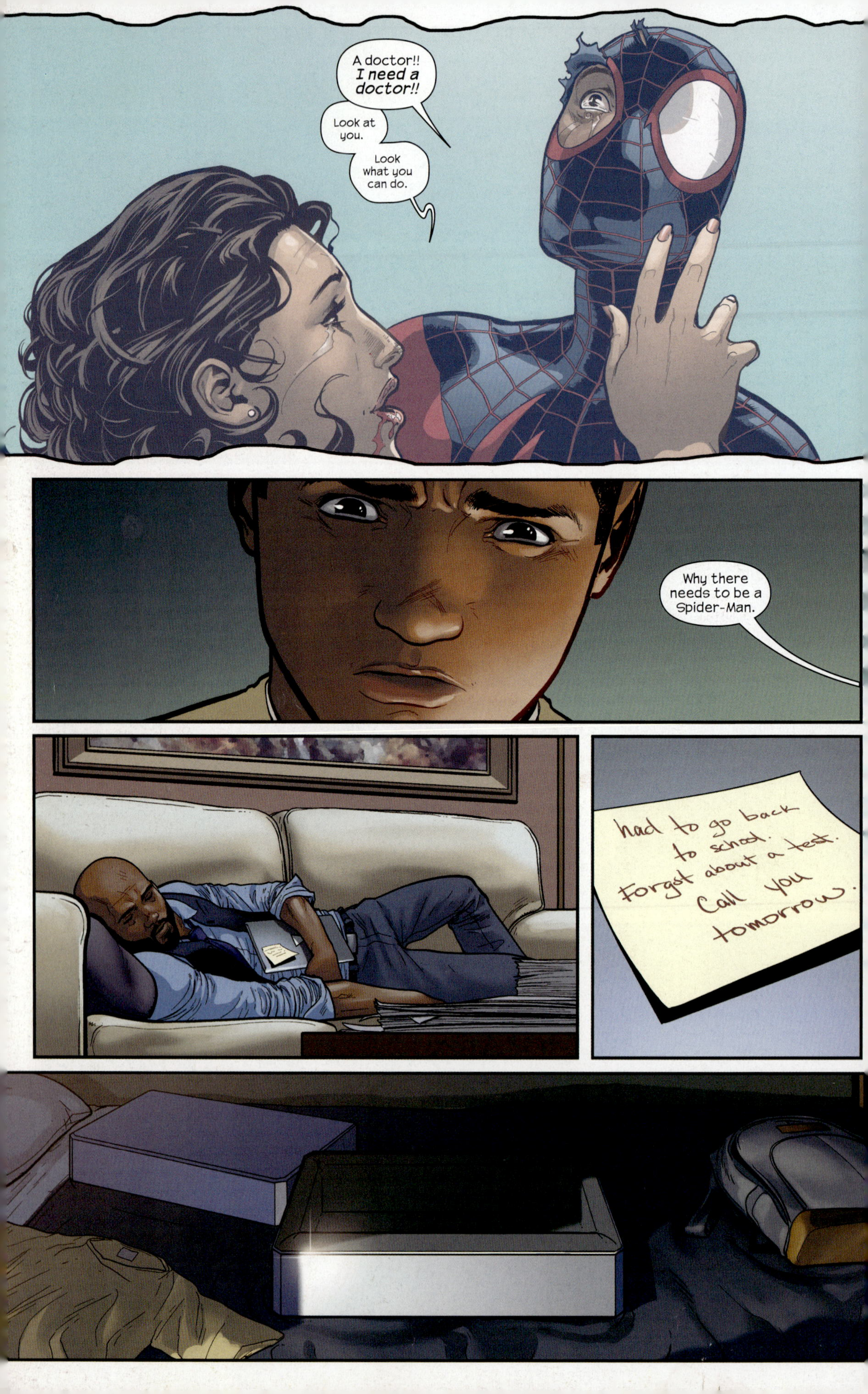
A doctor!! *I need a doctor!!*
Look at you.
Look what you can do.
Why there needs to be a Spider-Man.
had to go back to school. Forgot about a test. Call you tomorrow.

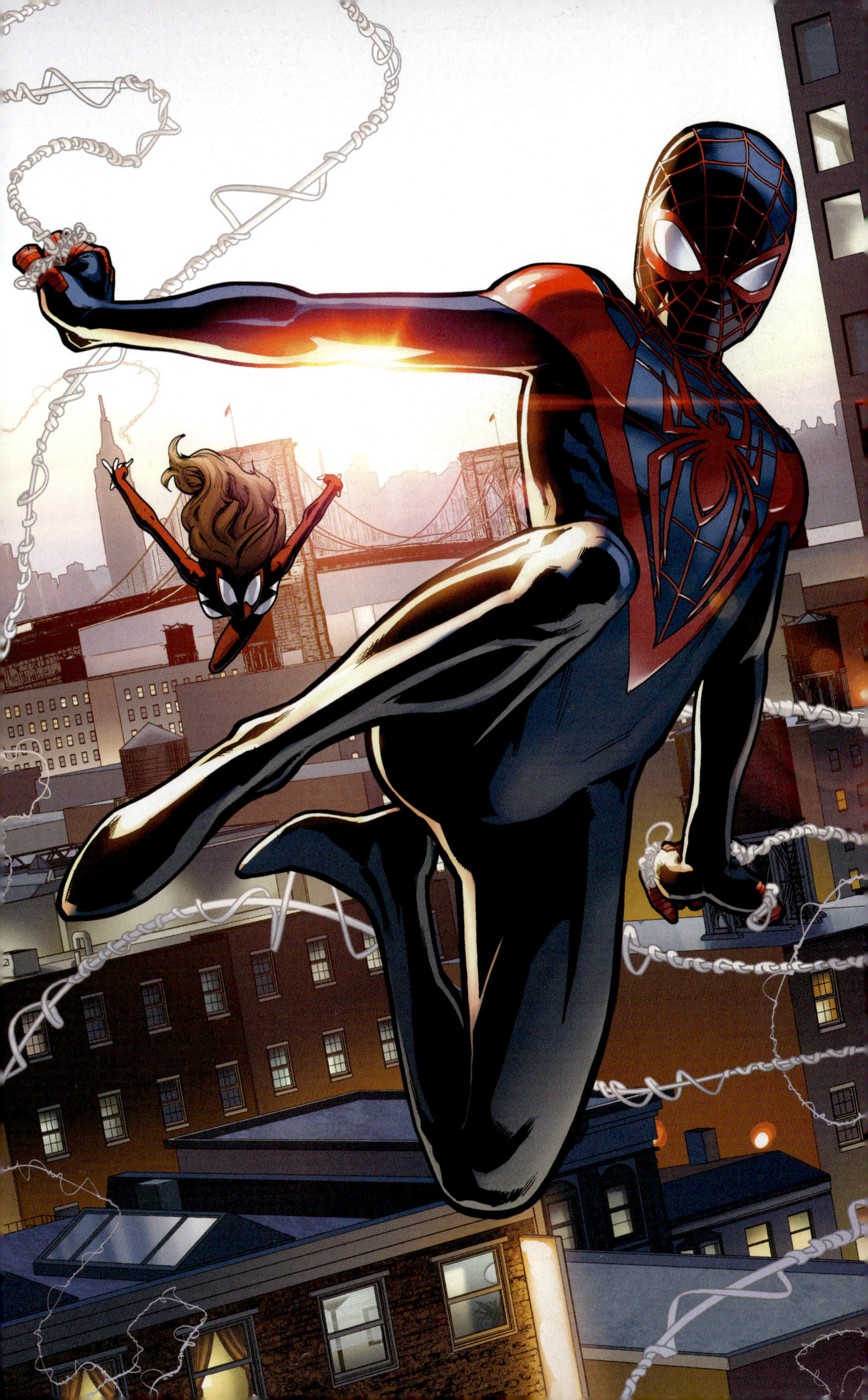

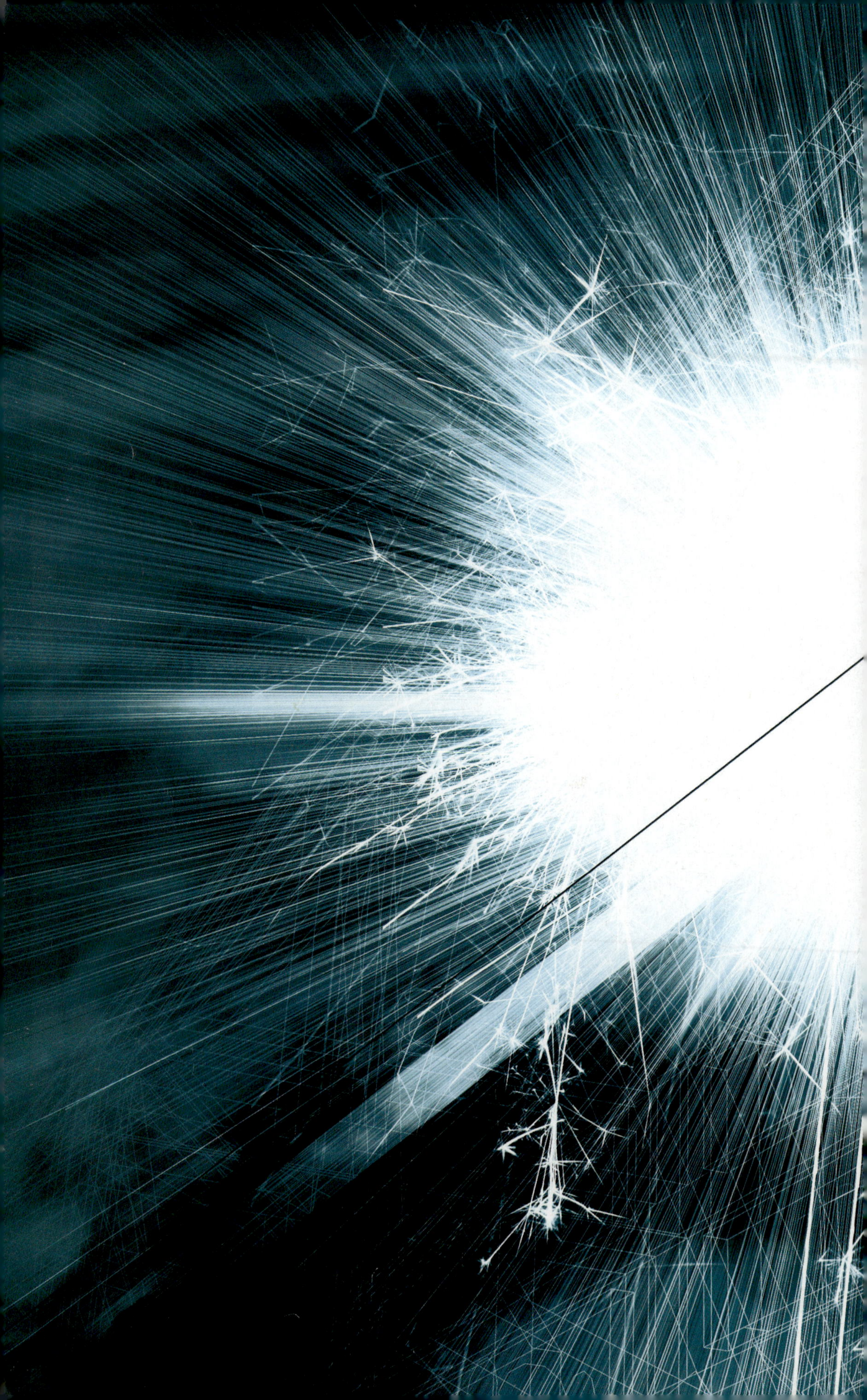

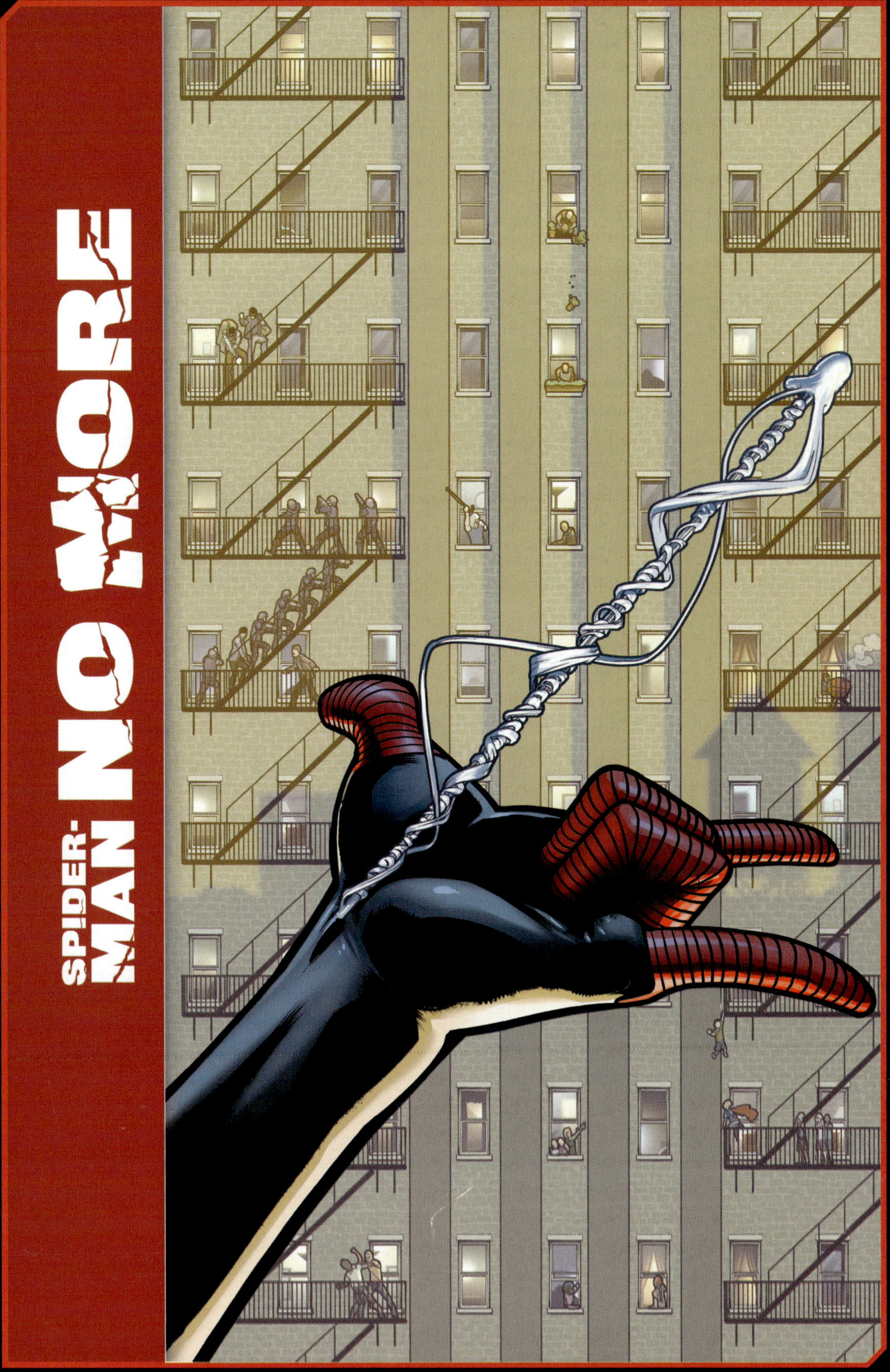
SPIDER-MAN
NO MORE

FINKLESTIEN
STRONG
LOIKA
ULTIMATE
AMAZING
FANTASY
#14
HERE COMES...
BOMBSHELL

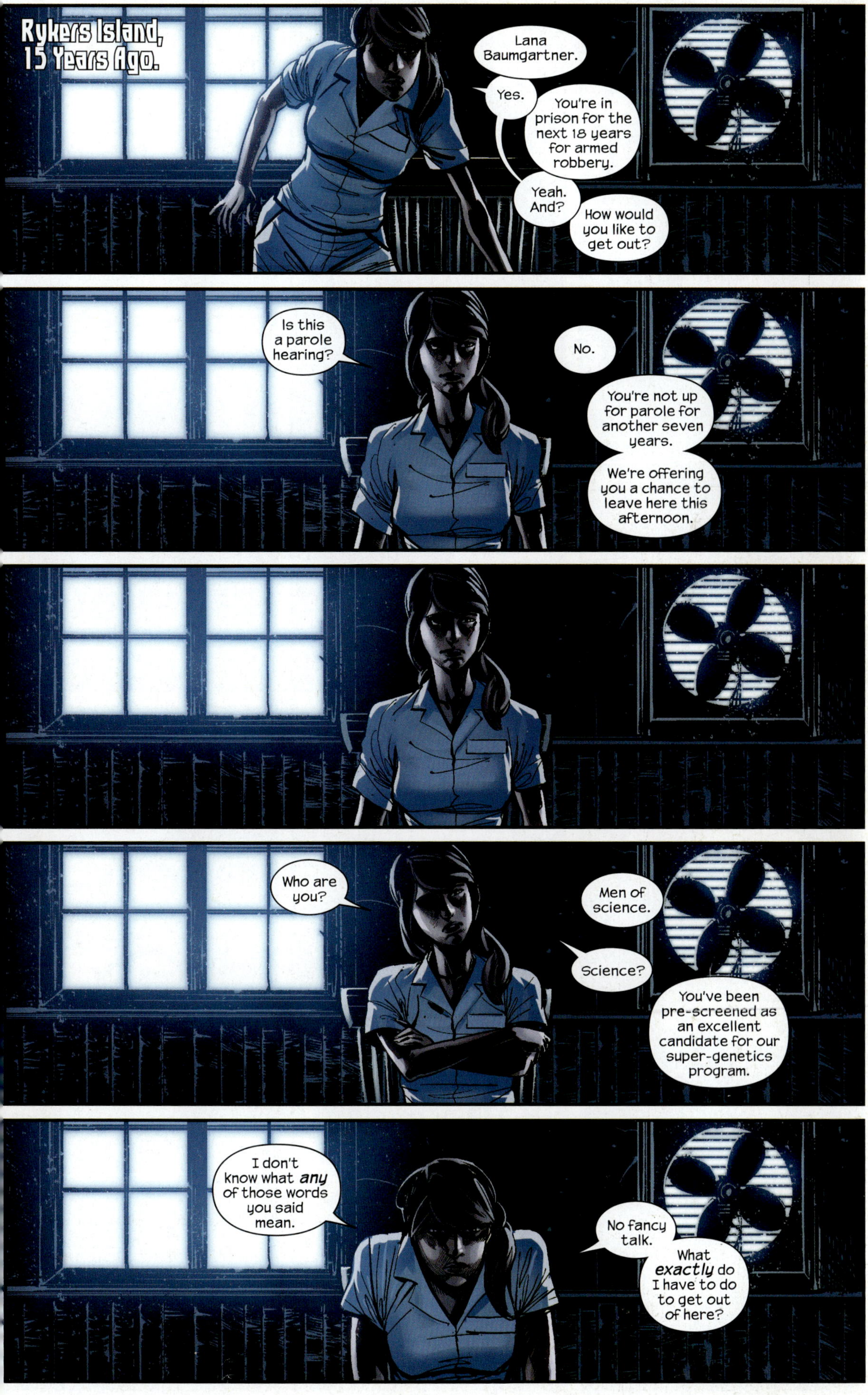

Rykers Island, 15 Years Ago.
Lana Baumgartner.
Yes.
You're in prison for the next 18 years for armed robbery.
Yeah. And?
How would you like to get out?
Is this a parole hearing?
No.
You're not up for parole for another seven years.
We're offering you a chance to leave here this afternoon.
Who are you?
Men of science.
Science?
You've been pre-screened as an excellent candidate for our super-genetics program.
I don't know what *any* of those words you said mean.
No fancy talk.
What *exactly* do I have to do to get out of here?

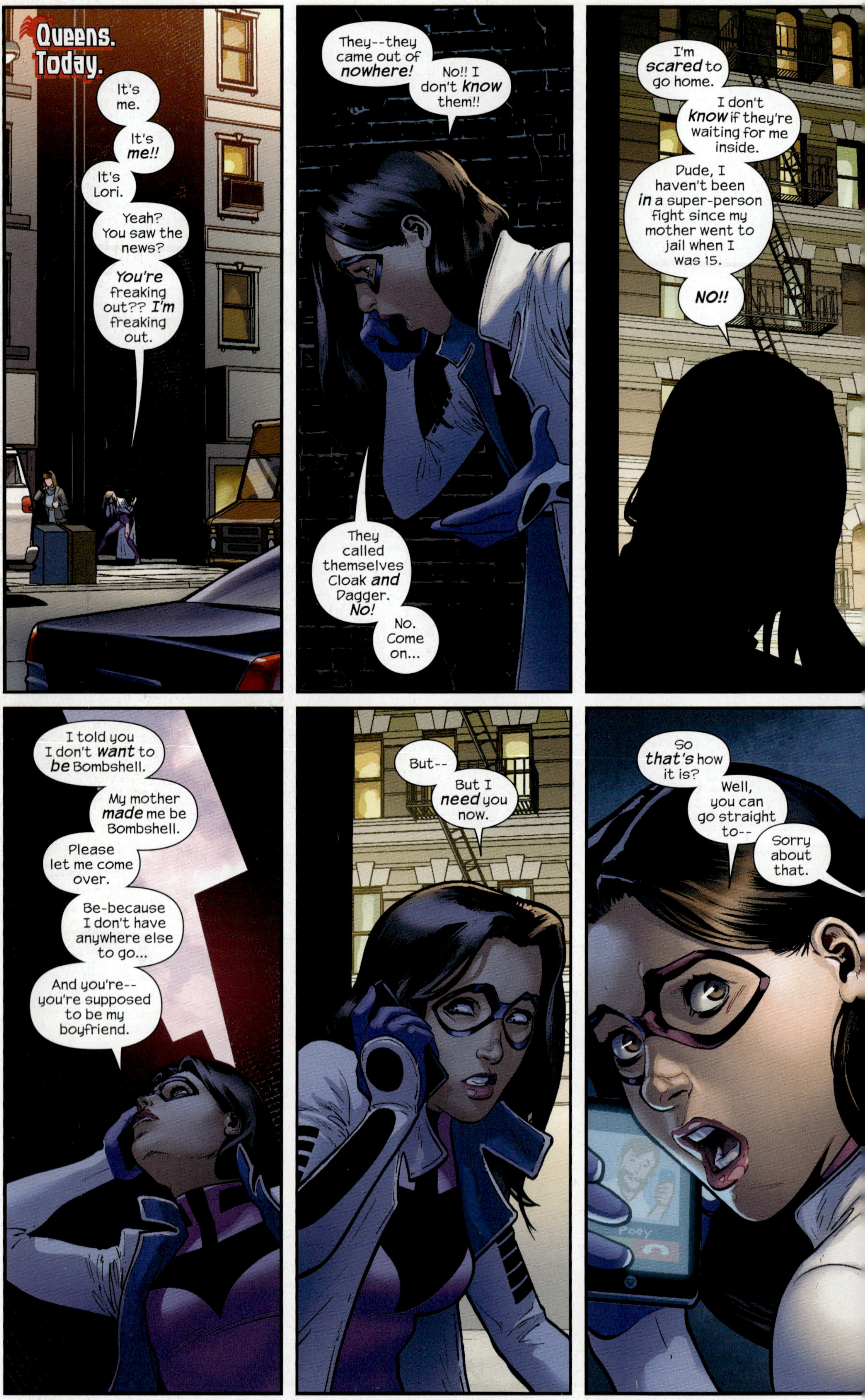
Queens. Today.
It's me.
It's me!!
It's Lori.
Yeah? You saw the news?
You're freaking out?? I'm freaking out.
They--they came out of nowhere!
No!! I don't know them!!
They called themselves Cloak and Dagger. No!
No. Come on...
I'm scared to go home.
I don't know if they're waiting for me inside.
Dude, I haven't been in a super-person fight since my mother went to jail when I was 15.
NO!!
I told you I don't want to be Bombshell.
My mother made me be Bombshell.
Please let me come over.
Be-because I don't have anywhere else to go...
And you're--you're supposed to be my boyfriend.
But--
But I need you now.
So that's how it is?
Well, you can go straight to--
Sorry about that.
Poey

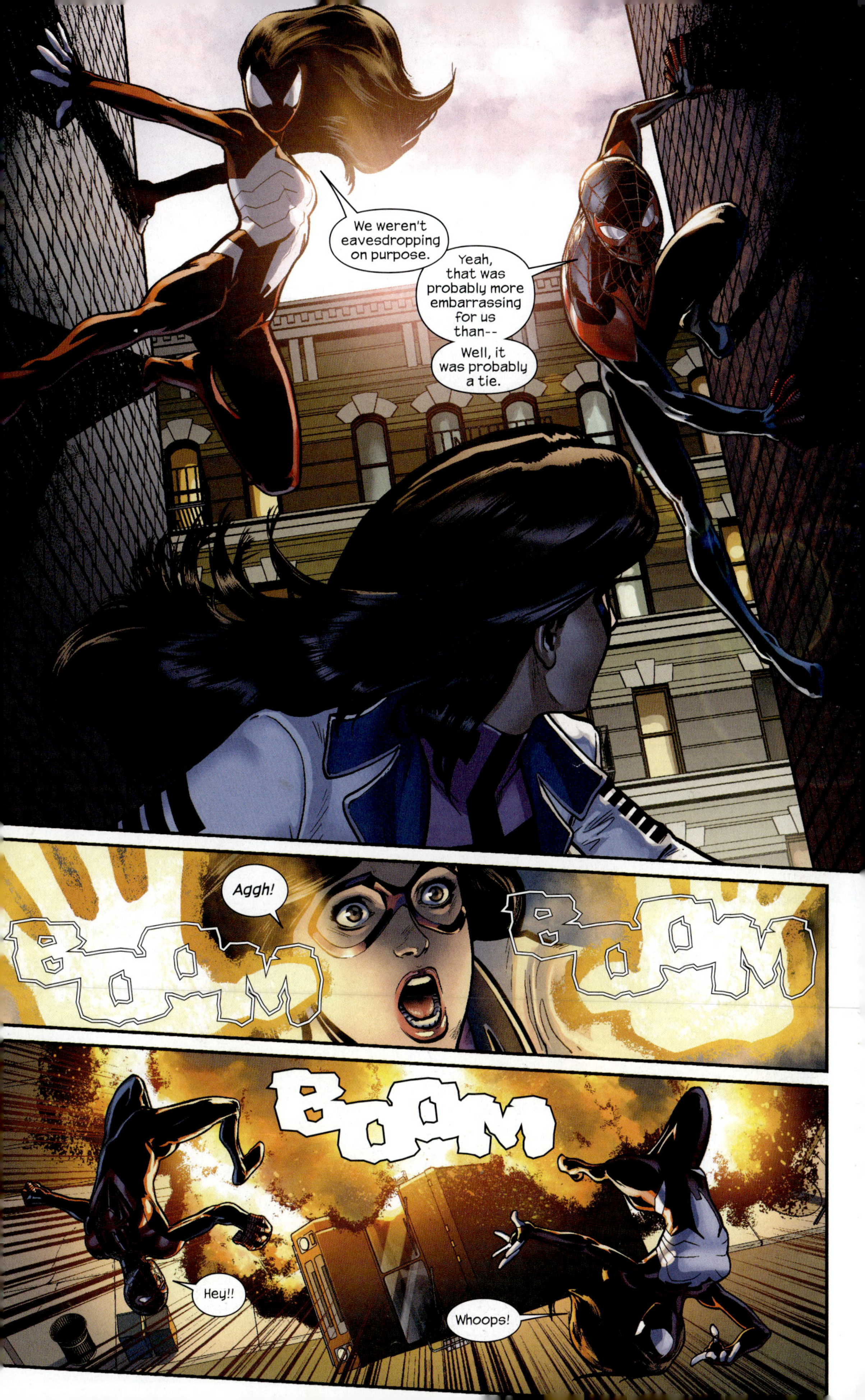

We weren't eavesdropping on purpose.
Yeah, that was probably more embarrassing for us than--
Well, it was probably a tie.
Aggh!
BOOM
BOOM
BOOM
Hey!!
Whoops!

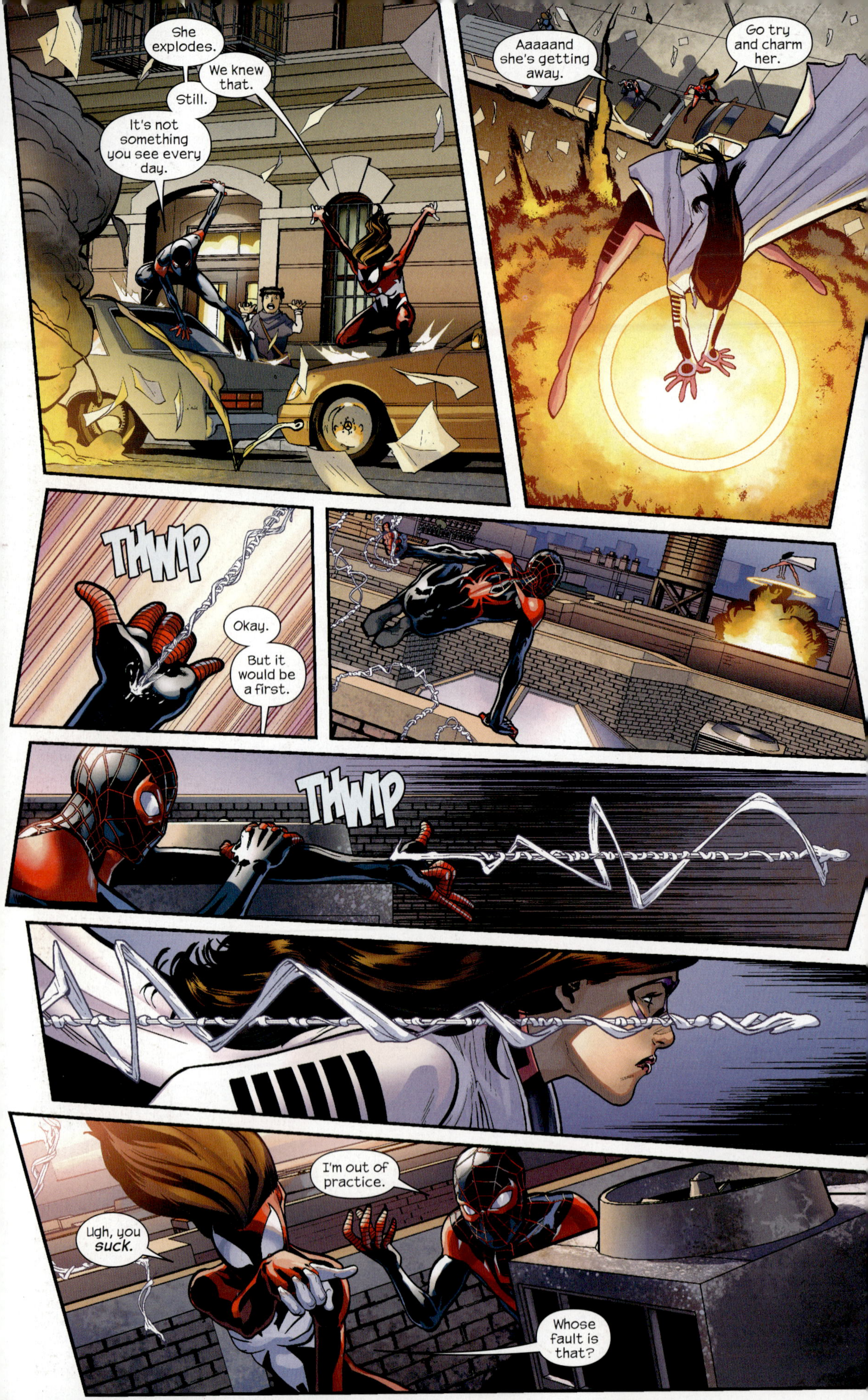

She explodes.
We knew that.
Still.
It's not something you see every day.
Aaaaand she's getting away.
Go try and charm her.
THWIP
Okay.
But it would be a first.
THWIP
Ugh, you *suck.*
I'm out of practice.
Whose fault is that?

Agh!

Oww!!

Stop running.

We're not here to toss around with you.

I--

We're here to help.

We're here, hey, we're here to help.

Lori, I know you're in trouble.

Get away!!

And I *think* I might know why.

You're-- wait, you're *both* Spider-people?

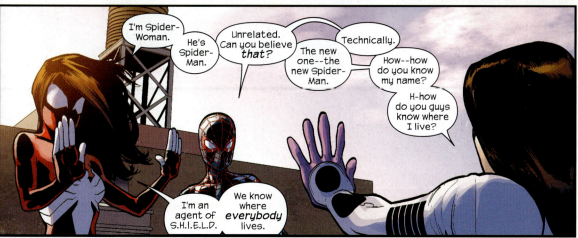

I'm Spider-Woman.

He's Spider-Man.

Unrelated. Can you believe *that?*

The new one--the new Spider-Man.

Technically.

How--how do you know my name?

H-how do you guys know where I live?

I'm an agent of S.H.I.E.L.D.

We know where *everybody* lives.

And you're here to help me?

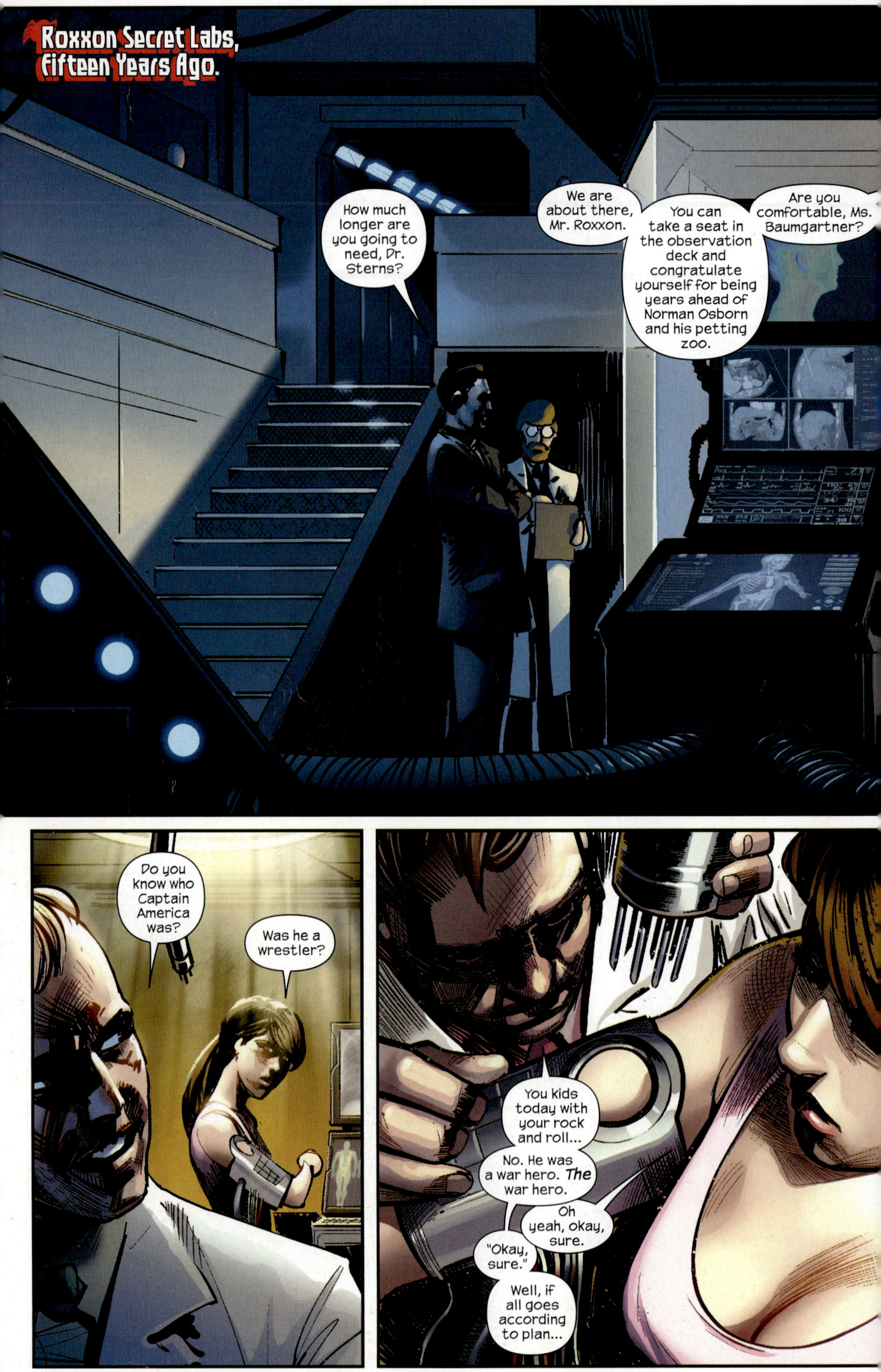
Roxxon Secret Labs, Fifteen Years Ago.
How much longer are you going to need, Dr. Sterns?
We are about there, Mr. Roxxon.
You can take a seat in the observation deck and congratulate yourself for being years ahead of Norman Osborn and his petting zoo.
Are you comfortable, Ms. Baumgartner?
Do you know who Captain America was?
Was he a wrestler?
You kids today with your rock and roll...
No. He was a war hero. *The* war hero.
Oh yeah, okay, sure.
"Okay, sure."
Well, if all goes according to plan...

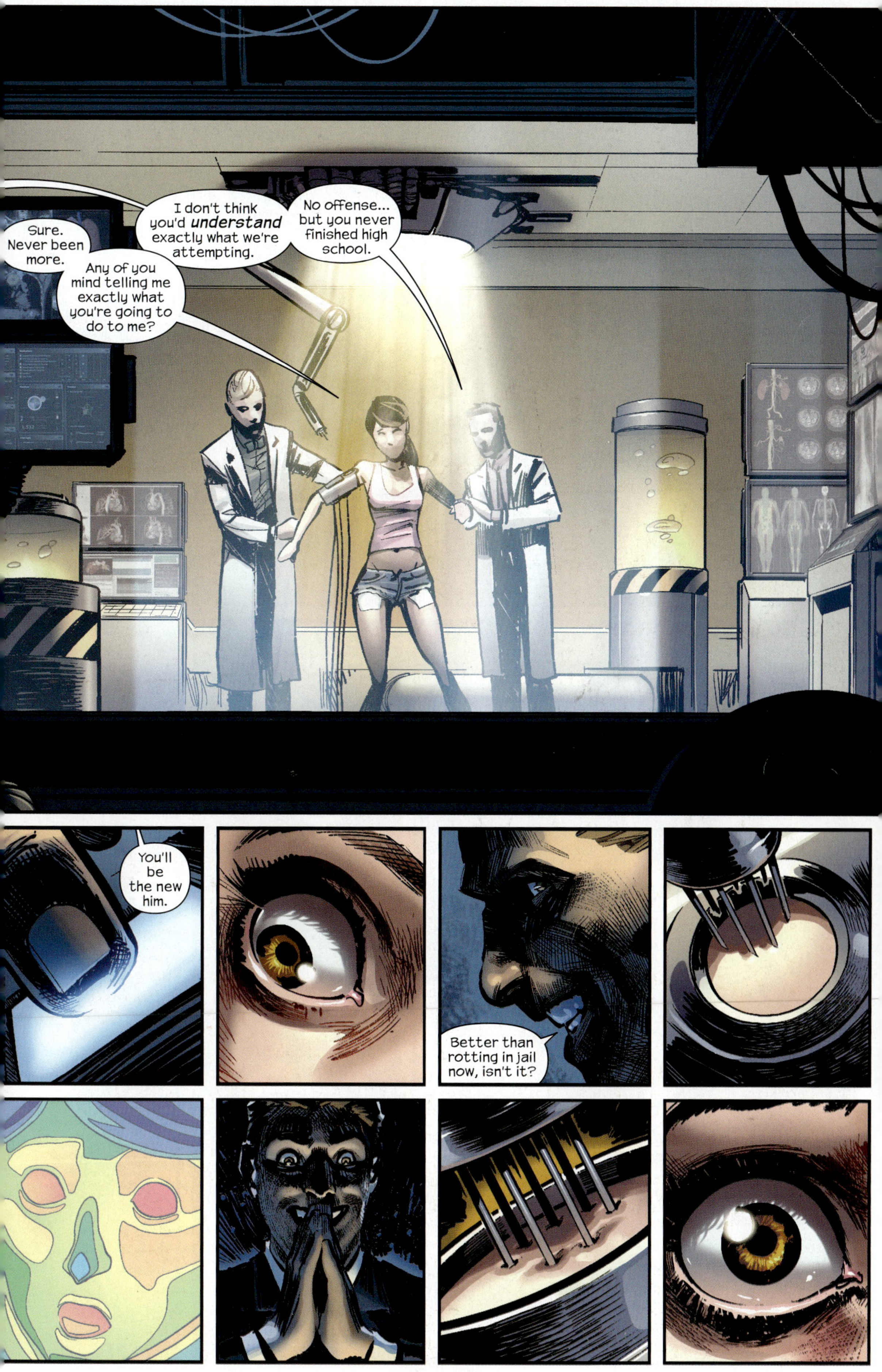
Any of you mind telling me exactly what you're going to do to me?
Sure. Never been more.
I don't think you'd **understand** exactly what we're attempting.
No offense... but you never finished high school.
You'll be the new him.
Better than rotting in jail now, isn't it?

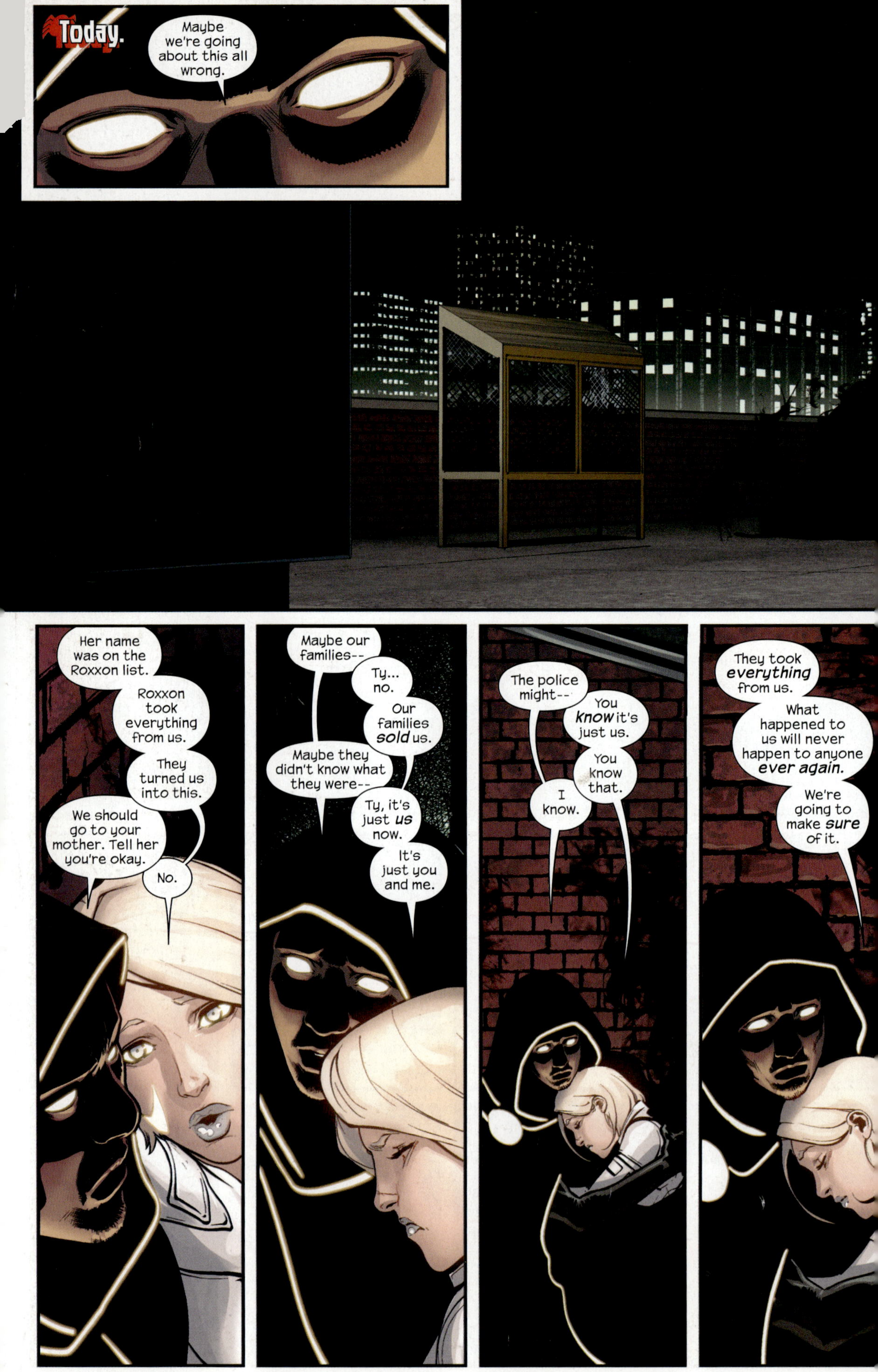
Today.
Maybe we're going about this all wrong.
Her name was on the Roxxon list.
Roxxon took everything from us.
They turned us into this.
We should go to your mother. Tell her you're okay.
No.
Maybe our families--
Ty... no.
Our families sold us.
Maybe they didn't know what they were--
Ty, it's just us now.
It's just you and me.
The police might--
You know it's just us.
You know that.
I know.
They took everything from us.
What happened to us will never happen to anyone ever again.
We're going to make sure of it.

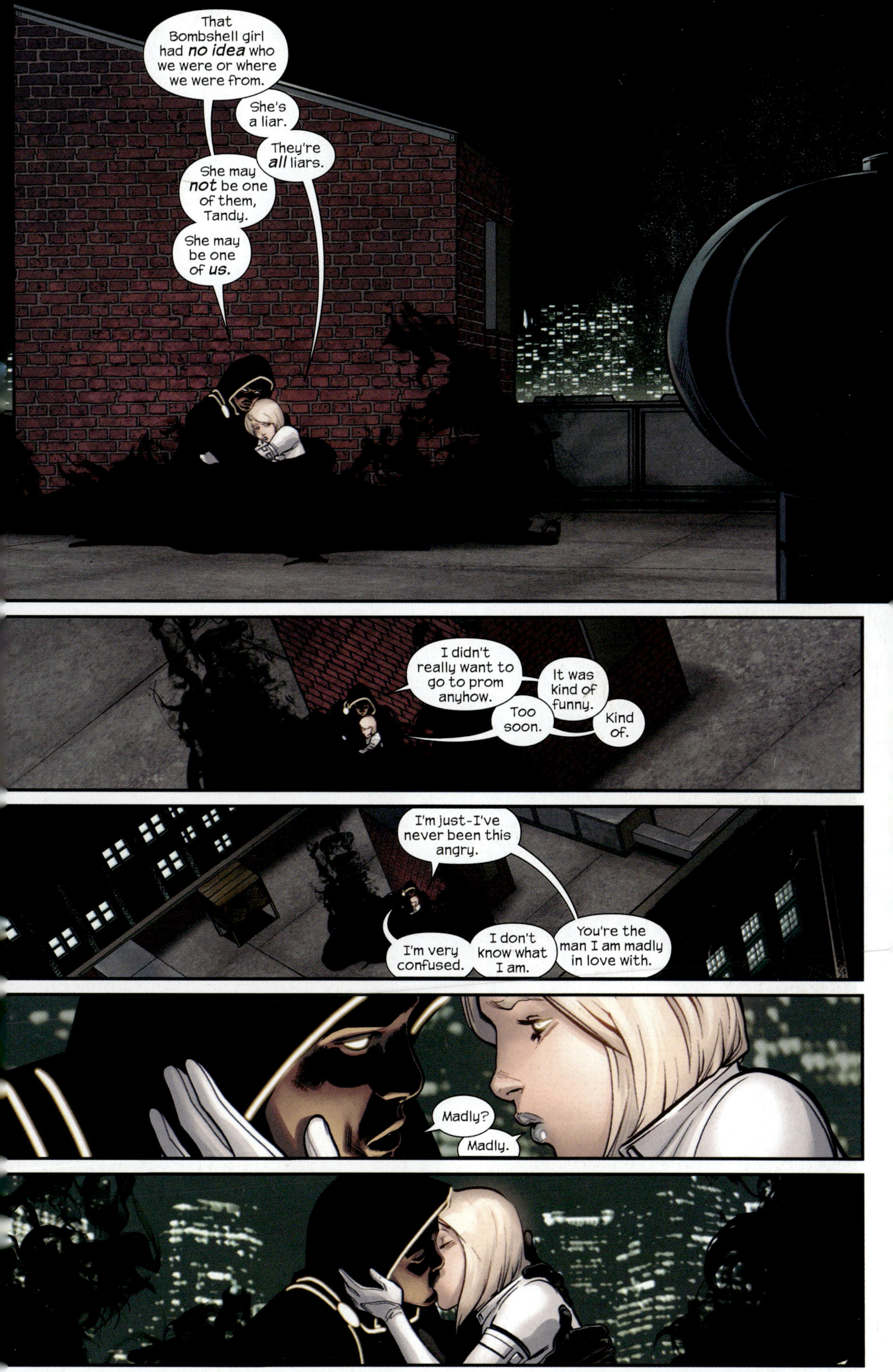
That Bombshell girl had *no idea* who we were or where we were from.
She's a liar.
They're *all* liars.
She may *not* be one of them, Tandy.
She may be one of *us.*
I didn't really want to go to prom anyhow.
It was kind of funny.
Too soon.
Kind of.
I'm just-I've never been this angry.
You're the man I am madly in love with.
I don't know what I am.
I'm very confused.
Madly?
Madly.

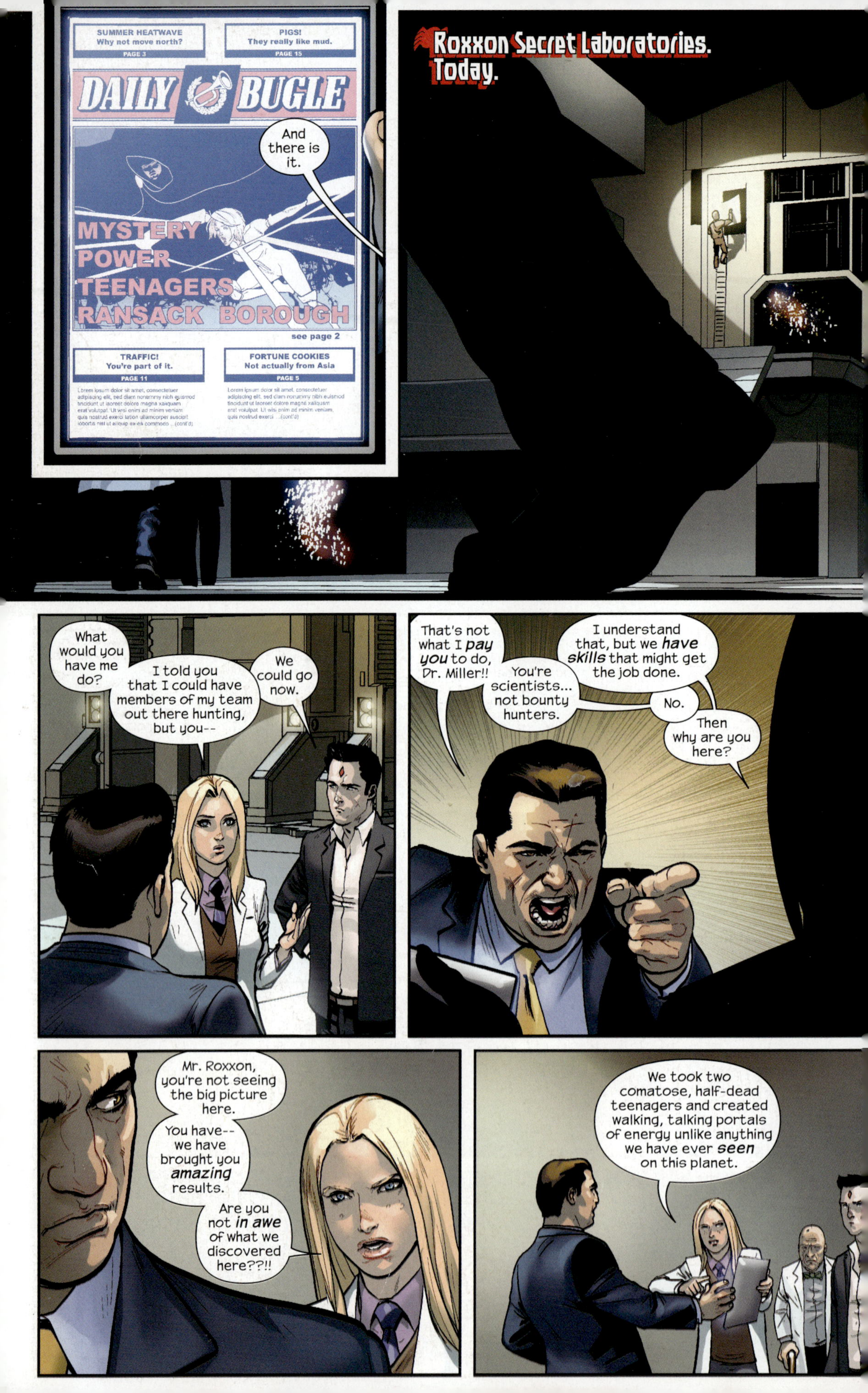
SUMMER HEATWAVE Why not move north? PAGE 3
PIGS! They really like mud. PAGE 15
DAILY BUGLE
MYSTERY POWER TEENAGERS RANSACK BOROUGH
see page 2
TRAFFIC! You're part of it. PAGE 11
FORTUNE COOKIES Not actually from Asia PAGE 5
And there is it.
Roxxon Secret Laboratories. Today.
What would you have me do?
I told you that I could have members of my team out there hunting, but you--
We could go now.
That's not what I pay you to do, Dr. Miller!!
I understand that, but we have skills that might get the job done.
You're scientists... not bounty hunters.
No.
Then why are you here?
Mr. Roxxon, you're not seeing the big picture here.
You have-- we have brought you amazing results.
Are you not in awe of what we discovered here??!!
We took two comatose, half-dead teenagers and created walking, talking portals of energy unlike anything we have ever seen on this planet.

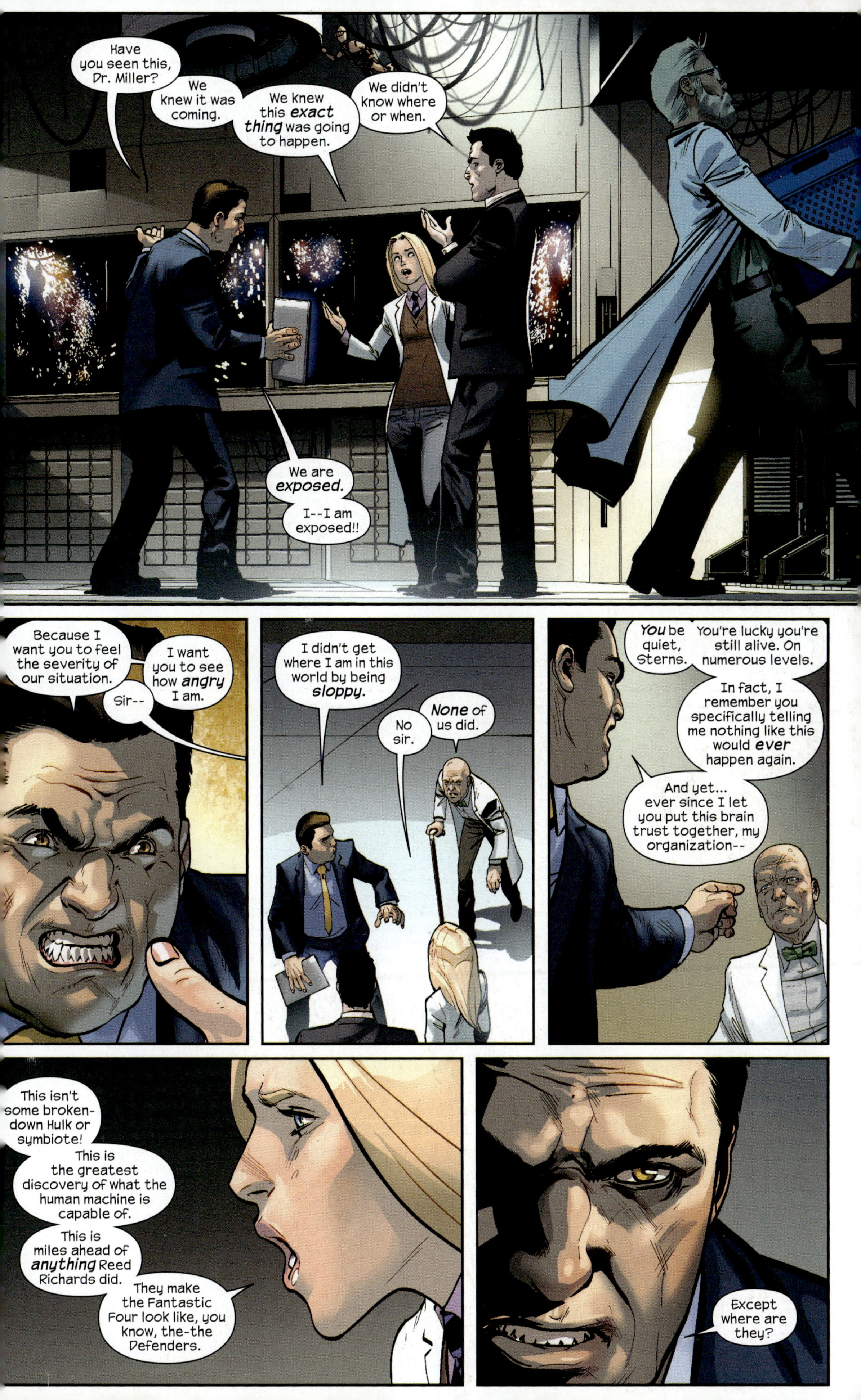

Have you seen this, Dr. Miller?
We knew it was coming.
We knew this *exact thing* was going to happen.
We didn't know where or when.
We are *exposed.*
I--I am exposed!!
Because I want you to feel the severity of our situation.
I want you to see how *angry* I am.
Sir--
I didn't get where I am in this world by being *sloppy.*
No sir.
None of us did.
You be quiet, Sterns.
You're lucky you're still alive. On numerous levels.
In fact, I remember you specifically telling me nothing like this would *ever* happen again.
And yet... ever since I let you put this brain trust together, my organization--
This isn't some broken-down Hulk or symbiote!
This is the greatest discovery of what the human machine is capable of.
This is miles ahead of *anything* Reed Richards did.
They make the Fantastic Four look like, you know, the-the Defenders.
Except where are they?

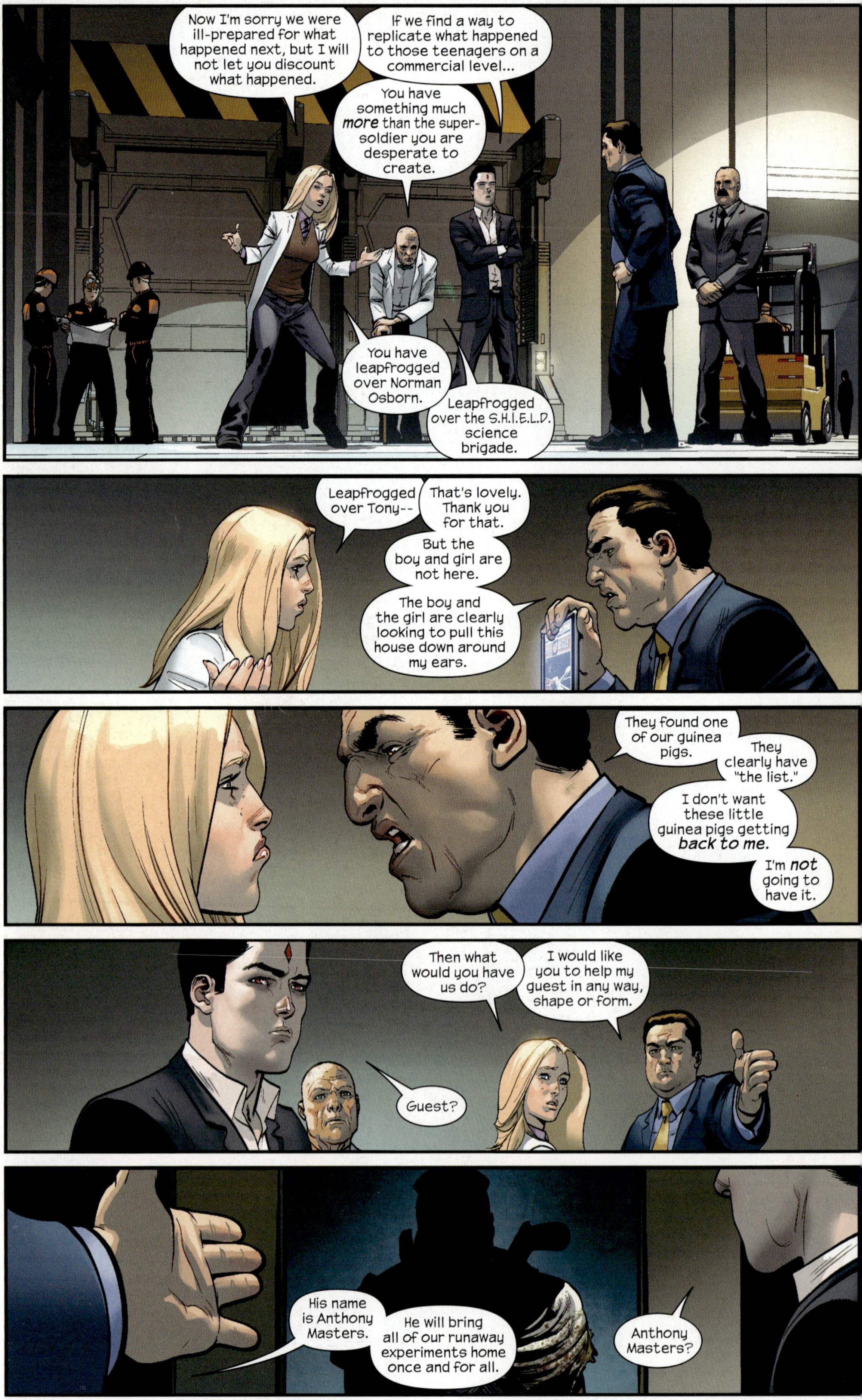
Now I'm sorry we were ill-prepared for what happened next, but I will not let you discount what happened.
If we find a way to replicate what happened to those teenagers on a commercial level...
You have something much *more* than the super-soldier you are desperate to create.
You have leapfrogged over Norman Osborn.
Leapfrogged over the S.H.I.E.L.D. science brigade.
Leapfrogged over Tony--
That's lovely. Thank you for that.
But the boy and girl are not here.
The boy and the girl are clearly looking to pull this house down around my ears.
They found one of our guinea pigs.
They clearly have "the list."
I don't want these little guinea pigs getting *back to me.*
I'm *not* going to have it.
Then what would you have us do?
I would like you to help my guest in any way, shape or form.
Guest?
His name is Anthony Masters.
He will bring all of our runaway experiments home once and for all.
Anthony Masters?

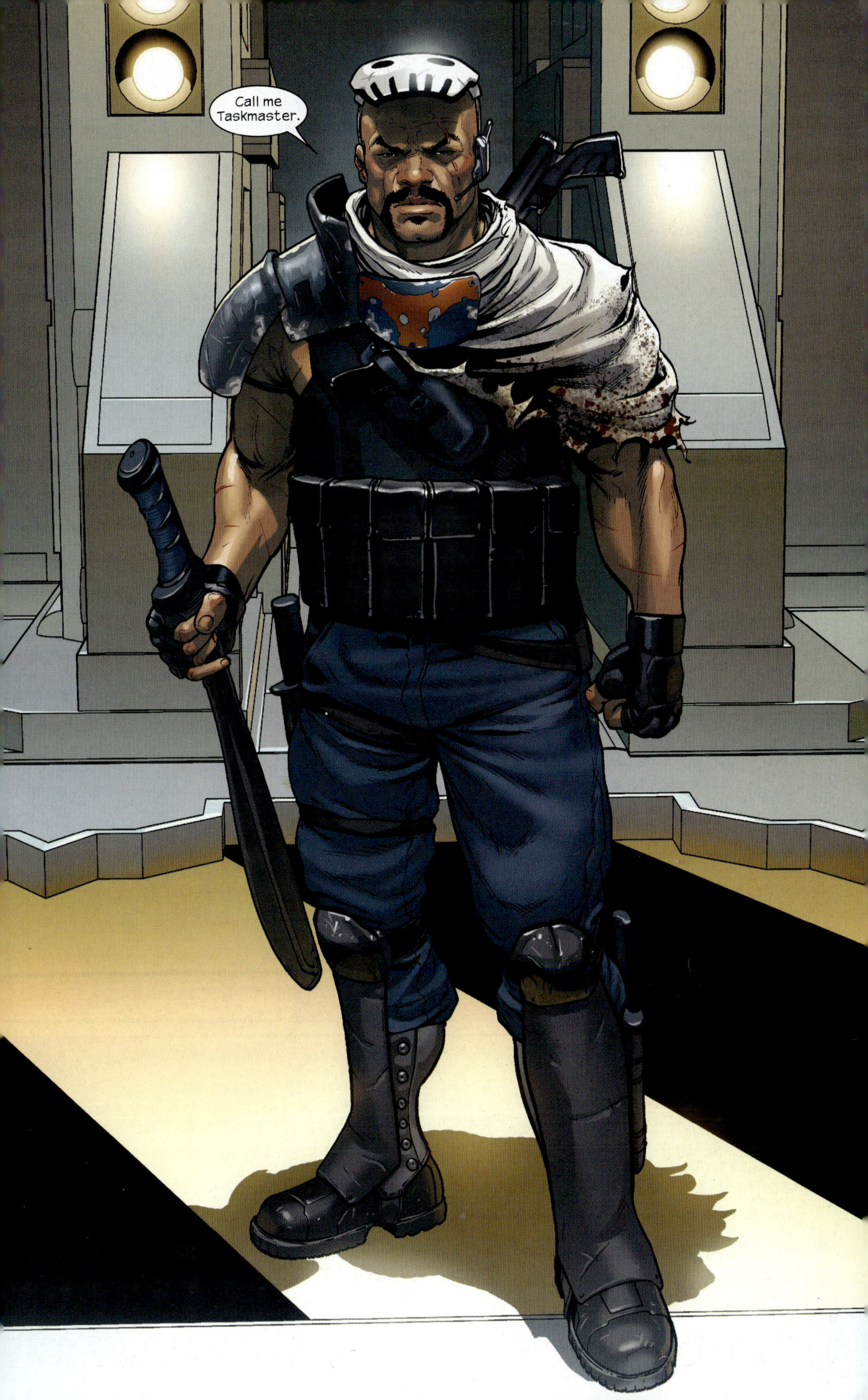
Call me Taskmaster.

Mmff...

Hello?

How are you feeling, Lana?

Where are you?

We're *observing* you.

So... Can I go now?

How are you *feeling*?

Creeped out. How would *you* feel?

Do you feel different?

How long have I been asleep?

Why are you looking at your hands?

They feel different.

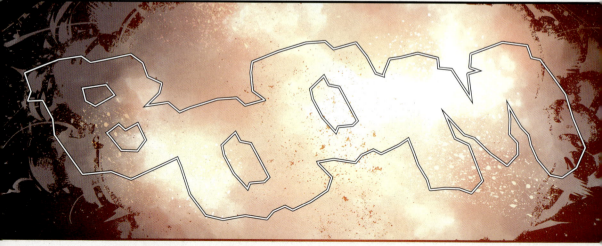

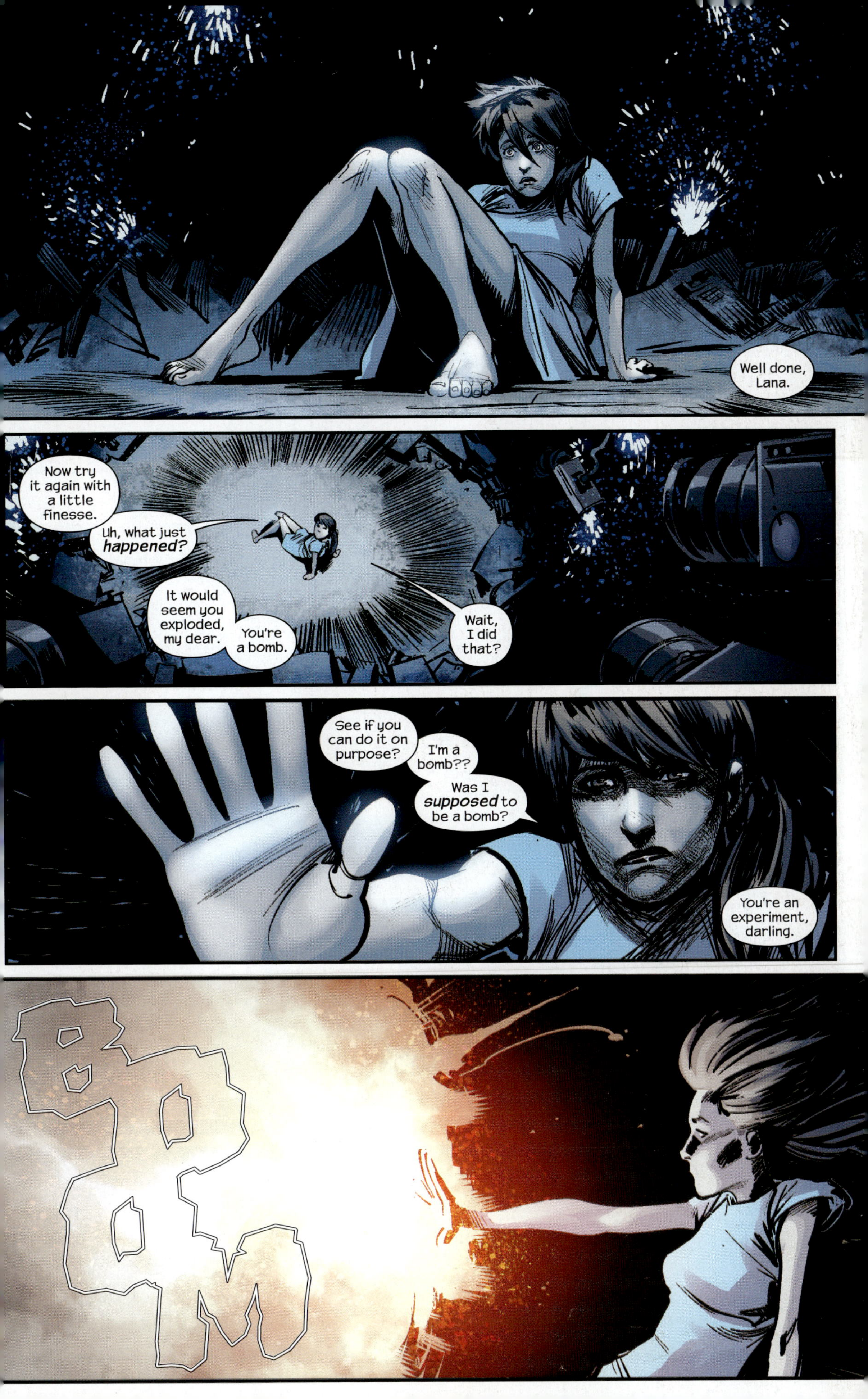
Well done, Lana.
Now try it again with a little finesse.
Uh, what just happened?
It would seem you exploded, my dear.
You're a bomb.
Wait, I did that?
See if you can do it on purpose?
I'm a bomb??
Was I supposed to be a bomb?
You're an experiment, darling.
BOM

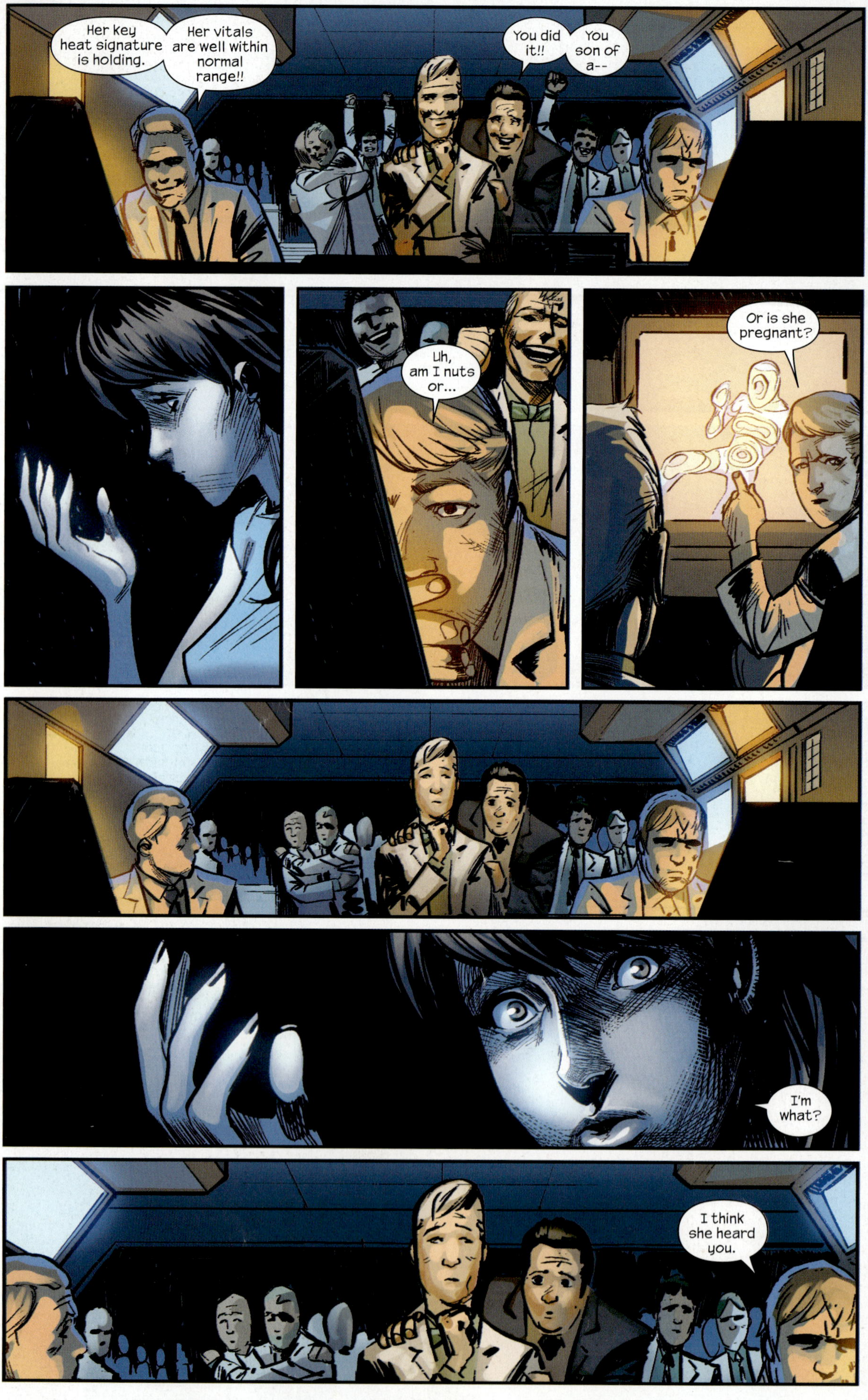
Her key heat signature is holding.
Her vitals are well within normal range!!
You did it!!
You son of a--
Uh, am I nuts or...
Or is she pregnant?
I'm what?
I think she heard you.

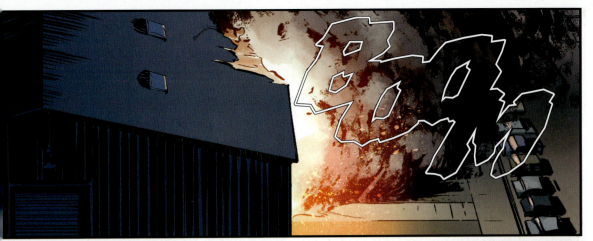

She has escaped! I repeat: the test subject has escaped!

If this gets back to me--

It *can't* get back to you!! She doesn't know who you are!

She doesn't know who *any* of us are.

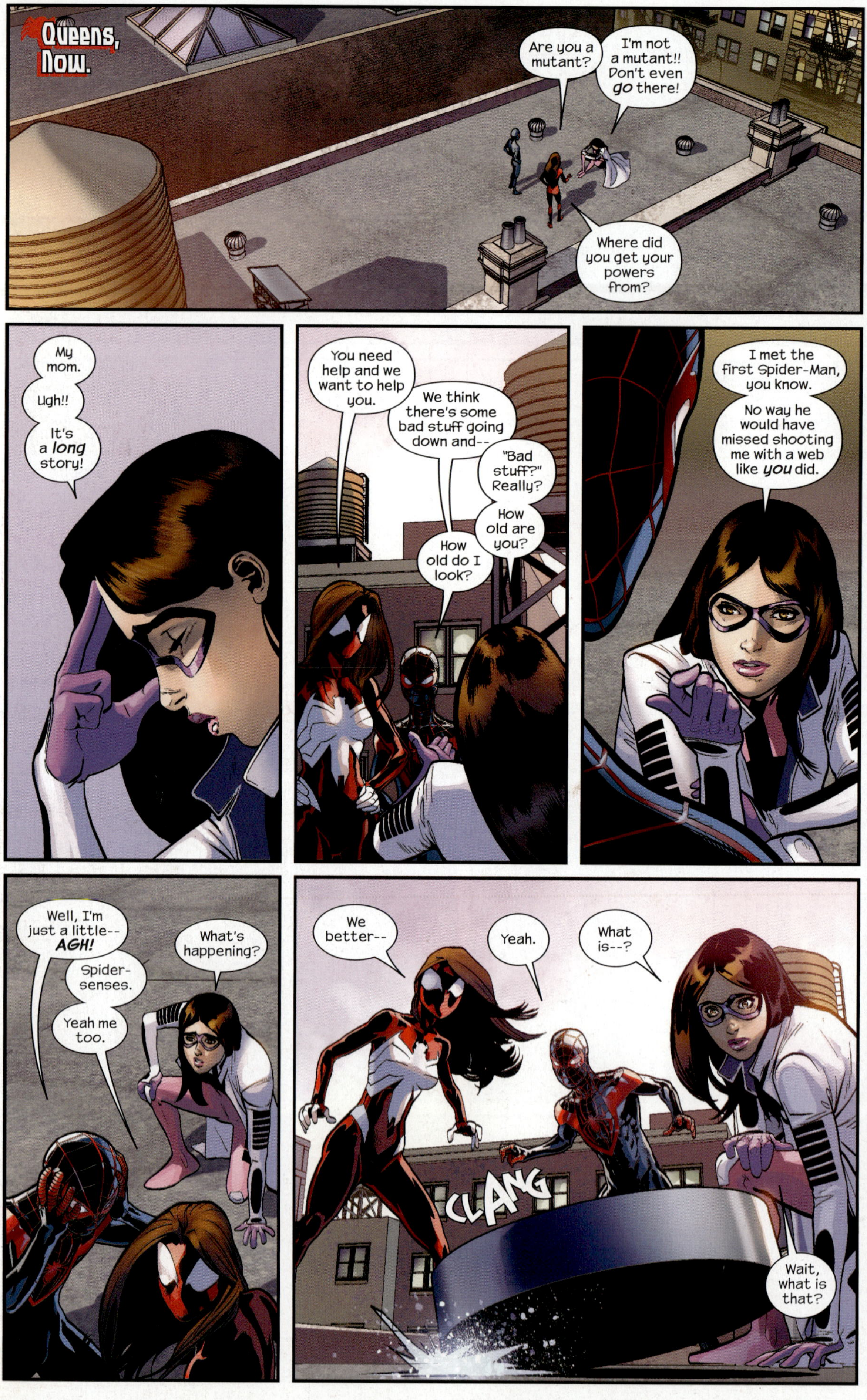
Queens, Now.
Are you a mutant?
I'm not a mutant!! Don't even go there!
Where did you get your powers from?
My mom.
Ugh!!
It's a long story!
You need help and we want to help you.
We think there's some bad stuff going down and--
"Bad stuff?" Really?
How old are you?
How old do I look?
I met the first Spider-Man, you know.
No way he would have missed shooting me with a web like you did.
Well, I'm just a little-- AGH!
What's happening?
Spider-senses.
Yeah me too.
We better--
Yeah.
What is--?
CLANG
Wait, what is that?

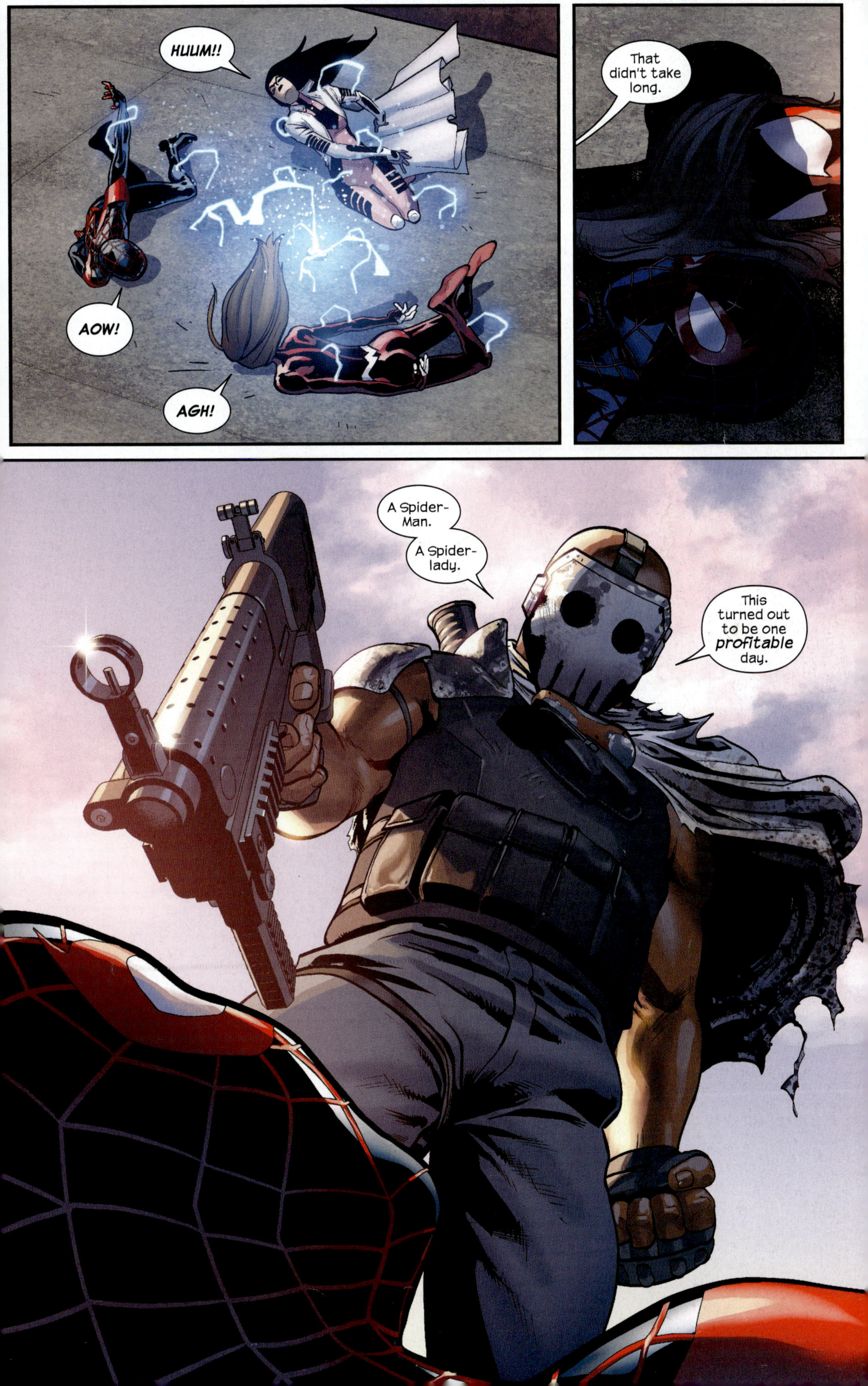
HUUM!!
AOW!
AGH!
That didn't take long.
A Spider-Man.
A Spider-lady.
This turned out to be one *profitable* day.

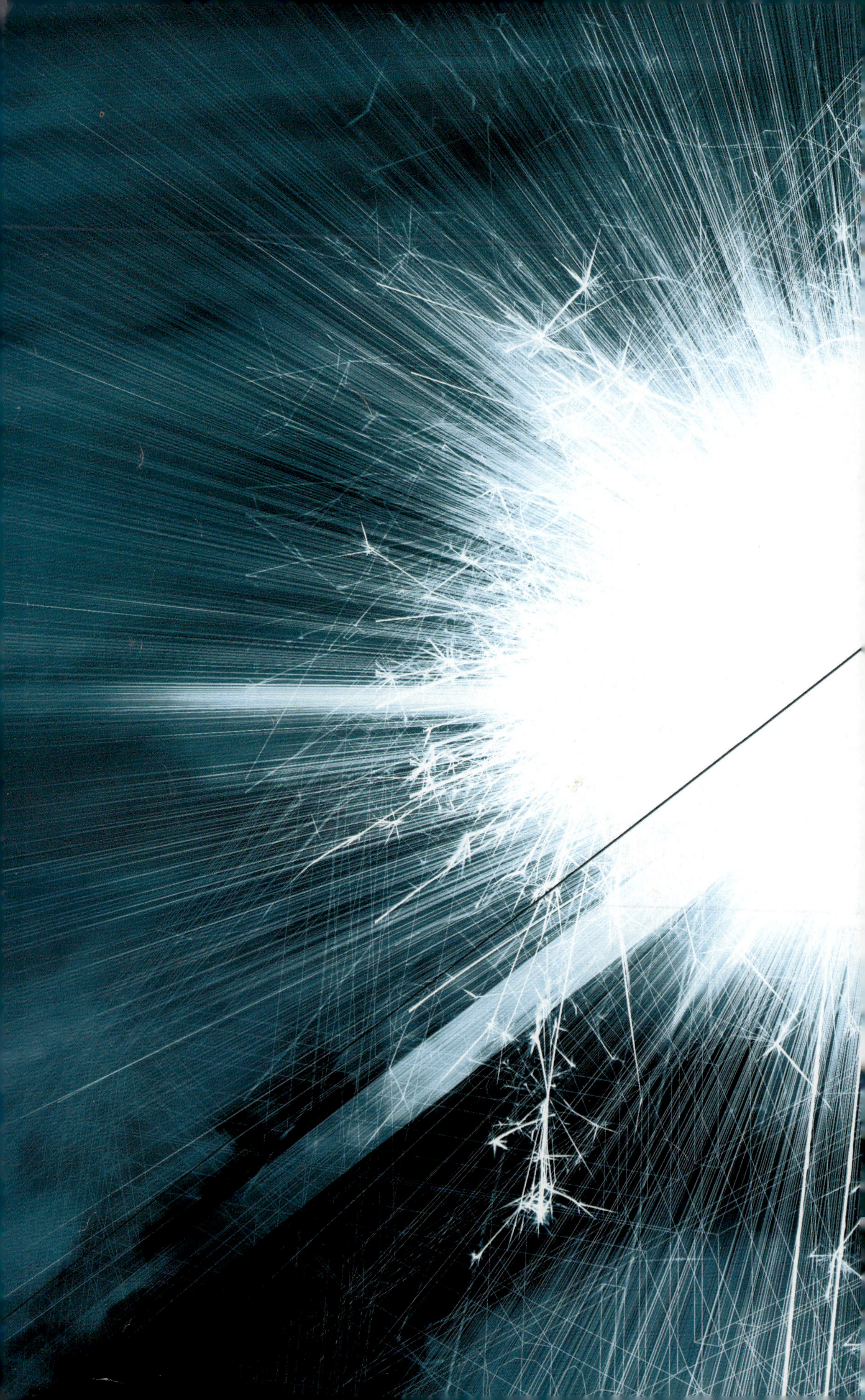

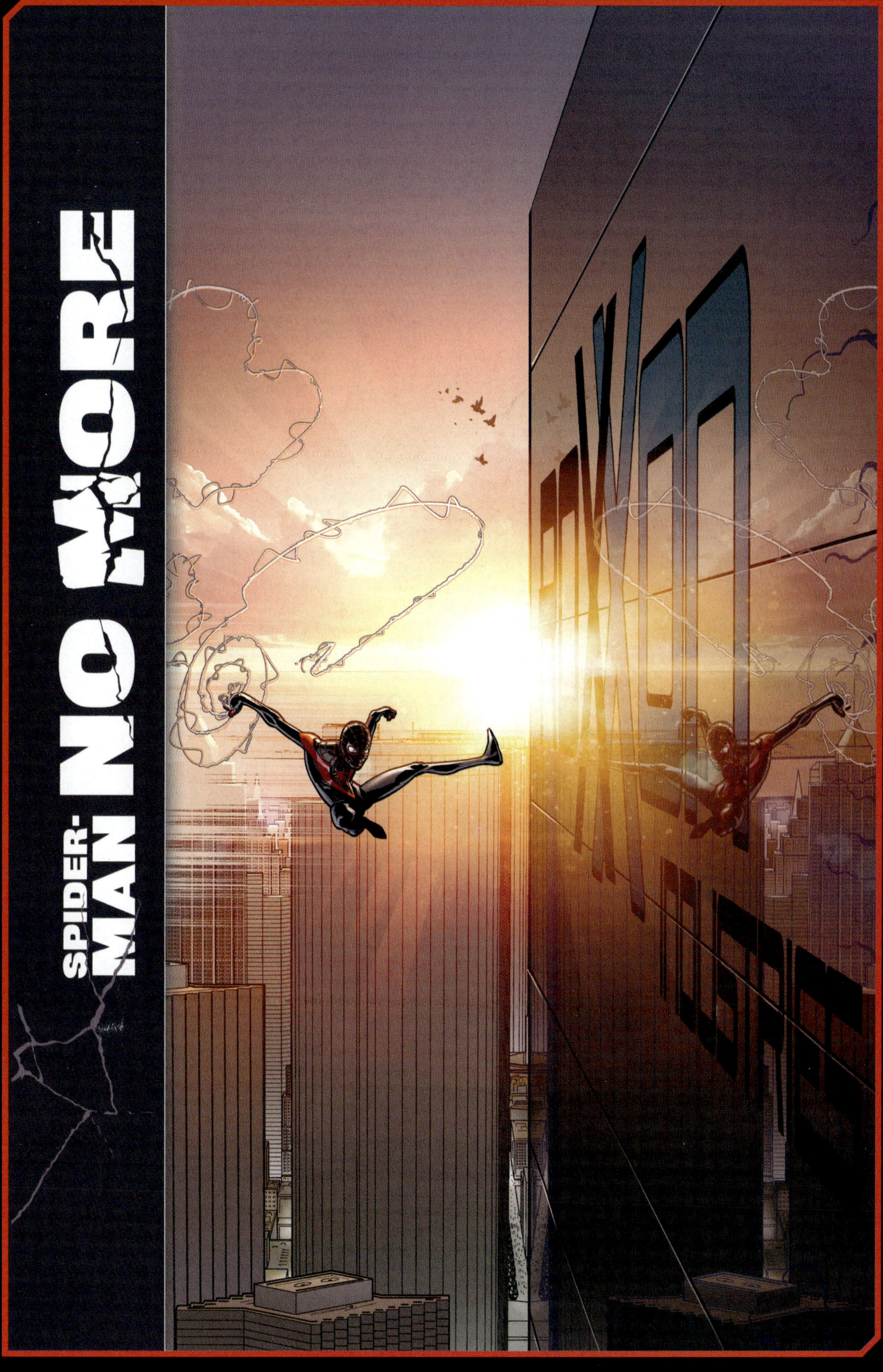
SPIDER-MAN NO MORE

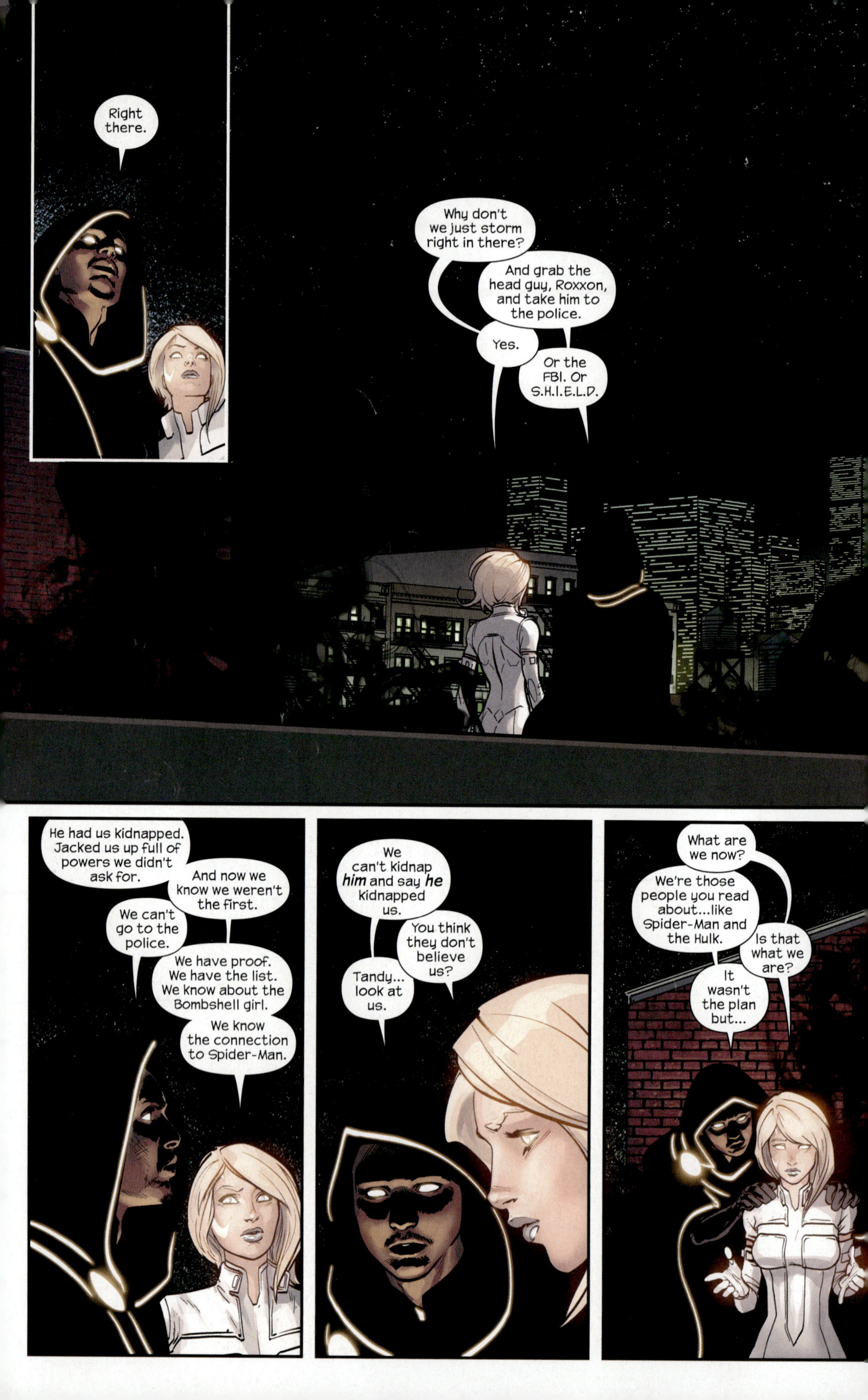
Right there.
Why don't we just storm right in there?
And grab the head guy, Roxxon, and take him to the police.
Yes.
Or the FBI. Or S.H.I.E.L.D.
He had us kidnapped. Jacked us up full of powers we didn't ask for.
And now we know we weren't the first.
We can't go to the police.
We have proof. We have the list. We know about the Bombshell girl.
We know the connection to Spider-Man.
We can't kidnap *him* and say *he* kidnapped us.
You think they don't believe us?
Tandy... look at us.
What are we now?
We're those people you read about...like Spider-Man and the Hulk.
Is that what we are?
It wasn't the plan but...

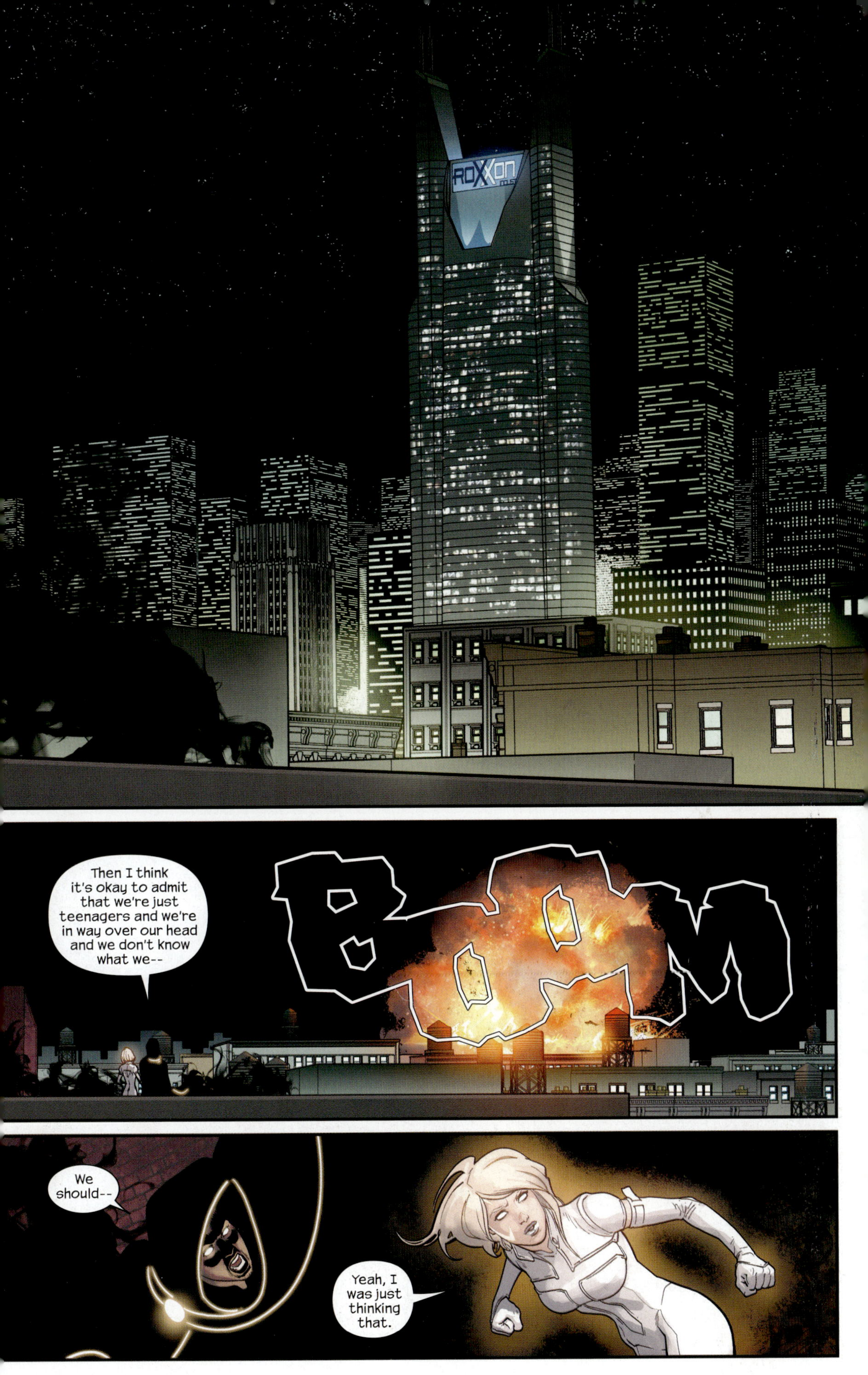
ROXXON
Then I think it's okay to admit that we're just teenagers and we're in way over our head and we don't know what we--
BOOM
We should--
Yeah, I was just thinking that.

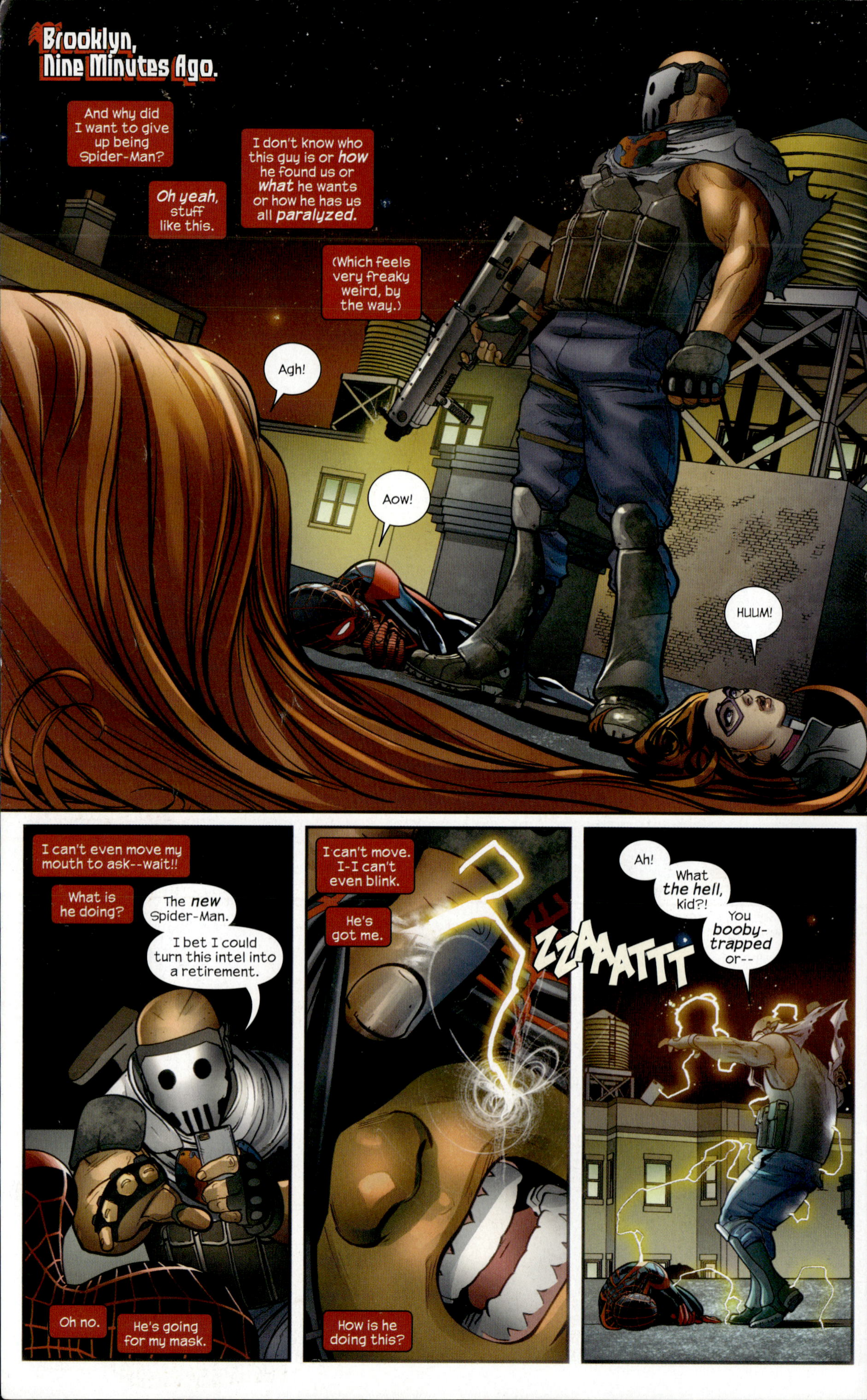

Brooklyn, Nine Minutes Ago.
And why did I want to give up being Spider-Man?
Oh yeah, stuff like this.
I don't know who this guy is or how he found us or what he wants or how he has us all paralyzed.
(Which feels very freaky weird, by the way.)
Agh!
Aow!
HUUM!
I can't even move my mouth to ask--wait!!
What is he doing?
The new Spider-Man.
I bet I could turn this intel into a retirement.
Oh no.
He's going for my mask.
I can't move. I-I can't even blink.
He's got me.
How is he doing this?
ZZAAATTT
Ah!
What the hell, kid?!
You booby-trapped or--

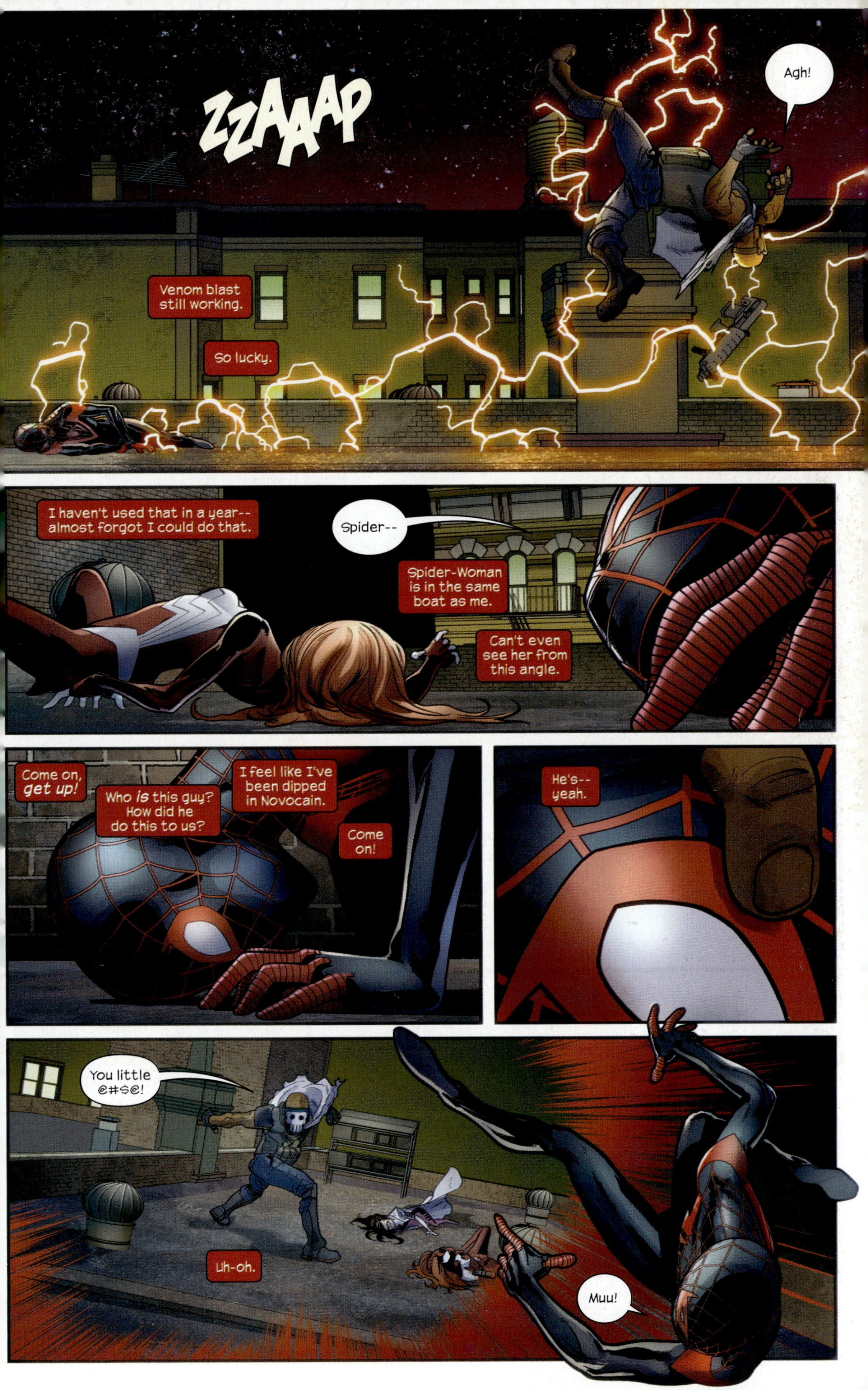

ZZAAAP
Agh!
Venom blast still working.
So lucky.
I haven't used that in a year-- almost forgot I could do that.
Spider--
Spider-Woman is in the same boat as me.
Can't even see her from this angle.
Come on, *get up!*
Who *is* this guy? How did he do this to us?
I feel like I've been dipped in Novocain.
Come on!
He's-- yeah.
You little @#$@!
Uh-oh.
Muu!

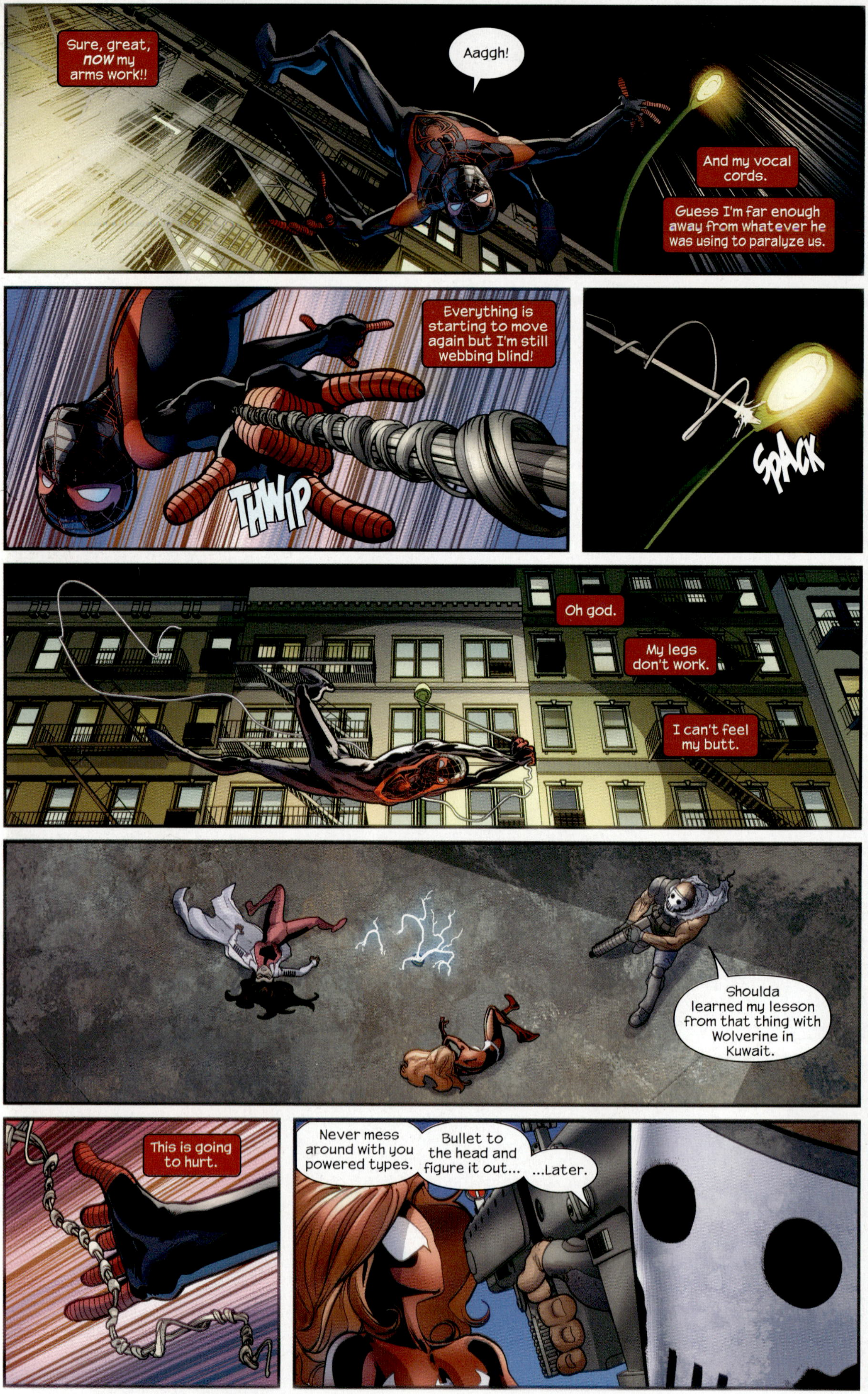

Sure, great, *now* my arms work!!
Aaggh!
And my vocal cords.
Guess I'm far enough away from whatever he was using to paralyze us.
Everything is starting to move again but I'm still webbing blind!
THWIP
SPACK
Oh god.
My legs don't work.
I can't feel my butt.
Shoulda learned my lesson from that thing with Wolverine in Kuwait.
This is going to hurt.
Never mess around with you powered types.
Bullet to the head and figure it out...
...Later.

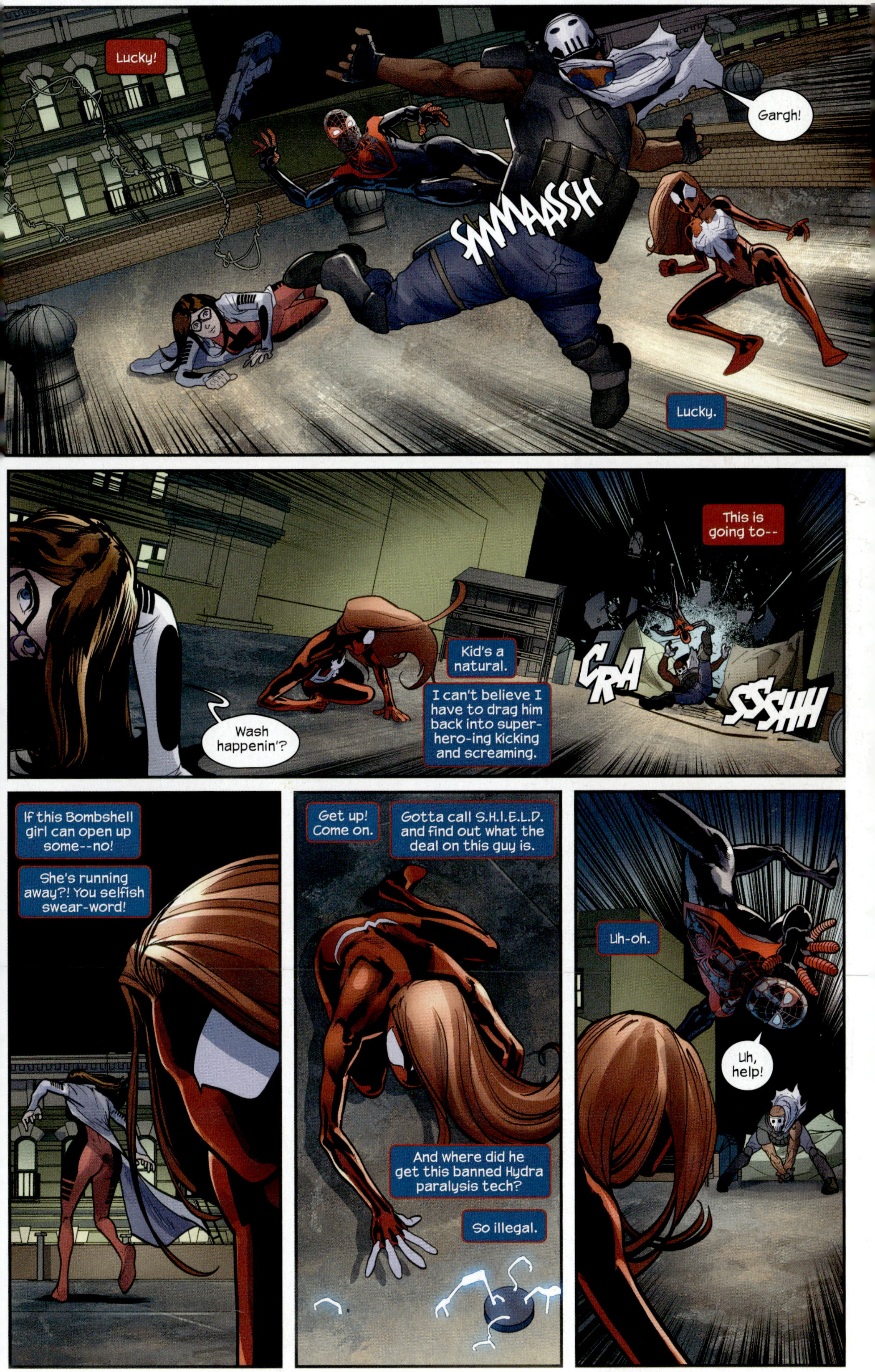
Lucky!
Gargh!
SMAASSH
Lucky.
This is going to--
Kid's a natural.
I can't believe I have to drag him back into super-hero-ing kicking and screaming.
CRA
SSHH
Wash happenin'?
If this Bombshell girl can open up some--no!
She's running away?! You selfish swear-word!
Get up! Come on.
Gotta call S.H.I.E.L.D. and find out what the deal on this guy is.
And where did he get this banned Hydra paralysis tech?
So illegal.
Uh-oh.
Uh, help!

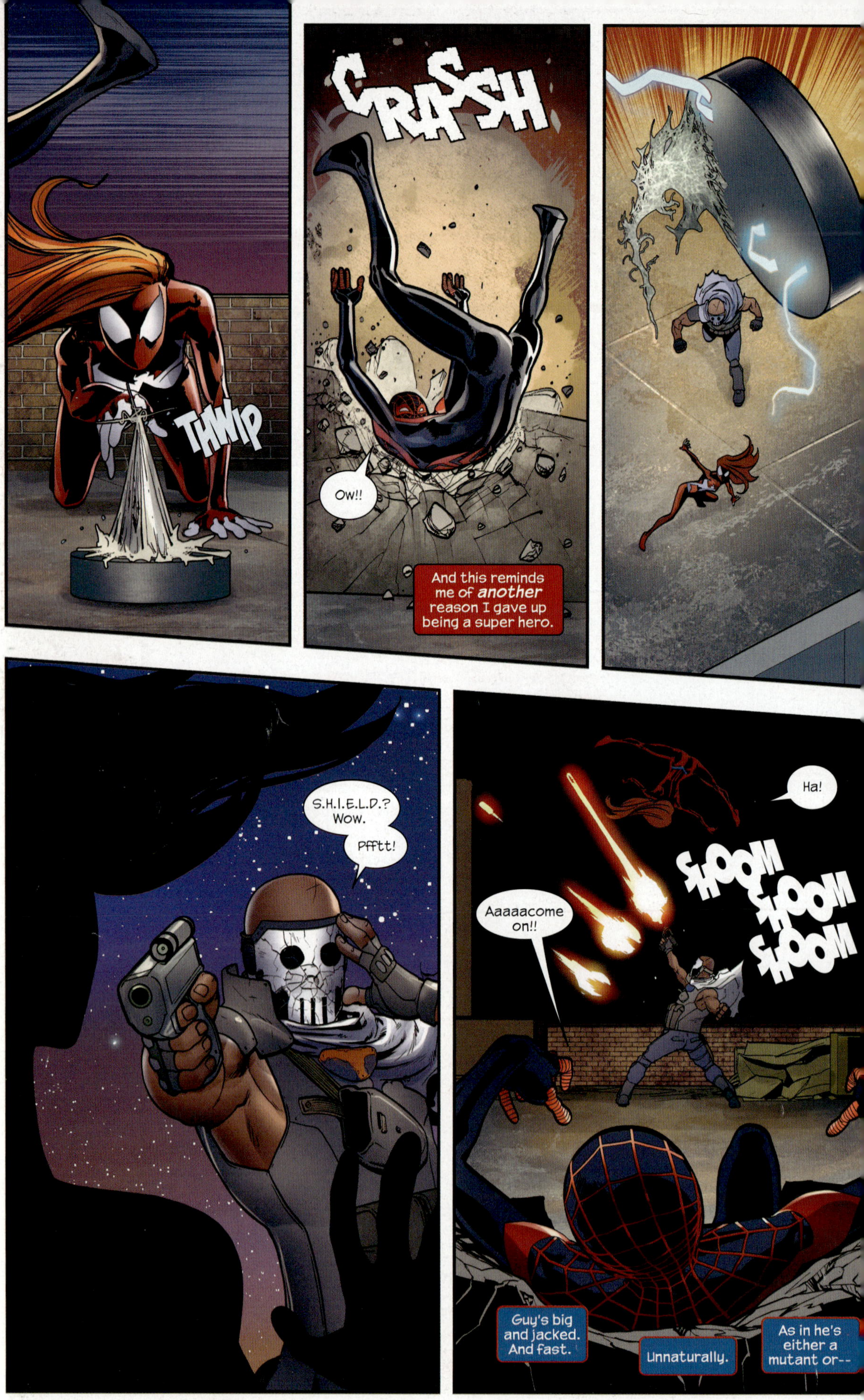
THWIP
CRASSH
Ow!!
And this reminds me of *another* reason I gave up being a super hero.
S.H.I.E.L.D.? Wow.
Pfftt!
Ha!
SHOOM SHOOM SHOOM
Aaaaacome on!!
Guy's big and jacked. And fast.
Unnaturally.
As in he's either a mutant or--

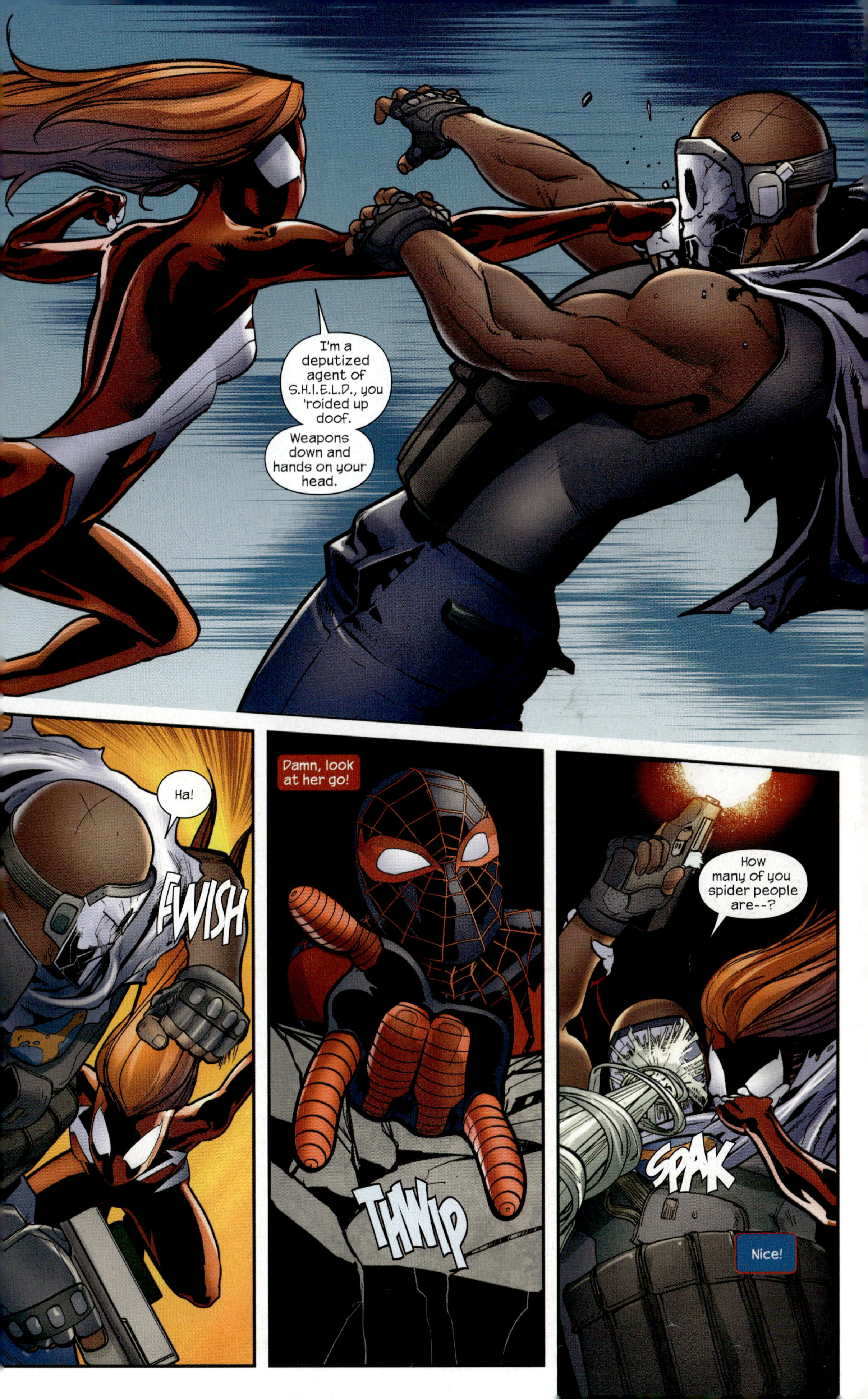
I'm a deputized agent of S.H.I.E.L.D., you 'roided up doof.
Weapons down and hands on your head.
Ha!
FWISH
Damn, look at her go!
THWIP
How many of you spider people are--?
SPAK
Nice!

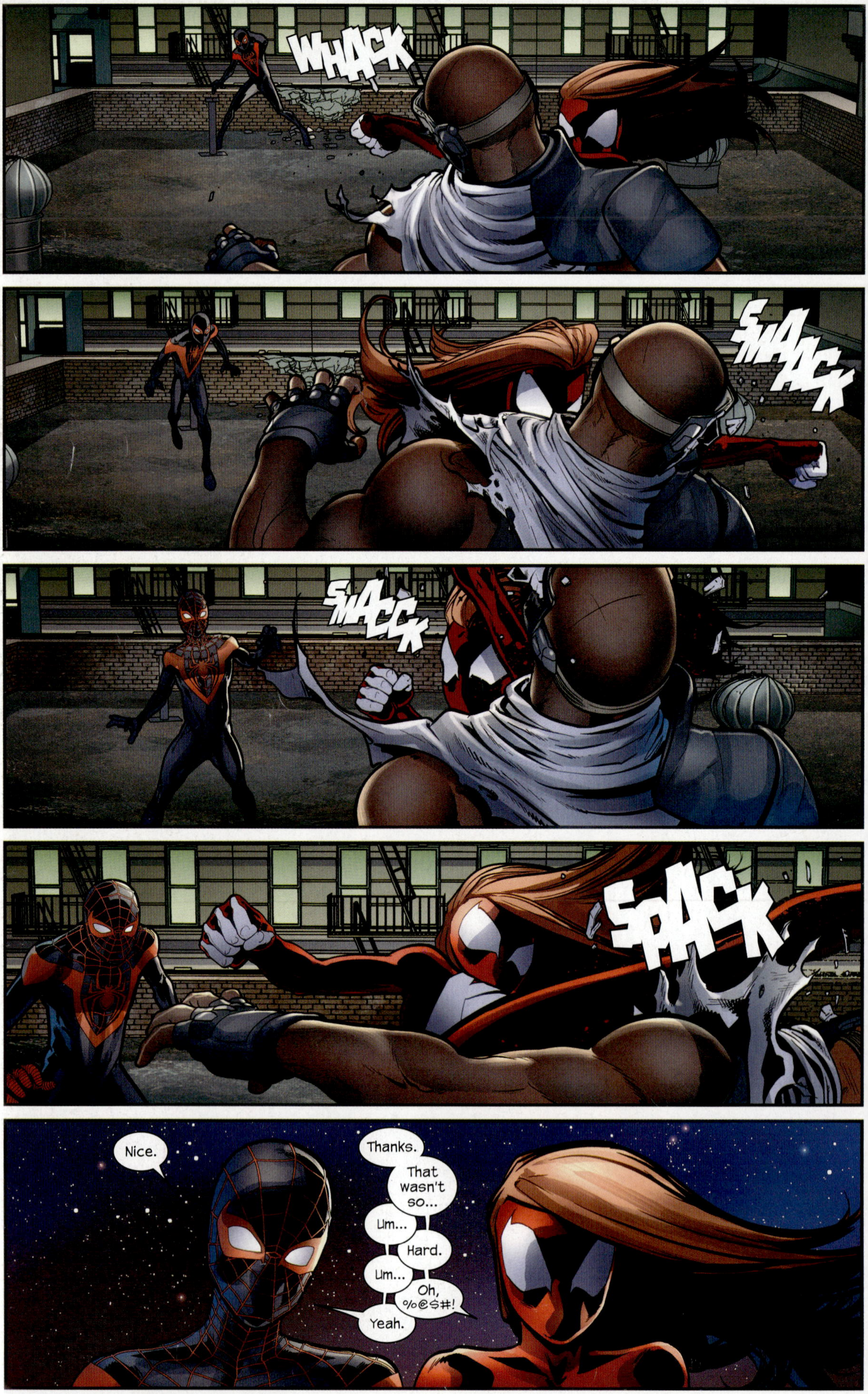
WHACK
SMAACK
SMACCK
SPACK
Nice.
Thanks.
That wasn't so...
Um...
Hard.
Um...
Oh, %@$#!
Yeah.

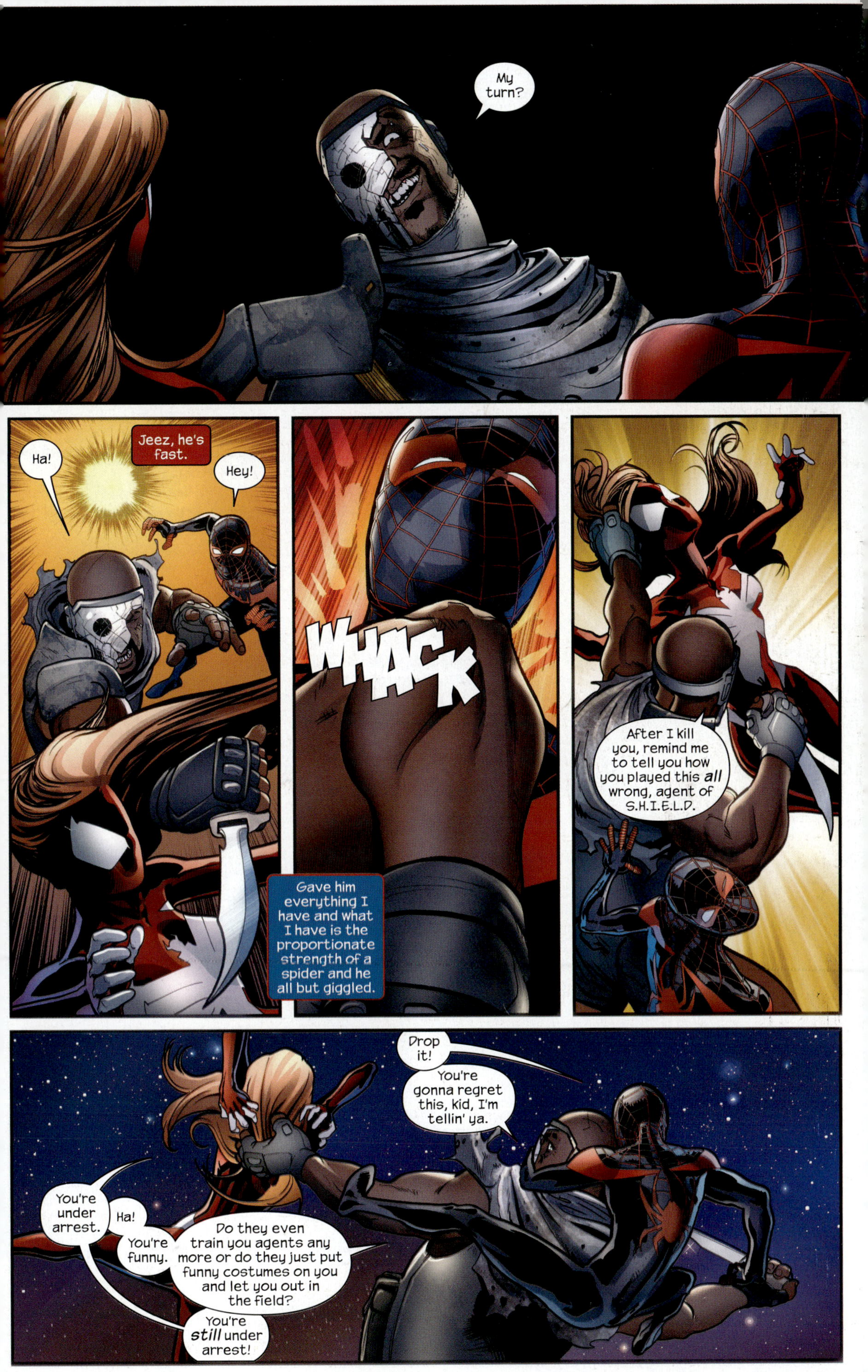
My turn?
Jeez, he's fast.
Ha!
Hey!
WHACK
Gave him everything I have and what I have is the proportionate strength of a spider and he all but giggled.
After I kill you, remind me to tell you how you played this *all* wrong, agent of S.H.I.E.L.D.
Drop it!
You're gonna regret this, kid, I'm tellin' ya.
You're under arrest.
Ha!
You're funny.
Do they even train you agents any more or do they just put funny costumes on you and let you out in the field?
You're *still* under arrest!

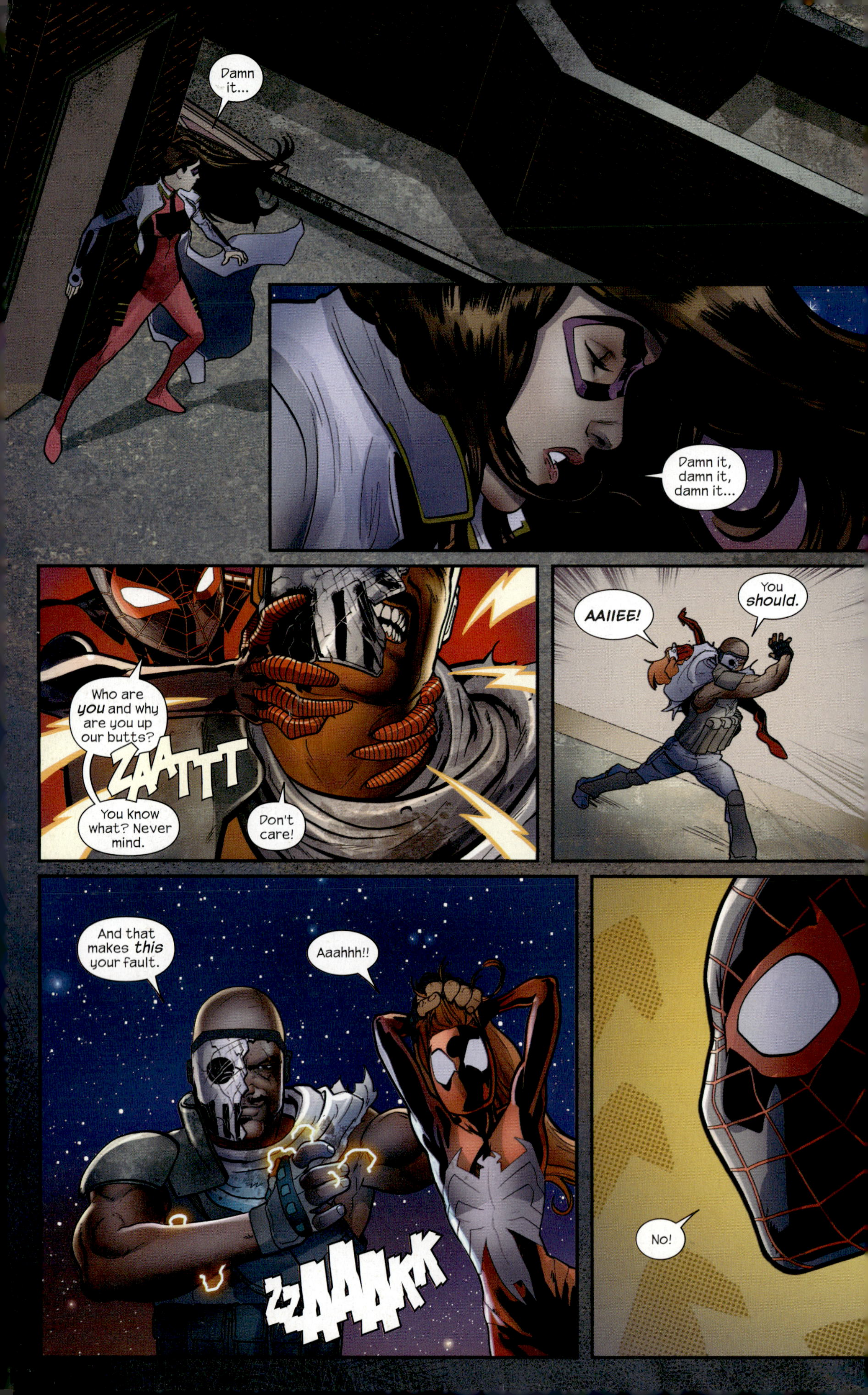
Damn it...
Damn it, damn it, damn it...
Who are *you* and why are you up our butts?
ZAATTT
You know what? Never mind.
Don't care!
AAIIEE!
You *should.*
And that makes *this* your fault.
Aaahhh!!
ZZAAAKKK
No!

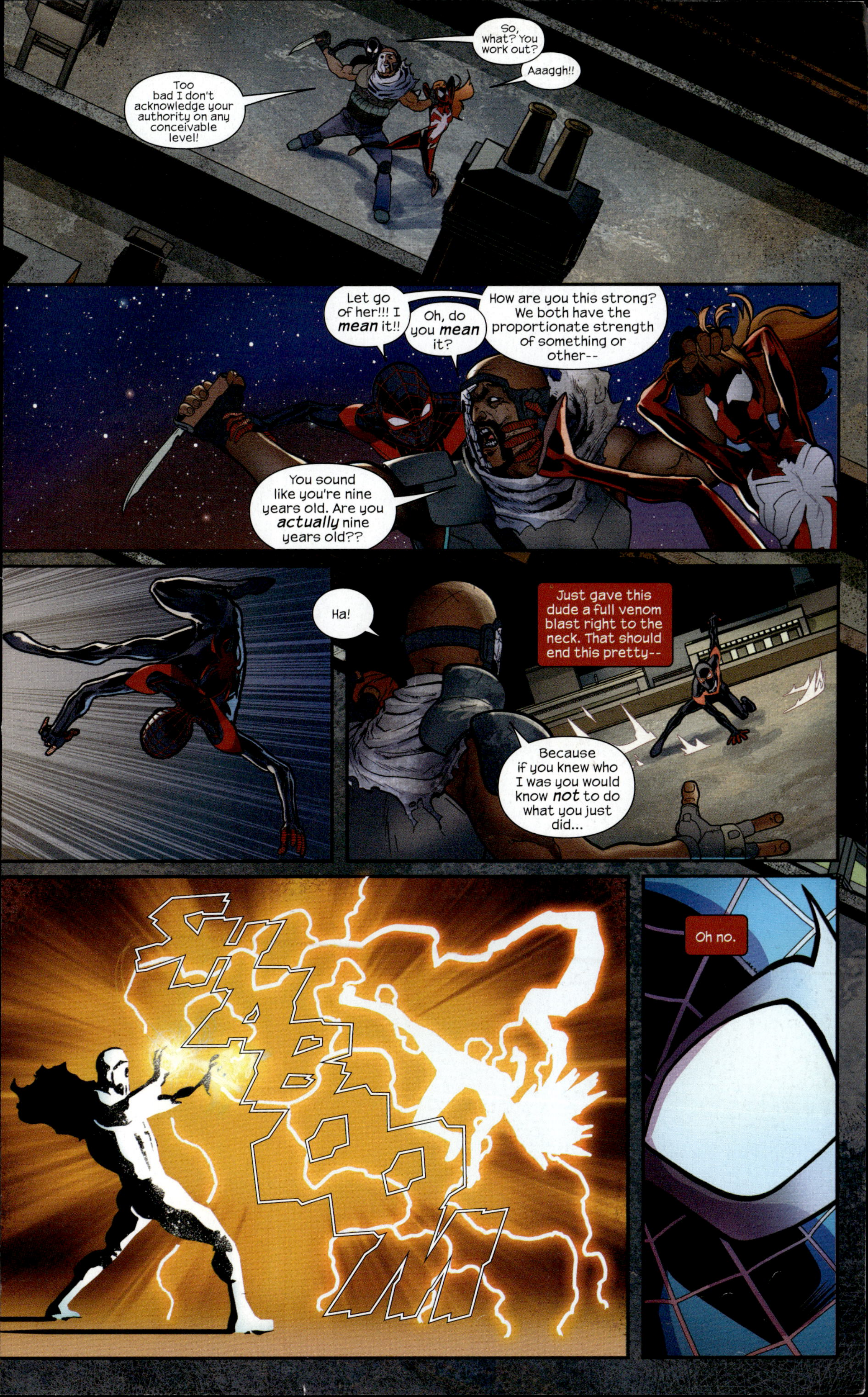
So, what? You work out?
Aaaggh!!
Too bad I don't acknowledge your authority on any conceivable level!
Let go of her!!! I **mean** it!!
Oh, do you **mean** it?
How are you this strong? We both have the proportionate strength of something or other--
You sound like you're nine years old. Are you **actually** nine years old??
Ha!
Just gave this dude a full venom blast right to the neck. That should end this pretty--
Because if you knew who I was you would know **not** to do what you just did...
Oh no.

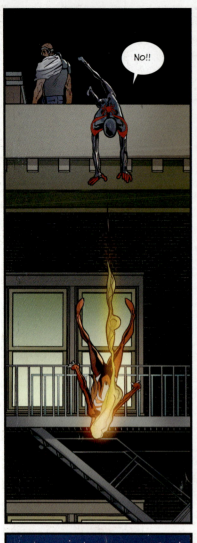

No!!

Please no, God!!

Please don't let her die anything like this.

This is my fault-- I had no idea he could do that.

One of the growing list of reasons why I didn't want to be a super hero in the first place!!

He took my power and slammed you with it.

THWIP

Nice save.

Kid's got real talent.

What a waste.

Come on.

Can you hear me?

Please don't be dead.

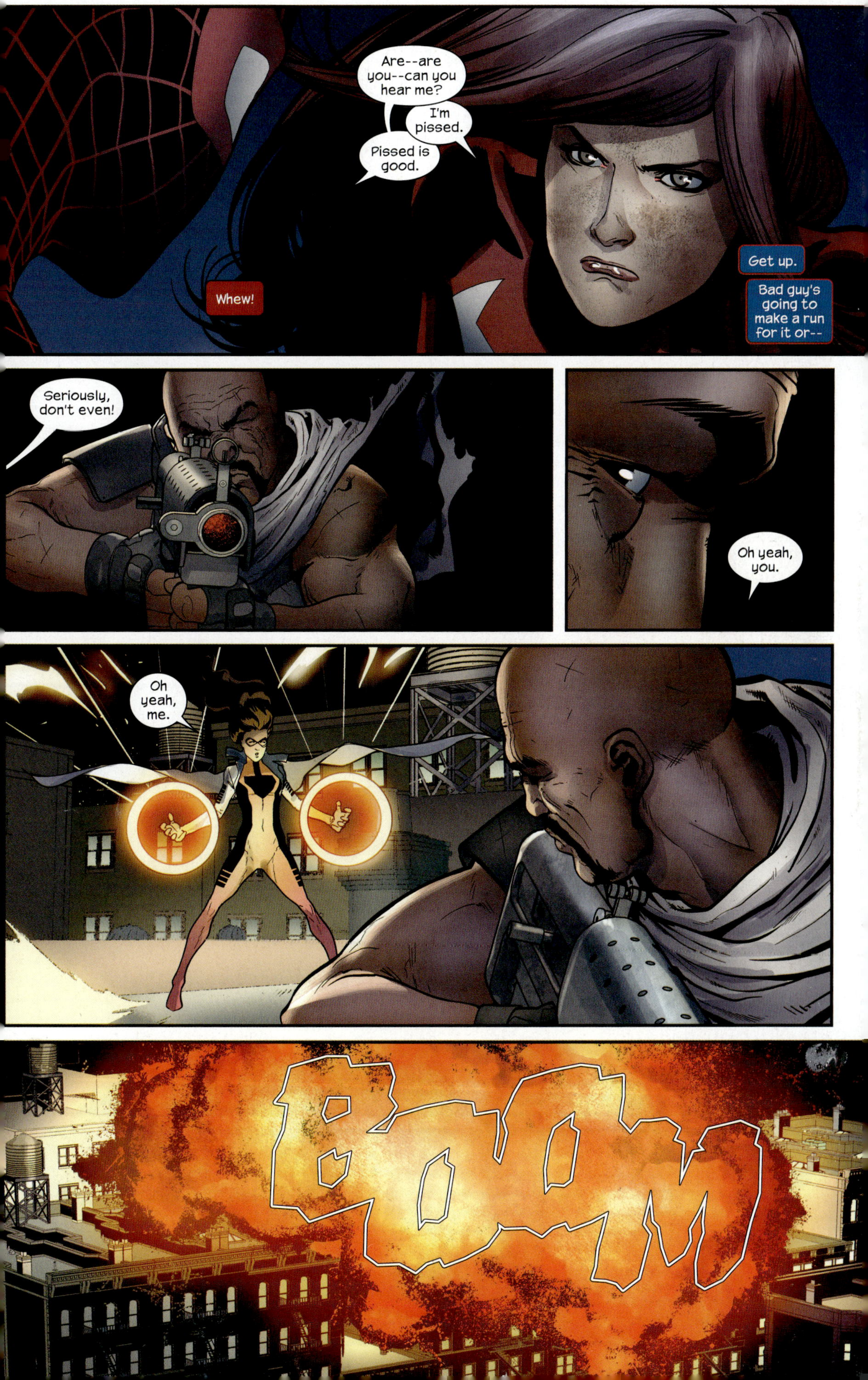
Are--are you--can you hear me?
I'm pissed.
Pissed is good.
Whew!
Get up.
Bad guy's going to make a run for it or--
Seriously, don't even!
Oh yeah, you.
Oh yeah, me.
BOOM

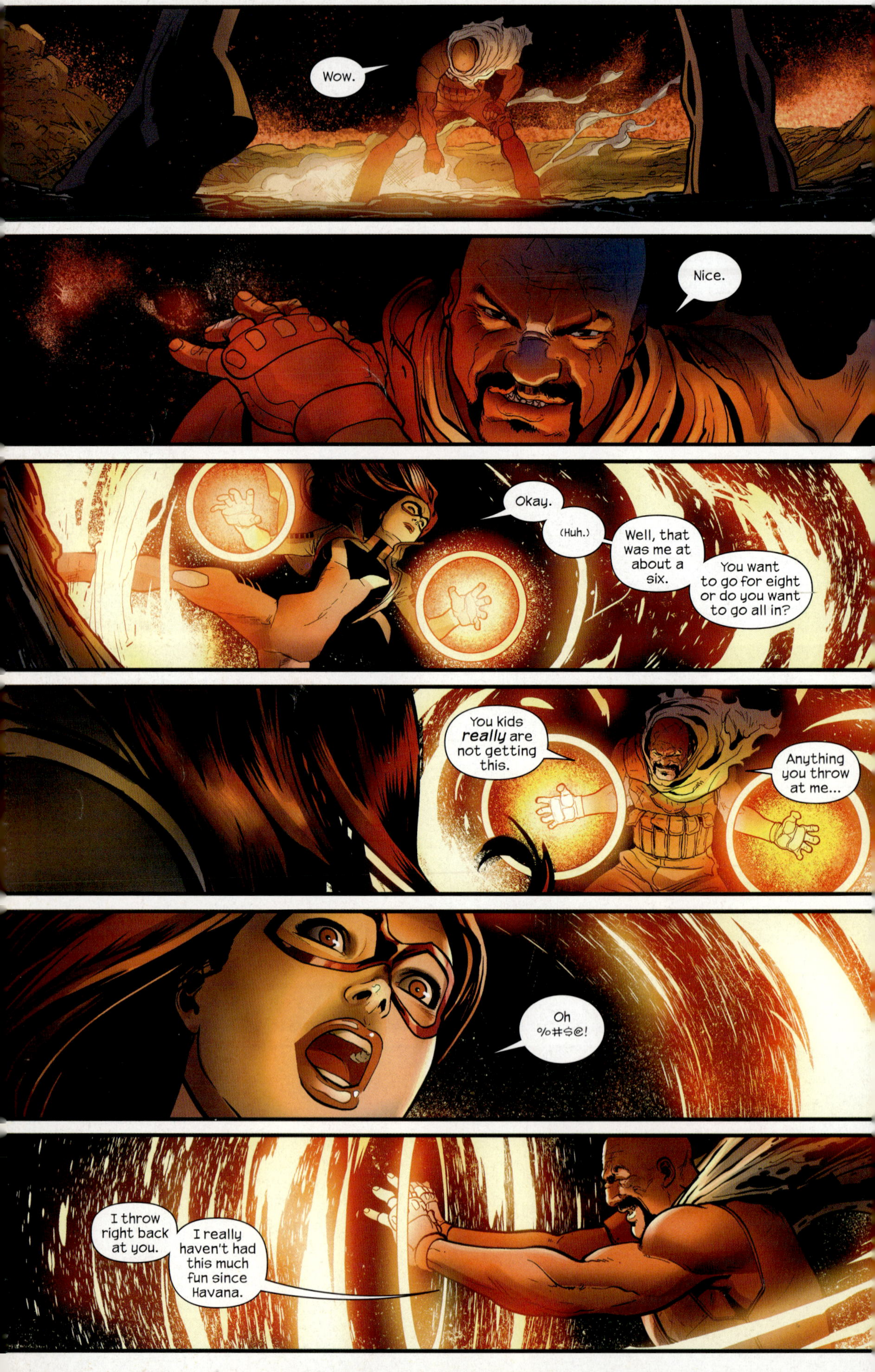
Wow.
Nice.
Okay.
(Huh.)
Well, that was me at about a six.
You want to go for eight or do you want to go all in?
You kids *really* are not getting this.
Anything you throw at me...
Oh %#$@!
I throw right back at you.
I really haven't had this much fun since Havana.

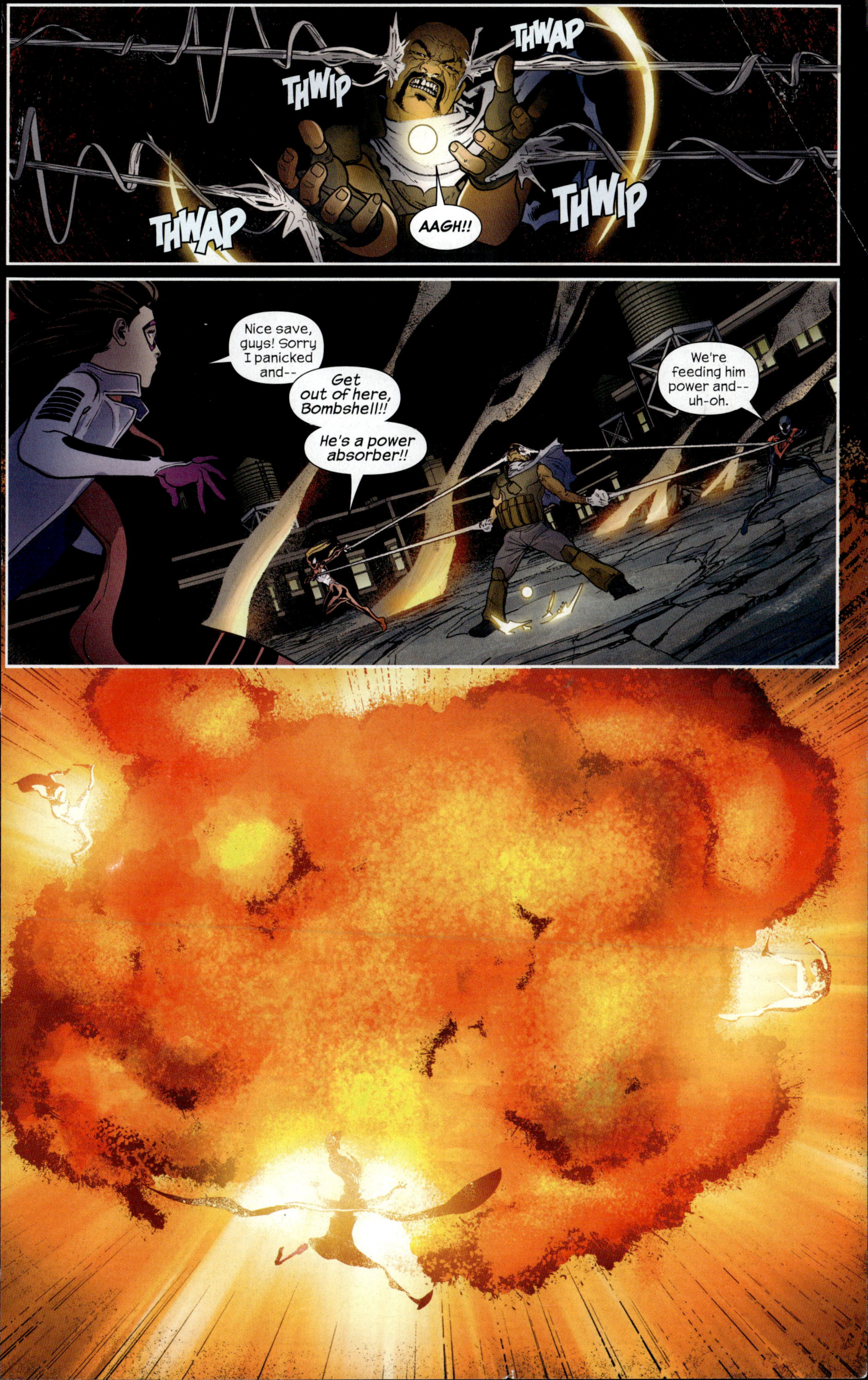
THWAP
THWIP
THWAP
THWIP
AAGH!!
Nice save, guys! Sorry I panicked and--
Get out of here, Bombshell!!
He's a power absorber!!
We're feeding him power and-- uh-oh.

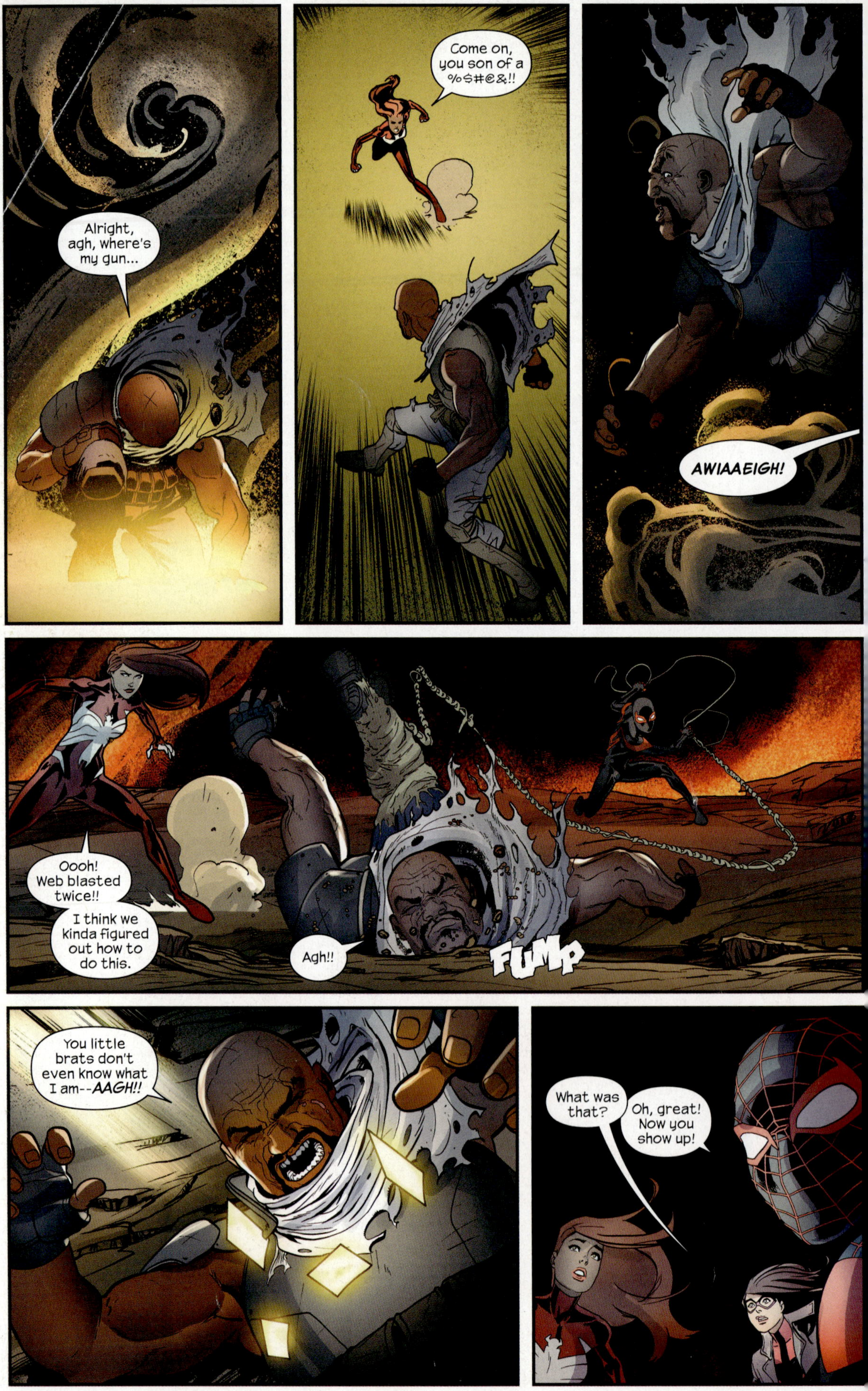

Alright, agh, where's my gun...
Come on, you son of a %$#@&!!
AWIAAEIGH!
Oooh! Web blasted twice!!
I think we kinda figured out how to do this.
Agh!!
FUMP
You little brats don't even know what I am--AAGH!!
What was that?
Oh, great! Now you show up!

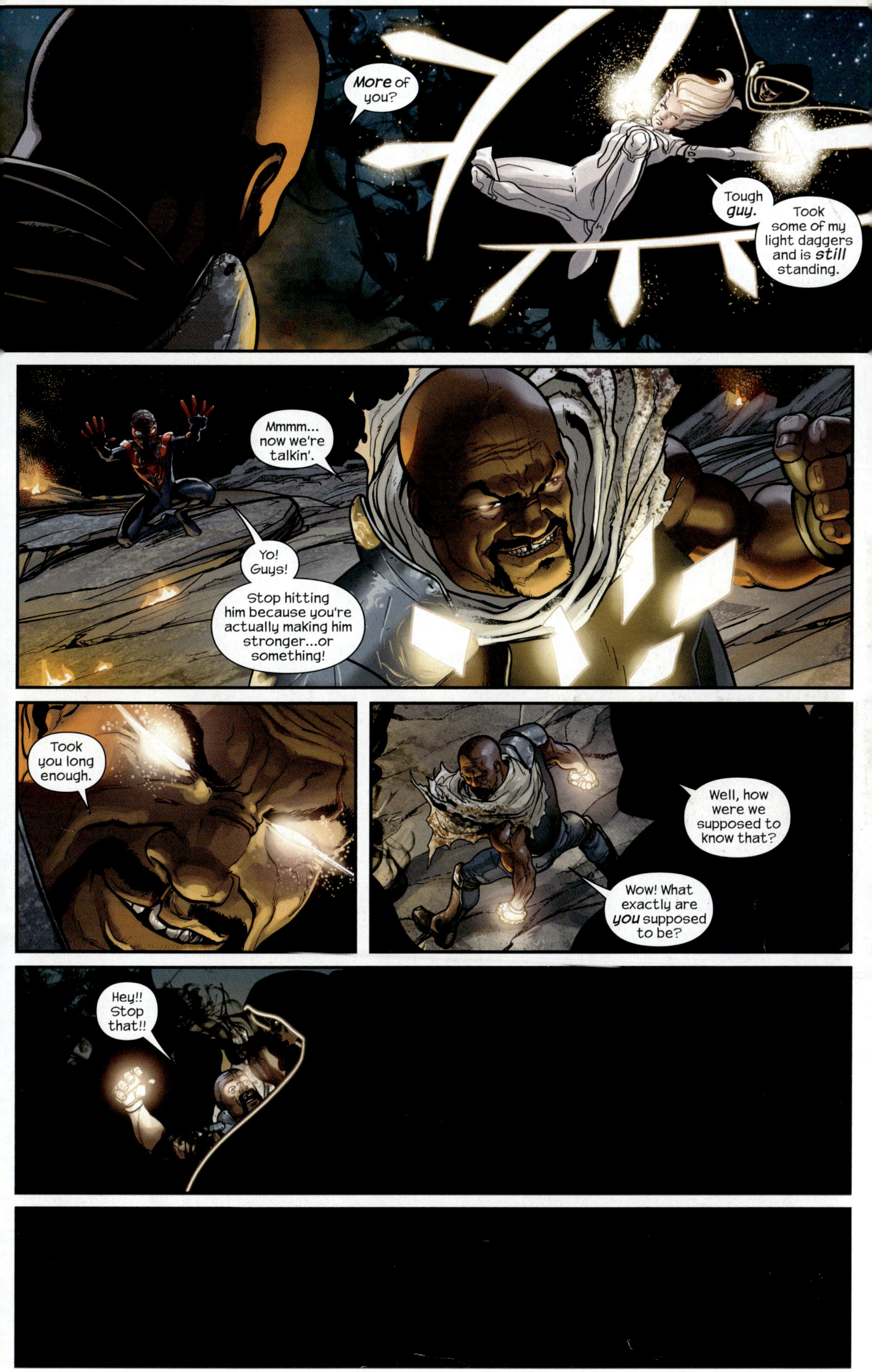
More of you?
Tough guy.
Took some of my light daggers and is still standing.
Mmmm... now we're talkin'.
Yo! Guys!
Stop hitting him because you're actually making him stronger...or something!
Took you long enough.
Well, how were we supposed to know that?
Wow! What exactly are you supposed to be?
Hey!! Stop that!!

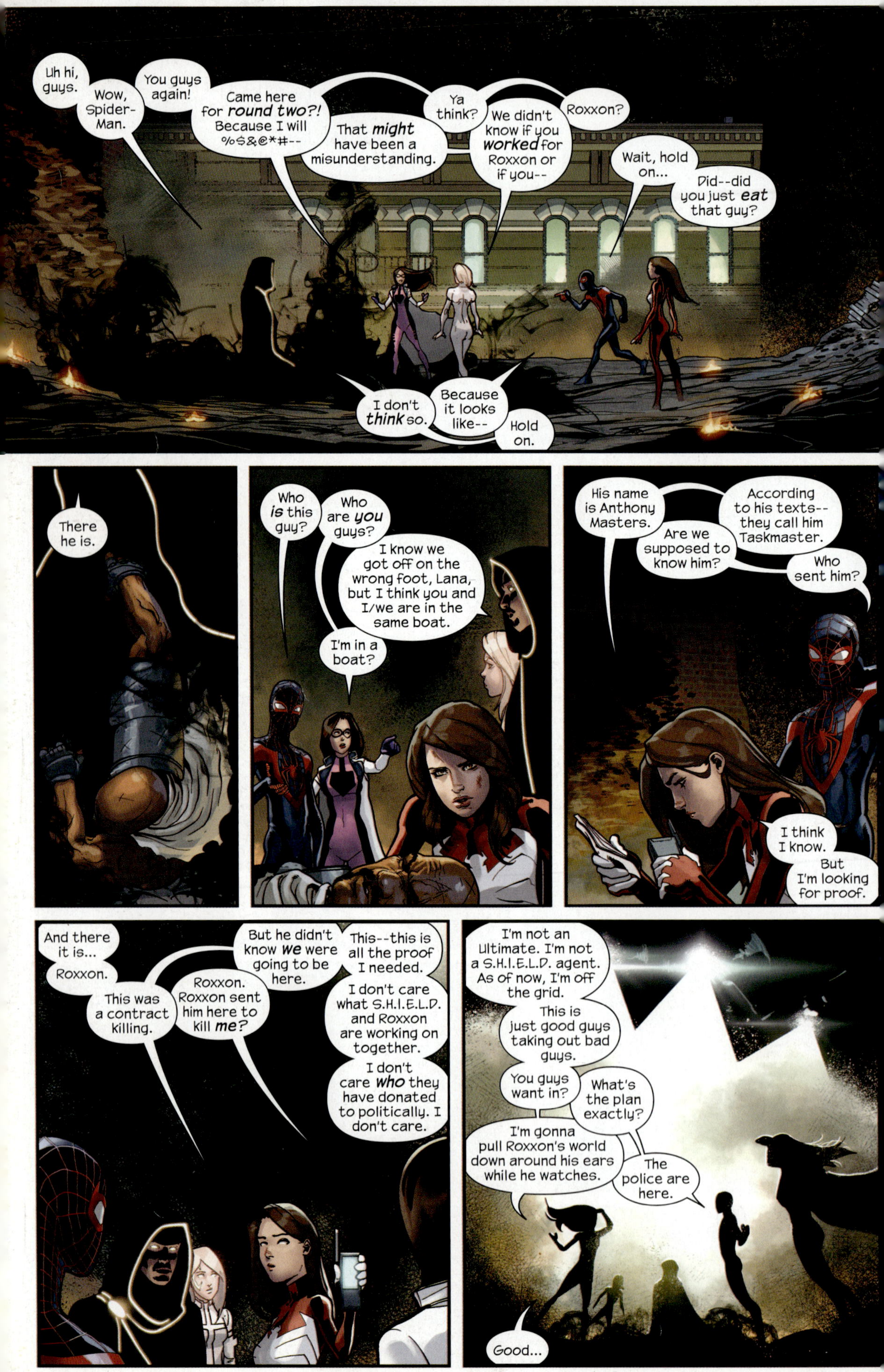

Uh hi, guys.
Wow, Spider-Man.
You guys again!
Came here for *round two?!* Because I will %$&@*#--
That *might* have been a misunderstanding.
Ya think?
We didn't know if you *worked* for Roxxon or if you--
Roxxon?
Wait, hold on...
Did--did you just *eat* that guy?
I don't *think* so.
Because it looks like--
Hold on.
There he is.
Who *is* this guy?
Who are *you* guys?
I know we got off on the wrong foot, Lana, but I think you and I/we are in the same boat.
I'm in a boat?
His name is Anthony Masters.
According to his texts--they call him Taskmaster.
Are we supposed to know him?
Who sent him?
I think I know.
But I'm looking for proof.
And there it is...
Roxxon.
This was a contract killing.
Roxxon. Roxxon sent him here to kill *me?*
But he didn't know *we* were going to be here.
This--this is all the proof I needed.
I don't care what S.H.I.E.L.D. and Roxxon are working on together.
I don't care *who* they have donated to politically. I don't care.
I'm not an Ultimate. I'm not a S.H.I.E.L.D. agent. As of now, I'm off the grid.
This is just good guys taking out bad guys.
You guys want in?
What's the plan exactly?
I'm gonna pull Roxxon's world down around his ears while he watches.
The police are here.
Good...

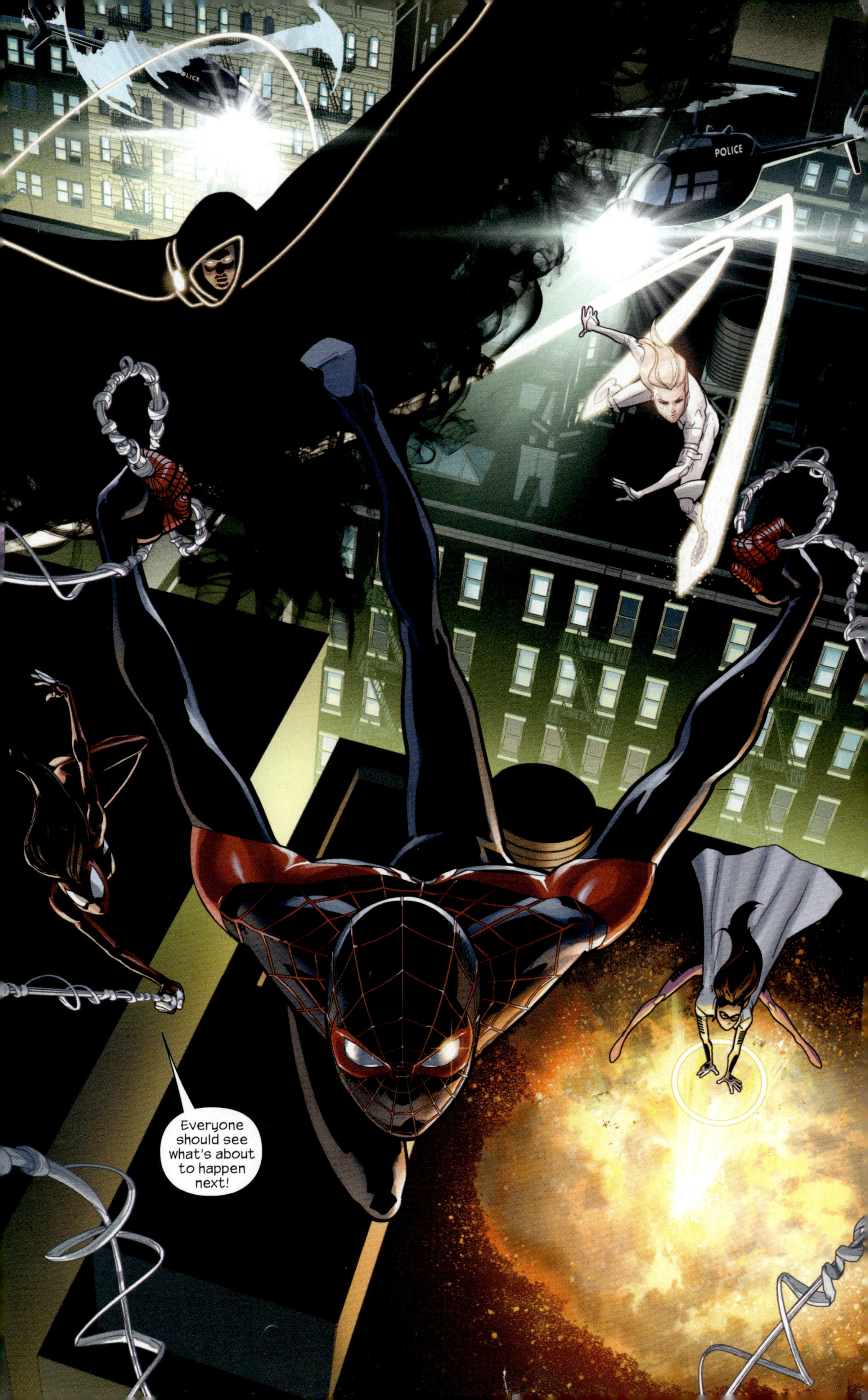
Everyone should see what's about to happen next!

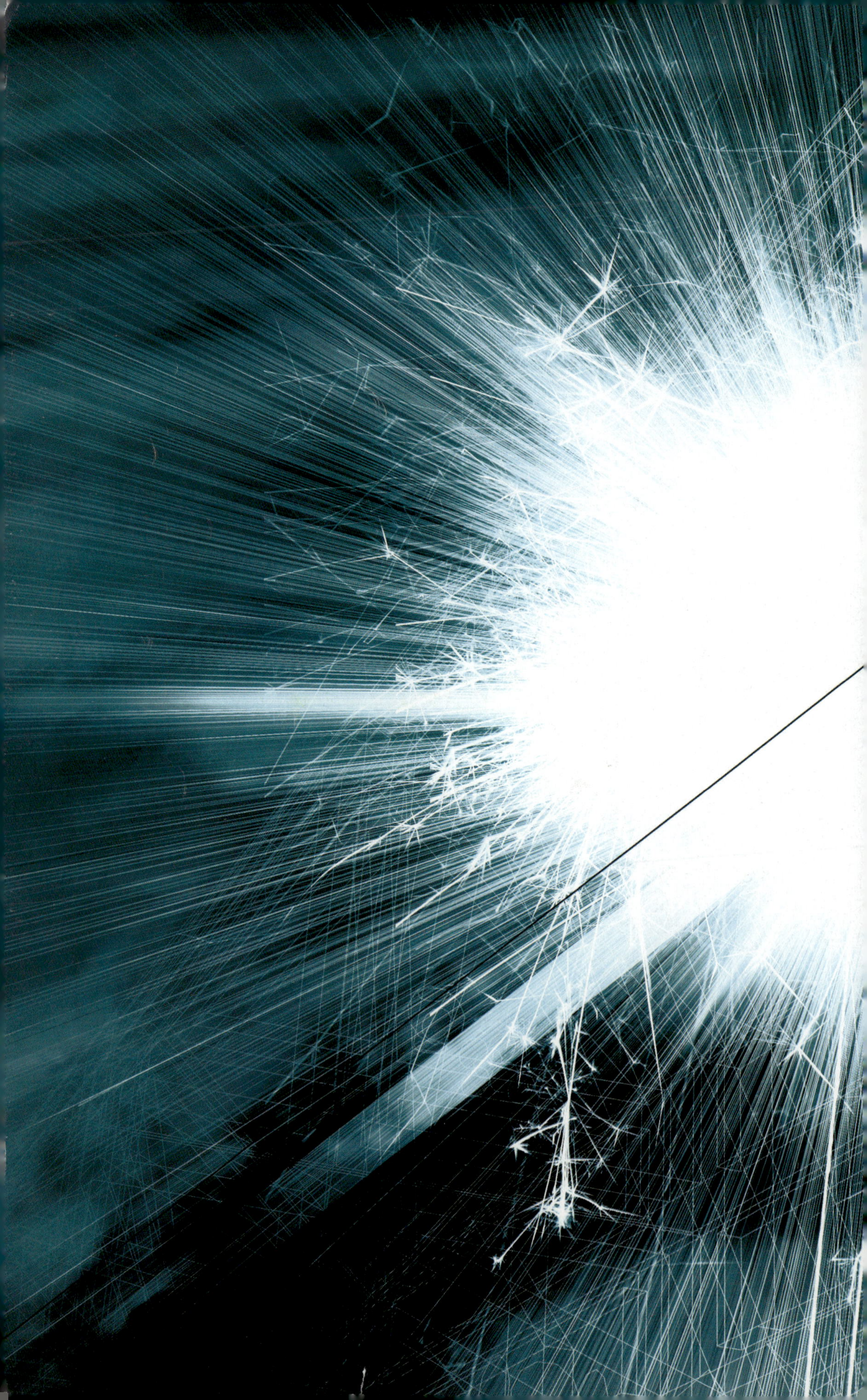

SPIDER-MAN NO MORE

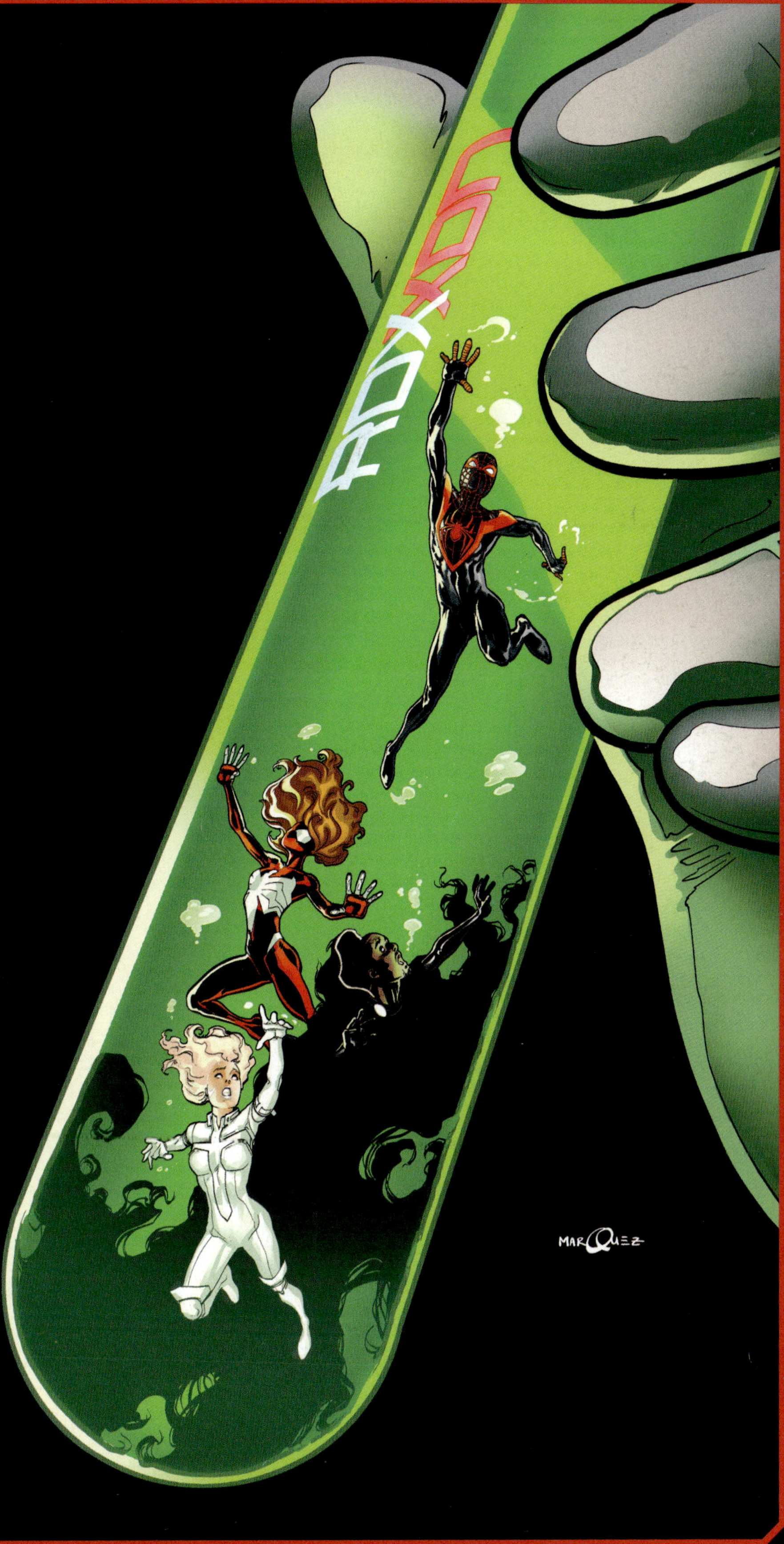
ROXXON

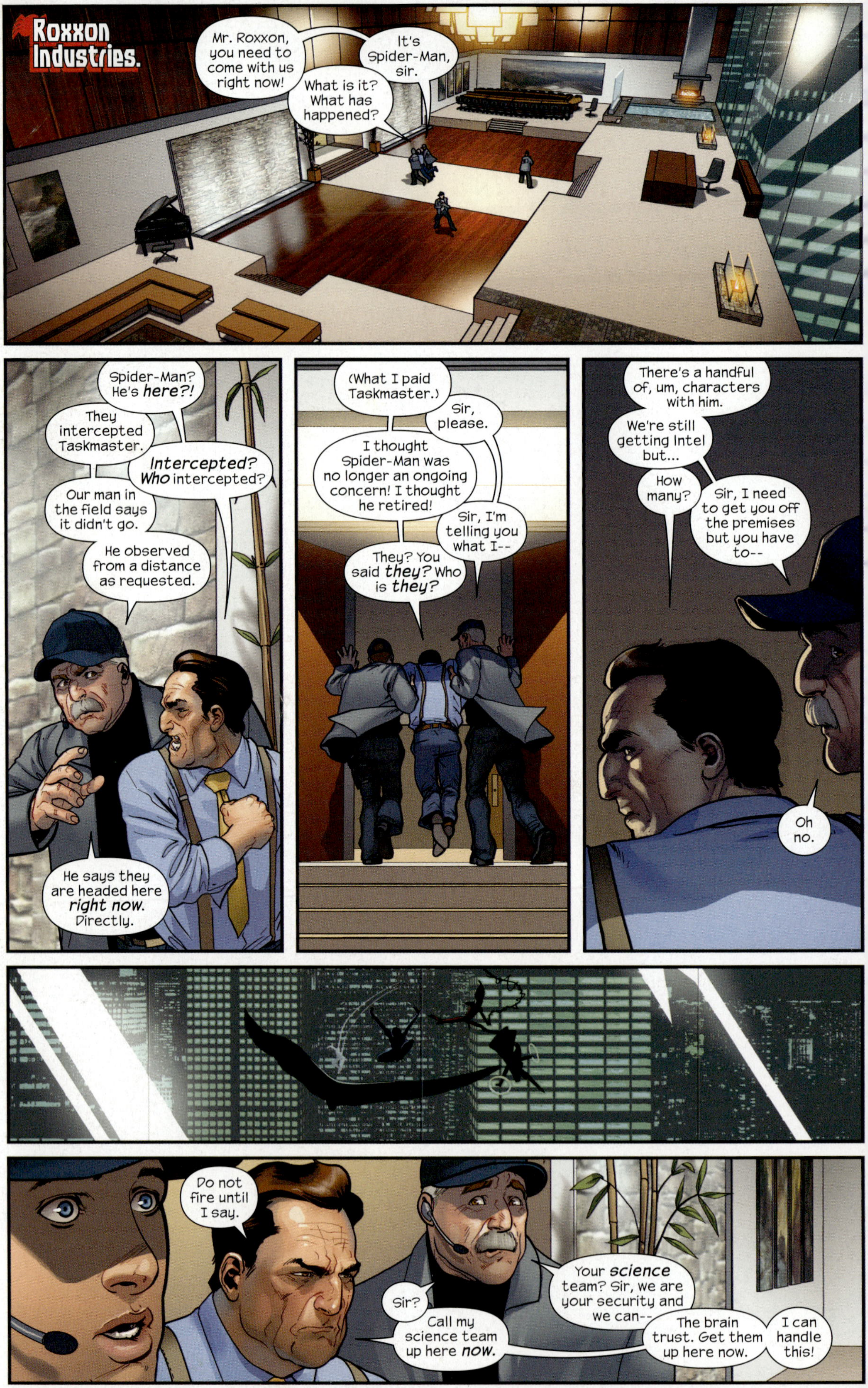
Roxxon Industries.
Mr. Roxxon, you need to come with us right now!
What is it? What has happened?
It's Spider-Man, sir.
Spider-Man? He's here?!
They intercepted Taskmaster.
Intercepted? Who intercepted?
Our man in the field says it didn't go.
He observed from a distance as requested.
He says they are headed here right now. Directly.
(What I paid Taskmaster.)
Sir, please.
I thought Spider-Man was no longer an ongoing concern! I thought he retired!
Sir, I'm telling you what I--
They? You said they? Who is they?
There's a handful of, um, characters with him.
We're still getting Intel but...
How many?
Sir, I need to get you off the premises but you have to--
Oh no.
Do not fire until I say.
Sir?
Call my science team up here now.
Your science team? Sir, we are your security and we can--
The brain trust. Get them up here now.
I can handle this!

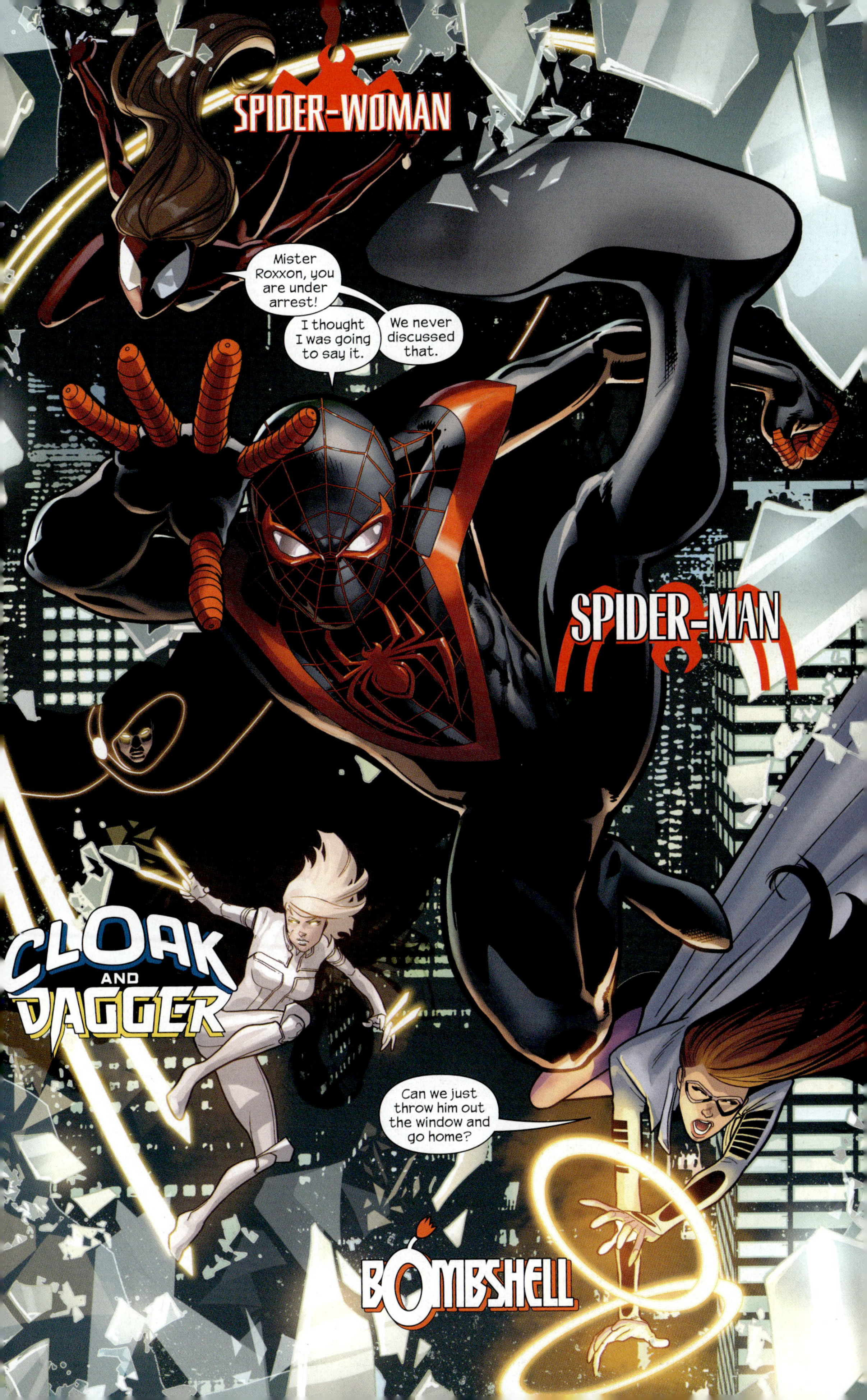
SPIDER-WOMAN
Mister Roxxon, you are under arrest!
I thought I was going to say it.
We never discussed that.
SPIDER-MAN
CLOAK AND DAGGER
Can we just throw him out the window and go home?
BOMBSHELL

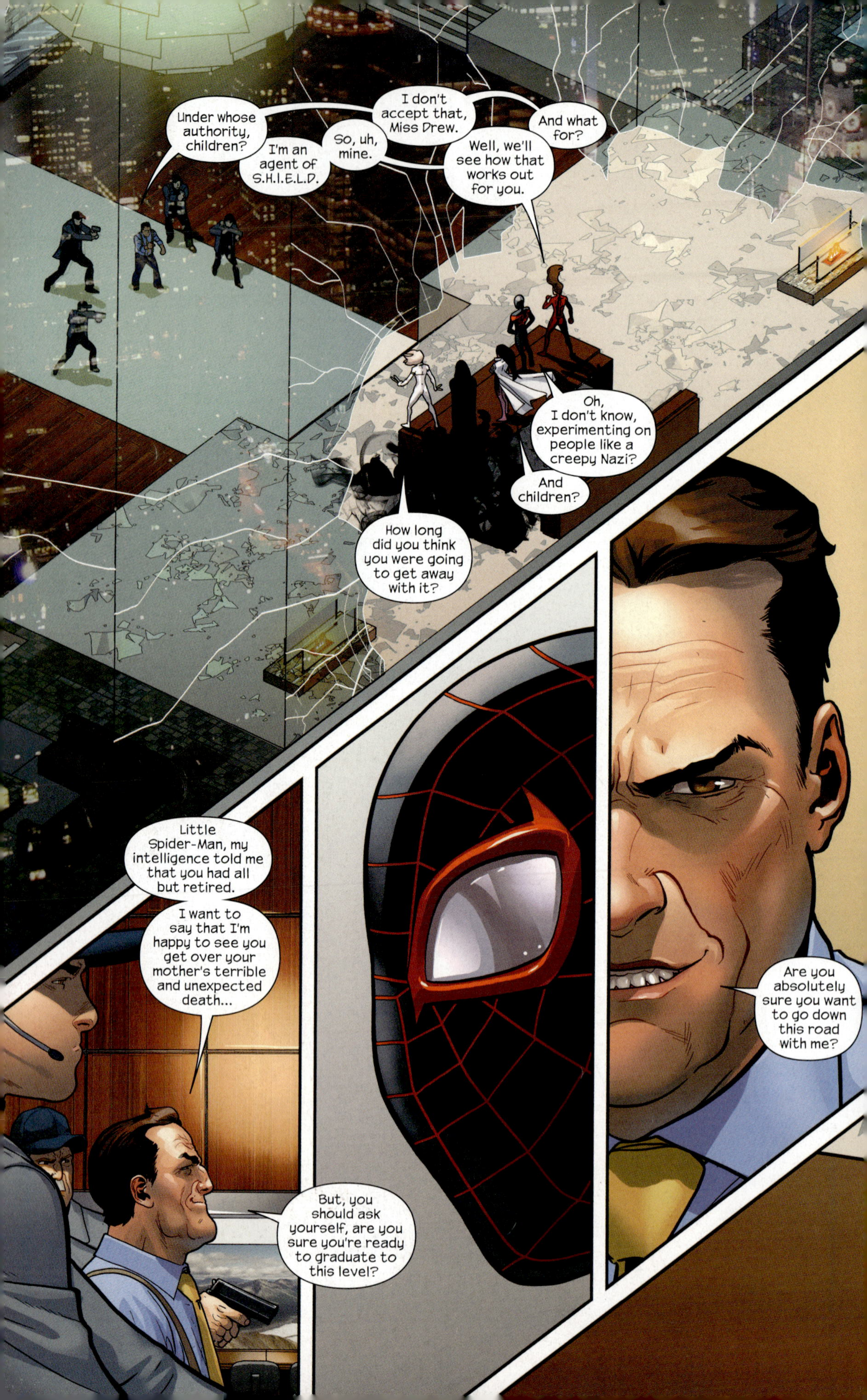
Under whose authority, children?
I'm an agent of S.H.I.E.L.D.
So, uh, mine.
I don't accept that, Miss Drew.
And what for?
Well, we'll see how that works out for you.
Oh, I don't know, experimenting on people like a creepy Nazi?
And children?
How long did you think you were going to get away with it?
Little Spider-Man, my intelligence told me that you had all but retired.
I want to say that I'm happy to see you get over your mother's terrible and unexpected death...
But, you should ask yourself, are you sure you're ready to graduate to this level?
Are you absolutely sure you want to go down this road with me?

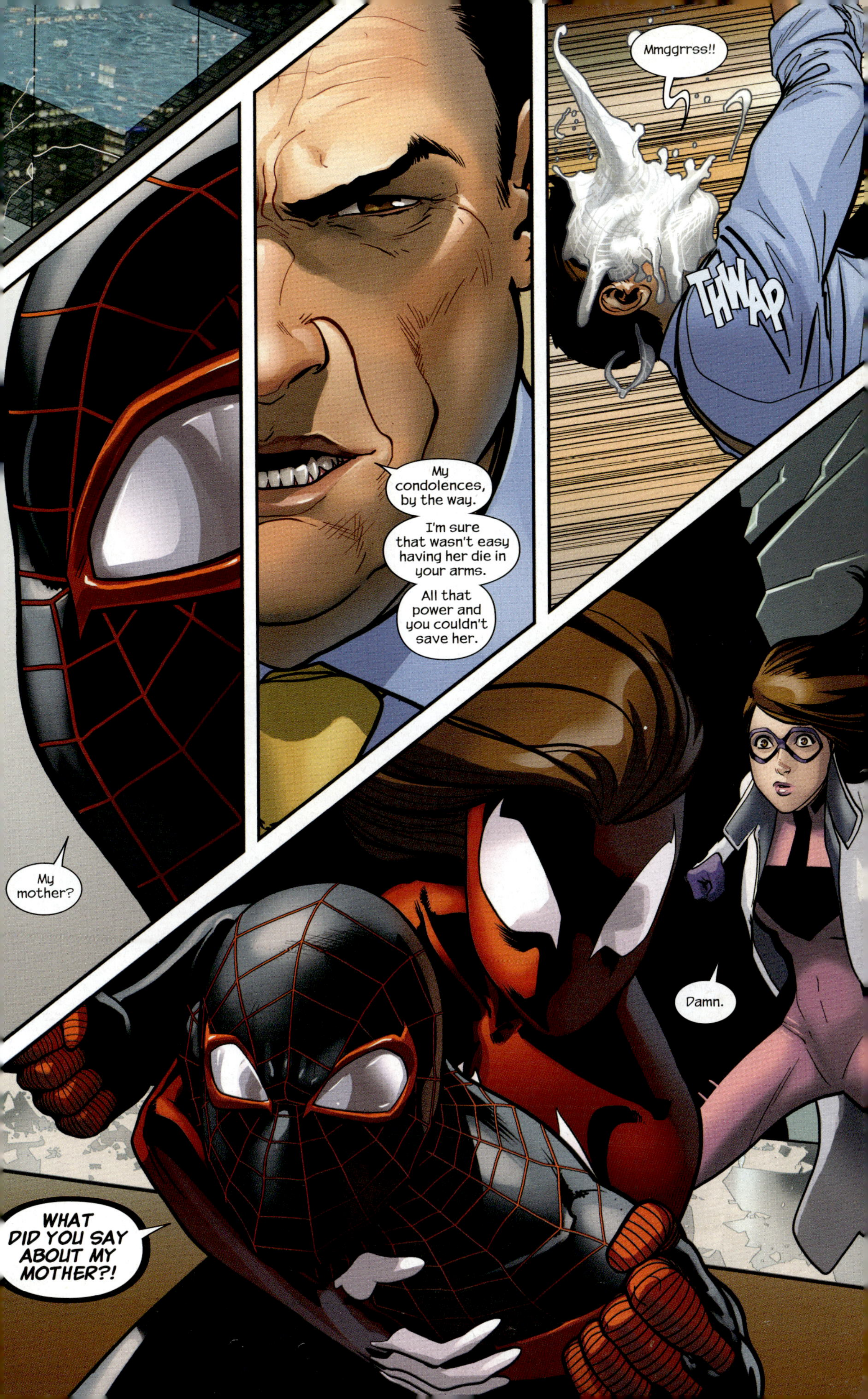
Mmggrrss!!
THWAP
My condolences, by the way.
I'm sure that wasn't easy having her die in your arms.
All that power and you couldn't save her.
My mother?
Damn.
WHAT DID YOU SAY ABOUT MY MOTHER?!

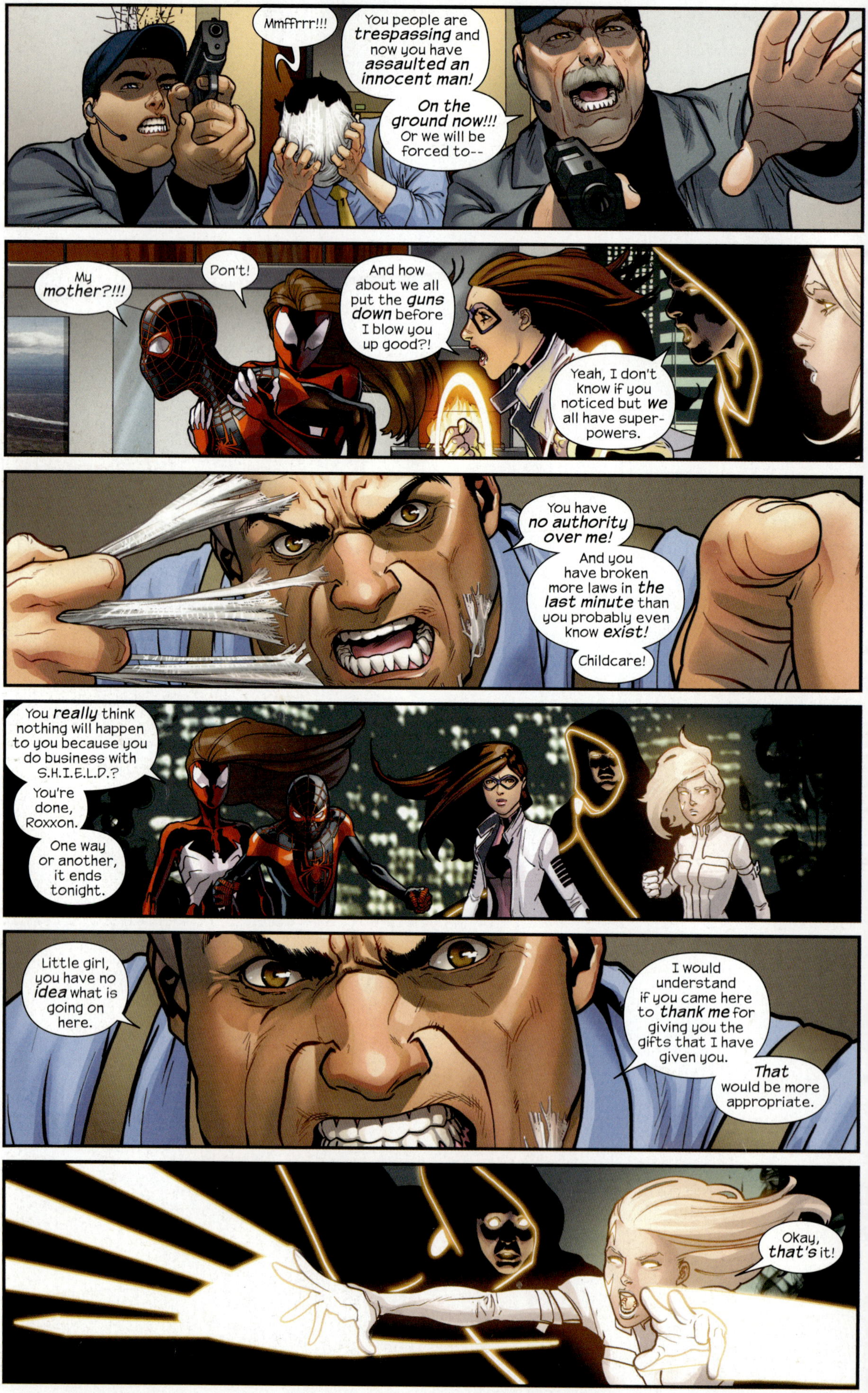
Mmffrrr!!!
You people are trespassing and now you have assaulted an innocent man!
On the ground now!!! Or we will be forced to--
My mother?!!!
Don't!
And how about we all put the guns down before I blow you up good?!
Yeah, I don't know if you noticed but we all have super-powers.
You have no authority over me!
And you have broken more laws in the last minute than you probably even know exist!
Childcare!
You really think nothing will happen to you because you do business with S.H.I.E.L.D.?
You're done, Roxxon.
One way or another, it ends tonight.
Little girl, you have no idea what is going on here.
I would understand if you came here to thank me for giving you the gifts that I have given you.
That would be more appropriate.
Okay, that's it!

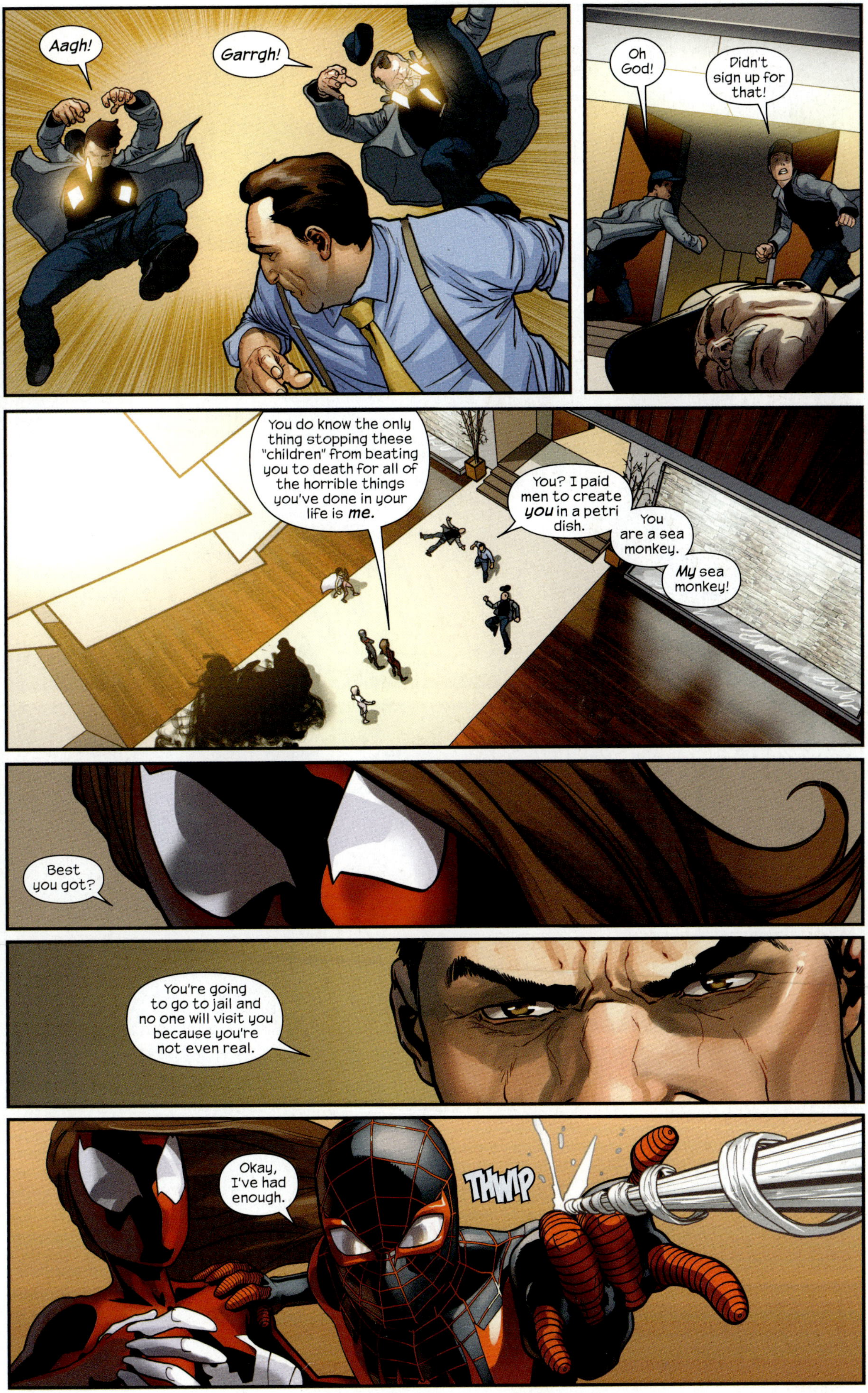
Aagh!
Garrgh!
Oh God!
Didn't sign up for that!
You do know the only thing stopping these "children" from beating you to death for all of the horrible things you've done in your life is *me.*
You? I paid men to create *you* in a petri dish.
You are a sea monkey.
My sea monkey!
Best you got?
You're going to go to jail and no one will visit you because you're not even real.
Okay, I've had enough.
THWIP

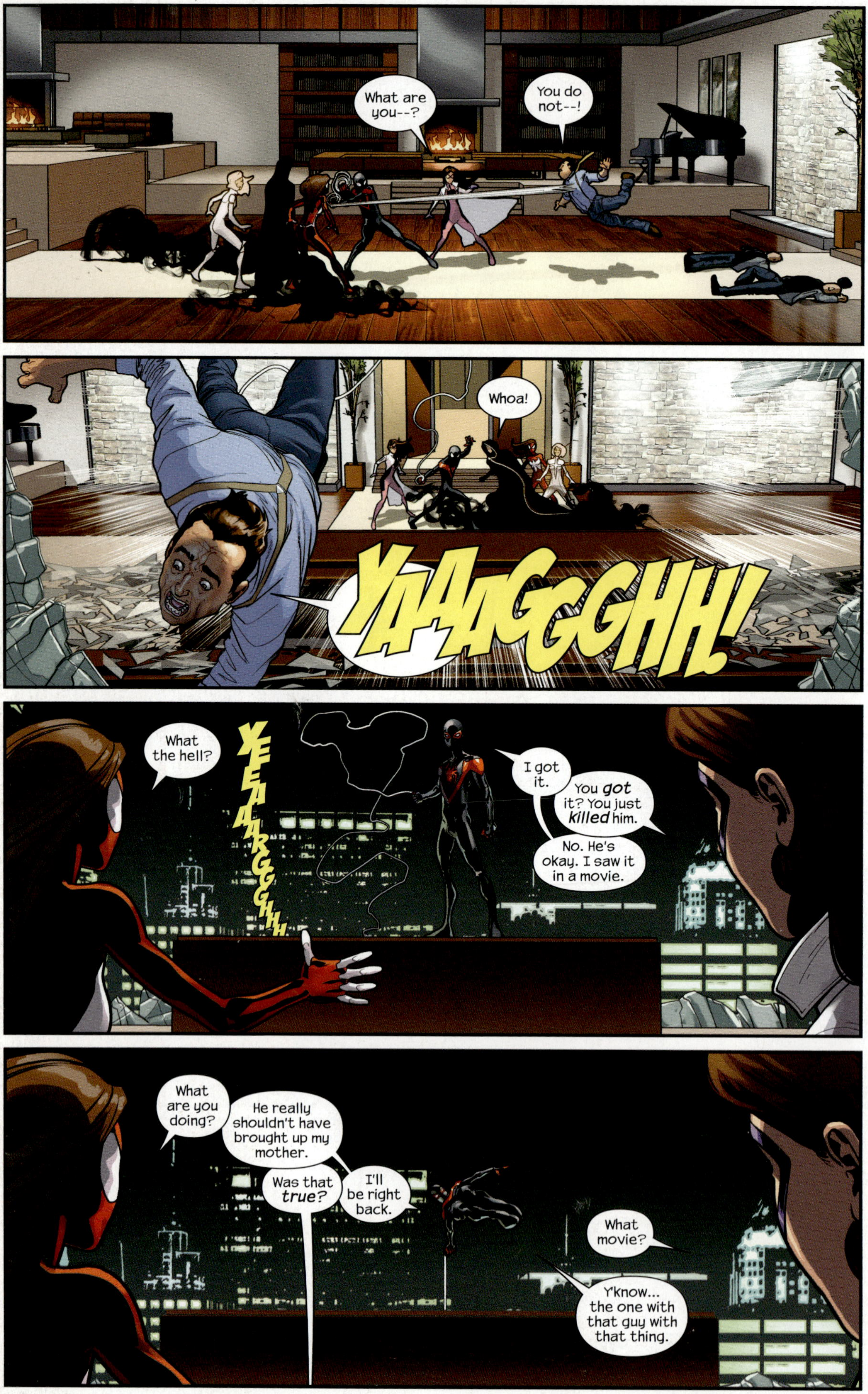
What are you--?
You do not--!
Whoa!
YAAAGGGHH!
What the hell?
YEEAAARGGGHHH
I got it.
You got it? You just killed him.
No. He's okay. I saw it in a movie.
What are you doing?
He really shouldn't have brought up my mother.
Was that true?
I'll be right back.
What movie?
Y'know... the one with that guy with that thing.

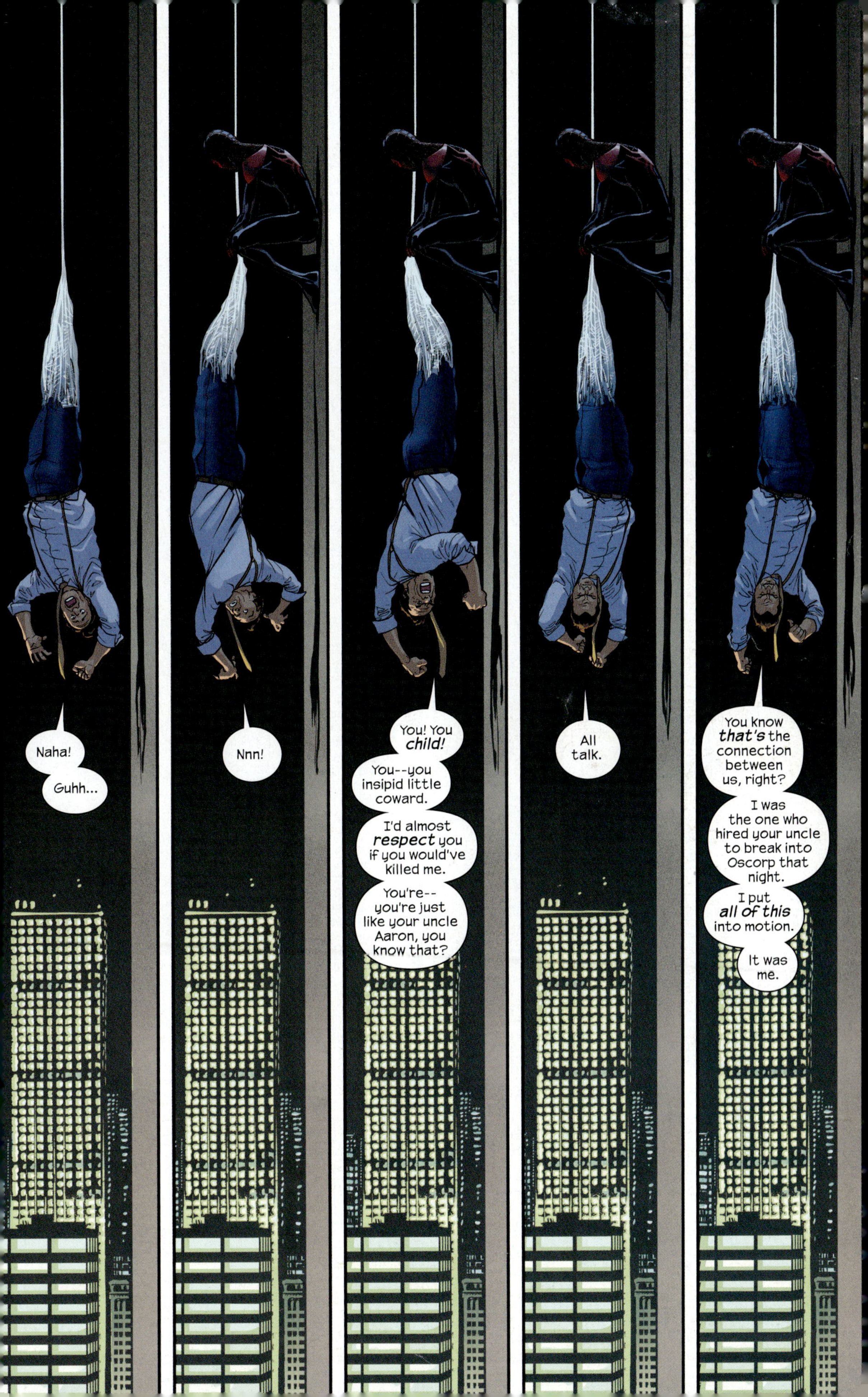
Naha!
Guhh...
Nnn!
You! You *child!*
You--you insipid little coward.
I'd almost *respect* you if you would've killed me.
You're-- you're just like your uncle Aaron, you know that?
All talk.
You know *that's* the connection between us, right?
I was the one who hired your uncle to break into Oscorp that night.
I put *all of this* into motion.
It was me.

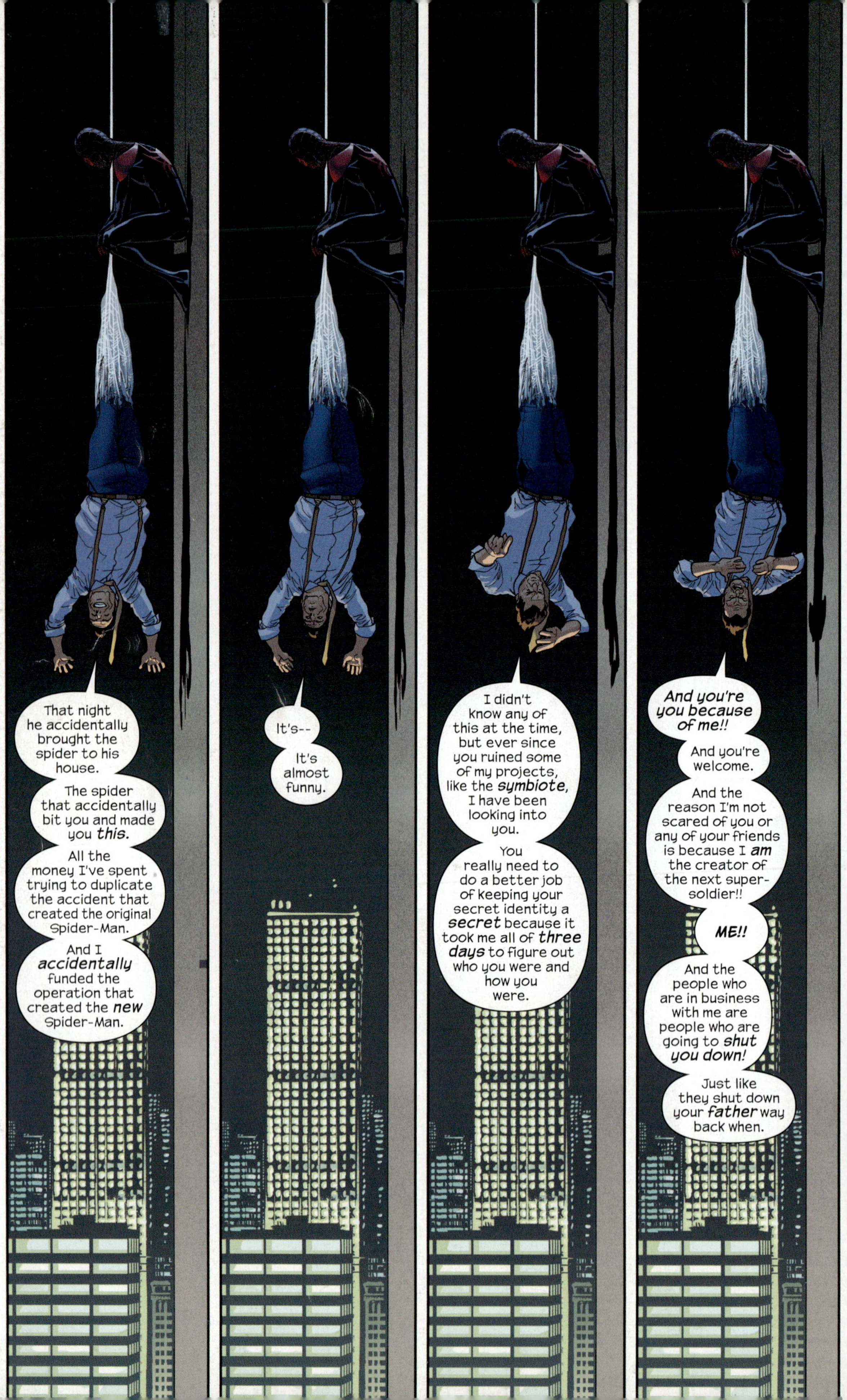
That night he accidentally brought the spider to his house.
The spider that accidentally bit you and made you *this.*
All the money I've spent trying to duplicate the accident that created the original Spider-Man.
And I *accidentally* funded the operation that created the *new* Spider-Man.
It's--
It's almost funny.
I didn't know any of this at the time, but ever since you ruined some of my projects, like the *symbiote*, I have been looking into you.
You really need to do a better job of keeping your secret identity a *secret* because it took me all of *three days* to figure out who you were and how you were.
And you're you because of me!!
And you're welcome.
And the reason I'm not scared of you or any of your friends is because I *am* the creator of the next super-soldier!!
ME!!
And the people who are in business with me are people who are going to *shut you down!*
Just like they shut down your *father* way back when.

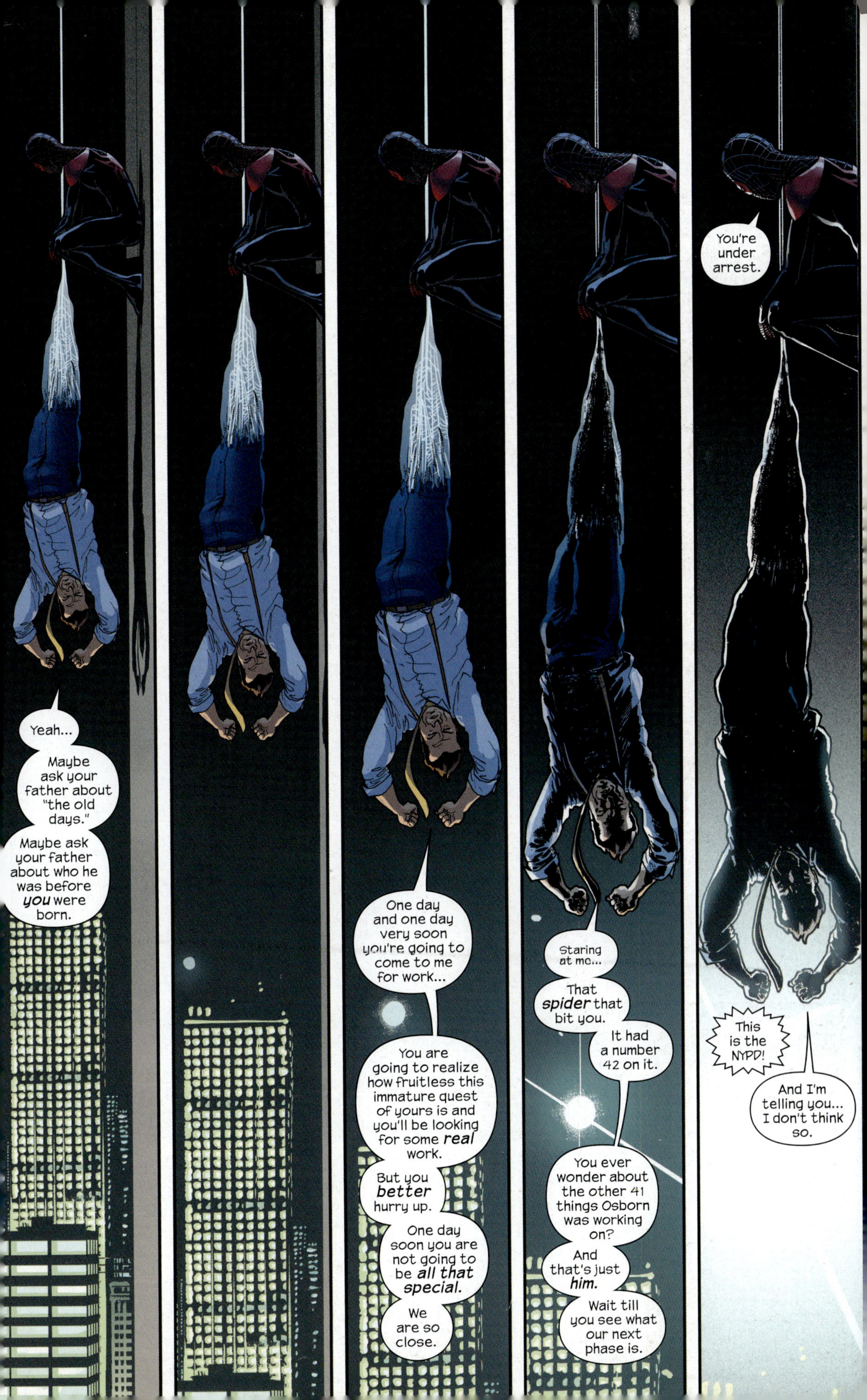
Yeah...
Maybe ask your father about "the old days."
Maybe ask your father about who he was before you were born.
One day and one day very soon you're going to come to me for work...
You are going to realize how fruitless this immature quest of yours is and you'll be looking for some real work.
But you better hurry up.
One day soon you are not going to be all that special.
We are so close.
Staring at me...
That spider that bit you.
It had a number 42 on it.
You ever wonder about the other 41 things Osborn was working on?
And that's just him.
Wait till you see what our next phase is.
You're under arrest.
This is the NYPD!
And I'm telling you... I don't think so.

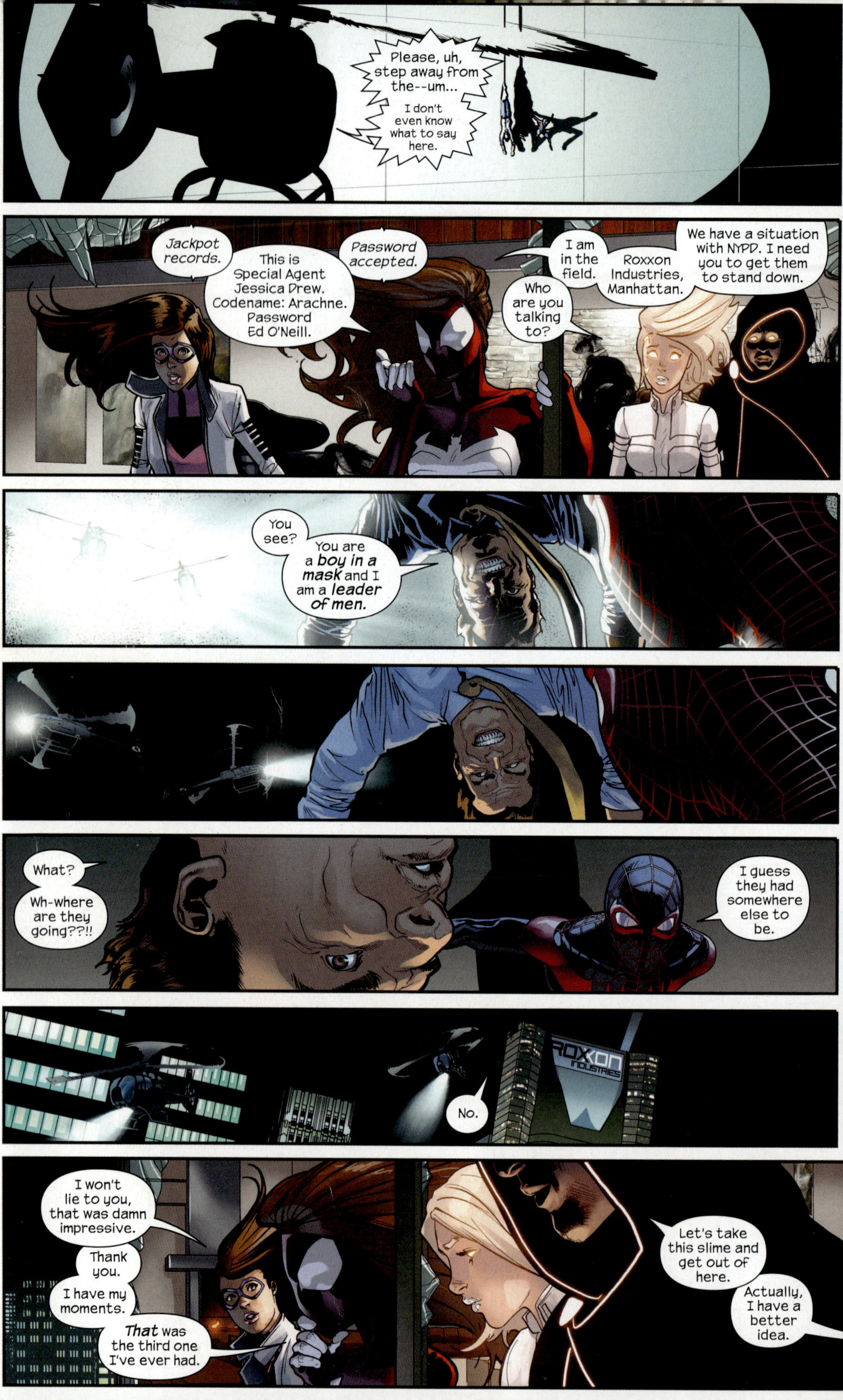
Please, uh, step away from the--um...
I don't even know what to say here.
Jackpot records.
This is Special Agent Jessica Drew. Codename: Arachne. Password Ed O'Neill.
Password accepted.
I am in the field.
Roxxon Industries, Manhattan.
We have a situation with NYPD. I need you to get them to stand down.
Who are you talking to?
You see?
You are a *boy in a mask* and I am a *leader of men.*
What?
Wh-where are they going??!!
I guess they had somewhere else to be.
ROXXON INDUSTRIES
No.
I won't lie to you, that was damn impressive.
Thank you.
I have my moments.
That was the third one I've ever had.
Let's take this slime and get out of here.
Actually, I have a better idea.

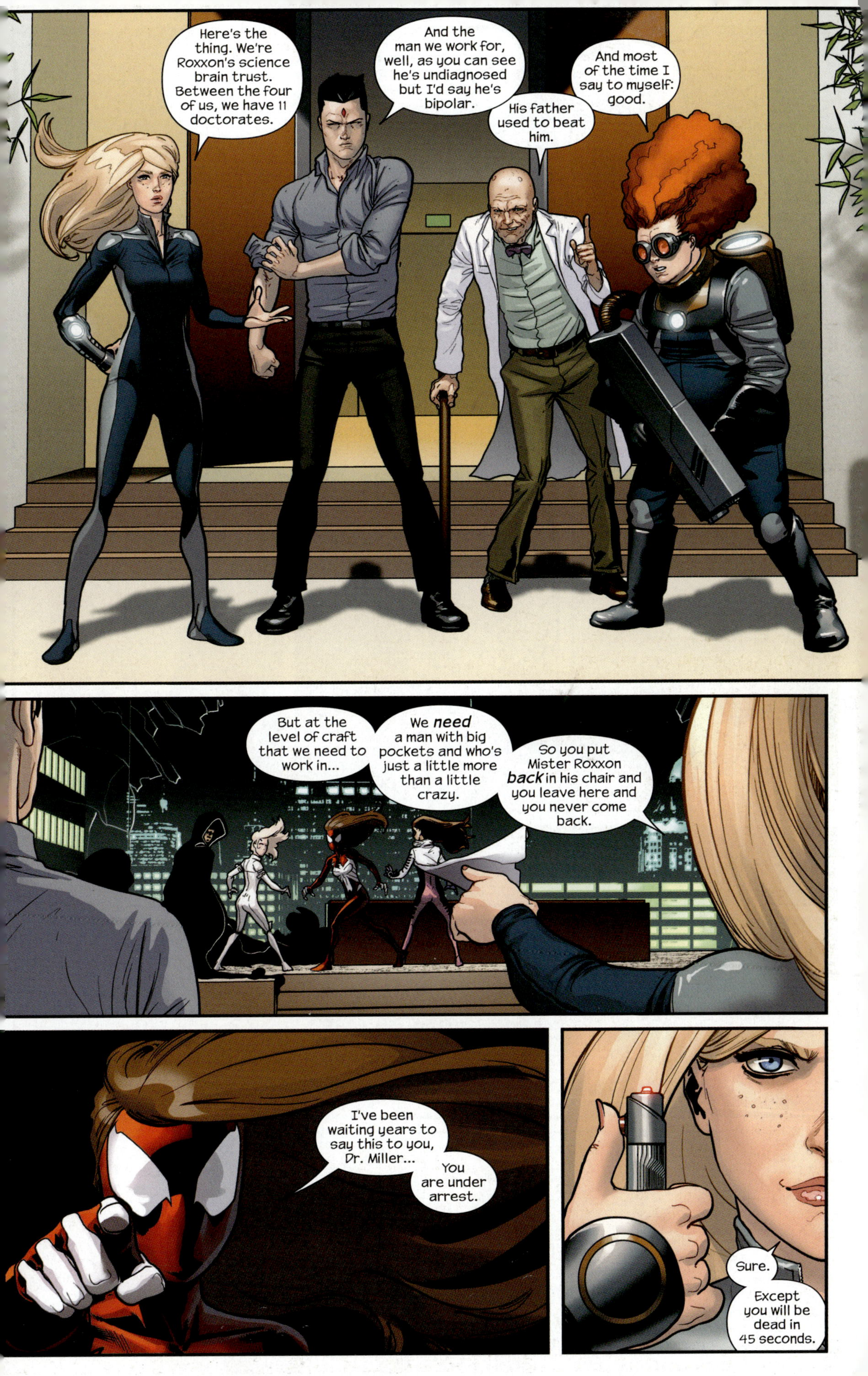
Here's the thing. We're Roxxon's science brain trust. Between the four of us, we have 11 doctorates.
And the man we work for, well, as you can see he's undiagnosed but I'd say he's bipolar.
His father used to beat him.
And most of the time I say to myself: good.
But at the level of craft that we need to work in...
We **need** a man with big pockets and who's just a little more than a little crazy.
So you put Mister Roxxon **back** in his chair and you leave here and you never come back.
I've been waiting years to say this to you, Dr. Miller...
You are under arrest.
Sure.
Except you will be dead in 45 seconds.

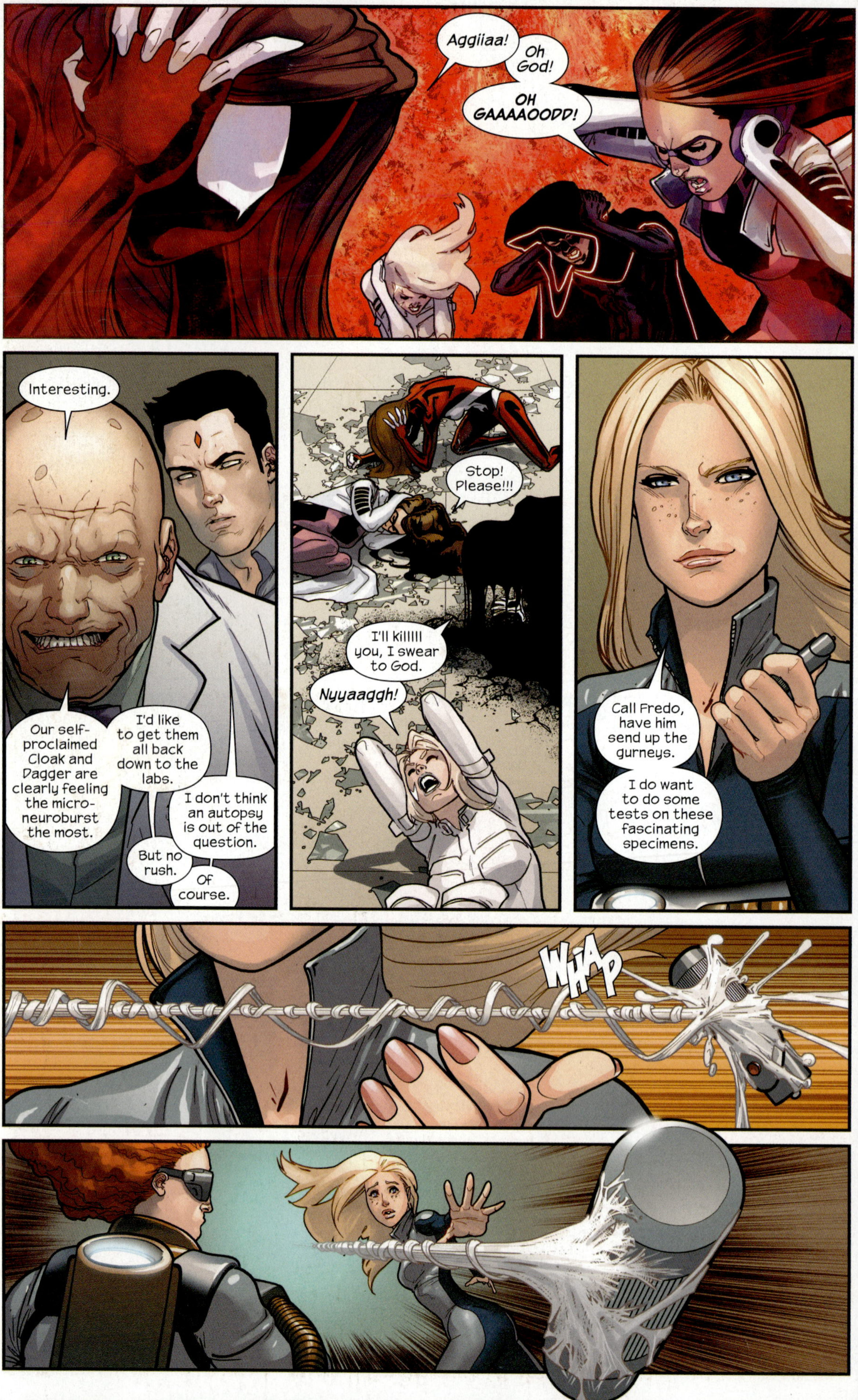
Aggiiaa!
Oh God!
OH GAAAAOODD!
Interesting.
Our self-proclaimed Cloak and Dagger are clearly feeling the micro-neuroburst the most.
I'd like to get them all back down to the labs.
But no rush.
I don't think an autopsy is out of the question.
Of course.
Stop! Please!!!
I'll killlll you, I swear to God.
Nyyaaggh!
Call Fredo, have him send up the gurneys.
I do want to do some tests on these fascinating specimens.
WHAP

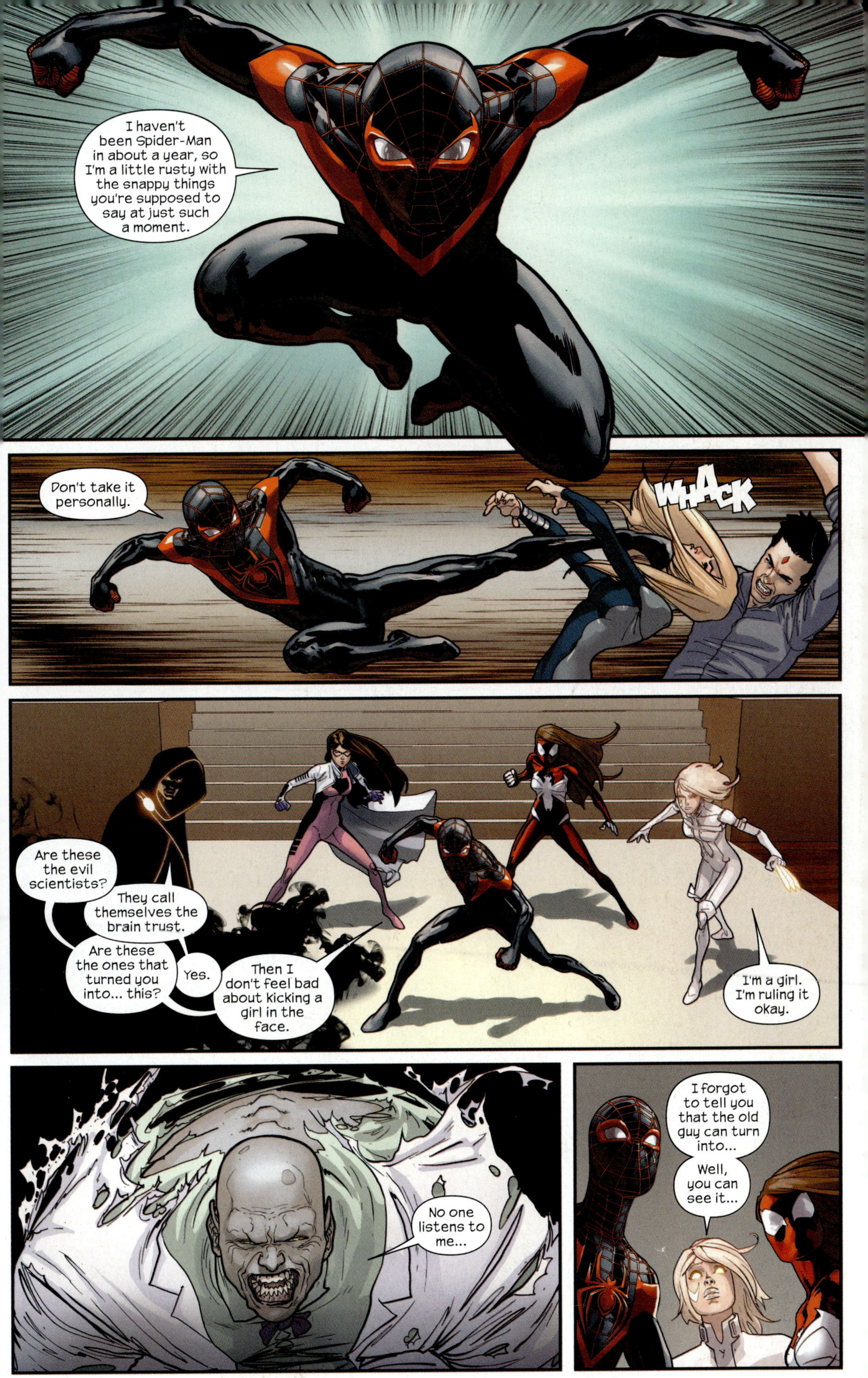
I haven't been Spider-Man in about a year, so I'm a little rusty with the snappy things you're supposed to say at just such a moment.
Don't take it personally.
WHACK
Are these the evil scientists?
They call themselves the brain trust.
Are these the ones that turned you into... this?
Yes.
Then I don't feel bad about kicking a girl in the face.
I'm a girl. I'm ruling it okay.
No one listens to me...
I forgot to tell you that the old guy can turn into...
Well, you can see it...

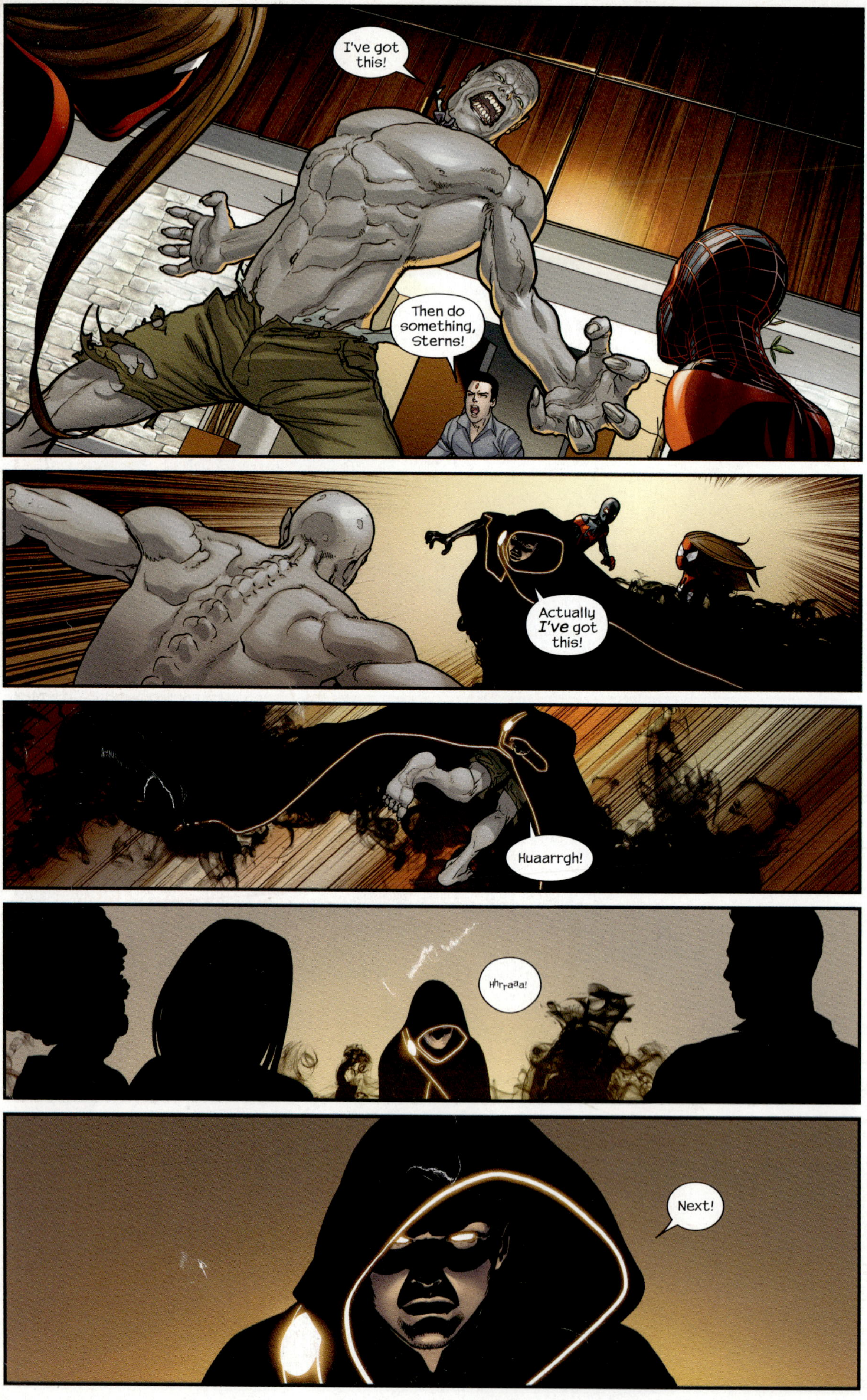
I've got this!
Then do something, Sterns!
Actually *I've* got this!
Huaarrgh!
Hhrraaa!
Next!

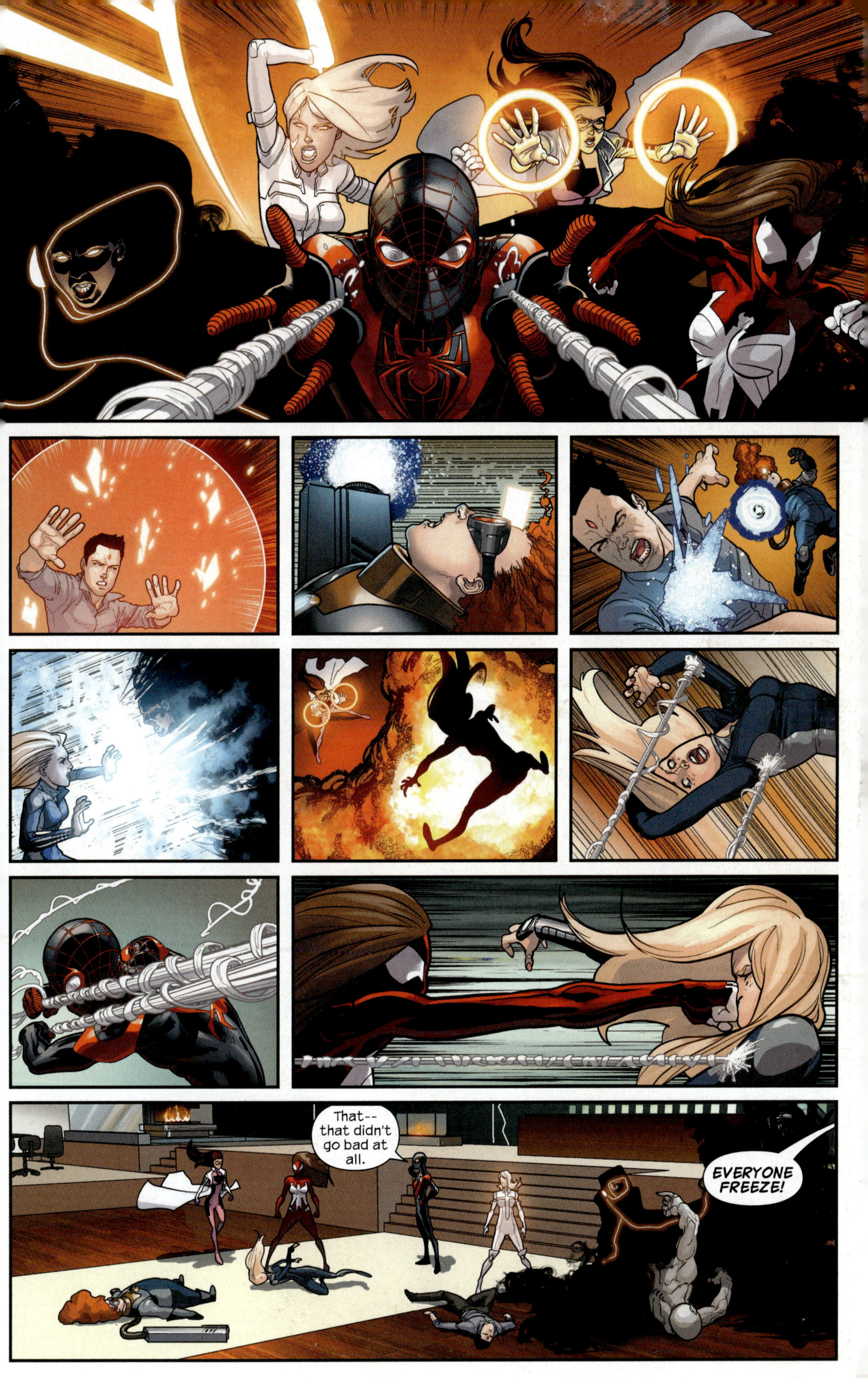
That--
that didn't
go bad at
all.
EVERYONE
FREEZE!

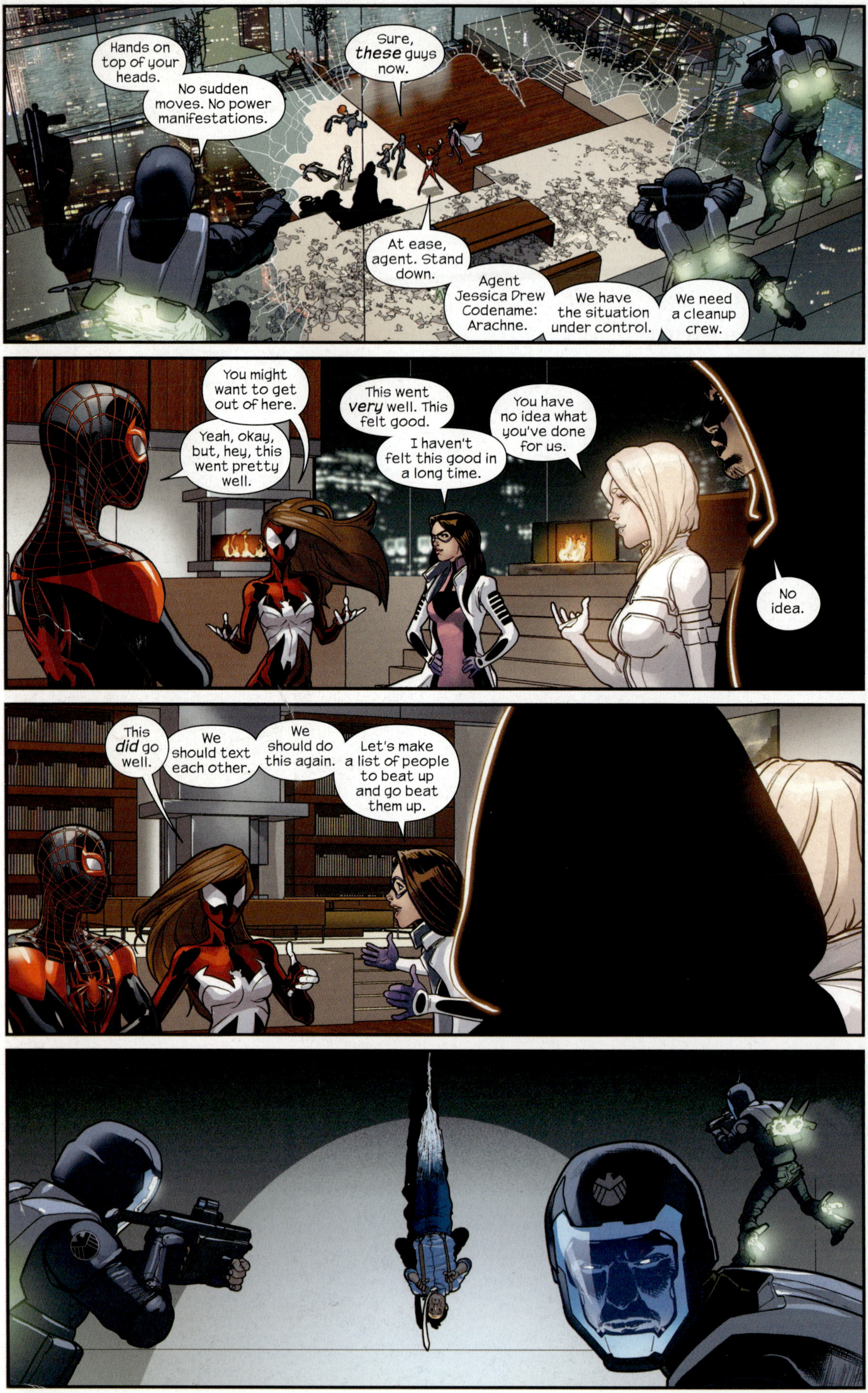
Hands on top of your heads.
No sudden moves. No power manifestations.
Sure, *these* guys now.
At ease, agent. Stand down.
Agent Jessica Drew Codename: Arachne.
We have the situation under control.
We need a cleanup crew.
You might want to get out of here.
Yeah, okay, but, hey, this went pretty well.
This went *very* well. This felt good.
I haven't felt this good in a long time.
You have no idea what you've done for us.
No idea.
This *did* go well.
We should text each other.
We should do this again.
Let's make a list of people to beat up and go beat them up.

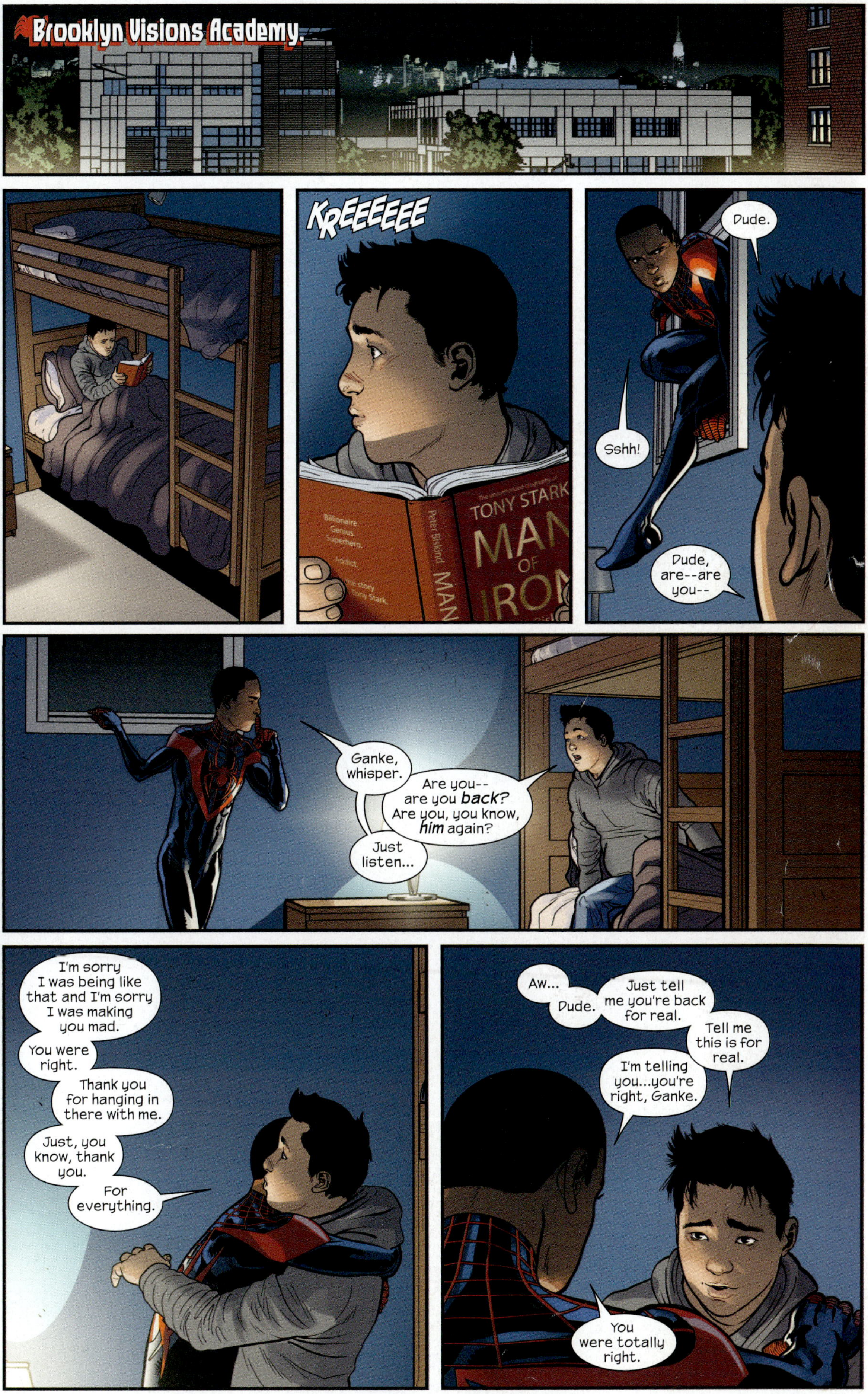

Brooklyn Visions Academy.
KREEEEEE
The unauthorized biography of
TONY STARK
MAN OF IRON
Peter Biskind
Billionaire. Genius. Superhero. Addict.
Dude.
Sshh!
Dude, are--are you--
Ganke, whisper.
Are you--are you back? Are you, you know, him again?
Just listen...
I'm sorry I was being like that and I'm sorry I was making you mad.
You were right.
Thank you for hanging in there with me.
Just, you know, thank you.
For everything.
Aw...
Dude.
Just tell me you're back for real.
Tell me this is for real.
I'm telling you...you're right, Ganke.
You were totally right.

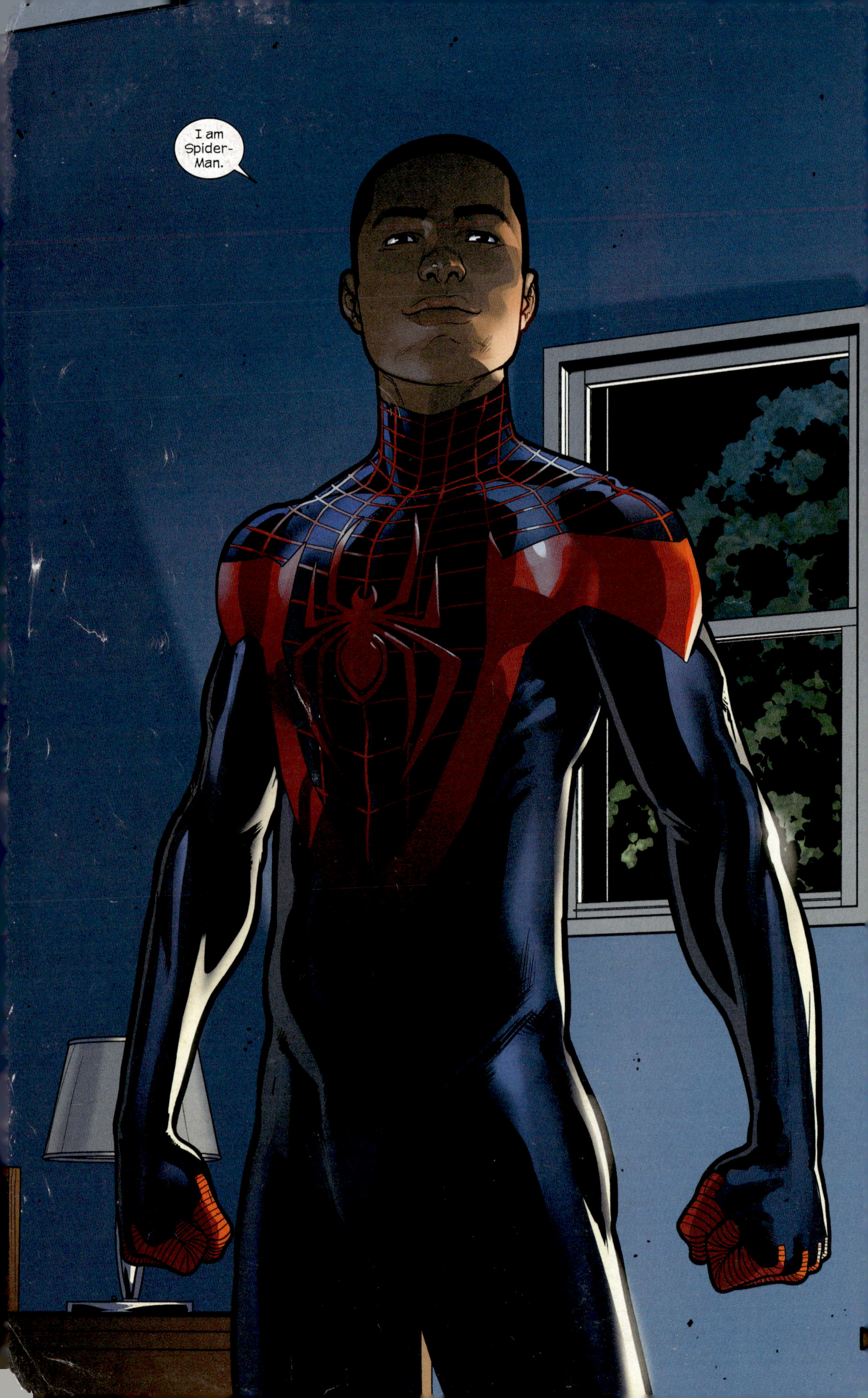
I am Spider-Man.

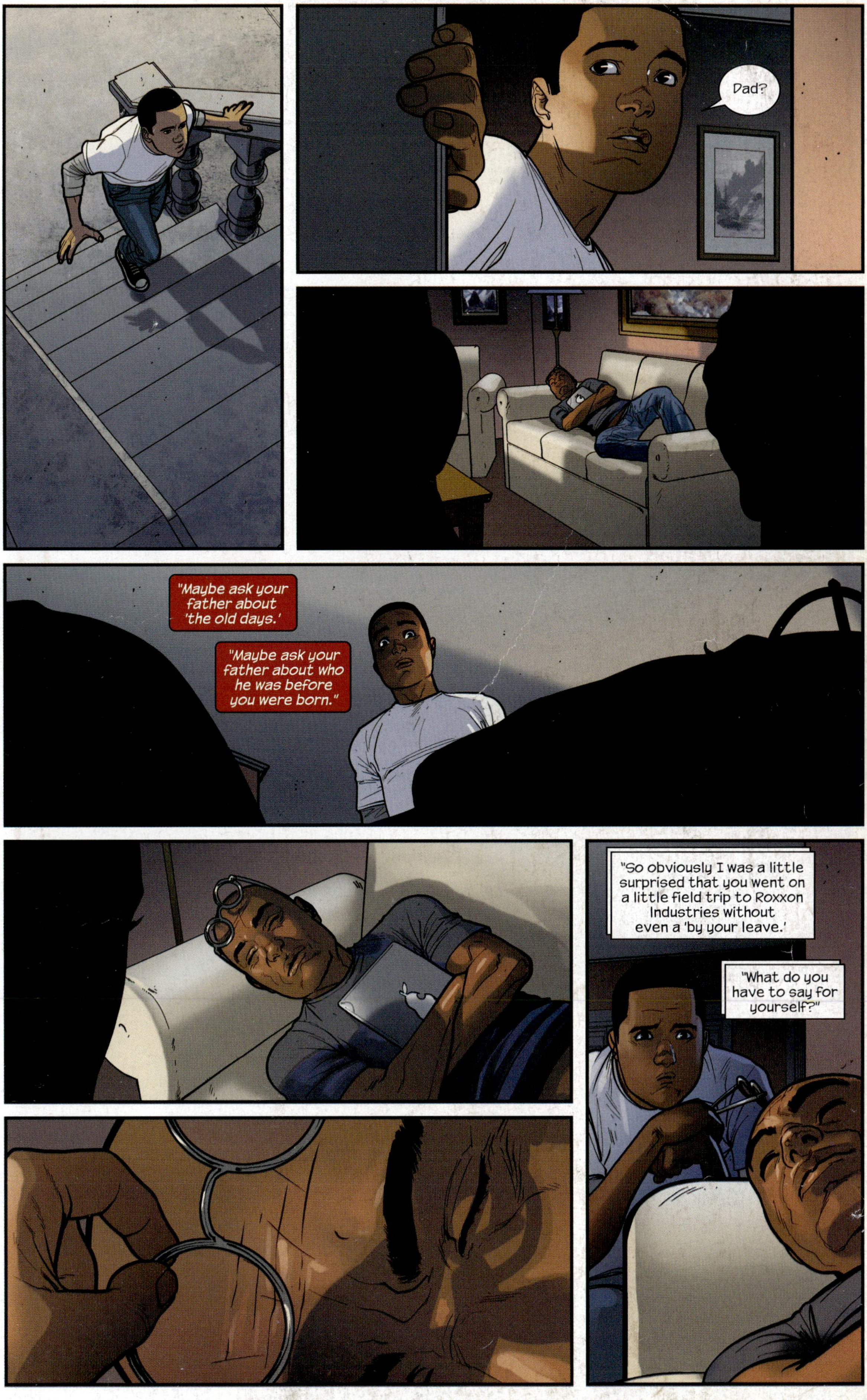
Dad?
"Maybe ask your father about 'the old days.'
"Maybe ask your father about who he was before you were born."
"So obviously I was a little surprised that you went on a little field trip to Roxxon Industries without even a 'by your leave.'
"What do you have to say for yourself?"

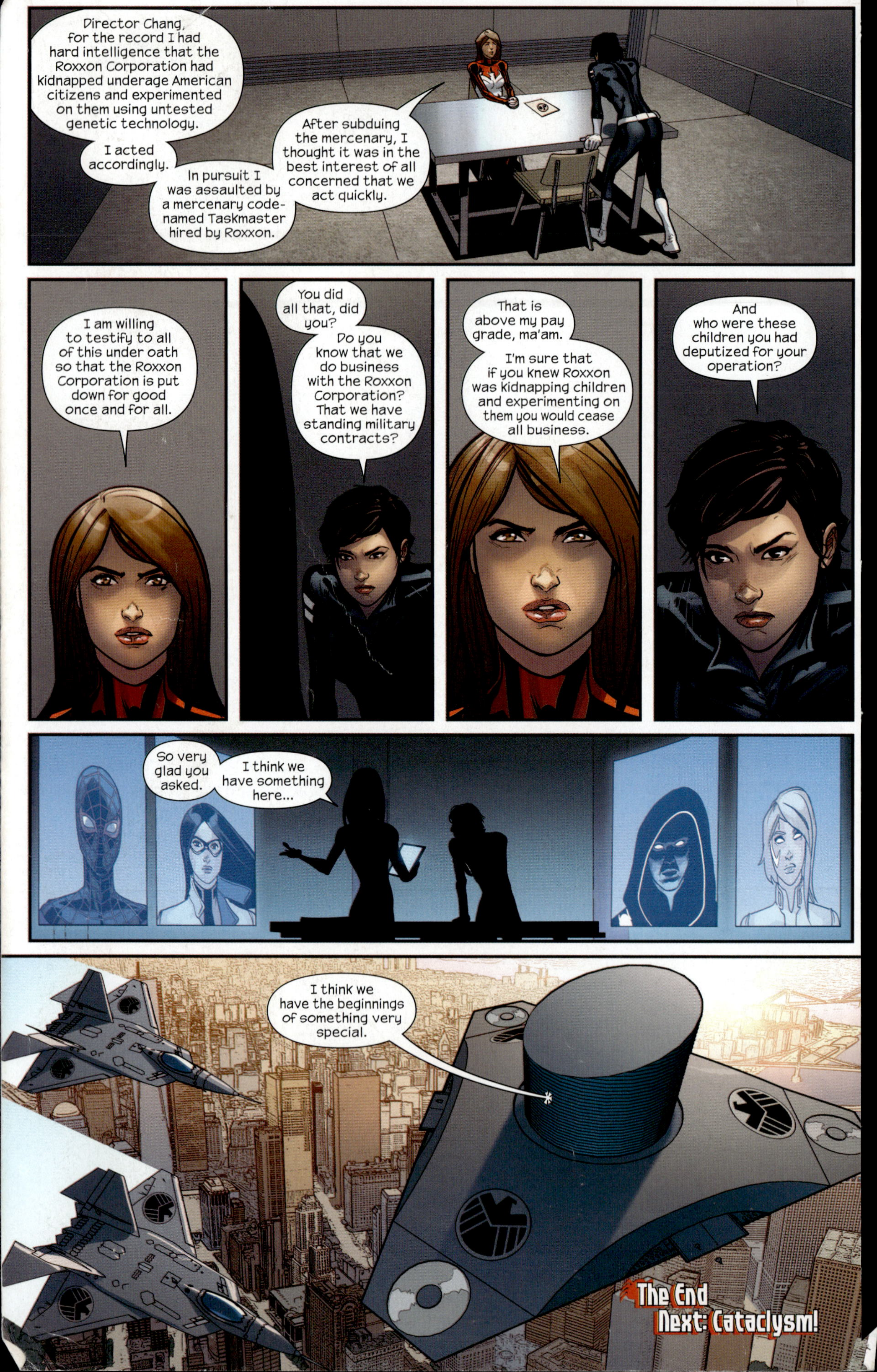
Director Chang, for the record I had hard intelligence that the Roxxon Corporation had kidnapped underage American citizens and experimented on them using untested genetic technology.
I acted accordingly.
In pursuit I was assaulted by a mercenary code-named Taskmaster hired by Roxxon.
After subduing the mercenary, I thought it was in the best interest of all concerned that we act quickly.
I am willing to testify to all of this under oath so that the Roxxon Corporation is put down for good once and for all.
You did all that, did you?
Do you know that we do business with the Roxxon Corporation? That we have standing military contracts?
That is above my pay grade, ma'am.
I'm sure that if you knew Roxxon was kidnapping children and experimenting on them you would cease all business.
And who were these children you had deputized for your operation?
So very glad you asked.
I think we have something here...
I think we have the beginnings of something very special.
The End
Next: Cataclysm!

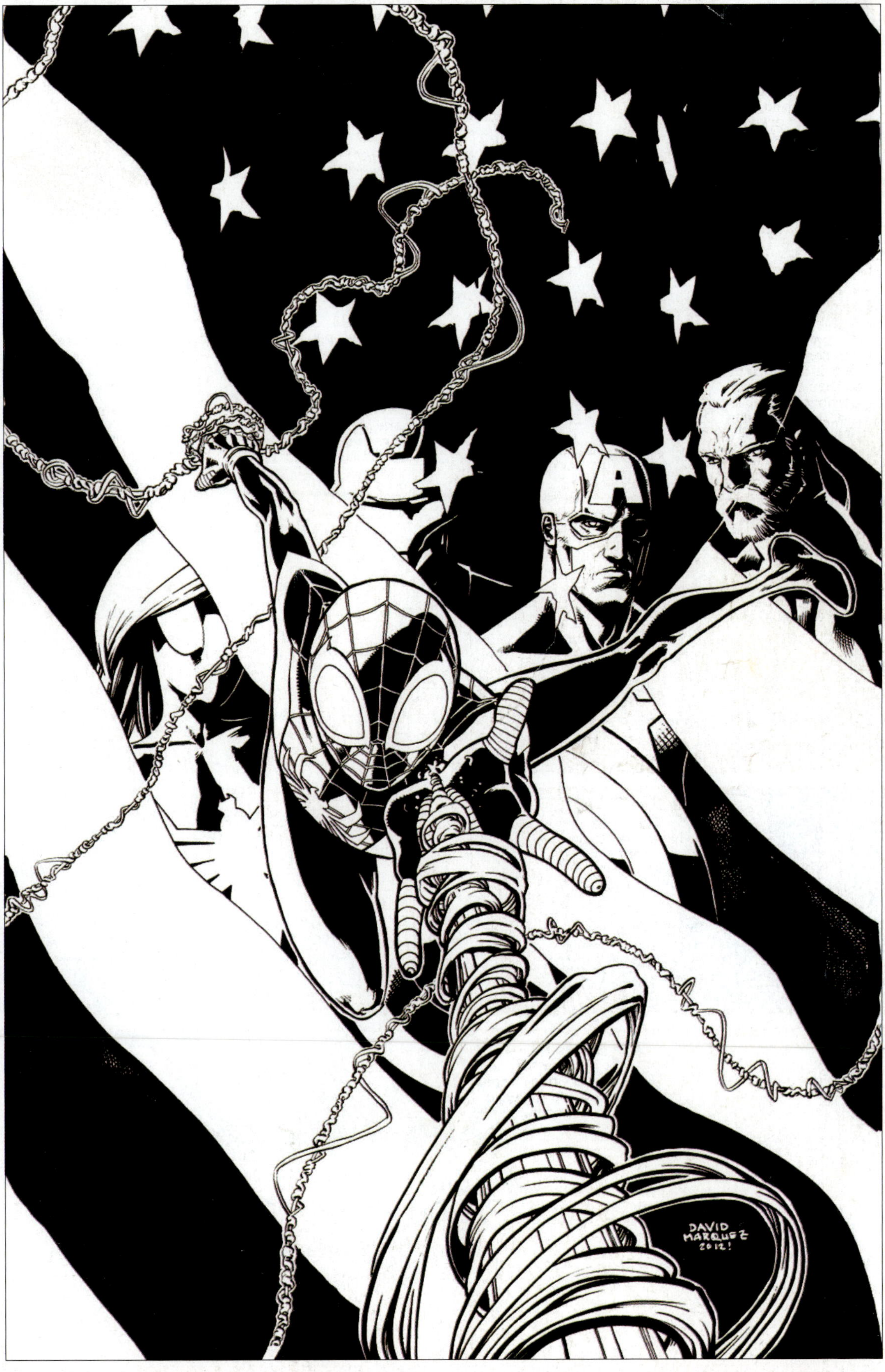
DAVID MARQUEZ 2012!

#16 COVER INKS BY DAVID MARQUEZ

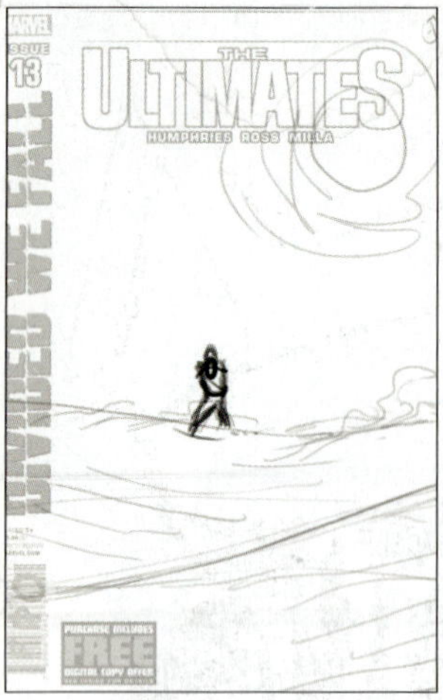
ISSUE 13
THE ULTIMATES
HUMPHRIES ROSS MILLA
DIVIDED WE FALL
PURCHASE INCLUDES
FREE
DIGITAL COPY OFFER

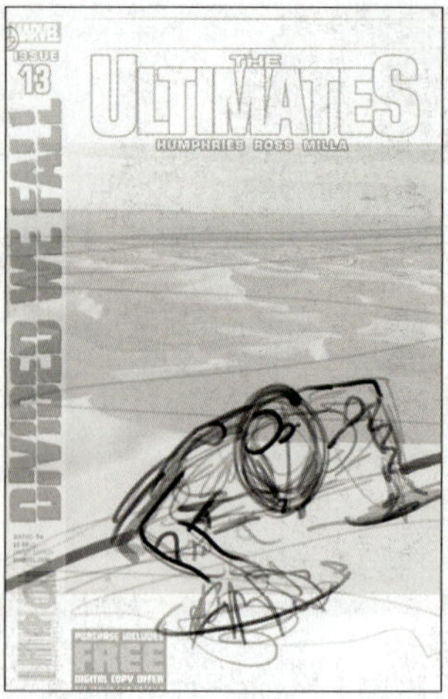
ISSUE 13
THE ULTIMATES
HUMPHRIES ROSS MILLA
DIVIDED WE FALL
PURCHASE INCLUDES
FREE
DIGITAL COPY OFFER

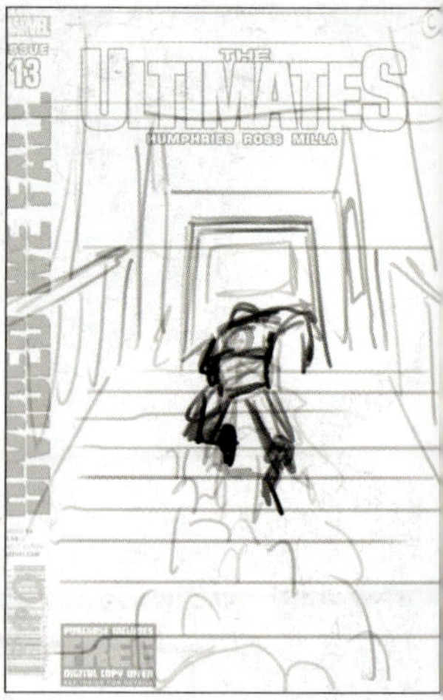
ISSUE 13
THE ULTIMATES
HUMPHRIES ROSS MILLA
DIVIDED WE FALL
PURCHASE INCLUDES
FREE
DIGITAL COPY OFFER

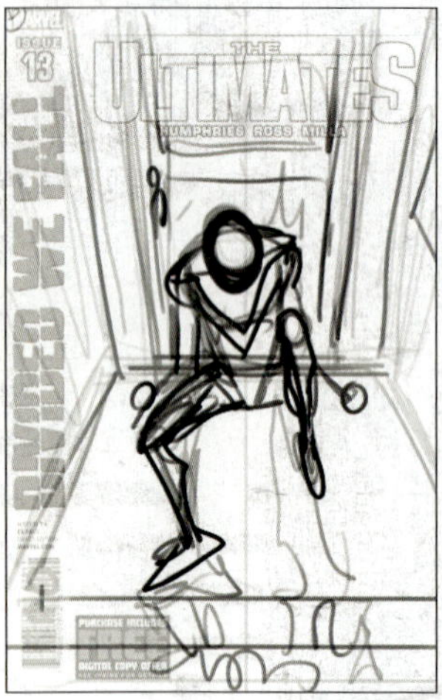
ISSUE 13
THE ULTIMATES
HUMPHRIES ROSS MILLA
DIVIDED WE FALL
PURCHASE INCLUDES
FREE
DIGITAL COPY OFFER

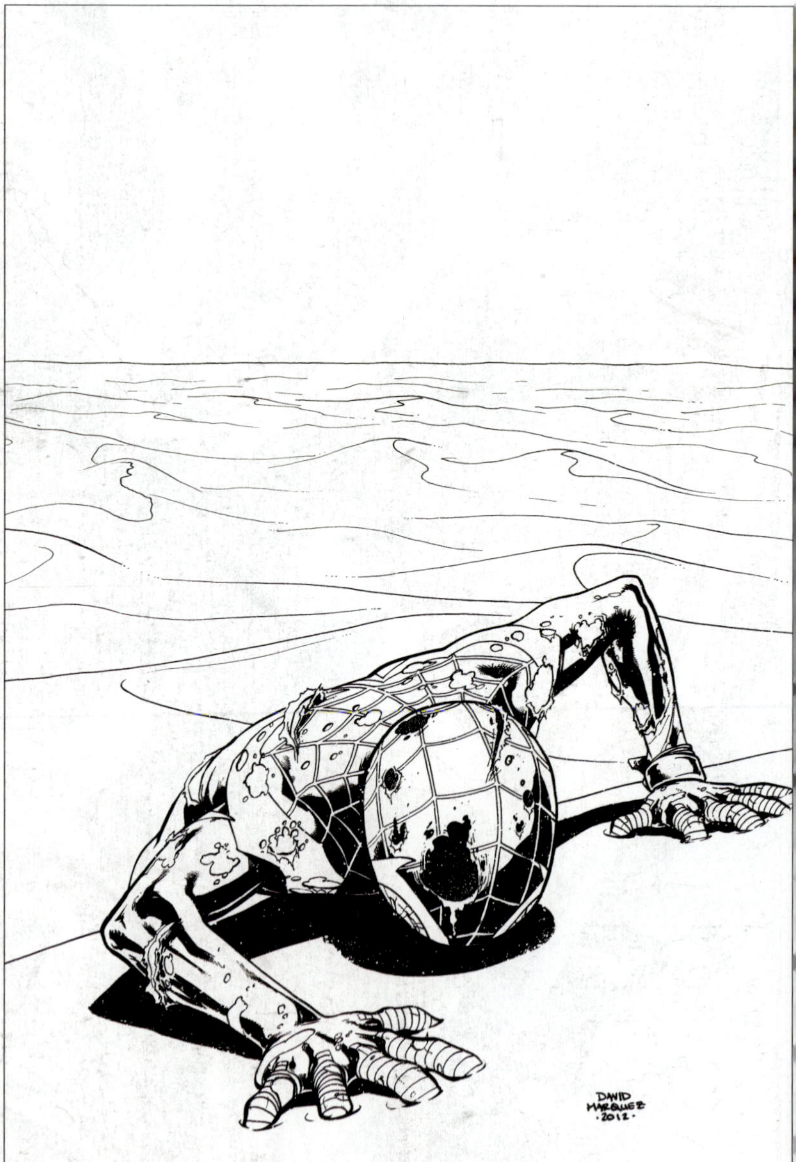
DAVID MARQUEZ ·2012·

#16 COVER PROCESS BY DAVID MARQUEZ

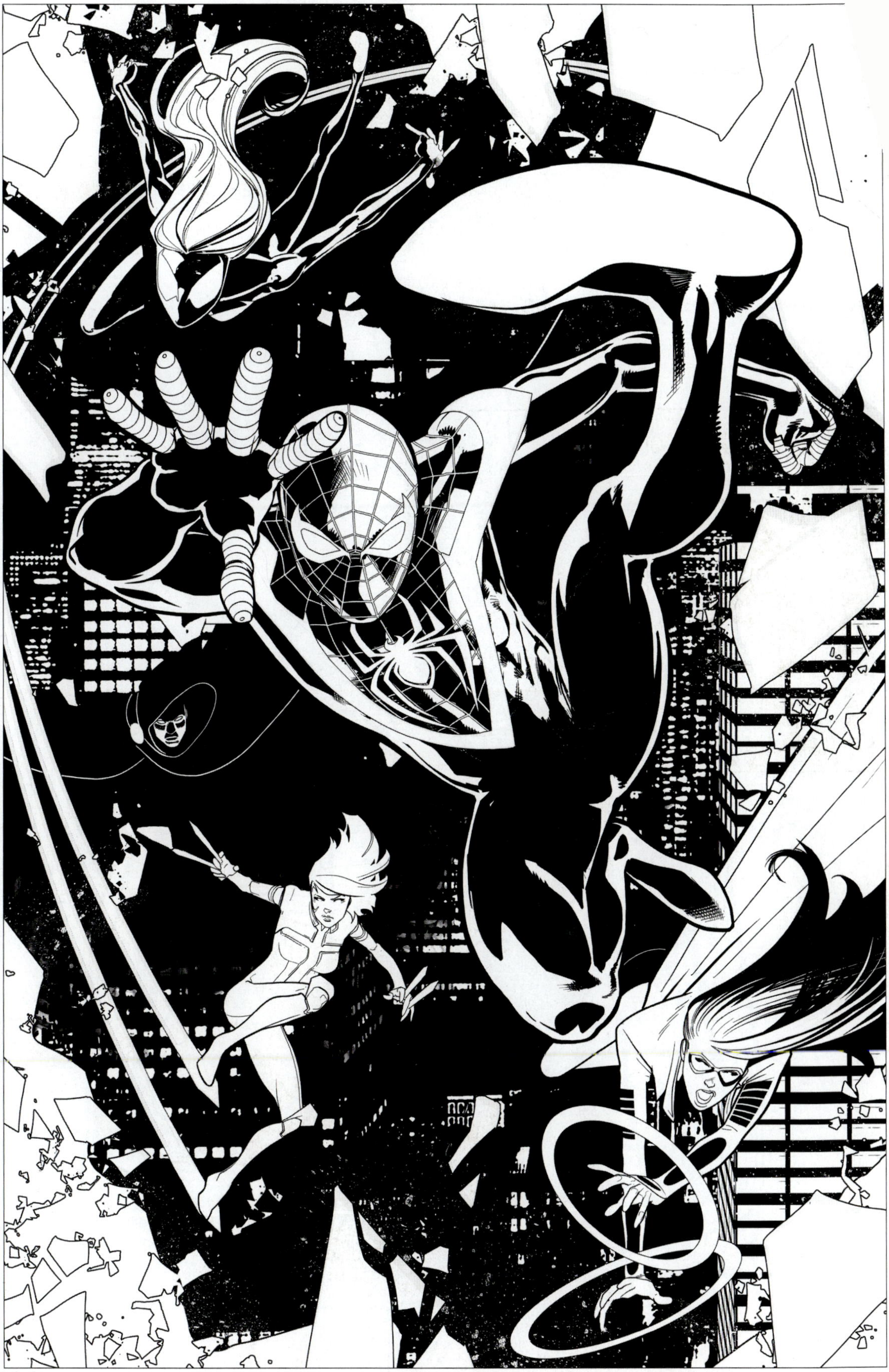

ULTIMATE SPIDER-MAN #28. PAGE 2 ART BY DAVID MARQUEZ

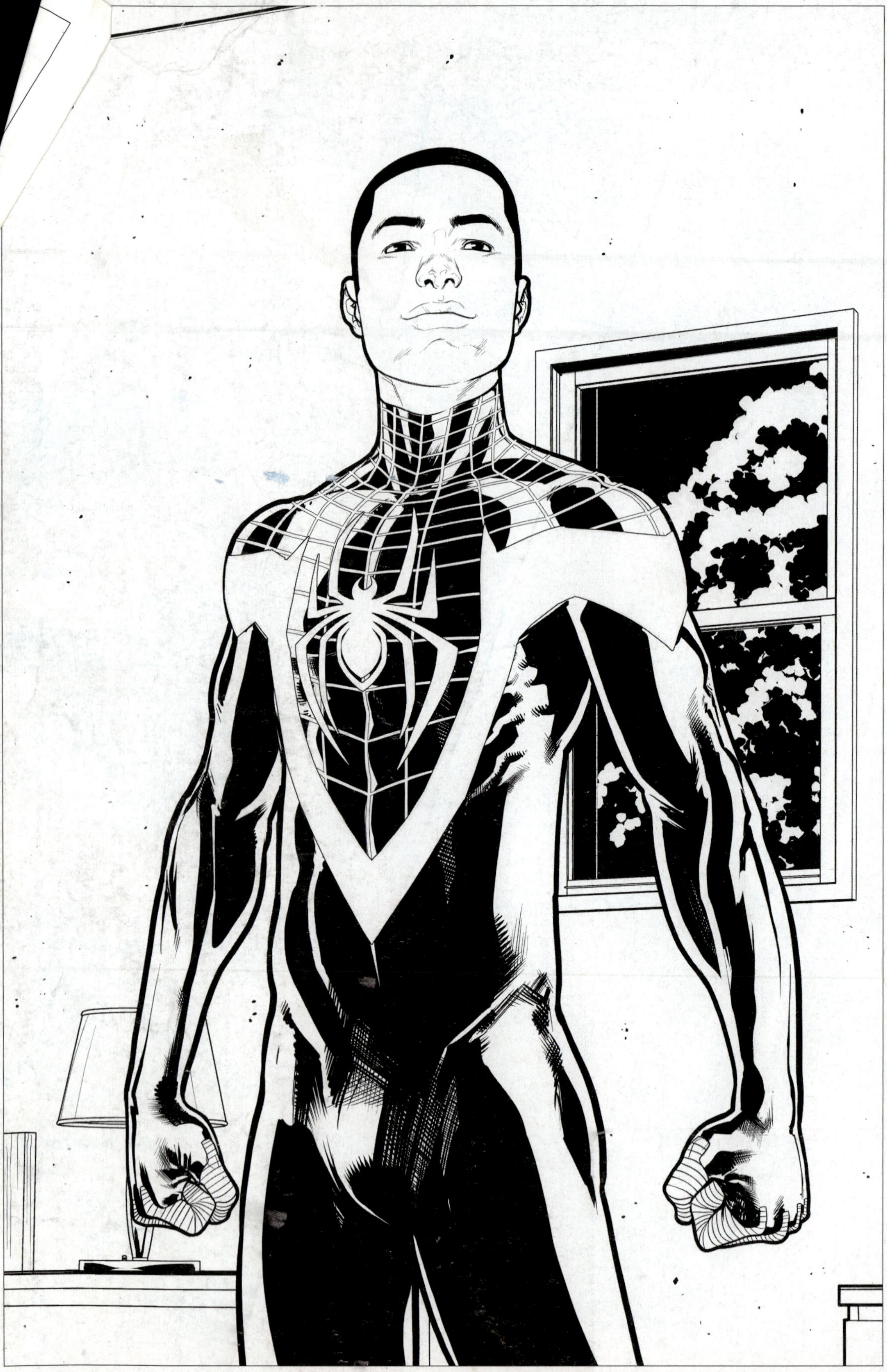

ULTIMATE SPIDER-MAN #28. PAGE 19 ART BY DAVID MARQUEZ